THE END TO END TRAIL

A LONG DISTANCE FOOTPATH FROM LAND'S END TO JOHN O'GROATS

ABOUT THE AUTHOR

Andy Robinson has been walking around the hills and mountains for more years than he cares to admit to, and is a mean hand with a map and compass. He has a habit of setting off on unreasonably optimistic expeditions and usually gets away with it. But not always. His family is very supportive and puts up with a lot, but he's not quite sure why.

THE END TO END TRAIL

A LONG DISTANCE FOOTPATH FROM LAND'S END TO JOHN O'GROATS

by
Andy Robinson

2 POLICE SQUARE, MILNTHORPE, CUMBRIA LA7 7PY
www.cicerone.co.uk

First edition 2007
ISBN-13: 978 185284 512 4

A catalogue record for this book is available from the British Library.

Photos by the author, mostly taken on an unsupported Land's End to John O'Groats walk.

DEDICATION

This route and this book have been inspired by the books of John Hillaby, A Wainwright and many others. It is dedicated to the memory of Elihu Burritt and of Robert and John Naylor, who seem to have started it all off.

ACKNOWLEDGEMENTS

I owe thanks to Ben MacGregor for his assistance with the route in Caithness, and to Ian Smith for his encouragement and his advice on photography. The End to End Trail borrows parts of its route from various sources, and in particular I am grateful to the late James Roberts (author of *Walking in Somerset*, Cicerone, 1997) for showing me the way out of Bridgwater, Denis Brook and Phil Hinchliffe for the Alternative Pennine Way, Hamish Brown for the route from Peebles to West Linton, and David Paterson for the Cape Wrath Trail, and of course all the people involved in the development of the more official routes the Trail uses.

Lastly and most importantly, I'd never have got away with so much walking, or completing this book, without an unreasonable amount of tolerance, encouragement and material support from my family. The biggest share of thanks therefore has to go to Nicola, Esther and Flossie.

Advice To Readers

Readers are advised that, while every effort has been made by the author to ensure the accuracy of this book, changes can occur that may affect the contents. It is advisable to check locally on any aspect that may affect your enjoyment of the services, facilities or routes mentioned. The publisher would welcome notification of any such changes, or you can inform the author via the website at www.longwalks.org.uk.

Front cover: Land's End (Day 1); the Stacks of Duncansby (Day 61)

CONTENTS

SECTION 3

Shropshire, Staffordshire and the Peak:

SECTION 4

The Pennines and Cheviots:

SECTION 5

Southern Scotland and the West Highland Way:

SECTION 6
The Northern Highlands and the Flow Country:

Appendix 1

Appendix 2

Appendix 3

Key to the symbols used in the strip maps

	End to End Trail on tarmac road, arrow indicating direction
	End to End Trail on untarred road or enclosed track
	End to End Trail on clear unenclosed path or track
	End to End Trail on intermittent path: not always clear
	End to End Trail following no visible path
	Other road or enclosed track
	Other clear unenclosed path or track
	Other intermittent path
	Stream or river, arrow showing direction of flow
Br37	Canal, with lock and a numbered bridge over it
	Sea, loch or lake
	Pond or pool
	Railway
Lairg	Town or village (named in bold)
□ +	Building or group of buildings, and a church or chapel
	Other visible feature (explained by accompanying text)
	Conifer or conifers, broad-leaved tree or trees
△	Summit of hill or mountain, often marked with height in metres
fb	Footbridge
A	Connector to elsewhere on the same map page
d5 m2	Connector to another map page (in this case Day 5 Map 2)
sw cp	Connector to another guidebook (e.g. South West Coast Path)
2	Links the map to the start of a route description paragraph

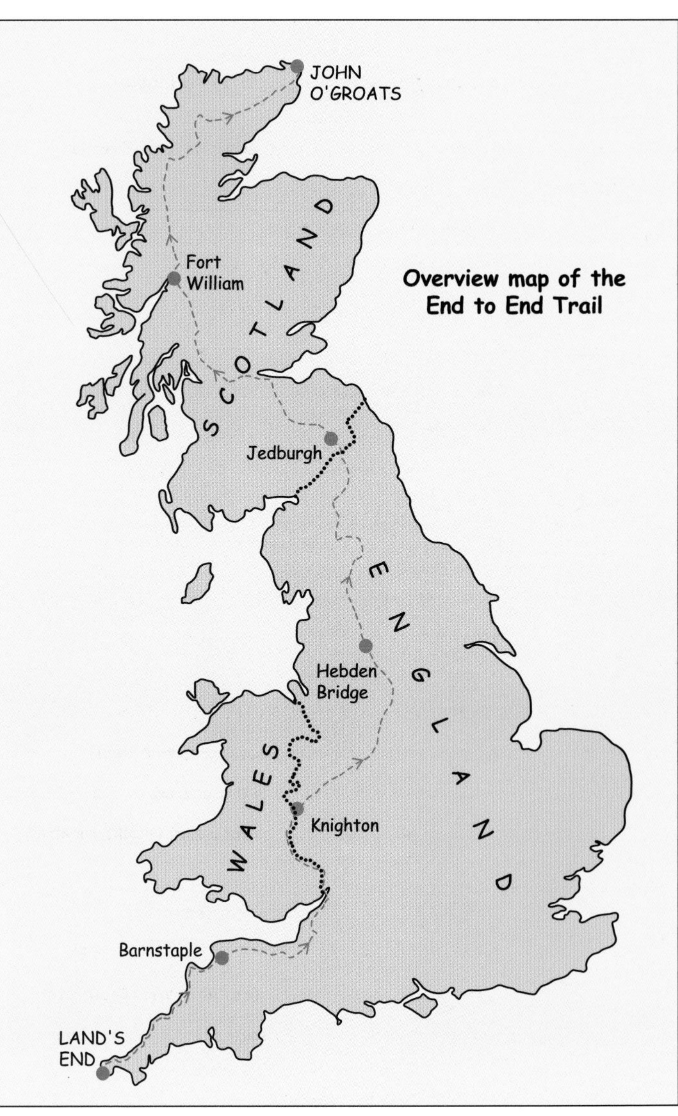
JOHN
O'GROATS
Fort
William
SCOTLAND
Jedburgh
Hebden
Bridge
ENGLAND
WALES
Knighton
Barnstaple
LAND'S
END
Overview map of the
End to End Trail

Pendeen Watch, Day 1

INTRODUCTION

> Where am I going? I don't quite know
> What does it matter where people go?
> Down to the wood where the blue-bells grow –
> Anywhere, anywhere. I don't know.
>
> 'Spring Morning', AA Milne

Land's End and John O'Groats are the two ends of the island of Great Britain – the two points that are the farthest apart from each other. As the crow flies they are 968km (602 miles) apart. Linking the two in a single, long off-road walk gives a magnificent expedition almost exactly twice that distance, and takes you through the very best that the British countryside can offer.

Such a walk is also a great challenge, one of the greatest that many walkers have the time to attempt, and unlike many great challenges, this one is also a great experience. As well as enjoying doing it, you will also enjoy looking back on it afterwards and thinking 'I walked all the way from Land's End to John O'Groats'. What more is there to say? Make your plans and go for it!

A lot of books have been written about getting from Land's End to John O'Groats, but good reading, inspirational and useful as many of them are, none is a guidebook describing a route with the level of detail that walkers expect from a guide to a long-distance path. This book does just that, and sets out to solve that perennial walker's problem: when walking in unfamiliar areas without a guide you are dependent on maps that can't always tell you whether the way you are thinking of going is practical or pleasant. Is it boggy? Is that path visible on the ground? Is the path blocked by barbed wire? Is that stream fordable? Is there an insurmountable deer fence in the way? In practice, what often happens is that you end up making too many mistakes and doing too much road walking. When you are walking a long-distance route you don't want to waste time trying to find the right way to go – it gets very frustrating. I've written this book because it's what I needed to walk from Land's End to John O'Groats the way I wanted to. I hope it will be of similar help to you.

The recommended 1941km (1206 mile) route is described using

Land's End from Mayon Cliff, Day 1

two resources. About 60% of the route is described in detail in this book, with accompanying strip maps at the end of each of the six sections. For the remainder you will be following established national trails, and will need guidebooks for the South West Coast Path, the Offa's Dyke Path, the Pennine Way and the West Highland Way. A number of variations on the recommended route of the Trail are described at the beginning of each section, and details of other guides you will need if you choose to follow them are given at the appropriate points.

The six sections of the route are divided into 61 daily stages, averaging just less than 32km (20 miles), allowing the walker to complete the journey in two months. The days are generally rather longer than those described in the average long-distance walk guidebook, and it will of course be up to you, the walker, to decide where to stop each night and how far to walk each day – the daily stage breaks are just suggestions.

A three-month Alternative Schedule can be found in Appendix 1. This is for those who prefer shorter days and can afford to take longer over the journey.

The route described is mainly a high-level one, avoiding roads and keeping to the hills where practical, and **is intended for experienced hill walkers**. If you can navigate safely in poor weather in the mountains of the Lake District, Snowdonia or the Scottish Highlands, then you should be able to follow this Trail. But a word of warning – don't assume that this means you will be safe whatever happens. The route takes you into some wild and remote areas, particularly in northern Scotland, and should not be undertaken lightly. In

Bannock Burn near Kinbrace, Day 59

particular the section north of Fort William should not be attempted unless you know how to navigate and survive in remote mountain areas in rough conditions (see introduction to Section 6).

Romany Hint for Hikers

A few years ago anyone walking long distances by choice – excepting the professional tramp – would have been considered insane.

Scattered through the book are quotations from *Romany Hints for Hikers* by Gipsy Petulengro, first published in 1936. This must have been one of the first books written about lightweight backpacking. The author knew what he was talking about, although I'm not sure I share his views on the essential nature of pyjamas or the dangers of wearing plus-fours.

There are also quotations from some of the early books written about Land's End to John O'Groats journeys. Some of these are classics, and many are more amateur affairs, but they nearly all provide insight into the challenge of an End to End journey, and make fascinating reading when you are planning your own trip. Details of all of them, and some more recent accounts, are found in the Bibliography in Appendix 2, and on the website www.longwalks.org.uk.

Finally, although the route is described from Land's End to John O'Groats, this book can also be used for a north to south walk, although the route-finding information has not been written with that in mind.

HOW TO USE THIS GUIDEBOOK

The guidebook is divided into an introduction, six Trail sections, each of which is further divided into day stages, and three appendices.

At the beginning of each section there is an information box describing distance in kilometres and miles, the proportion of route requiring road walking, number of days (for both two-month and three-month schedules), and a sketch map of the area covered by that section. A short summary of the general nature of each of the six sections is followed by details of recommended published maps and guidebooks, then information about accommodation and equipment shops, and alternative routes where relevant.

For each day stage of the walk the length of the route is given (for more details of each day stage see Appendix 1), and there is a description, including facilities and points of interest along the way. Where the day is covered by a published guidebook (e.g. the South West Coast Path), the description is usually brief, as all the information you need will be in your guidebook, and there is not much point in covering the same ground twice.

For the days not covered by published guidebooks, detailed annotated strip maps are included at the end of the section to make the route as easy as possible to follow. There are 163 of these maps altogether.

Appendix 1 consists of two route summary tables, one for the two-month Main Schedule, and a three-month Alternative Schedule. Day lengths and the facilities available at the end of each day are summarised here.

Appendix 2 is a bibliography listing some of the best books about Land's End to John O'Groats, as well as other titles that are not essential but could be useful.

Appendix 3 has details of organisations that are useful sources of information.

Other Guidebooks

In addition to this guidebook and a suitable set of Ordnance Survey maps (see Maps box, at the beginning of each section), guidebooks to four long-distance paths will be needed:

- The South West Coast Path
- The Offa's Dyke Path
- The Pennine Way
- The West Highland Way.

I have made recommendations under Guidebooks at the beginning of each section, and these are also listed in Appendix 2.

Where alternative routes are sugggested for parts of the Trail (e.g. Section 2, where the Limestone Link/ Cotswold Way/Heart of England Way can be followed instead of the Offa's Dyke Path), the guidebooks you will need are described under Alternative Routes at the beginning of that section.

In most cases there are several alternative guidebooks, but if one is published by Cicerone, that's the one I've recommended. (I wouldn't be recommending them if they weren't good guides, although of course many of the alternatives are worth looking at.)

For Section 6 it is worth reading *North to the Cape* by Denis Brook and Phil Hinchliffe (Cicerone, 1999), as the authors include details of some additional alternative routes that are useful in the Highlands during bad weather.

Finally, check the website www.longwalks.org.uk, where updates and corrections to this guidebook will be published.

Maps

Romany Hint for Hikers

If you are hiking through strange places do not forget the map.

Ordnance Survey maps

With the possible exception of the South West Coast Path, **neither this guidebook nor any other should be relied on without having relevant Ordnance Survey or equivalent maps with you as well**. Guidebooks are fine while you are on the right path, but rarely give you the information you need to find it again when you have lost it. At least when you have a map and get lost, you are probably still on the map.

The relevant OS maps are listed in the Maps box at the beginning of each section, and under the heading Recommendations are my suggestions for what to actually take.

Strip maps

When some or all of the day's walking is not covered by another guidebook, my own strip maps are provided (grouped together at the end of each section), annotated with useful information to help you to follow the route without going astray.

The strip maps are not intended to be a substitute for Ordnance Survey maps, however. There are no contours marked, so they do not show the lie of the land, and they only show the recommended route and a narrow strip on either side. The strip maps should be used *alongside* OS maps, and one way of doing this is to transfer the route onto your OS maps with a soft pencil (2B or 3B), which can easily be erased later.

Many walkers will be relieved to hear that all the maps are oriented with north at the top of the page. This makes navigation easier, and since the Trail is overall south to north, for quite a lot of the time you will be holding the book the right way up as you follow the route.

Each map page has a named start and end point, and these are intended to let you know approximately where the walking starts and ends on the page. Not every page actually starts and ends exactly in a spot named on a map, so the name given reflects the nearest significant place with a name – this place could be just before or just after the actual page end point, or slightly off to the left or right. The named location is usually shown on one or other of the map pages (before or after the page break), but not always.

The text on the maps is usually in a series of numbered paragraphs on each page, and each paragraph is as close as it can be to the part of the map it relates to. This means that when looking at the map pages, expect to start reading paragraph number 1 near the bottom. If there are a number of strips of the map on one page, where practical the first is lowest down, and the higher ones follow on.

Scale The strip maps are on a scale of 1:25000 as far as the point where the Trail joins the Pennine Way, then at 1:50000 from the Scottish border onwards. The reason for using two different scales is that on a 1:50000 map it is almost impossible to show the detailed route-finding information needed to navigate intensive farming areas, such as you will meet in Somerset and Staffordshire. On the other hand, in the Highlands of Scotland there are generally far fewer features to show on a map, and using a 1:25000 scale would have resulted in many map sections showing nothing but a dotted line across a featureless page, which would be of little use for navigation.

Key There is a key to the symbols on the strip maps on the page after the

Derwent and Howden Reservoirs, Day 27

contents list, but they include nothing revolutionary and should be easy to use.

'We decided to reduce our equipment to the lowest possible limit...even maps were voted off as encumbrances.'
From John O'Groat's to Land's End
by R and J Naylor

Distances and Daily Stage Lengths

Distances given in the text have been measured from Ordnance Survey maps, so may differ slightly from the distances given in other guidebooks. (Other people's estimates were not taken on trust, and one or two daily stage distances given in other guides turned out to be surprisingly inaccurate when re-measured.) Distances for each daily stage are given to the nearest kilometre and nearest mile. Estimates from maps can't reproduce all the wiggles you really walk, so the distances quoted are more likely to be underestimates than overestimates. (See Appendix 1 for Route Summary Tables.)

Daily stage lengths are a matter of personal choice and ability on long-distance walks, depending on how much of the time you want to walk each day, how fast you walk, how fit you are, and how flexible you are in your accommodation requirements. On the two-month Main Schedule, the daily stages are usually between 25 and 40km long (15 to 25 miles), and the end points usually have some sort of accommodation either on or near the route (for most of the Trail there are plenty of alternative overnight staging points). The three-month Alternative Schedule keeps to an average of 23km (14 miles) a day (see Appendix 1).

Where there is a particularly short or long daily stage there is always a reason, and the guide makes it clear what that reason is (usually a shortage of accommodation options at what would be the ideal stage end).

Where the End to End Trail follows an existing long-distance footpath, the route doesn't keep to the stages described in the recommended guidebooks, since many of the stages are too short to meet the Trail's 25 to 40km yardstick. So although you will be following the route as described in the recommended guidebook, refer to *this* book for daily stage lengths.

The Trail is described in six roughly equal sections. If you want to split it into a number of separate holidays, two sections can be completed in three weeks following the Main Schedule, so three such holidays should see you at John O'Groats. Alternatively, each of the six sections can be walked in about a fortnight using the three-month Alternative Schedule. Each of the section ends is easily accessible by public transport.

Distances are given in kilometres, usually with the equivalent in miles in brackets, but not always. I know this may not be everyone's preference, but as OS maps use a 1km grid, perhaps it's time we started to get used to it. Distances are usually quoted to the nearest kilometre or half kilometre. Heights are all given in metres.

THE ROUTE

The End to End Trail aims to join up as much of Britain's high ground as possible, while still keeping to a reasonably direct route from Cornwall to Caithness, and it follows existing, published long-distance paths where they fit the bill.

The South West Coast Path (SWCP) is followed, for the most part, from Land's End to Barnstaple in Devon. This is one of the national trails, so right-of-way problems have been solved, and the path follows the coast closely and usually avoids roads. This part of the route includes a lot of spectacular cliff scenery, and is definitely the most enjoyable way to start a Land's End to John O'Groats walk.

At Barnstaple the End to End Trail leaves the SWCP (which continues along the coast on a long detour to reach Minehead). Instead, the Trail heads inland to the hills – across Exmoor, over the Quantocks, on past Bristol and across the Severn, to Chepstow in South Wales.

From Chepstow the Trail follows the first half of the Offa's Dyke Path, along the River Wye and the England–Wales border.

The Wrekin from Wenlock Edge, Day 21

At Knighton, halfway up the border, the Trail cuts across northeast, along Wenlock Edge and south of Telford, to join the Staffordshire Way near Penkridge, a few miles south of Stafford. The Staffordshire Way and the Limestone Way follow the River Dove north into the heart of the Peak District.

Then, rather than follow the Pennine Way on its initial purgatory over the Dark Peak peat bogs, the route of the Alternative Pennine Way is taken instead. This follows deep limestone valleys, then the gritstone edges and moors to the east of the Pennine Way.

Near Hebden Bridge in West Yorkshire the Trail joins the Pennine Way and follows it up the Pennines to the Cheviots and the Scottish borders.

The Trail now turns northwest. St Cuthbert's Way is followed to Melrose, then the Southern Upland Way to Traquair. Paths and tracks to Peebles and across the Pentland Hills lead to canal towpaths and a disused railway line to get you through to the hills again, northwest of Glasgow, avoiding most of the urban sprawl around Edinburgh and Glasgow. From Loch Lomond you follow the West Highland Way to Fort William. After Fort William the Trail heads north into more remote areas of the Highlands: Glen Garry, Glen Affric, Kinlochewe, Oykel Bridge. Eventually the Highlands are left behind, and the

Malham Cove, Day 30

route heads northeast to the upper waters of the River Thurso, and then up the east coast to Duncansby Head and John O'Groats.

Why This Way?

Romany Hint for Hikers
Keep away from the dust and smells of cars and lorries.

Since my first holidays in the Lake District, when I was little, I've loved the hills and wilder areas of Great Britain, so that's where the End to End Trail goes. It passes through much of the best hill country (although for geographical reasons misses out Snowdonia and the Lake District), and generally follows hills and dales rather than flat plains and other vertically challenged areas. On the other hand, it is not a 'peak-bagging' exercise. Passes and valleys are usually preferred to peaks and ridges, but of course there are plenty of opportunities to visit the tops on the way if you want.

The End to End Trail is not the quickest or shortest way of getting from Land's End to John O'Groats, but it's as close as I could get to being what I consider to be the best way. It does keep to a reasonably direct route – most people will only have a limited amount of time, so extending the walk to pick off Snowdon or tick all the Munros is out – and if a route is not direct it removes some of the focus of the whole expedition – every day, every mile should take you closer to your objective.

The route does go past the foot of Ben Nevis, however. The symmetry of walking the length of Britain via the top of Britain's highest mountain is appealing, and although Ben Nevis is not 'officially' part of the route, it seems a shame not to climb it on the way (particularly if the weather is unusually good and you can actually see the damned thing).

Intensive agriculture tends to be avoided along the Trail, since ploughed fields and crops can be difficult and frustrating walking country, and often turn into unpleasant navigation and bushwhacking exercises. In one or two areas they are unavoidable (Somerset and Staffordshire, for example), and I have done my best to find a reasonable route through.

Most backpackers dislike walking on tarmac roads, and the route avoids them as far as is practical. Where they are unavoidable, as when crossing the Somerset Levels, the lanes followed are quiet ones. There is hardly any walking on busy roads, and large towns and cities are also avoided – this is a walk in the country, not in the suburbs. The route is intended to be entirely on either rights of way, established walking routes, or land with established open access. (Access law is different in England and Scotland – for the Countryside Code and maps of

Open Access land in England see countrysideaccess.gov.uk; for Scotland's Outdoor Access Code see www.outdooraccess-scotland.com).

A guiding principle is that the route is a *walking* route, and that every inch from Land's End to John O'Groats must be walked under your own steam. This means that every river and estuary is crossed *on foot*, i.e. by bridge or by wading (in the Highlands, for example).

So ferries are out (otherwise someone could claim to have walked from End to End by hitching a lift on a boat round the bits they didn't want to walk), and this has implications in southwest England and the Scottish Highlands. The South West Coast Path takes ferries (e.g. between Rock and Padstow in Cornwall), and some of the possible routes up the west coast of the Highlands involve crossing arms of the sea. But by following alternative routes in the southwest and keeping a bit further east in the Highlands, the need for such assistance is removed.

Bridges are of course perfectly OK, since the only alternatives would be (a) to follow the watershed all the way, which would probably be a good route but is not this one, or (b) to try to swim countless rivers and probably drown in the attempt. (Many of the routes through the Highlands described in other books feature boat trips, including John Hillaby's *Journey Through Britain* and Denis Brook and Phil Hinchliffe's *North To The Cape*.)

Near Hartland Point, Day 8

Designing Your Own Route

If you want to devise your own route, for part or even all of the way, here are a few tips on how to do it. I would be surprised if many of the walkers using this guidebook were to follow the route described here in its entirety. Use it to help you with the bits where you don't already have a route in mind, rather than to dictate your whole journey.

1 In England and Wales it is not worth considering routes that don't follow rights of way marked on OS maps (unless you already know there's easy walking without obstacles). Pathless ground is usually slow to walk on, right to roam or no right to roam.
2 In Scotland the same applies, but of course the rights of way are largely undefined and so are not marked on maps. This means you need more local knowledge.
3 In parts of the country where there is a lot of walking (e.g. the Peak District), you can usually follow all rights of way with little or no obstruction.
4 In other parts of the country, don't assume that a right of way marked on an OS map can be walked along unless you have a good reason to believe it is in regular use. Crops may block it, it may be overgrown with nettles or brambles, or it may simply be untraceable. This is considerably worse in summer than spring.
5 Waymarked routes are usually clear enough to walk, but there are exceptions.
6 As far as you can, rely on other walkers' knowledge about where the best walking is to be found. Local walking guidebooks are a very good source of information.
7 Study OS maps. For planning routes, 1:25000 Explorer maps are much better than 1:50000 maps, as they have a lot more detail. Most importantly, they include fences, walls and hedges, meaning that you can distinguish between unenclosed land and small fields. This is invaluable for planning routes in Scotland.
8 You can buy a complete set of 1:50000 maps for Great Britain on computer CDs at a far lower price than the paper versions.
9 Don't assume any route is either possible or impossible unless you or somebody else has tried it to see. It was very tempting to assume that the only way to get through Caithness to John O'Groats was on roads, just because all the published Land's End to John O'Groats accounts followed roads. When I went to have a look, it turned out not to be the case at all.
10 Avoid cities and large towns, however much you may like the centre of them. Suburbs are no fun to walk through.
11 Plan your route through villages to give you plenty of opportunities to

resupply and get a few home comforts.

GEOGRAPHY AND HISTORY

Land's End is not the most southerly point in England, and John O'Groats is not the most northerly point in Scotland – these honours belong to the Lizard and Dunnet Head respectively. The reason Land's End and John O'Groats are regarded as the end points of Great Britain is that they are the two points on the mainland of Britain that are the furthest apart from each other. To be more precise, it is actually Duncansby Head, rather than John O'Groats, that is the true furthest point – the John O'Groats Hotel and the rest of the village are about 2.5km (1½ miles) west of Duncansby Head, where there is a lighthouse but no other habitation.

The most *direct* route from Land's End to John O'Groats is not a practical proposition for anyone. It is 967km (601 miles) long, and at its halfway point is about 18km underground below the northwest coast of the Isle of Man.

The most direct *above-ground* route is only 1km further, and by contrast is entirely practical – although it's mostly a sea journey. Until you reach Scotland the only bits of dry land you cross are the tip of Pembrokeshire and the Isle of Man. (Anyone interested in following such a beeline route across country is recommended to read *Two Degrees West* by Nicholas Crane, in which he describes walking within a 2km-wide corridor from Berwick-upon-Tweed to Swanage on the south coast.)

The less direct route recommended in this guidebook sticks to the British mainland. It crosses the main watershed a number of times, and when this happens it is pointed out in the book. There is a watershed between any two points on the shore of an island: it is the line that divides the water flowing to one side of the island from that flowing to the other side. The watershed between Land's End and John O'Groats is essentially the line between the streams and rivers flowing west into the Atlantic and the Irish Sea, and those flowing south and east into the English Channel and the North Sea.

I haven't been able to find out definitively when Land's End and John O'Groats first became associated with the idea of being the two extremes of Great Britain. It was certainly in the mind of the American Elihu Burritt, in 1846, when he first arrived in Britain, having been appointed US Consul to Birmingham by Abraham Lincoln. Burritt eventually walked from London to John O'Groats in 1863, and in the following year from London to Land's End and back. He believed he may have been the first person to connect the two places on foot (or at all).

Elihu Burritt was an interesting character. Born in New Britain, Connecticut, he started his working life as a blacksmith's apprentice. Subsequently he learned 50 languages, and campaigned on many humanitarian issues, including the abolition of slavery, relief from the Irish potato famine, and cheap international postage rates, and when he walked to John O'Groats and Land's End he was in his 50s. He wrote accounts of both walks, and these are listed in the bibliography in Appendix 2.

Probably the first people to walk a continuous journey between Land's End and John O'Groats were Robert and John Naylor, well-to-do brothers from near Warrington, Cheshire, who set off in September 1871. It took them eight days to get to John O'Groats just to start the walk. On their arrival they read an entry in the visitors' book at the Huna Inn, near John O'Groats, as follows: 'Elihu Burrit of New Britain, Connecticut, U.S. America, on a walk from Land's End to John o'Groat's, arrived at Huna Inn, upon Monday Sep 28th 1863'. The visitors' book contained entries dating back to 1839. The Huna Inn the Naylors stayed in no longer survives, but a Victorian replacement, built in 1878, still stands, although it has been a burnt-out shell since about 1980.

The Naylors walked the whole journey in one push, taking no ferries or other transport. They covered 1372 miles (2208km) and completed the walk in nine weeks. They didn't walk on Sundays, so in 54 walking days they averaged 25 miles, or 41km, a day. Much of their route was on what are now main roads, but at that time roads were of course not surfaced with tarmac, and as there were no cars or lorries, the walking environment must have been more like a modern long-distance bridleway.

The brothers sought out the best countryside to walk through, including the Great Glen, the summit of Ben Nevis, the Lake District, the Yorkshire Dales and the Peak District. To a large degree their approach to their walk was similar to today's long-distance walkers. John Naylor wrote up the walk 45 years later, from the notes they had made at the time, and the result, *From John O'Groats to Land's End*, makes fascinating reading.

The End to End journey has been a popular endurance route for cyclists since the late 19th century, the first recorded ride, in July 1880, taking H Blackwell and CA Harman 13 days. The Vegetarian Cycling and Athletic Club records one of its members breaking the cycling record in 1907 and again in 1908, and another member, George Allen, walked from Land's End to John O'Groats in 1904 and again in 1908 (he published an account of his record-breaking 1904 walk). Early in the same year a certain Dr Deighton also walked south to north, getting a fair amount of local publicity as he went. EW Fox wrote an account of his walks from his home in Harrogate – to Land's End in 1905, and to John O'Groats four years later. Arnold Binns, a champion roller-skater from Hebden Bridge in West Yorkshire, skated from End to End in July 1930.

The next accounts are post-Second World War. Theo Lang, then a young journalist, walked from Land's End to John O'Groats in 1946 to provide a running story for the newspaper he worked for, and he subsequently published an entertaining book (*Cross Country* – see Appendix 2) based on his articles. In the First and Last Inn near Land's End he was told about someone who had arrived from John O'Groats pushing a wheelbarrow – stunt trips are nothing new! (This was possibly a memory of Robert Carlyle, a Cornishman who pushed a wheelbarrow End to End three times, the first being in 1879.)

Interest in walking between Land's End and John O'Groats was revitalised in 1960. At the start of the year Dr Barbara Moore walked a road route from John O'Groats to Land's End in 22 days, to promote her belief in subsisting on a diet of juice, raw tomatoes, grass, oranges and herbs. She gained a good deal of national publicity, and this inspired Billy Butlin, the holiday camp entrepreneur, to organise a challenge walk shortly afterwards, to give his business some publicity too. In February, in bad weather, 715 optimistic competitors set off from John O'Groats, of whom 138 managed to reach Land's End.

Since then the End to End business has never looked back, with

Woodland near Clovelly, Day 9

many novelty approaches, often undertaken for charity-fundraising purposes. Most of them have been along the roads, however, aiming at a fast time, fundraising or publicity, rather than enjoying the journey for its own sake. This is far from the relaxed, adventure approach of the Naylor brothers, or of most modern-day walkers on long-distance paths.

The inspiration for regarding Land's End and John O'Groats as two ends of a modern, long-distance footpath, and working out the best cross-country footpath between the two, must be attributed largely to John Hillaby. His book *Journey Through Britain*, published in 1968, is an extremely entertaining account of his walk in the mid-1960s (see Appendix 2). The rest of us are walking in his footsteps, sometimes literally.

SAFETY

Survival Tactics

Every guidebook to walking that includes remote areas should include a section on safety, so here is mine.

The main safety considerations relate to walking in remote areas, and as is made clear at the beginning of this introduction, you should not even consider following certain parts of this route if you are not competent at navigating in bad weather in the mountains, so this section doesn't spell out all the obvious basics. In the Scottish Highlands in particular you must not rely on there being anyone nearby to help if you get into trouble, and neither must you assume that if something goes wrong you will be close to shelter. Solo walking is an increased risk, as there will be nobody to hand to help if something goes wrong. This doesn't mean you shouldn't walk alone, but it does mean that you should take greater precautions if you do, to reduce the risk.

Some tips are as follows.

1 **Always make sure that someone knows where you are going**, and that they will know you are missing if you don't arrive where and when you expect to. As with just about every safety issue, this point is most important when going into remote areas and when walking alone. Be realistic about how likely you are to be delayed, and about any difficulty you may have in contacting them to let them know you are OK. Don't risk false alarms. Telephoning someone who has a copy of your route every day or so is a simple way of doing this. Make sure they know what to do if you don't report in.
2 **Take suitable equipment.** A tent or a Gore-Tex bivi bag and a sleeping bag are not only useful for overnight accommodation, but will also keep you alive with a broken leg in bad weather. (Plastic survival bags are of limited value, as once inside you get wet through

Port Isaac, Day 9

in no time from condensation.) Trekking poles will help you get out of a remote place with a sprained ankle. They will also help with river crossings, and take some of the strain off your knees when things are going well. Get good equipment and clothes, and be sure you will be warm enough even if you are soaked to the skin.

3 **Take suitable companions.** At least half your party should have a map and compass, and be capable of navigation on their own in bad weather.

4 **In remote areas take enough food** to last significantly longer than you expect to be away – say a couple of days extra. This emergency food should not need a stove in order to be eaten, since your stove going wrong may be the problem you hit. Also, if your emergency food is too nice, it won't be there when you have an emergency. If you don't like Kendal Mint Cake, for example, it makes a perfect emergency food supply – high energy for its weight, easy to eat, and unlikely to be eaten before everything else has gone.

5 **Don't rely on anything complicated or anything with a battery in it.** For example, your mobile phone probably won't work in much of the Highlands (at the time

of writing), and if you drop your GPS on a rock it may stop working, so if you don't know where you are without it, and can't use a compass, you could be in trouble.

6 **Don't rely on isolated accommodation or shelters being open, or an isolated phone box being in working order.** Pay phones in pubs and hotels are rapidly becoming rarer, since mobile phones have taken most of their business. Don't assume that any phone mentioned in this (or any other) guidebook will still be there when you want it.

7 **Be careful crossing rivers.** In the Scottish Highlands beyond Fort William the Trail crosses a number of streams and rivers that can be dangerous in flood. The danger is not the depth, but the current. If you can't stand up you will be washed downstream, possibly to a bad end, as many people have died trying to cross streams and rivers in the Highlands in spate conditions. If you are in any doubt, don't try to cross. There is usually an alternative 'long way round', although in very wet weather even a usually insignificant stream can become impossible to negotiate safely. I have given warnings for those that seemed to me to pose the greatest risk, and included alternatives where practical.

Crossing is safer if you keep your boots on (you can take your socks off though!). Crossing is safer with trekking poles or a stick, but make sure your poles are not going to telescope on you halfway across.

Crossing is safer in company – hold hands facing each other to give a broad base and better stability.

All the crossings on the End to End Trail are easy enough in normal conditions, but you are likely to get wet feet from time to time.

8 **Be careful when drinking water from streams.** It is still relatively safe to drink from streams in the British hills and moors, provided you are sure there is no human habitation or farming activity in the gathering grounds of the stream. Never drink from streams below significant cattle populations. You could still be unlucky and pick up a stomach bug, but it's never happened to me, and whenever I can I drink from streams rather than carry water.

Hazardous Wildlife

Romany Hint for Hikers

To ward off gnats and mosquitoes, boil a handful of elder leaves...add a few drops of oil of lavender and rub a drop on the arms, legs and face.
Watch for weasels and stoats.

The wildlife in Britain is not really very dangerous.

You may see snakes, particularly adders, from the first day onwards, but although they are poisonous, the chances of serious injury or death are very small. The other serious danger is from Lyme Disease, which can be carried by ticks in deer country. This can be a very unpleasant long-term illness, but again it is rare. (The majority of Lyme Disease cases in the UK actually occur in the southwest of England – comparatively few cases have been reported in northern England or Scotland, although that may be just because there are fewer people there, rather than fewer infected ticks.)

Ticks are a real nuisance in the Scottish Highlands, though, and it is a good idea to keep your legs covered while you are walking. If you don't, you will probably end up with a number of little black ticks firmly attached to your legs, digging in for a good meal. They are difficult to remove, and the old remedy of burning them off with a cigarette is now reckoned to be a bad idea, as it leaves the tick's mouthparts under your skin, which can lead to infection (also, fewer of us smoke these days). Ticks are reputed to be easier to get off if you unscrew them anticlockwise (but don't take that as gospel).

So much for the dangerous stuff. Now for the really annoying ones: mosquitoes, clegs and the dreaded midge.

Midges and mosquitoes are worst at dawn and dusk, can occur anywhere in the summer months, and although Keld on the Pennine Way is notorious for midges, they are principally a problem in the Scottish Highlands. Clegs (horseflies) can turn up at any time of day. DEET-based repellents such as Jungle Formula discourage most insects, and although DEET is not particularly good for humans either, you do need to carry it with you in the Highlands. Nothing will really keep off the midges completely though, so try to avoid the Highlands in July and August, and be equipped to cover up, even in hot weather.

PREPARATION

When to Go

Romany Hint for Hikers

Do not start camping too early in the year. The middle of April is quite soon enough to begin sleeping out, and even then you are likely to experience some cold nights.

Apart from whatever personal constraints there are on when you can set out, some objective considerations that will affect your decision are as follows.

1 There are restrictions on access to the Scottish hills in the deer-stalking and grouse-shooting seasons. In practice this means it is difficult to plan walking in many areas between 12 August and the end of October, and the best advice is to avoid the Scottish part of the route

during this period. If you do go then, you are likely to find yourself chasing round for permission to cross land and being diverted from your route. **Do not assume that any of the route in the Scottish hills is possible between 12 August and the end of October unless you have checked first**.

2 The midges and clegs in the hills, particularly in Scotland, are much worse in July and August than the rest of the year, and are likely to make your life a misery during that period. For this reason, **avoid the Scottish uplands during July and August**.

3 The Scottish Highlands in winter constitute a hostile environment requiring suitable experience and equipment, and this is outside the scope of anything normally described as a long-distance walk. Winter in this context stretches from October to April – extreme weather and ground conditions can occur throughout these months (and sometimes outside them). **Avoid the Highlands from October to April unless you are absolutely sure you know what you are doing**.

4 To walk a long way each day you need long days. The longest days are in June, but from April to September the days are long enough for most walkers to get tired before the daylight runs out.

The Wheel Stones and White Tor, Derwent Edge, Day 27

Taking all this into account, the recommended time of year for this walk is to start in April and finish before the end of June.

If you have to walk in the summer, then consider starting at the beginning of June at John O'Groats and walking north to south. If you do this, however, this guidebook will of course be describing the walk in the wrong direction, and be prepared for warm weather, crowds, and paths blocked by crops towards the end of the walk in the southwest.

If you intend to do the walk in separate chunks rather than all at once (see Distances and Daily Stage Lengths, above), your scheduling will be more flexible. This guidebook doesn't include any information on how to get to intermediate staging points, but this should not be difficult to arrange, as all the section ends are easily accessible by public transport.

Equipment

Romany Hint for Hikers

You should carry a pair of pyjamas, stockings, mackintosh and one spare shirt.
Do not wear collars and ties when you are hiking.
Never wear plus-fours. Not only are they insanitary through lack of ventilation, but the straps round the leg hinder the free flow of blood and cause varicose veins.

There should be no need to spell out what equipment you need for a long-distance walk, as it is assumed that if you are contemplating this route, you will be experienced enough to know already (and the other guidebooks you will need for parts of the route also include this kind of information), so again here are just a few tips.

1 **Travel light.** Nearly every guidebook says this, but the number of walkers with huge packs on long-distance paths makes it clear that a lot of people really find it difficult to separate what is necessary from what is 'nice to have'. What is not nice to have is a great weight on your shoulders, and as long as you are (i) warm enough during the day, (ii) warm and dry at night, (iii) able to find food and drink, and (iv) prepared for emergencies, then everything else should be regarded as optional. Weigh everything you're thinking of taking, think over whether you really need it at all, then if you do need it, try to find the lightest possible version. (See Packing List, at the end of this section.)

2 Remember that **things you can expect to last out a two-week walk won't necessarily last a two- or three-month one**. This doesn't matter so much for things that are easy to replace on the way (a list of equipment shops is given at the start of each section), but it is a

Constantine Bay, Day 5

good idea to have spare funds available just in case, and a replacement pair of boots, already broken in, ready to be sent to you if needed.

Plan what you are going to do if your tent disintegrates – have someone ready to post you a new one or lend you theirs.

John Merrill (author of *Turn Right at Land's End*) found that leather boots lasted about 2500 miles, and socks about three weeks. Hamish Brown (author of *Hamish's Groat's End Walk*) reckoned on 1000 miles for a pair of socks.

If you are keeping things in lightweight plastic bags, expect the bags to disintegrate within a couple of weeks at most.

3 **Don't take anything for your feet apart from your boots and your walking socks.** Search the shops for the lightest flip-flops you can find, then leave them out of your pack at the last moment (there speaks experience). Leave your boots at the door of pubs and bed and breakfasts and you are unlikely to be turned away. (Some hotels may have a different attitude, so avoid those that do.)

4 **Don't take too many spare clothes.** As long as you've got something dry to wear in the evening, and enough for the worst weather you can expect, then any more is luxury.

'Three socks – two to wear and one to wash' may sound a bit

extreme, but wash clothes whenever you can, and dry them overnight if you are in hostels or bed and breakfasts, or hang them from your rucksack when it's not raining.

John Merrill wore the same shorts for eight months on his coastal walk, and the same shirt for longer. They were each washed only once. I've done a week's walking in the Highlands with only one pair of socks – it was so wet they got washed continuously all day every day, and I kept them on in the evening since it was the best way to dry them out.

5 **Take big strong plastic bags to keep things dry in your rucksack.** You could consider a waterproof rucksack cover instead, but when I tried this I found it a real nuisance, as it's so hard to get into your bag when you need to.

6 **Don't carry things** from Land's End to John O'Groats that you only need for a fraction of the journey. Post maps ahead and post them home again when finished with (see Posting Ahead, later in this introduction).

If you are planning to eat in pubs and cafés whenever practical, you can manage without cooking equipment until you get to Fort William, so either buy equipment in Fort William, or post it on.

7 **Cut up your maps and guidebooks** (including this one) and carry the parts you need for the trip, leaving behind what you only need for planning.

8 Camping does not necessarily mean carrying a huge amount of extra weight, as long as you can afford **good-quality, lightweight equipment**. Consider carrying a Gore-Tex bivi bag rather than a tent, and if you are sure you want a tent then get a very lightweight one. Until you get to Fort William, if you are going to use bed and breakfasts and hostels for most nights, a tent is not really needed. From Fort William you should equip yourself for camping and cooking anyway, even if you think you have solved all your accommodation requirements without needing to sleep out. You will often be a long way from help, and may not reach your objective every night, so one option is to buy a tent in Fort William and post your bivi bag home if you have one. A tent rather than a bivi bag enables you to shelter from the weather and the midges while you cook. You may also need a bigger rucksack from Fort William onwards.

9 If you regard taking **reading matter** as essential (some of us do and some of us don't), then go for maximum words per ounce – books are heavy. The best value I've found so far is an Oxford World's Classic edition of Herman Melville's *Moby Dick* – nearly 600

pages for only 250g (9oz), once the hard cover was cut off.

10 It is possible you may encounter driving **sleet or snow**, even in June, when crossing the higher passes in the Scottish Highlands. Be prepared for such conditions.

Packing List

Below is a list of things I set off with on an unsupported walk from Land's End. I have included it as a practical example of how to keep the weight of your pack down.

To this needs to be added the weight of whatever cash, food and drink I happened to be carrying each day. I didn't generally carry much food, but since the pack was so light I found I could afford to carry a full water bottle if need be, as even with this the pack was so light I didn't

Item	g	oz
Rucksack (Lowe Contour Event 35 litre)	870	30.7
Rucksack liner (strong plastic bag)	60	2.1
Sleeping bag (PHD Minim 400) in compression sack	790	27.9
Sleeping mat (cut down)	180	6.3
Gore-Tex bivi bag	560	19.8
Anorak (Gore-Tex Paclite)	490	17.3
Gaiters (light but leaky)	150	5.3
One pair of trousers	330	11.6
One spare pair of underpants	60	2.1
One spare T-shirt	115	4.1
One spare pair of liner socks	30	1.1
One spare handkerchief (silk)	10	0.4
Silk headscarf (to protect bald head)	10	0.4
Toilet bag	10	0.4
Soap	35	1.2

Item	g	oz
Toothbrush (disposable hotel freebie)	5	0.2
Toothpaste	20	0.7
Disposable razor	10	0.4
Towel (small 'Packtowl')	50	1.8
Compeed blister patches in box	25	0.9
Vaseline (small tin) – for feet	30	1.1
Toilet paper	20	0.7
Maps (days 1 to 18, cut down)	340	12.0
Reference notes, including draft maps for this book	80	2.8
Extra writing materials (to make notes for this book)	55	1.9
Wallet (Ortlieb), bank cards, stamps & YHA card	25	0.9
Knife (Opinel – these are very light)	15	0.5
Platypus water container (1 litre)	30	1.1
Plastic bags and ties	60	2.1
Camera (Ricoh GR1S) and accessories	235	8.3
Films (professional quality, not easy to restock en route)	310	10.9
Book to read (*Moby Dick*)	250	8.8
Total pack weight	**5.3kg**	**11lb 9oz**

really notice it. The only things I needed to add on the way were sun-screen and Ibuprofen tablets. I also carried a map case (with a compass in it) and a pair of trekking poles, and set off in shorts and a fleece. I wore the lightest waterproof walking boots I could find (Brasher Supalites –1200g the pair).

At Fort William I switched to a larger rucksack, swapped the bivi bag for an ultra-lightweight Macpac tent (1570g), and added a lightweight gas stove, a pan, a Lexan spoon and some

Uisge Dubh and Bendronaig Lodge, Day 53

insect repellent. This put the weight without food and drink up to 7.7kg, or 17lb. I also had to add a lot of dried food, so for the first time I was feeling the weight. It was still a pretty light pack under the circumstances though. Everything turned out to be needed except the blister patches!

Romany Hint for Hikers

Cut your tent pegs
from the hedges.
If you do not wish to go to the
trouble of making a pack, you
can purchase a rucksack very
cheaply nowadays.

Companions

Whether you go on your own or with companions is of course up to you. Most people walking Land's End to John O'Groats seem to go on their own (presumably this is due to an inability to find anyone else daft enough to want to), and if you do so, don't forget to take extra safety precautions in case you get lost or injured in the hills (see Safety, above).

Please don't use this guide to take large numbers along all or part of the route. Much of it is on land that will be damaged by too much of that sort of treatment, so no mass sponsored relays please!

Planning Your Schedule

When walking day after day, you are capable of less per day than for a big, one-off effort. Remember that a lot of the walk involves climbing and descending, and difficult terrain, and that includes the first section along the Cornish coast (although for the

Romany Hint for Hikers

If you really want to enjoy the sport of hiking, you must first get yourself into good condition. Do not be tempted to rush out and buy a nice-looking pair of brogues with which to start your hike...Do not wear new boots or shoes of any description.

first week the daily stage lengths have been kept to below 32km (20 miles) a day, to give a fairly steady start to the journey), so don't start a walk like the End to End Trail unless your basic physical fitness is good. If you can get in a few days' walking before you start, that will help, particularly by hardening up your feet, but you will mainly get walking fit by starting the walk.

There should be no reason why anyone capable of walking, say, the Pennine Way cannot complete this walk, although you need to be confident you can maintain the daily mileage of your planned schedule, so don't set off at an unrealistic pace. If you haven't done any training beforehand, you are unlikely to be able to follow the Main Schedule given in this guide until you have been walking for a couple of weeks at least. Keep to a lower daily distance until your fitness has improved.

Angel's Wings shelter near Clovelly, Day 8

Walking long days

Romany Hint for Hikers
Hikers are usually early risers.
Do not try to exceed twenty miles
in a day, especially for the
first few hikes.

The day stages suggested in the two-month Main Schedule are significantly longer than those normally proposed in walking guides – an average of 32km (20 miles) a day. This is in order to get the walk finished in a reasonable length of time (if you can consider two months to be a reasonable length of time).

Following the three-month Alternative Schedule, summarised in Appendix 1, or one of your own devising, you can of course make the daily stages shorter, and stretch the walk to 12 weeks or more, but it is difficult enough for most people to get more than three weeks' holiday at a time, never mind three months. A three-month trip will also cost a lot more than a two-month trip.

'For all would-be walkers I've only three pieces of advice. Make sure you're in good condition, have a good pair of feet, and know how to take care of them.'
Jim Musgrave, winner of the 1960 Billy Butlin race, from the foreword to *The Big Walk* by A Walker, 1961.

You need to do three things to be able to walk long days: the first is to get reasonably fit, the second is to look after your feet, and the third is to set out early each morning.

Fitness If you can confidently set off for a day walk of 50km (30 mile) on footpaths in reasonably hilly country, then you are probably fit enough to follow the Main Schedule in this book from Day 1. To get to this state of fitness (assuming you are not already there) you will need to practise. Make up your own routes, or follow published routes, and go on your own or in company. There are many organised walking events that can help, usually with refreshments provided at checkpoints around the route. If you want to find out more about these, join the Long Distance Walkers' Association (LDWA) – see Appendix 3 for details. The LDWA organises many events and publishes details in their newsletters.

Feet and Boots It is more important to have comfortable, broken-in boots than to be at your absolute best at the start of the walk (you will soon either be fit or have given up). Your feet are likely to need more looking after if you are walking longer days than usual. Boots that give no trouble on 25km walks can give serious blisters over 40km, so before you set out, be sure that you have proven the capabilities of your boots and socks on a number of long days.

Setting Out Early Each Morning Do this to maximise the amount of time available for walking. If you are camping, get up and set off straight away, eating your breakfast on the move. If you are staying in bed and breakfast, ask for an early breakfast, or pay the previous night and skip a sit-down breakfast altogether, if necessary. Try to avoid running out of daylight before you run out of walking.

Romany Hint for Hikers
It is better to stop an hour before fatigue than an hour after.

Allowing for Contingencies

Allow some extra days for contingency – some things will inevitably go wrong. Your feet may need a day or two to rest; you may get lost and lose a day; you may encounter weather so bad that you lose several days; your equipment may fail – boots disintegrate, tents rip. Try not to run out of time to complete the walk.

To put this into perspective, many of the authors of accounts of End to End walks (see Appendix 2) were stopped temporarily due to stress injuries to their feet or legs (as was I on my walk). One of the Naylor brothers (*From John O'Groat's to Land's End*) was unable to walk properly for many days due to a swollen ankle; John Hillaby (*Journey Through Britain*) was laid up in Bristol with swollen and painful calves for a while; Chris Townsend (*The Great Backpacking Adventure*) had to stop for four days in Stafford with a badly bruised ankle; John Merrill (*Turn Right at Land's End*) suffered a stress fracture to his foot that put him out of action for weeks. They also all experienced equipment failure of one sort or another, and all were delayed by the need to wait for shops to open, or to collect a parcel from a post office – this should be enough evidence to persuade you to factor into your plans at least a week's contingency.

Mental strain

Something that is not always acknowledged is that undertaking a walk of this length can be a mental strain as well as a physical one. Many authors of accounts of End to End walks describe episodes during which they were on the point of giving up – it is difficult for most people to stay positive and single-minded for such a long time. This is one of the reasons for reading some of these accounts before you go, as they give a good picture of the mental challenge as well as the physical one.

Written Information

Access to a photocopier is useful, as it allows you to copy parts of books rather than carrying the whole thing (including this one), and to photoreduce both printed and handwritten information to get it to weigh less (use both sides of the paper!). Don't go overboard on the copying, though –

please do buy the guidebooks you need (the usual guidance is that it is acceptable to make a single photocopy of something 'for research or private study').

Posting Ahead

The main reason for having parcels posted on to you is that the maps and guidebooks you will need for the whole journey are too heavy to consider carrying all at the same time (although the fewer parcels you have, the less you will be delayed by waiting for post offices to open, or worse, by the failure of a parcel to arrive). Getting a supply of clean clothes by post is more of a luxury, but you might as well take advantage of the opportunity for this. (Include spare wrapping paper and sticky tape in each parcel to make it easy to send back the stuff you no longer need.)

A package at the end of each of the first five sections is not a bad approach: Bridgwater, Knighton, Hebden Bridge, Jedburgh and Fort William. But don't forget that parcels sometimes get lost or delayed in the post, so have a contingency plan for this.

You can get a leaflet from post offices explaining how to collect post from main post offices at no extra charge. Addresses of individual post offices can be found on the web at www.postoffice.co.uk. Alternatively, you can make arrangements with the places you are planning to stay at, such as youth hostels.

Money

Plan your finances well in advance – it is likely to cost a lot of money to complete the trip. Two months on holiday costs four times as much as a two-week holiday, and if you have to take unpaid time off work, make sure you have worked out the financial implications. (Also, don't forget the cost of getting to Land's End and getting home from John O'Groats.)

Having made sure you've got the money to finance the walk, you need to make sure you can spend it. In some areas banks and cash machines (ATMs) are few and far between, and carrying enough cash for the whole trip is too risky in my opinion, although it is an option. If you have a credit card, use this to pay whenever you can (but don't forget to pay it off as you go along, if you haven't got a direct debit to do this automatically). If your bank card won't work in a cash machine because it's the wrong bank, then your credit card may; you will pay a charge, but at least you will get your cash. Another option to consider is opening an account that allows you to withdraw cash at any post office. As the Royal Mail adapts to the commercial world, these arrangements keep changing – ask at your local post office well before you set off to find out what services are available.

When there is a bank and/or cash machine at the end of a daily stage, I have included this information. Where there is an ATM but no bank,

Union Canal, Linlithgow, Day 43/44

the machine is often inside a shop (often a Co-op), in which case it will only be accessible when the shop is open.

Carrying Food

Romany Hint for Hikers
Keep to wholesome plain food and an abundance of it.
Keep a supply of potatoes on hand.

As far as Fort William you should be able to manage carrying food for just a day or two at most – there are shops on most days, and pubs where food is available.

From Fort William onwards the situation changes, as there are far fewer opportunities to restock and eat out, so stock up at Fort William with what you need for the rest of the trip (you don't generally need to carry water, as there is no shortage of it in the Highlands). Since you are likely to need to carry enough food to last a few days, the best option is dried food, which is light for its nutritional value. It is also a good idea to carry food that needs little or no cooking, so you that don't need to carry so much fuel. If you already have experience of backpacking on long-distance paths, you will know what you like to take, and it is of course up to you and your personal tastes. (I don't take ready-prepared dried meals, for example, as I don't really like them much, and they are quite expensive.) Some suggestions are as follows.

- **Instant mashed potato** Just add to boiling water and it's done (it even includes salt, so you don't need to add any).
- **Couscous** Again you only need to mix with boiling water and leave for a few minutes – no need to cook (although you will need to add salt).
- **Polenta** Instant polenta takes 1 minute to cook. Again, add salt, and preferably some fat – cheese, butter or oil.
- **Pasta** Get the sort that cooks quickly so that you use less fuel. Quick-cook macaroni is usually easy to find, although it does need boiling for a few minutes, so uses more fuel than other carbohydrates.
- **Dried vegetables** Supermarkets usually carry a range of dried vegetables – onions, peppers, and mixtures including aubergines, mushrooms, etc. Anything that needs only a few minutes to cook will do (so avoid dried peas, for example). Add the dried vegetables to the water you are heating for your potato, couscous or polenta, and by the time the stodge is ready, the veg will be ready as well.
- **Dried herbs and spices** Take some mixed herbs or oregano to add flavour to whatever you're cooking. Chilli powder is good value too.
- **Instant soup** This already includes dried veg and herbs (and often other less natural ingredients as well). You can use it to flavour your stodge, not just as soup.
- **Cheese** Some strong hard cheese, stored in a plastic bag, will keep for a long time provided the weather isn't too hot. Strong cheese means you need to carry less to get the flavour, and the fat will improve whatever you're cooking. Parmesan or strong cheddar works well.
- **Biscuits, chocolate, etc** These keep you going through the day, but always run out sooner than you expect!
- **Dried fruit and nuts** These are good food value for the weight, and easy to eat on the march.
- **Fresh food** Whatever you fancy for the first day or two after restocking – bread, fruit, etc. (keep the dried stuff for when you really need it).

ACCOMMODATION AND SERVICES

This guide doesn't include a complete list of accommodation, as such lists quickly become out-of-date. Instead it includes the information you will need to collect together your own up-to-date lists. At the beginning of each section there is advice on how to get hold of accommodation information, and some general background about the accommodation situation along that section. The only times specific addresses are given are where the options are particularly limited.

Although local tourist information centres (TICs) are listed along with accommodation, it is worth pointing out that from any TIC you can get an up-to-date map giving the locations, addresses and phone numbers of all the TICs in the country.

Bed and Breakfast

Bed and breakfast can be found on or close to the route just about everywhere, apart from the Scottish Highlands beyond Fort William. Bed and breakfast in a pub has the obvious advantage of being close to an evening meal and a drink, but on the other hand there is often noise from the bar when you are trying to get to sleep. Also, an early breakfast is less likely to be an option in a pub, as people running pubs tend not to get early nights, so can't be expected to be up too early in the morning.

It is not a good idea to book your accommodation too far ahead, since on a journey of this length there are too many things that could happen to force a change of plan. It is at least four times as likely that something will go wrong on a two-month walk than on a two-week walk. Boots disintegrate, feet and legs may need first aid and a rest, the weather may slow you down, a parcel of maps may not arrive when you expect it. Take accommodation information, and if you want to book ahead do it no more than a week in advance. A day in advance is usually enough, particularly if you have the option of camping if you need to.

If you are walking alone, bed and breakfast can be easier to find at the last minute anyway, since many bed and breakfasts are reluctant to let a double room out to a single person until they have given up on getting a booking for two.

Having said all this, accommodation on the West Highland Way and the last day or two approaching John O'Groats is often insufficient to meet demand, so booking in advance is advisable on these two sections if you can.

Youth Hostels

Youth Hostels provide cheap accommodation for walkers, usually in shared dormitories. There are some on the route along the South West Coast Path, some along the Pennine Way, and a few at other places on the route, all referred to in the daily stage summaries. Unfortunately the YHA has recently closed down some of those that would have been useful in following the trail.

Youth hostels can be busy with noisy school parties at times, but provide a good alternative to bed and breakfast, particularly for solo walkers. Facilities for cooking your own food and drying clothes are usually pretty good. Join beforehand to get the latest handbook, or you can join at the first hostel you use on the route. The YHA operates those in England and Wales, and the SYHA those in Scotland (see Appendix 3). (**Note** Most youth hostels have limited opening seasons, and are often closed one or two nights a week.)

Campsites

Romany Hint for Hikers
Generally permission to camp is given free of charge, but if a charge is made it is usually only a shilling or one and sixpence per week. If more than one and sixpence is asked refuse to pay.

Camping is cheap, but campsites tend to be mainly in areas that holiday-makers frequent, which means, for example, that there are plenty on the South West Coast Path and in the Pennines, but not around Bristol and Glasgow. If you want to camp where there are no campsites, ask at any of the farms you pass.

If the weather is too wet, camping gets miserable, since everything you have gradually gets wetter, with little chance to dry out (apart from possibly a couple of hours in a pub in the evening). Unless you are particularly hardy and your budget is tight, combining camping with bed and breakfast or youth hostels is probably the best approach. It gives you the flexibility of always having a shelter for the night, plus the chance to dry out and get clean when you need it.

Levant Tin Mine, Trewellard, Day 1

Bunkhouses and Camping Barns

There are a number of bunkhouses and camping barns on or close to the route, varying from basic to fully equipped. You generally need to take your own sleeping bag, and typically there will be a bunk, mattress or sleeping platform in a communal room. There may or may not be cooking and drying facilities. If you plan to use these, get hold of the Independent Hostel Guide (see Appendix 2), and join the YHA (Appendix 3), as they manage a number of camping barns.

Bothies

A bothy is a building in a remote location, suitable and available for an overnight stay. Facilities are basic – there are usually bare boards to sleep on, a table to eat off, and a fireplace to burn any fuel you can find legitimately. They are mostly in the Scottish hills, and a number are potentially useful places to stay on this walk.

They are free to stay in, and usually maintained by generous estate owners, or the Mountain Bothies Association (MBA), a voluntary organisation dedicated to the maintenance of bothies. The catch, from the reader's point of view, is that I'm not usually going to tell you where they are. The reason for this is that the MBA has a policy of discouraging publicity about the location of bothies, to discourage too many people from using them. The logic behind this is that a proportion of users are vandals, so the more users the more vandalism (and they are, unfortunately, frequently vandalised). (Until recently this policy extended to not even telling MBA members where the bothies were, and one odd effect of this was that you were more likely to meet Germans than Scots in some bothies, since the location of at least

USING BOTHIES

If you use bothies, whether MBA bothies or not, then please observe the MBA Bothy Code.

'The bothies maintained by the MBA are available by courtesy of their owners. Please respect this privilege. Please record your visit in the Bothy Log Book.

Respect Other Users

- Please leave the bothy clean and tidy with dry kindling for the next visitors.
- Make other visitors welcome. If they are not MBA members set a good example.

cont. p46

Respect the Bothy

- Tell us about any accidental damage. Don't leave graffiti or vandalise the bothy.
- Please take out ALL rubbish that you can't burn.
- Avoid burying rubbish – this pollutes the environment.
- Please don't leave perishable food as this attracts vermin.
- Guard against fire risk and ensure the fire is out before your leave.
- Make sure the doors and windows are properly closed when you leave.

Respect the Surroundings

- If there is no toilet at the bothy, please bury human waste out of sight. Use the spade provided, keep well away from the water supply and never use the vicinity of the bothy as a toilet.
- Never cut live wood or damage estate property. Use fuel sparingly.

Respect our Agreement with the Estate

- Please observe any restrictions on use of the bothy, for example, during stag stalking or at lambing time.
- Please remember bothies are available for short stays only. The owner's permission must be obtained if you intend an extended stay.
- Unless the safety of the group requires the use of shelter in bad weather, bothies are not available for large groups of 6 or more because of overcrowding and the lack of facilities such as toilets. For the same reasons groups are asked not to camp outside bothies. Groups wishing to use a bothy should first seek permission from the estate.

Respect the Restrictions on Numbers

- Because of overcrowding and lack of facilities, large groups (6 or more) should not use a bothy or camp near a bothy without first seeking permission from the owner.
- Bothies are not available for commercial groups.

Bothies are used entirely at your own risk.'

some of them appears to have been published in a German guidebook.)

So how do you find out where the bothies are? The first thing is to join the MBA (see Appendix 3). Even if you can't find the time to help on maintenance working parties, at least your subscription will go into the pot. For your money you will get the locations of all the bothies the MBA maintains, and a regular newsletter. The second thing to do is talk to people you meet when walking in the Highlands – many of them will know where the bothies are.

Equipment Shops

There is a good chance you will need to replace equipment as you go along, since the walk is such a long one. A list of shops that sell walking equipment is given at the start of each section, but shops come and go of course. For the latest information the websites www.yell.com and www.ramblers.org.uk are good places to start.

Food Shops

In Section 6, beyond Fort William, there are few opportunities to buy food. For this reason there is a list of food shops included in that section. (See also Carrying Food, earlier in this introduction.)

Pubs

> **Romany Hint for Hikers**
> If you are tramping through a village, make a meal off a nice piece of new bread and cheese washed down with a tankard of foaming ale.

For many walkers, pubs are of great importance, and I have pointed out many of those that are on or near the route. Pubs are often the only places where there is any chance of finding food and drink out in the country – there is much more chance of finding a pub than a village shop, for instance. If you are camping they are often the only places you can spend a warm and dry evening in bad weather (and of course they also serve beer, which is an essential part of the diet of many walkers, including mine).

Any pub or hotel I've described as 'recommended' means I've been there, and would go back again given half a chance. Most, but not all, of the pubs mentioned serve food, and some have accommodation as well.

Real ale enthusiasts will find they are well provided for as far as the Scottish border, after which prospects become patchy as far as Fort William, although you will still be able to find some excellent beer. Don't expect to find much traditional foaming ale in the Scottish Highlands, though – things are improving, but unfortunately it's still rare.

White Castle, Monmouthshire, Day 17

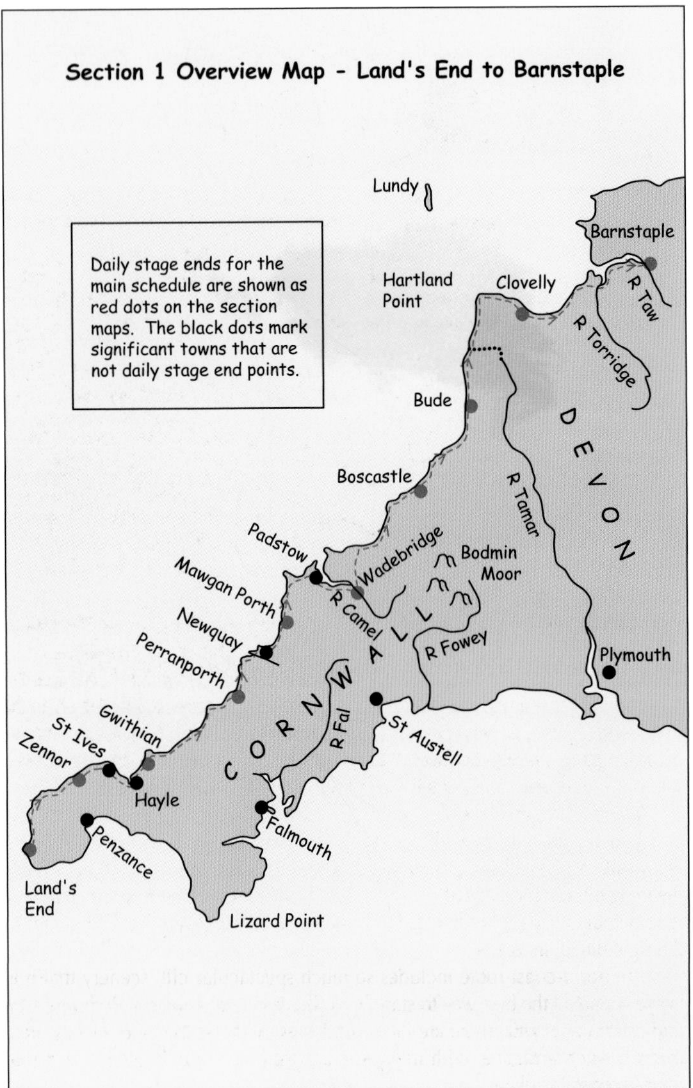
Section 1 Overview Map - Land's End to Barnstaple
Daily stage ends for the main schedule are shown as red dots on the section maps. The black dots mark significant towns that are not daily stage end points.
Lundy
Barnstaple
Hartland Point
Clovelly
R Taw
R Torridge
Bude
DEVON
Boscastle
R Tamar
Padstow
Wadebridge
Bodmin Moor
Mawgan Porth
R Camel
Newquay
CORNWALL
R Fowey
Plymouth
Perranporth
R Fal
St Austell
Gwithian
St Ives
Zennor
Hayle
Falmouth
Penzance
Land's End
Lizard Point

SECTION 1
The South West Coast Path: Land's End to Barnstaple

Distance 268km (166 miles)

Road Walking 13%. This is mainly through coastal towns such as St Ives, Hayle and Newquay, plus the private Hobby Drive through the woods near Clovelly.

Days 9 (Main Schedule), or 13 (Alternative Schedule)

Maps and Guides

- *Land's End to Constantine Bay*: South West Coast Path guide
- *Constantine Bay to Port Isaac:* this guide, strip maps Day 5 Map 1 to Day 6 Map 2
- *Port Isaac to Kipling Tors*: South West Coast Path guide
- *Kipling Tors to Bideford*: this guide, strip map Day 9 Map 1
- *Bideford to Barnstaple*: South West Coast Path guide

From Land's End in Cornwall to Barnstaple in Devon the Trail follows the South West Coast Path (SWCP). This is a national trail, so rights of way have been created where they were previously missing, and the route follows the coast closely.

The coastal scenery along the north coast of southwest England is so good that it seems a bit perverse to try to go any other way, although by its very nature a coastal path is rarely the most direct possible route between A and B, and this one is no exception, following the coast round headlands and bays.

Inland routes are possible, but footpaths going in the right direction are few, and you would end up walking many miles on tarmac. The south coast of Cornwall has considerably more deep estuaries and indentations to get round, meaning either taking ferries (which is not allowed on this End to End walk!) or long detours inland, often on roads. Also, the south coast doesn't really point in the right direction anyway.

The north-coast route includes so much spectacular cliff scenery that it is unquestionably the best way to start the walk (despite missing out Bodmin Moor and Dartmoor). While there are many tourist resorts in this popular holiday area, it is still very attractive, with many small seaside communities and plenty of remote coastal walking.

The north coast is rocky for much of the way, and there is rarely a road along it, apart from where the path passes through coastal towns such as Newquay and St Ives. This makes for mostly excellent walking on good paths, except for occasional areas of sand dunes (often avoidable by walking on the beach). In common with many coastal walks there are plenty of steep climbs, but none is very long.

There are opportunities for short cuts and variations, but only four places where it seemed worth recommending an alternative to the official national trail, which is after all an excellent route. Between Padstow and Rock the SWCP takes a ferry, so the alternative via Wadebridge is necessary to avoid cheating if you want to be able to claim you *walked* all the way.

Maps

1:25000 Explorer maps
102 Land's End
104 Redruth & St Agnes
106 Newquay & Padstow
111 Bude, Boscastle & Tintagel
126 Clovelly & Hartland
139 Bideford, Ilfracombe & Barnstaple

1:50000 Landranger maps
203 Land's End & Isles of Scilly
200 Newquay & Bodmin
190 Bude & Clovelly
180 Barnstaple & Ilfracombe

Guidebooks

The South West Coast Path by Paddy Dillon (Cicerone, 2003)
This guide includes 1:50000 OS strip maps. Unfortunately it describes the route in the wrong direction for the End to End Trail, but then so do most of the alternatives (see *South West Coast Path National Trail: Poole Harbour to Minehead*, below, for the exception).

The South West Coast Path, South West Coast Path Association (revised annually)
This annual publication includes details of the latest changes to the route and has a comprehensive accommodation guide, although it too describes the route in the wrong direction for the Trail. Available from the SWCPA (see Appendix 3), and free to SWCPA members.

South West Coast Path National Trail: Poole Harbour to Minehead, South West Coast Path Association (2004)
This gives a route description in the right direction, but doesn't include all the other useful information in the annual guide.

Recommendations

For this part of the Trail you are not really in any danger of getting seriously lost, even if you rely only on the guidebook maps – the trick is to keep the sea on your left. The detailed route finding can be surprisingly tricky at times, though, so hints from guidebooks are significant time-savers, and the SWCPA's *Poole Harbour to Minehead* guide in particular gives you warning of where you are likely to go astray. The guidebooks are all well written and researched, and give plenty of information about the route, and points of interest along the way.

My suggestion is to get the Cicerone guide (or an alternative that also includes OS strip maps) and the two SWCPA guides, to save you time in getting accommodation lists and for the other useful information they contain. Get Explorer 106 to cover the Trevone to Port Isaac shortcuts (Days 5 and 6), unless you already have Landranger 200. Get Explorer 139 to cover the shortcut from Westward Ho! to Bideford (Day 9), unless you already have Landranger 180. You should be able to manage without other maps.

To Help You on Your Way

Accommodation

Because this area is so popular for seaside holidays, accommodation is plentiful, although it can fill up in the summer and the Easter holidays. Apart from the most remote section, between Bude and Clovelly, there are plenty of alternative places to halt, with many bed and breakfasts and campsites. Not all campsites provide for backpackers though – some will charge the same rate as for a frame tent and a car. The annual South West Coast Path Association guide (see above) includes a comprehensive accommodation list, so is recommended. The only additional information you may need, apart from that in your YHA handbook, is a bit more about accommodation near Land's End and around Wadebridge. TICs for Land's End and Wadebridge are as follows.

Station Road, Penzance, tel 01736 362207 www.go-cornwall.com
The Rotunda, Eddystone Road, Wadebridge, tel 0870 122 3337
www.wadebridgelive.com

Equipment Shops

Day 1 Millets, 105 Market Jew Street, Penzance, tel 01736 363204
Day 3 Aztec Leisure, Old Garage, Trevellas, St Agnes, tel 01872 552372
Day 3 County Leisure, Hurling Barrow, Sevenmilestone, St Agnes, tel 01872 554406 (GR727490, about 3km inland)
Day 4 Camping Shop, Morfa Halls, 22a Cliff Road, Newquay, tel 01637 877619
Day 5 Country Wise, 5 Eddystone Rd, Wadebridge, tel 01208 812423
Day 6 Cycle Sport & Leisure, Fore Street, Tintagel, tel 01840 770060
Day 7 Tracks, 20 Queen Street, Bude, tel 01288 356689
Day 8 Clovelly Clothing Co, The Car Park, Clovelly, tel 01237 431070
Day 9 Mountain Warehouse, Atlantic Village, Bideford, tel 01237 429100
Day 9 RNS Marine & Leisure, Old School Rooms, Bridge Street, Bideford, tel 01237 474167
Day 9 Millets, 91 High Street, Barnstaple, tel 01271 342937
Day 9 Cassies Camping & Leisure, Rolle Quay, Barnstaple, tel 01271 346198

The Start: Land's End

'It would be difficult to conceive of any battle-ground on the face of earth or ocean, where the clutch and conflict of the elements could be more terribly grand than at Land's End.' Elihu Burritt, *A Walk from London to Land's End and Back*, 1865

Land's End can be found at the end of the A30, 12km (8 miles) beyond Penzance. Penzance can be reached by train, and from there you can either walk or hitch-hike to Land's End, or catch a bus – contact Western National on 01209 719988 for times.

'The first sight of Land's End Hotel, a low, drab-coloured building standing on the bleak headland, is apt to beget in the wayfarer who approaches it at sunset a feeling of regret that he passed through Penzance without stopping for the night.' Thos D Murphy, *On Old-World Highways*, 1914

There has been a hotel at Land's End for a long time – Elihu Burritt stayed there in 1864 after walking from London. More recently it has expanded into a small theme park, which is a good place to take children for a day out, but not a hiker's natural habitat. The Land's End complex usually gets a bad press from walkers, with the national press, outdoor magazines and walkers' guidebooks referring to it as an awful eyesore despoiling the whole area.

If you're there on a sunny weekend in summer you are likely to get that impression as well, but it's different when it's quieter. There are still big car parks and some ugly buildings, but the buildings are mainly together in a compact group, with the garish bits facing inwards rather than outwards. It's the number of visitors that makes it unpleasant, not the facilities. I'd much rather visit Land's End than Newquay, for example, provided it's out of season, or in the evening when it's quiet.

'At Sennen the inhabitants are most primitive, and there are those amongst them who believe in witchcraft, sorcery, snake-charming and other fables of bygone generations.' Evelyn Burnaby, *A Ride from Land's End to John O'Groats*, 1893

'Sennen, a forlorn collection of stone huts...' Thos D Murphy again

Sennen, which is the last village on the A30, 1.5km (1 mile) before Land's End, is a bit more respectable these days, and the place to stay the night before you set off, rather than Land's End itself, which is only a short walk along the A30. At Sennen there's an independent hostel (www.whitesandslodge.co.uk), a campsite, bed and breakfasts and a pub. (Land's End youth hostel is actually 8km (5 miles) north of Land's End.)

Walkers are permitted through the grounds of the Land's End complex without charge. If you plan to collect evidence of your walk, don't forget to pick up a form and get it stamped, signed and dated at the visitor centre, if it's open, otherwise at the hotel reception. Five minutes from Land's End and the theme park is forgotten – you're on your way.

DAY 1

The Game's Afoot

Land's End to Zennor (26km, 16 miles)

I see you stand like greyhounds in the slips,
Straining upon the start. The game's afoot:
Follow your spirit; and upon this charge
Cry 'God for Harry! England and Saint George!'

Henry V, *William Shakespeare*

For most of Section 1 you will be following the route description in your chosen guidebook, so it is not repeated here. The recommended variations from the national trail are described in full, however, on the accompanying strip maps (see end of Section 1).

The Main Schedule daily stage lengths for the first week have been kept down to below 32km (20 miles) a day (32km is the average for the whole Trail). This is to give a reasonably gentle start to the walk, although it has to be said that coastal cliff walking is often steep and rough, so it won't feel that gentle.

You may want to perform some kind of ceremony to mark the start of your expedition, and for most of the year there should be no shortage of people to take photos of you. (This will probably have to be with *your* camera, however, as your trip is unlikely to be taken very seriously when you haven't even started.)

Head for the cliff top and turn right, in the direction of Sennen Cove, following your South West Coast Path guidebook. On the way round to Sennen Cove the cliff-top path gives superb walking from the very start. From Sennen Cove, as long as the tide isn't in too far, the sands of Whitesand Bay give much easier walking than the official SWCP route through the dunes.

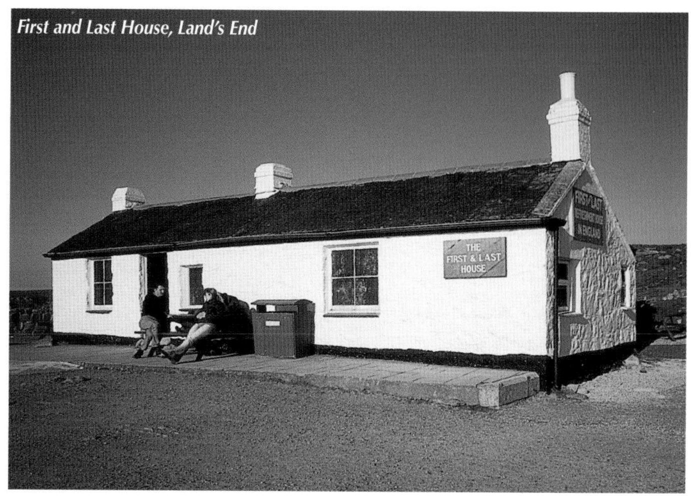

First and Last House, Land's End

At the far side of Whitesand Bay it's back to the cliff tops all the way to Cape Cornwall. Wild flowers are everywhere in spring: violets, squills, primroses, thrift, celandines, kidney vetch, campions, white bluebells, and even an area of escaped hottentot fig. There is also golden gorse in abundance.

Cape Cornwall is a small peninsula with a hill on top and an old tin mine chimney. From here all the way to Zennor there is evidence of the old tin mining industry, with many ruined buildings, tracks and spoil heaps. The Geevor mine was the last operational tin mine in Cornwall, closing in 1990, and is a scene of absolute devastation, but it is soon passed, and for the rest of the day it is back to spectacular cliff scenery. (It makes one wonder what a coastal walk would have been like when the mining was in full production – probably a lot less pleasant than it is now.)

From Cape Cornwall, continue along the SWCP to Pendeen Watch and Zennor. If you are breaking overnight at Pendeen Watch, 15km (9 miles) from Land's End, you will have to head inland to find accommodation. The road from the Pendeen Watch car park leads to Pendeen village, which has bed and breakfasts, and camping at the North Inn.

To reach Zennor itself, continue on the coastal path, crossing the footbridge in Pendour Cove (before Zennor Head), then going steeply up (steps) past a house on the right to a T-junction of paths and a National Trust signpost for Zennor

Cape Cornwall

Head. The SWCP continues by turning left here, but turn right and the track reaches Zennor in about 10 minutes.

Zennor has a very good pub, the Tinner's Arms (recommended), with a coal fire, and excellent food and beer. It's a tiny hamlet, and accommodation is restricted to an independent hostel, where you can also camp, and a bed and breakfast just outside the village.

DAY 2

St Ives Bay

Zennor to Gwithian (26km, 16 miles)

Today the Trail follows the SWCP through St Ives and round the Hayle estuary. It's 2km further if you go right round the Island – also known as St Ives Head – in St Ives and don't cut the corner.

Return to the point where you left the SWCP yesterday. The high point of the day is a tour of Zennor Head, glorious and remote. The Trail continues to be wild and adventurous until the descent to St Ives, and the first seaside resort of the walk. St Ives isn't a bad place, considering it's so dependent on income from tourism, but it marks the start of a pretty poor section of walking through to Carbis Bay – stick to the beach in Carbis Bay if the tide permits.

Soon after this, a frustrating trudge round the Hayle estuary starts. It gets progressively grimmer – through a golf course, along busy roads, and through abandoned industrial wasteland on the way out of Hayle.

At last you reach Hayle Towans and the open coastline again. Walk on the beach from here if you can – it's much easier than the path through the dunes. Eventually you reach the bay by Gwithian.

If you are heading for Gwithian itself, turn right when you reach the bay and follow the path to the village, which is a pretty place with thatched cottages. There is no shop, but there are two campsites in the village centre, bed and breakfasts, a café and the Red River Inn.

If you are not stopping overnight at Gwithian, you can cross the silted-up bay, then go over a footbridge over the stream to reach the car park at Godrevy (GR585422). The café will not necessarily be open, though, and the pub marked close by on maps has closed down.

Gurnard's Head from Zennor Head

DAY 3

More Tin Mining

Gwithian to Perranporth (31km, 19 miles)

Continuing along the South West Coast Path, the cliff-top path round Godrevy Point and along to Portreath gives another very good stretch of walking. There is a lot more evidence of the tin mining industry beyond Portreath.

Portreath itself is a good place to stop, with a surfers' beach, cafés, pubs, shops, bed and breakfasts, a youth hostel and a post office. The pasties from the bakery (by the post office) are particularly good.

Droskyn Point, near Perranporth

From Portreath to St Agnes Head the path follows the cliffs again, with brief and steep descents into Porthtowan and then Chapel Porth, followed by the inevitable climbs back out of the valleys.

You don't see much of St Agnes village from the coastal path, apart from a few houses at Trevaunance Cove, and the Driftwood Spars Hotel. The hotel is a recommended halt – they brew their own beer on the premises, and the cosy bar has an open fire and a collection of fascinating photographs of local shipwrecks.

There is much evidence of tin and tungsten mining on the final stretch along the cliffs and round Cligga Head to Perranporth. The cliff faces show the vivid colours characteristic of metal ores, including green streaks of copper sulphate.

Perranporth has plenty of facilities, including bed and breakfasts, a youth hostel, shops and pubs.

DAY 4

The Gannel and Watergate Bay

Perranporth to Mawgan Porth (27km, 17 miles)

Day 4 follows the South West Coast Path through dunes, across the River Gannel and through Newquay. Don't be tempted to take a ferry across the Gannel estuary – the recommended guidebooks give full details of the four tidal and non-tidal bridges. The distance of 27km assumes you can take the shortest route across the Gannel (the longest alternative is 4km (2½ miles) further).

There is a long stretch of dunes north of Perranporth, and as long as the tide isn't right in, the easiest walking by far is on the beach rather than in the dunes themselves (look out for the dancing shrimps though). At the end of the beach, climb up to round the cliffs on Ligger Point and Penhale Point, and descend again to Holywell Bay. You can avoid Holywell village altogether by crossing the stream by a footbridge in the dunes (a SWCP alternative route).

Newquay beach, unusually deserted

'New Quay is pretty, and is not yet overbuilt' – EW Fox, *2000 Miles On Foot*, 1911

In Crantock, just off-route before the Gannel crossing, there is a café (which closes when it rains) and also a very good pub, the Old Albion (good food, recommended). If the tide isn't yet low enough to use the tidal footbridge across the Gannel, this is all the excuse you need to visit Crantock.

Next comes Newquay, a big holiday resort stretching along the coast, and certainly not a rambler's paradise – things have moved on a bit since 1911. If the tide is out the best thing to do is avoid most of Newquay – get onto the beach at the first opportunity and follow that instead of the road through the town. Newquay stretches a long way, but eventually you reach the far end, and it's back to quiet cliff tops above Watergate Beach until the descent into the cove at Mawgan Porth.

At Mawgan Porth there is accommodation, including a campsite, and by the bridge is the Merrymoor Inn, which is welcoming and is recommended.

DAY 5

The Camel Estuary

Mawgan Porth to Wadebridge (28km, 17 miles)

'After a walk of about thirty miles, reached Wadebridge for tea' Elihu Burritt

For the first part of the day, until Treyarnon Bay, the Trail continues northwards along the South West Coast Path. Between Treyarnon Bay and Padstow you can shortcut two headlands if you want (see below) to save some distance (the SWCP takes the long way round). At Padstow the coast path meets its first major obstacle since Land's End – the estuary of the River Camel. The SWCP takes a ferry across the estuary to Rock, so the End to End Trail follows an alternative route via Wadebridge, rejoining the coast path at Port Isaac on Day 6.

The cliffs from Mawgan Porth north to Porthcothan and beyond to Treyarnon Bay are particularly spectacular, and worth taking your time over. There are narrow headlands and inlets, and offshore stacks and islands, and it's surprising the walking itself isn't more strenuous.

There's a youth hostel at Treyarnon Bay, and shortly after this you pass the end of the road up to the village of Constantine Bay. Don't go up the road, but follow either the coastal path in the dunes, or go along the beach, and turn right two or three minutes later, immediately behind a white coastguard hut on the beach. This is the start of a short cut along the golf course to Harlyn Bridge – strip map Day 5 Map 1 shows the way. (If you want to stay with the SWCP instead, and go the long way round via Trevose Head, this will add another 4km (2½ miles) to the day.)

About 1km after Harlyn Bridge, on the SWCP again, you reach the village of Trevone (if you are staying here overnight there are bed and breakfasts, a shop and a pub). Leave the Coast Path here and head up the road through the village, where another End to End Trail short cut takes you eastward directly to Padstow – see strip map Day 5 Map 2. (Again, you can stick to the Coast Path via Kellan Head if you wish – it is about 5km (3 miles) further.)

Mawgan Porth from Trenance Point

The short cut makes a beeline for Padstow across the fields, and is pleasant enough, descending to Padstow Harbour along Church Street and its continuation, Duke Street.

Padstow has all services, including a tourist information centre, and Rick Stein's fish restaurant (for which you will need to book well in advance).

Turn right at Padstow Harbour, and across a car park pick up the start of the Camel Trail, which the End to End Trail follows all the way to Wadebridge (Day 5 Map 3).

The Camel Trail is a popular waymarked Cornwall County Council route for cyclists and walkers. It follows a disused railway line along the River Camel from Padstow to Wadebridge, and then goes on to Bodmin. The cycle track can be unpleasantly busy during peak holiday times (another good reason for doing this walk in the spring), and the walking to Wadebridge is monotonous underfoot, but fast, with the estuary full of birdlife.

Wadebridge is the first proper town on the route since Newquay. It has a TIC, plenty of accommodation, and there is a campsite at Little Bodieve Holiday

Will's Rock and Park Head from above the Minnows Islands

Park (GR990735 – see Day 6 Map 1), although there have been mixed reports of how well it provides for backpackers.

DAY 6

Port Isaac Bay

Wadebridge to Boscastle (30km, 19 miles)

The Trail leaves the Camel Trail in Wadebridge to cross the River Camel, then goes northwards, following the River Amble. It climbs up to cross the hills that line the north coast and descends again to rejoin the SWCP at Port Isaac.

Looking north from Jacket's Point

The route is a good one (Day 6 Map 1). It enters meadows almost as soon as it has crossed the River Camel in Wadebridge, which is not yet entirely surrounded by suburbs. Once the busy B3314 has been left behind, more pleasant fields and meadows above the River Amble lead to the pretty village of Chapel Amble, which has an excellent pub, the Maltsters Arms, serving very good meals.

From Chapel Amble the dwindling stream is followed north, along wooded paths and through meadows, until the hills come close (Day 6 Map 2). These are tamed and cultivated hills, and the Trail climbs up through fields to cross the B3314 again at the old church of St Endellion, and descend gradually towards the coast, now laid out before you. The last kilometre to the coast is along a minor road that becomes steeper and steeper as it drops down into the quaint and typically Cornish fishing village of Port Isaac. (There is a grocery shop at the top of the hill at the eastern end of the village if you need it.)

From Port Isaac follow your South West Coast Path guidebook again, eastward round Port Isaac Bay then north to Tintagel Head. This is not such a wild stretch – rather than rough moorland cliff tops, the path follows field edges for part of the time. The first bit is still hard work though, with a number of steep descents to cross streams, the last one by Jacket's Point being the biggest.

Jacket's Point switchback

Trebarwith Strand is a pretty cove to pause at for lunch, and the Port William Inn here has tables right by the shore (recommended).

Continuing towards Tintagel Head, the path passes Tintagel youth hostel, and then you'll probably start meeting tourists visiting the ruins on the Island at Tintagel Head. Pay to go in and look round if you wish, but don't expect to see convincing evidence that King Arthur was ever here. Tintagel village is inland from here. It's very touristy, and in my opinion not worth going out of your way for.

'As for the story of King Arthur being both born and killed there, 'tis a piece of tradition, only on oral history, and not any authority to be produced for it' – Daniel Defoe, *A Tour Through the Whole Land of Great Britain*, 1724–6

The cliff path soon loses most of the tourists as it bends east again past two headlands, both called Willapark, with the chasm of Grower Gut in between. The day finishes by following the narrow, winding rock channel into Boscastle Harbour.

Boscastle is a lovely spot, with a small youth hostel by the harbour, and shops and pubs nearby. It suffered a devastating flash flood in storms in August 2004, but has not lost its character as a result.

'Squeezed into this gorge, there was one of the neatest, most romantic little harbours in the world' – Elihu Burritt on Boscastle

DAY 7

Bude Bay

Boscastle to Bude (25km, 16 miles)

Today, follow the South West Coast Path around the gradual curve of Bude Bay. There is quite a bit more walking along field edges, and a lot of up and down. From Boscastle to Bude (and on to Hartland Point – Day 8) is one of the most strenuous stretches of the whole End to End Trail, so don't underestimate it.

The Coombe Barton Inn at Crackington Haven, 10km (6 miles) from Boscastle, is recommended.

To cross the valley at Millook, 7km (4 miles) beyond Crackington Haven, the SWCP follows the road for the descent, and after this the road remains close by for most of the way to Bude. The approach to Bude is along a pretty dreary stretch of coastline, without the high cliffs that have, up till now, been bringing a lot of the drama to the views. Even the sand is dark brown. Eventually the path rounds Compass Point and takes you east into Bude, which has all services and plenty of accommodation.

'They tell me that Bude is a place that grows on you the more you see it. Well, I have seen it four times, now, and if I found it growing on me I should have it amputated.' – Colin Howard, *From Land's End to John O'Groats*, 1939

Bude is not that bad, but it's a full-time holiday resort, and admittedly a bit short on 'olde worlde' elements. The pasty shop is highly recommended, though, and this is your last chance of a genuine Cornish pasty, because tomorrow you'll be in Devon, so stock up here.

DAY 8

Hartland Point

Bude to Clovelly (37km, 23 miles)

It's the South West Coast Path all day again today, but not for much longer, so make the most of it. This is a very strenuous day, with a lot more climbing than any other day on the entire Trail (about 2400m), so you should only attempt to complete it in a day if you have found the preceding days well within your abilities, and can get an early start. The alternative is to split this stage into two days, with a break near Hartland Quay (see below).

Hartland Point, with Lundy in the distance

There is superb scenery again on the remote stretch north to Hartland Point, where a taxing series of switchbacks leads down one flight of steps then back up another, then good, fairly level walking east to Clovelly.

Heading north from Bude, the coast follows a pretty straight line. There are steep descents to Northcott Mouth and Duckpool, then comes Lower Sharpnose Point, where the path passes Cleave Camp signalling station, with its high fences and military warning notices.

At Higher Sharpnose Point a stream, the Tidna, runs out almost to the end of the point rather than into a bay – a curious geographical feature. At Morwenstow, a short distance inland from here, the eccentric poet Robert Hawker was vicar for 40 years in the mid-19th century. The path passes his cliff-top hut, built from driftwood, and the beautiful Norman parish church is well worth visiting.

Continuing north, as you cross the stream at Marsland Mouth, you finally leave Cornwall and enter Devon. This is after more than a week of hard walking, and no other county on the Trail takes anything like this long to traverse, until the huge Highlands and Islands region at the end of the journey.

This part of the coastline is remote, with few amenities. There is a campsite at Elmscott, a hotel at Hartland Quay, a couple of bed and breakfasts and another campsite just inland at Stoke, and that's about it until you get to Clovelly.

Bluebells in Brownsham Wood

The path from Hartland Quay to Hartland Point is dramatic, with wild cliff scenery and strenuous walking. Flat-topped Lundy Island is usually clearly in view out in the Bristol Channel. Lundy is a great place to visit if you want bird-watching, rock climbing or peace and quiet. The boat to Lundy sails from Bideford or Ilfracombe, depending on how high the tide is at Bideford. Hartland Point is a headland of savage cliffs with a lighthouse perched precariously on the end.

The walking from Hartland Point to Clovelly is good, and mostly reasonably level. There is a delightful bluebell wood at Brownsham, near the end of the day.

Clovelly itself is the classic 'chocolate box' fishing village, with a main street too steep for cars. It is a magnet for day-trippers, but in the evening they're nearly all gone, and it's a lot more pleasant. Don't make the mistake of going through the car park turnstiles – if you don't have a car you don't have to pay to get into the village. If you're staying in Clovelly, try to get accommodation in Clovelly itself, rather than in Higher Clovelly, so that you see the ridiculously picturesque old fishing village properly. Alternatively, there is a campsite at Dyke Green Farm by the A39 roundabout (GR314234).

'Talking to an old sea-dog at the inn, he tells me Clovelly is his native place, where all the inhabitants are related, so great was the custom of intermarriage' – EW Fox

DAY 9

Barnstaple Bay

Clovelly to Barnstaple (37km, 23 miles)

This is the Trail's last day on the South West Coast Path, and only the first part, as far as Westward Ho!, is really coastal. The scenery is good, but not as good as much of what has gone before. The cliffs are lower, the farmland tamer, and the coves fewer.

Clovelly village

At Kipling Tors, just before Westward Ho!, you need to make a decision. The route crosses the River Torridge today. One of the two official alternatives – the ferry from Appledore to Instow at the mouth of the river – is out of bounds, so you have to reach the Long Bridge at Bideford. To do this you can *either* follow the SWCP all along the coast and the estuary, via Northam Burrows and Appledore, *or* take the End to End Trail shortcut from Kipling Tors, saving about 8km (5 miles) – see Day 9 Map 1.

For the short cut, follow the SWCP until you see Westward Ho! ahead, then cut off right up the slope of Kipling Tors, an attractive hillside overlooking the sea that gives a good start to this stretch. The rest of the shortcut is less inspiring, but it does pass the Pig on the Hill at Pusehill, a pub that brews its own beer nearby (recommended). (If you are planning to stop overnight hereabouts, there is accommodation in Westward Ho! and in Bideford, but not currently at Pusehill.)

The short cut rejoins the SWCP at the quay in Bideford. Cross the Long Bridge over the River Torridge and follow the SWCP to Barnstaple, mainly along a disused railway track that makes for easy and fast walking. (For part of the way there is an alternative route across the marshes, which is slower but more interesting.)

There is plenty of accommodation in Barnstaple, and on the way out of the town the Trail passes the Reform Inn at Pilton, which brews its own beer in a brewery behind the pub (recommended, but doesn't serve meals).

Day 5 Map 1: Constantine Bay to Trevone

3. Turn left off the road after crossing Harlyn Bridge & follow the coast path again round St Cadoc's Point until you reach the next village (Trevone).

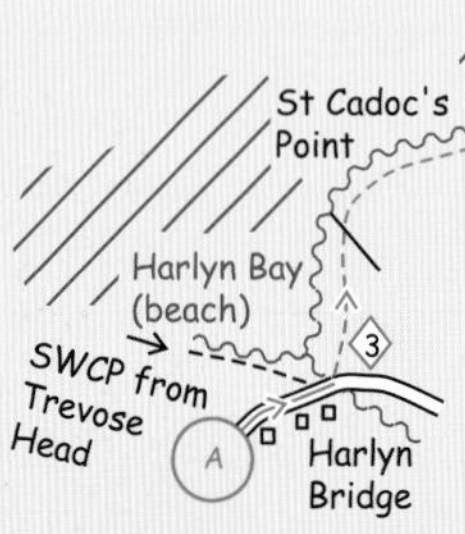

2. Pass a minor road to Trevose Head, then when the road bends slightly left take a signed footpath up steps to the right. Keep left to a stile, then slightly right to a gap in the hedge to join a drive. Go through the gate ahead, then after a few metres turn left off the drive to cross the road & follow the signed footpath across the field opposite. This leads to a residential road. Turn right along this, then left at a T-junction & follow this road down to cross Harlyn Bridge & rejoin the coast path.

1. Walk past the road end at the south end of Constantine Bay to the white coastguard hut (on the beach). Immediately behind this a path strikes inland over the dunes: follow it & it becomes a hedged path along the edge of Trevone Golf Club. It ends at a road junction: turn sharp left on the road towards Harlyn.

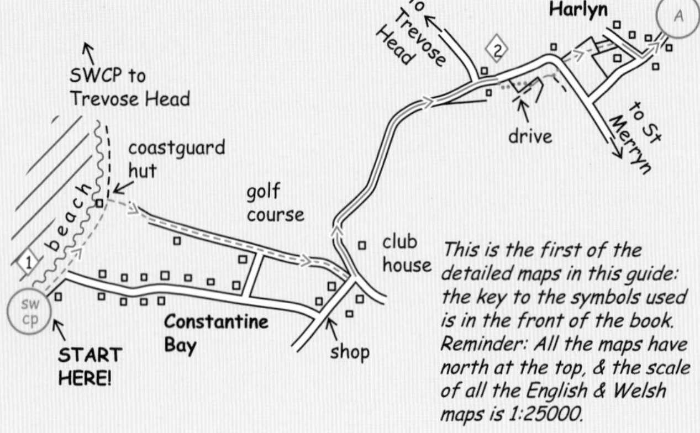

This is the first of the detailed maps in this guide: the key to the symbols used is in the front of the book. Reminder: All the maps have north at the top, & the scale of all the English & Welsh maps is 1:25000.

Day 5 Map 2: Trevone to Padstow

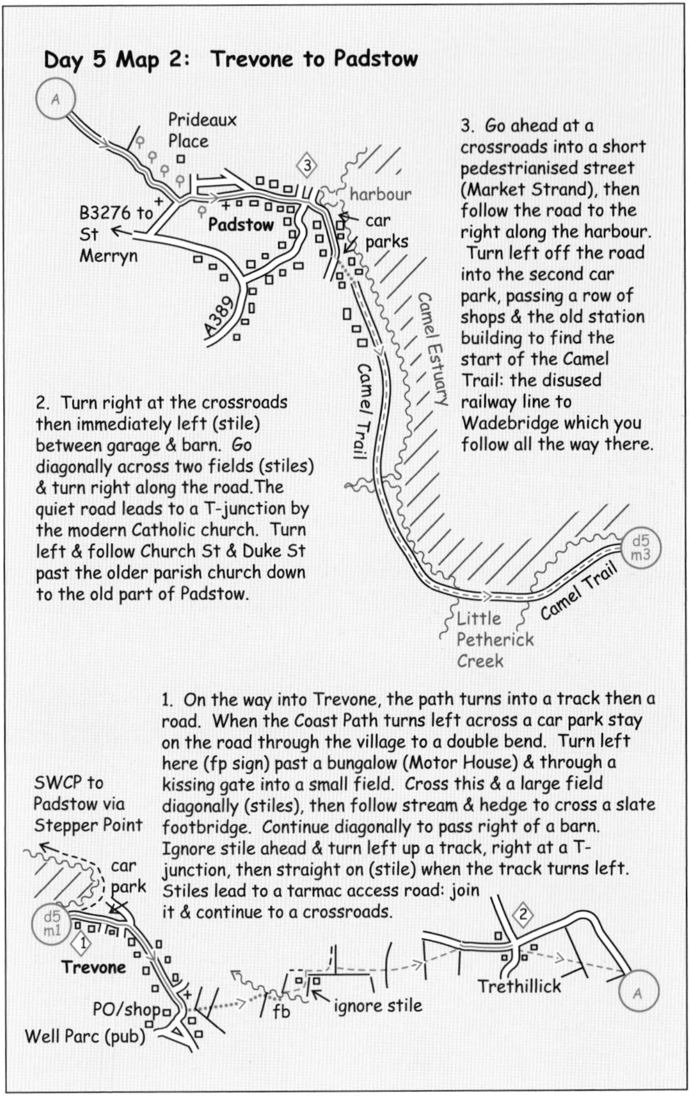

A

Prideaux Place

B3276 to St Merryn

Padstow

A389

3

harbour

car parks

Camel Estuary

Camel Trail

3. Go ahead at a crossroads into a short pedestrianised street (Market Strand), then follow the road to the right along the harbour. Turn left off the road into the second car park, passing a row of shops & the old station building to find the start of the Camel Trail: the disused railway line to Wadebridge which you follow all the way there.

2. Turn right at the crossroads then immediately left (stile) between garage & barn. Go diagonally across two fields (stiles) & turn right along the road. The quiet road leads to a T-junction by the modern Catholic church. Turn left & follow Church St & Duke St past the older parish church down to the old part of Padstow.

d5 m3

Camel Trail

Little Petherick Creek

1. On the way into Trevone, the path turns into a track then a road. When the Coast Path turns left across a car park stay on the road through the village to a double bend. Turn left here (fp sign) past a bungalow (Motor House) & through a kissing gate into a small field. Cross this & a large field diagonally (stiles), then follow stream & hedge to cross a slate footbridge. Continue diagonally to pass right of a barn. Ignore stile ahead & turn left up a track, right at a T-junction, then straight on (stile) when the track turns left. Stiles lead to a tarmac access road: join it & continue to a crossroads.

SWCP to Padstow via Stepper Point

car park

d5 m1

1

Trevone

PO/shop

Well Parc (pub)

fb

ignore stile

2

Trethillick

A

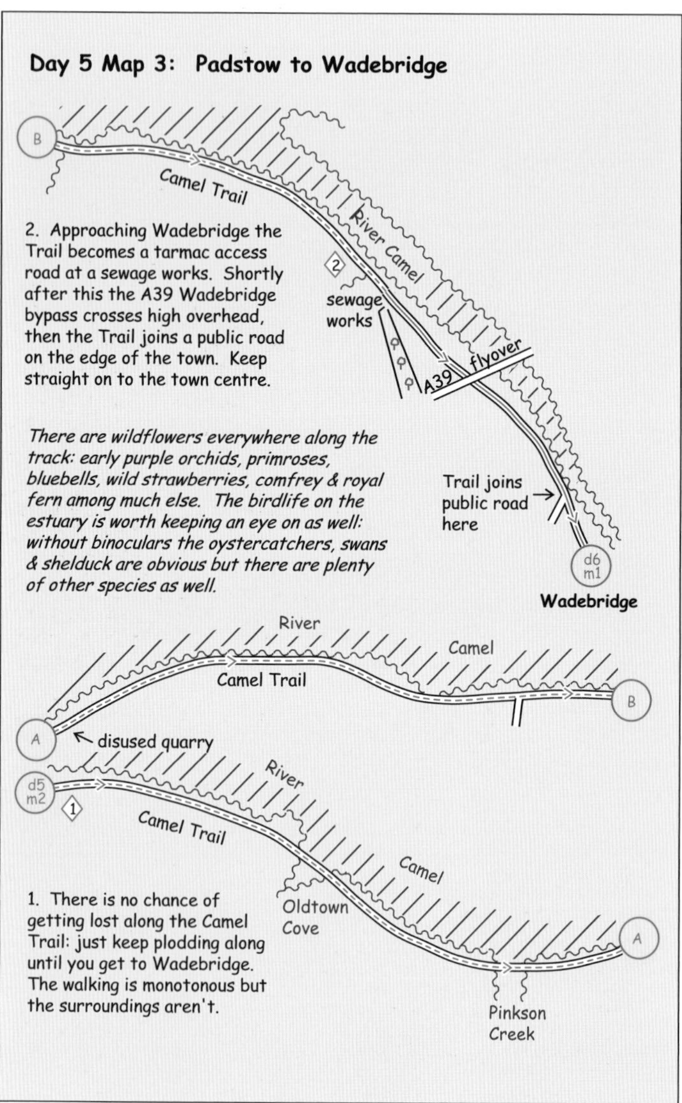
Day 5 Map 3: Padstow to Wadebridge
B
Camel Trail
River Camel
2
sewage works
A39
flyover
2. Approaching Wadebridge the Trail becomes a tarmac access road at a sewage works. Shortly after this the A39 Wadebridge bypass crosses high overhead, then the Trail joins a public road on the edge of the town. Keep straight on to the town centre.
There are wildflowers everywhere along the track: early purple orchids, primroses, bluebells, wild strawberries, comfrey & royal fern among much else. The birdlife on the estuary is worth keeping an eye on as well: without binoculars the oystercatchers, swans & shelduck are obvious but there are plenty of other species as well.
Trail joins public road here
d6 m1
Wadebridge
River
Camel
Camel Trail
B
A
disused quarry
d5 m2
1
River
Camel Trail
Camel
Oldtown Cove
A
1. There is no chance of getting lost along the Camel Trail: just keep plodding along until you get to Wadebridge. The walking is monotonous but the surroundings aren't.
Pinkson Creek

Day 6 Map 1: Wadebridge to Chapel Amble

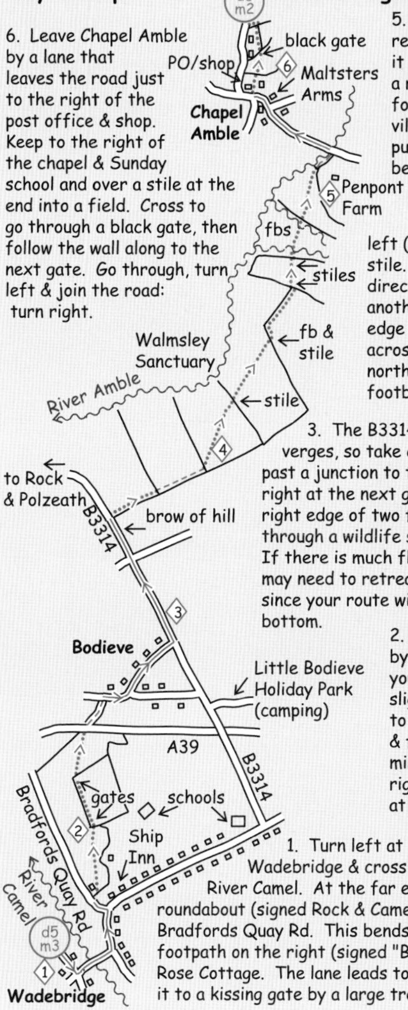

6. Leave Chapel Amble by a lane that leaves the road just to the right of the post office & shop. Keep to the right of the chapel & Sunday school and over a stile at the end into a field. Cross to go through a black gate, then follow the wall along to the next gate. Go through, turn left & join the road: turn right.

5. Keep left of Penpont Farm to reach the River Amble & follow it upstream on a clear path to a road bridge. Turn left & follow the road into the pretty village of Chapel Amble. The pub is recommended for both beer & food.

4. In the third field after leaving the B3314 turn half left (no path) down the field to a stile. Continue in the same direction across the next field to another stile then along the left edge of the next. Aim slightly left across the next field & continue north following stiles & footbridges.

3. The B3314 is busy, narrow, & has no verges, so take care: it is dangerous! Follow it past a junction to the brow of the hill. Turn right at the next gate (fp sign) & follow the right edge of two fields. The River Amble winds through a wildlife sanctuary down to the left. If there is much flooding in the valley then you may need to retreat & take an alternative route since your route will soon descend to the valley bottom.

2. Go through the kissing gate by the tree & keep the hedge on your left to a second gate. Aim slightly right in the next field to gates & the busy A39. Cross & follow the lane opposite to a minor road at Bodieve. Turn right, then left, then left again at the B3314.

1. Turn left at the mini-roundabout in Wadebridge & cross the Old Bridge over the River Camel. At the far end turn left at another mini-roundabout (signed Rock & Camelford), then turn left into Bradfords Quay Rd. This bends right, then take the footpath on the right (signed "Bodieve 1/2") to the right of Rose Cottage. The lane leads to a field: cut half right across it to a kissing gate by a large tree (no visible path).

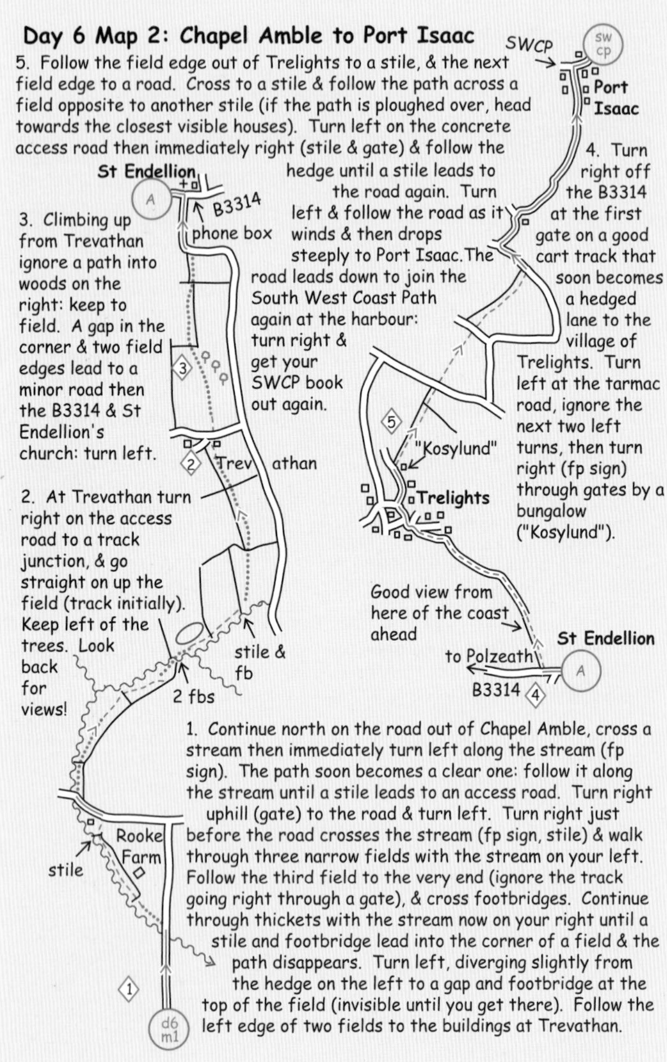
Day 6 Map 2: Chapel Amble to Port Isaac
5. Follow the field edge out of Trelights to a stile, & the next field edge to a road. Cross to a stile & follow the path across a field opposite to another stile (if the path is ploughed over, head towards the closest visible houses). Turn left on the concrete access road then immediately right (stile & gate) & follow the hedge until a stile leads to the road again. Turn left & follow the road as it winds & then drops steeply to Port Isaac. The road leads down to join the South West Coast Path again at the harbour: turn right & get your SWCP book out again.
SWCP
sw cp
Port Isaac
4. Turn right off the B3314 at the first gate on a good cart track that soon becomes a hedged lane to the village of Trelights. Turn left at the tarmac road, ignore the next two left turns, then turn right (fp sign) through gates by a bungalow ("Kosylund").
St Endellion
A
B3314
phone box
3. Climbing up from Trevathan ignore a path into woods on the right: keep to field. A gap in the corner & two field edges lead to a minor road then the B3314 & St Endellion's church: turn left.
3
5
"Kosylund"
Trelights
2
Trev athan
2. At Trevathan turn right on the access road to a track junction, & go straight on up the field (track initially). Keep left of the trees. Look back for views!
Good view from here of the coast ahead
St Endellion
to Polzeath
A
B3314
4
stile & fb
2 fbs
1. Continue north on the road out of Chapel Amble, cross a stream then immediately turn left along the stream (fp sign). The path soon becomes a clear one: follow it along the stream until a stile leads to an access road. Turn right uphill (gate) to the road & turn left. Turn right just before the road crosses the stream (fp sign, stile) & walk through three narrow fields with the stream on your left. Follow the third field to the very end (ignore the track going right through a gate), & cross footbridges. Continue through thickets with the stream now on your right until a stile and footbridge lead into the corner of a field & the path disappears. Turn left, diverging slightly from the hedge on the left to a gap and footbridge at the top of the field (invisible until you get there). Follow the left edge of two fields to the buildings at Trevathan.
Rooke Farm
stile
1
d6 m1

Day 9 Map 1: Kipling Tors to Bideford

3. The right of way between the A39 & A386 shown on OS maps does not coincide with the actual paths. Follow the overgrown fenced path until you can escape into the field on the right (straight on is more overgrown). Join path in this field and follow it through a gap into the next field & on to the road. Turn left, then right, then fork right (signed to Catholic Church). Follow the road into Bideford, turn left into North Rd, & right at the quay: you are now back on the SWCP, about to cross Bideford Long Bridge.

2. At Pusehill turn left (fp sign) before the first house on the left. Follow the fence to the field corner (no path), turn right, then left through the righthand of two gates. Go straight on with the "hedge" on your left until a stile leads to a surfaced path. Follow this to the road junction at Silford Cross and go straight on along a minor road. Fork right in Silford ("no through road" sign), then turn left over a stile (fp sign) opposite the drive to "Syringa". Keep hedge on your left through the field, and leave it through a gate into a minor road. Turn right & go under the busy A39. Turn left immediately up steps (fp sign) into an overgrown fenced path.

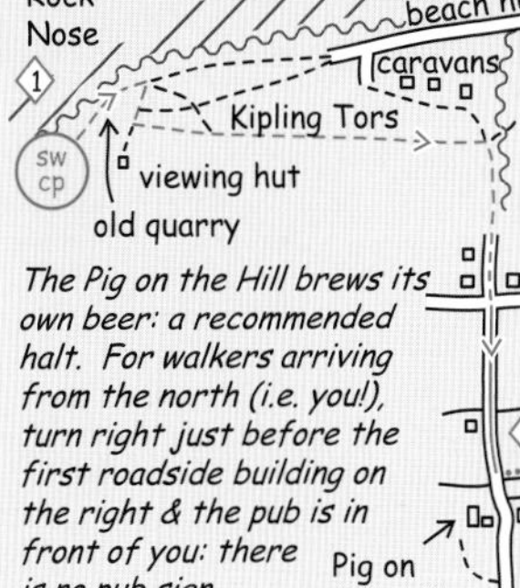

The Pig on the Hill brews its own beer: a recommended halt. For walkers arriving from the north (i.e. you!), turn right just before the first roadside building on the right & the pub is in front of you: there is no pub sign.

1. As the South West Coast Path approaches Westward Ho! it passes a small quarry on the right & the first buildings & caravans become visible as the path bends right. Look out for a smaller path to the right (sign "The National Trust Kipling Tors") & leave the coast path here. Turn immediately sharp right uphill & then take the second path on the left (trending uphill). Follow this path through gorse high above the caravans & beach huts: good views of Lundy & the coast. When the path drops down to a crossroads of paths turn right, follow the path to a road junction, & go down the road straight ahead.

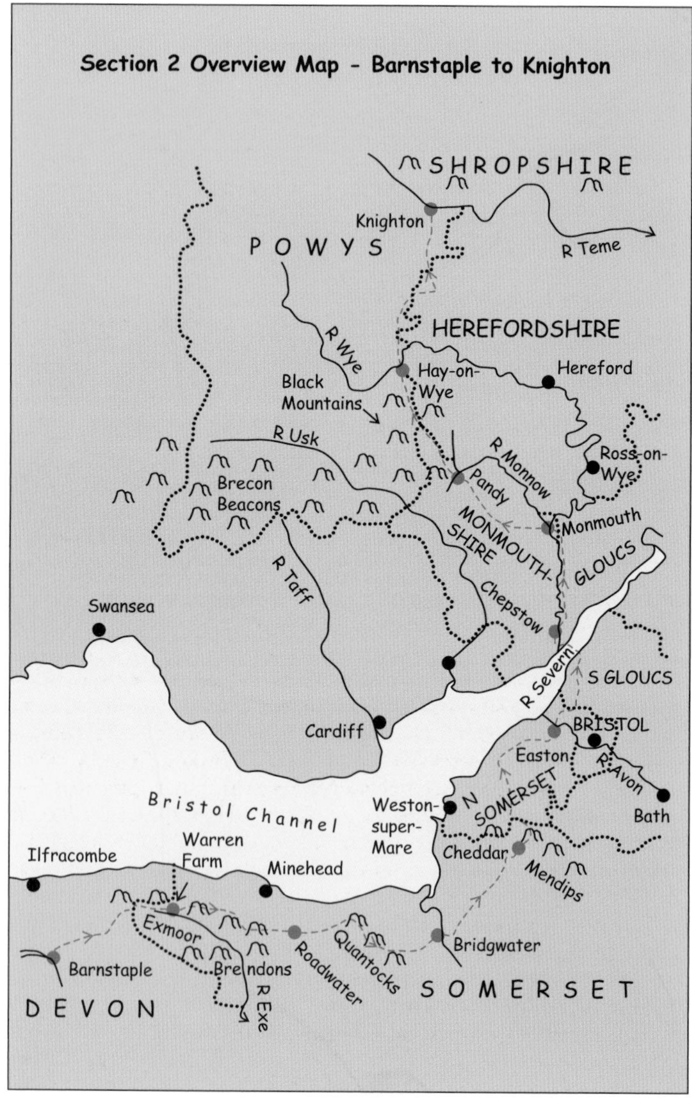
Section 2 Overview Map - Barnstaple to Knighton
SHROPSHIRE
Knighton
POWYS
R Teme
HEREFORDSHIRE
R Wye
Hay-on-Wye
Hereford
Black Mountains
R Usk
R Monnow
Ross-on-Wye
Brecon Beacons
Pandy
Monmouth
MONMOUTH-SHIRE
GLOUCS
R Taff
Chepstow
Swansea
R Severn
S GLOUCS
Cardiff
BRISTOL
Easton
R Avon
N SOMERSET
Bristol Channel
Weston-super-Mare
Bath
Warren Farm
Cheddar
Ilfracombe
Minehead
Mendips
Exmoor
Roadwater
Quantocks
Bridgwater
Barnstaple
Brendons
R Exe
SOMERSET
DEVON

SECTION 2

The Bristol Channel and the Welsh Border: Barnstaple to Knighton

Distance	330km (205 miles)
Road Walking	23%. This section has the highest proportion of road walking, mainly due to a shortage of footpaths in the low-lying farmland and Levels of Somerset, and the crossing of two long motorway bridges.
Days	10 (Main Schedule), or 14 (Alternative Schedule)
Maps and Guides	Barnstaple to Chepstow: this guide, strip maps Day 10 Map 1 to Day 15 Map 7 Chepstow to Knighton: Offa's Dyke Path guide

A number of published routes fill the gap between the South West Coast Path and Offa's Dyke Path (or the Cotswold Way, if you plan to follow this alternative, see below), but none quite fits the Trail bill, being either too indirect or missing some obvious walking opportunities, so we leave the SWCP at Barnstaple (rather than following it all the way to Minehead, which involves a long detour round the north Devon coast). Instead, the Trail goes inland and heads for the ranges of hills that overlook the Bristol Channel, taking in the highest points of Exmoor, the Brendon Hills and the Quantocks, before descending to cross the River Parrett in Bridgwater. The flat Somerset Levels are crossed to Cheddar and the Mendips, which again are crossed at their highest point. Once back on the plain we follow disused railways and little-used footpaths before taking to a series of low ridges to avoid, as far as practical, the urban sprawl around Bristol. The River Avon is crossed on the M5 bridge, which has a footpath/cycleway alongside it, and more low ridges take you past Bristol and back to the coastal plain. More quiet paths lead to the original motorway bridge (now the M48) across the Severn and Wye estuaries to Chepstow in Wales on Day 15. From Chepstow the route follows the excellent Offa's Dyke Path national trail northwards to Knighton (which is nearly halfway to its end at Prestatyn on the North Wales coast).

Exmoor and the Quantocks are popular places. The walking is generally easy, and in good weather the views can be wonderful, with the paths and tracks along the ridges well used and easy to follow. After the Quantocks the rights of way are often little used and not obvious on the ground. Invisible paths lead into Bridgwater, where the Trail has to go right through the town to cross the River Parrett. From Bridgwater the flat, former salt marshes of the Somerset Levels have to be crossed, and with few footpaths to follow, minor roads must be walked for sections of the way to Cheddar.

From Cheddar the Trail climbs to cross the Mendips, then drops back down to the plain, following footpaths and disused railway lines to the M5 crossing over the Avon. There is a foot and cycle path across this bridge, which avoids the need to walk into the centre of Bristol. (A route round to the east of Bristol would be too circuitous, and walking through the middle of the city would mean walking through miles of suburbia as well, so the route squeezes between the city and the Bristol Channel.) Rather than follow the rather industrialised coast of the Bristol Channel, the Trail goes back inland along the ridges of Kings Weston Hill, Coombe Hill and Spaniorum Hill, before crossing the flat farmland north to Aust, and the old Severn Bridge carrying the M48. This bridge also has a path for bikes and walkers, and leads to Chepstow and the start of the Offa's Dyke Path.

All the paths in the section preceding the Offa's Dyke Path can be followed in reasonable comfort, although there may be a few nettles occasionally, and not all the stiles are up to Lake District standard. Gates may not open, footpath signs are rare, and fences are sometimes electric, but paths that can't be followed while also enjoying yourself are not included in the route. (Detailed route-finding information from Barnstaple to Chepstow is on the End to End Trail strip map pages at the end of Section 2.)

From Chepstow the route along the Offa's Dyke Path roughly follows the Welsh border. The first day follows the River Wye through a lovely pastoral valley, with steep sides and limestone cliffs in places – the river has carved an impressive home for itself. Sometimes the path follows woods along the valley's edge, sometimes the riverbank, and this is a delightful stretch.

At Monmouth there is an abrupt change of direction, to follow the much smaller River Trothy west and then northwest through quiet farmland to the foot of the Black Mountains at Pandy. The mountains loom ahead alarmingly, but once the initial steep climb up from Pandy is over, the walking is easy, on good tracks along the whaleback Hatterall ridge. When the ridge comes to an abrupt end the path drops steeply down and into Hay-on-Wye. This is a very attractive old border town that is well worth pottering round, particularly if you like second-hand bookshops, of which the town is famously full.

From Hay the path follows the bank of the Wye again for a while, until the river meanders off east towards Hereford. The path continues north to Hergest Ridge, a smaller whaleback hill, and descends to Kington. From Kington to Knighton the path follows the old dyke itself, usually visible as a ridge through the fields.

Maps

1:25000 Explorer maps

9 Exmoor
140 Quantock Hills
141 Cheddar Gorge
154 Bristol West and Portishead
14 Wye Valley & Forest of Dean
13 Brecon Beacons National Park (Eastern area)
201 Knighton & Presteigne

1:50000 Landranger maps

180 Barnstaple & Ilfracombe
181 Minehead & Brendon Hills
182 Weston-super-Mare, Bridgwater & Wells
172 Bristol & Bath
162 Gloucester & Forest of Dean
161 Abergavenny & the Black Mountains
148 Presteigne & Hay-on-Wye area

Guidebooks

There are no suitable guidebooks covering the route in Section 2 preceding Offa's Dyke, although local walking guides are available covering most of the areas walked through. The strip maps at the end of this section, used in conjunction with OS maps, should be enough to keep you on the Trail.

Walking Offa's Dyke Path by David Hunter, Cicerone, 2001

This guide includes basic hand-drawn maps. It is easy to follow (and this time the route is described in the right direction for us).

Where to Stay – Offa's Dyke Path and Glendwr's Way, Offa's Dyke Association

Offa's Dyke Path Backpackers' and Camping List, Offa's Dyke Association

These are, respectively, comprehensive lists of bed and breakfasts and campsites on or near Offa's Dyke path, and revised annually. They are available from the Offa's Dyke Association, and the lists are also published on their website at www.offasdyke.demon.co.uk.

Recommendations

Get David Hunter's *Walking Offa's Dyke Path* (or one of the alternatives) and the Offa's Dyke Association accommodation lists. Buy all the

1:25000 Explorer maps listed, except for Explorer 201, unless you already have some of the 1:50000 alternatives. Buy Landranger 148 rather than Explorer 201 to avoid buying an additional 1:25000 map for Section 3. The number of maps in both series is the same, and the additional detail on the Explorer maps is useful in areas where the route finding is complex. Don't rely only on a guidebook with strip maps when walking Offa's Dyke, however – you do need OS maps as well.

To Help You On Your Way

Accommodation

Accommodation on Exmoor and around the Quantocks is sometimes limited, as in places the route is quite remote. Information is available from the following tourist information centres.

Museum of North Devon, The Square, Barnstaple, Devon, tel 01271 375000, www.staynorthdevon.co.uk.

Exmoor National Park, Fore Street, Dulverton, tel 01398 323841, www.exmoorholidayguide.co.uk.

50 High Street, Bridgwater, tel 01278 427652, www.somersetbythesea.co.uk.

The Gorge, Cheddar, tel 01934 744071, www.somersetbythesea.co.uk.

Beach Lawns, Weston-super-Mare, tel 01934 888800, www.somersetcoast.com.

The Annexe, Wildscreen Walk, Harbourside, Bristol, tel 0906 711 2191 (note – expensive to call), www.visitbristol.co.uk.

For accommodation in and near the Quantocks (including Bicknoller) you should also visit www.quantockonline.co.uk.

For Offa's Dyke you should get the Offa's Dyke Association's comprehensive accommodation guides (see Recommendations, above), which make life a lot easier.

Equipment Shops

Day 10	The Farmers Den, Simonsbath, tel 01643 831151
Day 12	Millets, 5 Fore Street, Bridgwater, tel 01278 422243
Day 13	The Gorge Outdoors, Hanlith House, The Cliffs, Cheddar, tel 01934 742688
Days 14/15	There are a couple of shops off-route in Weston-super-Mare, and plenty in Bristol
Day 16	Millets, 21 Monnow Street, Monmouth, tel 01600 719187

Alternative Routes

There are many possible alternative routes for parts of this section. I have picked out a few that are particularly worth considering.

Alternatives from Barnstaple to the Quantocks

1 The Minehead Alternative. Follow the South West Coast Path all the way to its end at Minehead, then take a waymarked Macmillan Way West link to meet the main Macmillan Way West at GR960439 on Knowle Hill, which will take you via Withycombe and Williton to rejoin the Trail at Bicknoller, at the foot of the Quantocks. The link is described in the Macmillan Way West guidebook, but you will be following it in reverse. This route is not very direct, and misses out the Exmoor hills, so it is not the recommended way.

2 From Barnstaple, cut off the 'corner' (i.e. avoiding a detour to Braunton and Ilfracombe) and rejoin the SWCP further along the north coast. You can then continue to Minehead and follow the Minehead Alternative (see above). One way to cut the corner would be via Bratton Fleming (which is on the Trail) and Parracombe, to rejoin the SWCP at Woody Bay, before Lynmouth. This route doesn't appear in a guidebook, so you would need to follow maps alone.

3 From Barnstaple, follow the waymarked Macmillan Way West/Tarka Trail (which coincide almost all the way from Barnstaple to Exmoor) to the crest of Exmoor – at either Woodbarrow Gate (Tarka Trail) or Chains Barrow (Macmillan Way West). You can then either continue on the End to End Trail across Exmoor, or descend from Exe Head on the Tarka Trail/Two Moors Way to rejoin the SWCP at Lynmouth, and then follow the Minehead Alternative (see above). Again, this route is rather indirect.

If you follow the main route of the End to End Trail from Barnstaple onto Exmoor, and the weather turns too bad for comfort, the Tarka Trail/Two Moors Way also gives you the option of heading north from Exe Head to the coast.

Guidebooks

Macmillan Way West, Macmillan Way Association, 2001

This guide describes the route of the Macmillan Way West from Castle Cary in Somerset to Barnstaple. It borrows a lot of the Tarka Trail at its western end. The guide is available from the Macmillan Way

Association, St Mary's Barn, Pillerton Priors, Warwick CV35 0PG, www.macmillanway.org.

The Tarka Trail – A Walker's Guide by Richard and Henry Williamson, Devon Books, 1992

The Cotswold Way and the Heart of England Way

This is an alternative to the End to End Trail's route via Bristol, Offa's Dyke and Shropshire. It involves leaving the main route in the Mendips, north of Cheddar (Day 14), and rejoining it on Cannock Chase in Staffordshire. The entire alternative route is on waymarked paths covered by guidebooks. The Limestone Link leads to Cold Ashton, north of Bath, then the Cotswold Way follows the Cotswolds to Chipping Campden. From Chipping Campden the Heart of England Way takes you between Birmingham and Coventry, then round north of Birmingham to Cannock Chase, where you join the Staffordshire Way, and the main End to End Trail route.

Despite the quality of the Cotswold Way, this is not the recommended route for two main reasons. First, it means missing out the Welsh mountains (and indeed missing out Wales entirely). Second, it involves a lot of lowland farmland – the Heart of England Way doesn't climb over a 250m contour for its whole length.

Guidebooks

The Limestone Link, Yatton Ramblers, 2001 (reprint)

Available from Yatton Ramblers, c/o 26 Moorside, Yatton, Bristol BS49 4RL

The Cotswold Way by Kev Reynolds, Cicerone, 2005

The Heart of England Way by Richard Sale, Aurum Press, 1998

Alternative Routes Along the Welsh Border

For anyone who has walked the Offa's Dyke path before, there are alternative routes for the first three of the four days. From Chepstow to Monmouth you can follow the Wye Valley Walk, which is waymarked and takes a parallel route up the Wye valley. From Monmouth to Hay-on-Wye the Offa's Dyke Castles Alternative provides a route somewhat east of the national trail, although it is not waymarked.

Guidebooks

The Wye Valley Walk by Anthony Burton, Aurum Press, 1998

Offa's Dyke Castles Alternative Route, Offa's Dyke Association
This was formerly available from the Offa's Dyke Association, but is unfortunately no longer in print. An updated version is however available to download from www.longwalks.org.uk (courtesy of the Offa's Dyke Association).

DAY 10

The River Yeo and Western Exmoor

Barnstaple to Warren Farm, Exmoor (34km, 21 miles)

From Barnstaple to Chepstow, detailed route-finding information is on the End to End Trail strip map pages at the end of this section, so you can now post your South West Coast Path guidebook home.

Today the Trail leaves the coast and heads for the hills for the first time. Pleasant wooded tracks lead inland from Barnstaple, following the River Yeo, then a gradual climb up to Bratton Fleming and a stretch of road walking bring you to the edge of Exmoor National Park. From the village of Challacombe, bridleways lead into the hills and true Exmoor moorland.

The way out of Barnstaple is a pleasant one (Day 10 Map 1), climbing up through the old village of Pilton, now a suburb of Barnstaple, and once the town has been left behind, so is the tarmac. An old lane, Smoky House Lane, runs east above the River Yeo. It is bounded by trees for much of the way and gives good walking, although it can be muddy in places. When it enters Raleigh Wood, an old wood of oaks and chestnuts, it gets even better.

When a minor road drops down into the valley from the west (Day 10 Map 2), you follow it briefly, then take to valley tracks through forestry and woodland, to cross the river and join the valley road at Chelfham.

Chelfham's most noticeable feature is its railway viaduct, which was restored in 2000, despite the fact that the railway, a narrow gauge line from Barnstaple to Lynton, has been closed since 1935.

Railway viaduct, Chelfham

After 1km of road northwards along the Yeo valley, you turn left at Loxhore Cross, then at Loxhore Bridge the Trail leaves the Yeo for a side valley. A track leads into woods, then you cross fields into forestry, and from Loxhore Mill take a short stretch of minor road, until the ascent to Exmoor starts with a stiff climb out of the valley (Day 10 Map 3) into the large village of Bratton Fleming.

Bratton Fleming is not very picturesque, but it does have two shops and a pub, the White Hart, which serves food and sells good beer (recommended). PG Wodehouse's uncle was rector in Bratton Fleming for nearly 40 years, and the author used to spend his school holidays here.

From Bratton Fleming onwards, for the first time on the Trail it feels as if you are on the hills rather than in valleys, with higher hills usually visible ahead. Three kilometres of road walking, mostly uphill, is unavoidable due to a shortage of footpaths, then an old bridleway crosses the Bray valley, and when it meets the road on the opposite side of the valley the route enters Exmoor National Park. A short stretch of road leads to Challacombe, the last village on the route for many miles (Day 10 Map 4).

Challacombe is a pretty little village, with an old packhorse bridge, a ford, a shop/post office and a pub, the Black Venus Inn, which is a recommended halt and serves meals. There are a number of bed and breakfasts in and near Challacombe, and a small campsite at Home Place Farm in the village, although this is only open in July and August. Fill your water bottle before leaving Challacombe. There are few obvious sources of clean water on Exmoor, largely due to cattle churning up the streams.

On Exmoor itself the hills are huge, rolling expanses, the higher parts still moorland, although much of the lower land has been 'improved' in terms of farming (i.e. made into richer pasture and poorer walking). Walking is not too difficult, as the gradients are mainly gentle, apart from where streams such as the Exe have carved a channel, and you also have to dodge the wetter parts.

A track leads east from Challacombe, south of and parallel to the B3358, up to the moorland of South Regis Common. As you climb, cultivation gradually gives way to moorland, with characteristic mounded field boundaries that often have a fence or hedge on top. Also to be seen along here are remnants of beech tree windbreaks, planted by Frederic Knight all over his Exmoor estate in the second half of the 19th century.

At the eastern end of South Regis Common the Trail turns north and crosses the B3358, now accompanied by the Devon/Somerset border and the Tarka Trail (waymarked with an otter's paw-print), which has followed a more circuitous route here from Barnstaple.

The Trail climbs (Day 10 Map 5) to the crest of the main Exmoor ridge at Woodbarrow Gate (476m), then turns east to enter Somerset and follow the ridge past Chains Barrow (487m) to the muddy source of the River Exe at Exe Head. (This is where you are glad you brought water with you – it may be moorland, but the cattle make the Exe too risky to drink from, even at its source.) At Exe Head the Trail crosses the Two Moors Way, and parts company with the Tarka Trail as well – both head north from here to Lynmouth, on the coast.

On the climb up from the B3358 to Woodbarrow Gate, the route follows the main watershed. Water to the west flows into the Bray, then into the Taw and to Barnstaple and the Bristol Channel. Water to the east flows into the Barle, which heads southeast and joins the Exe flowing south to Exmouth, on the south coast. From Woodbarrow Gate, despite being less than 8km (5 miles) from the Bristol Channel, the Trail's route is in the gathering grounds of the Exe.

The River Exe and Warren Farm

A path follows the infant River Exe to meet the B3223 at Exe Head Bridge (Day 10 Map 6). Following the road south for about a kilometre, the Trail climbs high above the deep valley the Exe has carved for itself, and at Preyway Head a decision needs to be made about where you are going to spend the night (unless you plan to camp out in the hills, in which case you will need to have carried water from Challacombe).

The first option is to go off-route to stay in the hamlet of Simonsbath, where accommodation is available at the Simonsbath House Hotel and the Exmoor Forest Hotel. If you want to head for Simonsbath, stay on the B3223 and descend for about 1.5km (1 mile). (Tomorrow you can climb back up to Warren Farm and rejoin the Trail by going via the B3223 to the east, and the bridleway north from Clovenrocks Bridge (GR786398), signed to Aldermans Barrow via Warren Bridge. The Postman's Path then takes you down to Warren Farm – see Day 10 Map 6.)

The second option is to head for Warren Farm, which is on the route and does bed and breakfast (tel 01643 831283). To reach Warren Farm more directly than the Simonsbath route, the Trail leaves the road at the crest of the ridge, at Preyway Head, and heads east across pathless, rough grazing land, parallel to the Exe but high above it to the south. When a gate on the right indicates a bridleway coming up from the B3223, and Warren Farm is visible on the opposite side of the valley, the Postman's Path drops down steeply to join the farm access road, which crosses the Exe and climbs up to the farm. Warren Farm is in a particularly isolated location, at nearly 400m in the middle of the hills.

DAY 11

High Exmoor and the Brendon Hills

Warren Farm, Exmoor to Roadwater (29km, 18 miles)

Today the route crosses the highest of the Exmoor hills, Dunkery Beacon (519m), then descends to Wheddon Cross and continues east through the farmland of the less wild Brendon Hills. The entire day is within the Exmoor National Park, and the farmland tends to be grazing land rather than crop cultivation, so the walking is generally good. There is no contest between Exmoor and the Brendons, though – after the ridge from Great Rowbarrow to Dunkery Beacon, the remainder of the day is an anticlimax. On the Rowbarrow to Dunkery ridge the views are extensive, the walking easy, and Dunkery Beacon is the highest point on the Trail before the Black Mountains in Wales.

From Warren Farm a good track crosses Elsworthy Moor to meet a minor road at Larkbarrow Corner (Day 11 Map 1). The road is lined with beech hedges, presumably another relic of Frederic Knight's estate management in the 19th century.

The route continues east across the high moors, over Almsworthy Common, where it meets the main watershed again (Day 11 Map 2). The watershed is followed, approximately, over Exford Common, then up to the highest of the Exmoor hills – Great Rowbarrow (510m) and, along the ridge, Dunkery Beacon (519m) (Day 11 Map 3).

(There is an alternative bad weather route to the south of the main Great Rowbarrow–Dunkery Beacon ridge that is probably a better idea if the hills are in cloud, but if there are any views to be had at all, the panorama from the tops is a must, particularly to the north across the Bristol Channel to South Wales.)

Dunkery Beacon is at the eastern end of the remaining true moors. The Trail now heads southeast, briefly on the northwest side of the watershed (River Avill), which is odd, since the Trail is going southeast from the watershed. The route

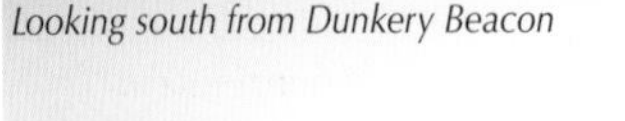

Looking south from Dunkery Beacon

quickly loses height, falling below 400m for the first time since shortly after leaving Warren Farm.

> 'A gallop over the wild moorlands of Exmoor, with sea breezes charged with ozone, will do more to recruit the health of the jaded and blanched Londoner, than quarts of the Elizabethan Brunnen at Homburg, or the waters of German Spas' – Evelyn Burnaby, *A Ride from Land's End to John O'Groats*, 1893

The descent by the River Avill is pleasant, rough pasture, followed by a riverside woodland path through Blagdon Wood. A steep climb up through Little Quarme Wood leads to the village of Wheddon Cross, the highest village on Exmoor at 300m (Day 11 Map 4).

At Wheddon Cross there is a pub, the Rest and Be Thankful (recommended), and there are a number of bed and breakfasts in and around the village.

From near Wheddon Cross a bridleway runs south then east up to White Moor and then Lype Hill, at 423m the highest point in the Brendon Hills. While the views are good, there is no moorland here, just improved pasture with little character.

The Trail follows the main watershed again over White Moor and Lype Hill, and from there you are back on its northwest side (and will remain so until you cross the Shropshire–Staffordshire border on Day 22.)

Paths lead down to Luxborough, a parish split between two villages – Churchtown has the church, Kingsbridge has the pub (Day 11 Map 5).

Luxborough used to provide accommodation for the iron-ore miners of the Brendon Hills (the mines were at their peak in the mid-19th century). The pub at Kingsbridge is the Royal Oak of Luxborough (recommended, particularly for its food), although it tends to be more of a restaurant at weekends, so booking is advisable if you want a meal (tel 01984 640319). The Royal Oak has the only accommodation in the area. It is not of the budget variety, but it is certainly very comfortable.

From Kingsbridge the walking improves again. A track climbs out of the Washford valley and along a ridge (Day 11 Map 6). The views are good and the immediate environment is quiet and pastoral. A path through Langridge Wood then descends back to the Washford river, and the quiet valley road leads to the village of Roadwater in about 1.5km (1 mile).

Roadwater has a pub (the Valiant Soldier, recommended), a shop/post office and bed and breakfasts. There is also a YHA camping barn at Woodadvent Farm, 1km beyond the village (see Day 12 Map 1).

DAY 12

The Quantocks

Roadwater to Bridgwater (36km, 22 miles)

Today the Trail leaves the Exmoor National Park to climb steeply up to the main Quantocks ridge. The Quantocks are a compact group of moorland hills running northwest to southeast for about 20km (12 miles) from the coast near Watchet. The highest point is Wills Neck, and the Trail follows the ridge and crosses the top of Wills Neck, before dropping down to cross the farmland between the hills and the large town of Bridgwater. The Trail goes through the middle of Bridgwater (reluctantly), as this is the lowest place the River Parrett can be crossed.

From Roadwater a minor road then field paths climb steeply up then down the other side of a hill to cross the B3190 (Day 12 Map 1). The descent from here is through parkland to Nettlecombe Court. (Nettlecombe Court, in a beautiful location and with its own church, used to be the seat of the Raleighs, and is now a field centre.) The main drive from Nettlecombe Court leads to a field path above a stream, leading southeast to the village of Monksilver, where the route leaves the national park.

Monksilver is not particularly pretty, but does have a pub, the Notley Arms, although there is no shop.

The West Somerset Railway near Bicknoller

From Monksilver to Bicknoller, at the foot of the Quantocks, the Trail follows an intricate course along field edges, often on invisible paths (Day12 Map 2). Thankfully it's only about 5km (3 miles), and it does have two features of interest. The first is the view ahead of the Quantocks, and the second is the West Somerset Railway, a preserved steam railway running between Minehead and Taunton. The Trail crosses the railway at stiles just before Bicknoller, but you are likely to hear train whistles long before you get there, and if you are lucky you will see a train steam past in front of you, with the Quantocks for a backdrop.

Bicknoller is a pretty little village with a pub, the Bicknoller Inn, a 15th-century church and a shop/post office. There is currently one bed and breakfast here, and there are others in the nearby villages of Stogumber and Crowcombe (see www.quantockonline.co.uk).

From Bicknoller a delightful, steep climb on a good track up Bicknoller Combe leads to the main north–south ridge of the Quantocks (Day 12 Map 3). The next 9km (5 miles) along the ridge, heading south then southeast, give an excellent moorland walk with a choice of paths – the Trail tries to avoid those used by the off-road vehicles that appear to be officially tolerated on the Quantocks tracks. (If you want to descend from the ridge for refreshment, there is a pub worth considering along the southwest foot of the hills – the Carew Arms in Crowcombe, 1.5km (1 mile) off-route from Crowcombe Combe Gate, though there is a stiff climb back up if you succumb to the temptation.)

From Crowcombe Combe Gate the Trail climbs past Triscombe Quarry to Wills Neck, at 386m the highest point in the Quantocks, and an exceptional viewpoint – Bridgwater and the Mendips come into view here (Day 12 Map 4). (If the weather is poor, an alternative route from the col at Triscombe Stone avoids the summit – see map).

About 2km (1½ miles) after Wills Neck the Trail skirts the summit of Lydeard Hill (Day 12 Map 5), then descends to the east, via Blaxhold Farm, Enmore and Goathurst (Day 12 Map 6), towards Bridgwater. The road walking between Blaxhold Farm and Goathurst is not very inspiring, but the last 3km (2 miles) into Bridgwater is a lot better, through the Meads (meadows) to the southwest of the town (Day 12 Map 7), although care with route finding is needed, as many of the paths are invisible.

At Enmore the Tynte Arms (recommended), just off-route (unless you are following the bad weather alternative, which takes you past it), has good beer and food, but there is no accommodation here or nearby. Enmore's school, passed on the way into Enmore, was the first free elementary school in England, opened in

1810 and still in use. Enmore church, just off-route to the north, has a Norman doorway and a tower dating from about 1500.

By the road just before Goathurst the Trail passes the Temple of Harmony, a folly completed in 1767 in the grounds of Halswell Park. The temple is based on the 1st-century temple of Fortuna Virilis in Rome, and is open to visitors on summer weekend afternoons.

'...Bridgwater, shabby little town on the slimy estuary Parrett, from whose mud bricks are made; a town of red brick buildings, billboards, and an absurdly lofty spire on a squat tower – hideous!' – Jessie Barker Gardner, *From Land's End to John O'Groats*, 1930

Bridgwater is not a pretty place, although it has a long history, since its strategic position at the crossing of the River Parrett has meant that a large proportion of traffic into and out of the southwest has come this way for centuries. Bridgwater was fortified in the 9th century, but 14th-century St Mary's church is now the only remaining medieval building. Bridgwater has all facilities, including a tourist information centre on your left on the way into town. This has an accommodation list in the window, so is useful even when closed.

DAY 13

The Somerset Levels

Bridgwater to Cheddar (32km, 20 miles)

Most of today's walking is only just above sea level on the Somerset Levels, land that was originally saltmarsh and frequently flooded. Drainage work probably started at least 1500 years ago, much of it done by the monks of Glastonbury, Athelney and Muchelney. Although there are still floods from time to time, the Levels are now drained by a crisscross pattern of straight ditches and wider rivers, with pumping stations at intervals, and a continuous maintenance programme is needed to keep the system operational. Seawater floods used to reach a long way inland – in 1607 Glastonbury was completely surrounded by water when a sea wall gave way at Burnham. In recent years a halt has been called to further drainage, to try to retain the traditional character of the Levels, which depends on seasonal freshwater flooding. The Levels will be allowed to continue to flood regularly, as they have done for hundreds of years.

The landscape is fascinating, but there are few public footpaths on the Levels, so the Trail follows quiet minor roads – you are likely to meet more tractors than cars.

Escape from Bridgwater (Day 13 Map 1) is not particularly pleasant, but the recommended route is a lot better than the more obvious one along the A372. A footbridge over the M5 motorway leads to the start of the Levels, where the land is flat and every field boundary is a drainage ditch. Walkers are scarce around here, so what footpaths there are tend to be invisible on the ground.

A footbridge over the wide King's Sedgemoor Drain leads to the village of Bawdrip (Day 13 Map 2), where there is a church, but no shop. The Knowle Inn (recommended) is 1km west of the village on the A39.

From Bawdrip, paths through the fields lead over a low ridge lead to Cossington, which has a church and a shop. On OS maps a right of way is marked heading north out of Cossington, but it is impassable, so instead you take a minor road north (Bell Lane), down the hill and over the Levels again, crossing the River Brue, to reach Westham (Day 13 Map 3). At Gold Corner Bridge a big pumping station at the end of the Huntspill river gives an idea of the scale of the technology that keeps the Levels drained.

At Westham the Trail leaves the road to cross fields to Blackford, where there is a pub, the Sexey's Arms. Accommodation is scarce around here, but there are bed and breakfasts and campsites in and around Mark, about 3km (2 miles) to the west of Blackford (or you can take a short cut to Mark from early on Day 13 Map 3 – see strip map). There is also bed and breakfast a bit closer to the route at Poplar Farm, 1km north of Blackford (GR415487, tel 01934 712087).

From Blackford a bridleway and invisible footpaths lead north, past Middle Staughton, along the edge of the steep escarpment of Brinscombe Hill (Day 13 Map 4), covered in orchards overlooking more Levels, and across to Axbridge and Cheddar.

Dropping down from Brinscombe Hill (Day 13 Map 5) you then reach a bridge and follow the Cheddar Yeo riverbank into Cheddar, emerging conveniently at a campsite. (If you are in a hurry there is an alternative way into Cheddar, *crossing* the bridge over the Cheddar Yeo and walking along the road.)

As well as campsites Cheddar has a youth hostel, shops, pubs, banks and plenty of other accommodation. Cheddar also has tourists who come to see the gorge, the caves and savour the Cheddar experience. It is the closest thing to Blackpool you will see on the route, surpassing even Land's End. The gorge is best seen from the road that winds up it, so if you are staying overnight, and the blisters are not too bad, take a walk up the B3135 for a couple of miles and back. The vertical limestone cliffs on either side of the narrow gorge are 120m high in places, and Cheddar Gorge is one of the most spectacular places in England. (In the summer months I'd leave it as late in the evening as you can, when the gorge will be less busy.)

'Here is a deep, frightful chasm in the mountain, in the hollow of which, the road goes, by which they travel towards Bristol; and out of the same hollow, springs a little river, which flows with such a full stream, that, it is said, it drives twelve mills within a quarter of a mile of the spring' – Daniel Defoe, letting you know what the tourist shops replaced.

DAY 14

The Mendips and Cadbury Camp

Cheddar to Easton-in-Gordano (44km, 27 miles)

Cheddar is on the 'shore' of the Levels, and Cheddar Gorge cuts deep into the edge of the Mendips, which stretch inland for about 40km (25 miles) from the Bristol Channel. The Trail climbs up from Cheddar to cross the Mendips at their highest point, Beacon Batch (325m), then follows a lower ridge westwards before descending to more levels north of the hills. The going is dead flat for most of the way north towards the coast, then a series of low ridges parallel to the coast gives good walking until the day's end, just before the mouth of the River Avon is reached at the edge of Bristol.

Long Wood Nature Reserve, Mendip Hills

The exit from Cheddar is a steep one, climbing up to follow the southern edge of the gorge (Day 14 Map 1). At the top of the climb you meet the top of Jacob's Ladder stairs, which is an alternative way, up steps, from Cheddar (for which privilege you have to pay an admission fee). There is a wooden observation tower here (free), which gives good views of Cheddar and the Levels. As you continue through scrubland along the top of the gorge, in places you can peer down into the bottom.

After crossing the B3135, above the gorge, there is very pretty walking through the wooded limestone valleys of Black Rock and Long Wood nature reserves. Once out of the woods it's a stiff climb up to the moorland and Beacon Batch (Day 14 Map 2).

Cotswold Way/Heart of England Way alternative route (see Alternative Routes at the beginning of Section 2). If you want to follow this alternative, you should leave the main route of the Trail at the summit of Beacon Batch, and head northeast to pick up the Limestone Link at the foot of the hill and follow it eastwards to Cold Ashton, north of Bath, where it joins the Cotswold Way. (The Limestone Link guidebook describes the route.)

The main Trail route continues west from the summit of Beacon Batch along the ridge for a bit, then descends north into North Somerset (formerly part of the county of Avon), to pick up more good walking along a lower ridge heading west again. This is Dolebury Warren, National Trust land with the remains of an Iron Age fort at the far end of the ridge, and fine views to the north. There is a short further stretch in the Mendip foothills before dropping down to the plain at Sandford (Day 14 Map 3).

At Sandford you pass a pub, the Railway Inn, and also Thatcher's cider brewery – in fact the path goes through the orchard next to the brewery. (There is a shop five minutes' walk along the main road to the right (east), and a couple of bed and breakfasts which may not appear in the TIC brochures.)

For the next 6km (4 miles) from Sandford the Trail takes advantage of another disused railway line, the Strawberry Line, which used to run from a junction at Yatton via Cheddar to Wells. It closed in 1965, and this section is now a footpath – the Cheddar Valley Railway Walk.

At Yatton (Day 14 Map 4) the disused railway joins the railway from Bristol to Weston-Super-Mare, so the Trail has to leave it to follow invisible paths through fields and meadows between the outskirts of Clevedon and Nailsea, towards Easton-in-Gordano and the Bristol Channel at the end of the day.

Before reaching the coast the Trail meets the M5 motorway again (Day 14 Map 5), shadowing it along a low wooded ridge to Cadbury Camp, a big Iron Age hill fort, then dropping down to Clapton-in-Gordano (Day 14 Map 6), a small village with an excellent pub, the Black Horse (highly recommended, but no food in the evenings), but no accommodation. Push on a bit further, climbing back up to the ridge and crossing the deep wooded valley of Bullock's Bottom (Day 14 Map 7). The walking is mostly pleasant farmland, until you cross the busy A369 to reach Easton-in-Gordano.

There is a handful of bed and breakfasts scattered around Easton and neighbouring Pill, and a pub and a bed and breakfast (Tynings, tel 01275 372608) where the route crosses the A369. Easton itself is entirely made up of housing estates – if you want shops, etc., head for the centre of Pill (see Day 15 Map 1).

DAY 15

Motorway Bridges and Other Follies

Easton-in-Gordano to Chepstow (30km, 19 miles)

From Easton-in-Gordano there are ahead of you three formidable obstacles to an enjoyable walk to the start of the Offa's Dyke Path at

Chepstow in Wales (the beginning of Section 3). These obstacles are the River Avon, the industrial and suburban sprawl in the City of Bristol, and the Bristol Channel.

The only bridge over the Avon downriver of the Clifton Suspension Bridge in Bristol is the M5 motorway bridge. (Admittedly, on OS maps there does appear to be a right of way that fords the Avon a little upriver from the motorway bridge, but the Avon is big, muddy and tidal, and it would be a shame to drown this early in the walk.) The bridge is reached through a housing estate in Easton (Day 15 Map 1), and there is a foot and cycle path alongside the motorway. While nobody could call this sort of proximity to so much traffic pleasant, there are at least some interesting views to be had of the river valley and some of the outskirts of Bristol. (There are shops near the north end of the bridge, and Shirehampton is only five minutes' walk away from here if you want banks, etc.)

The bridge brings you out of North Somerset into the City of Bristol's territory – the second obstacle before the Bristol Channel. Following the coast to avoid the

Blaise Hamlet

sprawl leads to a lot of road walking and a lot of industry, and is not very pleasant; further inland than the M5, and the industry gives way to housing estates, which are little better as walking territory. There is, however, a narrow green corridor through much of this, along Kings Weston Hill, after which only a short stretch in the housing estates leads to the edge of the city and countryside once more.

The climb up to Kings Weston Hill starts from a residential road near the north end of the bridge, and immediately you are in wooded parkland, with the city forgotten (Day 15 Map 2). This continues along the ridge and on to climb up to the Blaise Castle folly, built by Thomas Farr in 1766 (it looks like a real castle at first glance). After this you drop down to the suburb of Henbury, where there is a hidden gem – the Hansel and Gretel cottages of Blaise Hamlet. These cottages, grouped round a green, were designed by John Nash in 1809, and housed pensioners from the Blaise Estate. The route passes a few metres from them and they shouldn't be missed.

As you cross the railway, leaving the last estate on the edge of Henbury (Day 15 Map 3), you enter the green belt land of South Gloucestershire (another part of the former county of Avon). The Trail now heads north to Aust, crossing the M5 for the last time before coming to the last hill of the day – Spaniorum Hill. (This is the last good viewpoint before Aust, as for the next few miles it's back to sea level on more drained land.) At the bottom of the hill is the village of Easter Compton (Day 15 Map 4), which has a welcoming pub, the Fox.

Little-used field paths and green lanes (Day 15 Map 5) lead past Pilning to Aust, where there is another pub and a motorway service station (Day 15 Map 6). The motorway used to be the M4, but is now the M48 (the new M4 bridge is further south). From Aust the M48 crosses the Bristol Channel, the third and greatest obstacle of the day, to reach Chepstow. Again, this bridge has a foot and cycleway.

'There is also...an ugly, dangerous, and very inconvenient ferry over the Severn, to the mouth of the Wye; namely, at Aust; the badness of the weather, and the sorry boats; at which, deterred us from crossing there' – Daniel Defoe (so be thankful for the bridge)

The M48 road bridge was constructed in the 1960s. It's a suspension bridge with a main span of 1000m, side spans of 300m, and its towers are about 130m above sea level. It can be dangerous in windy weather, and sometimes has to

The M48 bridge over the Severn Estuary

be closed to traffic – this is one of the reasons the second crossing, the new M4 bridge, had to be built. Walking across it can be hard work if the weather is poor.

Halfway across the main span of the bridge is a county boundary – the Trail leaves South Gloucestershire and enters Gloucestershire proper. The bridge continues high above Beachley Point, and 2km after entering Gloucestershire, still on the bridge, the Trail enters Monmouthshire, Wales, as it crosses the River Wye.

After the path leaves the bridge (Day 15 Map 7), it roughly shadows the line of the River Wye, along the edge of housing estates and under the A48, for the short distance to the centre of Chepstow and the beginning of the Offa's Dyke Path.

Chepstow is a historic town on the Wye with accommodation and all the services you would expect of a small town. Camping is possible in Chepstow – see the Offa's Dyke Association camping list, under Guidebooks at the beginning of this section.

For the next four days you will be using your Offa's Dyke Path guidebook, so this is the end of the strip maps until Day 20.

DAY 16

The River Wye

Chepstow to Monmouth (27km, 17 miles)

The Trail follows the Offa's Dyke Path up the beautiful Wye Valley all day today, and if you walk it on a sunny day in spring, the woodland is magical, covered in bluebells, wood anemones and other flowers. There are other bluebell woods on the route from Cornwall to Sutherland, but there are none to match the Wye Valley. There are also stretches of the old dyke along the valley edge, and the impressive ruins of Tintern Abbey below.

Leave Chepstow by crossing the old bridge over the Wye back into Gloucestershire and go straight on (without following the road round to the left). After a few yards the Offa's Dyke Path comes in from the right – keep straight on, following your guidebook.

The Trail follows the wooded valley edge on the eastern side of the Wye, passing high above Tintern Abbey. There is a riverside option from Brockweir to Bigsweir Bridge, which adds an extra 1km to the walk, but it is worth it scenically, and walking by the river is very easy. Whichever route you choose, about halfway between the two bridges you reach an important (but invisible) milestone – this point marks 25% of your journey completed.

For most of the way to the town of Monmouth you are in Gloucestershire, the River Wye forming the boundary between Wales and England, but in Redbrook, about 5km (3 miles) before reaching Monmouth, you leave Gloucestershire for good and re-enter Wales.

Monmouth ("tis rather a decayed than a flourishing town' – Defoe) is an ancient and attractive place, and has shops, banks and plenty of accommodation, including a campsite nearby (GR502129, on the B4233).

DAY 17

The River Trothy

Monmouth to Pandy (26km, 16 miles)

Follow your Offa's Dyke Path guidebook for a second day, now in rolling hills through farmland up the River Trothy. It's a pleasant enough day's walking, but there's nothing to compare to yesterday's delights, or tomorrow's for that matter. Even Offa's Dyke itself is elsewhere – it heads north from Monmouth and you don't meet it again until Kington, on Day 19.

Today is best seen as a link between the Wye Valley and the Black Mountains – farmland walking with only the spectacular ruins of 12th-century White Castle to enliven the day. White Castle is well worth exploring, with most of the walls still standing and the moat full of water, and it drives home very effectively how impregnable these Norman fortresses must have been in their time.

At Llangattock Lingoed, 3.5 km (2 miles) from Pandy, the Hunter's Moon Inn has accommodation. There is no longer a pub in Llantilio Crossenny.

White Castle, Monmouthshire

As the day progresses the whaleback mountains ahead beckon, until you reach the foot of them at the day's end at Pandy.

Pandy is a scattered community, stretched along the A465 trunk road, in the shadow of the Black Mountains. There are a few bed and breakfasts here and three pubs. The Old Pandy Inn (1km north along the A465) has a bunkhouse, and the Rising Sun (0.5km south) has a campsite. There is a public phone halfway to the Old Pandy Inn, where the old road rejoins the new.

DAY 18

The Black Mountains

Pandy to Hay-on-Wye (26km, 16 miles)

This is the third of four days on the Offa's Dyke Path, and you're in the hills all day. These hills are the Black Mountains, part of the Brecon Beacons National Park, although the Brecon Beacons proper are further west, separated from the Black Mountains by the River Usk. The Black Mountains are much higher than any hills so far encountered, but the day is an easy one if the weather is reasonable. After the initial climb up from Pandy the route follows the Hatterrall ridge all day – the path is clear and the ridge gentle. The views are also very good, as you would expect from a high ridge along the edge of the hills, with a height of 703m attained at the highest point, approaching Hay-on-Wye. This is the highest on the End to End Trail so far, and the highest reached in Wales.

The day starts in Monmouthshire, then follows the border between Monmouthshire and Herefordshire along the ridge. Before the high point of the ridge, the northern-most corner of Monmouthshire is reached, and from here you have Powys on your left and Herefordshire on your right. Hay-on-Wye is in Powys (just), and also marks the northern tip of the national park.

There are all facilities and plenty of accommodation in Hay-on-Wye, which is a small town of great character, the main danger being the second-hand book-shops. (Remember that you will have to carry anything you buy, unless you can get the shop to post it home for you.) There is a campsite on the B4351 about 1km to the northwest of Hay.

DAY 19

Hergest Ridge and the Dyke

Hay-on-Wye to Knighton (45km, 28 miles)

This is a long day, and a stop in Kington is an option, splitting this leg into sections of 23km (15 miles) and 22km (13 miles). Alternatively, camping is possible at Evenjobb or at Discoed near Presteigne. Staying here would split the 68km (42 miles) between Hay and Craven Arms (Day 20) into two reasonable days instead of a long and a short one.

The Trail follows the Offa's Dyke Path again all day. The way out of Hay-on-Wye crosses the River Wye for the last time, and briefly follows it north (downstream!) before leaving it to strike north across farmland to Newchurch and Gladestry. The stretch to Kington is more interesting, climbing up to over 400m along Hergest Ridge, crossing the old racecourse on the summit plateau.

Kington is another border town, this time on the English side. It has rather less character than Monmouth, Hay and Knighton, however, although it has a youth hostel and some good pubs, including the Swan Hotel. Camping is also possible – see the Offa's Dyke Association list.

From Kington to Knighton the line of the ancient dyke is followed across hilly farmland – the dyke's direction is indicated by a ditch and ridges through the fields, often with a line of trees growing along it. The route crosses the border between Powys and Herefordshire four times during the day.

Knighton is just on the Powys side of the border, and has a station, pubs, bed and breakfasts, shops, post office, banks and even an Indian restaurant. There is a tourist information centre on the edge of the town, and camping is available nearby.

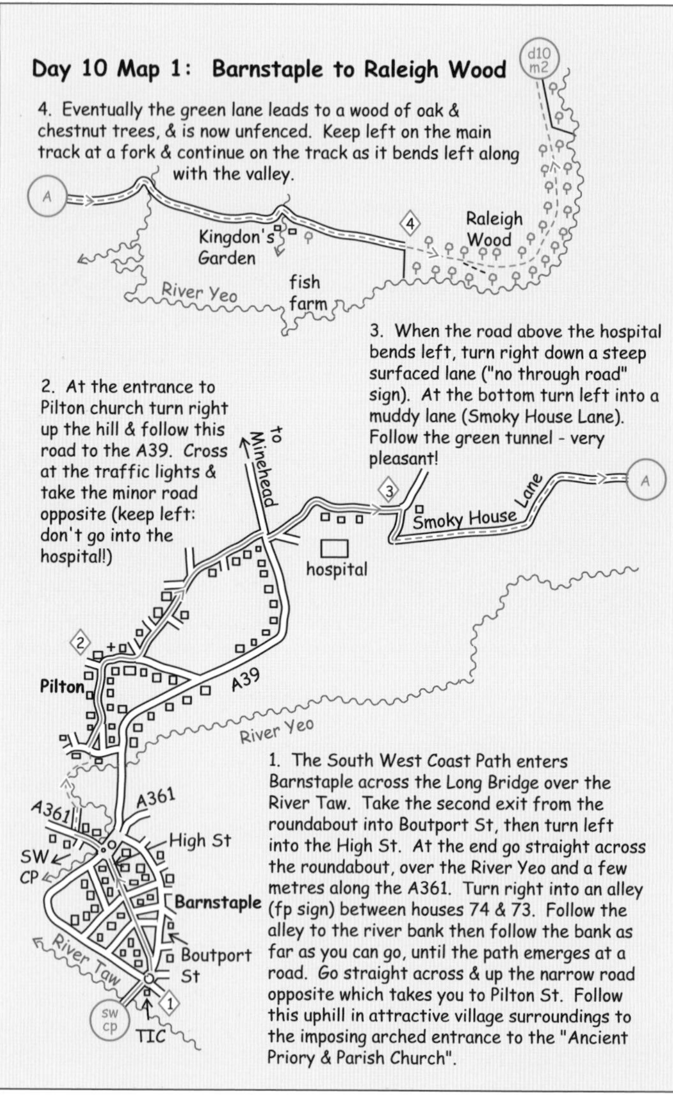
Day 10 Map 1: Barnstaple to Raleigh Wood
d10 m2
4. Eventually the green lane leads to a wood of oak & chestnut trees, & is now unfenced. Keep left on the main track at a fork & continue on the track as it bends left along with the valley.
A
Kingdon's Garden
4
Raleigh Wood
River Yeo
fish farm
3. When the road above the hospital bends left, turn right down a steep surfaced lane ("no through road" sign). At the bottom turn left into a muddy lane (Smoky House Lane). Follow the green tunnel - very pleasant!
2. At the entrance to Pilton church turn right up the hill & follow this road to the A39. Cross at the traffic lights & take the minor road opposite (keep left: don't go into the hospital!)
to Minehead
3
Smoky House Lane
A
hospital
2
Pilton
A39
River Yeo
1. The South West Coast Path enters Barnstaple across the Long Bridge over the River Taw. Take the second exit from the roundabout into Boutport St, then turn left into the High St. At the end go straight across the roundabout, over the River Yeo and a few metres along the A361. Turn right into an alley (fp sign) between houses 74 & 73. Follow the alley to the river bank then follow the bank as far as you can go, until the path emerges at a road. Go straight across & up the narrow road opposite which takes you to Pilton St. Follow this uphill in attractive village surroundings to the imposing arched entrance to the "Ancient Priory & Parish Church".
A361
A361
High St
SW
CP
Barnstaple
River Taw
Boutport St
1
SW cp
TIC

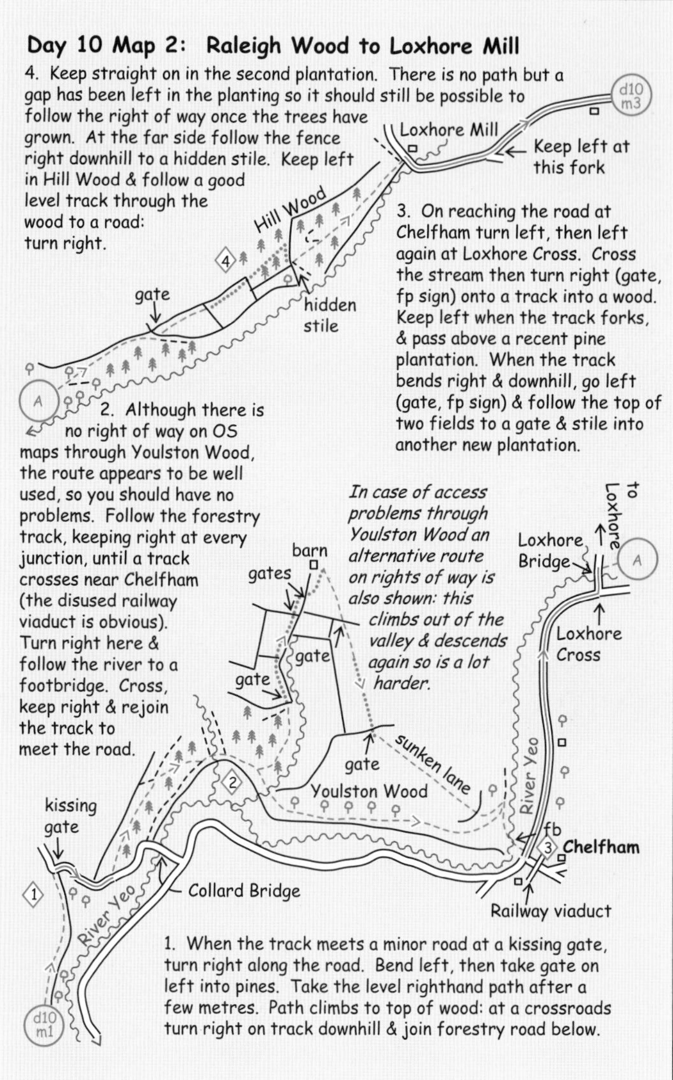
Day 10 Map 2: Raleigh Wood to Loxhore Mill
4. Keep straight on in the second plantation. There is no path but a gap has been left in the planting so it should still be possible to follow the right of way once the trees have grown. At the far side follow the fence right downhill to a hidden stile. Keep left in Hill Wood & follow a good level track through the wood to a road: turn right.
d10 m3
Loxhore Mill
Keep left at this fork
Hill Wood
4
3. On reaching the road at Chelfham turn left, then left again at Loxhore Cross. Cross the stream then turn right (gate, fp sign) onto a track into a wood. Keep left when the track forks, & pass above a recent pine plantation. When the track bends right & downhill, go left (gate, fp sign) & follow the top of two fields to a gate & stile into another new plantation.
gate
hidden stile
A
2. Although there is no right of way on OS maps through Youlston Wood, the route appears to be well used, so you should have no problems. Follow the forestry track, keeping right at every junction, until a track crosses near Chelfham (the disused railway viaduct is obvious). Turn right here & follow the river to a footbridge. Cross, keep right & rejoin the track to meet the road.
In case of access problems through Youlston Wood an alternative route on rights of way is also shown: this climbs out of the valley & descends again so is a lot harder.
to Loxhore
Loxhore Bridge
A
barn
gates
gate
gate
Loxhore Cross
River Yeo
gate
sunken lane
2
Youlston Wood
kissing gate
fb
3
Chelfham
1
River Yeo
Collard Bridge
Railway viaduct
1. When the track meets a minor road at a kissing gate, turn right along the road. Bend left, then take gate on left into pines. Take the level righthand path after a few metres. Path climbs to top of wood: at a crossroads turn right on track downhill & join forestry road below.
d10 m1

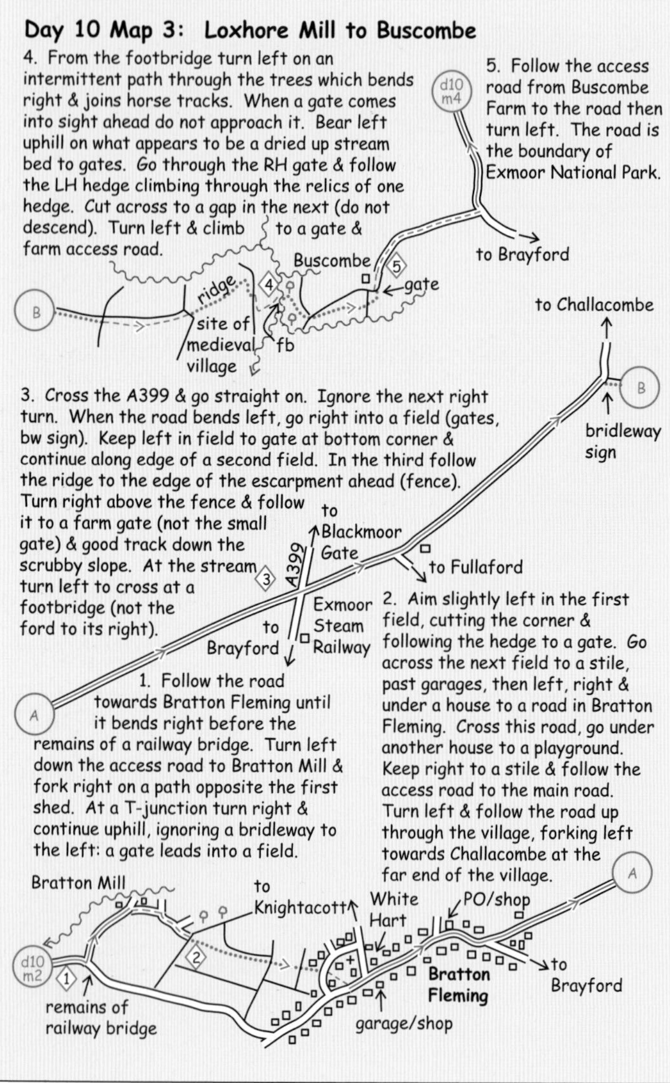
Day 10 Map 3: Loxhore Mill to Buscombe
4. From the footbridge turn left on an intermittent path through the trees which bends right & joins horse tracks. When a gate comes into sight ahead do not approach it. Bear left uphill on what appears to be a dried up stream bed to gates. Go through the RH gate & follow the LH hedge climbing through the relics of one hedge. Cut across to a gap in the next (do not descend). Turn left & climb to a gate & farm access road.
d10 m4
5. Follow the access road from Buscombe Farm to the road then turn left. The road is the boundary of Exmoor National Park.
to Brayford
Buscombe
5
gate
ridge
4
B
site of medieval village
fb
to Challacombe
B
bridleway sign
3. Cross the A399 & go straight on. Ignore the next right turn. When the road bends left, go right into a field (gates, bw sign). Keep left in field to gate at bottom corner & continue along edge of a second field. In the third follow the ridge to the edge of the escarpment ahead (fence). Turn right above the fence & follow it to a farm gate (not the small gate) & good track down the scrubby slope. At the stream turn left to cross at a footbridge (not the ford to its right).
to Blackmoor Gate
A399
3
to Fullaford
Exmoor Steam Railway
to Brayford
2. Aim slightly left in the first field, cutting the corner & following the hedge to a gate. Go across the next field to a stile, past garages, then left, right & under a house to a road in Bratton Fleming. Cross this road, go under another house to a playground. Keep right to a stile & follow the access road to the main road. Turn left & follow the road up through the village, forking left towards Challacombe at the far end of the village.
A
1. Follow the road towards Bratton Fleming until it bends right before the remains of a railway bridge. Turn left down the access road to Bratton Mill & fork right on a path opposite the first shed. At a T-junction turn right & continue uphill, ignoring a bridleway to the left: a gate leads into a field.
A
Bratton Mill
to Knightacott
White Hart
PO/shop
d10 m2
1
2
remains of railway bridge
Bratton Fleming
to Brayford
garage/shop

Day 10 Map 4: Buscombe to South Regis Common

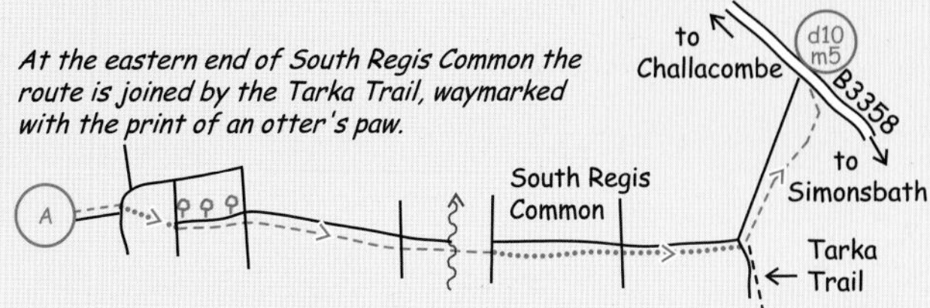

2. The track out of Challacombe climbs up along a ridge & then along the flank of South Regis Common: the first Exmoor moorland on the walk. The route is clear for a while, passing a shed, then following the right edge of a field. At the field corner go through the righthand gate then aim slightly right to a gate at the near end of a line of mature beech trees: there is no clear path. Follow an old track with the line of trees on your left. From here the route over South Regis Common is easy to follow: just keep the field boundary on your left. The boundary is an old "mound" hedge, some of it with a fence, some with trees, but always easy to follow. The path sometimes wanders right to avoid wet areas. When the end of the east-west boundary is reached, turn left on a good track to cross the B3358 at gates.

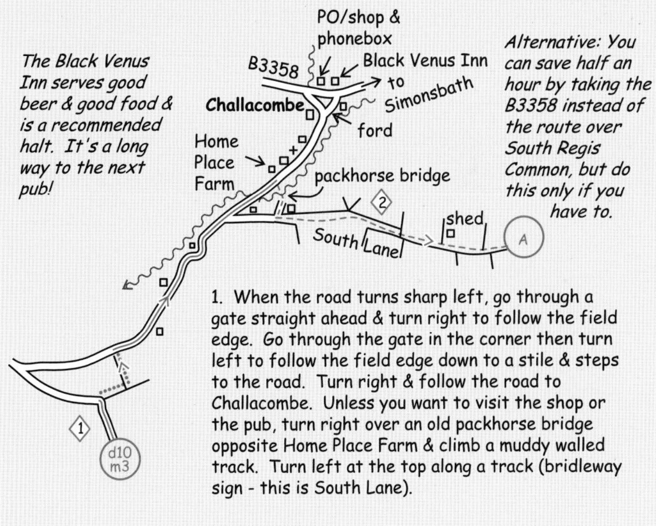

The Black Venus Inn serves good beer & good food & is a recommended halt. It's a long way to the next pub!

Alternative: You can save half an hour by taking the B3358 instead of the route over South Regis Common, but do this only if you have to.

1. When the road turns sharp left, go through a gate straight ahead & turn right to follow the field edge. Go through the gate in the corner then turn left to follow the field edge down to a stile & steps to the road. Turn right & follow the road to Challacombe. Unless you want to visit the shop or the pub, turn right over an old packhorse bridge opposite Home Place Farm & climb a muddy walled track. Turn left at the top along a track (bridleway sign - this is South Lane).

Day 10 Map 5: South Regis Common to Exe Head

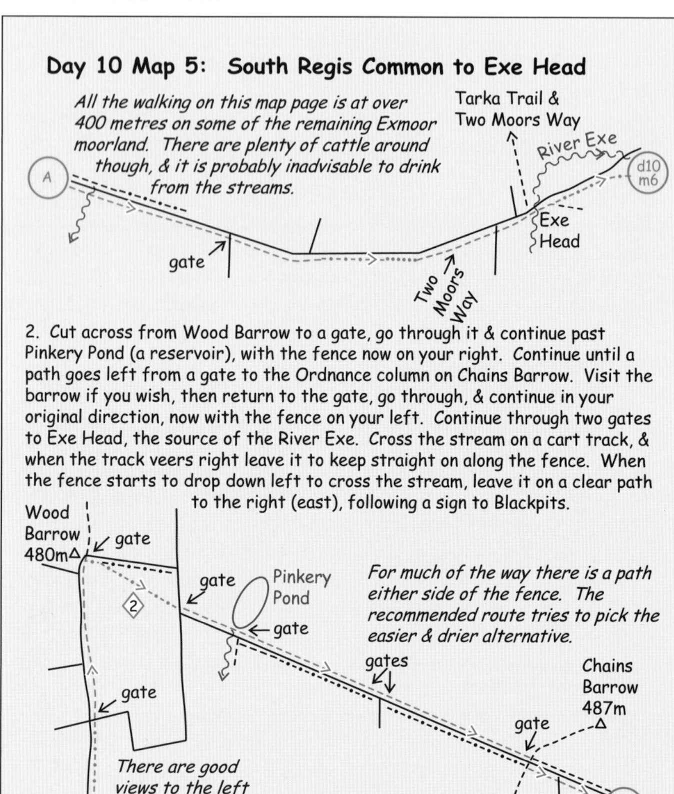

2. Cut across from Wood Barrow to a gate, go through it & continue past Pinkery Pond (a reservoir), with the fence now on your right. Continue until a path goes left from a gate to the Ordnance column on Chains Barrow. Visit the barrow if you wish, then return to the gate, go through, & continue in your original direction, now with the fence on your left. Continue through two gates to Exe Head, the source of the River Exe. Cross the stream on a cart track, & when the track veers right leave it to keep straight on along the fence. When the fence starts to drop down left to cross the stream, leave it on a clear path to the right (east), following a sign to Blackpits.

1. Cross the B3358 (gates) & head north up the moor. The path gradually approaches the hedge on the left then runs alongside it. There is one stretch of the old made track remaining, but mostly the path is a wet & peaty one. At the crest of the ridge is a gate (Woodbarrow Gate), & through the gate on the left is the Wood Barrow mound. To continue the route don't go through the gate: turn right when you get to it & try to spot a vague path diverging from the fence.

Day 10 Map 6: Exe Head to Warren Farm

3. Turn sharp left (north) from the gate down the steep slope (sign "Warren Bridge Postman's Path"). The path is unclear initially but there are one or two marker posts. The path keeps well to the left of the stream & its gorge. The Postman's Path reaches the Warren Farm access road near the bridge. Turn left, cross the bridge & follow the road up to the farm.

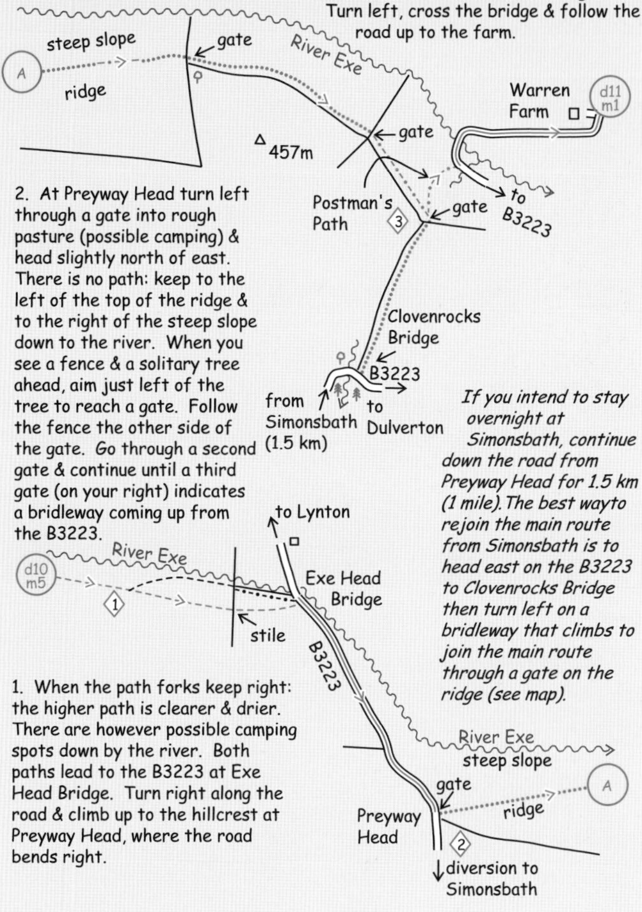

steep slope
gate
River Exe
A
ridge
Warren Farm
d11 m1
gate
457m
to B3223
Postman's Path
3
gate

2. At Preyway Head turn left through a gate into rough pasture (possible camping) & head slightly north of east. There is no path: keep to the left of the top of the ridge & to the right of the steep slope down to the river. When you see a fence & a solitary tree ahead, aim just left of the tree to reach a gate. Follow the fence the other side of the gate. Go through a second gate & continue until a third gate (on your right) indicates a bridleway coming up from the B3223.

Clovenrocks Bridge
B3223
from Simonsbath (1.5 km)
to Dulverton

If you intend to stay overnight at Simonsbath, continue down the road from Preyway Head for 1.5 km (1 mile).The best wayto rejoin the main route from Simonsbath is to head east on the B3223 to Clovenrocks Bridge then turn left on a bridleway that climbs to join the main route through a gate on the ridge (see map).

to Lynton
River Exe
d10 m5
1
Exe Head Bridge
stile
B3223

1. When the path forks keep right: the higher path is clearer & drier. There are however possible camping spots down by the river. Both paths lead to the B3223 at Exe Head Bridge. Turn right along the road & climb up to the hillcrest at Preyway Head, where the road bends right.

River Exe
steep slope
gate
A
ridge
Preyway Head
2
diversion to Simonsbath

Day 11 Map 1: Warren Farm to Almsworthy Common

2. At Larkbarrow Corner turn left & follow the road as far as a cattle grid. Turn right after the cattle grid on a good track signposted "Exford 3 1/2" with a field boundary on the right.

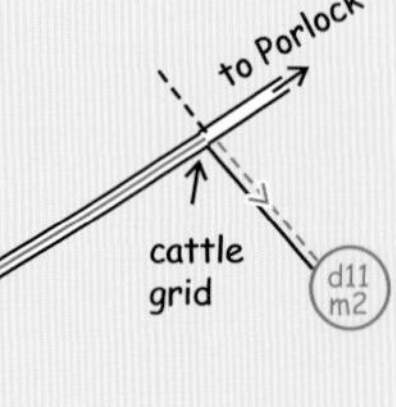

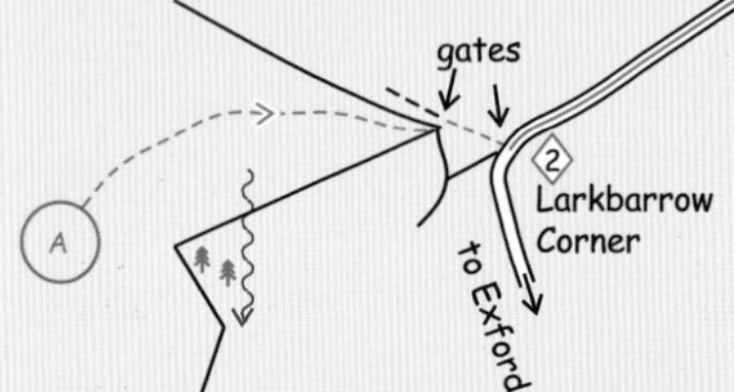

You should by now be getting used to the constant singing of skylarks above you. These birds are much more difficult to spot on the ground.

1. When the access road turns left into the Warren Farm farmyard, go through the gate ahead ("Bridleway to Larkbarrow Corner"). Follow the cart track through another gate, then about 100 metres further on leave the cart track through a gate on the left. Continue in your original direction on a good track, now with the field boundary on the right. Just after the next gate there is a water trough on the left with what appears to be a supply of clean water: the first for a long way. Follow the path along the field boundary, cutting the corner at one point. At the head of Rams Combe the path heads off across the moor of Elsworthy to the northeast: follow it to meet the road at Larkbarrow Corner. The path is easy to follow.

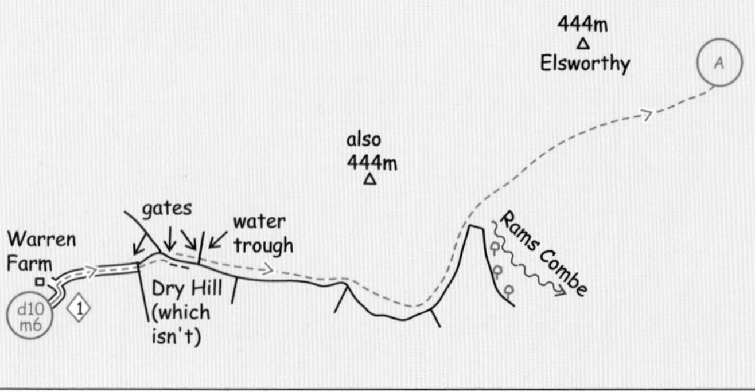

Day 11 Map 2: Almsworthy Common to Little Rowbarrow

Sign on Great Rowbarrow: "Bronze Age Cairns 3500-4000 years old. Please respect." The views from here & along the ridge are extensive & very fine indeed: a great place to be on a clear day.

Great Rowbarrow 510m
Little Rowbarrow
d11 m3
to Porlock
to Stoke Pero
A
ridge
ridge
cairn
bad weather route
d11 m3*
gates

2. The path crosses the northern slope of Exford Common on a bearing averaging about 110 degrees, although it follows the contours of the slope. Cross two minor unfenced roads to turn left along a good track alongside the hedge that forms the southern boundary of the unenclosed moorland. Follow this track past a slight bend to the right, then turn left up a small path through the heather opposite the second gate. There is also a path opposite the first gate: ignore this as it quickly peters out. The second path leads to the ridge & along it to the cairn on Great Rowbarrow. From here a good track eastwards gives a glorious ridge walk to Dunkery Beacon.

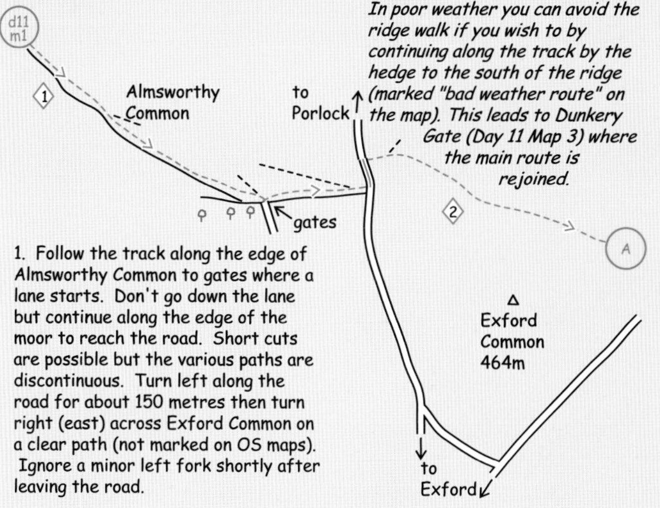

In poor weather you can avoid the ridge walk if you wish to by continuing along the track by the hedge to the south of the ridge (marked "bad weather route" on the map). This leads to Dunkery Gate (Day 11 Map 3) where the main route is rejoined.

1. Follow the track along the edge of Almsworthy Common to gates where a lane starts. Don't go down the lane but continue along the edge of the moor to reach the road. Short cuts are possible but the various paths are discontinuous. Turn left along the road for about 150 metres then turn right (east) across Exford Common on a clear path (not marked on OS maps). Ignore a minor left fork shortly after leaving the road.

Day 11 Map 3: Little Rowbarrow to Little Quarme Wood

3. When the track down the Avill valley leaves the wood at a gate continue along it until it crosses a side stream, then immediately leave the main track for an old sunken path that forks right (uphill). At the road, cross & follow a good track climbing steeply through Little Quarme Wood ("Bridleway to Wheddon Cross").

2. At Dunkery Gate turn right down the road for a few metres, then before the bridge turn left on a cart track (sign "Wheddon Cross 2 1/2"). Go through a gate into rough pasture. When a ruined hedge bank comes up from the right, fork right off the main track, go through the gap in the hedge bank & follow it ahead to a stream. Cross the stream then turn right to follow it down to a gate (no path). Go through the gate & turn left to follow the hedge bank. Go through a gap in a decrepit field boundary (trees & mound), & continue for a few metres until you can join a track that descends to the right. As the track nears the valley bottom it enters the trees. When a bridleway signed to Spangate goes left across a side stream keep straight on (signed "Drapers Way") to ford the River Avill & follow a good track through the woods down the valley. Ignore a bridleway to Combeshead a bit further on: keep to the valley track.

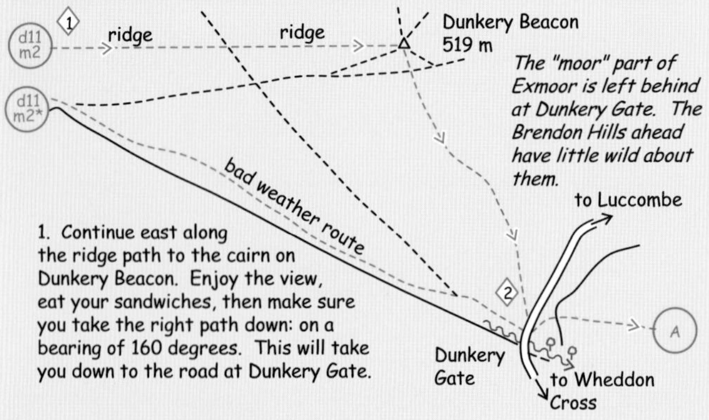

The "moor" part of Exmoor is left behind at Dunkery Gate. The Brendon Hills ahead have little wild about them.

1. Continue east along the ridge path to the cairn on Dunkery Beacon. Enjoy the view, eat your sandwiches, then make sure you take the right path down: on a bearing of 160 degrees. This will take you down to the road at Dunkery Gate.

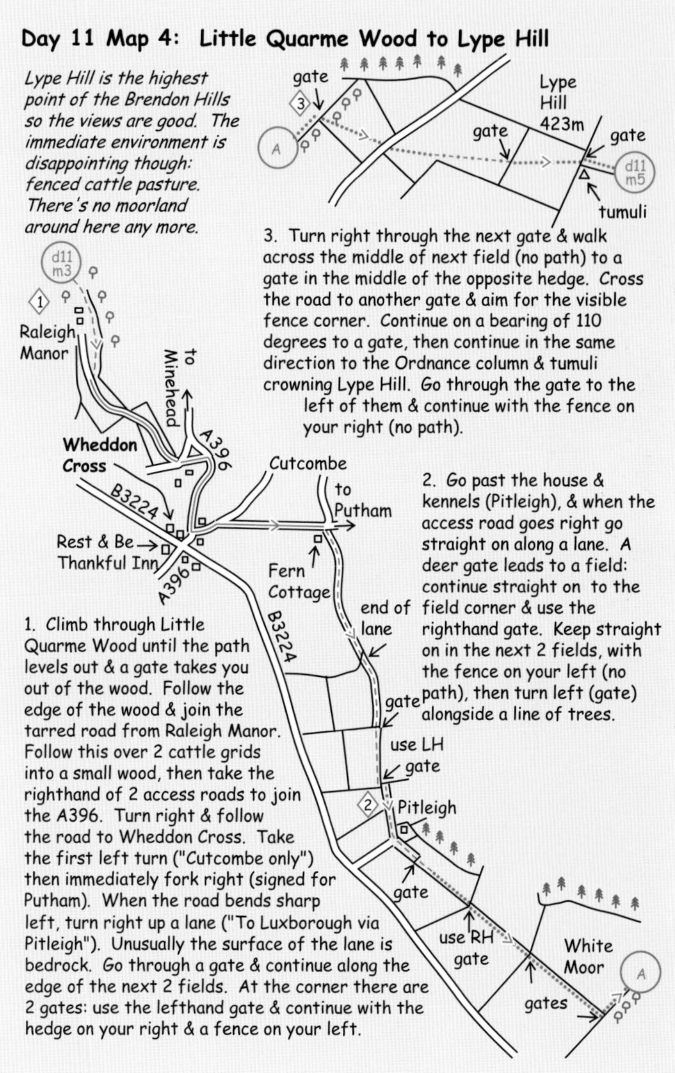

Day 11 Map 4: Little Quarme Wood to Lype Hill
Lype Hill is the highest point of the Brendon Hills so the views are good. The immediate environment is disappointing though: fenced cattle pasture. There's no moorland around here any more.
gate
3
A
Lype Hill 423m
gate
gate
d11 m5
tumuli
3. Turn right through the next gate & walk across the middle of next field (no path) to a gate in the middle of the opposite hedge. Cross the road to another gate & aim for the visible fence corner. Continue on a bearing of 110 degrees to a gate, then continue in the same direction to the Ordnance column & tumuli crowning Lype Hill. Go through the gate to the left of them & continue with the fence on your right (no path).
d11 m3
1
Raleigh Manor
to Minehead
Wheddon Cross
A396
B3224
Cutcombe
to Putham
Rest & Be Thankful Inn
A396
Fern Cottage
2. Go past the house & kennels (Pitleigh), & when the access road goes right go straight on along a lane. A deer gate leads to a field: continue straight on to the field corner & use the righthand gate. Keep straight on in the next 2 fields, with the fence on your left (no path), then turn left (gate) alongside a line of trees.
B3224
end of lane
gate
use LH gate
2
Pitleigh
1. Climb through Little Quarme Wood until the path levels out & a gate takes you out of the wood. Follow the edge of the wood & join the tarred road from Raleigh Manor. Follow this over 2 cattle grids into a small wood, then take the righthand of 2 access roads to join the A396. Turn right & follow the road to Wheddon Cross. Take the first left turn ("Cutcombe only") then immediately fork right (signed for Putham). When the road bends sharp left, turn right up a lane ("To Luxborough via Pitleigh"). Unusually the surface of the lane is bedrock. Go through a gate & continue along the edge of the next 2 fields. At the corner there are 2 gates: use the lefthand gate & continue with the hedge on your right & a fence on your left.
gate
use RH gate
White Moor
gates
A

Day 11 Map 5: Lype Hill to Kingsbridge

2. Pass the Royal Oak on your left then turn right at the T-junction. Afew metres further on, fork left uphill into a lane signed "Bridleway Lower Court Farm & Treborough". Continue up this lane (gates) over the crest of the hill until it ends at a field corner (gate). Continue along the ridge (no path) with the hedge on your left: a lovely stretch of walking with good views.

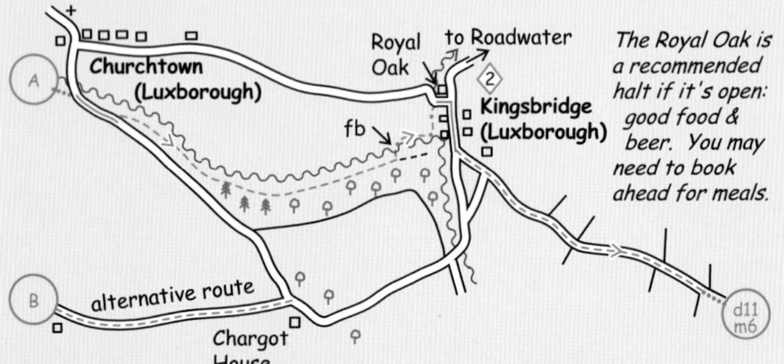

1. From Lype Hill the paths are invisible: gates show the way. Go ahead to a gate, then ahead (east) across a field to another. Aim slightly left (bearing 80 degrees) to another gate, go through & follow the fence on your right to another gate. Go through & head right (east) to the bottom field corner where an old track heads down towards the valley. Take care on the descent, as the rocky surface can be very slippery in the wet. A good track goes right almost immediately: this is a faster but inferior route to Kingsbridge. The main route continues down the old lane to meet another in the valley. Turn right, then right again into a field just before a ford. Cross 2 fields to a road, turn right along the road, then left along the drive to Thorney Cottage. Continue on the path through the woods past the cottage, eventually turning left off it over a footbridge into a field on the left. Keep by the stream initially, then at the end climb to a stile, a house, a short access road & the Royal Oak.

road route to Churchtown & Kingsbridge

ford

A

Lype Hill

d11 m4

1

Newcombe Farm

alternative (inferior) route to Kingsbridge

B

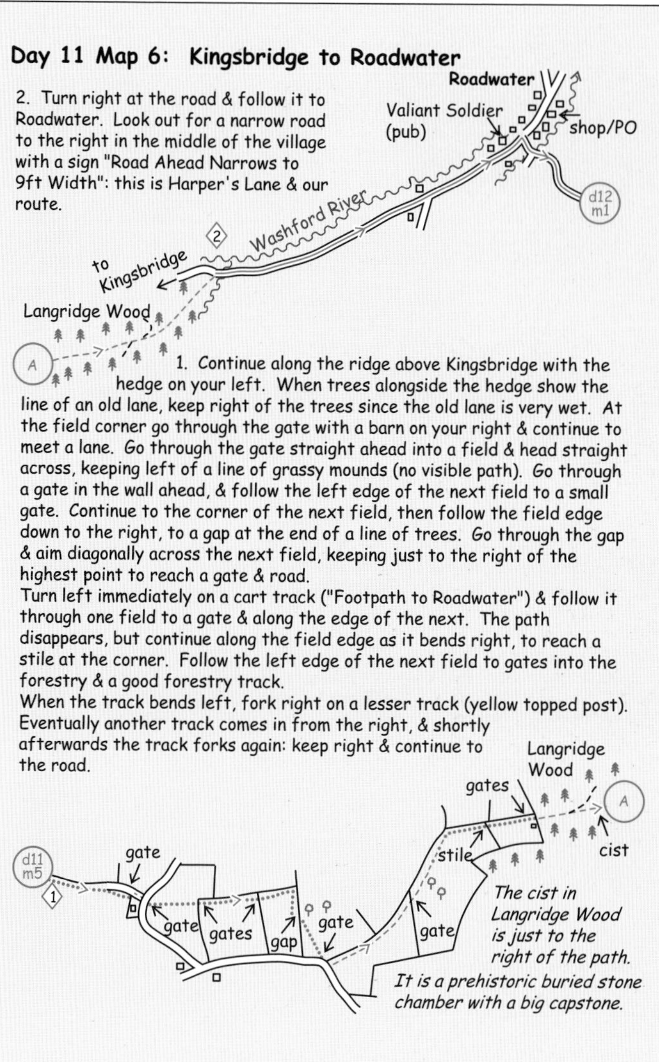
Day 11 Map 6: Kingsbridge to Roadwater
2. Turn right at the road & follow it to Roadwater. Look out for a narrow road to the right in the middle of the village with a sign "Road Ahead Narrows to 9ft Width": this is Harper's Lane & our route.
Roadwater
Valiant Soldier (pub)
shop/PO
d12 m1
Washford River
2
to Kingsbridge
Langridge Wood
A
1. Continue along the ridge above Kingsbridge with the hedge on your left. When trees alongside the hedge show the line of an old lane, keep right of the trees since the old lane is very wet. At the field corner go through the gate with a barn on your right & continue to meet a lane. Go through the gate straight ahead into a field & head straight across, keeping left of a line of grassy mounds (no visible path). Go through a gate in the wall ahead, & follow the left edge of the next field to a small gate. Continue to the corner of the next field, then follow the field edge down to the right, to a gap at the end of a line of trees. Go through the gap & aim diagonally across the next field, keeping just to the right of the highest point to reach a gate & road.
Turn left immediately on a cart track ("Footpath to Roadwater") & follow it through one field to a gate & along the edge of the next. The path disappears, but continue along the field edge as it bends right, to reach a stile at the corner. Follow the left edge of the next field to gates into the forestry & a good forestry track.
When the track bends left, fork right on a lesser track (yellow topped post). Eventually another track comes in from the right, & shortly afterwards the track forks again: keep right & continue to the road.
Langridge Wood
gates
A
cist
stile
d11 m5
1
gate
gate
gates
gap
gate
gate
The cist in Langridge Wood is just to the right of the path.
It is a prehistoric buried stone chamber with a big capstone.

Day 12 Map 1: Roadwater to Monksilver

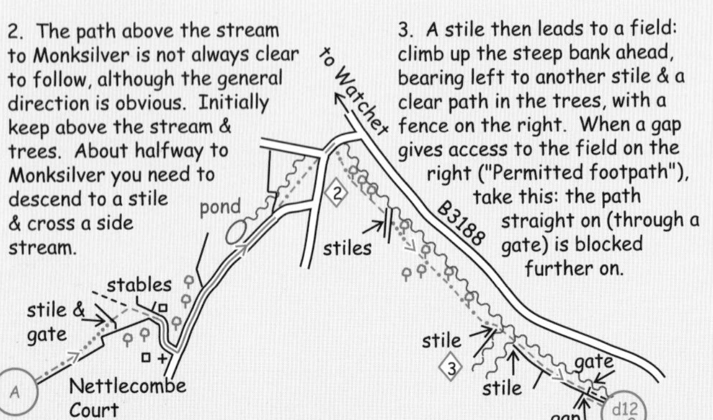

2. The path above the stream to Monksilver is not always clear to follow, although the general direction is obvious. Initially keep above the stream & trees. About halfway to Monksilver you need to descend to a stile & cross a side stream.

3. A stile then leads to a field: climb up the steep bank ahead, bearing left to another stile & a clear path in the trees, with a fence on the right. When a gap gives access to the field on the right ("Permitted footpath"), take this: the path straight on (through a gate) is blocked further on.

1. Climb steeply up the road from Roadwater. Turn left at a stile into a wood ("Chidgley via Kingsdown 2") & follow the path through the top of the wood. A stile leads to a field: turn left & cross another stile immediately. Follow the hedge round to the right (no path) & uphill, over stiles, through a gate & along the edge of a wood to the road. Turn left along the road then right at a gateway to follow a cart track up the field. A gap leads through trees, then continue uphill with a hedge on the left. The field levels out: cut the final corner to a stile (fp junction & sign: head for Nettlecombe). Continue straight on along the right edge of 2 fields (excellent views ahead & to the left), then a fenced track leads to the B3190. Cross to a stile ("Footpath to Nettlecombe") & make your way down as best you can to a gate & stile at the bottom of the small wood (paths indistinct). Follow the field edge down parkland until a stile leads to one of the drives of Nettlecombe Court (now a field centre). Follow the drive to the right through a gate & down to the main access road by the house & church. Turn left along the road. When the road bends right after a pond, go straight on (gate) along the original line of the road, now a grassy track. A gate leads to a road: go straight on then right over a stile ("Footpath to Monksilver").

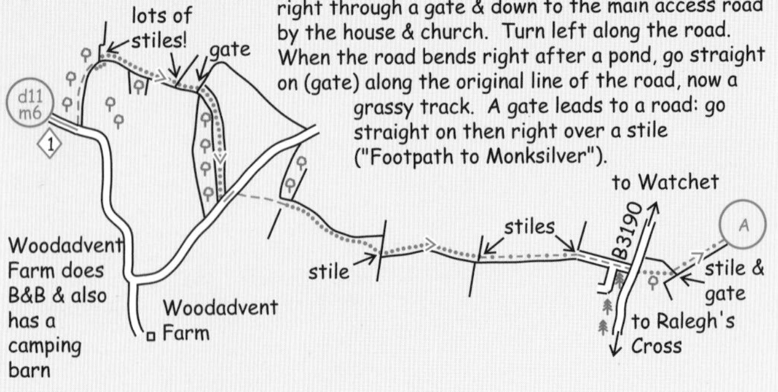

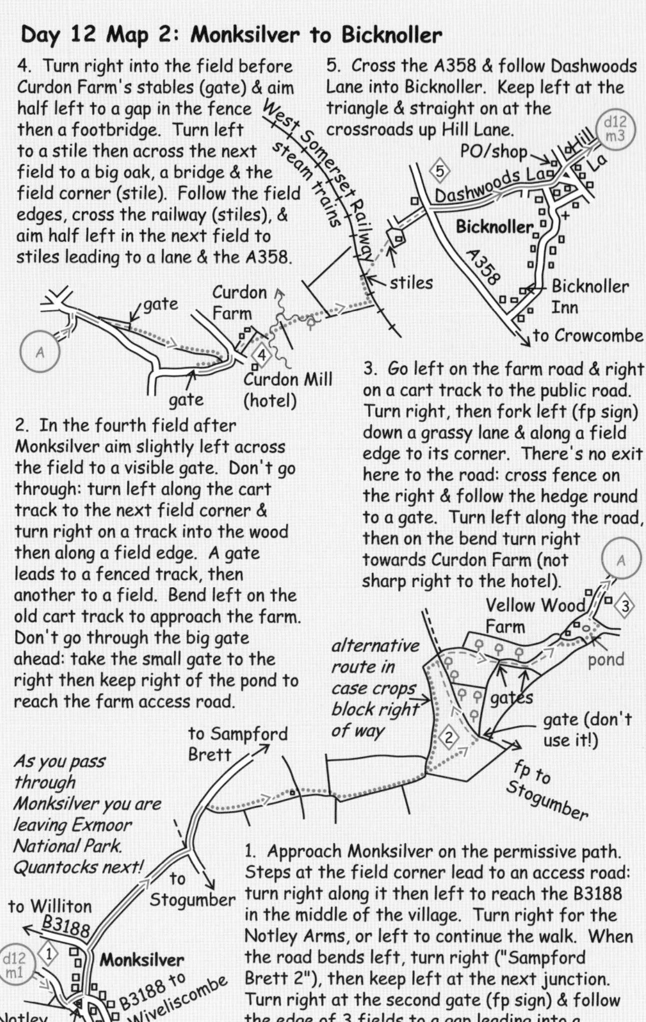

Day 12 Map 2: Monksilver to Bicknoller
4. Turn right into the field before Curdon Farm's stables (gate) & aim half left to a gap in the fence then a footbridge. Turn left to a stile then across the next field to a big oak, a bridge & the field corner (stile). Follow the field edges, cross the railway (stiles), & aim half left in the next field to stiles leading to a lane & the A358.
5. Cross the A358 & follow Dashwoods Lane into Bicknoller. Keep left at the triangle & straight on at the crossroads up Hill Lane.
West Somerset Railway
steam trains
d12 m3
PO/shop
Hill La
Dashwoods La
Bicknoller
A358
stiles
Bicknoller Inn
to Crowcombe
gate
Curdon Farm
A
gate
Curdon Mill (hotel)
3. Go left on the farm road & right on a cart track to the public road. Turn right, then fork left (fp sign) down a grassy lane & along a field edge to its corner. There's no exit here to the road: cross fence on the right & follow the hedge round to a gate. Turn left along the road, then on the bend turn right towards Curdon Farm (not sharp right to the hotel).
2. In the fourth field after Monksilver aim slightly left across the field to a visible gate. Don't go through: turn left along the cart track to the next field corner & turn right on a track into the wood then along a field edge. A gate leads to a fenced track, then another to a field. Bend left on the old cart track to approach the farm. Don't go through the big gate ahead: take the small gate to the right then keep right of the pond to reach the farm access road.
Vellow Wood Farm
pond
alternative route in case crops block right of way
gates
gate (don't use it!)
fp to Stogumber
to Sampford Brett
As you pass through Monksilver you are leaving Exmoor National Park. Quantocks next!
to Stogumber
to Williton
B3188
d12 m1
Monksilver
B3188 to Wiveliscombe
Notley Arms (pub)
1. Approach Monksilver on the permissive path. Steps at the field corner lead to an access road: turn right along it then left to reach the B3188 in the middle of the village. Turn right for the Notley Arms, or left to continue the walk. When the road bends left, turn right ("Sampford Brett 2"), then keep left at the next junction. Turn right at the second gate (fp sign) & follow the edge of 3 fields to a gap leading into a fourth.

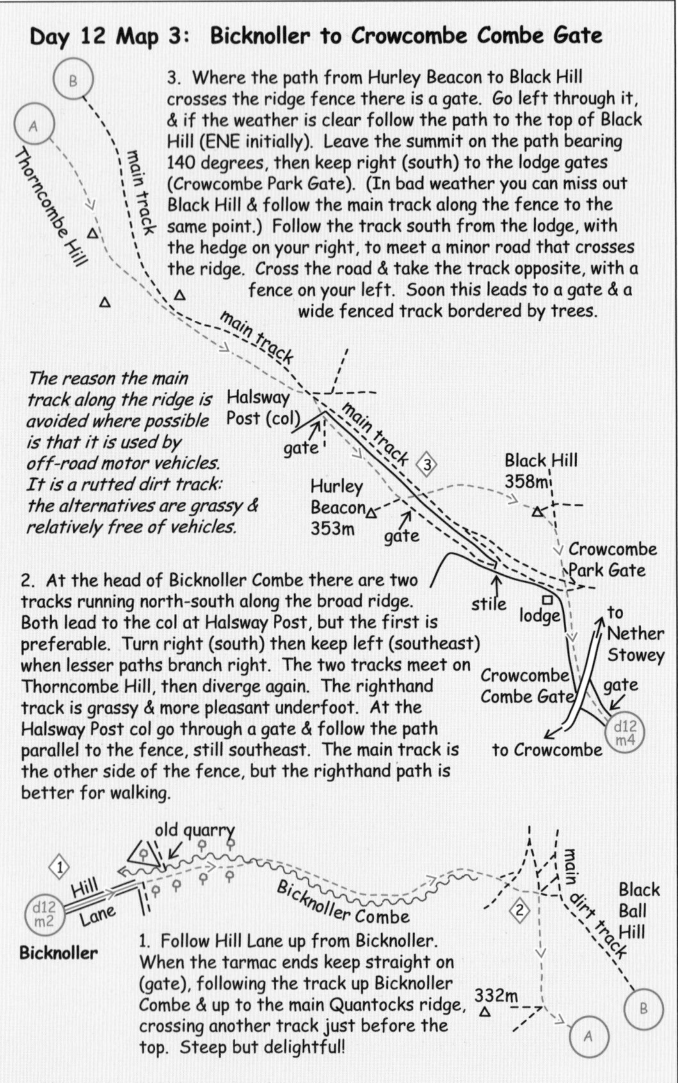
Day 12 Map 3: Bicknoller to Crowcombe Combe Gate
3. Where the path from Hurley Beacon to Black Hill crosses the ridge fence there is a gate. Go left through it, & if the weather is clear follow the path to the top of Black Hill (ENE initially). Leave the summit on the path bearing 140 degrees, then keep right (south) to the lodge gates (Crowcombe Park Gate). (In bad weather you can miss out Black Hill & follow the main track along the fence to the same point.) Follow the track south from the lodge, with the hedge on your right, to meet a minor road that crosses the ridge. Cross the road & take the track opposite, with a fence on your left. Soon this leads to a gate & a wide fenced track bordered by trees.
B
A
Thorncombe Hill
main track
main track
The reason the main track along the ridge is avoided where possible is that it is used by off-road motor vehicles. It is a rutted dirt track: the alternatives are grassy & relatively free of vehicles.
Halsway Post (col)
gate
main track
3
Black Hill 358m
Hurley Beacon 353m
gate
Crowcombe Park Gate
2. At the head of Bicknoller Combe there are two tracks running north-south along the broad ridge. Both lead to the col at Halsway Post, but the first is preferable. Turn right (south) then keep left (southeast) when lesser paths branch right. The two tracks meet on Thorncombe Hill, then diverge again. The righthand track is grassy & more pleasant underfoot. At the Halsway Post col go through a gate & follow the path parallel to the fence, still southeast. The main track is the other side of the fence, but the righthand path is better for walking.
stile
lodge
to Nether Stowey
Crowcombe Combe Gate
gate
d12 m4
to Crowcombe
old quarry
1
Hill Lane
d12 m2
Bicknoller
Bicknoller Combe
main dirt track
2
Black Ball Hill
1. Follow Hill Lane up from Bicknoller. When the tarmac ends keep straight on (gate), following the track up Bicknoller Combe & up to the main Quantocks ridge, crossing another track just before the top. Steep but delightful!
332m
B
A

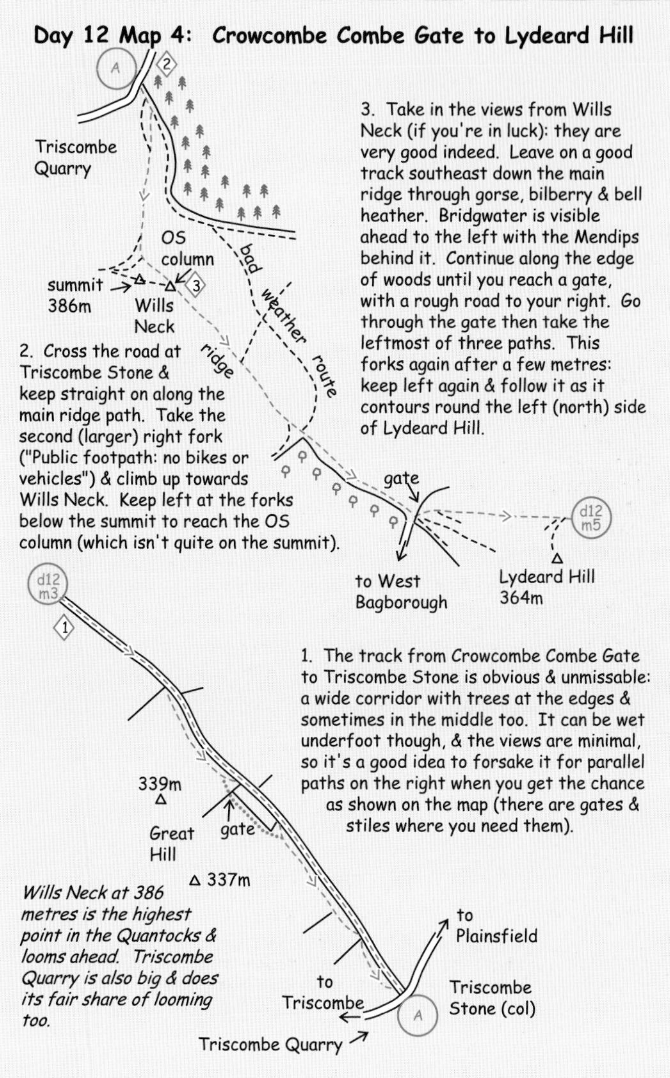
Day 12 Map 4: Crowcombe Combe Gate to Lydeard Hill
A
2
Triscombe
Quarry
3. Take in the views from Wills Neck (if you're in luck): they are very good indeed. Leave on a good track southeast down the main ridge through gorse, bilberry & bell heather. Bridgwater is visible ahead to the left with the Mendips behind it. Continue along the edge of woods until you reach a gate, with a rough road to your right. Go through the gate then take the leftmost of three paths. This forks again after a few metres: keep left again & follow it as it contours round the left (north) side of Lydeard Hill.
OS
column
bad
weather
route
summit
386m
Wills
Neck
3
ridge
2. Cross the road at Triscombe Stone & keep straight on along the main ridge path. Take the second (larger) right fork ("Public footpath: no bikes or vehicles") & climb up towards Wills Neck. Keep left at the forks below the summit to reach the OS column (which isn't quite on the summit).
gate
d12
m5
to West
Bagborough
Lydeard Hill
364m
d12
m3
1
1. The track from Crowcombe Combe Gate to Triscombe Stone is obvious & unmissable: a wide corridor with trees at the edges & sometimes in the middle too. It can be wet underfoot though, & the views are minimal, so it's a good idea to forsake it for parallel paths on the right when you get the chance as shown on the map (there are gates & stiles where you need them).
339m
Great
Hill
gate
337m
Wills Neck at 386 metres is the highest point in the Quantocks & looms ahead. Triscombe Quarry is also big & does its fair share of looming too.
to
Plainsfield
to
Triscombe
A
Triscombe
Stone (col)
Triscombe Quarry

Day 12 Map 5: Lydeard Hill to Blaxhold Farm

3. Turn right at the road then immediately left (fp sign). Follow the hedge up the field to a gap in the top right corner. Go through & continue, now with a hedge on your left. At the end of the field there is no exit (despite this being a right of way) so you will have to go right to a gate in the other corner. Almost opposite, a footpath sign indicates the way into a farmyard then along a good access track at right angles to the road (don't head for the farm). Pass a bungalow, then at the next farm (Great Holwell) turn left through the farmyard then right through a gate into a field. A track diverges gradually from the hedge on the left: follow it through a gate & above a covert. The track peters out here: climb steeply up right to an electricity pole & then a stile on the right at the top of the field. Cross this, then go left through a gate & continue with the hedge on your left.

2. Turn right over the stile & follow the field edge. The second field is a big cultivated prairie: follow its edge past one gate on the right, then just after the hedge bends slightly to the left there is a second gate. Turn right through this gate & go ahead with a hedge on your left. Turn right at the road, then when it bends right turn left into the farmyard (gate, fp sign). Bear left to a shiny gate (fp sign) into a field. Cross a fence (stile) then follow the hedge round to the left until you see a gate ahead: cut across to it (bearing 60 degrees). Don't go through the gate: turn right & follow the edge of the big field downhill to a stile, ford & short lane leading to a road.

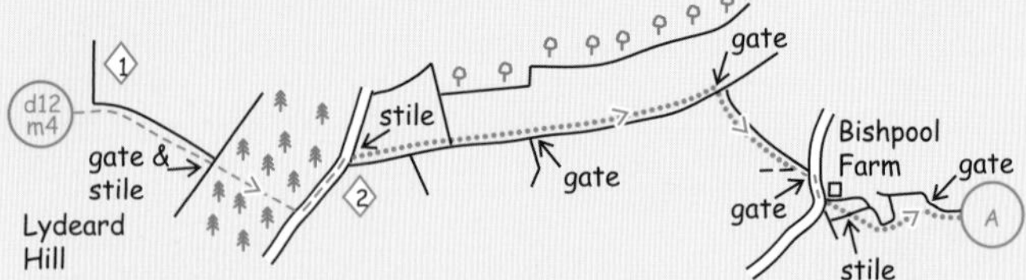

1. Follow the path round the north of Lydeard Hill: it is joined by a fence on the left. A gate leads to a forestry plantation & a good track through the trees. You have now left the Quantocks moorland behind you. At the far edge of the wood turn left along a lane then look out for a stile & footpath sign on the right.

Day 12 Map 6: Blaxhold Farm to Goathurst

3. Follow the road from Cobb's Cross Farm round a righthand bend, then turn left at the next junction (signed to Bridgwater). Turn left in the middle of Goathurst, towards Bridgwater again. The road bends left, then just before a cottage on the left, turn right (stile & fp sign) & follow the field edge, with a wood & a lane on your left.

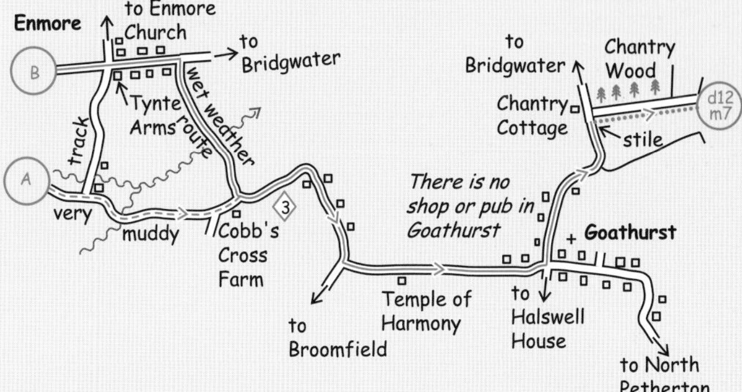

2. Continue on the road for just over 1 km (3/4 mile) to a school & a right turn. Here you have a choice to make. If the weather is dry & you don't want to visit the pub, then turn right & follow the road down, across a stream & round a lefthand bend. When the road bends right, turn left along a lane in a green tunnel. This leads to Cobb's Cross Farm where you keep straight on to regain tarmac. Unfortunately the lane is classified as a "road used as a public path", which allows motor vehicles to use it. Offroad motorbikes have turned it into an awful quagmire, so in wet weather stick to the main road, past the pub (Tynte Arms), then take the next right turn to rejoin the main route at a bend in the road by Cobb's Cross Farm.

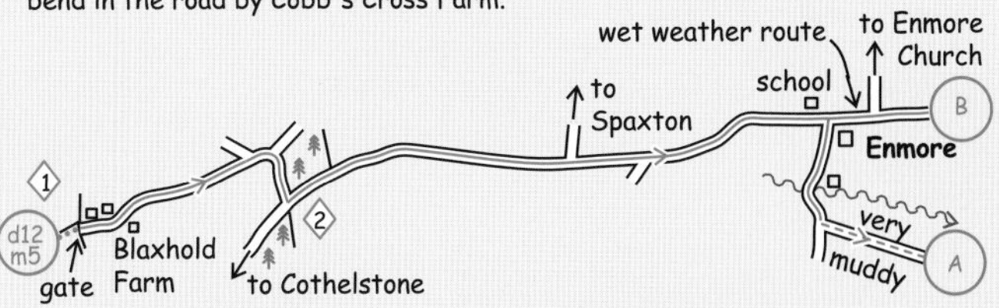

1. Follow the hedge to the field corner, where a gate leads to the end of a tarmac road & a house. Follow the tarmac past Blaxhold Farm to the public road & turn sharp left. Take care: although it is a narrow unclassified road it is busy & the traffic is fast.

Day 12 Map 7: Goathurst to Bridgwater

Bridgwater is not a pretty place: you need to go through it as it is the lowest point at which the River Parrett is bridged. Luckily you can get quite close to the town centre before joining a road or meeting houses.

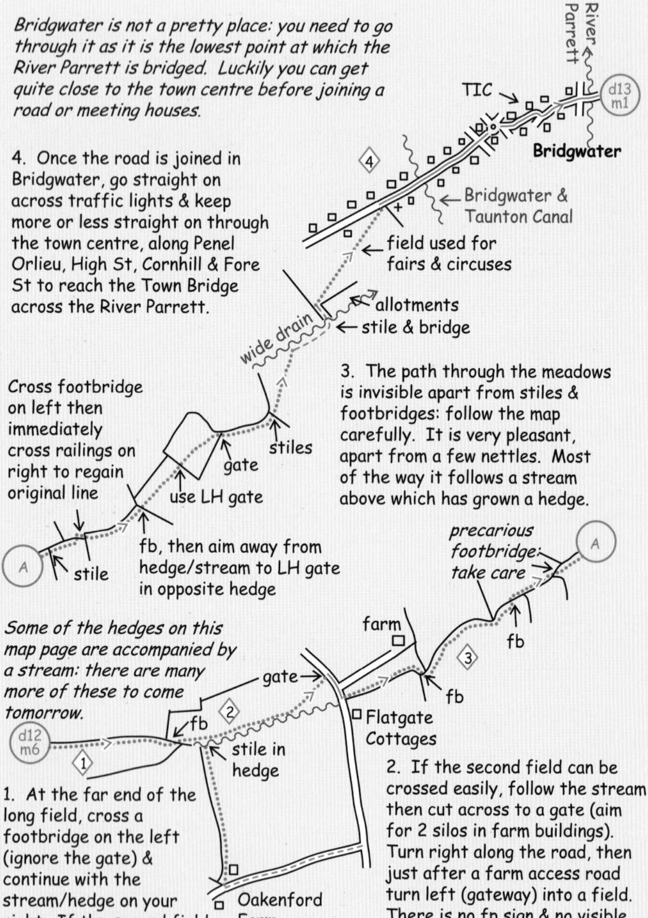

River Parrett

TIC

d13 m1

Bridgwater

4. Once the road is joined in Bridgwater, go straight on across traffic lights & keep more or less straight on through the town centre, along Penel Orlieu, High St, Cornhill & Fore St to reach the Town Bridge across the River Parrett.

Bridgwater & Taunton Canal

field used for fairs & circuses

allotments

stile & bridge

wide drain

Cross footbridge on left then immediately cross railings on right to regain original line

gate

stiles

use LH gate

3. The path through the meadows is invisible apart from stiles & footbridges: follow the map carefully. It is very pleasant, apart from a few nettles. Most of the way it follows a stream above which has grown a hedge.

A

stile

fb, then aim away from hedge/stream to LH gate in opposite hedge

precarious footbridge: take care

A

Some of the hedges on this map page are accompanied by a stream: there are many more of these to come tomorrow.

farm

fb

gate

fb

Flatgate Cottages

d12 m6

fb

stile in hedge

1. At the far end of the long field, cross a footbridge on the left (ignore the gate) & continue with the stream/hedge on your right. If the second field is blocked with crops, take the alternative route via Oakenford Farm.

Oakenford Farm

2. If the second field can be crossed easily, follow the stream then cut across to a gate (aim for 2 silos in farm buildings). Turn right along the road, then just after a farm access road turn left (gateway) into a field. There is no fp sign & no visible path. Follow the right edge of the field to a footbridge.

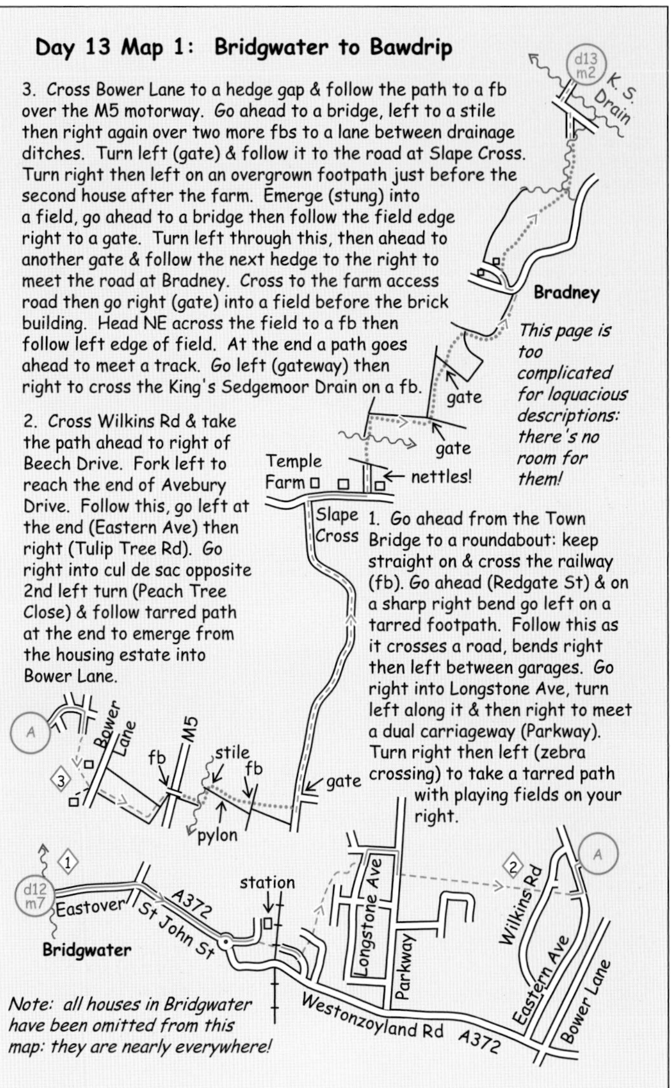
Day 13 Map 1: Bridgwater to Bawdrip
3. Cross Bower Lane to a hedge gap & follow the path to a fb over the M5 motorway. Go ahead to a bridge, left to a stile then right again over two more fbs to a lane between drainage ditches. Turn left (gate) & follow it to the road at Slape Cross. Turn right then left on an overgrown footpath just before the second house after the farm. Emerge (stung) into a field, go ahead to a bridge then follow the field edge right to a gate. Turn left through this, then ahead to another gate & follow the next hedge to the right to meet the road at Bradney. Cross to the farm access road then go right (gate) into a field before the brick building. Head NE across the field to a fb then follow left edge of field. At the end a path goes ahead to meet a track. Go left (gateway) then right to cross the King's Sedgemoor Drain on a fb.
2. Cross Wilkins Rd & take the path ahead to right of Beech Drive. Fork left to reach the end of Avebury Drive. Follow this, go left at the end (Eastern Ave) then right (Tulip Tree Rd). Go right into cul de sac opposite 2nd left turn (Peach Tree Close) & follow tarred path at the end to emerge from the housing estate into Bower Lane.
1. Go ahead from the Town Bridge to a roundabout: keep straight on & cross the railway (fb). Go ahead (Redgate St) & on a sharp right bend go left on a tarred footpath. Follow this as it crosses a road, bends right then left between garages. Go right into Longstone Ave, turn left along it & then right to meet a dual carriageway (Parkway). Turn right then left (zebra crossing) to take a tarred path with playing fields on your right.
This page is too complicated for loquacious descriptions: there's no room for them!
d13 m2
K. S. Drain
Bradney
gate
gate
Temple Farm
nettles!
Slape Cross
A
Bower Lane
M5
fb
stile
fb
3
gate
pylon
1
d12 m7
Eastover
A372
St John St
Bridgwater
station
Longstone Ave
Parkway
2
Wilkins Rd
A
Eastern Ave
Bower Lane
Westonzoyland Rd
A372
Note: all houses in Bridgwater have been omitted from this map: they are nearly everywhere!

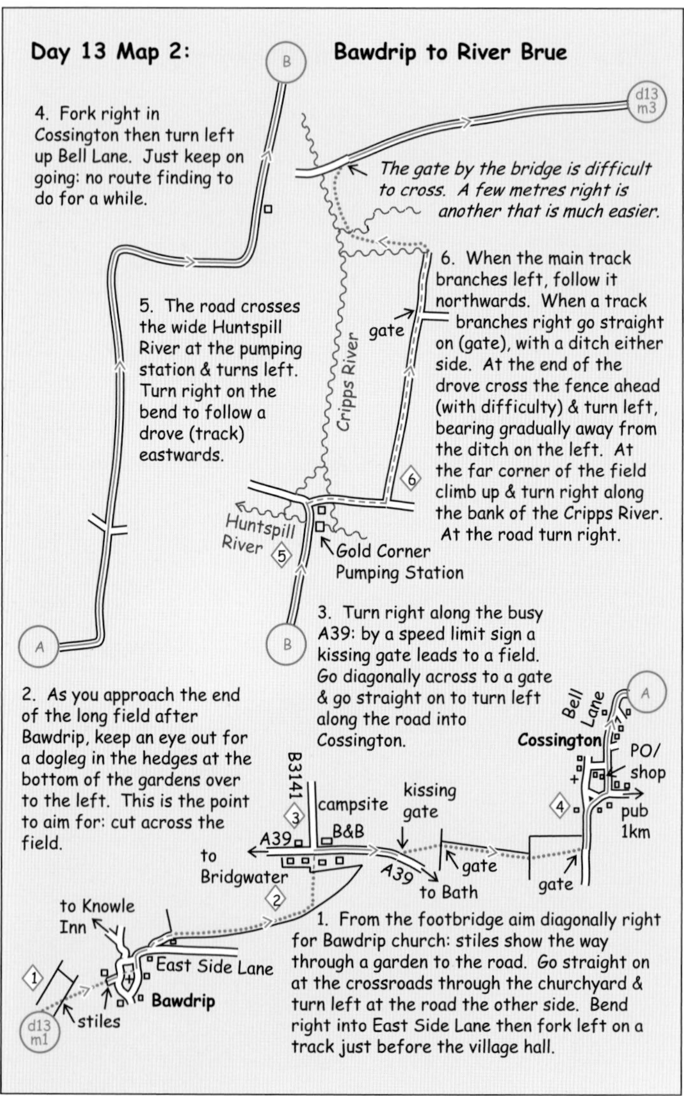

Day 13 Map 2:
Bawdrip to River Brue
B
d13 m3
4. Fork right in Cossington then turn left up Bell Lane. Just keep on going: no route finding to do for a while.
The gate by the bridge is difficult to cross. A few metres right is another that is much easier.
6. When the main track branches left, follow it northwards. When a track branches right go straight on (gate), with a ditch either side. At the end of the drove cross the fence ahead (with difficulty) & turn left, bearing gradually away from the ditch on the left. At the far corner of the field climb up & turn right along the bank of the Cripps River. At the road turn right.
5. The road crosses the wide Huntspill River at the pumping station & turns left. Turn right on the bend to follow a drove (track) eastwards.
gate
Cripps River
6
Huntspill River
5
Gold Corner Pumping Station
A
B
3. Turn right along the busy A39: by a speed limit sign a kissing gate leads to a field. Go diagonally across to a gate & go straight on to turn left along the road into Cossington.
A
Bell Lane
Cossington
PO/ shop
4
pub 1km
2. As you approach the end of the long field after Bawdrip, keep an eye out for a dogleg in the hedges at the bottom of the gardens over to the left. This is the point to aim for: cut across the field.
B3141
3
campsite
kissing gate
B&B
A39
to Bridgwater
A39
to Bath
gate
gate
2
to Knowle Inn
East Side Lane
1
Bawdrip
stiles
d13 m1
1. From the footbridge aim diagonally right for Bawdrip church: stiles show the way through a garden to the road. Go straight on at the crossroads through the churchyard & turn left at the road the other side. Bend right into East Side Lane then fork left on a track just before the village hall.

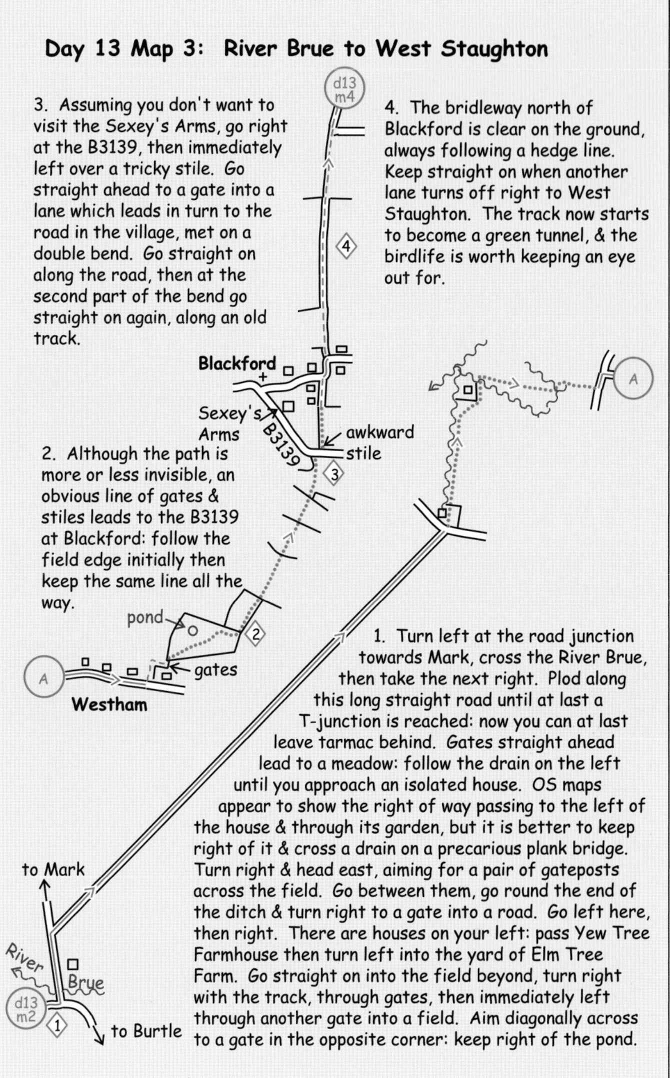
Day 13 Map 3: River Brue to West Staughton
d13 m4
3. Assuming you don't want to visit the Sexey's Arms, go right at the B3139, then immediately left over a tricky stile. Go straight ahead to a gate into a lane which leads in turn to the road in the village, met on a double bend. Go straight on along the road, then at the second part of the bend go straight on again, along an old track.
4. The bridleway north of Blackford is clear on the ground, always following a hedge line. Keep straight on when another lane turns off right to West Staughton. The track now starts to become a green tunnel, & the birdlife is worth keeping an eye out for.
4
Blackford
A
Sexey's Arms
B3139
awkward stile
3
2. Although the path is more or less invisible, an obvious line of gates & stiles leads to the B3139 at Blackford: follow the field edge initially then keep the same line all the way.
pond
2
A
gates
Westham
1. Turn left at the road junction towards Mark, cross the River Brue, then take the next right. Plod along this long straight road until at last a T-junction is reached: now you can at last leave tarmac behind. Gates straight ahead lead to a meadow: follow the drain on the left until you approach an isolated house. OS maps appear to show the right of way passing to the left of the house & through its garden, but it is better to keep right of it & cross a drain on a precarious plank bridge. Turn right & head east, aiming for a pair of gateposts across the field. Go between them, go round the end of the ditch & turn right to a gate into a road. Go left here, then right. There are houses on your left: pass Yew Tree Farmhouse then turn left into the yard of Elm Tree Farm. Go straight on into the field beyond, turn right with the track, through gates, then immediately left through another gate into a field. Aim diagonally across to a gate in the opposite corner: keep right of the pond.
to Mark
River Brue
d13 m2
1
to Burtle

Day 13 Map 4: West Staughton to Brinscombe Hill

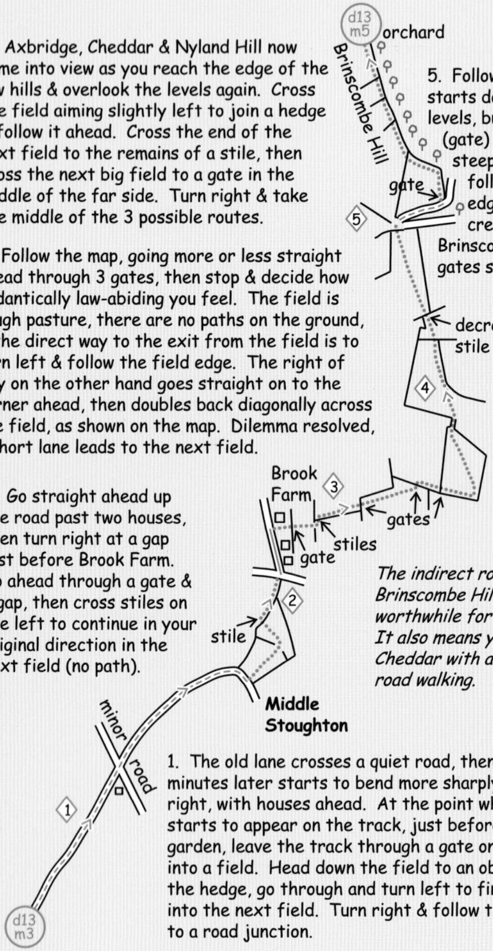

4. Axbridge, Cheddar & Nyland Hill now come into view as you reach the edge of the low hills & overlook the levels again. Cross the field aiming slightly left to join a hedge & follow it ahead. Cross the end of the next field to the remains of a stile, then cross the next big field to a gate in the middle of the far side. Turn right & take the middle of the 3 possible routes.

5. Follow the lane as it starts downhill to the levels, but turn left (gate) before it gets steep, & climb up to follow the field edges along the crest of Brinscombe Hill: gates show the way.

3. Follow the map, going more or less straight ahead through 3 gates, then stop & decide how pedantically law-abiding you feel. The field is rough pasture, there are no paths on the ground, & the direct way to the exit from the field is to turn left & follow the field edge. The right of way on the other hand goes straight on to the corner ahead, then doubles back diagonally across the field, as shown on the map. Dilemma resolved, a short lane leads to the next field.

2. Go straight ahead up the road past two houses, then turn right at a gap just before Brook Farm. Go ahead through a gate & a gap, then cross stiles on the left to continue in your original direction in the next field (no path).

The indirect route along Brinscombe Hill is well worthwhile for the views. It also means you can reach Cheddar with almost no road walking.

1. The old lane crosses a quiet road, then a few minutes later starts to bend more sharply to the right, with houses ahead. At the point where tarmac starts to appear on the track, just before the first garden, leave the track through a gate on the left into a field. Head down the field to an obvious gap in the hedge, go through and turn left to find a stile into the next field. Turn right & follow the hedge up to a road junction.

Day 13 Map 5: Brinscombe Hill to Cheddar

3. Go straight on over the bridge if you are in a hurry to get to Cheddar, but this isn't the recommended route as there is better walking along the river bank. Instead of crossing the bridge, turn right along the bank of the river & follow it all the way to Cheddar. Turn left along the A371 into the town, then turn right along the road towards the Gorge.

Cheddar
to YH & Axbridge
d14 m1
A371
to Gorge
camp site
camp site
A371
to Wells
old railway bridge
Cheddar Yeo
B3151
Hythe Bow Bridge
B3151
to Wedmore
A

2. The track crosses bridges over a stream then the River Axe by a pumping station. Continue to its end (gate) then go straight an along the drain to reach the Cheddar Yeo (river) at a bridge.

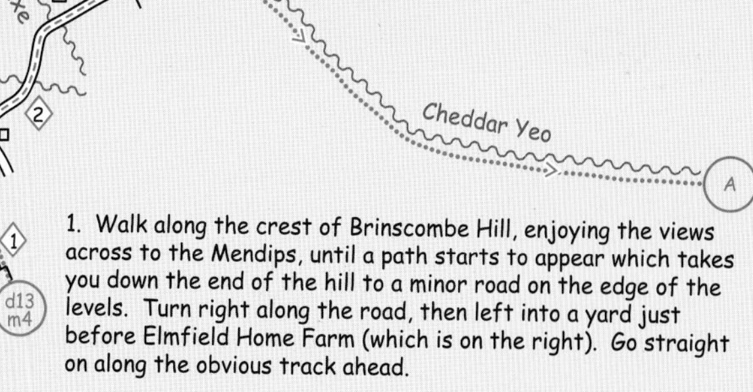

1. Walk along the crest of Brinscombe Hill, enjoying the views across to the Mendips, until a path starts to appear which takes you down the end of the hill to a minor road on the edge of the levels. Turn right along the road, then left into a yard just before Elmfield Home Farm (which is on the right). Go straight on along the obvious track ahead.

Day 14 Map 1: Cheddar to Beacon Batch

1. Follow the road to the Gorge past a mini-roundabout by the Riverside Inn, then turn right into The Lippiatt. Near the top of the hill turn left into Lynch Lane, then at the top, with the gate into Glen View in front of you, turn left (fp sign) on a good footpath uphill in bramble thickets to reach the lookout tower & the top of the Jacob's Ladder stairs. Turn right & follow a clear path along the top of the gorge, still climbing steeply.

2. The path above the gorge reaches a gate in the fence on the right near its high point: don't go through. Instead follow the path ahead, which starts to descend into the trees, crosses a stile, & then goes through a gate. Continue down, keeping right when the path forks, to cross the B3135 into Black Rock Nature Reserve: a wooded dry valley. Follow the main valley path until the valley forks.

3. At the valley fork don't go through the gate ahead into the Velvet Bottom Nature Reserve: turn left instead, go through the next gate then fork right (gate & stile) to follow a permissive path through Long Wood Nature Reserve. These wooded valleys are lovely to walk along.

4. Shortly after passing the water sink where the stream disappears, cross a footbridge on the right & climb out of the valley to a stile. Keep left along the top of the wood & join a track which leads to a tarmac lane. Turn right, then right again at the road.

5. Cross a stream then turn left (stile) & follow the field edge up to a stile into the trees by the stream. A good path leads up through the trees to a stile at the far end. Follow the fence ahead: the path peters out but keep going (up!).

d14 m2
fb
stile
water sink
Rhino Rift
Long Wood
gate & stile
gate
gate
Velvet Bottom
Black Rock
B3135
stile
A
gate (don't use)
255m
A
gate
Cheddar Gorge
tower
B3135
to YH
Riverside Inn
Cheddar
d13 m5

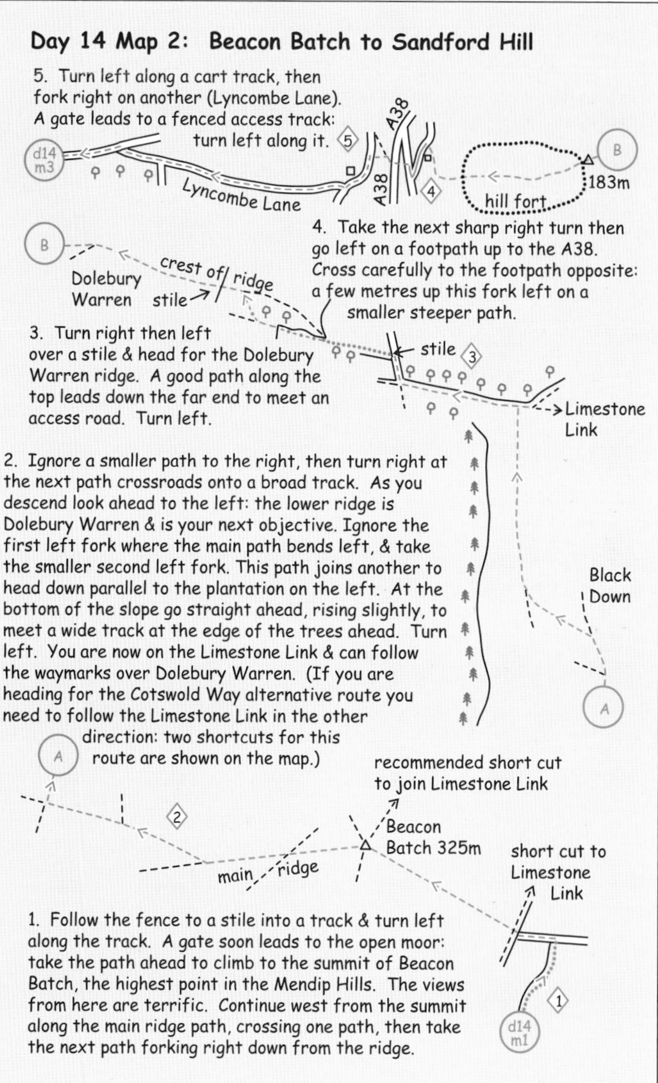
Day 14 Map 2: Beacon Batch to Sandford Hill
5. Turn left along a cart track, then fork right on another (Lyncombe Lane). A gate leads to a fenced access track: turn left along it.
d14 m3
5
Lyncombe Lane
A38
A38
4
hill fort
183m
B
4. Take the next sharp right turn then go left on a footpath up to the A38. Cross carefully to the footpath opposite: a few metres up this fork left on a smaller steeper path.
B
Dolebury Warren
crest of ridge
stile
3. Turn right then left over a stile & head for the Dolebury Warren ridge. A good path along the top leads down the far end to meet an access road. Turn left.
stile
3
Limestone Link
2. Ignore a smaller path to the right, then turn right at the next path crossroads onto a broad track. As you descend look ahead to the left: the lower ridge is Dolebury Warren & is your next objective. Ignore the first left fork where the main path bends left, & take the smaller second left fork. This path joins another to head down parallel to the plantation on the left. At the bottom of the slope go straight ahead, rising slightly, to meet a wide track at the edge of the trees ahead. Turn left. You are now on the Limestone Link & can follow the waymarks over Dolebury Warren. (If you are heading for the Cotswold Way alternative route you need to follow the Limestone Link in the other direction: two shortcuts for this route are shown on the map.)
Black Down
A
A
recommended short cut to join Limestone Link
2
Beacon Batch 325m
main ridge
short cut to Limestone Link
1. Follow the fence to a stile into a track & turn left along the track. A gate soon leads to the open moor: take the path ahead to climb to the summit of Beacon Batch, the highest point in the Mendip Hills. The views from here are terrific. Continue west from the summit along the main ridge path, crossing one path, then take the next path forking right down from the ridge.
1
d14 m1

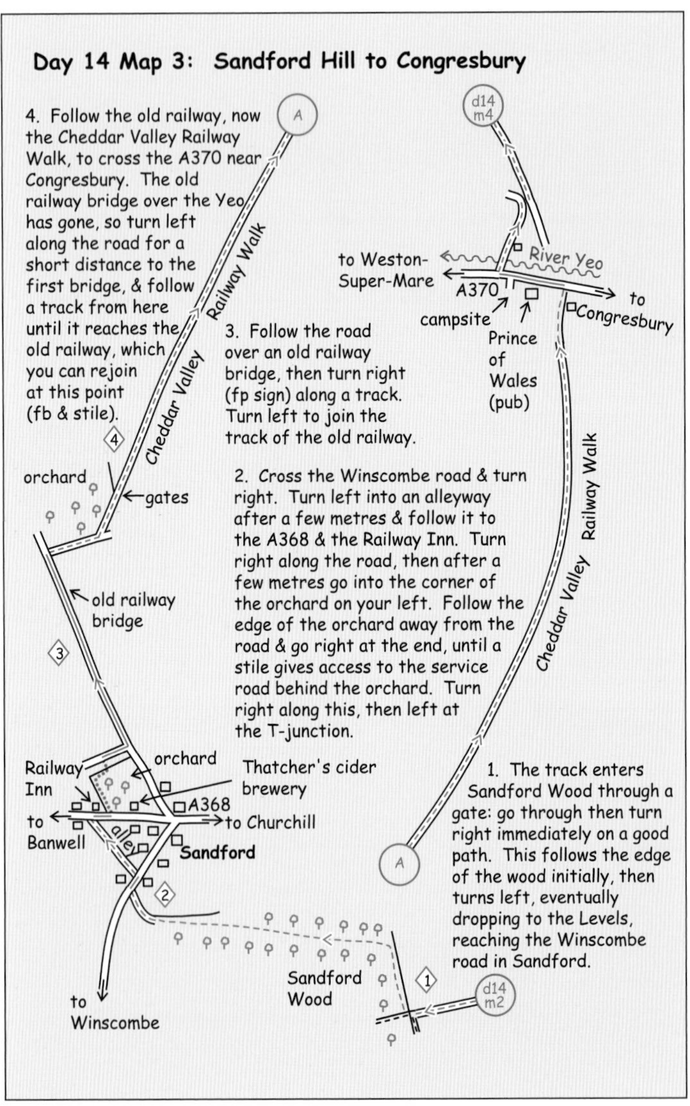
Day 14 Map 3: Sandford Hill to Congresbury
4. Follow the old railway, now the Cheddar Valley Railway Walk, to cross the A370 near Congresbury. The old railway bridge over the Yeo has gone, so turn left along the road for a short distance to the first bridge, & follow a track from here until it reaches the old railway, which you can rejoin at this point (fb & stile).
A
d14 m4
Cheddar Valley Railway Walk
to Weston-Super-Mare
River Yeo
A370
campsite
Prince of Wales (pub)
to Congresbury
3. Follow the road over an old railway bridge, then turn right (fp sign) along a track. Turn left to join the track of the old railway.
4
orchard
gates
2. Cross the Winscombe road & turn right. Turn left into an alleyway after a few metres & follow it to the A368 & the Railway Inn. Turn right along the road, then after a few metres go into the corner of the orchard on your left. Follow the edge of the orchard away from the road & go right at the end, until a stile gives access to the service road behind the orchard. Turn right along this, then left at the T-junction.
Cheddar Valley Railway Walk
old railway bridge
3
Railway Inn
orchard
Thatcher's cider brewery
A368
to Churchill
to Banwell
alley
Sandford
2
A
1. The track enters Sandford Wood through a gate: go through then turn right immediately on a good path. This follows the edge of the wood initially, then turns left, eventually dropping to the Levels, reaching the Winscombe road in Sandford.
Sandford Wood
1
d14 m2
to Winscombe

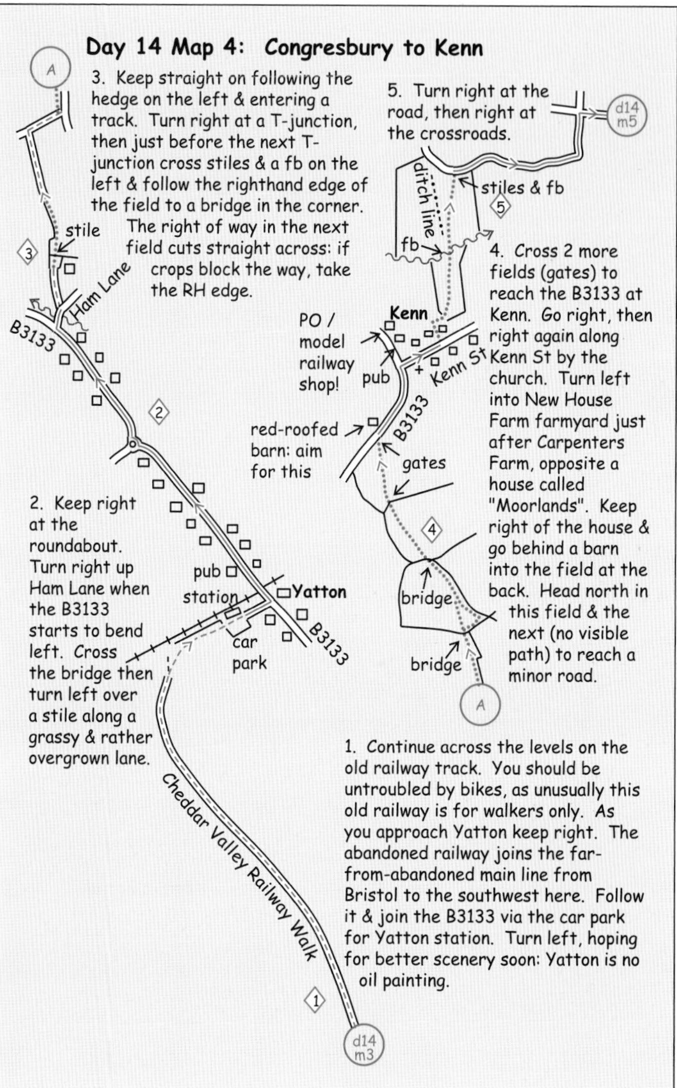
Day 14 Map 4: Congresbury to Kenn
3. Keep straight on following the hedge on the left & entering a track. Turn right at a T-junction, then just before the next T-junction cross stiles & a fb on the left & follow the righthand edge of the field to a bridge in the corner. The right of way in the next field cuts straight across: if crops block the way, take the RH edge.
5. Turn right at the road, then right at the crossroads.
d14 m5
A
stile
3
Ham Lane
B3133
ditch line
stiles & fb
5
fb
4. Cross 2 more fields (gates) to reach the B3133 at Kenn. Go right, then right again along Kenn St by the church. Turn left into New House Farm farmyard just after Carpenters Farm, opposite a house called "Moorlands". Keep right of the house & go behind a barn into the field at the back. Head north in this field & the next (no visible path) to reach a minor road.
Kenn
PO / model railway shop!
pub
Kenn St
B3133
2
red-roofed barn: aim for this
gates
4
2. Keep right at the roundabout. Turn right up Ham Lane when the B3133 starts to bend left. Cross the bridge then turn left over a stile along a grassy & rather overgrown lane.
pub
station
Yatton
bridge
car park
B3133
bridge
A
1. Continue across the levels on the old railway track. You should be untroubled by bikes, as unusually this old railway is for walkers only. As you approach Yatton keep right. The abandoned railway joins the far-from-abandoned main line from Bristol to the southwest here. Follow it & join the B3133 via the car park for Yatton station. Turn left, hoping for better scenery soon: Yatton is no oil painting.
Cheddar Valley Railway Walk
1
d14 m3

Day 14 Map 5: Kenn to Cadbury Camp

Wherever the trees permit, the views both left & right from Tickenham Hill are extensive, varied & interesting. Portishead, the Avonmouth Docks & the Bristol Channel are laid out before you.

5. Turn right along Cadbury Camp Lane West & follow it up Tickenham Hill towards Cadbury Camp. Much of the route from here to Easton-in-Gordano follows a waymarked route: the Gordano Round.

d14 m6

Tickenham Hill

Cadbury Camp Lane West

A

Ignore this turning to Rockshelter & Baye Cottage

4. Turn right at the B3130, then left into Golden Acres Nursery & Fruit Farm. Go straight up the fruit field ahead (no path) into the top left corner to find the path up to the road.

A

5

Cadbury Camp Lane West

3. Cross the Land Yeo at the second bridge, then use a stile on the right to join a fenced path by the hedge that leads to the B3130. If it's too overgrown, escape into the field on the left.

fruit farm

cafe

B3130

4

M5

escape route

bridge

stile

Land Yeo

3

bridge

wooden fb

metal fb

2. Turn left off the road to cross a bridge over the Blind Yeo, turn left again (stile) following the Yeo to another bridge crossing a rhyne (big drainage ditch) coming in from the north. Cross & turn right, following the rhyne north. As you walk, two landmarks become gradually nearer. The first is the M5 motorway, which will be your intermittent companion until Spaniorum Hill north of Bristol. The second is the ridge of hills running eastward. These are the first hills since the Mendips: you will follow them almost to the Avon, & they will shield you from the motorway for most of the way there. A field before reaching the M5 turn right over a metal footbridge & follow the Land Yeo to the east.

Triangle Farm

bridges

Blind Yeo

d14 m4

1

2

1. Walking eastward along this road, two things strike you: the amount of traffic & the amount of litter. The outskirts of Clifton are less than a mile away behind you, which must explain both.

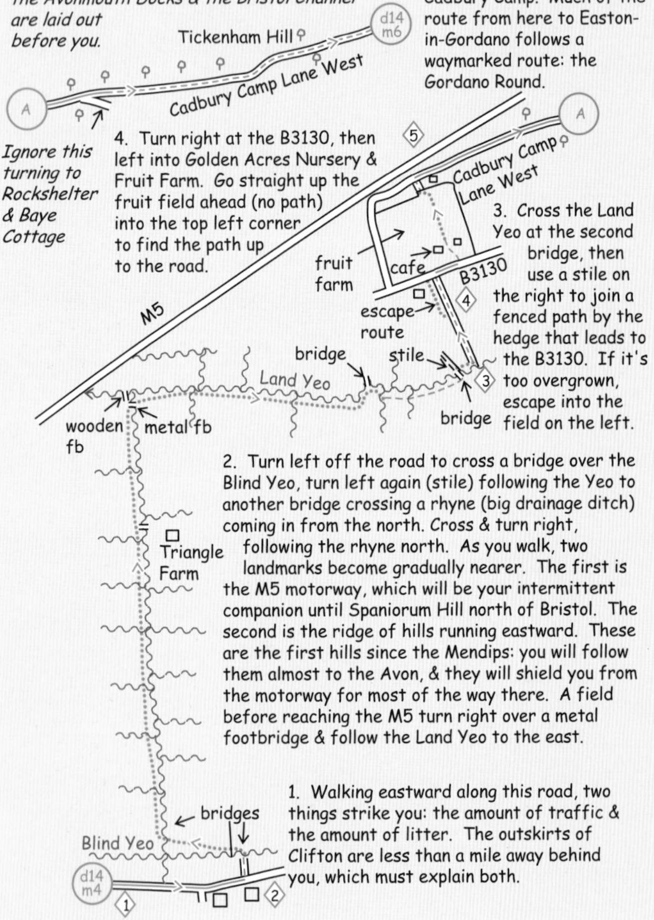

Day 14 Map 6: Cadbury Camp to Bullock's Bottom

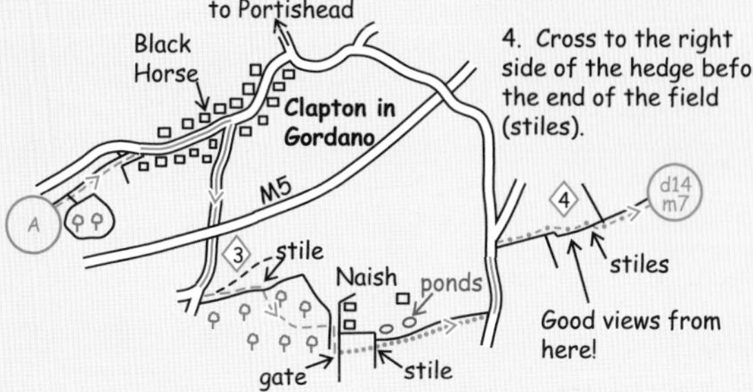

4. Cross to the right side of the hedge before the end of the field (stiles).

2. Turn right along the road at Clapton Court & follow it round a double bend. Fork right up the access road to St Michael's church, then opposite the church entrance a gate on the left leads to a good path through fields to Clapton. Continue along the road past (or via) the Black Horse, then turn sharp right uphill & under the M5. When the road bends right turn sharp left (gate & stile).

3. Don't follow the track: instead follow the edge of the wood to the right. A stile gives access to a path up through the woods to Naish Farm. Turn right at the track by the farm, go past the buildings, then turn left through a gate & over a stile, passing ponds to reach a minor road. Turn left along it. Turn right just before the road forks & follow field edges.

Continuing along Cadbury Camp Lane looks a good option on OS maps, but it's a tarmac access road with no views & too many BMWs & Mercedes' heading for the exclusive houses.

1. At the top of the hill, the remains of Cadbury Camp Iron Age fort are obvious on the right. A stile a bit further down the track gives access to it. After looking round, return to the track & continue along it. Just after the second house on the right ("Bridleways"), take a narrow fenced footpath on the left (fp sign). This leads to another lane: cross it & follow the signed path opposite to cross a footbridge over the M5. An overgrown path along the edge of a small wood leads to a field, then stiles indicate the line of an invisible footpath diverging gradually from the M5 to reach the road by Clapton Court farm.

Day 14 Map 7: Bullock's Bottom to Easton-in-Gordano

5. Continue ahead on the road until the tarmac ends, then along the unmade lane beyond (gate). Just before the track enters a wood, leave it for a parallel path in the field to the right (avoiding the wet bridleway). A stile gives access to the wood: continue, then turn right at a junction (fp sign). Follow field edges & cross an old lane to reach the A369 & Easton-in-Gordano.

4. The path continues down the other side of the hill, crosses a stile into a field, & descends to a stile into an old lane & the tarmac of Failand Lane. Cross into the field opposite (gate & stile) & go half left to a stile by the LH of two visible gates & a tarred access road.

3. Follow the path through the wood & past a ruin to descend to a gate into Mill Lane. Cross the tarmac to a gate & stile, & follow a clear path slightly right & up to turn left on a concrete access road. After a gate & stile in the corner the concrete turns right: leave it to keep left by the fence (fp sign) to a stile in the next corner. Continue in the same direction in the next field to reach a stile into the pines ahead on Windmill Hill.

2. A gate & stile lead into a large field. Aim half left across it (slightly E of NE), & when buildings come into sight aim between the shed & the house. Join an access road at a gate & turn right along it until you can turn left along a track that curves round school buildings. Ignore a stile & fp sign on your left. & go through gates into a cricket field. Go diagonally across this to a stile (no path), then keep left in the next field, cutting the corner (if practical) to a gap into a scrubby wood on a path that gets rather overgrown with bracken as summer progresses.

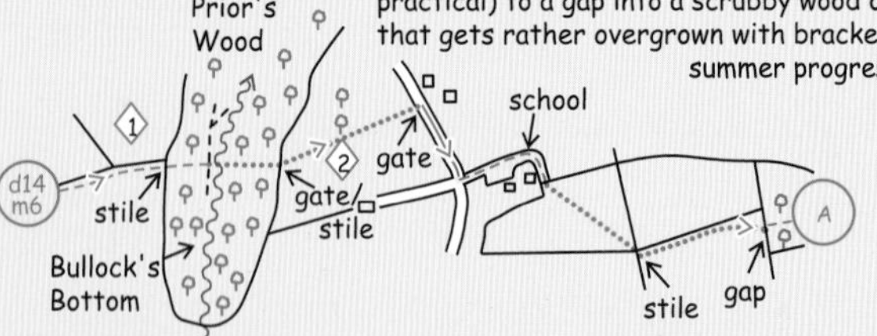

1. Follow field edges, then enter the woods & descend on a clear path into Bullock's Bottom (!). At the valley floor go straight across a track, cross the stream & climb steeply straight up through the wood eastwards. There is no path: just be thankful the wood is narrow & the undergrowth sparse.

Day 15 Map 1: Easton-in-Gordano to Shirehampton

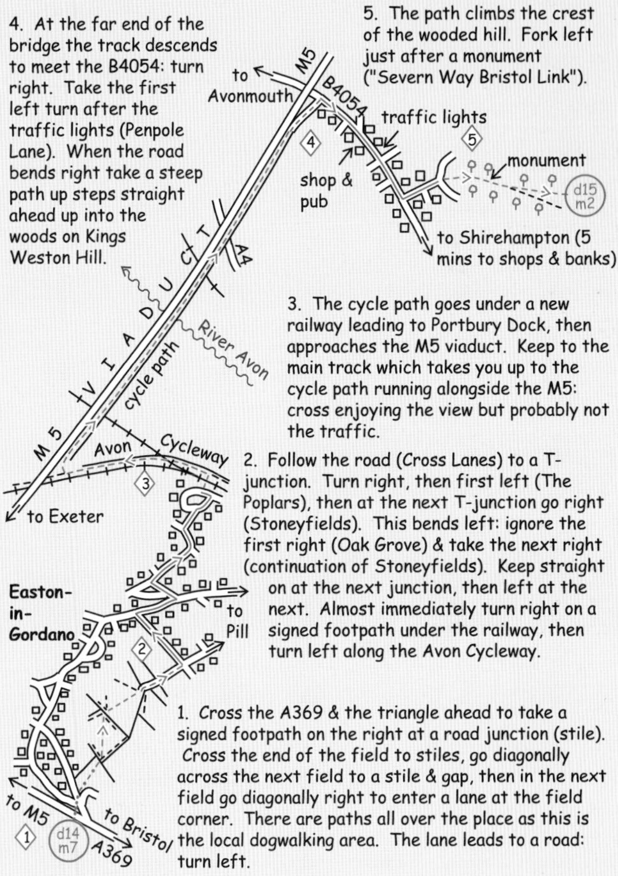
4. At the far end of the bridge the track descends to meet the B4054: turn right. Take the first left turn after the traffic lights (Penpole Lane). When the road bends right take a steep path up steps straight ahead up into the woods on Kings Weston Hill.
5. The path climbs the crest of the wooded hill. Fork left just after a monument ("Severn Way Bristol Link").
to Avonmouth
M5
B4054
traffic lights
4
5
shop & pub
monument
d15 m2
to Shirehampton (5 mins to shops & banks)
A4
VIADUCT
River Avon
cycle path
M 5
3. The cycle path goes under a new railway leading to Portbury Dock, then approaches the M5 viaduct. Keep to the main track which takes you up to the cycle path running alongside the M5: cross enjoying the view but probably not the traffic.
Avon Cycleway
3
to Exeter
2. Follow the road (Cross Lanes) to a T-junction. Turn right, then first left (The Poplars), then at the next T-junction go right (Stoneyfields). This bends left: ignore the first right (Oak Grove) & take the next right (continuation of Stoneyfields). Keep straight on at the next junction, then left at the next. Almost immediately turn right on a signed footpath under the railway, then turn left along the Avon Cycleway.
Easton-in-Gordano
to Pill
2
1. Cross the A369 & the triangle ahead to take a signed footpath on the right at a road junction (stile). Cross the end of the field to stiles, go diagonally across the next field to a stile & gap, then in the next field go diagonally right to enter a lane at the field corner. There are paths all over the place as this is the local dogwalking area. The lane leads to a road: turn left.
to M5
to Bristol
1
d14 m7
A369

Day 15 Map 2: Shirehampton to Henbury

4. Follow the drive round the left side of the museum to join the road in Henbury. Turn left, then right downhill (Hallen Rd). Look for a gate in the wall on the left, & a sign. This is the entrance to Blaise Hamlet, which should not be passed by without a visit.

5. After visiting Blaise Hamlet, continue down Hallen Rd, turn right at the end, then left along the B4055 (Station Rd). A shop/PO on the left is the last general store the Trail passes before Chepstow.

3. Blaise Castle is a picturesque folly built in 1766: get the camera out! There is no path on the hilltop: keep right of the castle & bear slightly right to the end of the clearing. Two paths descend through the trees from here: take the left one & drop steeply through the trees (crossing the other path), emerging into parkland at the bottom of the hill. Cross the park to the museum (the obvious big house).

2. After crossing the B4057 keep straight on (to right of the house) to regain the path along the ridge. Keep left when the path forks. Follow this path along the clearing on the ridge until, just before the end of the clearing, it descends left down steps through the wood. Cross a track near the bottom of the hill & bend slightly left to follow the right edge of the parkland (briefly). Re-enter the wood & go straight across a bigger track. Ignore the first right fork (a dead end), & take the second (fp sign). Climb steeply up to a hilltop clearing & Blaise Castle.

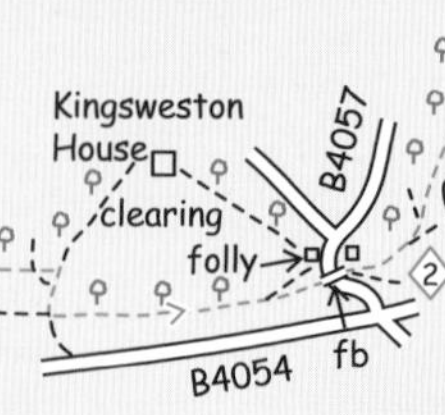

1. The ridge path meets a track from Kingsweston House just before a large clearing. Follow another good track from here in the trees on the right edge of the clearing, heading east. When the track forks, keep right: steps lead to a footbridge over the B4057.

Day 15 Map 3: Henbury to Easter Compton

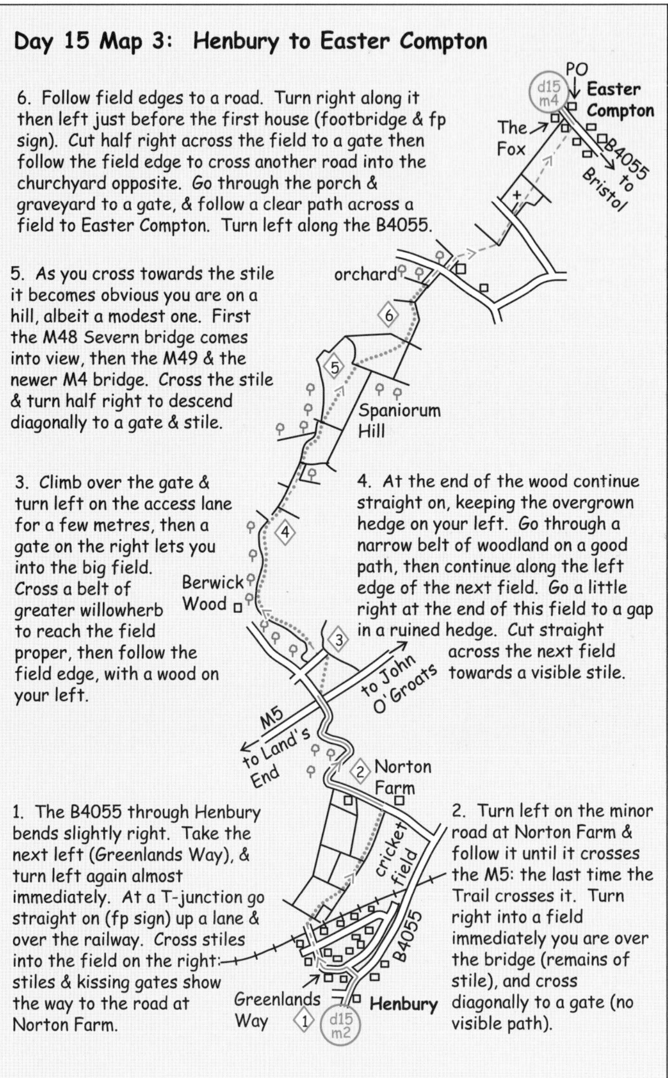

6. Follow field edges to a road. Turn right along it then left just before the first house (footbridge & fp sign). Cut half right across the field to a gate then follow the field edge to cross another road into the churchyard opposite. Go through the porch & graveyard to a gate, & follow a clear path across a field to Easter Compton. Turn left along the B4055.

5. As you cross towards the stile it becomes obvious you are on a hill, albeit a modest one. First the M48 Severn bridge comes into view, then the M49 & the newer M4 bridge. Cross the stile & turn half right to descend diagonally to a gate & stile.

3. Climb over the gate & turn left on the access lane for a few metres, then a gate on the right lets you into the big field. Cross a belt of greater willowherb to reach the field proper, then follow the field edge, with a wood on your left.

4. At the end of the wood continue straight on, keeping the overgrown hedge on your left. Go through a narrow belt of woodland on a good path, then continue along the left edge of the next field. Go a little right at the end of this field to a gap in a ruined hedge. Cut straight across the next field towards a visible stile.

1. The B4055 through Henbury bends slightly right. Take the next left (Greenlands Way), & turn left again almost immediately. At a T-junction go straight on (fp sign) up a lane & over the railway. Cross stiles into the field on the right: stiles & kissing gates show the way to the road at Norton Farm.

2. Turn left on the minor road at Norton Farm & follow it until it crosses the M5: the last time the Trail crosses it. Turn right into a field immediately you are over the bridge (remains of stile), and cross diagonally to a gate (no visible path).

Day 15 Map 4: Easter Compton to Pilning

Depending on how active the local council and/or amenity volunteers have been, the section from Easter Compton to the railway can be a bit awkward to follow. The paths are little-used & mostly invisible, the cattle can be worryingly inquisitive, and the footbridges overgrown and thorny. An alternative route on minor roads is possible to the west if you need it.

1. Pass (or pass through) the Fox in Easter Compton then turn right up the drive to "Collingwood" (fp sign). A stile leads to a field: aim half left to a stile & continue in the same direction past an electricity pole to a gate. Cross the short end of the next field to a gate (ignore the two gates on the right). Cut diagonally across the next field to a stile. Cross & follow the hedge & drain to a footbridge.

2. Cross the footbridge & aim half left, crossing a concrete track to a second footbridge. The main line railway to South Wales is now visible ahead. Keep straight on (north) to cross two more footbridges, then turn right to a gate. Go through this then keep left to skirt the buildings of Brynleaze Farm.

3. Past Brynleaze Farm keep right of the barn ahead to join a minor road (gates). Go under the railway & turn left at the first opportunity along a grassy lane leading to Rookery Farm. Turn right at a track junction, then at the end of the field on the left cross a stile into the field, then a footbridge and on to stiles in the field corner.

4. Keep straight on along the edges of two more fields then cross a stile and footbridge & follow the hedge on the right to meet a farm access road. Turn left to meet a minor road by Torrs Farm. Cross straight over onto the access road opposite.

5. Keep right when the tarmac ends and the track divides (left goes to Gumhurn Farm). Continue along a grassy lane.

The route is now back on flat drained seamarsh: maps have no contours on them here & you have no hills to climb.

Day 15 Map 5: Pilning to Aust

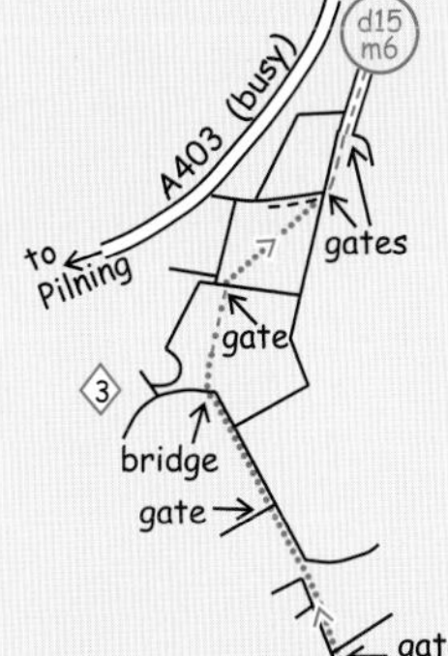

3. Cross the bridge over the rhine & cut across the big field to a visible gate. The Severn bridge is in sight again now, not that far away. In the next field aim diagonally across the field to the right (NE), not straight ahead (N) to the more obvious gate. Join a farm track & follow it through a gate & round to the left until another gate leads to a hedged lane, with Aust church now visible ahead to the left.

2. Aim right of the buildings of Bilsham Farm, & go through the righthand of the two gates ahead of you. Keep the hedge on your left for two fields, then go through a wide gap ahead & continue, now with the hedge & Lords Rhine (a drainage ditch) on the right. Continue in the next field until you reach a bridge across the rhine (note they spell rhine with an "i" around here - it was a "y" earlier).

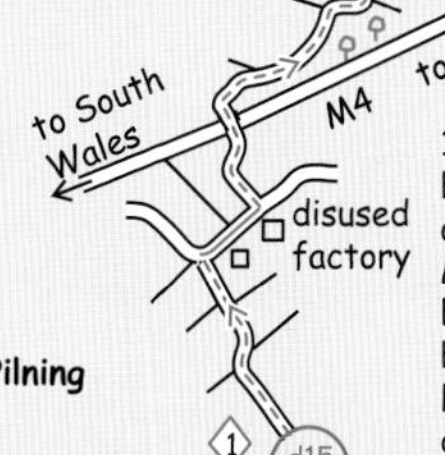

1. Follow the grassy lane until it meets a road on a bend. Turn right, then left on an access road opposite a disused factory. Follow this lane over the M4 motorway & round two double bends. It gets a bit overgrown but is still navigable despite the bamboo! On the next righthand bend, approaching Holm Farm, turn left over a footbridge & cut diagonally across the field to a gateway. Continue with a hedge on your left until stiles on the left let you cross a road to the field opposite.

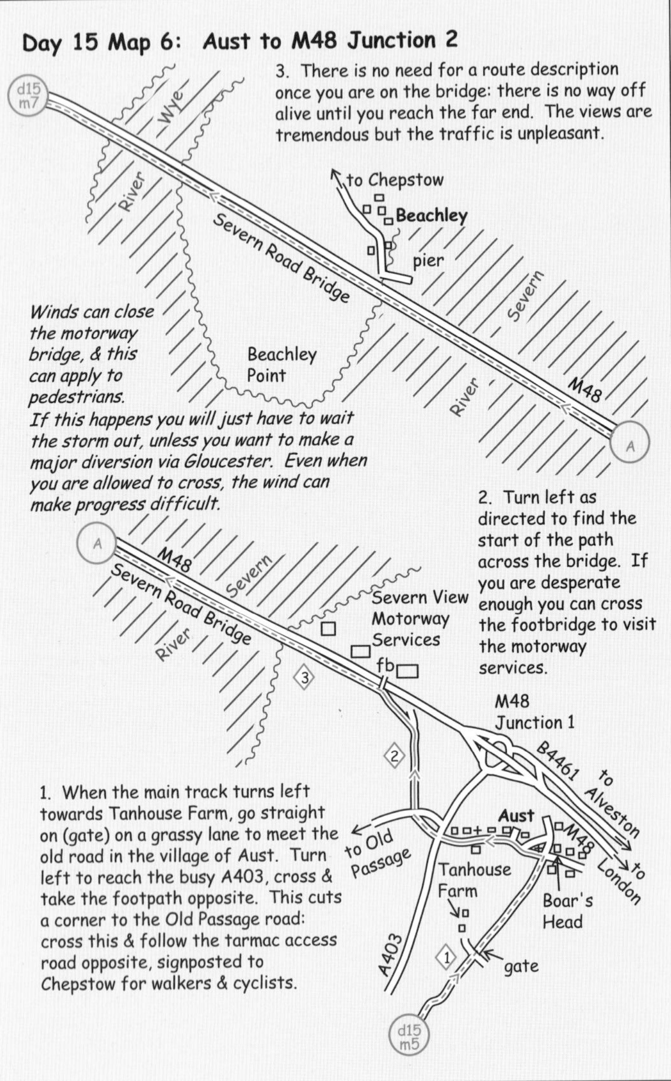

Day 15 Map 6: Aust to M48 Junction 2
3. There is no need for a route description once you are on the bridge: there is no way off alive until you reach the far end. The views are tremendous but the traffic is unpleasant.
d15 m7
River Wye
to Chepstow
Beachley
pier
Severn Road Bridge
River Severn
M48
Winds can close the motorway bridge, & this can apply to pedestrians.
If this happens you will just have to wait the storm out, unless you want to make a major diversion via Gloucester. Even when you are allowed to cross, the wind can make progress difficult.
Beachley Point
A
2. Turn left as directed to find the start of the path across the bridge. If you are desperate enough you can cross the footbridge to visit the motorway services.
A
M48
Severn Road Bridge
Severn
River
Severn View Motorway Services
fb
3
M48 Junction 1
B4461 to Alveston
2
1. When the main track turns left towards Tanhouse Farm, go straight on (gate) on a grassy lane to meet the old road in the village of Aust. Turn left to reach the busy A403, cross & take the footpath opposite. This cuts a corner to the Old Passage road: cross this & follow the tarmac access road opposite, signposted to Chepstow for walkers & cyclists.
to Old Passage
Aust
M48
to London
Tanhouse Farm
Boar's Head
A403
1
gate
d15 m5

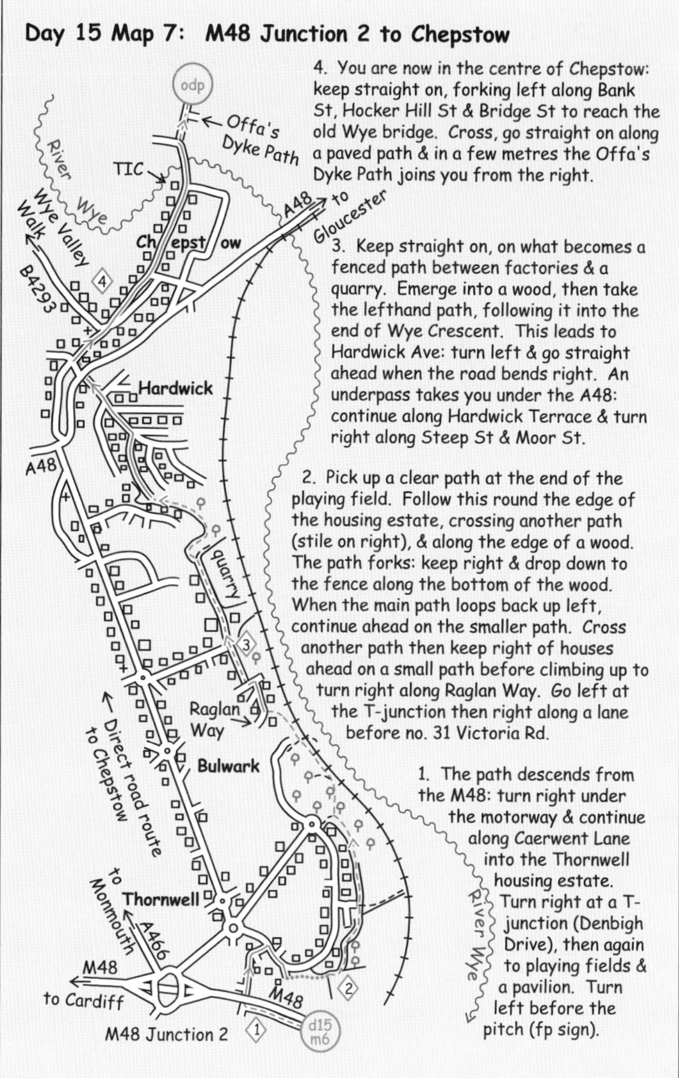
Day 15 Map 7: M48 Junction 2 to Chepstow
4. You are now in the centre of Chepstow: keep straight on, forking left along Bank St, Hocker Hill St & Bridge St to reach the old Wye bridge. Cross, go straight on along a paved path & in a few metres the Offa's Dyke Path joins you from the right.
3. Keep straight on, on what becomes a fenced path between factories & a quarry. Emerge into a wood, then take the lefthand path, following it into the end of Wye Crescent. This leads to Hardwick Ave: turn left & go straight ahead when the road bends right. An underpass takes you under the A48: continue along Hardwick Terrace & turn right along Steep St & Moor St.
2. Pick up a clear path at the end of the playing field. Follow this round the edge of the housing estate, crossing another path (stile on right), & along the edge of a wood. The path forks: keep right & drop down to the fence along the bottom of the wood. When the main path loops back up left, continue ahead on the smaller path. Cross another path then keep right of houses ahead on a small path before climbing up to turn right along Raglan Way. Go left at the T-junction then right along a lane before no. 31 Victoria Rd.
1. The path descends from the M48: turn right under the motorway & continue along Caerwent Lane into the Thornwell housing estate. Turn right at a T-junction (Denbigh Drive), then again to playing fields & a pavilion. Turn left before the pitch (fp sign).
odp
Offa's Dyke Path
River Wye
TIC
Wye Valley Walk
Chepstow
A48 to Gloucester
B4293
Hardwick
A48
quarry
Raglan Way
Bulwark
Direct road route to Chepstow
to Monmouth
Thornwell
A466
M48
to Cardiff
M48
M48 Junction 2
d15 m6
River Wye

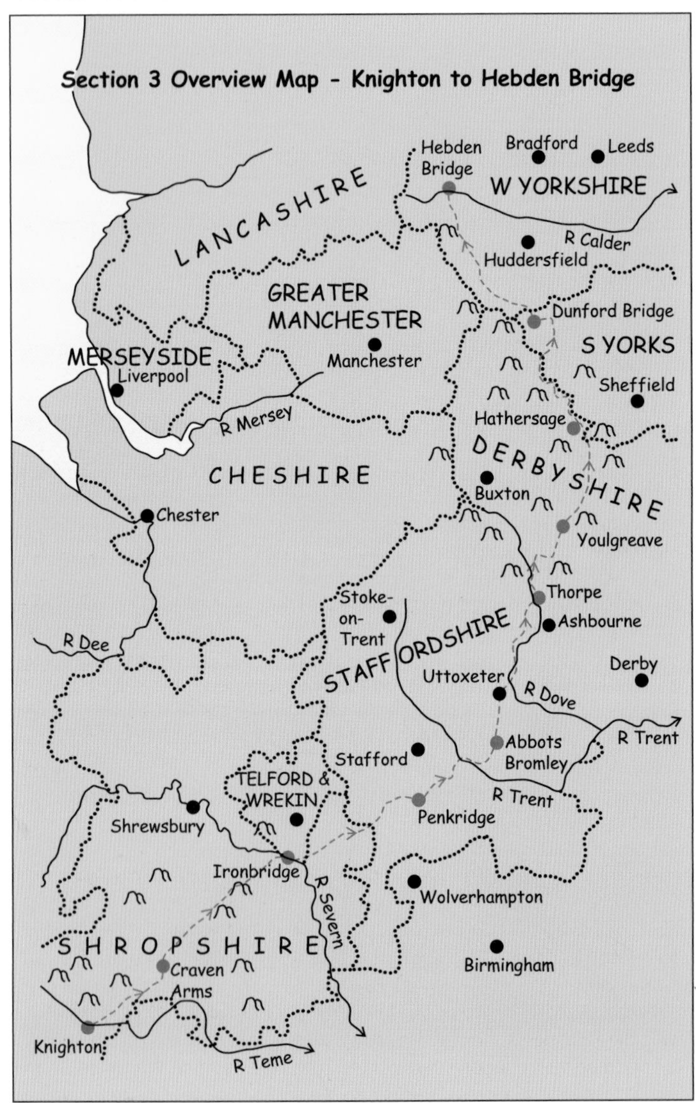
Section 3 Overview Map - Knighton to Hebden Bridge
Hebden Bridge
Bradford
Leeds
W YORKSHIRE
LANCASHIRE
R Calder
Huddersfield
GREATER MANCHESTER
Dunford Bridge
S YORKS
MERSEYSIDE
Manchester
Liverpool
Sheffield
R Mersey
Hathersage
DERBYSHIRE
CHESHIRE
Buxton
Chester
Youlgreave
Thorpe
Stoke-on-Trent
Ashbourne
R Dee
STAFFORDSHIRE
Derby
Uttoxeter
R Dove
R Trent
Abbots Bromley
Stafford
TELFORD & WREKIN
R Trent
Shrewsbury
Penkridge
Ironbridge
R Severn
Wolverhampton
SHROPSHIRE
Birmingham
Craven Arms
Knighton
R Teme

SECTION 3
Shropshire, Staffordshire and the Peak: Knighton to Hebden Bridge

Distance	291km (181 miles)
Road Walking	16%. The longest stretches are along minor lanes crossing low-lying farmland in Shropshire and Staffordshire, including quite a lot on the Staffordshire Way.
Days	9 (Main Schedule), or 11 (Alternative Schedule)
Maps and Guides	The whole section: this guide, strip maps.

To reach the southern Pennines from the Welsh border hills means crossing a stretch of lowland farming country wherever you cut across. The route chosen for the Trail heads diagonally northeastwards from Knighton through the Shropshire hills, crossing the Clun and the Onny (tributaries of the River Teme that itself feeds the Severn near Worcester). It then follows the long ridge of Wenlock Edge to Much Wenlock, crosses the River Severn at Coalport just below Ironbridge, and continues east-northeast across farmland to meet the waymarked Staffordshire Way by the Shropshire Union Canal near Penkridge, south of Stafford.

The Staffordshire Way crosses Cannock Chase (where the Cotswold Way/Heart of England Way alternative – see Section 2, Alternative Routes – rejoins the route), and continues northeast to Uttoxeter. Here you meet the River Dove, which the Trail follows upstream (northwards) for over 30km (20 miles) to Rocester in the Peak District. At Rocester the Staffordshire Way is abandoned for the Limestone Way – again a waymarked route. At Thorpe, 5km (3 miles) north of Ashbourne, the Trail leaves the Limestone Way to join the line of the Alternative Pennine Way (not waymarked), and follows it all the way to Hebden Bridge in West Yorkshire.

If you want to keep to the hills from Land's End to John O'Groats, then following the Pennines is the only way to go through the north of England. Until recently there was only one waymarked path, the Pennine Way, starting in Edale and finishing at Kirk Yetholm, in Scotland. This is a good route, but there are horrendous peat bogs at both ends, and serious erosion problems that don't need adding to. It can be busy as well (and there's a good chance you've already done it).

A second waymarked route, the Pennine Bridleway, is being opened progressively, and will run from near Ashbourne in Derbyshire to Byrness in Northumberland. This route has been designed principally for cyclists and horseriders, though, and it involves a fair amount of road walking and made surfaces.

The only other complete documented route is the Alternative Pennine Way (APW), devised by Denis Brook and Phil Hinchliffe. This avoids most of the peat bogs of the Dark Peak and the Cheviots, at either end of the Pennine Way, and while it tends not to follow the highest ground, it generally keeps to hilly country and avoids the Pennine Way crowds. Although it is not waymarked, surely this is an advantage rather than a disadvantage, and the APW would be the recommended route all the way to Jedburgh in Scotland, if the guidebook to it were generally available. Unfortunately it is now out of print, so the End to End Trail uses just the two ends to avoid the main Pennine Way peat bog areas, and joins the Pennine Way at Hebden Bridge, now safely beyond the Peak District morasses.

Maps

1:25000 Explorer maps
201 Knighton & Presteigne
203 Ludlow (very briefly)
217 The Long Mynd & Wenlock Edge
242 Telford, Ironbridge & The Wrekin
244 (formerly 6) Cannock Chase
259 Derby
24 The Peak District – White Peak Area
1 The Peak District – Dark Peak area (later two-sided editions)
21 South Pennines (later two-sided editions)

1:50000 Landranger maps
148 Presteigne & Hay-on-Wye area
137 Ludlow & Wenlock Edge
138 Kidderminster & Wyre Forest (briefly)
127 Stafford & Telford
128 Derby & Burton upon Trent
119 Buxton, Matlock & Dove Dale
110 Sheffield
104 Leeds & Bradford (briefly)
103 Blackburn & Burnley

Guidebooks

The Alternative Pennine Way by Denis Brook and Phil Hinchliffe, Cicerone, 1992
(Out of print)

Recommendations

Get Landranger 148 (see Recommendations, Section 2), and Explorers 217, 242, 244, 259, 24, 1 and 21. This minimises the number of maps and gives good detail for most of Section 3.

To Help You on Your Way

Accommodation

The best sources of accommodation information are the following tourist information centres.

The Library, Church Street, Church Stretton, tel 01694 723133 (seasonal)
Ironbridge Gorge Museum Trust, Coalbrookdale, tel 01952 884391 www.ironbridge.org.uk
The Museum, High Street, Much Wenlock, tel 01952 727679 (seasonal) www.bridgnorthshropshire.com
Market Sreet, Stafford, tel 01785 619619 www.staffordbc.gov.uk
Coors Visitor Centre, Horninglow Street, Burton upon Trent (for the Abbots Bromley area, Days 23 and 24), tel 01283 508111 www.eaststaffsbc.gov.uk
13 Market Place, Ashbourne, tel 01335 343666
The Crescent, Buxton, tel 01298 25106 www.highpeak.gov.uk
The Gatehouse, Victoria Street, Glossop, tel 01457 855920
49–51 Huddersfield Road, Holmfirth, tel 01484 222444
Visitor & Canal Centre, New Road, Hebden Bridge, tel 01422 843831 www.pennineyorkshire.co.uk

Additionally, for Penkridge you should visit www.penkridge.org.uk, since the local TICs have little or nothing in Penkridge (Day 22). Similarly www.shifnal.com is the best source of information about accommodation in Shifnal (Day 22), and www.abbotsbromley.com has information about some of the accommodation around Abbots Bromley, but not all of it (Day 23). For an update on the situation in and around Dunford Bridge (Day 27) try www.kirklees.gov.uk.

Equipment Shops

Day 22 (off-route) Millets, 207 Dean Street, Telford, tel 01952 201002
Day 22 (off-route) Stafford Outdoor Leisure, 38 Mill Street, Stafford, tel 01785 240594
Day 22 (off-route) Millets, 13 Gaolgate Street, Stafford, tel 01785 251912
Day 23 (off-route) The Beaten Track, Unit 6, Newhall Street, Cannock, tel 01543 578412
Day 24 (off-route) Track & Trail, 32 St John Street, Ashbourne, tel 01335 346403
Day 24 (off-route) Yeomans, 3 Victoria Square, Ashbourne, tel 01335 342468
Day 26 There are a number of shops in Bakewell (off-route)
Day 26 Outside, Main Road, Hathersage, tel 01433 651936
Day 26 Cotswold Camping, 6 Main Road, Hathersage, tel 01433 659870
Day 26 Nevisport, 26 The Square, Hathersage, tel 01433 659666
Day 26 Hitch 'n' Hike, Mytham Bridge, Bamford, tel 01433 651013
Day 28 Kebcote Country Wear, Albert Street, Hebden Bridge, tel 01422 842248

Alternative Routes

Whitchurch and Macclesfield

The principal alternative direct link between Offa's Dyke and the Pennines is further north than the Trail route through Ironbridge and Cannock Chase. The Whitchurch and Macclesfield alternative means you get to walk about 80% of the Offa's Dyke Path rather than 50%, but miss out on the Peak limestone country and gritstone edges. It only grazes the edge of the Peak District, which is its main disadvantage, although it doesn't make a significant difference to the distance covered.

If you want to take the Whitchurch and Macclesfield alternative, you leave the Offa's Dyke Path at Bronygarth near Chirk, taking the waymarked Maelor Way (see below) east across farmland to Grindley Brook near Whitchurch, on the Cheshire–Shropshire border (a major crossroads of little-walked footpaths). From Grindley Brook another waymarked route, the South Cheshire Way (see below), enables you to maintain your easterly direction to just short of its end at Mow Cop, north of Stoke-on-Trent. Just before Mow Cop, the South Cheshire Way crosses the Macclesfield Canal, which you follow north through Macclesfield and on to Marple. At Marple you pick up the Etherow-Goyt Valley Way, another waymarked route (see below), and at its end in Hadfield join the Trans Pennine Trail, a waymarked long-distance bridleway that follows the disused railway line east up Longdendale to meet the Pennine Way at Crowden, near Glossop in Derbyshire. Alternatively, you can continue along the Trans Pennine Trail from here to meet the End to End Trail at Dunford Bridge (Days 27/28).

Guidebooks

Walking Offa's Dyke Path by David Hunter, Cicerone, 2001

Guide to the Maelor Way, by Gordon Emery, 2003, available from Wrexham TIC, Lambpit Street, Wrexham LL11 1AY, tel 01978 292015 www.wrexham.gov.uk

The South Cheshire Way: Grindley Brook to Mow Cop, Mid-Cheshire Footpath Society, available via www.mcfs.org.uk

Etherow-Goyt Valley Way, published by Tameside Countryside Warden Service, Chief Warden's Office, Park Bridge Visitor Centre, The Stables, Park Bridge, Ashton-under-Lyne OL6 8AQ, www.tameside.gov.uk

Trans Pennine Trail Map 1 West – Southport to Penistone, published by Trans Pennine Trail Office, Barnsley MBC, Central Offices, Kendray Street, Barnsley S70 2TN, www.transpenninetrail.org.uk

Offa's Dyke to Its End, Then Across to the Pennines

The Offa's Dyke Path ends at Prestatyn on the North Wales coast, so if you want to walk the whole of it, you need a route that will take you east from Prestatyn to the Pennines, where you can link either to the main Trail route, or the start of the Pennine Way at Edale. Most of this link will be through lowland farmland across northeast Wales and Cheshire, and it adds significantly to the distance covered – Knighton to Hebden Bridge via Prestatyn and Edale is almost exactly 400km (250 miles), which is about 110km (70 miles) further than the main route of the End to End Trail.

One option is to find a copy of the out-of-print guidebook to the Cestrian Link Walk (see below), which describes a good route between Prestatyn and Edale. It goes through Mold, south of Chester, then through Tattenhall and Gawsworth, meeting the Pennines around

Wildboarclough. This route isn't waymarked, and follows some little-used paths that can be difficult to follow in places.

The second option is to follow the Dee estuary southeast from Prestatyn to Connah's Quay, making use of National Cycle Network Route 5, which is waymarked, and preferably taking alternative footpaths where the cycle route follows busy roads. The section between Prestatyn and Connah's Quay isn't particularly pretty, as there's a lot of industry along the coast here. From Connah's Quay follow the same cycle route, now on a disused railway line, into Chester. Approaching Chester city centre the old railway crosses the Shropshire Union Canal, and here turn left to follow the canal north. You are now on the waymarked North Cheshire Way, which you follow for 110km (70 miles) – along the River Weaver, through Knutsford, past Manchester Airport and over Alderley Edge – to its end at Disley, at the edge of the Peak District southeast of Stockport. From Disley follow the Peak Forest Canal towpath 3km (2 miles) east to New Mills, and at the other side of the town another disused railway, the Seth Valley Trail, takes you on to Hayfield. 5km (3 miles) of footpaths climbing east from Hayfield lead you to the edge of the Kinder plateau at Edale Cross, which is where you meet the Pennine Way, about 5km (3 miles) from its start at Edale.

If you want to switch between one of these routes and the Whitchurch and Macclesfield alternative, they both cross that route as it follows the Macclesfield Canal. The Cestrian Link crosses it just south of Macclesfield, and the North Cheshire Way crosses it (and follows the towpath briefly) just north of Bollington.

Additional alternative routes through Cheshire between the Offa's Dyke Path and the Pennine Way are outlined in an e-mail or leaflet entitled *The Cheshire Link*, available from Cheshire County Council's Public Rights of Way Unit – see www.cheshire.gov.uk.

Guidebooks

Walking Offa's Dyke Path by David Hunter, Cicerone, 2001

A Cestrian Link Walk by John N Davenport, Westmorland Gazette, 1983 with 1986 amendment sheet

This has been available until recently, but is now out of print, so try libraries or the second-hand market if you want to walk this route.

The North Cheshire Way, Mid-Cheshire Footpath Society, 2006

Available via www.mcfs.org.uk

The Complete Pennine Way

If you haven't already walked the Pennine Way, and walking every inch of it is a 'must' for your Land's End to John O'Groats walk, then it is quite straightforward to vary the route to accommodate this. Leave the Alternative Pennine Way at Youlgreave and rejoin the Limestone Way, which has taken a much longer route between Thorpe and Youlgreave than the Trail. Follow the Limestone Way to its end at Castleton, then climb the tourist path over Mam Tor ridge to the start of the Pennine Way at Edale. It's about 33km (21 miles) from Youlgreave to Edale. From Edale the Pennine Way will take you to Kirk Yetholm in the Scottish borders, and from there the waymarked St Cuthbert's Way allows you to rejoin the main route of the End to End Trail near Jedburgh.

Guidebooks

Walking the Limestone Way by Ron and Elizabeth Haydock and Bill and Dorothy Allen, Scarthin Books, 1997

The Pennine Way by Martin Collins, Cicerone, 2003

St Cuthbert's Way Official Trail Guide by Roger Smith and Ron Shaw, The Stationery Office, 1997

The Complete Alternative Pennine Way

The Alternative Pennine Way is a good route and a lot quieter than the Pennine Way, but to follow the whole of it, from Ashbourne to Jedburgh, you will need a copy of the out-of-print (at the time of writing) guidebook, since the route is not waymarked. Although it favours valleys rather than the high moorland, this doesn't mean it is easier – there are plenty of hills to climb to get from one valley to the next. (If you want to start at the very beginning of the APW, you will also have to find your way into Ashbourne.)

Guidebook

The Alternative Pennine Way by Denis Brook and Phil Hinchliffe, Cicerone, 1992

(Out of print)

DAY 20

The Shropshire Hills

Knighton to Craven Arms (21km, 13 miles)

This is a short day through the hills of southwest Shropshire. The Trail follows pleasant, quiet paths and tracks, over hummocky hills and through forestry plantations, before meeting the River Onny near picturesque Stokesay Castle and following the river to the small town of Craven Arms. There are no shops or pubs between the beginning and the end of the stage – the only home comforts to be found are at the Bird on the Rock Tea Rooms at Abcott.

As you cross the railway bridge at Knighton station the path leaves Wales for the last time and enters Shropshire (Day 20 Map 1). Initially a woodland track follows the Teme valley downstream, but soon you head into the hills, over a shoulder to the hamlet of Stowe, with its wooden church tower, and then over Stow Hill and down to the quiet Redlake valley (Day 20 Map 2). A steep climb up the other side of the valley leads to tracks through the forestry on Hopton Titterhill and down to the village of Hopton Castle, the ruined castle being clearly visible ahead (Day 20 Map 3).

There are no facilities at Hopton Castle apart from a public telephone. The castle itself was originally built in the 13th century, and added to in the 14th and 16th centuries, although the mound it was built on is a 'motte', more typical of 11th and 12th century castles. The castle was attacked and ruined during the Civil War, and never rebuilt.

After Hopton Castle invisible footpaths lead over a low ridge to Abcott, whose Bird on the Rock Tea Room is in all the 'best teashop' guides, and your only chance of refreshments before Craven Arms.

The Bird on the Rock is a faithful recreation of a 1930s tearoom – there isn't a teabag in sight, and the home-baked cakes are fabulous. It is the best café between Land's End and John O'Groats, and highly recommended. (It's closed on Mondays and Tuesdays, though, and very popular, so book ahead if you can, tel 01588 660631.)

From Abcott continue to Clungunford. Climb up the road out of Clungunford and turn left at the T-junction. You are now heading north on a minor road that used to be the line of a major Roman highway – now called Welsh Watling Street – which ran from Caerleon near Cardiff via Usk, Monmouth and Leintwardine to Wroxeter, and on to Chester. (The other Watling Street, mostly transformed by Thomas Telford into what is now the A5, ran from London to meet up with Welsh Watling Street at Wroxeter. The Trail crosses that Watling Street the day after tomorrow.)

After a short walk on the Roman road (Day 20 Map 4) the Trail turns right and crosses a broad, wooded shoulder on paths to descend towards Stokesay Castle.

Stokesay Castle is a spectacular 13th-century fortified manor house with an equally spectacular timber-framed gatehouse. The castle was sympathetically restored in the 19th century, and is open to the public daily except winter Mondays and Tuesdays, courtesy of English Heritage.

Before reaching Stokesay Castle the route is joined at Clapping Wicket by the Marches Way, which runs from Cardiff to Chester. The two paths coincide for most of the next 10km (6 miles), until the Marches Way leaves Wenlock Edge to head north to Church Stretton, but you won't notice this much, as despite being marked on OS Explorer maps, this section of the Marches Way is not waymarked. At Stokesay Castle you also cross the waymarked Shropshire Way, a route you will meet again (and follow) later on tomorrow.

From Stokesay Castle you cross the A49 and follow the River Onny to Craven Arms.

Craven Arms is a small town that grew up around what was once a major railway junction, and is now a minor railway junction (the Heart of Wales line branches off here). It has shops, a bank, a station and accommodation, and information is available at the Paper Shop in Corvedale Road, which is an official tourist information point.

DAY 21

Wenlock Edge

Craven Arms to Ironbridge (37km, 23 miles)

Wenlock Edge, formed by a tilted layer of limestone, is a wooded escarpment facing northwest and running for 30km (18 miles). Today's route follows it virtually all day, mainly through woods or along the edge of woods at the crest of the escarpment. There are extensive views all day, although along some stretches you can only spot them occasionally through gaps in the trees. The Long Mynd and the neighbouring hills east and northeast of Church Stretton dominate on the left for the first half of the day; later the views open out a long way across Shropshire. On the right the mass of Brown Clee Hill, with its radio masts, is the most obvious landmark. Underfoot there is a clear path virtually all day. There are many paths on Wenlock Edge, and plenty of visitors, and the Trail's route has been selected to try to give the best combination of pleasant immediate environment and views.

There are two waymarked long-distance paths that follow part of the Edge – the Shropshire Way and the Jack Mytton Way. From Craven Arms the Trail coincides with a third route – the Marches Way, with minor variations to avoid road walking and an unnecessary hill climb, until just before the first road crosses the Edge at Burwood (Day 21 Map 2). The Marches Way is marked on the OS Explorer map, but not waymarked on the ground, and follows the valley to the west of the Edge to the hamlet of Strefford, then climbing to follow the top of the Edge.

If you are walking this part in the middle of the day, the Plough at Wistanstow is recommended. It is the brewery tap of Wood's brewery and is 1km off-route from the footbridge over Quinny Brook near Strefford. Apart from the Wenlock Edge Inn there are no other shops or sources of refreshment close to the route between Craven Arms and Much Wenlock (Day 21 Map 6), 29km (18 miles) away.

Between Craven Arms (Day 21 Map 1) and Ironbridge there is only one real climb all day, which is the initial stiff pull from Strefford, diagonally up a muddy track from the bottom to the top of the Edge. This initial stretch along

'No hammering no climbing', Ippikins Rock, Wenlock Edge

the top follows a good track and is easy underfoot. As with the rest of the day, the woods are delightful – ancient woodland that used to be coppiced, full of woodland flowers and birdlife.

When the Marches Way leaves the Edge (Day 21 Map 2), the Trail continues along the Edge. Cross the two roads at Burwood and continue along a quieter path along the top, initially in the woods and later along field edges at the top of the woods.

Before reaching the next road at Roman Bank (Day 21 Map 3), a track rises up through the woods to join the Trail – along this runs the Jack Mytton Way, a waymarked long-distance bridleway that attracts many horseriders.

The Jack Mytton Way has been very successful, and as a result many stretches have turned into deep mudbaths, which is probably unpleasant for horses, and certainly not what walkers have in mind when they head out to the country. Horses have churned up other paths along the Edge, but it is the Jack Mytton Way that seems to have suffered the most. Work has been done on the worst stretches, although this itself has left a very rough, stony surface.

The Trail follows the Jack Mytton Way only where it has to – from just before Roman Bank, through Coats Wood, to the next road near Wilderhope Manor (Day 21 Map 4), there is no real alternative. (This section has recently been rebuilt from a narrow trench full of mud into an ugly, stony track, as wide as a road – with luck the passage of time will mellow it.)

From Wilderhope Manor to Presthope and beyond the Edge is National Trust property, with open access for walkers, which means you can follow any path, not just rights of way. Although there are still a few muddy bits, from here the Trail avoids most of the paths most frequented by horseriders, finding lesser-used ones rather than the main highways. The route passes close to Wilderhope Manor youth hostel, and even if you are not staying there you may want to have a look at this historic manor house.

At Wilderhope the Shropshire Way approaches the Edge, running parallel to it for a while before joining and following it and the Jack Mytton Way to Much Wenlock.

For much of the way from Wilderhope to Presthope (Day 21 Map 5) the obvious line along the top of the Edge is taken by the B4371, so the Trail follows paths lower down the escarpment.

Along this section the Jack Mytton Way mostly follows the disused railway line that used to run from Craven Arms to Much Wenlock, and on to Buildwas near Ironbridge. This is the fastest option, and not muddy, as the trackbed is well ballasted, as you would expect of a railway. (The trains stopped rumbling in 1962, after taking a Beeching's Powder – thank you Maurice Dodd and his 'Perishers' cartoon for that old joke.) Although this option is included on the strip maps and is a good walk, the old railway bed is not the best route, unless you are in a hurry, as there other paths that are quieter and prettier – as shown on the strip maps.

Above the path between Easthope and Presthope is a limestone outcrop called Ippikin's Rock (Day 21 Map 4), on which you may see the occasional rock climber, although the rocks are not of any great height. Above Ippikin's Rock, on the B4371, is the Wenlock Edge Inn (recommended), the only pub on the Edge, and conveniently placed for lunch (it also has accommodation). A little further along, the Trail passes the access road to Lower Hill Farm, where there is a very good little campsite (GR581977).

From the small car park at Presthope (Day 21 Map 5) the B4371 leaves the top of the Edge, so the Trail reclaims it, and follows it until rejoining the Jack Mytton Way and the Shropshire Way and leaving the Edge along a lane into Much Wenlock, following the narrow High Street to the16th-century Guildhall and past the 12th- and 13th-century ruins of Wenlock Priory.

The priory was built on the site of the 7th-century Milburga's Abbey – Much Wenlock is an ancient market town that grew around the priory. There are many

Much Wenlock

other old buildings worth looking at in this pretty little town, and it has plenty of shops, banks and other facilities. If you have the time a good town trail leaflet can be bought at the bookshop in the High Street. There is a campsite a short distance along the A458 towards Shrewsbury (GR615001).

From Much Wenlock to Ironbridge the route follows the Shropshire Way, apart from a short stretch on the way out of Much Wenlock, to avoid unnecessary road walking. The Shropshire Way takes you through farmland and then along Benthall Edge (Day 21 Map 7), the last stretch of the continuation to the northeast of Wenlock Edge before the Severn Gorge outside Ironbridge (the motorway bridge over the Severn estuary seems a world away).

The final part of the day follows another disused railway through the woods alongside the Severn to end at the historic Iron Bridge. Across the bridge is the small town of Ironbridge, with accommodation and many old houses, shops and pubs, although the Trail itself does not go over the bridge. (There is a youth hostel at Coalport, 2.5km (1½ miles) further along the route (see Day 22 Map 1).)

The Iron Bridge was completed in 1779, and was the first bridge in the world to use cast iron structurally, crossing the Severn in a single arch with a span of over

River Severn from the Iron Bridge

30m. It was built when the area was one of the most important of the Industrial Revolution, pioneering the use of coke instead of charcoal for iron smelting on an industrial scale. There were also a lot of pottery, tile and brick works, although virtually all the heavy industry has gone now, leaving a valley full of fascinating relics of its industrial past in an attractive wooded setting.

DAY 22

Crossing the Watershed

Ironbridge to Penkridge (37km, 23 miles)

Although today features the first time the main watershed is crossed since Exmoor, it is mostly easy walking through flat farmland, apart from a short section where you have to follow an invisible bridleway across cultivated fields. After leaving the interesting and atmospheric Severn

Gorge at the beginning of the day, much of the countryside is pleasant enough, but not inspiring. The high point is King Charles's Wood near Kemberton, and the rest is really just the farmland you need to cross to bridge the gap between Wenlock Edge and Cannock Chase on your way to the southern end of the Peak District.

From the outskirts of Ironbridge you follow the disused railway along the valley on the south bank of the Severn for a couple of kilometres to a pub by a footbridge over the river (Day 22 Map 1).

The Boat Inn (recommended) is a basic and traditional pub that presumably used to serve the needs of the workers in the tile works. The footbridge was originally put up in 1922, replacing Coalport Ferry (a boat sank here in 1799, drowning 29 people), and commemorates the dead of World War 1. It was taken away by road for renovation in 2000 and put back later in the year.

Across the river and then the canal, and the path climbs up alongside the Hay Inclined Plane.

The Iron Bridge

The Hay Inclined Plane

The Inclined Plane is a steep railway line up the valley side, used to transport boats down to the River Severn from a canal leading from coalmines. Boats were floated onto a cradle, which was then winched out of the water and down the rails. The height difference between canal and river was 63m, which would have needed 27 locks to connect them in a more orthodox manner. The Plane was operational from 1793 until 1894. (Coalport youth hostel is just along the road to the right from here.)

Once past the Inclined Plane and through the woods up the hillside the interest fades (Day 22 Map 2). There is a pub in Kemberton, a delightful walk up by the stream in King Charles's Wood, then lanes and cart tracks take you quickly east (Day 22 Map 3), under the M54 and across the A41 to Tong Norton (Day 22 Map 4).

At Tong Norton there is the Bell Inn and a petrol station with a limited shop – the only shop before Penkridge. If you want an overnight stay around here your options are limited, and unfortunately the Bell Inn has no accommodation. Your best bet, if you are not camping courtesy of a friendly farm, is to divert to Shifnal, where bed and breakfast is available (see Day 22 Map 3).

Paths and lanes lead from Tong Norton to the dormitory village of Bishop's Wood, where there is a pub, but no shop, despite the size of the village.

On the road into Bishop's Wood there is a hill, at the top of which you cross the main watershed of Britain for the first time since Exmoor. On the west side the streams flow into the River Worfe, which joins the Severn to the south; on the east side the streams flow into the River Penk (which you meet at the end of the day), which flows north into the Sow, which flows east into the Trent, which eventually makes up its mind and flows north into the Humber. It is an unlikely place to be so significant, but at least there is an official height of 154m marked on the OS Landranger map (oddly it is missing from 1:25000 Explorer maps). In fact the route from here lies entirely on the eastern side of the watershed all the way to the end of this section at Hebden Bridge and beyond. On the way into Bishop's Wood, just before the crossroads, you cross the county boundary from Shropshire into Staffordshire.

The Trail reaches Lapley via lanes, the aforementioned invisible bridleway, and more lanes leading northeast, past Belvide Reservoir, across the A5 (the more famous Roman Watling Street, as opposed to the Welsh Watling Street, encountered on Day 20), to meet the Staffordshire Way at the Shropshire Union Canal (Day 22 Map 5).

For the rest of the day, to Penkridge (Day 22 Map 6), the Trail follows the Staffordshire Way (waymarked with the symbol of a knot), and continues to follow it all day the next day and part of the next, to eventually leave it on Day 24 at Rocester.

At Lapley there is a pub (the Vaughan Arms), then route finding is easy to the small town of Penkridge (although there is rather too much road walking).

Penkridge is on an old coaching route, and this ancient market town was given its charter in 1244 by Henry III. Defoe called it 'a small but ancient town', and was surprised at the size of the horse fair there when he arrived for a three-day stay. The old coaching route is now the busy A449 connecting Stafford to Wolverhampton, so the west side of the town is rather dominated by traffic. Penkridge has a station, shops, banks and pubs. Accommodation is limited to the Bridge House Hotel (tel 01785 714426) and the more expensive Quality Hotel, but for the latest information check www.penkridge.org.uk before you set out.

DAY 23

Towpaths and Cannock Chase

Penkridge to Abbots Bromley (26km, 16 miles)

Today's walking along the Staffordshire Way starts off on one canal towpath, crosses some farmland to get to Cannock Chase (what is left of an ancient Royal Forest), then at the other side of the Chase takes you to a second canal, this time heading southeast – not often on the Trail does the route head so blatantly in the wrong direction. When the towpath is left for more fields and lanes, you head more or less northeast to Abbots Bromley. The canal towpaths are very pleasant to walk, easy underfoot, and the narrowboats provide a bit of colour and companionship. Cannock Chase is a big expanse of woodland, plantations and heathland that is very popular with walkers and mountain bikers, and fortunately the Staffordshire Way takes you through some of the best of it, avoiding forestry plantations. The remaining farmland is pleasant enough on the whole, but not what I go on walking holidays for.

The Trail leaves Penkridge along the Staffordshire and Worcestershire Canal (Day 23 Map 1). This is a classic narrowboat canal, completed in 1772, and running from the Severn at Stourport to join the Trent and Mersey Canal north of Cannock Chase. Despite the noise of the M6 motorway that crosses the canal, this is a beautiful stretch of water to walk along, overhung by trees, and some of the old canal bridges ought to be in paintings.

The towpath walking is over all too soon, and followed by a less pleasant trudge along the edges of huge cultivated fields. Lanes lead to Bednall, which has little worth stopping for apart from the shop/post office (it is mainly a dormitory village with many modern houses), but, thankfully, just across the A34 is Cannock Chase, where you meet much better walking country (Day 23 Map 2). The last bit of the Heart of England Way crosses the Trail on the Chase, so this is where the Cotswold Way/Heart of England Way alternative – see Section 2, Alternative Routes – rejoins the main Trail.

Cannock Chase is entered at a wood of tall pines, but this is atypical of what the route sees of the Chase. After crossing a road you are on heathland –

Staffordshire and Worcestershire Canal, near Penkridge

a mixture of heather, bracken and birch trees that is more characteristic of the next few miles.

The Trail descends into the Oldacre Valley, then climbs up again and crosses over to the Sherbrook Valley, which you follow north on a popular track until you reach the Stepping Stones (Day 23 Map 2, number 3), where you have a choice.

You can either take the recommended route of the Trail, leaving the Staffordshire Way here and going via the Seven Springs car park (Day 23 Map 3) to reach the Trent and Mersey Canal at Bridge 72. Alternatively, you can take the longer Shugborough alternative route. This keeps to the Staffordshire Way from the Stepping Stones, going north to visit Shugborough Hall before turning back southeast along the Trent and Mersey Canal to reach Bridge 72. The Shugborough route is included on the strip maps, but is not the recommended route because it involves an extra 2km of unnecessary road walking, both on the busy A513 and the busy Shugborough estate roads.

Shugborough Hall, built in the 1690s and the home of the Earl of Lichfield, is probably worth a visit if you like country houses, but in my opinion the view of it from the route doesn't justify the additional road walking. The ancient Essex Bridge over the River Trent, used by the Staffordshire Way near Shugborough, is the longest packhorse bridge in England, and the best thing to be seen on the Shugborough route.

Whether you choose the main Trail route or the Shugborough alternative, you end up at Bridge 72, heading the 'wrong way' along the Trent and Mersey Canal (Day 23 Map 3). Opportunities just off-route for lunch stops include pubs in Little Haywood, near Bridge 72, and the Wolseley Arms near Bridge 70.

The Trent and Mersey Canal was built at the same time as the Staffordshire and Worcestershire Canal, linking Merseyside with the Trent Navigation. It runs through Stoke-on-Trent and the Cheshire salt mining area (characterised by towns ending in 'wich', such as Northwich and Middlewich), and the key drivers for its construction were the pottery and salt industries that wanted cheaper transportation of their raw materials, such as coal and iron, and of their products. Josiah Wedgwood cut the first sod in 1766, the canal was completed in 1777, and it was financially very successful. Like the Staffs and Worcs, it is a narrow-boat canal, with locks only 7 feet (2m) wide.

The canal starts to become drearier as the trees disappear and the power station at Rugeley starts to loom near. With relief leave the canal at Bridge 68 (Day

Colwich Lock, Trent and Mersey Canal

23 Map 4) and start heading in the right direction again. The Staffordshire Way bypasses most of the village of Colton through fields to its west, but there are two pubs in the village, both just off-route.

Intricate route finding is the order of the day all the way from Colton to Abbots Bromley. Although stiles help to make the route relatively easy to follow, there are few Staffordshire Way signs, and for much of the way there is no visible path through the fields (follow the strip maps closely to trace the route).

Cross a ridge at Medleywood Barn (Day 23 Map 5), and suddenly Blithfield Reservoir is spread out ahead, covered with small boats if it is a weekend. More bobbing and weaving through the fields leads to Abbots Bromley.

Abbots Bromley is a pretty little village with shops and pubs. Its main claim to fame is the Horn Dance, enacted each September, when six local men wearing ancient reindeer antlers dance round the parish all day, drinking beer to keep them going. (The antlers are kept in the church for the rest of the year.) There is some bed and breakfast accommodation in and around Abbots Bromley, but it's limited, so you need to plan ahead to be sure of a bed.

DAY 24

The River Dove

Abbots Bromley to Thorpe (34km, 21 miles)

Today the Trail follows the Staffordshire Way north across farmland to Uttoxeter, then up the broad floodplain of the River Dove to Rocester. At Rocester the Trail leaves the Staffordshire Way (which follows the River Churnet northwest instead) to continue up the Dove, then follows a tributary stream parallel to and west of the Dove, mostly following the waymarked Limestone Way. The day ends by crossing the Dove again and entering the Peak District National Park, just before the village of Thorpe, close to the tourist haunt of Dovedale.

The section from Abbots Bromley to Uttoxeter is not the best of walking, particularly the section through Bagot's Park (Day 24 Maps 1 and 2). The path here follows the edge of huge, prairie-like fields of crops, and it seems to take forever to get anywhere. It's possibly the low point of the whole Trail, and Uttoxeter is likely to be reached with some relief.

> Uttoxeter has a station, banks, shops and accommodation. If you are there at the time of a horseracing meeting, accommodation may be difficult to find – try to plan ahead.

From Uttoxeter the day improves, although it is not until Thorpe, at the end of the day, that any real sign of the Peak District raises the curtain on what is to come. The Staffordshire Way leaves Uttoxeter via a small industrial estate and car parks for the racecourse, then crosses floodplain meadows to meet the River Dove and the A50 trunk road (Day 24 Map 3). This is a very busy dual carriageway linking the M6 and M1 motorways, but a pedestrian underpass spares walkers any physical danger (although that doesn't make the road any more pleasant – the old Dove Bridge next to the modern one is a reminder of when driving was a less frenetic business).

All the way from its source on Axe Edge near Buxton, to its confluence with the Trent near Burton, the Dove forms the boundary between Staffordshire and Derbyshire, and crossing the A50 bridge the Trail enters Derbyshire for the first time. From here you follow the river north, up to field edges at the top of the escarpment, then back down past a shooting club to follow quiet farm tracks and riverside paths towards Rocester (Day 24 Map 4).

Rocester's JCB factory is prominent ahead on the left as you near the village, with the Weaver Hills beyond. These hills are the start of limestone country, and being outside the Peak National Park have been quarried extensively.

At Rocester Bridge the Trail re-enters Staffordshire and heads along the road towards the village, leaving the Staffordshire Way by turning right into West View immediately after Tutbury Mill. This is the start of the Limestone Way, although there are no waymarks to indicate this. From here, bypassing the centre of Rocester, the Trail follows the Limestone Way to Thorpe, at the end of this day. (The Limestone Way is generally poorly waymarked – every now and then you may spot a faded sign with a cream arrow on a grey-green background, but that's about all.)

> Rocester is dominated by the JCB factory; most of the buildings are post-war, and the village centre is worth visiting only if you need the pub, a shop or accommodation. There are virtually no visible signs of the Roman settlement or the old abbey, but the Trail does pass Tutbury Mill, one of many early textile mills set up by Richard Arkwright in and around the Peak District.

The Trail is invisible for most of the next 2km (1½ miles), through fields on the ridge between the Churnet and Dove valleys, before descending to the Dove again, where the riverside path is very pleasant (Day 24 Map 5).

At the B5033 bridge you leave the Dove, heading up towards Ellastone along a tributary running parallel to it (Day 24 Map 6).

Before turning left up the road towards Ellastone, it is worth considering visiting the ancient church and manor house at Norbury, a few hundred metres along the road to the right. Norbury Manor is a 13th-century medieval hall, and next to it is the 14th-century church of St Mary and St Barlok. You will probably only be able to view them from the outside, as the church is usually locked. The Naylor brothers visited the church here in 1871: 'On arrival at Ellastone we left our luggage at the substantially built inn there while we went to visit Norbury Church, which was well worth seeing.'

At Ellastone as at Rocester the Trail misses the centre of the village, but there is a shop very close to the route, and a pub, the Duncombe Arms, a bit further off-route (see Day 24 Map 6).

Ellastone isn't particularly picturesque, but it is the setting for George Eliot's *Adam Bede*, renamed Hayslope in the novel. Adam Bede himself was based on George Eliot's grandfather, who was the local blacksmith and wheelwright.

West of Ellastone the Trail passes through Calwich Park, the former grounds of Calwich Abbey, and shortly afterwards leaves the Limestone Way for a while for a better alternative. The Limestone Way follows field edges above Ordley Brook valley, but there is an excellent route along the wooded valley bottom that is a lot better (Day 24 Map 7). Although it is occasionally wet underfoot, the wood is delightful to walk through and mostly very easy walking.

The path emerges from the trees briefly to descend a minor road down Ordley Bank and rejoin the stream – this is the first time the flavour of the Peak District is tasted, with steep slopes, bracken and stone walls. The path up the stream from here is less frequented and a bit overgrown, but eventually climbs out of the valley to Ellishill Farm.

Tricky route finding on invisible field paths leads up over the ridge, crossing the A52 at Swinscoe, where there is a pub, the Dog and Partridge. From the top of the next ridge the cone of Thorpe Cloud and the narrow exit from Dovedale are clearly visible ahead – something to look forward to for tomorrow.

Dropping down from the ridge you rejoin the Limestone Way (Day 24 Map 8), then a switchback down and up again onto a second ridge leads to Coldwall

Farm, where an old road is joined, now just a track, which leads down to cross the River Dove into Derbyshire again at Coldwall Bridge. This is also where you enter the Peak District National Park, and it's another place worth lingering, if you have time.

A riverside footpath to the left just before the bridge is the best way to Ilam youth hostel, otherwise Thorpe village is just ahead, with a pub and a number of bed and breakfasts. There is also a campsite about 1.5km (1 mile) from Thorpe at Highfields Farm. (If you are camping here, there is another pub, the Bluebell Inn, on the A515 at GR172516, which is closer to the campsite than the Dog and Partridge in Thorpe.)

Thorpe is a strangely scattered village – it has attractive stone houses, a church, a pub, a hotel, and even used to have a station, but it doesn't seem to have a village centre.

DAY 25

The Limestone Dales

Thorpe to Youlgreave (26km, 16 miles)

Today the Trail follows the Alternative Pennine Way all day (and continues to do so until the end of Day 28), but remember that this is not a waymarked route, and if you don't have a copy of the out-of-print guidebook, you will need to follow carefully the OS maps and the strip maps at the end of this section.

For much of the day the route is along the bottom of some of the Peak District's many limestone dales, and these valley bottoms are usually the best places to walk in the Peak limestone areas. The higher ground above them is usually not particularly high in absolute terms, and provides good farmland, which means that paths mainly follow field edges. The valleys, on the other hand, are typically steep sided and U shaped, with a bottom not wide enough to bother with intensive farming. In addition, the more spectacular dales have outcrops, and sometimes high cliffs of pale-grey limestone lining their sides, and they tend to be quieter and wilder than the uplands, and used for pasture or left to woodland. Often they are dry, since the streams that carved them through ice-age permafrost have long since gone underground in the porous limestone. These valleys make excellent walking country, and what they lack in distant views is more than made up for by the immediate surroundings. Inevitably they are popular with walkers and day-trippers, and the first on the route, Dovedale (a Site of Special Scientific Interest), is the busiest of them all, with a huge car park at the southern end that has been known to experience gridlock on sunny summer Sundays.

The route from Thorpe, for the next three and a half days as far as Marsden (Day 28), is almost entirely within or along the boundary of the Peak District National Park. The environment here is traditionally rural and well protected – of all the national parks, only the Peak District and Lake District authorities have direct control of the planning permission process in their areas.

There is an alternative route from Thorpe to Biggin following the Tissington Trail, a disused railway line, but although quicker, it's far inferior scenically, and disused railways are monotonous underfoot. The start is shown on Day 24 Map 8, and its junction with the recommended route of the Trail is shown on Day 25 Map 2.

The recommended route of the Trail takes a short walk from Thorpe down Lin Dale to reach the stepping stones in Dovedale (Day 25 Map 1). Thorpe Cloud is an excellent viewpoint, and well repays the short but brutally steep climb up the path from the stepping stones. From the stepping stones the Trail follows Dovedale north to Milldale.

Dovedale is a classic limestone valley, perhaps the most spectacular in the country, and draws large numbers of visitors. It has attracted people for centuries – Isaac Walton was here in the 17th century, and Samuel Johnson and Byron also visited. The valley is deep and wooded, between limestone cliffs and pinnacles covered in rock climbs, with the River Dove playing its full part as an archetypal sparkling limestone stream (apart from staying resolutely above ground). There is a small shop at Milldale, selling essentials such as ice cream and chocolate, and there is a youth hostel at Alstonefield, about 1km to the northwest.

'If I ever regretted being a cyclist it was along this section. The sweet pastoral Dove has an irresistible pulling power after the slightest introduction. But it is only for the walker, and it would be excusable for the cyclist and the motorist to throw their machines over the hedge, take to shoe leather and sample the exquisite walk from Alsop-on-le-Dale to Thorpe Cloud by the riverside' – William Dawson, *Land's End to John O'Groats*, 1934

The route continues north up Mill Dale, the continuation of the Dove valley above Milldale village (Day 25, Map 2). It is slightly quieter now, but there are still plenty of hikers at weekends. The valley eventually forks, and you turn right to follow the dry side valley of Biggin Dale, still immaculate walking country.

Biggin Dale gradually becomes shallower, until a small sewage works presages the less scenic middle part of the day. A minor road leads east through the small village of Biggin, where the Waterloo Inn is nicely placed for lunchtime (recommended), with a spacious beer garden at the front and a campsite at the back.

From Biggin the Trail continues east along lanes and field paths (Day 25 Map 3). There is a seasonal café at the higher of the two Gotham Granges, then at Gotham Curve the route briefly joins the High Peak Trail, which follows the trackbed of the Cromford and High Peak Railway, with Gotham Curve reputed to have been the tightest railway curve in Britain.

The Cromford and High Peak was one of the earliest railways, opened in 1831. It was designed as part of the canal network, joining the Cromford Canal to the Peak Forest Canal at Whaley Bridge, and incorporated a number of steep inclines up which trucks had to be winched.

A pleasant kilometre along the High Peak Trail, then a less inspiring stretch on roads, and you drop down on a footpath into Gratton Dale, another fascinating, deep, wooded limestone valley.

At the foot of the dale a short climb up the hillside along a minor road (Day 25 Map 4) leads to very different type of country, with an invisible path crossing a gritstone boulder field towards Youlgreave (there will be plenty more grit tomorrow!). The gritstone area is soon passed, and the last limestone dale of the day, Bradford Dale, leads to the pretty village of Youlgreave.

(If you are heading for Edale and the start of the Pennine Way, you don't need to go through the centre of Youlgreave unless you need its facilities. See Day 25 Map 4 for the recommended point at which to leave the Alternative Pennine Way in Bradford Dale and rejoin the Limestone Way to Castleton, from where a climb over the Mam Tor Ridge leads to Edale.)

Bradford Dale, near Youlgreave

Youlgreave (it appears to be a matter of opinion whether the name of the village is spelled Youlgreave or Youlgrave – I've used the former to be consistent with the Ordnance Survey) is a classic Peak District village with old stone cottages crowded together and hugging the narrow roads. It has accommodation, including a youth hostel and the George Hotel, and there is a camping barn at Castle Farm, just over a kilometre to the west (the nearest campsite is at Hopping Farm (GR204631), close to where the route enters Bradford Dale). There is also a post office, a couple of shops, and what looks like a monument opposite the youth hostel, but is actually the original water supply to the village, piped to here in 1829.

DAY 26

The Gritstone Edges

Youlgreave to Hathersage (29km, 18 miles)

Today the Trail continues to follow the Alternative Pennine Way north-east out of limestone country. At Baslow it picks up the line of gritstone edges that runs northwards for the rest of the day, above the east side of the Derwent valley, to Hathersage and Stanage Edge. A diversion from Stanage Edge down to the village of Hathersage is necessary at the end of the day to find accommodation, returning to the edge the next morning.

From Youlgreave the route crosses Lathkill Dale, then through farmland to cross the River Wye close to Haddon Hall (Day 26 Map 1), and continues over low hills and through woods, via Calton Pastures, to descend to Edensor and the parklands of Chatsworth House (Day 26 Map 2).

Haddon Hall dates back to the Norman Conquest, and was the home of William Peverel, the illegitimate son of William the Conqueror. The hall was never allowed to fall into ruin, and was sympathetically restored by the Duke of Rutland between the wars.

Chatsworth is principally an 18th-century creation, built for the first Duke of Devonshire, and designed for show rather than defence, with an extensive landscaped park. Defoe expressed his astonishment that anyone would attempt to

Edensor

create something like the Chatsworth Estate in such a place, 'where the mountains insult the clouds, intercept the sun, and would threaten, were earthquakes frequent here, to bury the very towns, much more the house, in their ruins'. Am I alone in thinking the Chatsworth House buildings are hideously ugly? From the hillside above Edensor they look to me more like a Victorian hospital than an elegant country house. By contrast, the buildings in the estate village of Edensor are delightful – all different, and all the woodwork painted in the same shade of Chatsworth Blue. The original Edensor village was largely demolished, resited and rebuilt when the park was landscaped.

Elihu Burritt visited both Haddon and Chatsworth on his walk to John O'Groats in 1863, and called them the 'two most representative buildings in the kingdom'. They are both open to visitors.

A stroll alongside the River Derwent through Chatsworth's parkland leads to the village of Baslow, which has pubs, shops and accommodation. The Devonshire Arms is recommended for a lunch stop (there is even a 'walkers welcome' sign).

From here the scenery changes. A steep climb up a rough lane brings you to Baslow Edge, the first of the gritstone edges, outcrops of hard, grey sandstone. By far the longest line of these in Britain runs due north from here for over 16km (10 miles), overlooking the River Derwent, from Baslow to Moscar. The edges vary from nothing to 25m or more in height, and include some of the most popular rock climbing in the country. The walking along the top of the edges is usually easy, as the gritty rock forms well-drained and even paths. The views, particularly to the west, are extensive.

After Baslow Edge come Curbar and Froggatt Edges (Day 26 Map 3), both important rock-climbing areas, so expect to hear the clanking of metal coming up from below. Shortly after the end of Froggatt Edge the Trail passes the excellent Grouse Inn, then diverges a bit from the top of the escarpment to cross, on an old estate road, what used to be the parkland of the Longshaw Estate (Day 26 Map 4). This used to be the Duke of Rutland's shooting land, but now belongs to the National Trust. (**Note** The road numbering in this area has been changed in recent years, so only newer maps will show the correct numbers.)

Crossing the A6187 by Burbage Bridge, a path climbs up the gritstone moorland to the outcrop of Carl Wark (there are various paths, but the Trail follows one that doesn't ford Burbage Brook). On Carl Wark there is an ancient boulder wall, thought to be part of the defences for an Iron Age fort.

Beyond Carl Wark the Trail ascends to the higher outcrop of Higger Tor, then crosses two moorland roads and climbs to follow the longest of the gritstone edges – Stanage Edge (Day 26 Map 5) – to round off the day.

If there is mist on the edge and you are planning to stay at Hathersage for the night, it is best to turn left along the second moorland road (Day 26 Map 4 – bad weather route) rather than continue the climb up to Stanage Edge. In mist it is difficult to identify the top of the descent from Stanage Edge to Hathersage.

Stanage Edge has been climbed on for a hundred years, although it wasn't until after the Second World War that it started to become popular. Now, justifiably, it is one of the most popular venues in the country, with nearly a thousand documented routes, and hundreds of climbers swarm all over it on dry summer weekends. Even when the edge is engulfed in mist, it is by no means unusual to hear the 'clank, clank' of climbers groping their way up the greasy rock below you.

The Trail route for the Main Schedule (i.e. the one reflected in the stage distances) drops down from Stanage Edge (just after Stanage Plantation and just before reaching the Long Causeway) to head for the North Lees campsite above Hathersage (GR235833), returning to the same point on the edge the next morning. The campsite is the closest legitimate accommodation to the Trail around here (unofficial camping is not allowed in the national park). The campsite is small and often full, so booking is recommended (tel 01433 650838).

An alternative is to continue beyond the campsite to Hathersage village and stay there (even if you stay at the campsite you are likely to want to visit Hathersage to eat, drink and/or shop). Hathersage has a youth hostel, bed and breakfasts, shops, a bank, and outdoor shops, including the excellent Outside and its equally excellent café upstairs. It is a pleasant village, though marred slightly by the busy road through the middle, and Robin Hood's Little John is supposed to be buried in the churchyard here. Descent to Hathersage adds about 2km (1½ miles) to the day, and the same again the next morning.

On the way down to Hathersage you pass North Lees Hall, reputed to be the model for Thornfield Hall, the home of Mr Rochester in Charlotte Brontë's *Jane Eyre*. In 1845 the author spent three weeks in Hathersage while writing the novel.

The Alternative Pennine Way as originally described doesn't drop down to Hathersage, but continues along Stanage Edge to a stage end at Moscar on the A57 (Day 27 Map 1). Unfortunately there is nowhere to stay at Moscar, and it is not a suitable place to camp (and again, wild camping isn't allowed in the national park), so if you don't want to stay at North Lees or Hathersage there are three options.

1. Drop down the Long Causeway from Stanage Edge to the village of Bamford (see Day 27 Map 1, number 1), which has accommodation and pubs, and camping at Swallow Holme Caravan Park. This adds about 3km (2 miles) to today's walk, and makes little difference to tomorrow's.
2. Continue to Moscar, follow the A57 west, then take a minor road to the Strines Inn (Day 27 Map 1, GR222906, tel 0114 285 1247). This 13th-century pub has excellent accommodation (four-poster bed, coal fire in your room), but is not cheap. If you stay there, you can take a short cut up to Derwent Edge tomorrow (Day 27 Map 2). This option adds nearly 7km (4 miles) to today, but reduces tomorrow's tally by 9km (6 miles).
3. Again continue to Moscar, follow the A57 west (or, better, a parallel track just north of the A57), this time until you reach the Ladybower Inn (tel 01433 651241, GR204865), which also has accommodation. (Again there is a route up to Derwent Edge to rejoin the Trail tomorrow.) This adds 6km (4 miles) to today and shortens tomorrow by the same distance.

DAY 27

The Yorkshire Peak

Hathersage to Dunford Bridge (33km, 20 miles)

Today's journey is quieter and less eventful, leaving Derbyshire and the busier areas of the Peak District for Yorkshire and the more industrialised region between the Manchester and West Yorkshire conurbations. There is no pub until Holme (tomorrow), and there are no shops until you reach Marsden (tomorrow), so stock up in Hathersage before you leave.

It's an excellent day's walking, along the rest of Stanage Edge, and then across Derwent Moor to follow Derwent Edge, high above the flooded Derwent valley, then dropping down to the valley and following the shore of Howden Reservoir. From the head of the valley, and now in a very remote spot, an excellent path climbs up onto the moorland and north over the undulating and featureless peat moors. This path descends from the moor to cross the A628 trunk road, then the route follows another disused railway line (the Trans Pennine Trail, a coast to coast cycling and horseriding route from Southport to Humberside) westwards to the isolated hamlet of Dunford Bridge.

From Hathersage there is a strenuous start to the day (Day 26 Map 5), climbing back up to rejoin the Trail following the Alternative Pennine Way along the top of Stanage Edge (Day 27 Map 1). It's worth the effort, though, to resume striding along the edge, past the ordnance column on High Neb (458m) to Stanage End, at the end of Stanage Edge, and across the moor to the A57 at Moscar. In fact wherever you spent the night, you will start by climbing back up to the moors.

Sheffield is only a few kilometres away to the right, and to the left the A57 drops down again to the Derwent valley before starting its long climb up to the notorious Snake Pass. This route to Glossop and Manchester is frequently closed by snow and ice in winter, and passes few houses between here and Glossop.

From Moscar there is another stiff climb through the grouse-shooting country of Derwent Moors, and you are on Derwent Edge, the last and highest of the line of gritstone edges (Day 27 Map 2). From here until you reach the Derwent valley reservoirs it is possible that you may be diverted from the main route by grouse shooting on certain days of the year – see Day 27 Maps 2 and 3 for alternative routes.

Back Tor, Derwent Edge

There are some grotesquely shaped gritstone pinnacles on and by Derwent Edge – the Wheelstones and the Cakes of Bread are particularly bizarre. As soon as you see them the reasons for the names are obvious!

The ridge climbs to 538m at Back Tor, and to reach the OS column there you will need to scramble up the rocky top. Back Tor is the highest point on the route since the Black Mountains near Hay-on-Wye, and won't be exceeded until Fountains Fell north of Malham on Day 30. Over to the left are the higher peat moors of Kinder Scout and the start of the Pennine Way – be thankful that you are not floundering in peat groughs in the middle of the Kinder plateau! – and the transmission mast on Holme Moss (passed on Day 28) is visible. Further along, by the cairn at Lost Lad, there is a brass panoramic plaque that identifies the rest of the hills around you.

After the descent from Derwent Edge, beyond Lost Lad (Day 27 Map 3), rather than continue along the moors north, where there are poor paths and boggy ground, the Trail descends with the Alternative Pennine Way into the Derwent valley, joining an untarred road up the valley past Howden Reservoir and on to a packhorse bridge at Slippery Stones.

The Derwent Reservoir was the scene for the testing of Barnes Wallace's bouncing bombs, both in reality and in the 1954 film *The Dam Busters*. The Derwent dam and the higher Howden dam were completed during the First World War. At Slippery Stones the old packhorse bridge looks as though it's been there for centuries, although in fact it was only rebuilt here in 1959, after being removed from Derwent village, now drowned in Ladybower Reservoir, which was completed in 1945.

From Slippery Stones an old packhorse track climbs up out of the valley to the northeast (Day 27 Maps 3 and 4), then over the moor via Mickleden Edge to the head of Langsett Reservoir and the A628 trunk road.

At Langsett village, 1.5km down the valley, at the foot of the reservoir, the Wagon and Horses (tel 01226 763147) has accommodation. To reach Langsett, turn right along either of the two paths in the wood after crossing the River Porter, and follow the reservoir shore (Day 27 Map 5).

From the point where you cross the A628, the 'Flouch Hotel' is a few minutes east along the line of the old road, but no longer has accommodation. What was a hotel has now been converted into three restaurants (Chinese, Indian and Italian). There is accommodation at the Dog and Partridge, 1.5km along the A628 to the west, but it's not cheap.

The head of Langsett Reservoir

A few minutes beyond the A628, across a low moor called Low Moor, you are in the Don valley. Alongside the River Don is the disused Woodhead railway line between Manchester and Sheffield. This section has been recycled as part of the Trans Pennine Trail, and our route follows it west up the valley to the hamlet of Dunford Bridge.

Dunford Bridge is where the railway used to disappear into the Woodhead Tunnels. The three tunnels are 5km (3 miles) long, and have all been closed to traffic since 1981. The first opened in 1845, at a cost of 26 men killed. The second opened in 1852, with 28 more dead, many from cholera. The third tunnel opened in 1954 as part of electrification of the line, and even this project resulted in the loss of six more lives.

Although this day stage ends at Dunford Bridge, there was at the time of writing no accommodation either here or at the next obvious stopping place, Holme village, 9km (5 miles) further on (Day 28 Map 2). The hotel in Holme has closed down permanently, and the Stanhope Arms at Dunford Bridge, which used to provide bed and breakfast and allow walkers to camp in the grounds, was 'closed for refurbishment' at the time of writing, and had been for some time. The best plan is to search the Web for the latest information (try www.kirklees.gov.uk)

before you set out (unless you are planning to ask a farmer for permission to camp). The most convenient bed and breakfast accommodation currently available is Ash House, 240 Dunford Road, Holmfirth (tel 01484 688244) at GR147071, just over 2km off-route from where you first join the Kirklees Way – see Day 28 Map 1, and at Corn Loft House, 146 Woodhead Road, Holmbridge (tel 01484 683147), 1km off-route – see Day 28 Map 1.

DAY 28

Reservoirs and Moor Edges

Dunford Bridge to Hebden Bridge (45km, 28 miles)

Today is the last day on the Alternative Pennine Way, which the Trail has been following since Day 25. This is the day you walk out of the Peak District and into the West Yorkshire Pennines, but rather than join the Pennine Way just yet, the route follows the APW on an intricate itinerary along the eastern flank of the Pennine spine (which separates Greater Manchester and south Lancashire from the West Yorkshire woollen mill towns of Huddersfield and Halifax). This means you avoid some of the more unsavoury peat bogs on the Pennine Way, such as the infamous Black Hill, and you also get better views.

There is a stiff climb up from Dunford Bridge to the dam of Winscar Reservoir (Day 28 Map 1). The reservoir was completed in 1975 and looms over the hamlet like a scene from a disaster movie. The dam started leaking in early 2001, and the reservoir had to be drained for emergency remedial work.

A short distance along a minor road, then on a path through old quarry workings, and the Holme valley comes into view ahead. (The town in the foreground is Holmfirth, with Huddersfield beyond it, and this is also the point where you enter West Yorkshire.) From here it is fairly hard work for a few kilometres, crossing the many minor valleys that feed into Holmfirth (Day 28 Map 2). The walking is good, though, past small reservoirs, and through plantations and typical West Yorkshire drystone wall hill country. There is a pub at Holme, where the route crosses the A6024.

At Wessenden Head (Day 28 Map 3), the highest point of the day at 451m, you cross the A635 Saddleworth Moor road, and meet the Pennine Way for the

Butterley Reservoir, approaching Marsden

first time, although you don't start following it yet. (If you're lucky there will be a tea van here as well.)

From Leyzing Clough (below Wessenden Head Reservoir) down to the small mill town of Marsden the Trail follows the Alternative Pennine Way along the line of Deer Hill Conduit (which feeds Deer Hill Reservoir), before dropping steeply down into Marsden (Day 28 Map 4). The path along the conduit is virtually level and gives marvellous views over the reservoirs in the valley and over Marsden.

> Marsden itself is an attractive old town, with shops, accommodation and pubs, including the Riverhead Brewery Tap in Peel Street, which brews its own beer. They don't serve food, but you can eat your own food, and there is a sandwich shop across the road. The nearest camping is behind the Carriage House pub, on the A62 (GR028102).

On the way out of Marsden you cross the Huddersfield Narrow Canal, and if you have time a short detour to the left brings you to the eastern end of the Standedge Tunnel, which has recently been reopened to narrowboats.

From Marsden to Hebden Bridge is a switchback across valley after valley. Some of the crossings are above the intake walls across moorland, and some are within the stone-walled pasture areas; it is all good walking, though, and the views are excellent. There are reservoirs all over the place, feeding the surrounding towns.

In the first valley the Trail drops steeply to cross the dam of Deanshead Reservoir. In the second, just before Booth Wood Reservoir, you cross the M62 at the point where it divides to run either side of Stott Hall Farm (Day 28 Map 5).

In the third valley (Day 28 Map 6) you diverge from the original line of the Alternative Pennine Way, which crosses the dam of Baitings Reservoir then skirts Great Manshead Hill on minor roads. The Trail follows a better route, along the south shore of the reservoir and straight over the top of Manshead Hill (417m) on what is now a permissive footpath. (Don't worry about this route missing the two pubs by the other side of Baitings dam, marked on old maps – they are now both private houses.) The route of the APW is shown on the strip map as a bad weather alternative.

After rejoining the APW at a crossroads of paths and descending again, the fourth valley is Cragg Vale (Day 28 Map 7), which has old stone terraced houses scattered along it, and also the Hinchliffe Arms (a pub with accommodation), whose door the route passes.

After crossing Bell House Moor, the fifth valley is the deep, narrow Calder valley, where the path drops steeply down to enter Hebden Bridge (Day 28 Map 8).

The Calder valley has been occupied ever since the valley bottom was drained when the Rochdale Canal was constructed. Mills were built in the main valley and the neighbouring side valleys in the early part of the Industrial Revolution, to avoid the regulations affecting less remote areas, and to exploit the water power of the streams. The valley is so narrow that there was little land to build on – the river, railway and canal use up the whole of the valley bottom in places. In Hebden Bridge, terraces of back-to-back houses were built on slopes so steep that there was room for a second terrace below the back-to-backs on the lower side of the slope, with a walkway giving access to the 'upstairs' houses. In the 1960s this was a rundown area, and houses could barely be given away. These days it is a thriving community of great character, and Hebden Bridge has all the services a walker needs except a campsite.

Day 20 Map 1: Knighton to Stow Hill

Say goodbye to Wales as you cross the railway bridge in Knighton & enter Shropshire. If you think you have escaped the hills at the same time you will be disappointed: this page is nearly all uphill.

5. The track through the woods emerges from the trees to meet a better track. Turn left (gate & stile) & follow the track uphill, ignoring the steeper track to the right. Keep left after the pond to the top of the field (gate & stile).

4. Turn right off the track (gate) just after a pair of cottages (the lefthand is called "Almshouse" which presumably explains how they came to be here). Climb steeply up the field past a ruin (no path) to a gate on the right. Follow the track uphill through the woods.

3. Go through the gate straight ahead & continue, now with the hedge on your right, climbing the shoulder of the hill. At the top cross a farm track & bear left downhill with a fence now on your left on what appears to be an old sunken lane. Stowe Church is ahead to the right with its distinctive wooden panelled tower. At the bottom, turn left along the access track.

2. Cross the Teme & the railway then bend right with the main road. After about 70m a broad signed path forks left into the woods: follow this until it forks as it nears the road again. Fork right, descend to a forestry track & turn left. After a few metres the track bends sharp left: at the apex turn right (steps & stile) into the field ahead. Bear gradually away from the road (no visible path) to a footbridge then a stile. Cross the road, go through the gate opposite & follow the hedge.

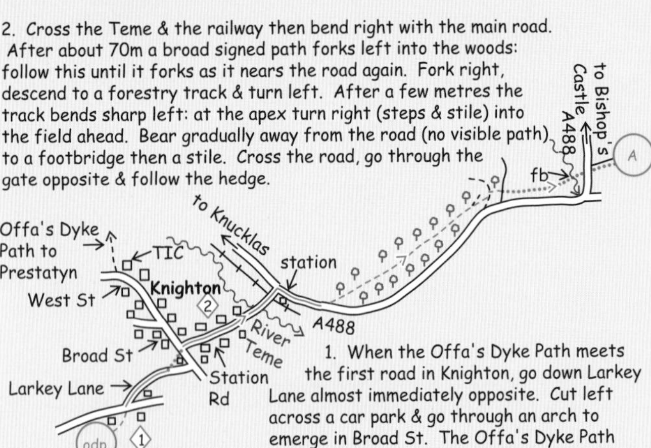

1. When the Offa's Dyke Path meets the first road in Knighton, go down Larkey Lane almost immediately opposite. Cut left across a car park & go through an arch to emerge in Broad St. The Offa's Dyke Path turns left here, but our route goes right then immediately left along Station Rd.

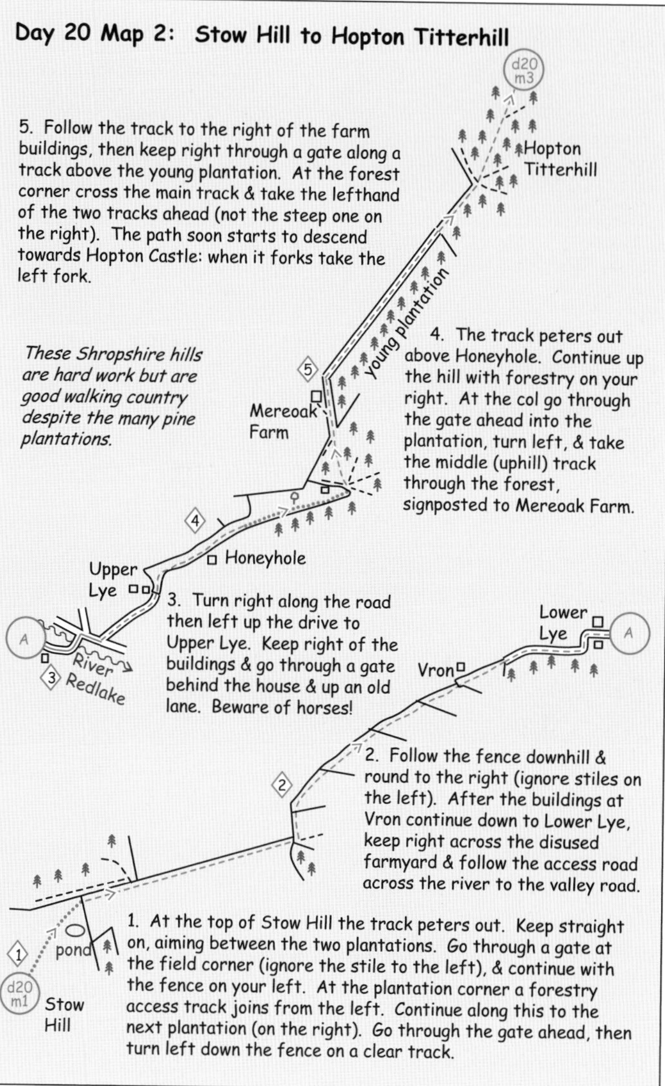
Day 20 Map 2: Stow Hill to Hopton Titterhill
d20 m3
Hopton Titterhill
5. Follow the track to the right of the farm buildings, then keep right through a gate along a track above the young plantation. At the forest corner cross the main track & take the lefthand of the two tracks ahead (not the steep one on the right). The path soon starts to descend towards Hopton Castle: when it forks take the left fork.
young plantation
These Shropshire hills are hard work but are good walking country despite the many pine plantations.
5
Mereoak Farm
4. The track peters out above Honeyhole. Continue up the hill with forestry on your right. At the col go through the gate ahead into the plantation, turn left, & take the middle (uphill) track through the forest, signposted to Mereoak Farm.
4
Honeyhole
Upper Lye
3. Turn right along the road then left up the drive to Upper Lye. Keep right of the buildings & go through a gate behind the house & up an old lane. Beware of horses!
A
River Redlake
3
Lower Lye
A
Vron
2
2. Follow the fence downhill & round to the right (ignore stiles on the left). After the buildings at Vron continue down to Lower Lye, keep right across the disused farmyard & follow the access road across the river to the valley road.
1
pond
d20 m1
Stow Hill
1. At the top of Stow Hill the track peters out. Keep straight on, aiming between the two plantations. Go through a gate at the field corner (ignore the stile to the left), & continue with the fence on your left. At the plantation corner a forestry access track joins from the left. Continue along this to the next plantation (on the right). Go through the gate ahead, then turn left down the fence on a clear track.

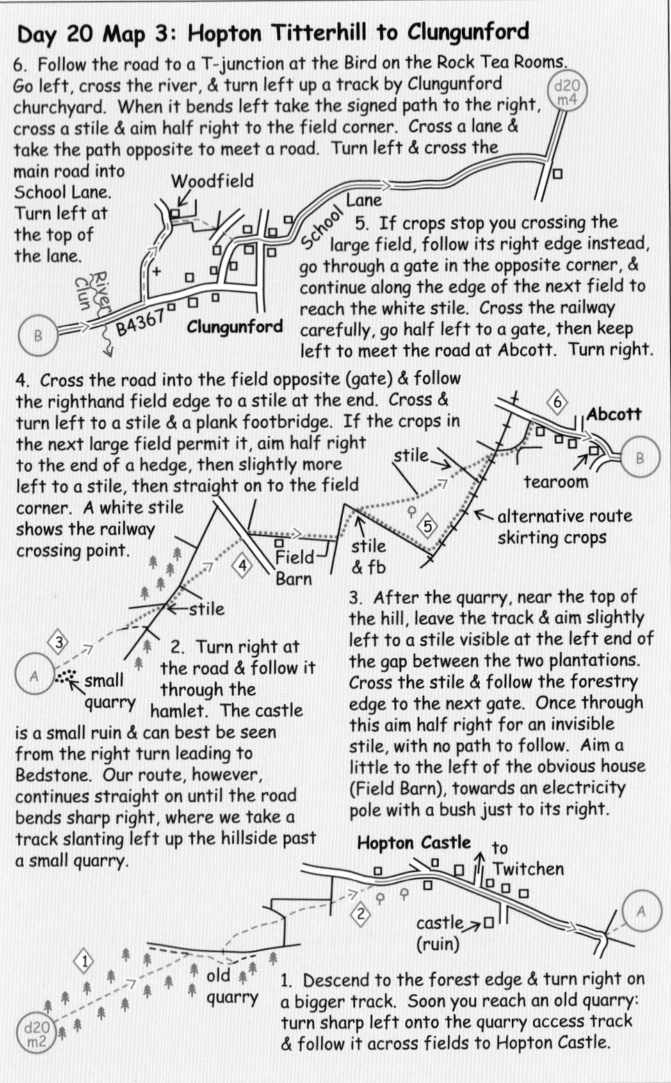
Day 20 Map 3: Hopton Titterhill to Clungunford
6. Follow the road to a T-junction at the Bird on the Rock Tea Rooms. Go left, cross the river, & turn left up a track by Clungunford churchyard. When it bends left take the signed path to the right, cross a stile & aim half right to the field corner. Cross a lane & take the path opposite to meet a road. Turn left & cross the main road into School Lane. Turn left at the top of the lane.
d20 m4
Woodfield
School Lane
River Clun
B4367
Clungunford
B
5. If crops stop you crossing the large field, follow its right edge instead, go through a gate in the opposite corner, & continue along the edge of the next field to reach the white stile. Cross the railway carefully, go half left to a gate, then keep left to meet the road at Abcott. Turn right.
4. Cross the road into the field opposite (gate) & follow the righthand field edge to a stile at the end. Cross & turn left to a stile & a plank footbridge. If the crops in the next large field permit it, aim half right to the end of a hedge, then slightly more left to a stile, then straight on to the field corner. A white stile shows the railway crossing point.
6
Abcott
B
stile
tearoom
5
alternative route skirting crops
4
Field Barn
stile & fb
stile
3
A
small quarry
2. Turn right at the road & follow it through the hamlet. The castle is a small ruin & can best be seen from the right turn leading to Bedstone. Our route, however, continues straight on until the road bends sharp right, where we take a track slanting left up the hillside past a small quarry.
3. After the quarry, near the top of the hill, leave the track & aim slightly left to a stile visible at the left end of the gap between the two plantations. Cross the stile & follow the forestry edge to the next gate. Once through this aim half right for an invisible stile, with no path to follow. Aim a little to the left of the obvious house (Field Barn), towards an electricity pole with a bush just to its right.
Hopton Castle
to Twitchen
2
castle (ruin)
A
1
old quarry
d20 m2
1. Descend to the forest edge & turn right on a bigger track. Soon you reach an old quarry: turn sharp left onto the quarry access track & follow it across fields to Hopton Castle.

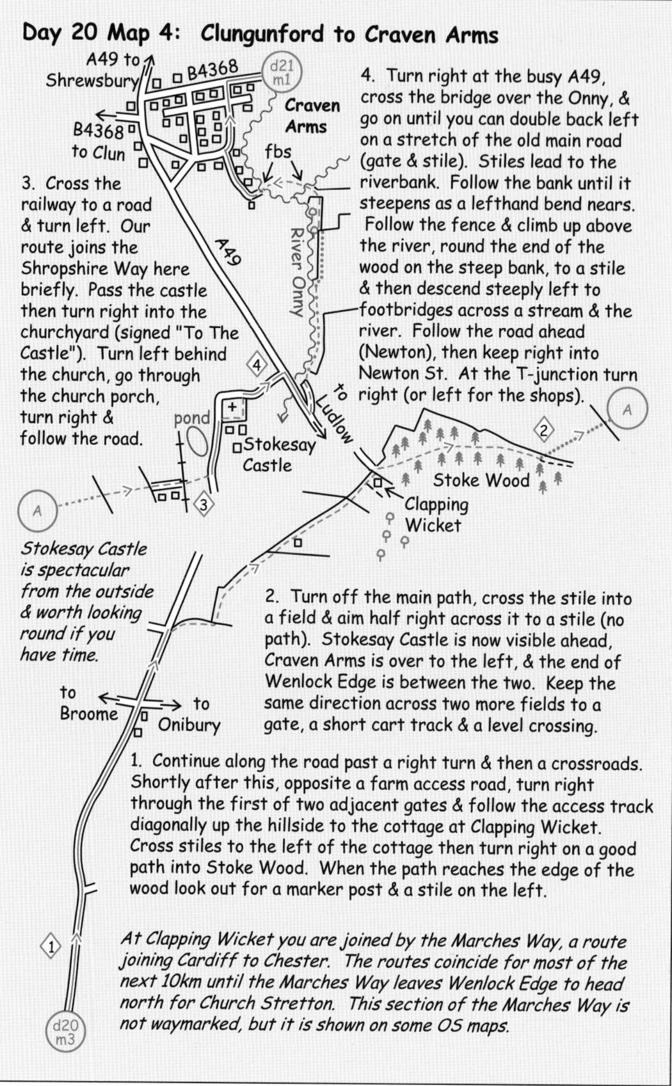
Day 20 Map 4: Clungunford to Craven Arms
A49 to Shrewsbury
B4368
d21 m1
Craven Arms
B4368 to Clun
fbs
3. Cross the railway to a road & turn left. Our route joins the Shropshire Way here briefly. Pass the castle then turn right into the churchyard (signed "To The Castle"). Turn left behind the church, go through the church porch, turn right & follow the road.
A49
River Onny
4. Turn right at the busy A49, cross the bridge over the Onny, & go on until you can double back left on a stretch of the old main road (gate & stile). Stiles lead to the riverbank. Follow the bank until it steepens as a lefthand bend nears. Follow the fence & climb up above the river, round the end of the wood on the steep bank, to a stile & then descend steeply left to footbridges across a stream & the river. Follow the road ahead (Newton), then keep right into Newton St. At the T-junction turn right (or left for the shops).
4
to Ludlow
pond
Stokesay Castle
A
2
A
3
Stoke Wood
Clapping Wicket
Stokesay Castle is spectacular from the outside & worth looking round if you have time.
2. Turn off the main path, cross the stile into a field & aim half right across it to a stile (no path). Stokesay Castle is now visible ahead, Craven Arms is over to the left, & the end of Wenlock Edge is between the two. Keep the same direction across two more fields to a gate, a short cart track & a level crossing.
to Broome
to Onibury
1. Continue along the road past a right turn & then a crossroads. Shortly after this, opposite a farm access road, turn right through the first of two adjacent gates & follow the access track diagonally up the hillside to the cottage at Clapping Wicket. Cross stiles to the left of the cottage then turn right on a good path into Stoke Wood. When the path reaches the edge of the wood look out for a marker post & a stile on the left.
1
At Clapping Wicket you are joined by the Marches Way, a route joining Cardiff to Chester. The routes coincide for most of the next 10km until the Marches Way leaves Wenlock Edge to head north for Church Stretton. This section of the Marches Way is not waymarked, but it is shown on some OS maps.
d20 m3

Day 21 Map 1: Craven Arms to Strefford

From the top of the Edge a ruined tower is prominent on Callow Hill to the southeast. This is Flounders Camp: a folly built in 1838.

4. Once in the woods the path becomes a muddy sunken lane slanting up the steep slope. Ignore left forks & continue up to join a good path along the top of the Edge.

Wistanstow is 1km off-route & is the home of the Plough Inn & Wood's brewery.

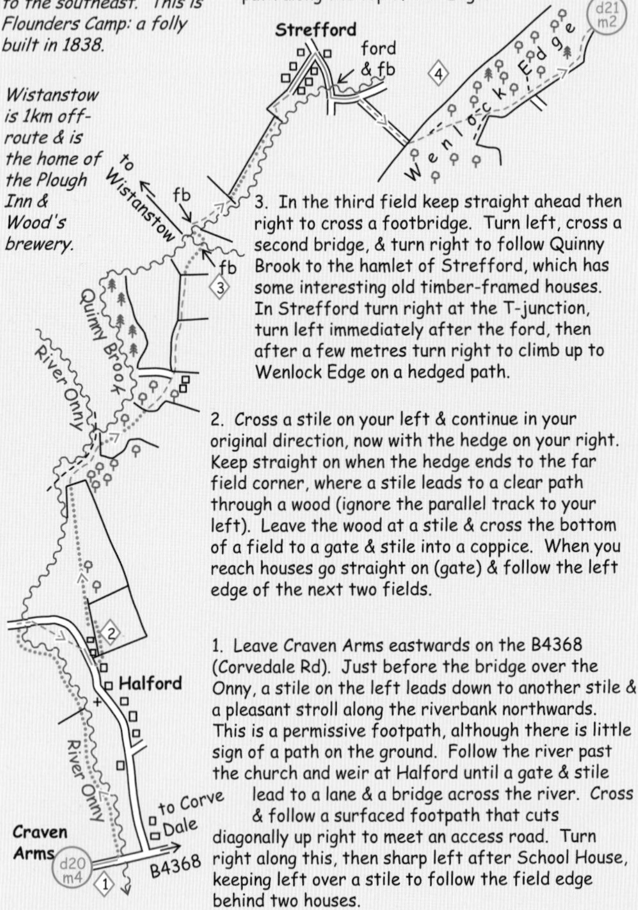

3. In the third field keep straight ahead then right to cross a footbridge. Turn left, cross a second bridge, & turn right to follow Quinny Brook to the hamlet of Strefford, which has some interesting old timber-framed houses. In Strefford turn right at the T-junction, turn left immediately after the ford, then after a few metres turn right to climb up to Wenlock Edge on a hedged path.

2. Cross a stile on your left & continue in your original direction, now with the hedge on your right. Keep straight on when the hedge ends to the far field corner, where a stile leads to a clear path through a wood (ignore the parallel track to your left). Leave the wood at a stile & cross the bottom of a field to a gate & stile into a coppice. When you reach houses go straight on (gate) & follow the left edge of the next two fields.

1. Leave Craven Arms eastwards on the B4368 (Corvedale Rd). Just before the bridge over the Onny, a stile on the left leads down to another stile & a pleasant stroll along the riverbank northwards. This is a permissive footpath, although there is little sign of a path on the ground. Follow the river past the church and weir at Halford until a gate & stile lead to a lane & a bridge across the river. Cross & follow a surfaced footpath that cuts diagonally up right to meet an access road. Turn right along this, then sharp left after School House, keeping left over a stile to follow the field edge behind two houses.

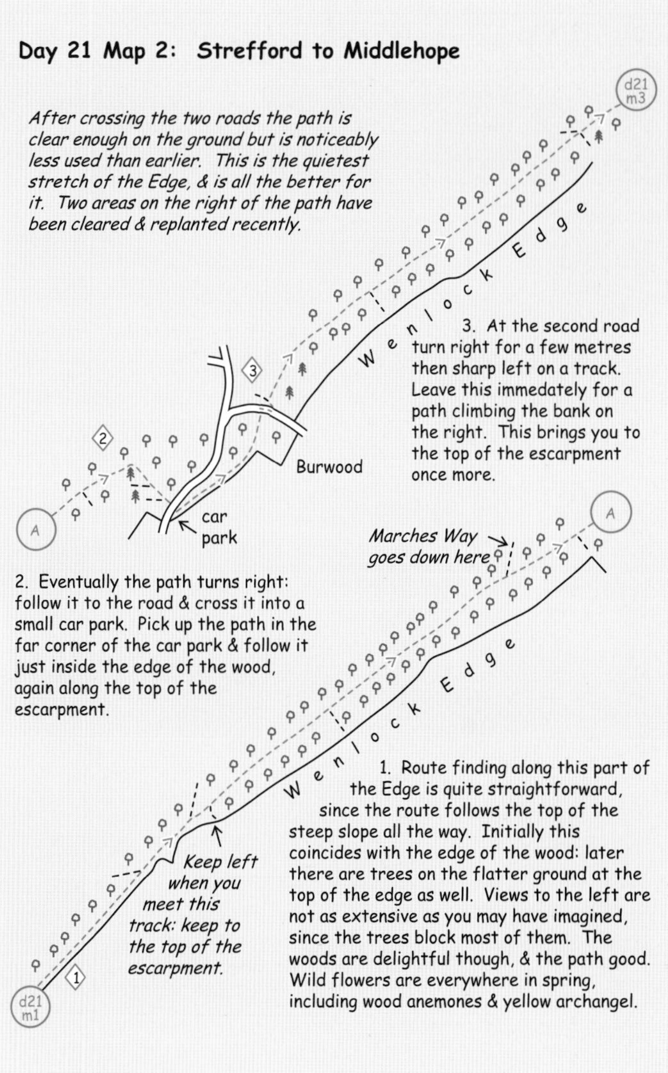

Day 21 Map 2: Strefford to Middlehope
d21 m3
After crossing the two roads the path is clear enough on the ground but is noticeably less used than earlier. This is the quietest stretch of the Edge, & is all the better for it. Two areas on the right of the path have been cleared & replanted recently.
Wenlock Edge
3. At the second road turn right for a few metres then sharp left on a track. Leave this immedately for a path climbing the bank on the right. This brings you to the top of the escarpment once more.
3
2
Burwood
A
car park
A
Marches Way goes down here
2. Eventually the path turns right: follow it to the road & cross it into a small car park. Pick up the path in the far corner of the car park & follow it just inside the edge of the wood, again along the top of the escarpment.
Wenlock Edge
1. Route finding along this part of the Edge is quite straightforward, since the route follows the top of the steep slope all the way. Initially this coincides with the edge of the wood: later there are trees on the flatter ground at the top of the edge as well. Views to the left are not as extensive as you may have imagined, since the trees block most of them. The woods are delightful though, & the path good. Wild flowers are everywhere in spring, including wood anemones & yellow archangel.
Keep left when you meet this track: keep to the top of the escarpment.
1
d21 m1

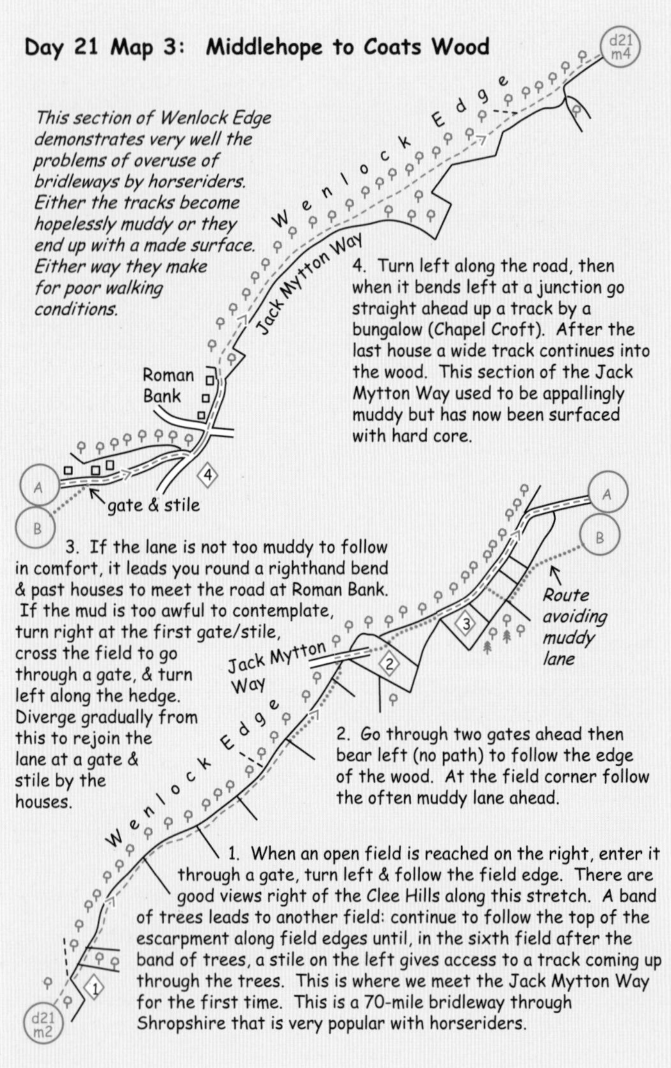
Day 21 Map 3: Middlehope to Coats Wood
d21 m4
This section of Wenlock Edge demonstrates very well the problems of overuse of bridleways by horseriders. Either the tracks become hopelessly muddy or they end up with a made surface. Either way they make for poor walking conditions.
Wenlock Edge
Jack Mytton Way
4. Turn left along the road, then when it bends left at a junction go straight ahead up a track by a bungalow (Chapel Croft). After the last house a wide track continues into the wood. This section of the Jack Mytton Way used to be appallingly muddy but has now been surfaced with hard core.
Roman Bank
4
A
B
gate & stile
3. If the lane is not too muddy to follow in comfort, it leads you round a righthand bend & past houses to meet the road at Roman Bank. If the mud is too awful to contemplate, turn right at the first gate/stile, cross the field to go through a gate, & turn left along the hedge. Diverge gradually from this to rejoin the lane at a gate & stile by the houses.
A
B
Route avoiding muddy lane
3
Jack Mytton Way
2
Wenlock Edge
2. Go through two gates ahead then bear left (no path) to follow the edge of the wood. At the field corner follow the often muddy lane ahead.
1. When an open field is reached on the right, enter it through a gate, turn left & follow the field edge. There are good views right of the Clee Hills along this stretch. A band of trees leads to another field: continue to follow the top of the escarpment along field edges until, in the sixth field after the band of trees, a stile on the left gives access to a track coming up through the trees. This is where we meet the Jack Mytton Way for the first time. This is a 70-mile bridleway through Shropshire that is very popular with horseriders.
1
d21 m2

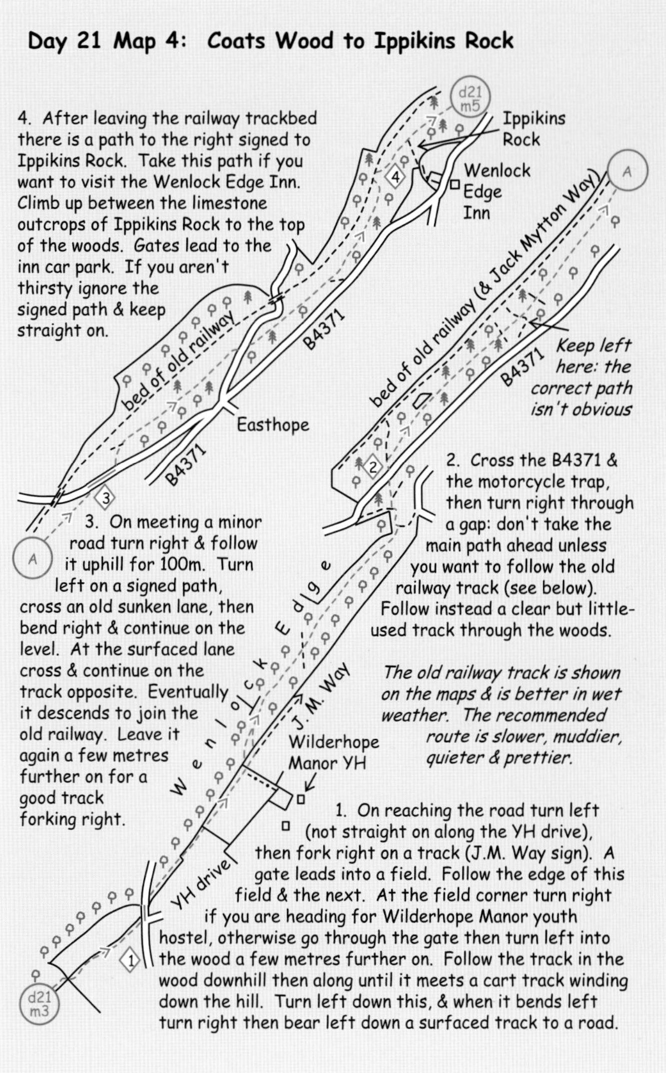
Day 21 Map 4: Coats Wood to Ippikins Rock
4. After leaving the railway trackbed there is a path to the right signed to Ippikins Rock. Take this path if you want to visit the Wenlock Edge Inn. Climb up between the limestone outcrops of Ippikins Rock to the top of the woods. Gates lead to the inn car park. If you aren't thirsty ignore the signed path & keep straight on.
d21
m5
Ippikins
Rock
Wenlock
Edge
Inn
A
bed of old railway (& Jack Mytton Way)
bed of old railway
B4371
B4371
Keep left here: the correct path isn't obvious
Easthope
B4371
2. Cross the B4371 & the motorcycle trap, then turn right through a gap: don't take the main path ahead unless you want to follow the old railway track (see below). Follow instead a clear but little-used track through the woods.
A
3. On meeting a minor road turn right & follow it uphill for 100m. Turn left on a signed path, cross an old sunken lane, then bend right & continue on the level. At the surfaced lane cross & continue on the track opposite. Eventually it descends to join the old railway. Leave it again a few metres further on for a good track forking right.
Wenlock Edge
The old railway track is shown on the maps & is better in wet weather. The recommended route is slower, muddier, quieter & prettier.
J.M. Way
Wilderhope
Manor YH
1. On reaching the road turn left (not straight on along the YH drive), then fork right on a track (J.M. Way sign). A gate leads into a field. Follow the edge of this field & the next. At the field corner turn right if you are heading for Wilderhope Manor youth hostel, otherwise go through the gate then turn left into the wood a few metres further on. Follow the track in the wood downhill then along until it meets a cart track winding down the hill. Turn left down this, & when it bends left turn right then bear left down a surfaced track to a road.
YH drive
d21
m3

Day 21 Map 5: Ippikins Rock to Blakeway Coppice

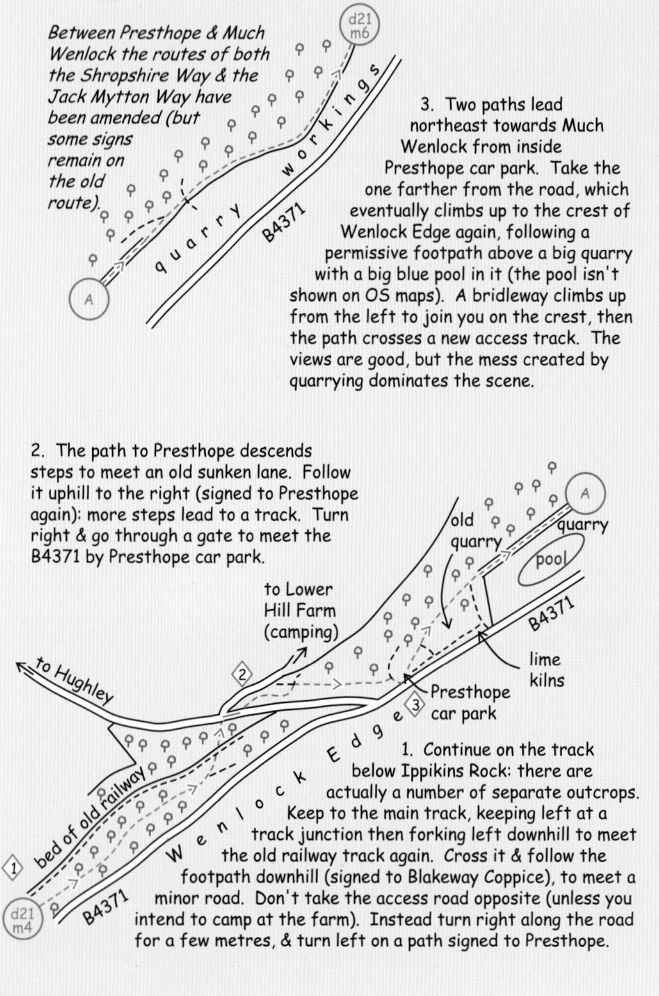

Between Presthope & Much Wenlock the routes of both the Shropshire Way & the Jack Mytton Way have been amended (but some signs remain on the old route).

3. Two paths lead northeast towards Much Wenlock from inside Presthope car park. Take the one farther from the road, which eventually climbs up to the crest of Wenlock Edge again, following a permissive footpath above a big quarry with a big blue pool in it (the pool isn't shown on OS maps). A bridleway climbs up from the left to join you on the crest, then the path crosses a new access track. The views are good, but the mess created by quarrying dominates the scene.

2. The path to Presthope descends steps to meet an old sunken lane. Follow it uphill to the right (signed to Presthope again): more steps lead to a track. Turn right & go through a gate to meet the B4371 by Presthope car park.

1. Continue on the track below Ippikins Rock: there are actually a number of separate outcrops. Keep to the main track, keeping left at a track junction then forking left downhill to meet the old railway track again. Cross it & follow the footpath downhill (signed to Blakeway Coppice), to meet a minor road. Don't take the access road opposite (unless you intend to camp at the farm). Instead turn right along the road for a few metres, & turn left on a path signed to Presthope.

Day 21 Map 6: Blakeway Coppice to Bradley Farm

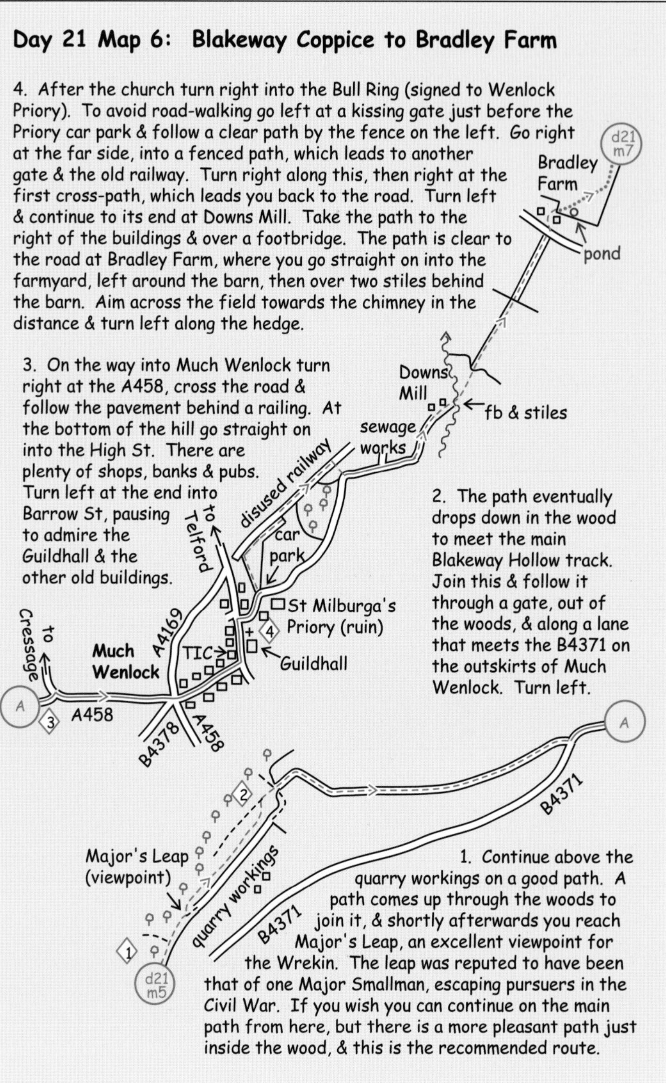

4. After the church turn right into the Bull Ring (signed to Wenlock Priory). To avoid road-walking go left at a kissing gate just before the Priory car park & follow a clear path by the fence on the left. Go right at the far side, into a fenced path, which leads to another gate & the old railway. Turn right along this, then right at the first cross-path, which leads you back to the road. Turn left & continue to its end at Downs Mill. Take the path to the right of the buildings & over a footbridge. The path is clear to the road at Bradley Farm, where you go straight on into the farmyard, left around the barn, then over two stiles behind the barn. Aim across the field towards the chimney in the distance & turn left along the hedge.

3. On the way into Much Wenlock turn right at the A458, cross the road & follow the pavement behind a railing. At the bottom of the hill go straight on into the High St. There are plenty of shops, banks & pubs. Turn left at the end into Barrow St, pausing to admire the Guildhall & the other old buildings.

2. The path eventually drops down in the wood to meet the main Blakeway Hollow track. Join this & follow it through a gate, out of the woods, & along a lane that meets the B4371 on the outskirts of Much Wenlock. Turn left.

1. Continue above the quarry workings on a good path. A path comes up through the woods to join it, & shortly afterwards you reach Major's Leap, an excellent viewpoint for the Wrekin. The leap was reputed to have been that of one Major Smallman, escaping pursuers in the Civil War. If you wish you can continue on the main path from here, but there is a more pleasant path just inside the wood, & this is the recommended route.

Day 21 Map 7: Bradley Farm to Ironbridge

There are a lot of paths on Benthall Edge. The route shown follows the Shropshire Way, so you can follow the waymarks.

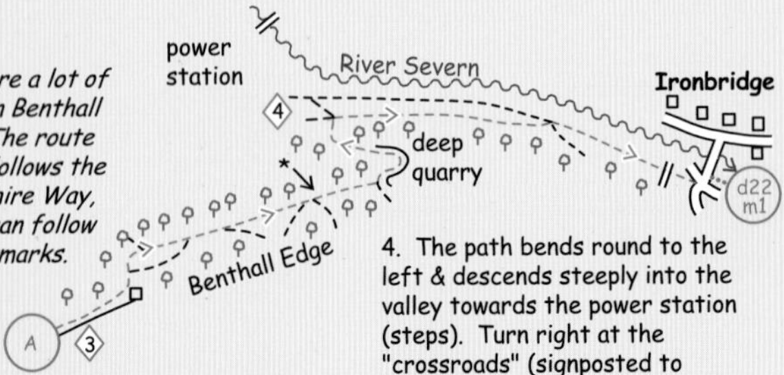

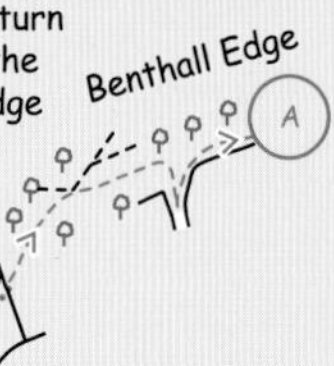

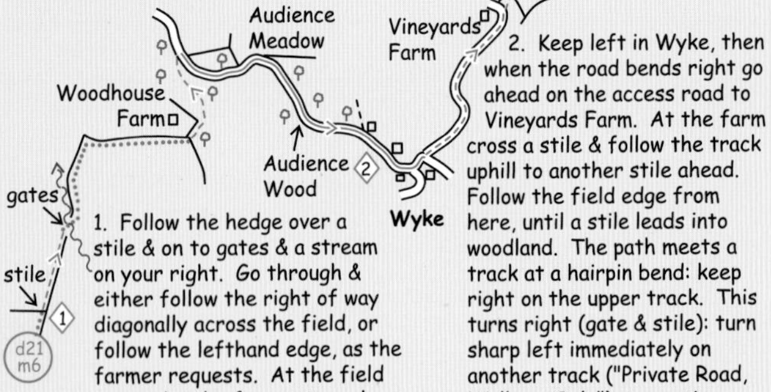

1. Follow the hedge over a stile & on to gates & a stream on your right. Go through & either follow the right of way diagonally across the field, or follow the lefthand edge, as the farmer requests. At the field corner by the farm enter a lane & follow the access road to turn right at the public road.

2. Keep left in Wyke, then when the road bends right go ahead on the access road to Vineyards Farm. At the farm cross a stile & follow the track uphill to another stile ahead. Follow the field edge from here, until a stile leads into woodland. The path meets a track at a hairpin bend: keep right on the upper track. This turns right (gate & stile): turn sharp left immediately on another track ("Private Road, Walkers Only"), to continue your original direction along the top of woods on Benthall Edge.

3. The general idea on Benthall Edge is to follow the top edge of the steep escarpment as far as the big quarry, then to zigzag down to the valley. At the cottage the path turns left. Ignore the smaller path on the right. At the first fork keep left. When the main path bends right (* on map), go straight on on a smaller path through a small dell (probably an old quarry working). At the fence turn left down steps then keep right. It soon becomes clear why the fence is there: a deep quarry comes into view.

4. The path bends round to the left & descends steeply into the valley towards the power station (steps). Turn right at the "crossroads" (signposted to Ironbridge). This path runs parallel to a disused railway & eventually descends to meet it. Join the railway & follow it to meet a road. To continue the route go straight on across the car park, or turn left across the old Iron Bridge to visit the town of Ironbridge.

Day 22 Map 1: Ironbridge to Brickkiln Coppice

3. Cross the river, then turn right along the canal to a footbridge over it: cross this & climb to the road. Ironbridge (Coalport) youth hostel is a short distance along the road to the right. To continue the walk turn left along the road, then turn right up a zigzag path just before the Shakespeare Inn, signed "Silkin Way". At a T-junction turn left (signed "Blists Hill"), then right up steps just before the bridge under the Hay Inclined Plane (signed "Sutton Hill"). Climb steeply alongside the railway incline until a stile on the right gives access to a field (signed "Upper Haywood"). Cut diagonally up the field (marker posts but no visible path) to a stile into the wood. Turn right & follow the path along the edge of the wood. When it forks in front of a fallen tree keep right. The path soon rises through the wood to meet a better track: join this. Keep straight on at a path junction (signed "S. Maddock") to emerge from the woods onto a golf course. Turn right (no path) & follow the edge of the golf course & Monarch's Way signs to a road: turn left.

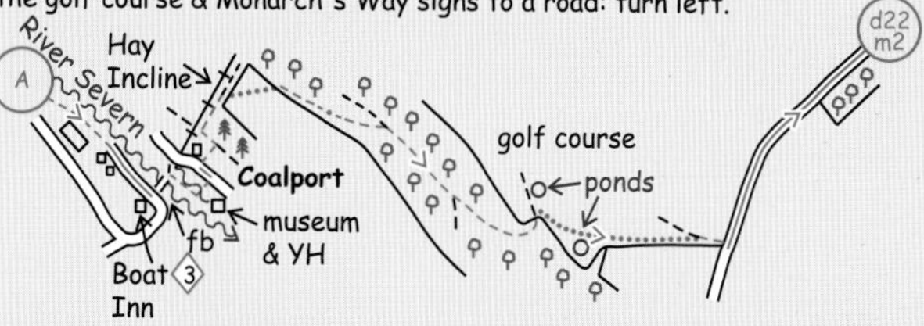

2. Follow the trackbed under two bridges to the restored level crossing gates at the road at Jackfield. From here the line of the railway has been taken into local gardens, so bear right (not sharp right) along the road, keeping straight on along Church Rd when the main road bends right. Just after the entrance to the Tile Museum fork left (still Church Rd), past the church to the end of the road then down a path to the riverbank. The path then climbs away from the river through a thicket. On reaching an access track go left along it: this leads to what used to be the Half Moon Inn: leave the track here for a riverbank footpath (fp sign) which leads into another thicket. The path emerges onto a grassy area behind an old mill: keep straight on to the end of Ferry Rd & follow this to the Boat Inn & a footbridge over the river.

1. To continue the walk, don't cross the Iron Bridge: go straight on into a car park across the road & find the continuation of the old railway track at the far left end of the car park. Cycle path & Severn Valley Way signs show the way.

Day 22 Map 2: Brickkiln Coppice to Evelith

3. From the tree bear slightly left to an electricity pole & beyond to the field edge. Turn right, cross a stile into a lane, & when the lane joins an untarred access road turn sharp left & follow it to Kemberton Mill. Follow the road round to the left (garages on the left), then cross two footbridges, the first of which incorporates a sluice. Turn left at a path junction to follow the stream up the pretty wooded valley: easily the best part of the day. Turn right at the road, but not before noticing the cave carved into the sandstone by the house straight ahead across the road.

If you want to find a bed in Shifnal, paths lead there heading north from Evelith Mill. (arrow on map)

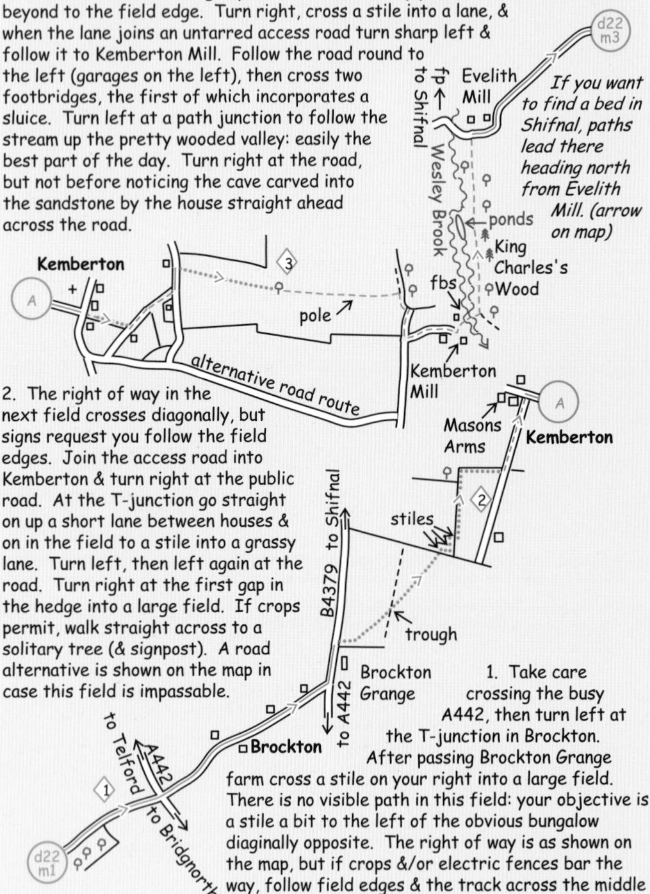

2. The right of way in the next field crosses diagonally, but signs request you follow the field edges. Join the access road into Kemberton & turn right at the public road. At the T-junction go straight on up a short lane between houses & on in the field to a stile into a grassy lane. Turn left, then left again at the road. Turn right at the first gap in the hedge into a large field. If crops permit, walk straight across to a solitary tree (& signpost). A road alternative is shown on the map in case this field is impassable.

1. Take care crossing the busy A442, then turn left at the T-junction in Brockton. After passing Brockton Grange farm cross a stile on your right into a large field. There is no visible path in this field: your objective is a stile a bit to the left of the obvious bungalow diaginally opposite. The right of way is as shown on the map, but if crops &/or electric fences bar the way, follow field edges & the track across the middle of the field. In the next field turn right to the field corner. Ignore the stile here: turn left for a few metres to a second stile & cross here instead.

Day 22 Map 3: Evelith to Tong Norton

3. Follow the road under the M54 motorway & continue until the road starts to emerge from its cutting & nears the top of the hill. Turn left on a metalled access road, & at its end go downhill on a track. Turn right before the bridge & follow this track through fields.

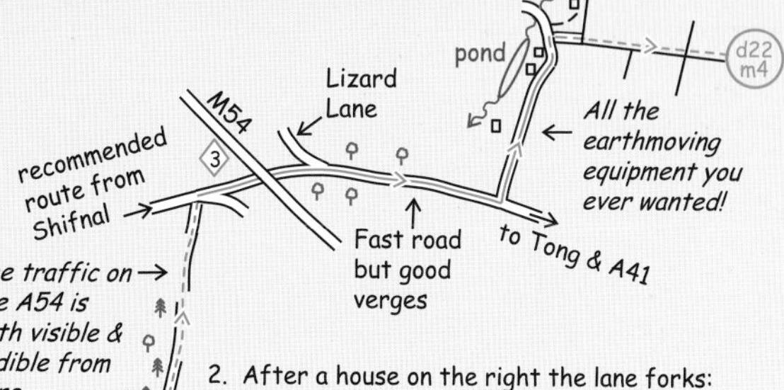

2. After a house on the right the lane forks: keep left. The right fork sports a gate with the slogan "Private Drive No Entry". Not to be outdone, the left fork passes another house then goes through a gate that carries the same welcoming message. It is however a public footpath, & a sign confirms this. Follow the track until it meets the busy road joining Shifnal to the A41, & turn right along it.

To rejoin the route from Shifnal you will need to follow the busy road heading east. There is no footpath link.

1. At the T-junction (Hinnington Rd) go straight ahead along a drive. Cross a stile into the grounds & follow the drive until it bends left to the house. Keep straight on here along a hedged path. When this meets the access road to Twyford Cottage turn left & follow it to the A464. Cross & take the road opposite, which turns into an untarred lane & crosses the Wolverhampton to Shrewsbury railway.

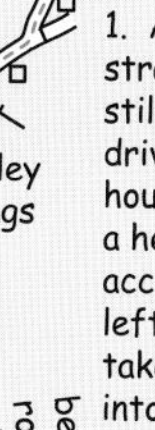

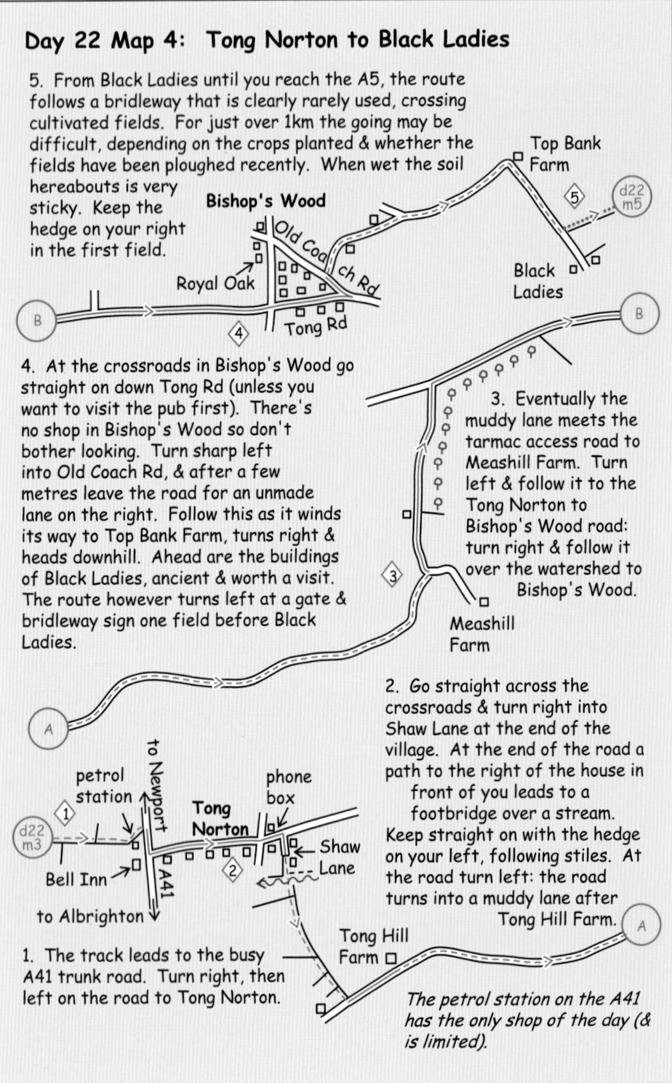
Day 22 Map 4: Tong Norton to Black Ladies
5. From Black Ladies until you reach the A5, the route follows a bridleway that is clearly rarely used, crossing cultivated fields. For just over 1km the going may be difficult, depending on the crops planted & whether the fields have been ploughed recently. When wet the soil hereabouts is very sticky. Keep the hedge on your right in the first field.
Top Bank Farm
Bishop's Wood
Old Coach Rd
Royal Oak
Black Ladies
Tong Rd
d22 m5
4. At the crossroads in Bishop's Wood go straight on down Tong Rd (unless you want to visit the pub first). There's no shop in Bishop's Wood so don't bother looking. Turn sharp left into Old Coach Rd, & after a few metres leave the road for an unmade lane on the right. Follow this as it winds its way to Top Bank Farm, turns right & heads downhill. Ahead are the buildings of Black Ladies, ancient & worth a visit. The route however turns left at a gate & bridleway sign one field before Black Ladies.
3. Eventually the muddy lane meets the tarmac access road to Meashill Farm. Turn left & follow it to the Tong Norton to Bishop's Wood road: turn right & follow it over the watershed to Bishop's Wood.
Meashill Farm
2. Go straight across the crossroads & turn right into Shaw Lane at the end of the village. At the end of the road a path to the right of the house in front of you leads to a footbridge over a stream. Keep straight on with the hedge on your left, following stiles. At the road turn left: the road turns into a muddy lane after Tong Hill Farm.
petrol station
to Newport
phone box
Tong Norton
d22 m3
Shaw Lane
Bell Inn
A41
to Albrighton
Tong Hill Farm
1. The track leads to the busy A41 trunk road. Turn right, then left on the road to Tong Norton.
The petrol station on the A41 has the only shop of the day (& is limited).

Day 22 Map 5: Black Ladies to Lapley

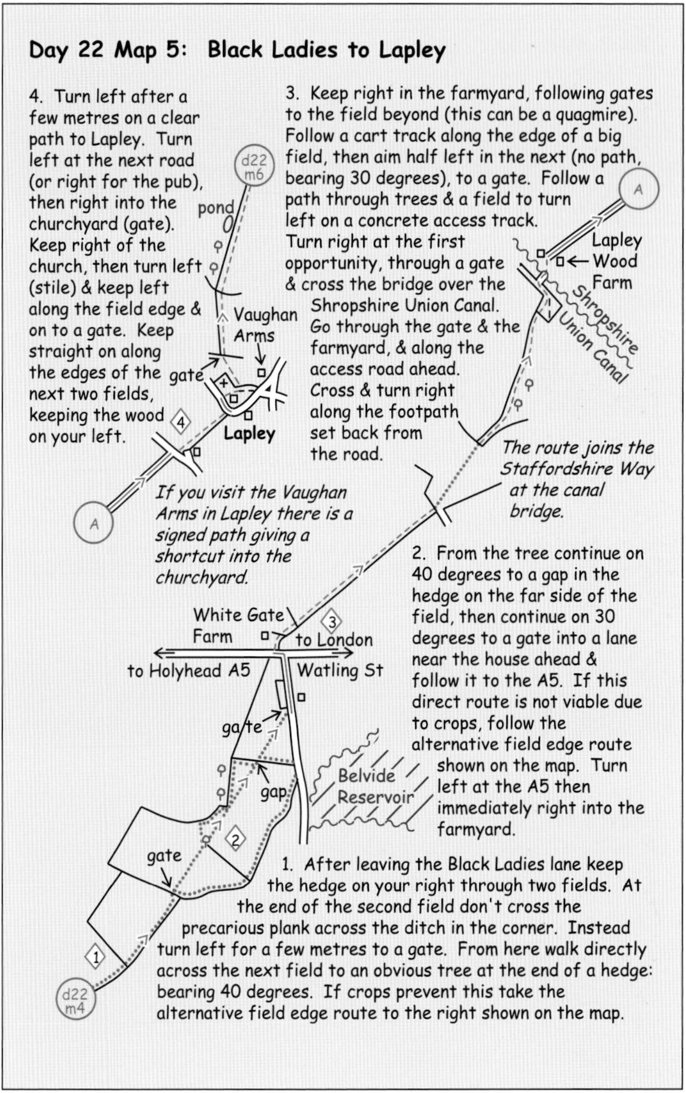

4. Turn left after a few metres on a clear path to Lapley. Turn left at the next road (or right for the pub), then right into the churchyard (gate). Keep right of the church, then turn left (stile) & keep left along the field edge & on to a gate. Keep straight on along the edges of the next two fields, keeping the wood on your left.

3. Keep right in the farmyard, following gates to the field beyond (this can be a quagmire). Follow a cart track along the edge of a big field, then aim half left in the next (no path, bearing 30 degrees), to a gate. Follow a path through trees & a field to turn left on a concrete access track. Turn right at the first opportunity, through a gate & cross the bridge over the Shropshire Union Canal. Go through the gate & the farmyard, & along the access road ahead. Cross & turn right along the footpath set back from the road.

d22 m6

pond

Vaughan Arms

gate

Lapley

A

Lapley Wood Farm

Shropshire Union Canal

The route joins the Staffordshire Way at the canal bridge.

If you visit the Vaughan Arms in Lapley there is a signed path giving a shortcut into the churchyard.

White Gate Farm

to London

to Holyhead A5

Watling St

gate

gap

Belvide Reservoir

gate

d22 m4

2. From the tree continue on 40 degrees to a gap in the hedge on the far side of the field, then continue on 30 degrees to a gate into a lane near the house ahead & follow it to the A5. If this direct route is not viable due to crops, follow the alternative field edge route shown on the map. Turn left at the A5 then immediately right into the farmyard.

1. After leaving the Black Ladies lane keep the hedge on your right through two fields. At the end of the second field don't cross the precarious plank across the ditch in the corner. Instead turn left for a few metres to a gate. From here walk directly across the next field to an obvious tree at the end of a hedge: bearing 40 degrees. If crops prevent this take the alternative field edge route to the right shown on the map.

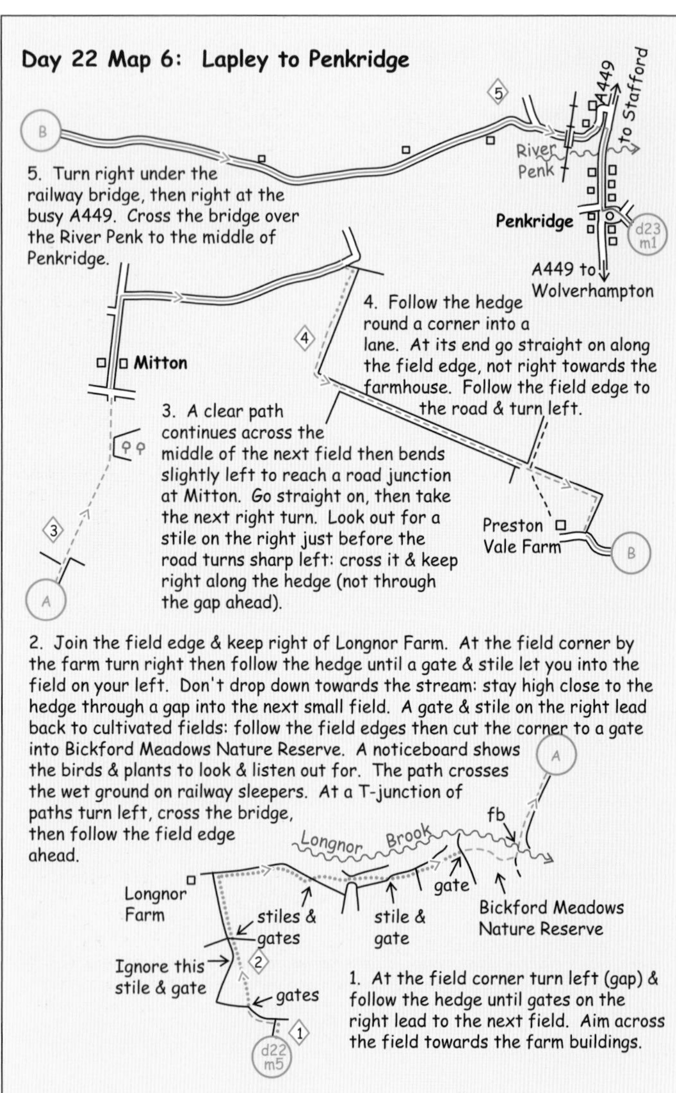
Day 22 Map 6: Lapley to Penkridge
5. Turn right under the railway bridge, then right at the busy A449. Cross the bridge over the River Penk to the middle of Penkridge.
A449
to Stafford
River Penk
Penkridge
d23 m1
A449 to Wolverhampton
4. Follow the hedge round a corner into a lane. At its end go straight on along the field edge, not right towards the farmhouse. Follow the field edge to the road & turn left.
Mitton
3. A clear path continues across the middle of the next field then bends slightly left to reach a road junction at Mitton. Go straight on, then take the next right turn. Look out for a stile on the right just before the road turns sharp left: cross it & keep right along the hedge (not through the gap ahead).
Preston Vale Farm
2. Join the field edge & keep right of Longnor Farm. At the field corner by the farm turn right then follow the hedge until a gate & stile let you into the field on your left. Don't drop down towards the stream: stay high close to the hedge through a gap into the next small field. A gate & stile on the right lead back to cultivated fields: follow the field edges then cut the corner to a gate into Bickford Meadows Nature Reserve. A noticeboard shows the birds & plants to look & listen out for. The path crosses the wet ground on railway sleepers. At a T-junction of paths turn left, cross the bridge, then follow the field edge ahead.
fb
Longnor Brook
Longnor Farm
stiles & gates
stile & gate
gate
Bickford Meadows Nature Reserve
Ignore this stile & gate
gates
d22 m5
1. At the field corner turn left (gap) & follow the hedge until gates on the right lead to the next field. Aim across the field towards the farm buildings.

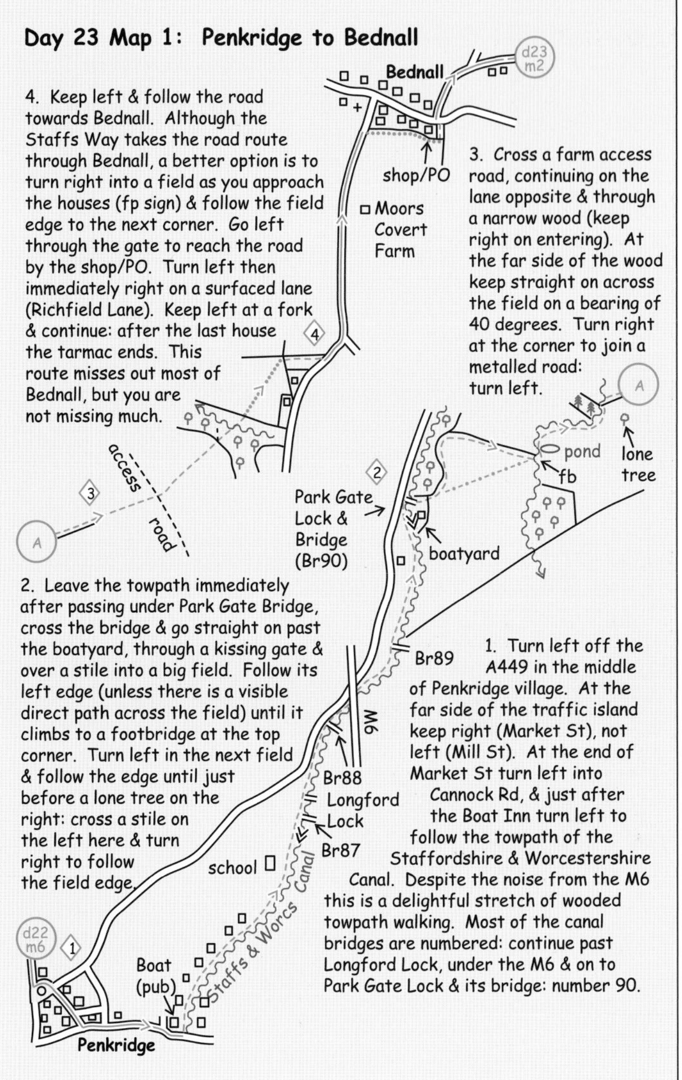

Day 23 Map 1: Penkridge to Bednall
Bednall
d23 m2
4. Keep left & follow the road towards Bednall. Although the Staffs Way takes the road route through Bednall, a better option is to turn right into a field as you approach the houses (fp sign) & follow the field edge to the next corner. Go left through the gate to reach the road by the shop/PO. Turn left then immediately right on a surfaced lane (Richfield Lane). Keep left at a fork & continue: after the last house the tarmac ends. This route misses out most of Bednall, but you are not missing much.
shop/PO
Moors Covert Farm
3. Cross a farm access road, continuing on the lane opposite & through a narrow wood (keep right on entering). At the far side of the wood keep straight on across the field on a bearing of 40 degrees. Turn right at the corner to join a metalled road: turn left.
4
A
pond
lone tree
fb
access road
3
A
2
Park Gate Lock & Bridge (Br90)
boatyard
2. Leave the towpath immediately after passing under Park Gate Bridge, cross the bridge & go straight on past the boatyard, through a kissing gate & over a stile into a big field. Follow its left edge (unless there is a visible direct path across the field) until it climbs to a footbridge at the top corner. Turn left in the next field & follow the edge until just before a lone tree on the right: cross a stile on the left here & turn right to follow the field edge.
Br89
1. Turn left off the A449 in the middle of Penkridge village. At the far side of the traffic island keep right (Market St), not left (Mill St). At the end of Market St turn left into Cannock Rd, & just after the Boat Inn turn left to follow the towpath of the Staffordshire & Worcestershire Canal. Despite the noise from the M6 this is a delightful stretch of wooded towpath walking. Most of the canal bridges are numbered: continue past Longford Lock, under the M6 & on to Park Gate Lock & its bridge: number 90.
M6
Br88
Longford Lock
Br87
school
Staffs & Worcs Canal
d22 m6
1
Boat (pub)
Penkridge

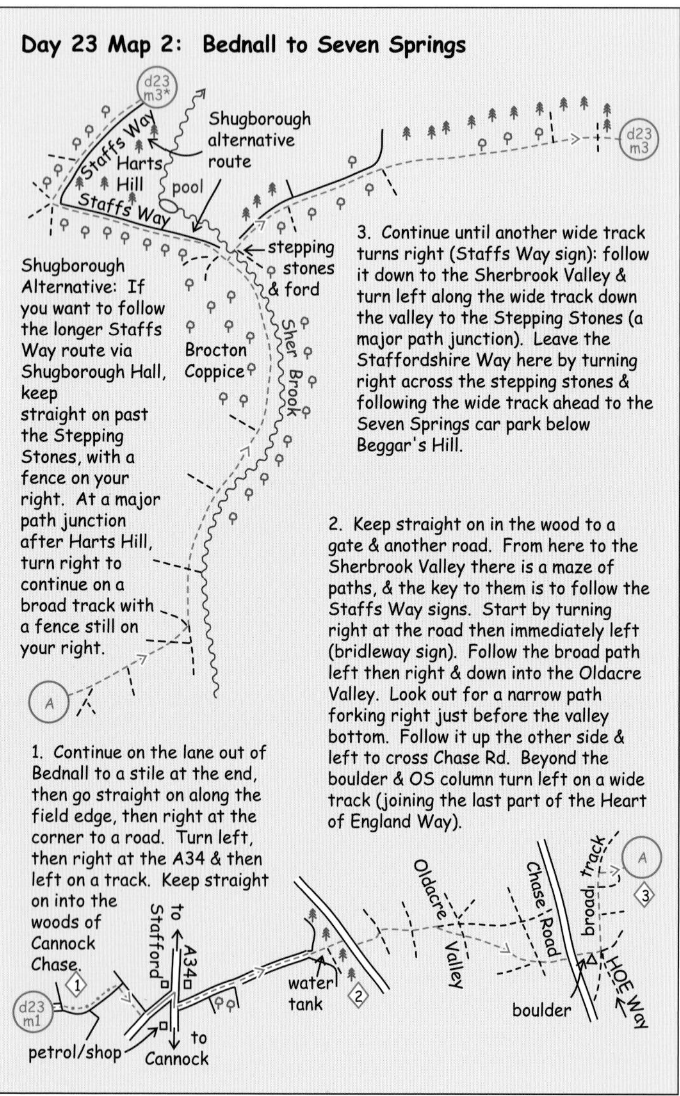
Day 23 Map 2: Bednall to Seven Springs
d23 m3*
Shugborough alternative route
Staffs Way
Harts Hill
pool
Staffs Way
stepping stones & ford
Sher Brook
Brocton Coppice
d23 m3
3. Continue until another wide track turns right (Staffs Way sign): follow it down to the Sherbrook Valley & turn left along the wide track down the valley to the Stepping Stones (a major path junction). Leave the Staffordshire Way here by turning right across the stepping stones & following the wide track ahead to the Seven Springs car park below Beggar's Hill.
Shugborough Alternative: If you want to follow the longer Staffs Way route via Shugborough Hall, keep straight on past the Stepping Stones, with a fence on your right. At a major path junction after Harts Hill, turn right to continue on a broad track with a fence still on your right.
A
2. Keep straight on in the wood to a gate & another road. From here to the Sherbrook Valley there is a maze of paths, & the key to them is to follow the Staffs Way signs. Start by turning right at the road then immediately left (bridleway sign). Follow the broad path left then right & down into the Oldacre Valley. Look out for a narrow path forking right just before the valley bottom. Follow it up the other side & left to cross Chase Rd. Beyond the boulder & OS column turn left on a wide track (joining the last part of the Heart of England Way).
1. Continue on the lane out of Bednall to a stile at the end, then go straight on along the field edge, then right at the corner to a road. Turn left, then right at the A34 & then left on a track. Keep straight on into the woods of Cannock Chase.
1
d23 m1
petrol/shop
to Stafford
A34
to Cannock
water tank
2
Oldacre Valley
Chase Road
broad track
A
3
boulder
HOE Way

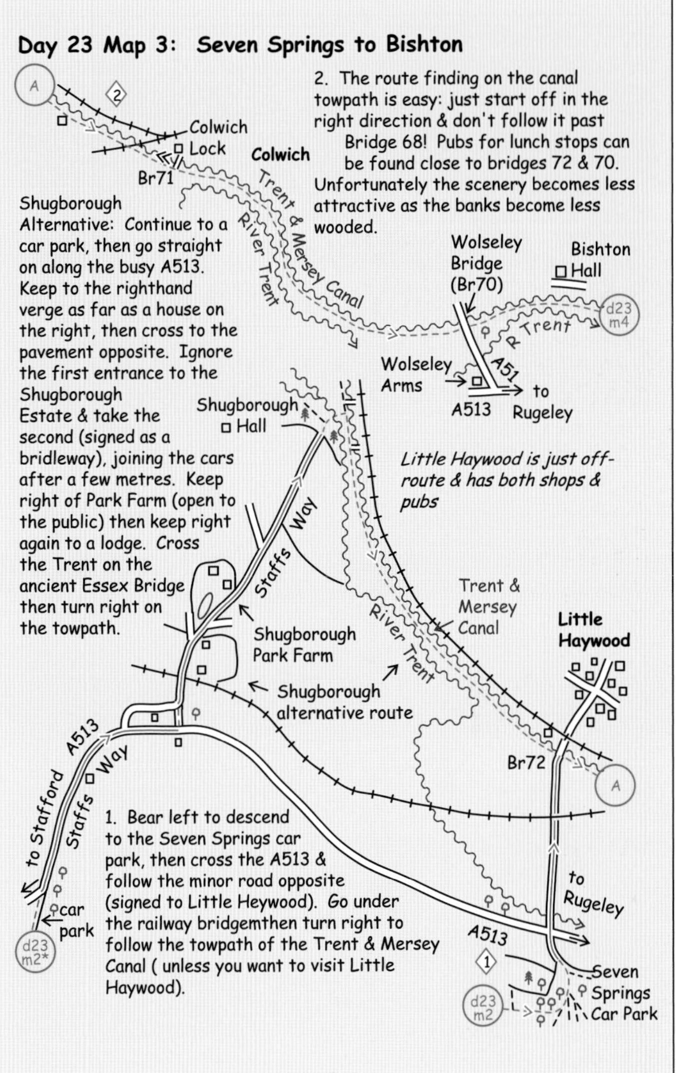
Day 23 Map 3: Seven Springs to Bishton
2. The route finding on the canal towpath is easy: just start off in the right direction & don't follow it past Bridge 68! Pubs for lunch stops can be found close to bridges 72 & 70. Unfortunately the scenery becomes less attractive as the banks become less wooded.
Shugborough Alternative: Continue to a car park, then go straight on along the busy A513. Keep to the righthand verge as far as a house on the right, then cross to the pavement opposite. Ignore the first entrance to the Shugborough Estate & take the second (signed as a bridleway), joining the cars after a few metres. Keep right of Park Farm (open to the public) then keep right again to a lodge. Cross the Trent on the ancient Essex Bridge then turn right on the towpath.
1. Bear left to descend to the Seven Springs car park, then cross the A513 & follow the minor road opposite (signed to Little Heywood). Go under the railway bridgemthen turn right to follow the towpath of the Trent & Mersey Canal (unless you want to visit Little Haywood).
Little Haywood is just off-route & has both shops & pubs
A
2
Colwich
Lock
Colwich
Br71
Trent & Mersey Canal
River Trent
Wolseley
Bridge
(Br70)
Bishton
Hall
d23
m4
R Trent
Wolseley
Arms
A51
to
Rugeley
A513
Shugborough
Hall
Staffs Way
Shugborough
Park Farm
Shugborough
alternative route
River Trent
Trent &
Mersey
Canal
Little
Haywood
Br72
A
A513
to Stafford
Staffs Way
car
park
d23
m2*
to
Rugeley
A513
1
Seven
Springs
Car Park
d23
m2

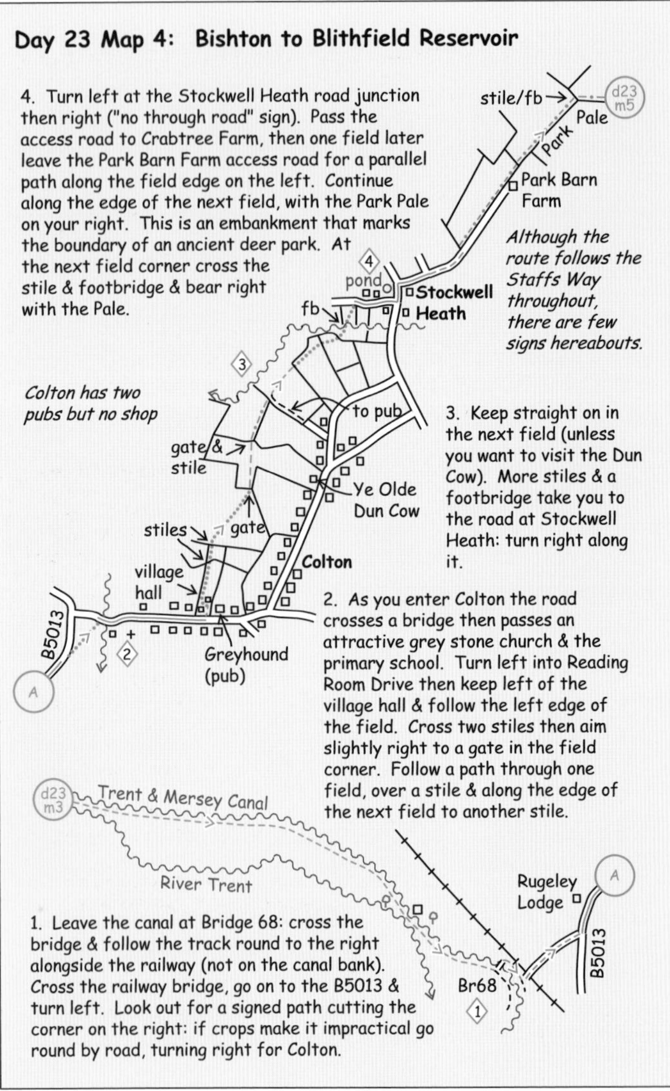
Day 23 Map 4: Bishton to Blithfield Reservoir
4. Turn left at the Stockwell Heath road junction then right ("no through road" sign). Pass the access road to Crabtree Farm, then one field later leave the Park Barn Farm access road for a parallel path along the field edge on the left. Continue along the edge of the next field, with the Park Pale on your right. This is an embankment that marks the boundary of an ancient deer park. At the next field corner cross the stile & footbridge & bear right with the Pale.
stile/fb
d23 m5
Pale
Park
Park Barn Farm
Although the route follows the Staffs Way throughout, there are few signs hereabouts.
4
pond
fb
Stockwell Heath
3
Colton has two pubs but no shop
to pub
3. Keep straight on in the next field (unless you want to visit the Dun Cow). More stiles & a footbridge take you to the road at Stockwell Heath: turn right along it.
gate & stile
Ye Olde Dun Cow
stiles
gate
Colton
village hall
B5013
2
Greyhound (pub)
A
2. As you enter Colton the road crosses a bridge then passes an attractive grey stone church & the primary school. Turn left into Reading Room Drive then keep left of the village hall & follow the left edge of the field. Cross two stiles then aim slightly right to a gate in the field corner. Follow a path through one field, over a stile & along the edge of the next field to another stile.
d23 m3
Trent & Mersey Canal
River Trent
Rugeley Lodge
A
B5013
1. Leave the canal at Bridge 68: cross the bridge & follow the track round to the right alongside the railway (not on the canal bank). Cross the railway bridge, go on to the B5013 & turn left. Look out for a signed path cutting the corner on the right: if crops make it impractical go round by road, turning right for Colton.
Br68
1

Day 23 Map 5: Blithfield Reservoir to Abbots Bromley

3. Follow the cart track below the dam until it approaches a gate & joins the road across the dam, by a water company building. Don't go through the gate: past water board policy has ensured no rights of way go past their water or their buildings. Instead leave the track for a stile to the right, walk dutifully between two pitifully pointless pairs of posts, then left along the hedge to join the road. Turn right, then left at the first opportunity along a track. At the end turn right (stile) & follow a decrepit lane then a footpath straight on through fields to a road junction. Turn right, then at the first opportunity sharp left (stile & gate) & follow the right edge of the field to a gate into a lane. Continue past the sewage works & cross a stile on the left into a field when the lane bends right. Keep the stream on your left, & aim for a stile to the right of the church. Keep right in the churchyard & exit through the porch. Take the first left turn which brings you out in the centre of Abbots Bromley, opposite Schoolhouse Lane.

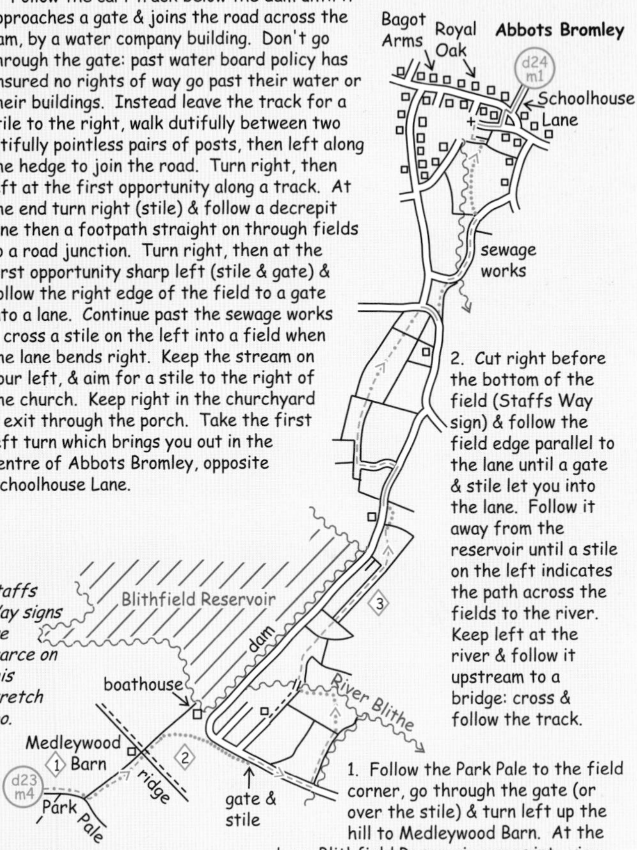

2. Cut right before the bottom of the field (Staffs Way sign) & follow the field edge parallel to the lane until a gate & stile let you into the lane. Follow it away from the reservoir until a stile on the left indicates the path across the fields to the river. Keep left at the river & follow it upstream to a bridge: cross & follow the track.

Staffs Way signs are scarce on this stretch too.

1. Follow the Park Pale to the field corner, go through the gate (or over the stile) & turn left up the hill to Medleywood Barn. At the barn Blithfield Reservoir comes into view, complete with sailing dinghies. Keep straight on down towards the dam & boathouse.

You could of course take a shortcut across the dam, but despite the volume of traffic it is probably not a right of way.

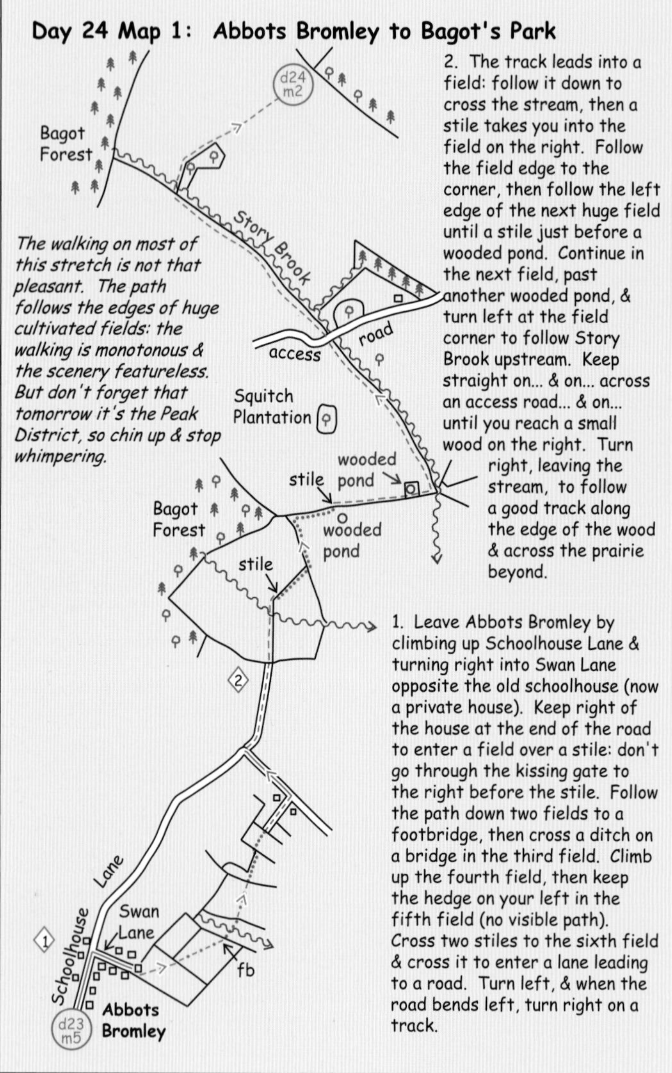

Day 24 Map 1: Abbots Bromley to Bagot's Park
d24
m2
Bagot
Forest
Story Brook
The walking on most of this stretch is not that pleasant. The path follows the edges of huge cultivated fields: the walking is monotonous & the scenery featureless. But don't forget that tomorrow it's the Peak District, so chin up & stop whimpering.
access
road
Squitch
Plantation
wooded
pond
stile
Bagot
Forest
wooded
pond
stile
2. The track leads into a field: follow it down to cross the stream, then a stile takes you into the field on the right. Follow the field edge to the corner, then follow the left edge of the next huge field until a stile just before a wooded pond. Continue in the next field, past another wooded pond, & turn left at the field corner to follow Story Brook upstream. Keep straight on... & on... across an access road... & on... until you reach a small wood on the right. Turn right, leaving the stream, to follow a good track along the edge of the wood & across the prairie beyond.
2
1. Leave Abbots Bromley by climbing up Schoolhouse Lane & turning right into Swan Lane opposite the old schoolhouse (now a private house). Keep right of the house at the end of the road to enter a field over a stile: don't go through the kissing gate to the right before the stile. Follow the path down two fields to a footbridge, then cross a ditch on a bridge in the third field. Climb up the fourth field, then keep the hedge on your left in the fifth field (no visible path). Cross two stiles to the sixth field & cross it to enter a lane leading to a road. Turn left, & when the road bends left, turn right on a track.
Schoolhouse
Lane
Swan
Lane
1
fb
d23
m5
Abbots
Bromley

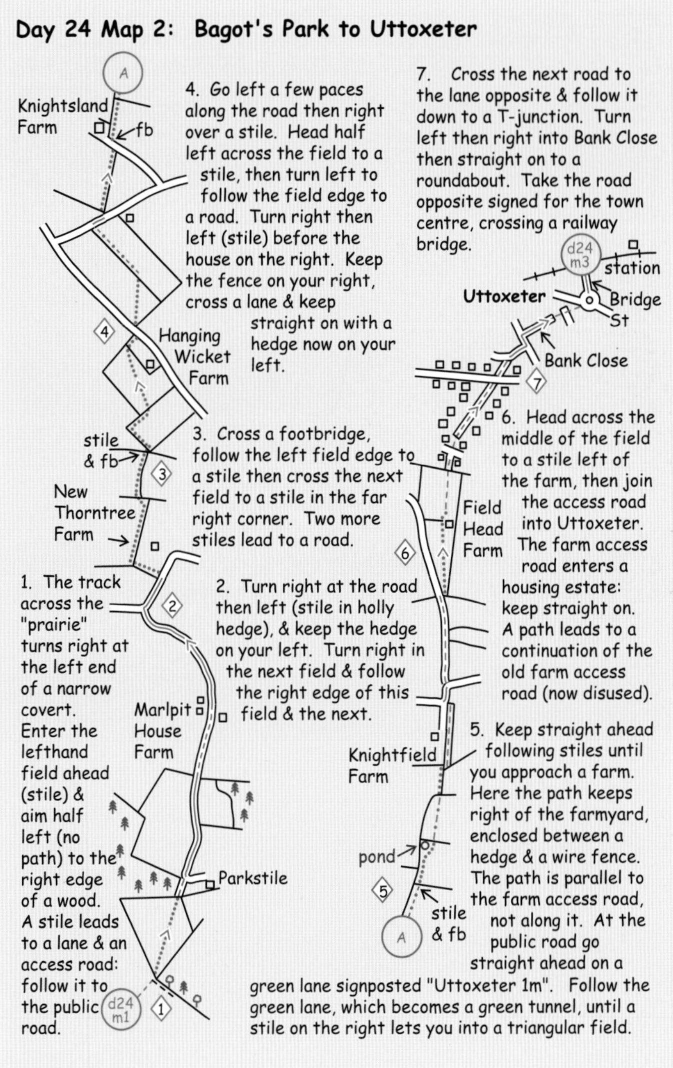
Day 24 Map 2: Bagot's Park to Uttoxeter
A
Knightsland Farm
fb
4. Go left a few paces along the road then right over a stile. Head half left across the field to a stile, then turn left to follow the field edge to a road. Turn right then left (stile) before the house on the right. Keep the fence on your right, cross a lane & keep straight on with a hedge now on your left.
7. Cross the next road to the lane opposite & follow it down to a T-junction. Turn left then right into Bank Close then straight on to a roundabout. Take the road opposite signed for the town centre, crossing a railway bridge.
d24 m3
station
Uttoxeter
Bridge St
Bank Close
4
Hanging Wicket Farm
7
stile & fb
3
3. Cross a footbridge, follow the left field edge to a stile then cross the next field to a stile in the far right corner. Two more stiles lead to a road.
6. Head across the middle of the field to a stile left of the farm, then join the access road into Uttoxeter. The farm access road enters a housing estate: keep straight on. A path leads to a continuation of the old farm access road (now disused).
New Thorntree Farm
Field Head Farm
6
1. The track across the "prairie" turns right at the left end of a narrow covert. Enter the lefthand field ahead (stile) & aim half left (no path) to the right edge of a wood. A stile leads to a lane & an access road: follow it to the public road.
2
2. Turn right at the road then left (stile in holly hedge), & keep the hedge on your left. Turn right in the next field & follow the right edge of this field & the next.
Marlpit House Farm
Knightfield Farm
5. Keep straight ahead following stiles until you approach a farm. Here the path keeps right of the farmyard, enclosed between a hedge & a wire fence. The path is parallel to the farm access road, not along it. At the public road go straight ahead on a green lane signposted "Uttoxeter 1m". Follow the green lane, which becomes a green tunnel, until a stile on the right lets you into a triangular field.
pond
Parkstile
5
stile & fb
A
d24 m1
1

Day 24 Map 3: Uttoxeter to Eaton Hall Farm

4. Cross the meadow to go through two gates & join a cart track. Follow it through a gate into a field above the river, and keep straight on to climb the rough ground ahead on a small path. At the top keep to the left edge of the hayfield & into a lane at its end. Turn left just before the corner of the next field (footpath sign), then cross into the field on the right & follow its left edge along the top of the escarpment. Turn left on the track to Doveridge Clay Sports Club & follow it down the slope.

3. Cross the rivers Tean & Dove on the cycle path, then leave it immediately to descend right to a pedestrian underpass by the Dove. In the wood the other side of the A50, turn right at a path junction (away from the A50), to reach a stile into a meadow.

2. At the end of the track go left (stile), not through the gate ahead. Keep left to the field corner (stile), then ignore the second stile on the left. Head across the field past a pylon to a stile just left of the end of the hedge on the right. Cross an access road, & another stile leads to the cycle path by the very busy A50: turn right.

1. Turn right at the roundabout after the railway bridge & follow Brookside Rd to its end. Green gates, a "Welcome to Uttoxeter Racecourse" sign & a footpath sign show the way on a track across grass - car parking for the racecourse. Bend left round a large industrial building then straight on to a stile into pasture. Cut across to a gate just left of the house. Turn right on the access road & the short track beyond.

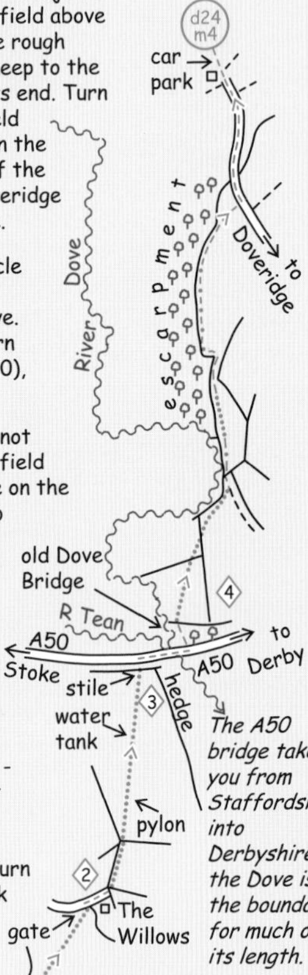

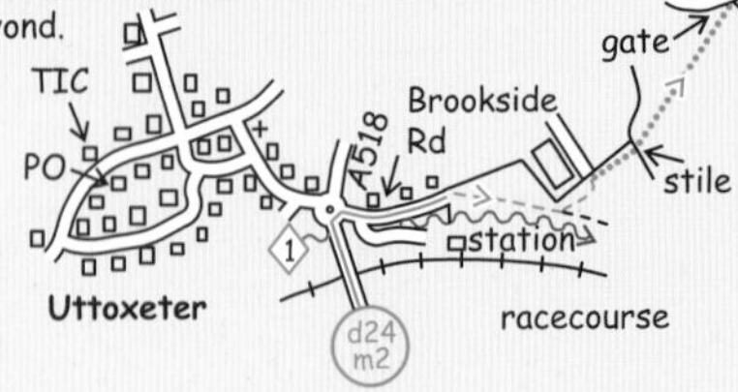

The A50 bridge takes you from Staffordshire into Derbyshire: the Dove is the boundary for much of its length.

If you want to visit Uttoxeter centre, turn left at the roundabout after the railway bridge, then second left brings you to the Market Place.

Day 24 Map 4: Eaton Hall Farm to Rocester

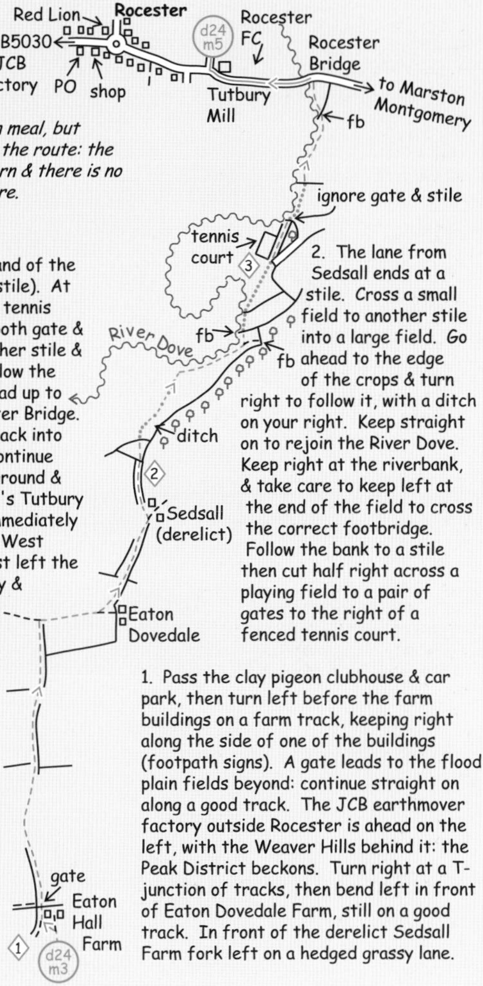

Red Lion
Rocester
Rocester FC
Rocester Bridge
to B5030 & JCB factory
PO
shop
d24 m5
Tutbury Mill
to Marston Montgomery
fb

Visit the centre of Rocester if you need a pub, a shop or an Indian meal, but otherwise stick to the route: the buildings are modern & there is no pretty village centre.

ignore gate & stile
tennis court
River Dove
fb
fb
ditch
Sedsall (derelict)
Eaton Dovedale
gate
Eaton Hall Farm
d24 m3

3. Take the lefthand of the two gates (or the stile). At the far end of the tennis court go right of both gate & stile to reach another stile & the riverbank. Follow the river until steps lead up to the road at Rocester Bridge. Cross the bridge back into Staffordshire & continue past the football ground & Richard Arkwright's Tutbury Mill. Turn right immediately after the mill into West View. You have just left the Staffordshire Way & started along the Limestone Way (although there are no signs to say so).

2. The lane from Sedsall ends at a stile. Cross a small field to another stile into a large field. Go ahead to the edge of the crops & turn right to follow it, with a ditch on your right. Keep straight on to rejoin the River Dove. Keep right at the riverbank, & take care to keep left at the end of the field to cross the correct footbridge. Follow the bank to a stile then cut half right across a playing field to a pair of gates to the right of a fenced tennis court.

1. Pass the clay pigeon clubhouse & car park, then turn left before the farm buildings on a farm track, keeping right along the side of one of the buildings (footpath signs). A gate leads to the flood plain fields beyond: continue straight on along a good track. The JCB earthmover factory outside Rocester is ahead on the left, with the Weaver Hills behind it: the Peak District beckons. Turn right at a T-junction of tracks, then bend left in front of Eaton Dovedale Farm, still on a good track. In front of the derelict Sedsall Farm fork left on a hedged grassy lane.

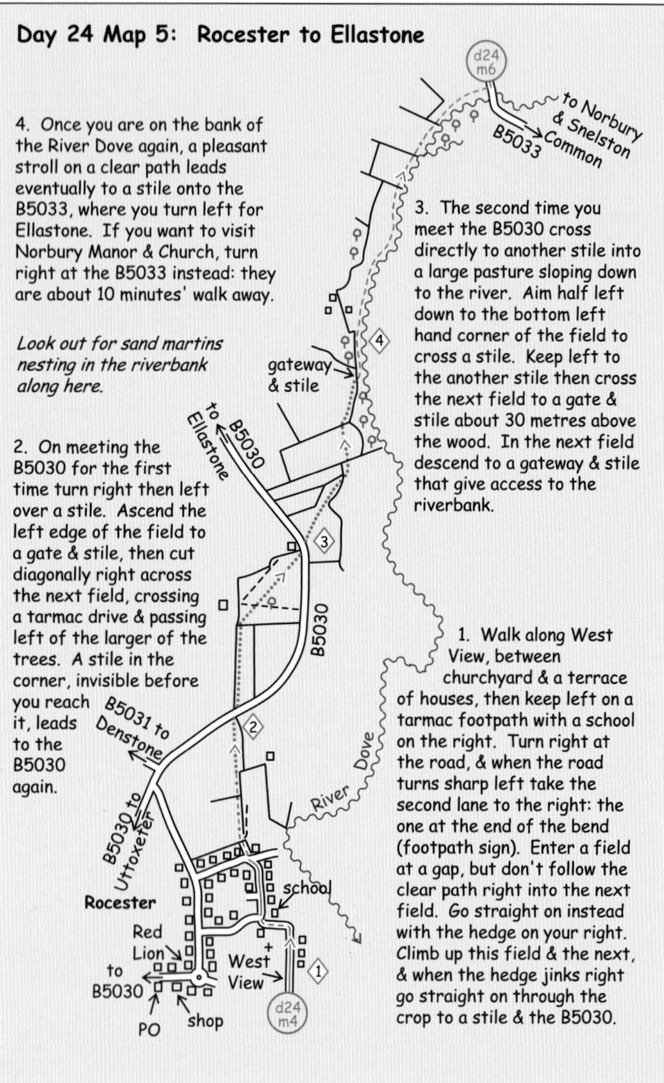
Day 24 Map 5: Rocester to Ellastone
d24 m6
to Norbury & Snelston Common
B5033
4. Once you are on the bank of the River Dove again, a pleasant stroll on a clear path leads eventually to a stile onto the B5033, where you turn left for Ellastone. If you want to visit Norbury Manor & Church, turn right at the B5033 instead: they are about 10 minutes' walk away.
Look out for sand martins nesting in the riverbank along here.
3. The second time you meet the B5030 cross directly to another stile into a large pasture sloping down to the river. Aim half left down to the bottom left hand corner of the field to cross a stile. Keep left to the another stile then cross the next field to a gate & stile about 30 metres above the wood. In the next field descend to a gateway & stile that give access to the riverbank.
4
gateway & stile
to Ellastone
B5030
2. On meeting the B5030 for the first time turn right then left over a stile. Ascend the left edge of the field to a gate & stile, then cut diagonally right across the next field, crossing a tarmac drive & passing left of the larger of the trees. A stile in the corner, invisible before you reach it, leads to the B5030 again.
3
B5030
1. Walk along West View, between churchyard & a terrace of houses, then keep left on a tarmac footpath with a school on the right. Turn right at the road, & when the road turns sharp left take the second lane to the right: the one at the end of the bend (footpath sign). Enter a field at a gap, but don't follow the clear path right into the next field. Go straight on instead with the hedge on your right. Climb up this field & the next, & when the hedge jinks right go straight on through the crop to a stile & the B5030.
B5031 to Denstone
2
River Dove
B5030 to Uttoxeter
school
Rocester
Red Lion
to B5030
West View
1
PO
shop
d24 m4

Day 24 Map 6: Ellastone to Motcarn Sprink

3. The access road down from the Hutts Farm doubles back on itself. There is a stile on this bend, indicating the line of the Limestone Way, which follows a ridge through fields for the next few kilometres. The End to End Trail follows the wooded valley instead: continue along the road for a short distance to a second stile. Descend the steep pathless slope to a footbridge & climb a clear path opposite to join a good track. Turn right & follow it up the valley & into the woods.

Motcarn Sprink, whatever it may be, is up in the woods to the left just before the end of this map page (according to the OS).

Ellastone has a PO/shop & a pub. The latter can be reached either by road or by using a right of way to cut the corner: turn right off the B5033 into the first garden after Mill Lane to locate its start.

2. Turn right along the B5032 until it starts to bend slightly right, then go left at a gate (footpath sign) into a field. Follow the left edge of the field, then cut across the next field to join a path coming up from the stream. Follow this along the top of the wood until it enters the wood at a stile. Don't cross this stile: instead climb up right to another stile, & aim half right in the next field past the corner of a wood & left of a barn. Bear right to a gate & stile, then keep left of the main farm buildings to join the access road down from the farm (The Hutts).

1. Follow the B5033 towards Ellastone, past the first isolated house on the right. Turn right between stone gateposts immediately before the next house on the right: this is a former entrance to the grounds of Calwich Abbey. Follow this track, possibly past a field of llamas, through a gate into unenclosed rough pasture, & on through a second gate to a junction of tracks, with a wooded pond to the left & a house to the right. Turn sharp left here on a fenced track that soon leads to another pasture. As the lodge & its enclosure grow nearer, look for a stile to the right: leave the track to cross this stile & cut the corner of the field beyond to another stile & the B5032.

Day 24 Map 7: Motcarn Sprink to Swinscoe

4. Join the road at Ellishill Farm, then go left through a small gate. Cross the field to a stile, turn half left to another, then half right to the next. From here aim between the barn & the house to join the access road at Leasow Farm.

5. Leave the Leasow Farm road almost immediately as it bends left, over a stile straight ahead. Cross the field to a stile visible in front of a group of houses at Swinscoe: keep left initially to avoid a marshy dip. An alley leads to a road: turn right to reach the A52 & then turn left.

3. Once you have found the path in the wood again it climbs gradually up from the stream to leave the wood at a gate & stile. Follow the top of the wood briefly, then slant up the steep field along the line of an old disused track, aiming right of Ellishill Farm, visible ahead. Join a track along the top of the field & follow it to the farm.

2. Turn right downhill on the minor road until it crosses the stream, then turn left (stile) to continue walking up by the stream. This section is less frequented & once back in the woods the path is rudimentary in places. It is close to the stream until it peters out at a bend in the stream, with bits of a wire fence ahead. At this point the path is actually up to your right: it left the "main" path obscurely a short distance behind you!

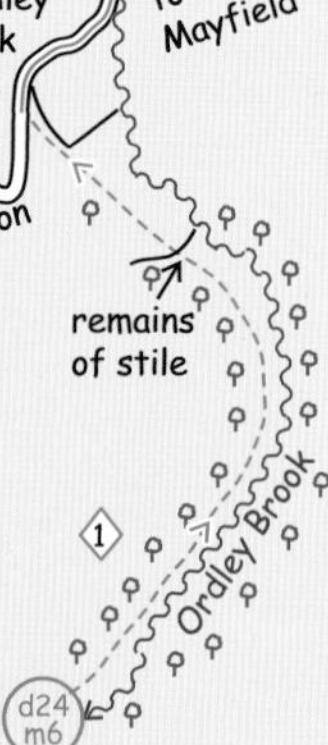

1. The path along Ordley Brook is mostly easy to follow, although there is one section that is very wet underfoot. Apart from this, the wood is a very pleasant place to walk, & far preferable to the Limestone Way route on the ridge to the right. Eventually a ruined stile marks the end of the wood & the path climbs slightly through wooded pasture with some recent plantings to meet a road.

Day 24 Map 8: Swinscoe to Thorpe

The map has been extended to show a connection to the Tissington Trail (an alternative route to Biggin) & the campsite at Highfields Farm.

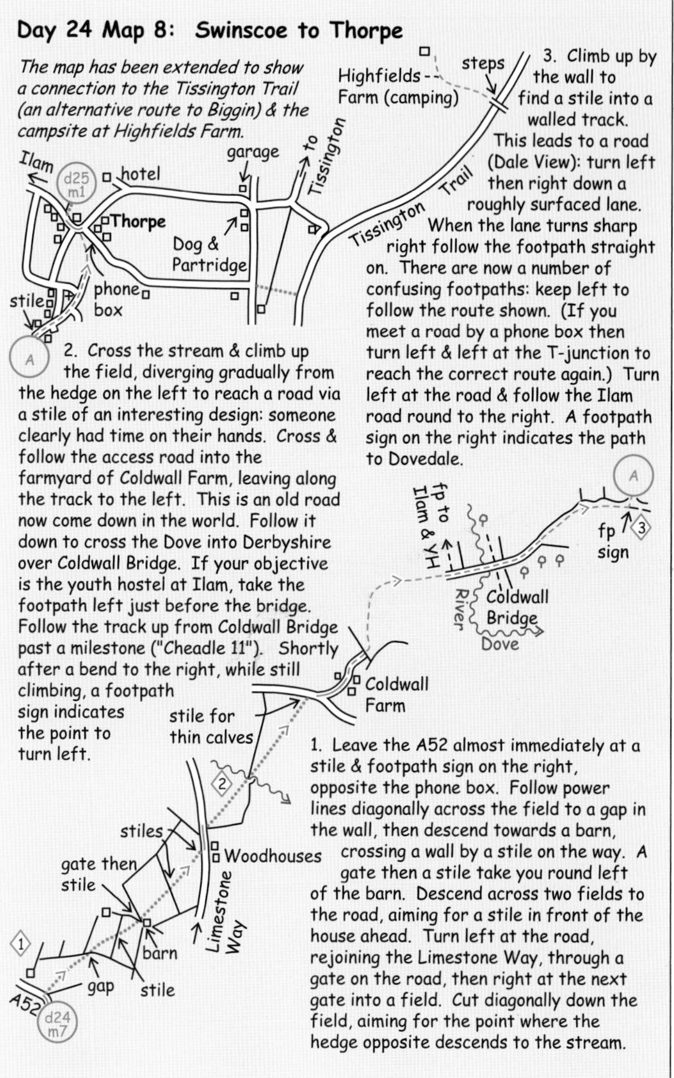

3. Climb up by the wall to find a stile into a walled track. This leads to a road (Dale View): turn left then right down a roughly surfaced lane. When the lane turns sharp right follow the footpath straight on. There are now a number of confusing footpaths: keep left to follow the route shown. (If you meet a road by a phone box then turn left & left at the T-junction to reach the correct route again.) Turn left at the road & follow the Ilam road round to the right. A footpath sign on the right indicates the path to Dovedale.

2. Cross the stream & climb up the field, diverging gradually from the hedge on the left to reach a road via a stile of an interesting design: someone clearly had time on their hands. Cross & follow the access road into the farmyard of Coldwall Farm, leaving along the track to the left. This is an old road now come down in the world. Follow it down to cross the Dove into Derbyshire over Coldwall Bridge. If your objective is the youth hostel at Ilam, take the footpath left just before the bridge. Follow the track up from Coldwall Bridge past a milestone ("Cheadle 11"). Shortly after a bend to the right, while still climbing, a footpath sign indicates the point to turn left.

1. Leave the A52 almost immediately at a stile & footpath sign on the right, opposite the phone box. Follow power lines diagonally across the field to a gap in the wall, then descend towards a barn, crossing a wall by a stile on the way. A gate then a stile take you round left of the barn. Descend across two fields to the road, aiming for a stile in front of the house ahead. Turn left at the road, rejoining the Limestone Way, through a gate on the road, then right at the next gate into a field. Cut diagonally down the field, aiming for the point where the hedge opposite descends to the stream.

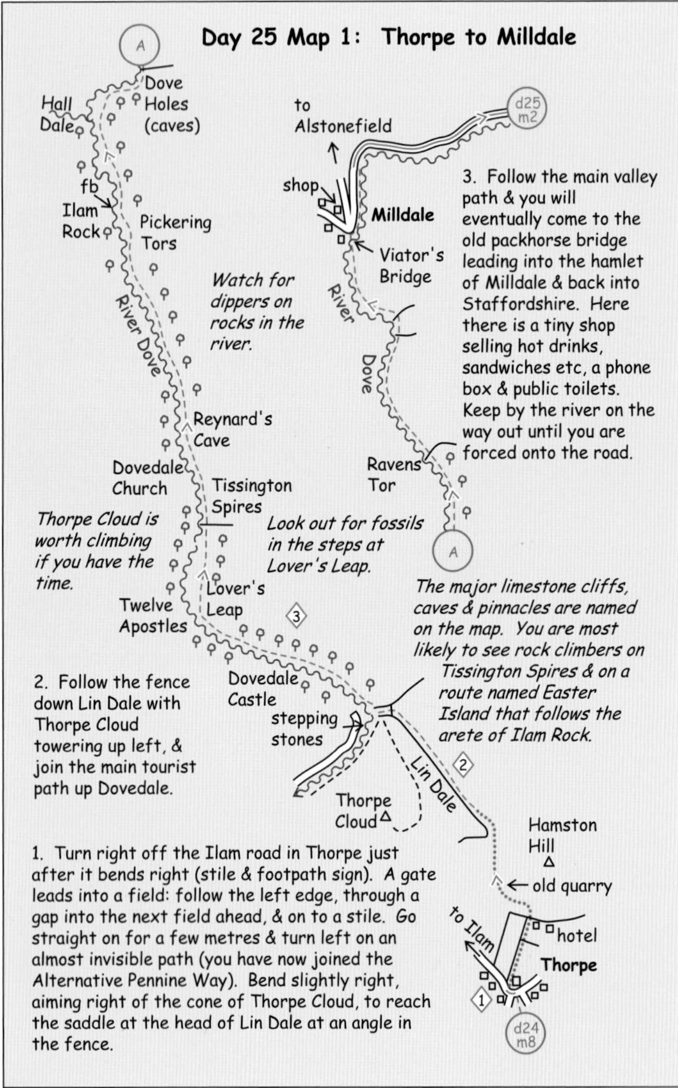

Day 25 Map 1: Thorpe to Milldale
A
Dove Holes (caves)
Hall Dale
fb
Ilam Rock
Pickering Tors
River Dove
Reynard's Cave
Dovedale Church
Tissington Spires
Thorpe Cloud is worth climbing if you have the time.
Twelve Apostles
Lover's Leap
Look out for fossils in the steps at Lover's Leap.
Watch for dippers on rocks in the river.
to Alstonefield
shop
Milldale
Viator's Bridge
River Dove
d25 m2
3. Follow the main valley path & you will eventually come to the old packhorse bridge leading into the hamlet of Milldale & back into Staffordshire. Here there is a tiny shop selling hot drinks, sandwiches etc, a phone box & public toilets. Keep by the river on the way out until you are forced onto the road.
Ravens Tor
A
The major limestone cliffs, caves & pinnacles are named on the map. You are most likely to see rock climbers on Tissington Spires & on a route named Easter Island that follows the arete of Ilam Rock.
3
2. Follow the fence down Lin Dale with Thorpe Cloud towering up left, & join the main tourist path up Dovedale.
Dovedale Castle
stepping stones
Thorpe Cloud
Lin Dale
2
Hamston Hill
old quarry
1. Turn right off the Ilam road in Thorpe just after it bends right (stile & footpath sign). A gate leads into a field: follow the left edge, through a gap into the next field ahead, & on to a stile. Go straight on for a few metres & turn left on an almost invisible path (you have now joined the Alternative Pennine Way). Bend slightly right, aiming right of the cone of Thorpe Cloud, to reach the saddle at the head of Lin Dale at an angle in the fence.
to Ilam
hotel
Thorpe
1
d24 m8

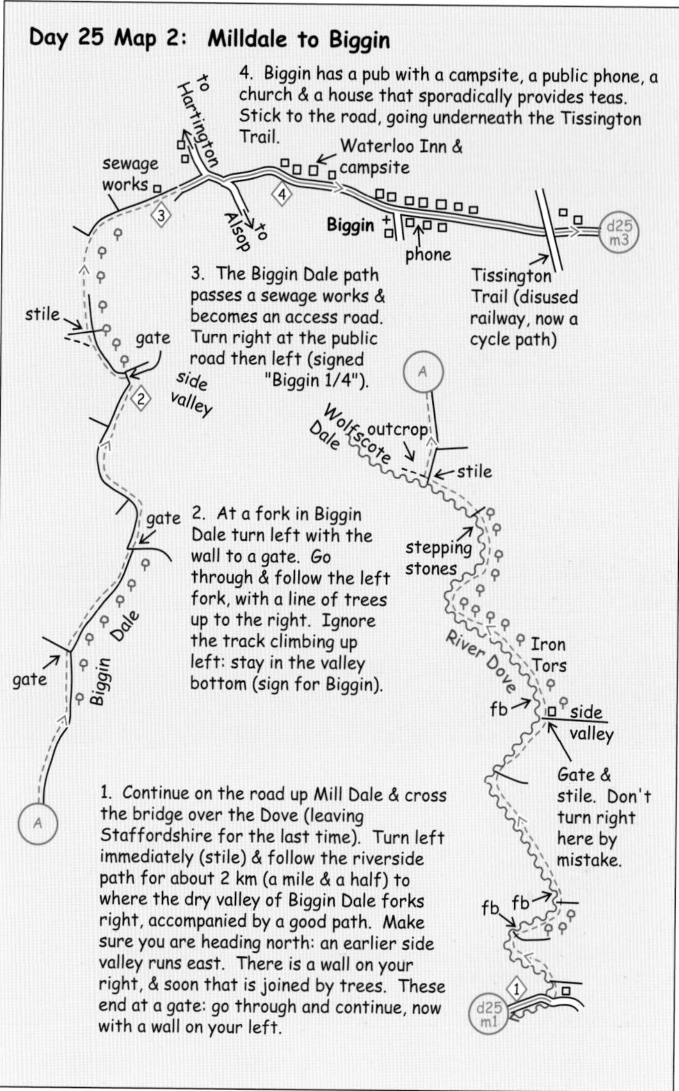
Day 25 Map 2: Milldale to Biggin
4. Biggin has a pub with a campsite, a public phone, a church & a house that sporadically provides teas. Stick to the road, going underneath the Tissington Trail.
to Hartington
Waterloo Inn & campsite
sewage works
Biggin
to Alsop
phone
d25 m3
3. The Biggin Dale path passes a sewage works & becomes an access road. Turn right at the public road then left (signed "Biggin 1/4").
Tissington Trail (disused railway, now a cycle path)
stile
gate
side valley
A
Wolfscote Dale
outcrop
stile
gate
2. At a fork in Biggin Dale turn left with the wall to a gate. Go through & follow the left fork, with a line of trees up to the right. Ignore the track climbing up left: stay in the valley bottom (sign for Biggin).
stepping stones
Biggin Dale
gate
River Dove
Iron Tors
fb
side valley
Gate & stile. Don't turn right here by mistake.
A
1. Continue on the road up Mill Dale & cross the bridge over the Dove (leaving Staffordshire for the last time). Turn left immediately (stile) & follow the riverside path for about 2 km (a mile & a half) to where the dry valley of Biggin Dale forks right, accompanied by a good path. Make sure you are heading north: an earlier side valley runs east. There is a wall on your right, & soon that is joined by trees. These end at a gate: go through and continue, now with a wall on your left.
fb
fb
d25 m1

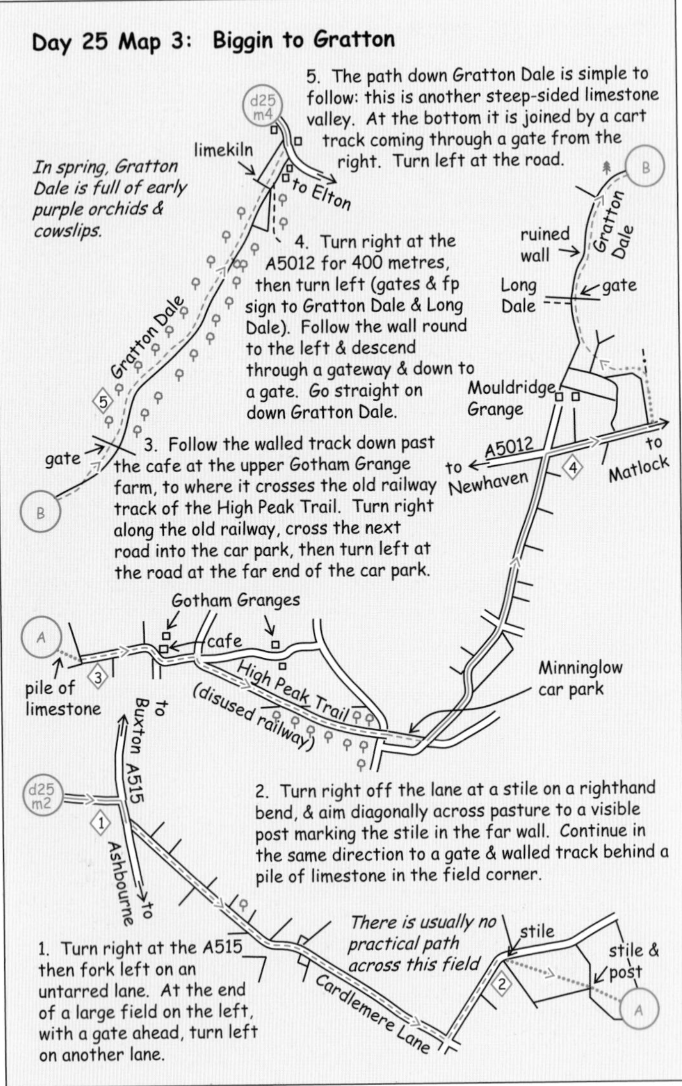
Day 25 Map 3: Biggin to Gratton
5. The path down Gratton Dale is simple to follow: this is another steep-sided limestone valley. At the bottom it is joined by a cart track coming through a gate from the right. Turn left at the road.
d25 m4
limekiln
to Elton
In spring, Gratton Dale is full of early purple orchids & cowslips.
B
ruined wall
Gratton Dale
Long Dale
gate
4. Turn right at the A5012 for 400 metres, then turn left (gates & fp sign to Gratton Dale & Long Dale). Follow the wall round to the left & descend through a gateway & down to a gate. Go straight on down Gratton Dale.
Gratton Dale
Mouldridge Grange
A5012
to Matlock
to Newhaven
gate
3. Follow the walled track down past the cafe at the upper Gotham Grange farm, to where it crosses the old railway track of the High Peak Trail. Turn right along the old railway, cross the next road into the car park, then turn left at the road at the far end of the car park.
B
Gotham Granges
A
cafe
pile of limestone
High Peak Trail
(disused railway)
Minninglow car park
to Buxton
A515
d25 m2
to Ashbourne
2. Turn right off the lane at a stile on a righthand bend, & aim diagonally across pasture to a visible post marking the stile in the far wall. Continue in the same direction to a gate & walled track behind a pile of limestone in the field corner.
There is usually no practical path across this field
stile
stile & post
A
1. Turn right at the A515 then fork left on an untarred lane. At the end of a large field on the left, with a gate ahead, turn left on another lane.
Cardlemere Lane

Day 25 Map 4: Gratton to Youlgreave

4. The path along the south bank of the River Bradford ends at a stone flag footbridge. Cross & climb the steep lane opposite (cafe) to reach the middle of Youlgreave. Turn right to the crossroads by the church & the George Hotel. Turn left here to continue the walk out of the village.

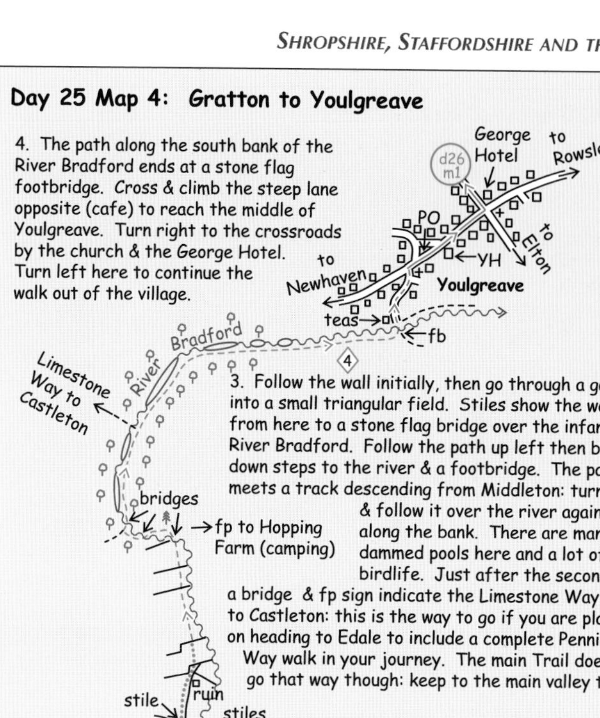

3. Follow the wall initially, then go through a gap into a small triangular field. Stiles show the way from here to a stone flag bridge over the infant River Bradford. Follow the path up left then back down steps to the river & a footbridge. The path meets a track descending from Middleton: turn right & follow it over the river again then along the bank. There are many dammed pools here and a lot of birdlife. Just after the second dam a bridge & fp sign indicate the Limestone Way route to Castleton: this is the way to go if you are planning on heading to Edale to include a complete Pennine Way walk in your journey. The main Trail doesn't go that way though: keep to the main valley track.

gate & stile

2

to Youlgreave

stiles

Gratton Grange Farm

1

to Middleton

d25 m3

1. Keep right when the road forks & climb up past Gratton Grange Farm to the start of a double bend where the road steepens: turn left off the road here on an overgrown walled path (fp sign). A stile leads to a field, with overhead power lines indicating the approximate direction. The next stile is slightly left of the power lines, although keeping right of them initially avoids wet ground. This is a gritstone boulder field: a brief taste of things to come tomorrow.

2. Go slightly right of the power lines again to a gate & stile. Go straight from here, with the power lines, & when they bend right follow the line of trees & ditch ahead to join a farm access road. Turn right along the road, then after a few metres leave it by a stile on the right.

Day 26 Map 1: Youlgreave to Calton Pastures

1. Leave Youlgreave along Conksbury Lane, then turn right on a tarred lane in front of Easter Cottage, before the end of the 30 mph zone. Pass the interesting building of Raper Lodge to cross the River Lathkill on an old packhorse bridge & climb up through woods on a clear zigzag path. At the top a gate leads to a large field: keep right by the fence to reach a gate by trees & farm buildings. Go on in the same direction with a wall on the right: a vague path appears by the wall. Keep straight on across Haddon Fields: eventually a farm track joins from the left & descends to the A6 by the gatehouse to Haddon Hall: turn left along the A6.

2. Walking along the A6 look out for a stile into the woods on the right (fp sign to Sheepbridge). This fenced path leads through the grounds of Haddon Hall & across & along the River Wye to meet a minor road. Turn right along the road, climb round the entrance of a disused railway tunnel, & after the bend go right (gate & fp sign), to follow a clear path up through fields to join an unmetalled lane by Bowling Green Farm. Turn left at the first T-junction, cross a col (valleys both sides), & leave the lane at the next junction for a steep path up through the wood half left (sign "Bridleway Chatsworth"). The path climbs to meet a broader track: keep left along it for a short distance.

3. Turn right at a track junction by a noticeboard & follow this path uphill into pines then alongside a wall. The path levels out then goes right through a gap in the wall & diverges from it. It briefly joins a ride with a power line along it, then diverges right from this as well to a wall corner. Go right through a gap & follow the wall to a stile, then slightly left on a narrow path through pasture: occasional marker posts show the way.

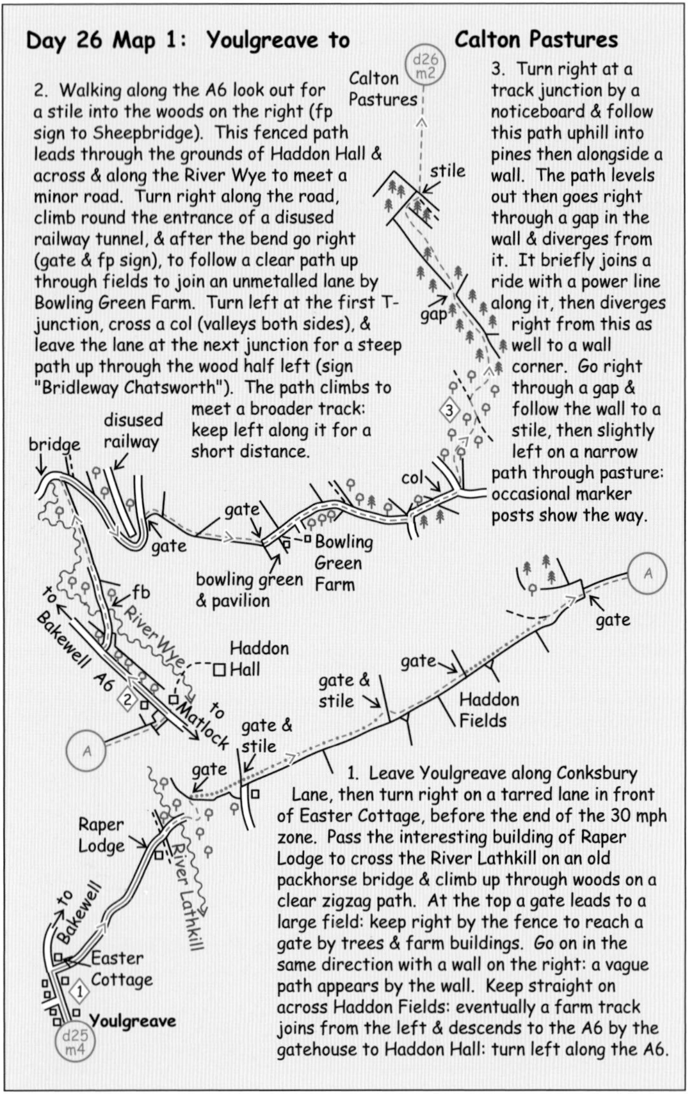

d26 m2
Calton Pastures
stile
gap
col
disused railway
bridge
gate
gate
Bowling Green Farm
bowling green & pavilion
fb
to Bakewell
River Wye
Haddon Hall
A6
to Matlock
A
A
gate
gate
gate & stile
Haddon Fields
gate & stile
gate
Raper Lodge
River Lathkill
to Bakewell
Easter Cottage
Youlgreave
d25 m4

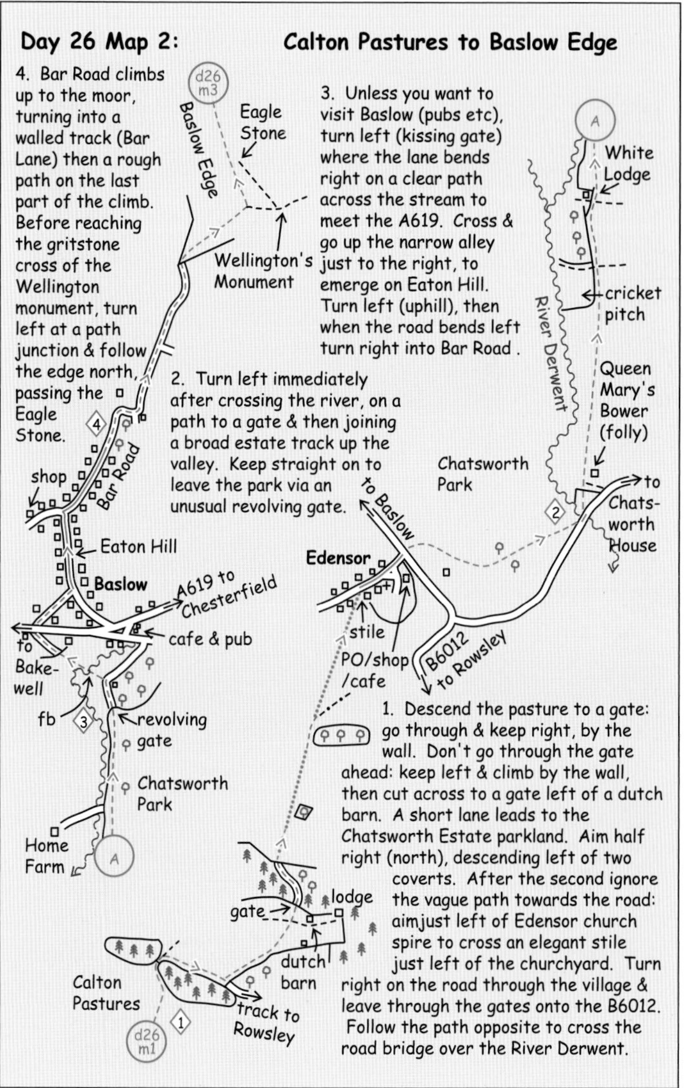
Day 26 Map 2: Calton Pastures to Baslow Edge
4. Bar Road climbs up to the moor, turning into a walled track (Bar Lane) then a rough path on the last part of the climb. Before reaching the gritstone cross of the Wellington monument, turn left at a path junction & follow the edge north, passing the Eagle Stone.
d26 m3
Baslow Edge
Eagle Stone
Wellington's Monument
3. Unless you want to visit Baslow (pubs etc), turn left (kissing gate) where the lane bends right on a clear path across the stream to meet the A619. Cross & go up the narrow alley just to the right, to emerge on Eaton Hill. Turn left (uphill), then when the road bends left turn right into Bar Road .
A
White Lodge
cricket pitch
River Derwent
Queen Mary's Bower (folly)
2. Turn left immediately after crossing the river, on a path to a gate & then joining a broad estate track up the valley. Keep straight on to leave the park via an unusual revolving gate.
4
shop
Bar Road
to Baslow
Chatsworth Park
2
to Chats-worth House
Eaton Hill
Edensor
Baslow
A619 to Chesterfield
to Bake-well
cafe & pub
stile
PO/shop /cafe
B6012 to Rowsley
fb
3
revolving gate
1. Descend the pasture to a gate: go through & keep right, by the wall. Don't go through the gate ahead: keep left & climb by the wall, then cut across to a gate left of a dutch barn. A short lane leads to the Chatsworth Estate parkland. Aim half right (north), descending left of two coverts. After the second ignore the vague path towards the road: aimjust left of Edensor church spire to cross an elegant stile just left of the churchyard. Turn right on the road through the village & leave through the gates onto the B6012. Follow the path opposite to cross the road bridge over the River Derwent.
Chatsworth Park
Home Farm
A
lodge
gate
dutch barn
Calton Pastures
track to Rowsley
1
d26 m1

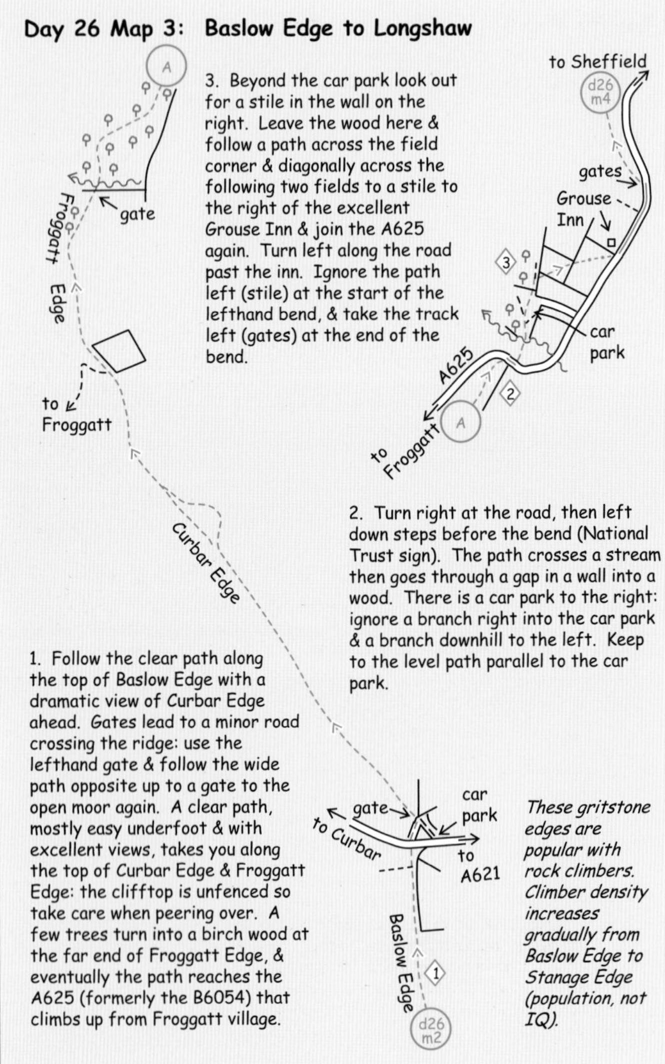

3. Beyond the car park look out for a stile in the wall on the right. Leave the wood here & follow a path across the field corner & diagonally across the following two fields to a stile to the right of the excellent Grouse Inn & join the A625 again. Turn left along the road past the inn. Ignore the path left (stile) at the start of the lefthand bend, & take the track left (gates) at the end of the bend.

2. Turn right at the road, then left down steps before the bend (National Trust sign). The path crosses a stream then goes through a gap in a wall into a wood. There is a car park to the right: ignore a branch right into the car park & a branch downhill to the left. Keep to the level path parallel to the car park.

1. Follow the clear path along the top of Baslow Edge with a dramatic view of Curbar Edge ahead. Gates lead to a minor road crossing the ridge: use the lefthand gate & follow the wide path opposite up to a gate to the open moor again. A clear path, mostly easy underfoot & with excellent views, takes you along the top of Curbar Edge & Froggatt Edge: the clifftop is unfenced so take care when peering over. A few trees turn into a birch wood at the far end of Froggatt Edge, & eventually the path reaches the A625 (formerly the B6054) that climbs up from Froggatt village.

These gritstone edges are popular with rock climbers. Climber density increases gradually from Baslow Edge to Stanage Edge (population, not IQ).

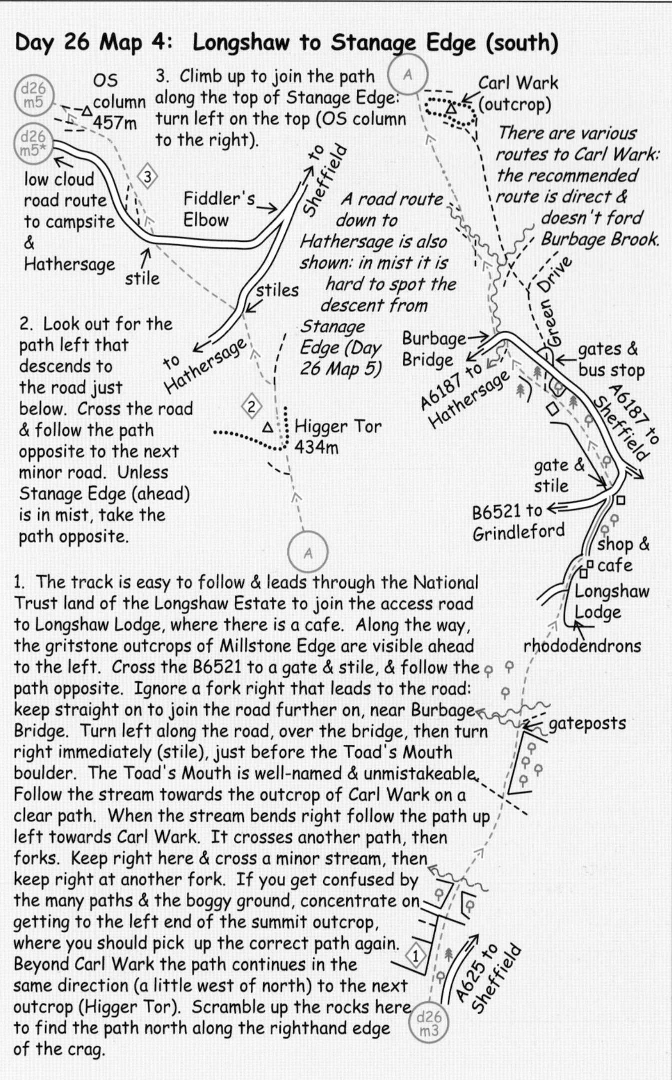
Day 26 Map 4: Longshaw to Stanage Edge (south)
d26 m5
OS column 457m
3. Climb up to join the path along the top of Stanage Edge: turn left on the top (OS column to the right).
A
Carl Wark (outcrop)
d26 m5*
There are various routes to Carl Wark: the recommended route is direct & doesn't ford Burbage Brook.
low cloud road route to campsite & Hathersage
3
Fiddler's Elbow
to Sheffield
A road route down to Hathersage is also shown: in mist it is hard to spot the descent from Stanage Edge (Day 26 Map 5)
stile
stiles
Green Drive
2. Look out for the path left that descends to the road just below. Cross the road & follow the path opposite to the next minor road. Unless Stanage Edge (ahead) is in mist, take the path opposite.
to Hathersage
Burbage Bridge
gates & bus stop
A6187 to Hathersage
A6187 to Sheffield
2
Higger Tor 434m
gate & stile
B6521 to Grindleford
A
shop & cafe
1. The track is easy to follow & leads through the National Trust land of the Longshaw Estate to join the access road to Longshaw Lodge, where there is a cafe. Along the way, the gritstone outcrops of Millstone Edge are visible ahead to the left. Cross the B6521 to a gate & stile, & follow the path opposite. Ignore a fork right that leads to the road: keep straight on to join the road further on, near Burbage Bridge. Turn left along the road, over the bridge, then turn right immediately (stile), just before the Toad's Mouth boulder. The Toad's Mouth is well-named & unmistakeable. Follow the stream towards the outcrop of Carl Wark on a clear path. When the stream bends right follow the path up left towards Carl Wark. It crosses another path, then forks. Keep right here & cross a minor stream, then keep right at another fork. If you get confused by the many paths & the boggy ground, concentrate on getting to the left end of the summit outcrop, where you should pick up the correct path again. Beyond Carl Wark the path continues in the same direction (a little west of north) to the next outcrop (Higger Tor). Scramble up the rocks here to find the path north along the righthand edge of the crag.
Longshaw Lodge
rhododendrons
gateposts
1
A625 to Sheffield
d26 m3

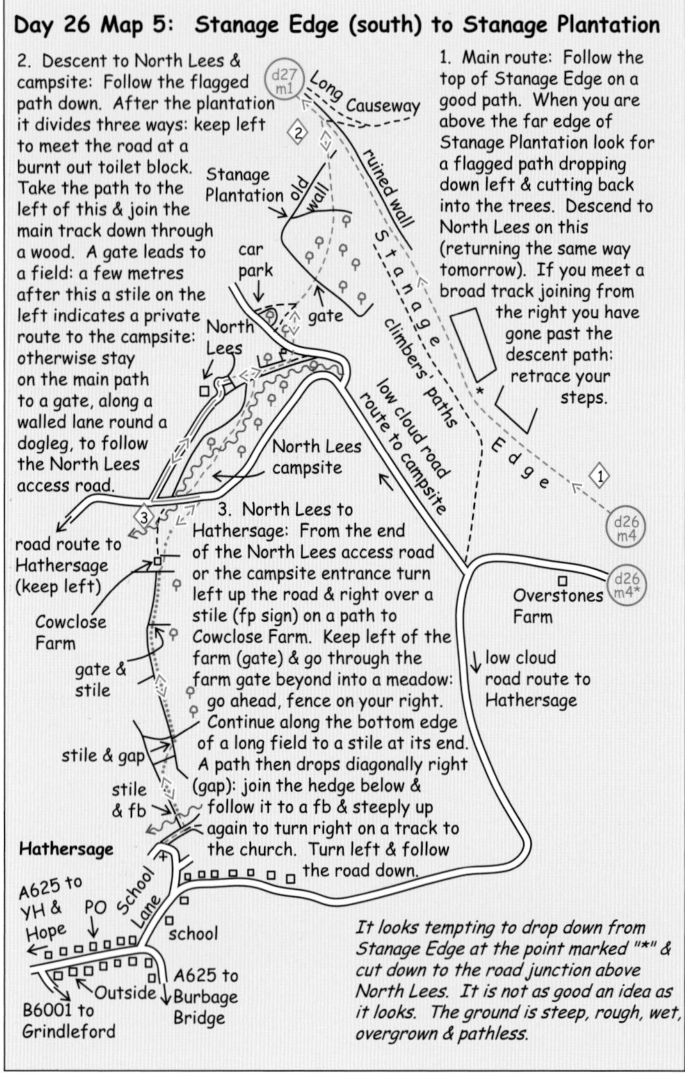

Day 26 Map 5: Stanage Edge (south) to Stanage Plantation
2. Descent to North Lees & campsite: Follow the flagged path down. After the plantation it divides three ways: keep left to meet the road at a burnt out toilet block. Take the path to the left of this & join the main track down through a wood. A gate leads to a field: a few metres after this a stile on the left indicates a private route to the campsite: otherwise stay on the main path to a gate, along a walled lane round a dogleg, to follow the North Lees access road.
1. Main route: Follow the top of Stanage Edge on a good path. When you are above the far edge of Stanage Plantation look for a flagged path dropping down left & cutting back into the trees. Descend to North Lees on this (returning the same way tomorrow). If you meet a broad track joining from the right you have gone past the descent path: retrace your steps.
d27 m1
Long Causeway
ruined wall
Stanage Plantation
old wall
car park
gate
North Lees
Stanage Edge
climbers' paths
low cloud road route to campsite
North Lees campsite
d26 m4
d26 m4*
Overstones Farm
road route to Hathersage (keep left)
Cowclose Farm
gate & stile
stile & gap
stile & fb
3. North Lees to Hathersage: From the end of the North Lees access road or the campsite entrance turn left up the road & right over a stile (fp sign) on a path to Cowclose Farm. Keep left of the farm (gate) & go through the farm gate beyond into a meadow: go ahead, fence on your right. Continue along the bottom edge of a long field to a stile at its end. A path then drops diagonally right (gap): join the hedge below & follow it to a fb & steeply up again to turn right on a track to the church. Turn left & follow the road down.
low cloud road route to Hathersage
Hathersage
A625 to YH & Hope
PO
School Lane
school
Outside
A625 to Burbage Bridge
B6001 to Grindleford
It looks tempting to drop down from Stanage Edge at the point marked "*" & cut down to the road junction above North Lees. It is not as good an idea as it looks. The ground is steep, rough, wet, overgrown & pathless.

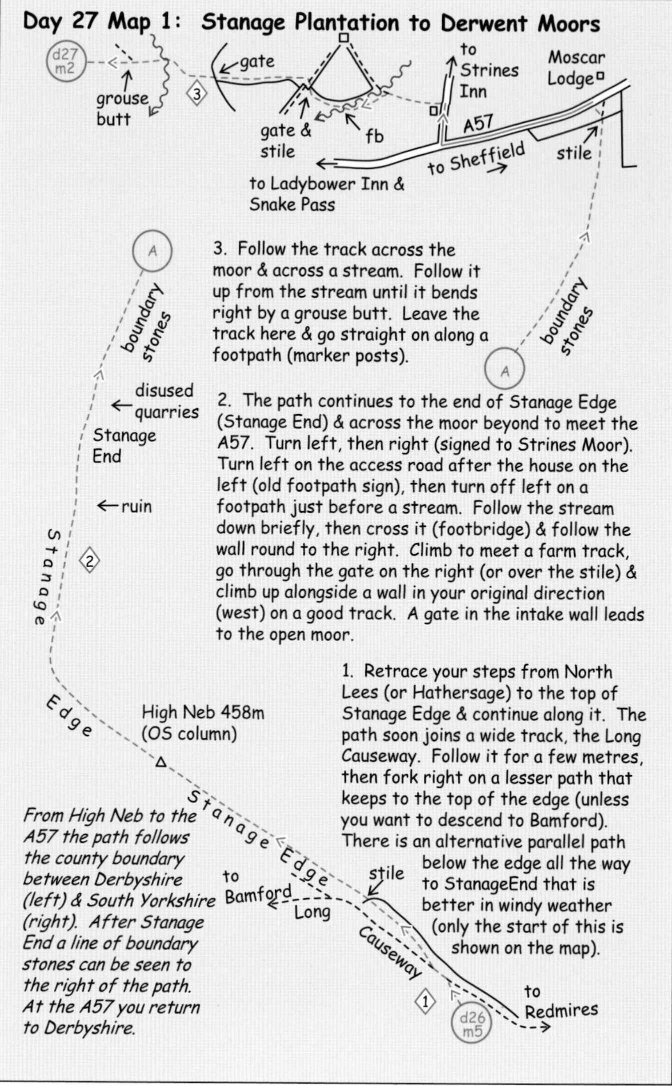
Day 27 Map 1: Stanage Plantation to Derwent Moors
d27 m2
grouse butt
3
gate
gate & stile
fb
to Strines Inn
Moscar Lodge
A57
stile
to Sheffield
to Ladybower Inn & Snake Pass
A
boundary stones
3. Follow the track across the moor & across a stream. Follow it up from the stream until it bends right by a grouse butt. Leave the track here & go straight on along a footpath (marker posts).
boundary stones
A
disused quarries
Stanage End
2. The path continues to the end of Stanage Edge (Stanage End) & across the moor beyond to meet the A57. Turn left, then right (signed to Strines Moor). Turn left on the access road after the house on the left (old footpath sign), then turn off left on a footpath just before a stream. Follow the stream down briefly, then cross it (footbridge) & follow the wall round to the right. Climb to meet a farm track, go through the gate on the right (or over the stile) & climb up alongside a wall in your original direction (west) on a good track. A gate in the intake wall leads to the open moor.
ruin
Stanage
2
Edge
High Neb 458m (OS column)
1. Retrace your steps from North Lees (or Hathersage) to the top of Stanage Edge & continue along it. The path soon joins a wide track, the Long Causeway. Follow it for a few metres, then fork right on a lesser path that keeps to the top of the edge (unless you want to descend to Bamford). There is an alternative parallel path below the edge all the way to StanageEnd that is better in windy weather (only the start of this is shown on the map).
Stanage Edge
From High Neb to the A57 the path follows the county boundary between Derbyshire (left) & South Yorkshire (right). After Stanage End a line of boundary stones can be seen to the right of the path. At the A57 you return to Derbyshire.
to Bamford
Long
Causeway
stile
1
d26 m5
to Redmires

Day 27 Map 2: Derwent Moors to Lost Lad

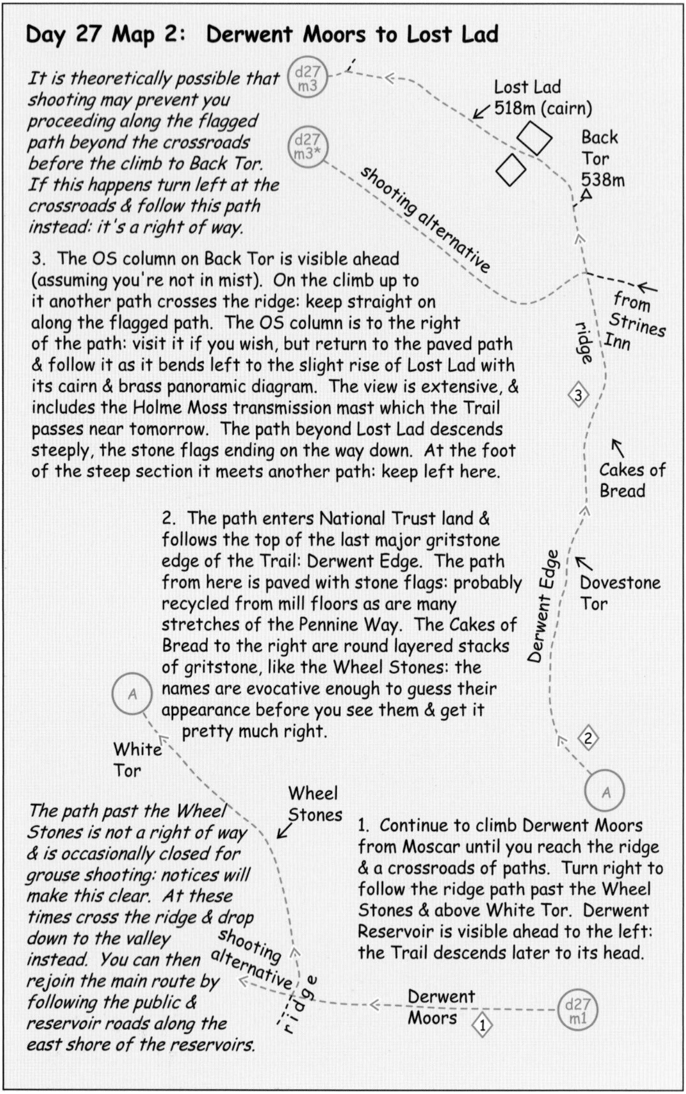

It is theoretically possible that shooting may prevent you proceeding along the flagged path beyond the crossroads before the climb to Back Tor. If this happens turn left at the crossroads & follow this path instead: it's a right of way.

3. The OS column on Back Tor is visible ahead (assuming you're not in mist). On the climb up to it another path crosses the ridge: keep straight on along the flagged path. The OS column is to the right of the path: visit it if you wish, but return to the paved path & follow it as it bends left to the slight rise of Lost Lad with its cairn & brass panoramic diagram. The view is extensive, & includes the Holme Moss transmission mast which the Trail passes near tomorrow. The path beyond Lost Lad descends steeply, the stone flags ending on the way down. At the foot of the steep section it meets another path: keep left here.

2. The path enters National Trust land & follows the top of the last major gritstone edge of the Trail: Derwent Edge. The path from here is paved with stone flags: probably recycled from mill floors as are many stretches of the Pennine Way. The Cakes of Bread to the right are round layered stacks of gritstone, like the Wheel Stones: the names are evocative enough to guess their appearance before you see them & get it pretty much right.

The path past the Wheel Stones is not a right of way & is occasionally closed for grouse shooting: notices will make this clear. At these times cross the ridge & drop down to the valley instead. You can then rejoin the main route by following the public & reservoir roads along the east shore of the reservoirs.

1. Continue to climb Derwent Moors from Moscar until you reach the ridge & a crossroads of paths. Turn right to follow the ridge path past the Wheel Stones & above White Tor. Derwent Reservoir is visible ahead to the left: the Trail descends later to its head.

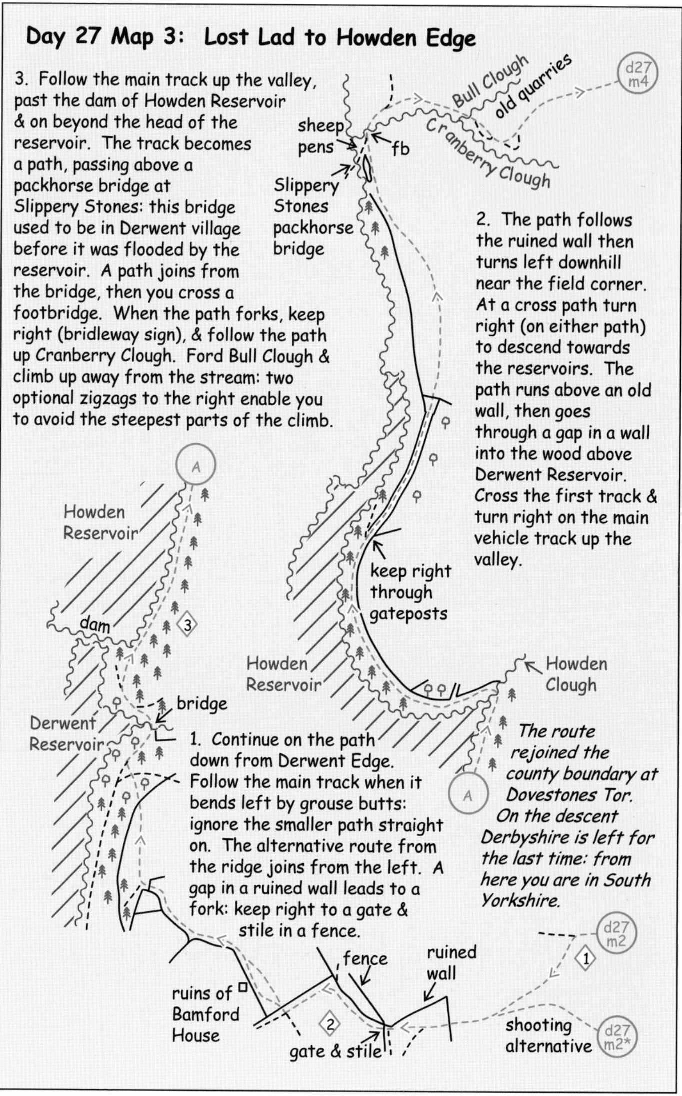
Day 27 Map 3: Lost Lad to Howden Edge
3. Follow the main track up the valley, past the dam of Howden Reservoir & on beyond the head of the reservoir. The track becomes a path, passing above a packhorse bridge at Slippery Stones: this bridge used to be in Derwent village before it was flooded by the reservoir. A path joins from the bridge, then you cross a footbridge. When the path forks, keep right (bridleway sign), & follow the path up Cranberry Clough. Ford Bull Clough & climb up away from the stream: two optional zigzags to the right enable you to avoid the steepest parts of the climb.
Bull Clough
old quarries
d27 m4
sheep pens
fb
Cranberry Clough
Slippery Stones packhorse bridge
2. The path follows the ruined wall then turns left downhill near the field corner. At a cross path turn right (on either path) to descend towards the reservoirs. The path runs above an old wall, then goes through a gap in a wall into the wood above Derwent Reservoir. Cross the first track & turn right on the main vehicle track up the valley.
A
Howden Reservoir
keep right through gateposts
dam
3
Howden Reservoir
Howden Clough
bridge
Derwent Reservoir
1. Continue on the path down from Derwent Edge. Follow the main track when it bends left by grouse butts: ignore the smaller path straight on. The alternative route from the ridge joins from the left. A gap in a ruined wall leads to a fork: keep right to a gate & stile in a fence.
The route rejoined the county boundary at Dovestones Tor. On the descent Derbyshire is left for the last time: from here you are in South Yorkshire.
A
d27 m2
1
fence
ruined wall
ruins of Bamford House
2
gate & stile
shooting alternative
d27 m2*

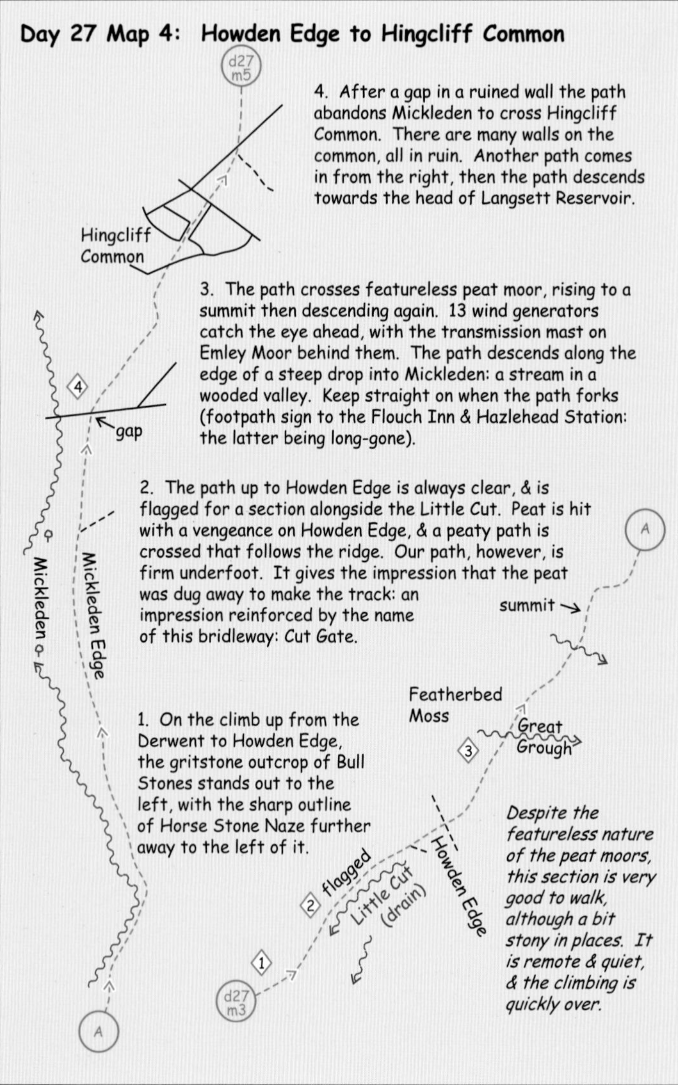
Day 27 Map 4: Howden Edge to Hingcliff Common
d27 m5
4. After a gap in a ruined wall the path abandons Mickleden to cross Hingcliff Common. There are many walls on the common, all in ruin. Another path comes in from the right, then the path descends towards the head of Langsett Reservoir.
Hingcliff Common
3. The path crosses featureless peat moor, rising to a summit then descending again. 13 wind generators catch the eye ahead, with the transmission mast on Emley Moor behind them. The path descends along the edge of a steep drop into Mickleden: a stream in a wooded valley. Keep straight on when the path forks (footpath sign to the Flouch Inn & Hazlehead Station: the latter being long-gone).
4
gap
2. The path up to Howden Edge is always clear, & is flagged for a section alongside the Little Cut. Peat is hit with a vengeance on Howden Edge, & a peaty path is crossed that follows the ridge. Our path, however, is firm underfoot. It gives the impression that the peat was dug away to make the track: an impression reinforced by the name of this bridleway: Cut Gate.
A
summit
Mickleden
Mickleden Edge
Featherbed Moss
1. On the climb up from the Derwent to Howden Edge, the gritstone outcrop of Bull Stones stands out to the left, with the sharp outline of Horse Stone Naze further away to the left of it.
3
Great Grough
Despite the featureless nature of the peat moors, this section is very good to walk, although a bit stony in places. It is remote & quiet, & the climbing is quickly over.
Howden Edge
flagged
Little Cut (drain)
2
1
d27 m3
A

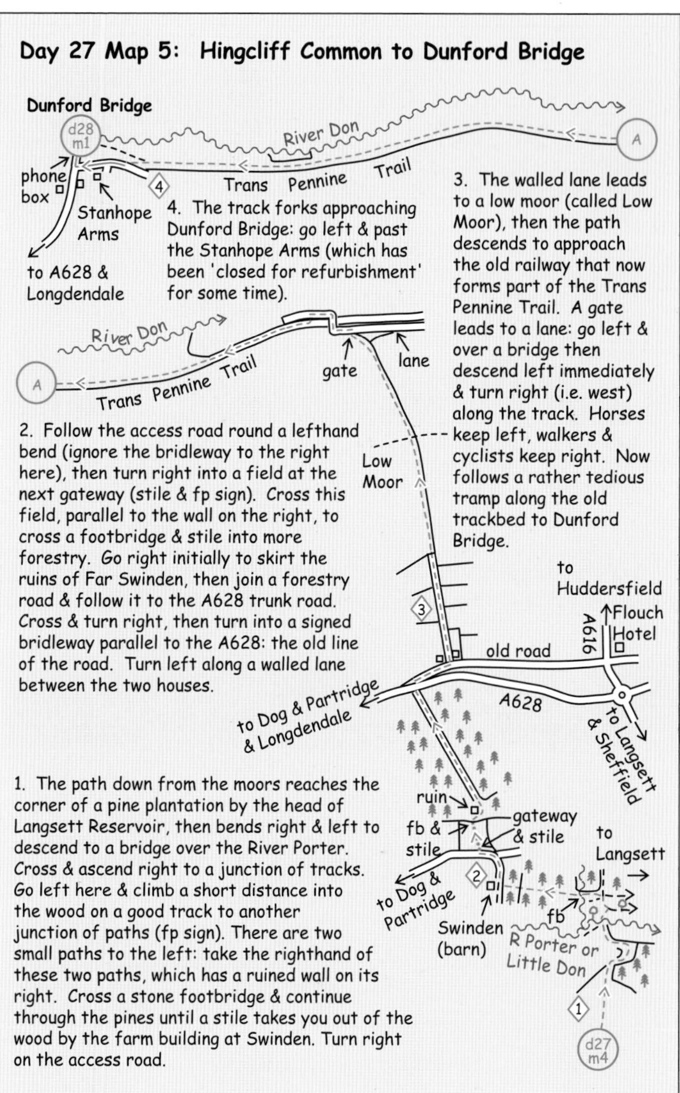
Day 27 Map 5: Hingcliff Common to Dunford Bridge
Dunford Bridge
d28 m1
River Don
A
phone box
Stanhope Arms
Trans Pennine Trail
to A628 & Longdendale
4. The track forks approaching Dunford Bridge: go left & past the Stanhope Arms (which has been 'closed for refurbishment' for some time).
3. The walled lane leads to a low moor (called Low Moor), then the path descends to approach the old railway that now forms part of the Trans Pennine Trail. A gate leads to a lane: go left & over a bridge then descend left immediately & turn right (i.e. west) along the track. Horses keep left, walkers & cyclists keep right. Now follows a rather tedious tramp along the old trackbed to Dunford Bridge.
River Don
A
Trans Pennine Trail
gate
lane
2. Follow the access road round a lefthand bend (ignore the bridleway to the right here), then turn right into a field at the next gateway (stile & fp sign). Cross this field, parallel to the wall on the right, to cross a footbridge & stile into more forestry. Go right initially to skirt the ruins of Far Swinden, then join a forestry road & follow it to the A628 trunk road. Cross & turn right, then turn into a signed bridleway parallel to the A628: the old line of the road. Turn left along a walled lane between the two houses.
Low Moor
to Huddersfield
Flouch Hotel
A616
old road
A628
to Dog & Partridge & Longdendale
to Langsett & Sheffield
1. The path down from the moors reaches the corner of a pine plantation by the head of Langsett Reservoir, then bends right & left to descend to a bridge over the River Porter. Cross & ascend right to a junction of tracks. Go left here & climb a short distance into the wood on a good track to another junction of paths (fp sign). There are two small paths to the left: take the righthand of these two paths, which has a ruined wall on its right. Cross a stone footbridge & continue through the pines until a stile takes you out of the wood by the farm building at Swinden. Turn right on the access road.
ruin
fb & stile
gateway & stile
to Langsett
to Dog & Partridge
Swinden (barn)
fb
R Porter or Little Don
d27 m4

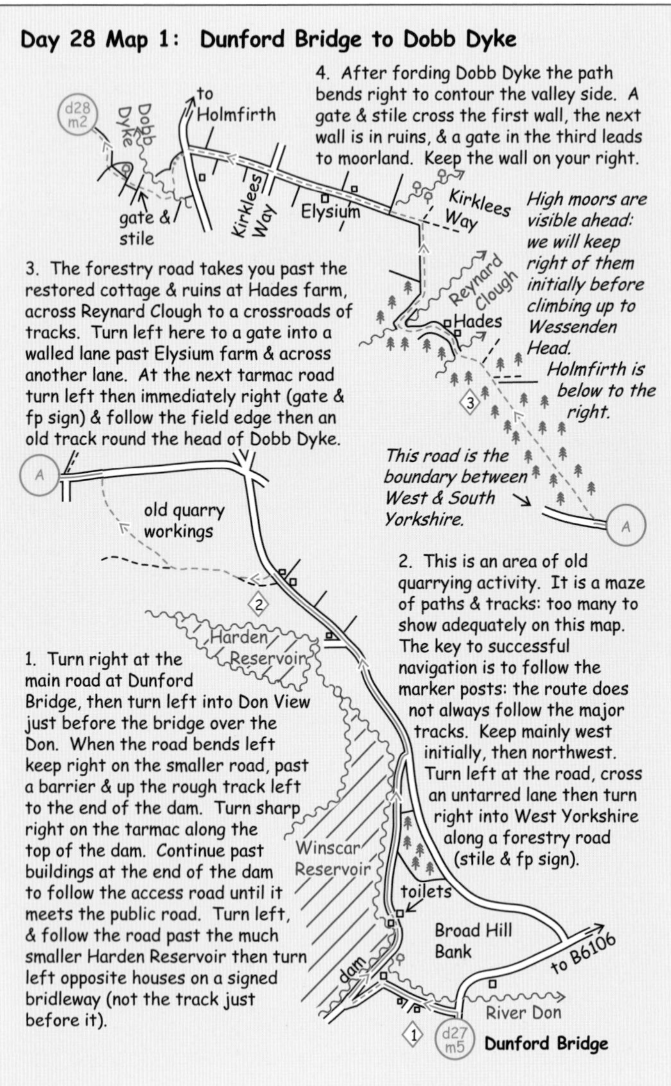
Day 28 Map 1: Dunford Bridge to Dobb Dyke
4. After fording Dobb Dyke the path bends right to contour the valley side. A gate & stile cross the first wall, the next wall is in ruins, & a gate in the third leads to moorland. Keep the wall on your right.
d28 m2
Dobb Dyke
to Holmfirth
Kirklees Way
Elysium
gate & stile
Kirklees Way
High moors are visible ahead: we will keep right of them initially before climbing up to Wessenden Head.
3. The forestry road takes you past the restored cottage & ruins at Hades farm, across Reynard Clough to a crossroads of tracks. Turn left here to a gate into a walled lane past Elysium farm & across another lane. At the next tarmac road turn left then immediately right (gate & fp sign) & follow the field edge then an old track round the head of Dobb Dyke.
Reynard Clough
Hades
Holmfirth is below to the right.
A
old quarry workings
This road is the boundary between West & South Yorkshire.
A
2. This is an area of old quarrying activity. It is a maze of paths & tracks: too many to show adequately on this map. The key to successful navigation is to follow the marker posts: the route does not always follow the major tracks. Keep mainly west initially, then northwest. Turn left at the road, cross an untarred lane then turn right into West Yorkshire along a forestry road (stile & fp sign).
Harden Reservoir
1. Turn right at the main road at Dunford Bridge, then turn left into Don View just before the bridge over the Don. When the road bends left keep right on the smaller road, past a barrier & up the rough track left to the end of the dam. Turn sharp right on the tarmac along the top of the dam. Continue past buildings at the end of the dam to follow the access road until it meets the public road. Turn left, & follow the road past the much smaller Harden Reservoir then turn left opposite houses on a signed bridleway (not the track just before it).
Winscar Reservoir
toilets
Broad Hill Bank
to B6106
dam
River Don
d27 m5
Dunford Bridge

Day 28 Map 2: Dobb Dyke to Marsden Clough

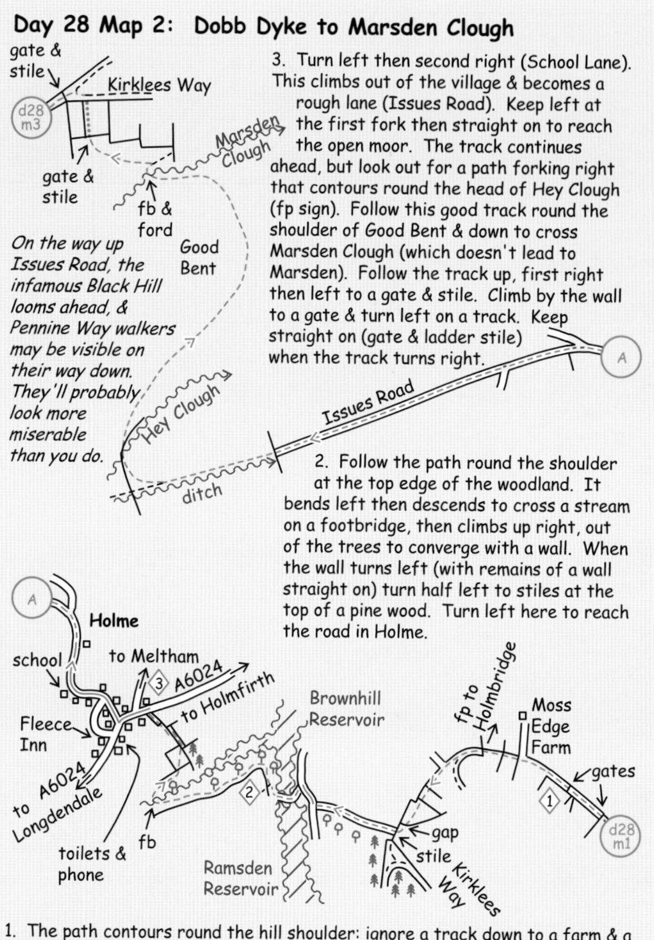

3. Turn left then second right (School Lane). This climbs out of the village & becomes a rough lane (Issues Road). Keep left at the first fork then straight on to reach the open moor. The track continues ahead, but look out for a path forking right that contours round the head of Hey Clough (fp sign). Follow this good track round the shoulder of Good Bent & down to cross Marsden Clough (which doesn't lead to Marsden). Follow the track up, first right then left to a gate & stile. Climb by the wall to a gate & turn left on a track. Keep straight on (gate & ladder stile) when the track turns right.

2. Follow the path round the shoulder at the top edge of the woodland. It bends left then descends to cross a stream on a footbridge, then climbs up right, out of the trees to converge with a wall. When the wall turns left (with remains of a wall straight on) turn half left to stiles at the top of a pine wood. Turn left here to reach the road in Holme.

1. The path contours round the hill shoulder: ignore a track down to a farm & a left fork that climbs uphill. On the descent the path leaves the righthand wall briefly then descends right to a gap & a stile. Go down the track (now on the Kirklees Way), with a stream on your right. Continue past a picnic area to turn right at the reservoir road, then turn left on a fenced footpath across the dam of Ramsden Reservoir. A clear path now slants up right through trees.

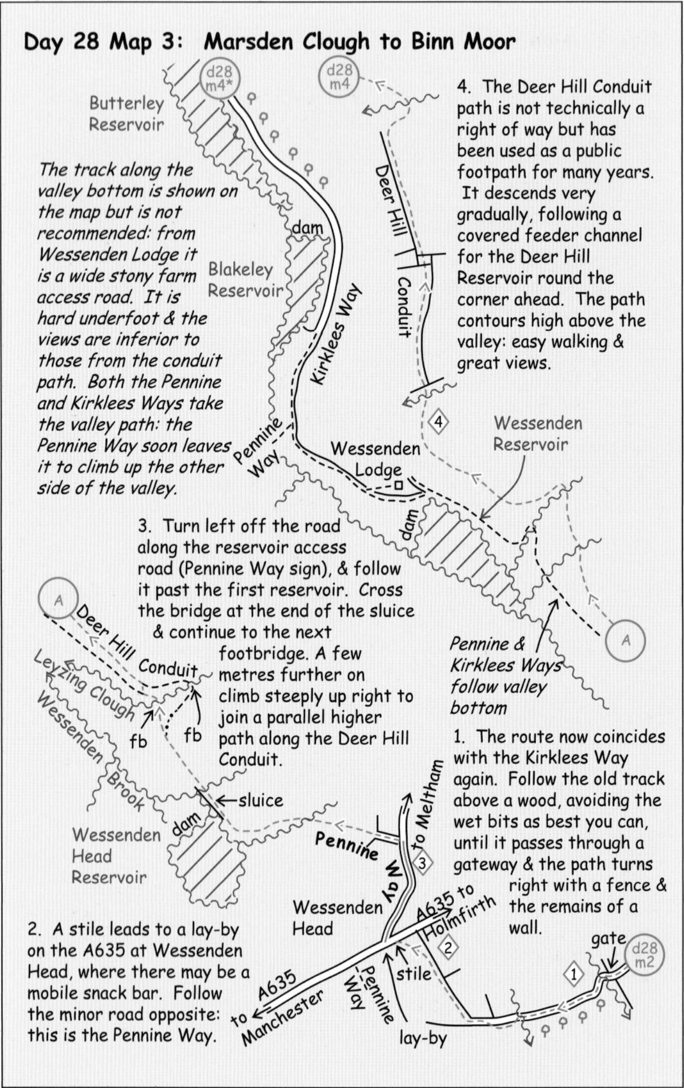
Day 28 Map 3: Marsden Clough to Binn Moor
d28 m4*
d28 m4
Butterley Reservoir
The track along the valley bottom is shown on the map but is not recommended: from Wessenden Lodge it is a wide stony farm access road. It is hard underfoot & the views are inferior to those from the conduit path. Both the Pennine and Kirklees Ways take the valley path: the Pennine Way soon leaves it to climb up the other side of the valley.
4. The Deer Hill Conduit path is not technically a right of way but has been used as a public footpath for many years. It descends very gradually, following a covered feeder channel for the Deer Hill Reservoir round the corner ahead. The path contours high above the valley: easy walking & great views.
Deer Hill
Conduit
dam
Blakeley Reservoir
Kirklees Way
Pennine Way
Wessenden Lodge
Wessenden Reservoir
dam
3. Turn left off the road along the reservoir access road (Pennine Way sign), & follow it past the first reservoir. Cross the bridge at the end of the sluice & continue to the next footbridge. A few metres further on climb steeply up right to join a parallel higher path along the Deer Hill Conduit.
A
Deer Hill
Conduit
Leyzing Clough
Wessenden Brook
fb
fb
sluice
Pennine & Kirklees Ways follow valley bottom
A
1. The route now coincides with the Kirklees Way again. Follow the old track above a wood, avoiding the wet bits as best you can, until it passes through a gateway & the path turns right with a fence & the remains of a wall.
to Meltham
Pennine Way
Wessenden Head Reservoir
dam
Wessenden Head
A635 to Holmfirth
gate
d28 m2
2. A stile leads to a lay-by on the A635 at Wessenden Head, where there may be a mobile snack bar. Follow the minor road opposite: this is the Pennine Way.
A635 to Manchester
Pennine Way
stile
lay-by

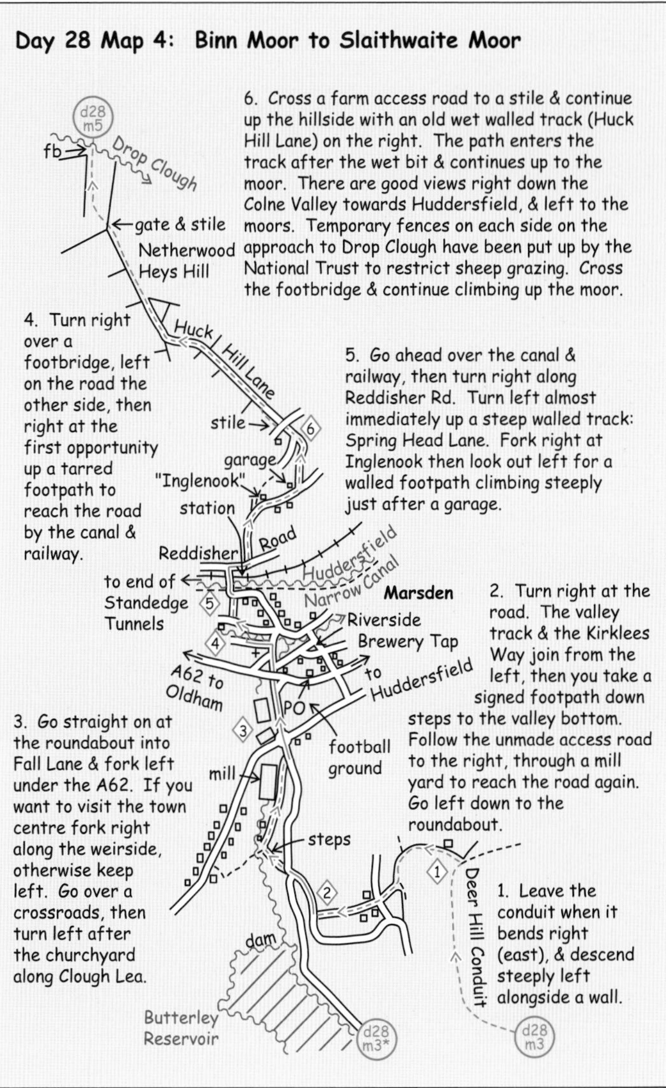
Day 28 Map 4: Binn Moor to Slaithwaite Moor
6. Cross a farm access road to a stile & continue up the hillside with an old wet walled track (Huck Hill Lane) on the right. The path enters the track after the wet bit & continues up to the moor. There are good views right down the Colne Valley towards Huddersfield, & left to the moors. Temporary fences on each side on the approach to Drop Clough have been put up by the National Trust to restrict sheep grazing. Cross the footbridge & continue climbing up the moor.
d28 m5
fb
Drop Clough
gate & stile
Netherwood Heys Hill
4. Turn right over a footbridge, left on the road the other side, then right at the first opportunity up a tarred footpath to reach the road by the canal & railway.
Huck Hill Lane
5. Go ahead over the canal & railway, then turn right along Reddisher Rd. Turn left almost immediately up a steep walled track: Spring Head Lane. Fork right at Inglenook then look out left for a walled footpath climbing steeply just after a garage.
stile
6
garage
"Inglenook"
station
Reddisher Road
Huddersfield Narrow Canal
to end of Standedge Tunnels
5
Marsden
2. Turn right at the road. The valley track & the Kirklees Way join from the left, then you take a signed footpath down steps to the valley bottom. Follow the unmade access road to the right, through a mill yard to reach the road again. Go left down to the roundabout.
Riverside Brewery Tap
4
A62 to Oldham
to Huddersfield
PO
3. Go straight on at the roundabout into Fall Lane & fork left under the A62. If you want to visit the town centre fork right along the weirside, otherwise keep left. Go over a crossroads, then turn left after the churchyard along Clough Lea.
3
football ground
mill
steps
1
2
Deer Hill Conduit
1. Leave the conduit when it bends right (east), & descend steeply left alongside a wall.
dam
Butterley Reservoir
d28 m3*
d28 m3

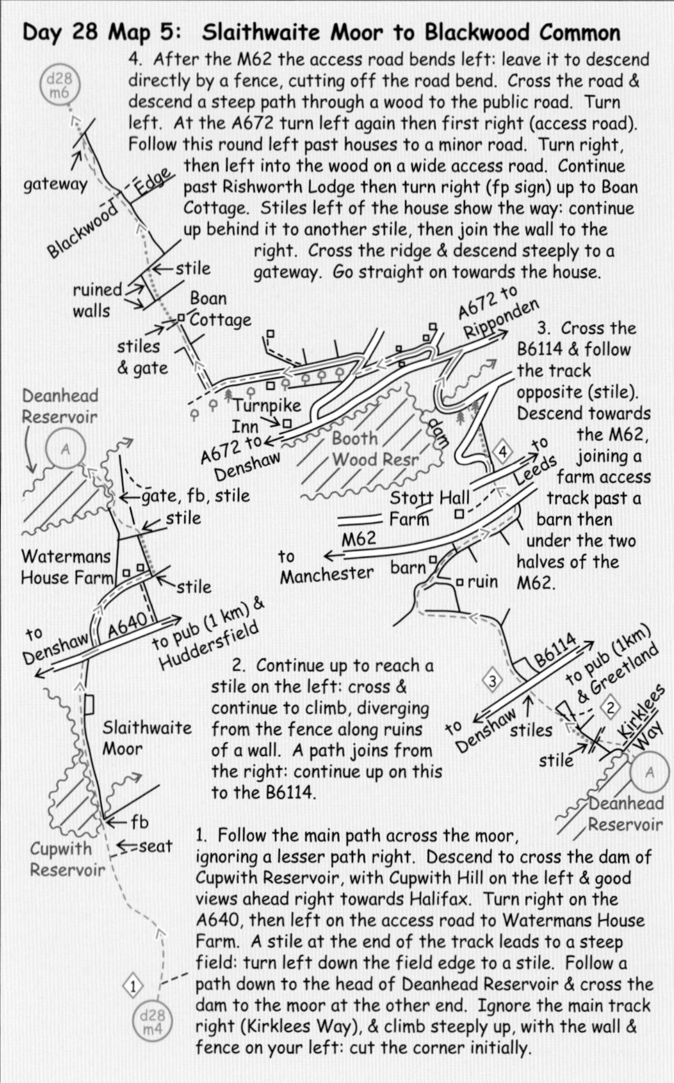

Day 28 Map 5: Slaithwaite Moor to Blackwood Common
4. After the M62 the access road bends left: leave it to descend directly by a fence, cutting off the road bend. Cross the road & descend a steep path through a wood to the public road. Turn left. At the A672 turn left again then first right (access road). Follow this round left past houses to a minor road. Turn right, then left into the wood on a wide access road. Continue past Rishworth Lodge then turn right (fp sign) up to Boan Cottage. Stiles left of the house show the way: continue up behind it to another stile, then join the wall to the right. Cross the ridge & descend steeply to a gateway. Go straight on towards the house.
d28 m6
gateway
Blackwood Edge
stile
ruined walls
Boan Cottage
stiles & gate
A672 to Ripponden
3. Cross the B6114 & follow the track opposite (stile). Descend towards the M62, joining a farm access track past a barn then under the two halves of the M62.
Deanhead Reservoir
Turnpike Inn
A672 to Denshaw
Booth Wood Resr
dam
4
to Leeds
gate, fb, stile
stile
Stott Hall Farm
Watermans House Farm
stile
M62
to Manchester
barn
ruin
to Denshaw
A640
to pub (1 km) & Huddersfield
2. Continue up to reach a stile on the left: cross & continue to climb, diverging from the fence along ruins of a wall. A path joins from the right: continue up on this to the B6114.
3
B6114
to pub (1km) & Greetland
2
to Denshaw
stiles
stile
Kirklees Way
Slaithwaite Moor
A
Deanhead Reservoir
fb
Cupwith Reservoir
seat
1. Follow the main path across the moor, ignoring a lesser path right. Descend to cross the dam of Cupwith Reservoir, with Cupwith Hill on the left & good views ahead right towards Halifax. Turn right on the A640, then left on the access road to Watermans House Farm. A stile at the end of the track leads to a steep field: turn left down the field edge to a stile. Follow a path down to the head of Deanhead Reservoir & cross the dam to the moor at the other end. Ignore the main track right (Kirklees Way), & climb steeply up, with the wall & fence on your left: cut the corner initially.
1
d28 m4

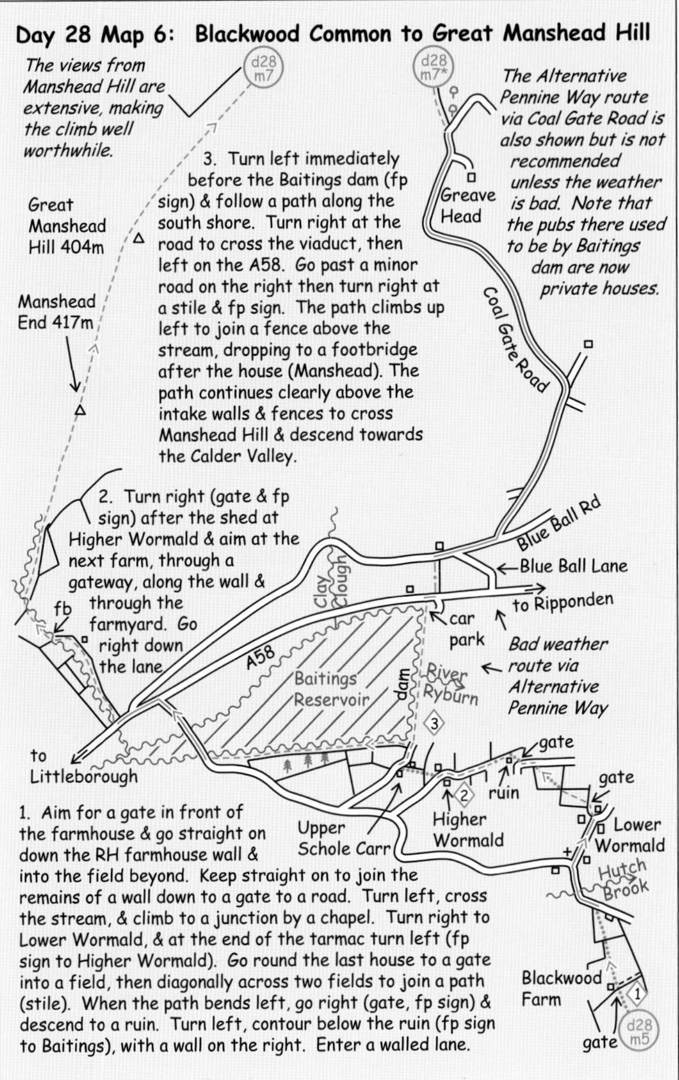

Day 28 Map 6: Blackwood Common to Great Manshead Hill
The views from Manshead Hill are extensive, making the climb well worthwhile.
d28 m7
d28 m7*
The Alternative Pennine Way route via Coal Gate Road is also shown but is not recommended unless the weather is bad. Note that the pubs there used to be by Baitings dam are now private houses.
3. Turn left immediately before the Baitings dam (fp sign) & follow a path along the south shore. Turn right at the road to cross the viaduct, then left on the A58. Go past a minor road on the right then turn right at a stile & fp sign. The path climbs up left to join a fence above the stream, dropping to a footbridge after the house (Manshead). The path continues clearly above the intake walls & fences to cross Manshead Hill & descend towards the Calder Valley.
Great Manshead Hill 404m
Greave Head
Manshead End 417m
Coal Gate Road
2. Turn right (gate & fp sign) after the shed at Higher Wormald & aim at the next farm, through a gateway, along the wall & through the farmyard. Go right down the lane
Blue Ball Rd
Blue Ball Lane
to Ripponden
Clay Clough
fb
car park
Bad weather route via Alternative Pennine Way
A58
Baitings Reservoir
dam
River Ryburn
3
to Littleborough
gate
gate
ruin
2
Higher Wormald
Upper Schole Carr
Lower Wormald
Hutch Brook
1. Aim for a gate in front of the farmhouse & go straight on down the RH farmhouse wall & into the field beyond. Keep straight on to join the remains of a wall down to a gate to a road. Turn left, cross the stream, & climb to a junction by a chapel. Turn right to Lower Wormald, & at the end of the tarmac turn left (fp sign to Higher Wormald). Go round the last house to a gate into a field, then diagonally across two fields to join a path (stile). When the path bends left, go right (gate, fp sign) & descend to a ruin. Turn left, contour below the ruin (fp sign to Baitings), with a wall on the right. Enter a walled lane.
Blackwood Farm
1
gate
d28 m5

Day 28 Map 7: Great Manshead Hill to Cragg Vale

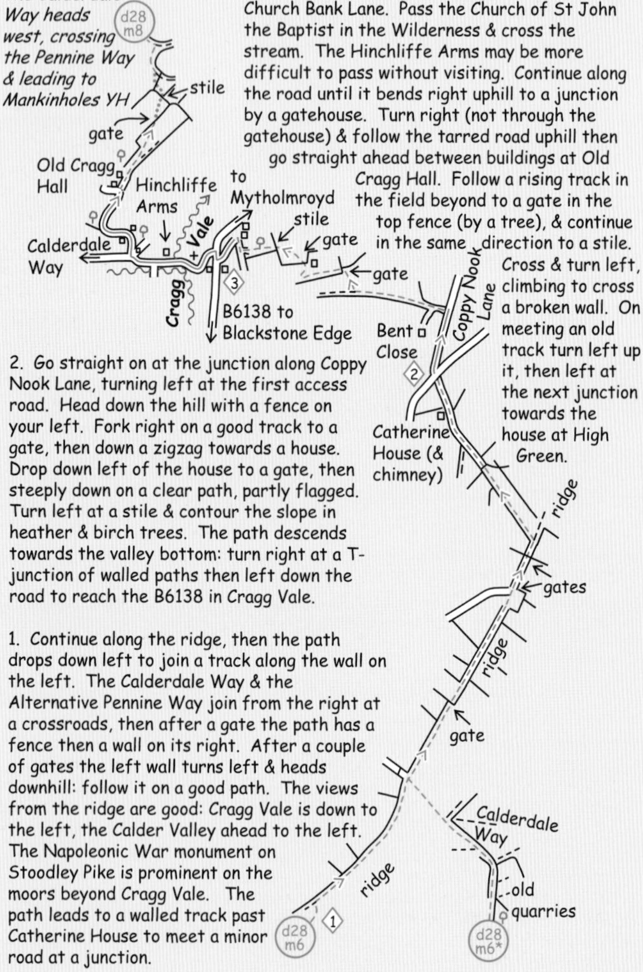

The Calderdale Way heads west, crossing the Pennine Way & leading to Mankinholes YH

3. Turn right on the B6138 then sharp left down Church Bank Lane. Pass the Church of St John the Baptist in the Wilderness & cross the stream. The Hinchliffe Arms may be more difficult to pass without visiting. Continue along the road until it bends right uphill to a junction by a gatehouse. Turn right (not through the gatehouse) & follow the tarred road uphill then go straight ahead between buildings at Old Cragg Hall. Follow a rising track in the field beyond to a gate in the top fence (by a tree), & continue in the same direction to a stile. Cross & turn left, climbing to cross a broken wall. On meeting an old track turn left up it, then left at the next junction towards the house at High Green.

2. Go straight on at the junction along Coppy Nook Lane, turning left at the first access road. Head down the hill with a fence on your left. Fork right on a good track to a gate, then down a zigzag towards a house. Drop down left of the house to a gate, then steeply down on a clear path, partly flagged. Turn left at a stile & contour the slope in heather & birch trees. The path descends towards the valley bottom: turn right at a T-junction of walled paths then left down the road to reach the B6138 in Cragg Vale.

1. Continue along the ridge, then the path drops down left to join a track along the wall on the left. The Calderdale Way & the Alternative Pennine Way join from the right at a crossroads, then after a gate the path has a fence then a wall on its right. After a couple of gates the left wall turns left & heads downhill: follow it on a good path. The views from the ridge are good: Cragg Vale is down to the left, the Calder Valley ahead to the left. The Napoleonic War monument on Stoodley Pike is prominent on the moors beyond Cragg Vale. The path leads to a walled track past Catherine House to meet a minor road at a junction.

Day 28 Map 8: Cragg Vale to Hebden Bridge

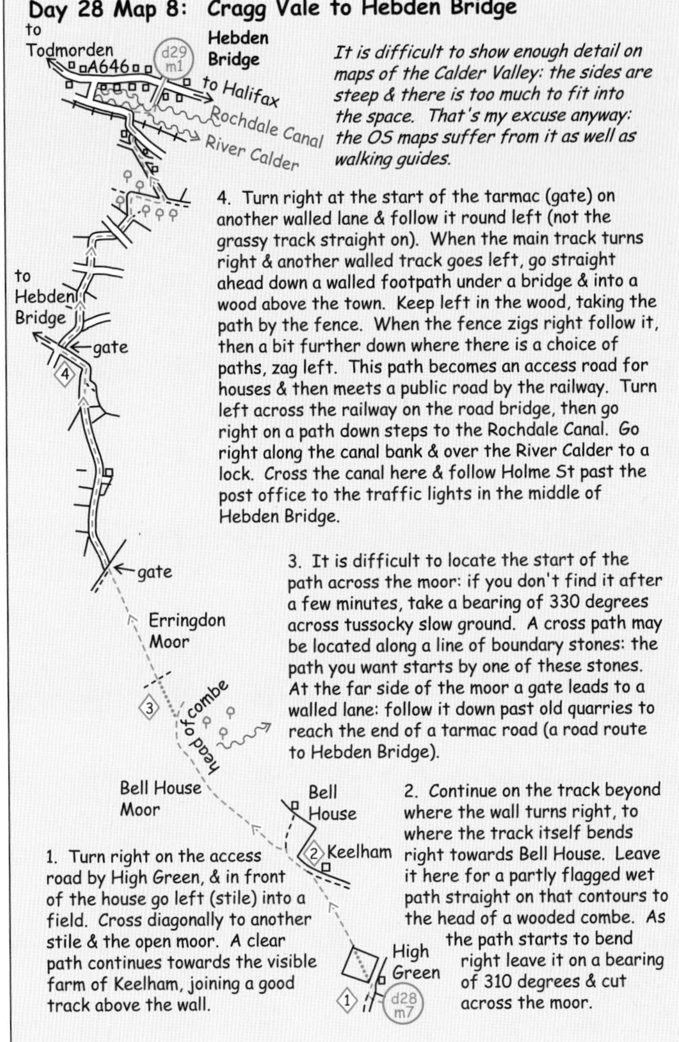

It is difficult to show enough detail on maps of the Calder Valley: the sides are steep & there is too much to fit into the space. That's my excuse anyway: the OS maps suffer from it as well as walking guides.

4. Turn right at the start of the tarmac (gate) on another walled lane & follow it round left (not the grassy track straight on). When the main track turns right & another walled track goes left, go straight ahead down a walled footpath under a bridge & into a wood above the town. Keep left in the wood, taking the path by the fence. When the fence zigs right follow it, then a bit further down where there is a choice of paths, zag left. This path becomes an access road for houses & then meets a public road by the railway. Turn left across the railway on the road bridge, then go right on a path down steps to the Rochdale Canal. Go right along the canal bank & over the River Calder to a lock. Cross the canal here & follow Holme St past the post office to the traffic lights in the middle of Hebden Bridge.

3. It is difficult to locate the start of the path across the moor: if you don't find it after a few minutes, take a bearing of 330 degrees across tussocky slow ground. A cross path may be located along a line of boundary stones: the path you want starts by one of these stones. At the far side of the moor a gate leads to a walled lane: follow it down past old quarries to reach the end of a tarmac road (a road route to Hebden Bridge).

2. Continue on the track beyond where the wall turns right, to where the track itself bends right towards Bell House. Leave it here for a partly flagged wet path straight on that contours to the head of a wooded combe. As the path starts to bend right leave it on a bearing of 310 degrees & cut across the moor.

1. Turn right on the access road by High Green, & in front of the house go left (stile) into a field. Cross diagonally to another stile & the open moor. A clear path continues towards the visible farm of Keelham, joining a good track above the wall.

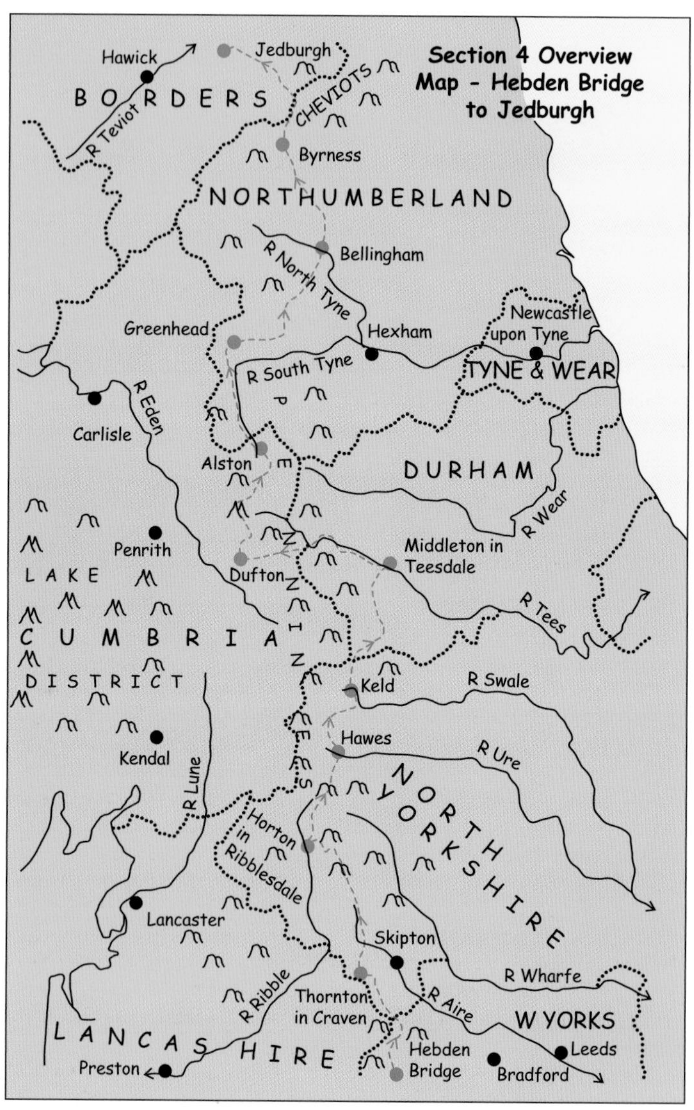
Section 4 Overview
Map - Hebden Bridge
to Jedburgh
Hawick
Jedburgh
BORDERS
R Teviot
CHEVIOTS
Byrness
NORTHUMBERLAND
Bellingham
R North Tyne
Greenhead
Hexham
Newcastle upon Tyne
TYNE & WEAR
R South Tyne
Carlisle
R Eden
Alston
DURHAM
R Wear
Penrith
Middleton in Teesdale
Dufton
LAKE
CUMBRIA
DISTRICT
PENNINES
R Tees
Keld
R Swale
Hawes
R Ure
Kendal
R Lune
NORTH YORKSHIRE
Horton in Ribblesdale
Lancaster
Skipton
R Wharfe
R Ribble
Thornton in Craven
R Aire
W YORKS
LANCASHIRE
Hebden Bridge
Bradford
Leeds
Preston

SECTION 4

The Pennines and Cheviots: Hebden Bridge to Jedburgh

Distance	330km (205 miles)
Road Walking	10%. This is not much for a long-distance footpath, reflecting the success of the Pennine Way in avoiding roads. The longest road stretches are along Roman Dere Street in Scotland on Day 39, the last day of this section.
Days	11 (Main Schedule), or 14 (Alternative Schedule)
Maps and Guides	Hebden Bridge to Widdop (Holme Ends): this guide, strip maps Day 29 Map 1 and Map 2 Widdop (Holme Ends) to Chew Green: Pennine Way guide Chew Green to Jedburgh: this guide, strip maps Day 39 Map 1 and Map 2

Note The map scale changes from 1:25000 to 1:50000 from Chew Green.

Just beyond Hebden Bridge the Trail joins the Pennine Way, and follows it for about 310km (190 miles) along the hills that form the spine of the north of England. The Pennine Way was the first official long-distance path in the UK, opened in 1965. These days it is not as popular as Wainwright's Coast to Coast Walk or the West Highland Way, but you will still meet many fellow walkers, and there is a good, clear path almost all the way.

The terrain is varied and nearly all very good to walk. The Yorkshire Dales are beautiful, with a contrast between the bleaker gritstone moorland and the green limestone areas. This is drystone wall country, and the valleys are intricately laid out with ancient small fields whose boundaries have been unchanged for centuries.

There is a lot of high moorland, and the weather up there can be poor – rain, mist and wind are normal. On the other hand, when the sun shines, nearly every day is magnificent. As you go further north, the scale of the scenery becomes bigger – the hills sprawl more and the villages are sparser, until you meet the fascinating remains of Hadrian's Wall, by far the most impressive Roman relic in Britain.

Continuing north the moors are even bleaker, habitation scarce, and much of what was moorland has been planted with pines to form the vast Kielder Forest.

Malham village, Day 30

In the Cheviot Hills, at the Scottish border, the Pennine Way crosses the Roman road Dere Street, and here the Trail leaves the Pennine Way and follows Dere Street into Scotland, and out of the hills to the border town of Jedburgh, and the end of Section 4.

This section is nearly all on the eastern side of the main watershed. Only twice, for overnight stops in Horton and Dufton, does the route cross to the western side.

Maps

1:25000 Explorer maps

21 South Pennines (later two-sided editions)
2 Yorkshire Dales–Southern & Western Areas
30 Yorkshire Dales – Northern & Central Areas
31 North Pennines –Teesdale & Weardale

1:50000 Landranger maps

103 Blackburn & Burnley
98 Wensleydale & Upper Wharfdale
91 Appleby-in-Westmorland
86 Haltwhistle
80 Cheviot Hills

Maps

1:25000 Explorer maps	**1:50000 Landranger maps**
43 Hadrian's Wall	74 Kelso & Coldstream
42 Kielder Water	
16 Cheviot Hills	

Guidebook

The Pennine Way by Martin Collins, Cicerone, 2nd edition, 2003
This is another good Cicerone guide, including a strip of 1:50000 OS mapping.

Recommendation

Get a Pennine Way guide, both accommodation guides (see below) and either set of maps. (Don't rely on guidebook strip maps alone on the Pennine Way – you need a set of maps to be safe in many areas.) There is little advantage in taking 1:25000 maps rather than 1:50000, unless you are doing without a guidebook altogether. The path is usually clear, and generally well waymarked in more complex valley farmland.

To Help You on Your Way

Accommodation

Since virtually all this section is on the Pennine Way, you can take advantage of other people's work in compiling accommodation lists. The Pennine Way Association publishes a booklet and also has information on its website www.pennineway.demon.co.uk. There is also an 'official' accommodation guide available from some TICs or via www.nationaltrail.co.uk. It's worth getting hold of both these guides. Hebden Bridge and Jedburgh aren't on the Pennine Way, so you may need these TICs.

Visitor and Canal Centre, New Road, Hebden Bridge, tel 01422 843831 www.pennineyorkshire.co.uk

Murrays Green, Jedburgh, tel 0870 608 0404 www.visitscottishborders.com

Equipment Shops

Day 30 Cove Centre, Wallbridge Mill, Cove Road, Malham, tel 01729 830432
Day 30 Pen-y-Ghent Café & Outdoor Shop, Horton in Ribblesdale, tel 01729 860333
Day 31 Three Peaks Outdoor Leisure, Riverside House, Bridge End, Hawes, tel 01969 667443
Day 31 Stewart R Cunningham Outdoor Centre, Market Place, Hawes, tel 01969 667595
Day 33 JE & V Winter, 7 Horsemarket, Middleton-in-Teesdale, tel 01833 640346
Day 35 Hi-Pennine Outdoor Shop, Market Square, Alston, tel 01434 381389
Day 39 Sanford's, 6–8 Canongate, Jedburgh, tel 01835 863019

Alternative Routes

The Pennine Way and the Alternative Pennine Way

As described at the beginning of Section 3, you can follow the Pennine Way all the way to its end at Kirk Yetholm, in the Scottish borders, if you wish, and from here the waymarked St Cuthbert's Way allows you to rejoin the main route of the Trail near Jedburgh.

From Day 30 to Day 38 the Trail follows the Pennine Way, but as the Alternative Pennine Way and the Pennine Way cross and approach each other frequently, there are also many points where you can switch between the two. For instance, if you decide to follow the APW, it could still be tempting to climb Cross Fell, which is the highest point in the Pennines, and on the Pennine Way.

DAY 29

Clog Country

Hebden Bridge to Thornton in Craven (36km, 22 miles)

Once Hebden Bridge has been left behind, the day follows side valleys, moorland and pasture up the western edge of the Yorkshire hills.

For the first 6km (4 miles) from Hebden Bridge the Trail follows the deep, wooded valley of Hebden Dale, an area known locally as Hardcastle Crags, although there aren't actually many crags (Day 29 Map 1). It is a lovely valley to walk along (although it gets busy on sunny weekends), and has been a local recreation area for generations. Much of it is owned by the National Trust. (The Pennine Way avoids Hardcastle Crags, presumably for fear of adding to the Sunday crowds.)

On emerging from the woods below Blake Dean (Day 29 Map 2), the Trail joins the Pennine Way on the reservoir track at Holme Ends, close to the Pack Horse Inn, an old and remote pub the locals call the Ridge (recommended).

The strip maps in this guide stop here for the time being, and you will need a Pennine Way guidebook as far as the Scottish border, just beyond Byrness on Day 39.

From Holme Ends the reservoir access road takes you up to the Walshaw Dean reservoirs, then a good path through heather crosses the moor over Dean Stones Edge to the Worth valley above Keighley – this is Bronte country. (The Old Silent Inn outside Stanbury is 1km off-route to the east, on Hob Lane in the Worth valley.)

From the Worth valley the Pennine Way climbs up onto Ickornshaw Moor, crossing into North Yorkshire near Wolf Stones. (Although the Trail doesn't enter Lancashire at all, you are only about 300m from it here – the Lancashire–Yorkshire border crosses Wolf Stones, as does the main watershed.)

Ickornshaw Moor is a featureless mound of moorland, and was one of the last parts of the Pennine Way along which a visible path was established. The descent from the moor to Cowling and Ickornshaw marks the end of the best part of the day. Although the farmland that follows is mainly pasture, and pleasant enough, it isn't a patch on Hardcastle Crags or the moors.

Cowling has accommodation, shops, pubs and takeaways, all along the main road to the right. Further along, at the end of the day, Thornton in Craven has limited accommodation (two bed and breakfasts), and there is bed and breakfast and camping at East Marton 3km (2 miles) further on. There is also a good youth hostel at Earby, 2km south of Thornton.

DAY 30

Airedale and Pen-y-Ghent

Thornton in Craven to Horton in Ribblesdale (41km, 25 miles)

This is a day of two halves, all but the start of it in the Yorkshire Dales National Park.

The first part potters merrily from Thornton in Craven up the River Aire to its source in the limestone playground of Malham. On the way you go through the pretty village of Gargrave, which has a cash machine and shops. The day gradually gets better and better as the limestone bones of the land come closer and closer to the surface, until around Malham they are exposed completely. Streams disappear and reappear, the vegetation is lush, and the rocks themselves break out, most spectacularly at the cliff of Malham Cove (on route) and the gorge of Goredale Scar (just off-route).

A59 bridge, Leeds & Liverpool Canal, East Marton

Pen-y-ghent

Malham is a wonderful place, but gets very busy on summer weekends. If you are there midweek and don't already know the area, break here overnight and spend some time exploring. There is a large youth hostel and two pubs, including the Lister Arms (accommodation, recommended), which in earlier days memorably discouraged walkers with a 'no boots, no stockinged feet' sign on the door. Also highly recommended is Beck Hall, a traditional tearoom by the stream.

The second half of the day, from Malham, climbs up above Malham Cove, across bare limestone pavements up to Malham Tarn, then on to the hills of Fountains Fell and Pen-y-Ghent. The first part is classic limestone country – spectacular stuff – walking across huge limestone blocks, round a dry waterfall, and past a stream that disappears under a wall. Malham Tarn is bleak by comparison, although the planted estate around Malham Tarn House makes up for this a bit.

There's no mercy after this, though. Fountains Fell is high (650m), big and bleak, and Pen-y-Ghent is even higher (694m), although a lot less extensive and much more interesting to climb. Pen-y-Ghent is also avoidable if you need a break – a path leads straight down into Horton from GR836728 on the shoulder of Pen-y-Ghent. Walking Land's End to John O'Groats entitles you to miss out bits of the Pennine Way in an emergency, although it would be a pity to miss out Pen-y-Ghent.

Horton in Ribblesdale is a small village largely dependent on walkers and cavers for its living. There are two pubs, and the Golden Lion (recommended) has a bunkhouse. The Pen-y-Ghent café acts as a TIC for walkers, and there are also bed and breakfasts and a good campsite.

DAY 31

Ribblesdale and Cam High Road

Horton in Ribblesdale to Hawes (21km, 13 miles)

This is a relatively short day, mainly on good tracks with easy gradients, and tomorrow is even shorter, so if you are going particularly well you could consider running the two days into one.

A cart track leads north out of Horton, gradually climbing up the east side of Ribblesdale, past a number of potholes. The track climbs to the summit of a pass over to Langstrothdale, where the Pennine Way and our Trail leave it to cut across west and join an old packhorse road bound for Hawes.

Ten minutes later you should pause briefly to take in the fact that, as you reach Old Ing farm, you have completed half your journey. This is the midpoint of the End to End Trail, and despite the fact that you'd have been in John O'Groats by now had you walked a direct route, you'll have to admit that the scenery here is probably rather better than that 18km underneath the Isle of Man.

Continuing north, the Pennine Way crosses Ling Gill and climbs onto Cam Fell to join Cam High Road for about 1500m (Cam High Road is a Roman road that rises to 588m). It then takes a track forking left off Cam High Road along a ridge to the north, and descends to Wensleydale and the small town of Hawes.

Hawes is a traditional Dales town, still acting as the focal point for a wide community (as well as tourists). It is a relaxing place to stop and has shops and banks.

There is plenty of accommodation, including a youth hostel, and a campsite nearby. (The local Wensleydale cheese is very good – buy some to help boost the local economy.)

DAY 32

Great Shunner Fell and Swaledale

Hawes to Keld (20km, 12 miles)

Today is really all about crossing Great Shunner Fell. This is a huge area of high moorland, and the Pennine Way crosses its summit, reaching your highest point so far at 716m. (Great Shunner Fell is just a few metres higher than is reached by the Offa's Dyke Path in the Black Mountains on Day 18.)

The climb starts a couple of kilometres from Hawes and is pretty unremitting. You climb higher and higher out of Wensleydale along a long, exposed ridge to the top of the fell, and the descent to the village of Thwaite is almost as long.

Thwaite is in Swaledale, a little way to the west of the main valley, and rather than follow Thwaite Beck east to the Swale, then follow the river upstream to Keld, the Pennine Way follows a far superior course, high above the river. This means a stiff climb up from Thwaite, but the views down to and across the valley bottom between here and Keld more than justify the effort. The walking is good as well, along terraces high on the steep valley side.

In due course the path descends gradually to meet the Swale at the hamlet of Keld – the nearest thing to a major crossroads in British long-distance walking. Here the Pennine Way crosses Wainwright's Coast to Coast Walk, and in summer the population of Keld seems to be made up mainly of long-distance walkers. As you near Keld, the waterfalls of Kisdon Force are below to your right, and are well worth the short diversion.

Keld is a lovely spot, unspoilt despite the walkers, who have in fact probably contributed a lot to keeping the old stone buildings in active use. There is plenty of accommodation here for such a small village, including a campsite (which is

Kisdon Force, Keld

notorious for midges, so beware). There is no pub, but the campsite shop sells beer and wine.

DAY 33

The Durham Moors

Keld to Middleton-in-Teesdale (33km, 21 miles)

It's farewell to the Yorkshire Dales, and hello to wet feet in all probability. It's moorland all day, and the first half is famously wet underfoot, not having (as yet) been paved with stone flags like the wet parts of the southern Pennine Way.

The first section as far as the Tan Hill Inn runs parallel to a road, so there is an alternative if needed. The Tan Hill Inn is the highest pub in

England, and is only there because there used to be a mining industry here, many traces of which can still be seen.

At Tan Hill the Pennine Way finally leaves the Yorkshire Dales National Park, and North Yorkshire, and enters Durham. Sodden Sleightholme Moor can also be avoided, if necessary, by following the road east from Tan Hill then forking left on the Sleightholme Moor Road.

The Trail meets a road at Sleightholme Farm, then crosses the River Greta and the A66 Penrith to Scotch Corner trunk road. It's still pretty remote moorland, though, and this is followed by another moorland crossing to Baldersdale. This section is a bit dryer underfoot than earlier in the day, and a bit more enjoyable. (Baldersdale itself has farms, reservoirs, a bed and breakfast, and a bunkhouse.)

There are two more climbs and descents to complete the day. As for Day 28 (around Huddersfield) the valleys run east–west across the route, so it's up out of Baldersdale, down into Lunedale, up again, then back down to Teesdale and the quiet town of Middleton.

Middleton has shops, pubs and accommodation, and there is a campsite on the right before you cross the river to the town. There's also a bunkhouse and campsite by the river at Low Way Farm, 4km (2½ miles) further up the valley (on route), with the excellent Strathmore Arms close by.

DAY 34

Upper Teesdale and High Cup

Middleton-in-Teesdale to Dufton (32km, 20 miles)

Admittedly we are going in the wrong direction all day, but believe me it's worth it – this is one of the best days of the whole Trail, and arguably the very best day on the Pennine Way.

It starts with a riverside walk along the River Tees – in spring and early summer there are wild flowers everywhere along here, including globe flowers, early purple orchids and fairy foxgloves. There also are waterfalls – Low Force and High

Low Force, River Tees

Force, the latter being spectacular in wet weather – and a youth hostel, a pub and a bed and breakfast at Langdon Beck, if you want to make an overnight stop hereabouts.

Continuing up the river heading west, the rural and pastoral gradually give way to upland scenery – look out for spring gentians in the turf. Just before reaching Cauldron Snout waterfall there is a short, difficult section across boulders, and this is a good excuse for a lunch stop by the waterfall, where the Tees tumbles down from Cow Green Reservoir.

The Trail leaves Durham for Cumbria as it crosses the river above the waterfall. Beyond here, past remote Birkdale Farm, it's back to the moors, climbing to nearly 600m above and beside Maize Beck.

The main watershed is eventually reached on a wide, flat rocky plateau, then suddenly you become aware of the huge U-shaped valley scooped out of the hillside ahead. This is High Cup, about 300m deep, 3km (2 miles) long, and with very steep sides topped off with a line of crags. If it is clear enough there is a terrific view across the Vale of Eden to the Lake District. This is a place to stop for a while and enjoy just being there. Once you can drag yourself away, an easy descent into Dufton follows.

Dufton is a small, unspoilt village on the edge of the wide Vale of Eden, clustering around a wide, tree-lined main-street-cum-green. It has a youth hostel, bed

High Cup

and breakfasts, campsites, a very good village shop and the excellent Stag Inn. The village economy is largely dependent on walkers, so spend your money here. (The YHA threatened to close the youth hostel rather than spend money on it, but it was reprieved with the aid of a local action committee and generous grants.)

DAY 35

Cross Fell

Dufton to Alston (31km, 19 miles)

Physically this is the high point of the Trail. The Pennine Way crosses the summit of Cross Fell, which at 893m is the highest point on the Pennine Way as well as the End to End Trail, and the highest mountain in England outside the Lake District.

In good weather this is a tremendous day, particularly the ascents, but if the weather is poor it could also be the psychological low point of your walk – Cross Fell is notorious for bad weather and strong winds.

Dufton

It is also big and remote, and can feel very bleak and exposed. Unlike most of the Pennine Way, there isn't a clear path all the way, and **you should not attempt this section in bad weather unless you know how to navigate by map and compass**.

The climb up from Dufton is steady and hard work. Gradually you haul your way up to Green Fell (800m), then Great Dun Fell (848m) (which has an ugly radar station on its summit), then across bleak, pathless terrain to Little Dun Fell (842m), and then up to Cross Fell. A short descent leads to an old track that heads eventually down past relics of old mining activity to Garrigill and the River South Tyne.

Garrigill is a quiet little village with a shop/post office and a pub, which may or may not be open when you expect it to be.

The last stretch follows the river north to Alston, an easy riverside stroll, but not as memorable as yesterday morning's walk up the Tees.

Alston is another unspoilt small town you don't want to leave. It has banks, shops, bed and breakfasts, a campsite, a bunkhouse and a youth hostel.

DAY 36

The South Tyne

Alston to Greenhead (26km, 16 miles)

This is a fairly easy day, not too long and not particularly hilly. Shortly after leaving Alston a footbridge across Gilderdale Burn takes you out of Cumbria and into Northumberland, the most northerly English county.

For most of the day the Pennine Way follows the River South Tyne northwards, mainly along the hillside on the west side of the valley, and briefly along the riverbank on the approach to Slaggyford – this bit is particularly good. (The Kirkstyle Inn is 5 minutes off-route due east from Burnstones, 2km (1½ miles) beyond Slaggyford.)

Soon after this, the Maiden Way is joined, an old Roman road heading for a fort near Greenhead, although the Pennine Way reaches Greenhead by a slightly more circuitous route, abandoning the Maiden Way for some featureless moors to the west. Here there is a rare opportunity to lose the Pennine Way on the descent, as the path disappears in places.

The Pennine Way doesn't go through Greenhead village, but an invisible footpath leads there across fields, from GR653644, where the Pennine Way turns sharp left. Get out your compass if you want to follow this footpath to Greenhead. (Walking along the A69 is best avoided, as it is a fast and busy trunk road connecting Carlisle and Newcastle.)

Greenhead is a small village with a range of accommodation in the village and nearby, including a campsite, a camping barn and the Greenhead Hotel. The hotel is largely a locals' haunt, but serves food and is welcoming to visitors. A hostel in the village has been sold by the YHA, but may re-open under new ownership.

DAY 37

Hadrian's Wall and Wark Forest

Greenhead to Bellingham (34km, 21 miles)

The Pennine Way changes direction at Greenhead to follow Hadrian's Wall eastwards. Even without the Roman wall this would be an excellent walk, as it follows the crests of a series of rock ridges. The views are good and the walking interesting, although it's a bit of a switchback, and when you add the Roman remains, the result is one of the best bits of the whole Trail.

Hadrian's Wall is well preserved along a lot of this stretch due to its remoteness – less of the stone has been taken for building. There are a number of milecastles along the part of Hadrian's Wall followed by the Pennine Way, and a lot of major ditch-work is obvious.

Hadrian's Wall was built by the Roman Emperor Hadrian around 120AD, and he visited Britain to oversee its construction. The objective was to protect the Roman Empire from marauding invaders from the north, and it was the high-water mark of the empire. The Romans had no control north of this line for any significant length of time, and it marked the boundary of the empire for nearly 300 years.

12km (8 miles) from Greenhead, and just off-route to the south, are the Twice Brewed Inn (recommended) and the Once Brewed youth hostel. The youth hostel is large and well equipped, but tends to be fully booked by school field parties. There is a campsite and bunkhouse close by, and there are bed and breakfasts not far away.

After following the wall a little further, the Pennine Way turns left at Cuddy's Crags to head north, and although the rest of the day is pleasant enough, it can't compete with Hadrian and his wall.

First there is a soggy section of rough pasture between Greenlee and Broomhead loughs, then the rest of the day follows pretty nondescript low moorland, three sections of which are planted with conifers. This is Wark Forest, part of the huge Kielder Forest Park.

Milecastle, Hadrian's Wall

There is a bunkhouse at Shitlington Crag Farm (GR829808), otherwise all the accommodation is in the small and quiet town of Bellingham, by the River North Tyne. Bellingham has campsites, bed and breakfasts, a bunkhouse, shops, a post office and a couple of banks.

DAY 38

Northumberland Moors and Kielder Forest

Bellingham to Byrness (24km, 15 miles)

This is a day of featureless, boggy moorland followed by a trudge on forestry roads. In bad weather it feels like typical Pennnine Way purgatory, and you may start wondering what you've done to deserve it.

The moors north of Bellingham are bleak. The Pennine Way gradually climbs up to around 370m across bog and heather, crossing the tops of Deer Play, Whitley Pike, Padon Hill and Brownrigg Head. All of these are wide, flat hills (the name 'Whitley Pike' giving entirely the wrong impression) and it's also wet underfoot in places.

Near Brownrigg Head the forestry is met again, and after following its edge for a while the Trail enters the trees of Kielder Forest – and that's it for scenery. The path joins a forestry road, and you'll see nothing but pine trees for the rest of the day.

The forestry road takes the Pennine Way down into Redesdale, then a riverside path heads up the valley to a campsite at Cottonshopeburnfoot. A bit further up the valley is the hamlet of Byrness on the A68 trunk road. Here there is a petrol station with an excellent café, and the Byrness Hotel also serves food and allows camping in its grounds.

DAY 39

The Cheviots and Dere Street

Byrness to Jedburgh (31km, 19 miles)

This is a significant day in your progress from End to End. It is the day you leave the Pennine Way, after following it for 10 days and 310km (190 miles), and also the day the Trail leaves England and enters Scotland. The journey will have a different feel from here on, the cultural and building traditions being quite distinct on the two sides of the border.

From Byrness to Chew Green continue to follow your Pennine Way guidebook. From Byrness there is a brutally steep climb up through the forestry to the top of Byrness Hill (427m). Just before the top of the hill the Pennine Way finally emerges from the pines and onto the Cheviot Hills, to follow a ridge north, over Houx Hill and Ravens Knowe (527m), but this is no rocky Lake District ridge – the Cheviots appear to be made of equal quantities of peat, water and bath sponges. Some of the wettest parts have now been paved, but some haven't, and it's still quite possible to end up in a morass up to your thighs (he said with feeling).

A little beyond Ravens Knowe the border fence is reached – go through the gate and you are in Scotland. The Pennine Way soon crosses back into Northumberland again at Chew Green (Day 39 Map 1), where there are the remains of a Roman army camp. Through the camp passes Dere Street, a Roman road older than Hadrian's Wall, and the Pennine Way follows Dere Street north for 2km (1½ miles) as far as another gate in the border fence at Black Halls, between Brownhart Law and Blackhall Hill, and this is where you finally leave the Pennine Way. (It stays on the English side of the fence, soon heading north-east, aiming for the Cheviot, and eventually descending into Scotland to end at the village of Kirk Yetholm.)

The Trail follows Dere Street to Jedburgh, instead, missing out most of the Cheviot peat bogs, so **put away your Pennine Way guidebook and turn to the strip map pages in this guide again**. (**Note** The strip maps are at a scale of 1:50000 from here on.)

Dere Street originally ran from York to the Forth near Edinburgh, via the fort at Trimontium near Melrose, and was built during the governorship of Agricola, who governed Roman Britain from AD79 to 83, 40 years before Hadrian built his wall. Agricola built the road as he advanced in AD81. This was a two-pronged advance, the other route being along the Western Way, which you cross above West Linton on Day 44.

Twise Hope and Streethouse Wood, Cheviot Hills

Pass through the gate at Black Halls and out of England for the last time on the Trail. Follow the path along the fence, and when it forks, keep right to follow the old road through another gate and round the back of Blackhall Hill (the other path ends up at the same place, but the line of Dere Street is clearly the right-hand path).

The track follows the crest of a saddle between White Hope and Twise Hope streams, then at the next saddle descends between Woden Law and Langside Law to the road junction at Tow Ford, and out of the Cheviot Hills. (On the descent the three hills – the Roman 'Trimontium' – of the Eildon Hills above Melrose can be seen straight ahead: the Trail crosses them at the end of tomorrow.)

From Tow Ford, Dere Street is a tarmac road for a short way, then at the next road junction becomes a path again, following a rough pasture ridge with good views of the Cheviots to the right and the Eildons to the left.

The track passes Cunzierton Hill (Day 39 Map 2), then meets a road just before Shibden Hill. Dere Street is covered in tarmac again for about 3km (2 miles), but luckily it's a quiet road. After that there is a delightful stretch of track up hill and down dale, in a dead straight line, some of it accompanied by a line of mature beech trees.

Dere Street doesn't visit Jedburgh, but the Trail does, so if you plan to do so also, you will need to turn left at the third road crossing (see strip map) and follow a minor road into town.

Jedburgh is one of the main border towns, and has all services and plenty of accommodation, as well as restaurants and takeaways. The town has plenty of history, and the ruins of the abbey are worth visiting if you have time. It was founded by King David I in 1118 for Augustinian canons, and destroyed by the Earl of Hertford in 1545.

'Historic Jedburgh I remember well because its castle looks so new that it might have been built by Marks and Spencer' – Theo Lang, *Cross Country*, 1948

The main alternative to staying in Jedburgh is to push on a bit further to Ancrum (2km off-route), where there is limited accommodation, but an excellent pub, the Cross Keys Inn, that serves food (although it doesn't open on weekday lunchtimes). There is also an excellent walkers' bed and breakfast at Lilliard, Harrietsfield (GR626263), which has its own access across a field from Dere Street.

Dere Street Roman Road, near Oxnam

Day 29 Map 1: Hebden Bridge to Gibson Mill

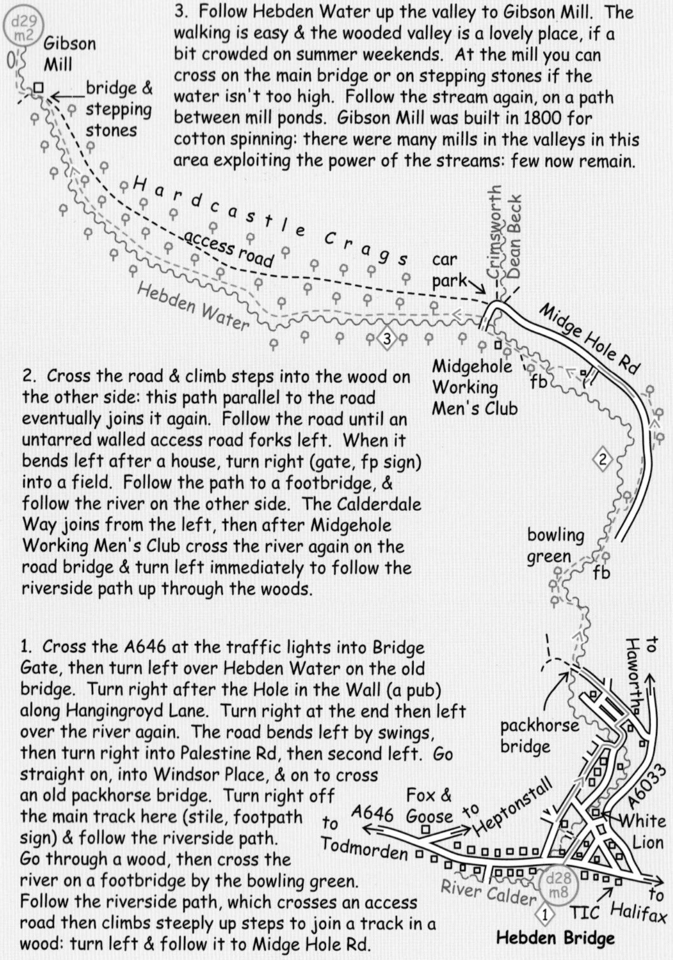

3. Follow Hebden Water up the valley to Gibson Mill. The walking is easy & the wooded valley is a lovely place, if a bit crowded on summer weekends. At the mill you can cross on the main bridge or on stepping stones if the water isn't too high. Follow the stream again, on a path between mill ponds. Gibson Mill was built in 1800 for cotton spinning: there were many mills in the valleys in this area exploiting the power of the streams: few now remain.

d29 m2
Gibson Mill
bridge & stepping stones
Hardcastle Crags
access road
Crimsworth Dean Beck
car park
Hebden Water
Midge Hole Rd
Midgehole Working Men's Club
fb

2. Cross the road & climb steps into the wood on the other side: this path parallel to the road eventually joins it again. Follow the road until an untarred walled access road forks left. When it bends left after a house, turn right (gate, fp sign) into a field. Follow the path to a footbridge, & follow the river on the other side. The Calderdale Way joins from the left, then after Midgehole Working Men's Club cross the river again on the road bridge & turn left immediately to follow the riverside path up through the woods.

bowling green
fb

1. Cross the A646 at the traffic lights into Bridge Gate, then turn left over Hebden Water on the old bridge. Turn right after the Hole in the Wall (a pub) along Hangingroyd Lane. Turn right at the end then left over the river again. The road bends left by swings, then turn right into Palestine Rd, then second left. Go straight on, into Windsor Place, & on to cross an old packhorse bridge. Turn right off the main track here (stile, footpath sign) & follow the riverside path. Go through a wood, then cross the river on a footbridge by the bowling green. Follow the riverside path, which crosses an access road then climbs steeply up steps to join a track in a wood: turn left & follow it to Midge Hole Rd.

to Haworth
packhorse bridge
A6033
Fox & Goose
A646 to Todmorden
to Heptonstall
White Lion
River Calder
d28 m8
TIC
to Halifax
Hebden Bridge

Day 29 Map 2: Gibson Mill to Widdop (Holme Ends)

2. After crossing the footbridge below Blake Dean you have a choice. To continue the direct route, turn right to follow the track up by Alcomden Water until it joins a reservoir access road. You can now put these maps away until you reach the Scottish border, & get out you Pennine Way guide, as the End to End Trail follows the Pennine Way for the rest of its time in England. If you are thirsty, & you have carefully planned to be here at a suitable time of day, climb very steeply up the bank ahead of you to reach the Widdop road on a hairpin bend. Follow the road up to reach the Packhorse Inn (known locally as the Ridge), which has accommodation & serves good food (but no chips). To regain your route afterwards continue along the road & turn right along the Pennine Way.

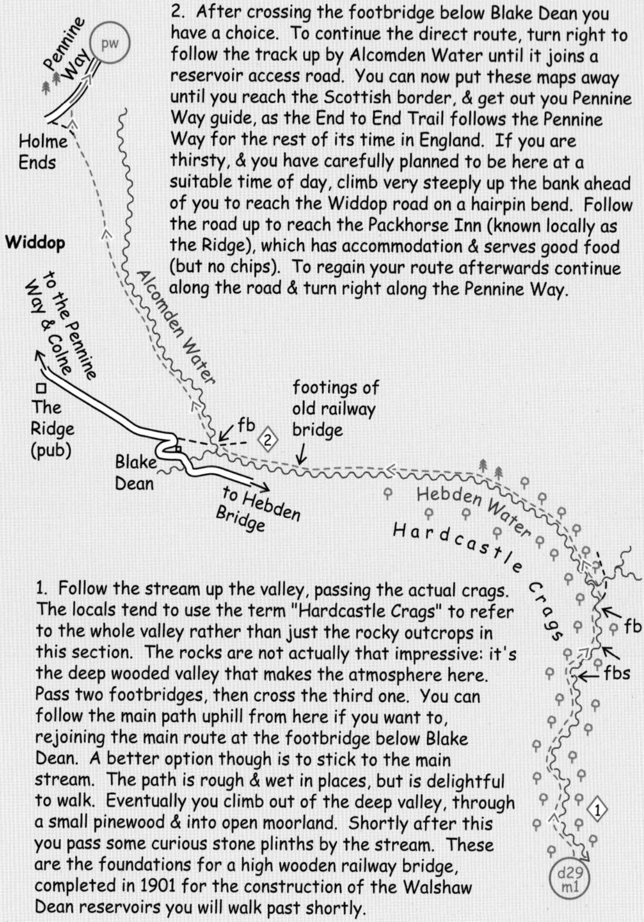

Pennine Way
pw
Holme Ends
Widdop
to the Pennine Way & Colne
Alcomden Water
The Ridge (pub)
Blake Dean
fb
2
footings of old railway bridge
to Hebden Bridge
Hebden Water
Hardcastle Crags
fb
fbs
1
d29 m1

1. Follow the stream up the valley, passing the actual crags. The locals tend to use the term "Hardcastle Crags" to refer to the whole valley rather than just the rocky outcrops in this section. The rocks are not actually that impressive: it's the deep wooded valley that makes the atmosphere here. Pass two footbridges, then cross the third one. You can follow the main path uphill from here if you want to, rejoining the main route at the footbridge below Blake Dean. A better option though is to stick to the main stream. The path is rough & wet in places, but is delightful to walk. Eventually you climb out of the deep valley, through a small pinewood & into open moorland. Shortly after this you pass some curious stone plinths by the stream. These are the foundations for a high wooden railway bridge, completed in 1901 for the construction of the Walshaw Dean reservoirs you will walk past shortly.

Day 39 Map 1: Chew Green to Cunzierton Hill

NOTE ON THE MAP SCALE
The Scottish map sections, of which this is the first, are mapped at a scale of 1:50000. Since the English & Welsh maps are 1:25000, it will take you twice as long to cross a map page from now on! The reason for the difference is that the Scottish sections have less complex route finding & fewer small fields.

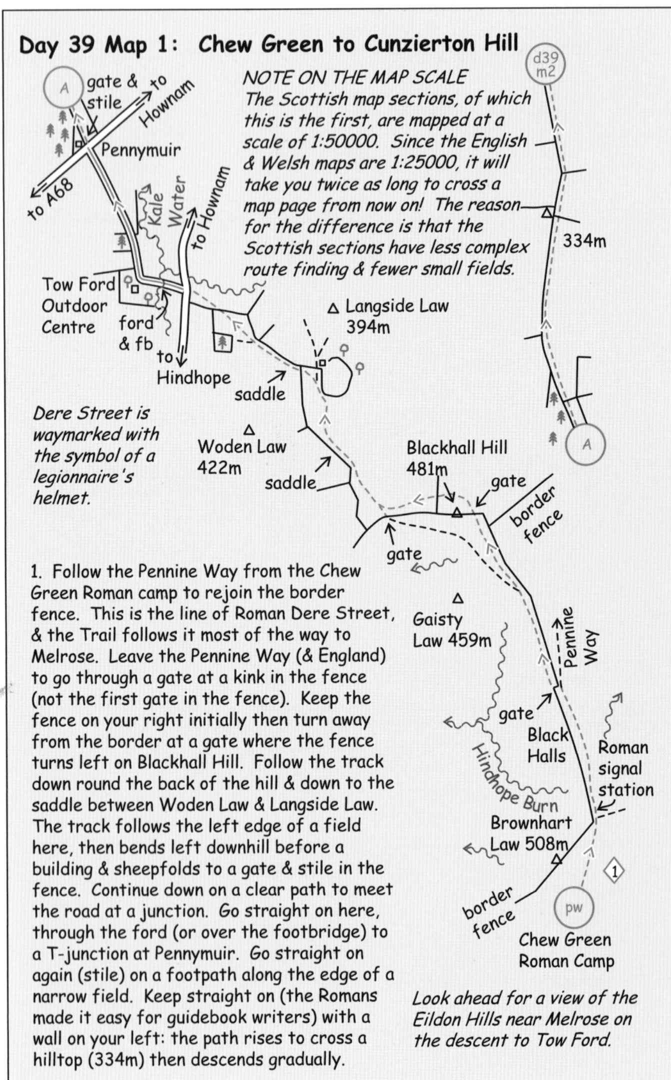

Dere Street is waymarked with the symbol of a legionnaire's helmet.

1. Follow the Pennine Way from the Chew Green Roman camp to rejoin the border fence. This is the line of Roman Dere Street, & the Trail follows it most of the way to Melrose. Leave the Pennine Way (& England) to go through a gate at a kink in the fence (not the first gate in the fence). Keep the fence on your right initially then turn away from the border at a gate where the fence turns left on Blackhall Hill. Follow the track down round the back of the hill & down to the saddle between Woden Law & Langside Law. The track follows the left edge of a field here, then bends left downhill before a building & sheepfolds to a gate & stile in the fence. Continue down on a clear path to meet the road at a junction. Go straight on here, through the ford (or over the footbridge) to a T-junction at Pennymuir. Go straight on again (stile) on a footpath along the edge of a narrow field. Keep straight on (the Romans made it easy for guidebook writers) with a wall on your left: the path rises to cross a hilltop (334m) then descends gradually.

Look ahead for a view of the Eildon Hills near Melrose on the descent to Tow Ford.

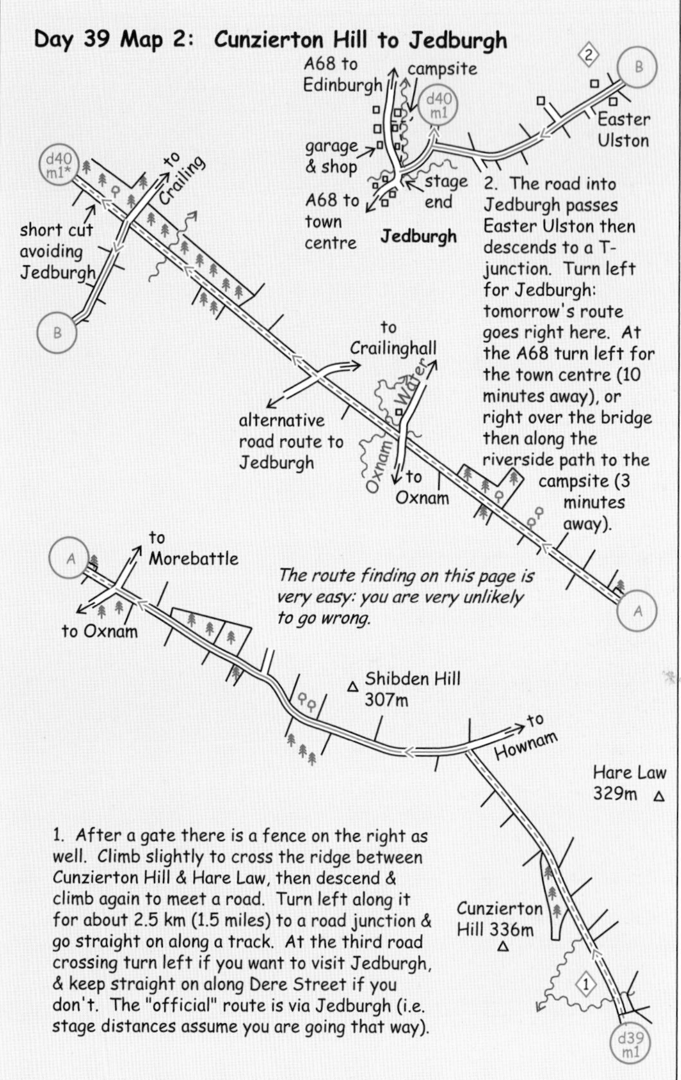
Day 39 Map 2: Cunzierton Hill to Jedburgh
A68 to Edinburgh
campsite
d40 m1
2
B
Easter Ulston
garage & shop
stage end
A68 to town centre
Jedburgh
2. The road into Jedburgh passes Easter Ulston then descends to a T-junction. Turn left for Jedburgh: tomorrow's route goes right here. At the A68 turn left for the town centre (10 minutes away), or right over the bridge then along the riverside path to the campsite (3 minutes away).
d40 m1*
to Crailing
short cut avoiding Jedburgh
B
to Crailinghall
Oxnam Water
alternative road route to Jedburgh
to Oxnam
A
to Morebattle
to Oxnam
A
The route finding on this page is very easy: you are very unlikely to go wrong.
Shibden Hill 307m
to Hownam
Hare Law 329m
Cunzierton Hill 336m
1
d39 m1
1. After a gate there is a fence on the right as well. Climb slightly to cross the ridge between Cunzierton Hill & Hare Law, then descend & climb again to meet a road. Turn left along it for about 2.5 km (1.5 miles) to a road junction & go straight on along a track. At the third road crossing turn left if you want to visit Jedburgh, & keep straight on along Dere Street if you don't. The "official" route is via Jedburgh (i.e. stage distances assume you are going that way).

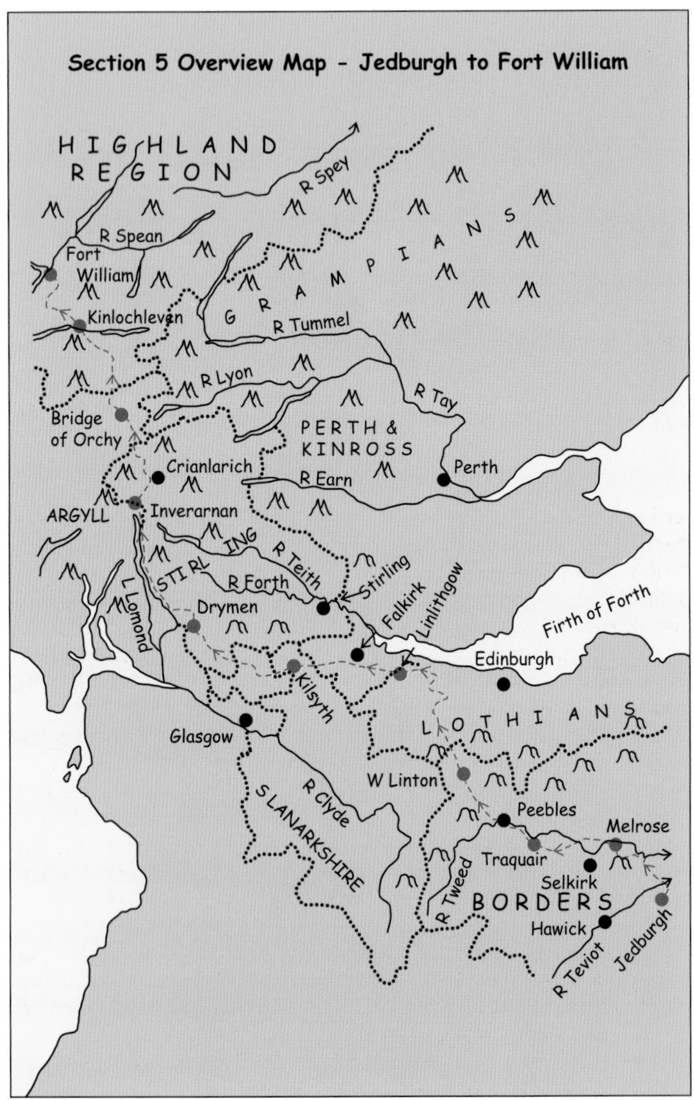
Section 5 Overview Map - Jedburgh to Fort William
HIGHLAND REGION
R Spey
R Spean
Fort William
GRAMPIANS
Kinlochleven
R Tummel
R Lyon
R Tay
Bridge of Orchy
PERTH & KINROSS
Crianlarich
R Earn
Perth
ARGYLL
Inverarnan
STIRLING
R Teith
R Forth
Stirling
Falkirk
Linlithgow
L Lomond
Drymen
Firth of Forth
Edinburgh
Kilsyth
Glasgow
LOTHIANS
W Linton
R Clyde
S LANARKSHIRE
Peebles
Melrose
Traquair
Selkirk
R Tweed
BORDERS
Hawick
Jedburgh
R Teviot

SECTION 5

Southern Scotland and the West Highland Way: Jedburgh to Fort William

Distance	332km (206 miles)
Road Walking	12%. The longest stretches of road are around Peebles and West Linton in the Tweed Valley, not (as you might have expected) in the Forth–Clyde lowlands.
Days	10 (Main Schedule), or 14 (Alternative Schedule)
Maps	Jedburgh to Dumgoyach: this guide, strip maps Day 40 Map 1 and Map 2 Dumgoyach to Fort William: West Highland Way guide

Section 5 takes the Trail from the Scottish border to Fort William in the heart of the Highlands. The general direction is northwest, initially parallel to or alongside the River Tweed, then crossing the rolling Southern Upland hills to descend to the Forth–Clyde lowlands. The lowlands have seen a lot of industrial development over the past 200 years, but the Trail misses the worst of this, threading its way between Edinburgh and Glasgow on canal towpaths and along a disused railway line to reach Loch Lomond, then follow the West Highland Way north into the mountains.

From Jedburgh to where it joins the West Highland Way, north of Glasgow, the Trail mainly follows documented routes, although only the first part is waymarked. On Day 40 St Cuthbert's Way follows Roman Dere Street into Tweeddale, then from Maxton follows the River Tweed itself to Newtown St Boswells, and then crosses the Eildon hills to end in Melrose. Here the Trail picks up the Southern Upland Way and heads westward for Day 41. The Southern Upland Way is a waymarked national trail, and it crosses the hills to Traquair, with the Tweed once more close by.

At Traquair you leave the Southern Upland Way and follow a road and forestry tracks up the valley to Peebles, from where the approximate line of an old drove road (recorded in 1755) is taken northwest over the Pentland Hills to meet the mid-Scotland sprawl at Mid Calder.

Here the character of the route changes – a patchwork of countryside and industrial Scotland lies between you and the West Highland Way. Walkers are not particularly provided for, and there are many signs of present and past industrial activity, although on the other hand there are plenty of small towns for restocking with provisions. From Mid Calder the Almondell Country Park takes you down the beautiful wooded Almond valley to meet the newly reopened Union Canal, linking Edinburgh to the Forth and Clyde Canal at Falkirk. The Union Canal towpath is followed to Falkirk, then the Forth and Clyde towpath on towards Glasgow. Until recently both these canals were in disrepair and closed to boats, but they have recently been reopened at a cost of £78 million, including building a unique new boatlift at Falkirk (the Falkirk Wheel) to link them once again.

You forsake the canals at Kirkintilloch for a disused railway track northwest along the valley to Lennoxtown and Strathblane, to join the West Highland Way at Dumgoyach Bridge, a few kilometres north of its start at Milngavie (thus avoiding going all the way into Glasgow).

The route then follows the West Highland Way up the east side of Loch Lomond and north to Glencoe and Fort William. The West Highland Way is the most northerly of the major national trails, and largely follows the same valleys and passes as the main road from Glasgow to Fort William as far as the Kingshouse above Glencoe. From here it cuts across the hills to Kinlochleven, then follows side valleys northwards to Fort William, the walkers' capital of the Highlands.

Ben Nevis looms above Fort William, or rather it does when the cloud is high enough to see it. Since this is the highest mountain in Great Britain it is worth taking a day off from the Trail to climb it. You will probably need to do some serious shopping in Fort William anyway, since it is the last chance to stock up properly. You will need plenty of fuel and food, particularly dried food. The only shops on or near the route after Fort William are at Kinlochewe (end of Day 53) and at Watten (end of Day 60). Ben Nevis in the morning and shopping in the afternoon could be a good plan.

Maps

1:25000 Explorer maps	**1:50000 Landranger maps**
16 Cheviot Hills	74 Kelso & Coldstream
44 Tweed Valley	73 Peebles, Galashiels
336 Biggar & Broughton (briefly)	72 Upper Clyde Valley
344 Pentland Hills	65 Falkirk & Linlithgow
	64 Glasgow

Maps

1:25000 Explorer maps
349 Falkirk, Cumbernauld & Livingston
342 Glasgow (briefly)
348 Campsie Fells
347 Loch Lomond South
364 Loch Lomond North
377 Loch Etive & Glen Orchy
384 Glen Coe & Glen Etive
392 Ben Nevis & Fort William

1:50000 Landranger maps
57 Stirling & the Trossachs
56 Loch Lomond & Inveraray
50 Glen Orchy
41 Ben Nevis, Fort William & Glen Coe

Guidebooks

Exploring the Edinburgh to Glasgow Canals by Hamish Brown, Mercat Press, 2nd edition 2006
The West Highland Way by Terry Marsh, Cicerone, 2nd edition 2003
This guidebook includes a strip of 1:50000 OS maps

Recommendations

Get Explorer maps 16, 44 and 336, and Landrangers 65 and 64. Take the old 1:25000 Outdoor Leisure maps 39 and 38 if you have them already, or Landrangers 57, 56, 50 and 41 if you haven't. There is little additional benefit in having the other 1:25000 maps. The West Highland Way used to need only Outdoor Leisure maps 39 and 38 (now out of print), whereas now you need four 1:50000 maps to cover it, or five of the new Explorer maps. You might want to consider getting the Harvey's strip map for the West Highland Way as an alternative to the OS maps.

Guidebooks are optional extras, provided you have maps with the West Highland Way marked on them – the WHW is very easy to follow. Hamish Brown's book about the canals adds a lot to the experience of walking them, and I recommended it highly.

Accommodation
These TICs are your best sources of information as far as the West Highland Way.
Murray's Green, Jedburgh, tel 0870 608 0404
www.visitscottishborders.com

Abbey House, Abbey Street, Melrose, tel 0870 608 0404 www.visitscottishborders.com
High Street, Peebles, tel 0870 608 0404 www.visitscottishborders.com
Burgh Halls, The Cross, Linlithgow (seasonal, expensive!), tel 0945 225 5721 www.edinburgh.org
2–4 Glebe Street, Falkirk, tel 0870 720 0614 www.visitscottishheartlands.org
11 George Square, Glasgow, tel 0141 204 4400 www.seeglasgow.com

Accommodation is limited in some areas, but there are bed and breakfasts where you need them. An accommodation guide to the Southern Upland Way is available from TICs – this contains the best information for Melrose and Traquair. The same information is available online at www.dumgal.gov.uk/southernuplandway. The best source for accommodation in and around Kilsyth is the town's website www.kilsyth.org.uk.

A West Highland Way accommodation list, the *West Highland Way Pocket Companion*, is available from TICs, and the WHW website www.west-highland-way.co.uk has a comprehensive accommodation list. Although there are bed and breakfasts and bunkhouses all the way, supply often cannot meet the demand. Either book ahead or carry camping equipment just in case. Note that the website includes the locations of recommended wild camping sites, information that isn't currently in the printed guide.

Equipment Shops

Day 42 CCW International, 74 High Street, Peebles, tel 01721 723055
Day 42 It's Great Outdoors, 12 High Street, Peebles, tel 01721 724263
Day 42 Out and About, 2 Elcho Street Brae, Peebles, tel 01721 723590
Day 43 (off-route) Outdoor Scene, McArthur Glen Design Outlet Centre, Almondvale Avenue, Livingston, tel 01506 429705 (near M8 junction 3). There are also lots of shops further off-route in Edinburgh…
Day 45 …and of course more shops off-route in Glasgow.
Day 45 It's Great Outdoors, 1 Stirling Road, Drymen, tel 01360 661148
Day 47 Green Welly Shop, Tyndrum, tel 01838 400271
Day 49 Fort William has plenty of shops, the highlight being Nevisport at the end of the High Street, tel 01397 704921

Alternative Routes

Via Milngavie

The recommended route of the End to End Trail misses out the first few kilometres of the West Highland Way. If you want to walk the whole of the WHW, then this alternative, between Kirkintilloch and Drymen via Milngavie, where the WHW starts, is recommended. It adds 7km (4 miles) in distance, and about half of that is additional road walking.

From Kirkintilloch, keep on the Forth and Clyde Canal towpath for another 7km (4 miles) towards Glasgow (Day 45 Map 1). You will pass the stables at Glasgow Bridge (now a restaurant), another bridge carrying the A807, then another at Calder (church on right). At the next bridge (GR605716) leave the canal and turn right on Balmuildy Road. Follow the road round three corners (the line of the Roman Antonine Wall is now on your right), to meet the main road (A879 Balmore Road). The site of Balmuildy Fort is on your right, although there isn't much to see. Turn right, cross the River Kelvin, then turn right off the road to follow the Kelvin Walkway, a waymarked path by the river. After 1km the River Allander joins from the left – the waymarked route (now the Allander Walkway) follows the Allander all the way to the centre of Milngavie and the start of the West Highland Way. Follow the West Highland Way to Drymen, where you rejoin the End to End Trail.

The Highland High Way

If the weather is good enough, an alternative route has been published that runs parallel to the West Highland Way, from Milngavie to Fort William, taking to the mountain tops rather than the valleys. The route is called the Highland High Way, and it follows the West Highland Way closely enough to allow you to mix and match days from each. The Ben Vorlich section of the Highland High Way is out of bounds if you are determined to walk every inch, however, as it involves taking a ferry across Loch Lomond (Day 46). The HHW is not a waymarked route, and follows remote mountain tops where there are not always well-defined paths. **It is not a route to follow if you are not experienced in such a mountain environment**.

Guidebook

The Highland High Way by Heather Connon and Paul Roper, Mainstream, 1996

Avoiding the West Highland Way: Alternative Routes from Drymen to Fort William

If you are feeling antisocial and want to avoid the West Highland Way altogether, there are alternative routes possible further to the east that will link Drymen with Fort William. There are a number of options to get from Drymen to Killin (about 3 days from Fort William) at the head of Loch Tay, in Perthshire, which should be possible in a couple of days if you are following the End to End Trail Main Schedule. The easiest option (excluding roads of course) is to follow the Rob Roy Way via Aberfoyle, Callander and Lochearnhead. This follows forestry tracks and valley paths. The route isn't waymarked, but a guidebook has been published, and there is a website, www.robroyway.com.

There are other alternative routes if you want to be more adventurous. The Menteith Hills, northeast of Loch Lomond, make a good hill route variation between Aberfoyle and Callander, or you could instead head from Aberfoyle through the forestry past Loch Drunkie and down to Brig o' Turk, then follow routes across the hills to Balquhidder and Killin. The route from Brig o' Turk to Killin is described in *Scottish Hill Tracks* (see below).

From Killin to Fort William, again there are routes described in *Scottish Hill Tracks* that should see you there in three days. The first day takes you over the Lairig Breisleich pass into Glen Lyon, then over another bealach from Innerwick to reach the head of Loch Rannoch. The second day takes the road west nearly to Rannoch station, then by Loch Eigheach and the historic Road to the Isles over to Loch Ossian and Corrour. The third day you can follow the popular route west along Glen Nevis to Fort William. Alternatively you could miss out Fort William altogether, and head north via the Lairig Leacach and down to Spean Bridge, which is about 6km (4 miles) by road from Gairlochy, where you can rejoin the main route of the Trail part way through Day 50.

All these alternatives will be a lot quieter than the West Highland Way, and will give a taste of what is to come beyond Fort William.

Guidebooks

The Rob Roy Way by Jacquetta Megarry, Rucksack Readers, 2002

Scottish Hill Tracks, edited by DJ Bennet and CD Stone, Scottish Rights of Way and Access Society, 2004 edition

Eastern Routes from the Lowlands to Inverness

There are many alternative routes possible through the Scottish Highlands, and in particular if you want to take an eastern route north from Inverness, there are more direct routes possible from the Edinburgh and Glasgow areas than via Fort William. You can cross the Forth road bridge west of Edinburgh, head north to Perth (mainly on roads), then northwest on hill tracks to Aberfeldy and on to Pitlochry. A short way up Glen Garry takes you to Blair Atholl and the start of the track up Glen Tilt and into the Cairngorms. From Linn of Dee you can continue north over the high pass of the Larig Ghru (833m), or alternatively take a lower route into Glen Feshie to the west. You can then follow what's left of one of General Wade's roads, parallel to the A9 as far as Tomatin, then minor roads to the west of the A9 enable you to reach Inverness with minimal main-road walking. To reach Dingwall or Evanton from Inverness you will need to cross the A9 Kessock Bridge, then follow minor roads.

You may also want to consider heading north from closer to Glasgow. Paths lead from Kilsyth across the Kilsyth and Gargunnock hills to Kippen on the River Forth. From there it's not far on the B822 to Callendar, and from there you can take a path northeast over to Glen Artney and down a track to Comrie in Strath Earn. Tracks north of the valley can be followed east to join the A822 at the Falls of Monzie, north of Crieff. Another of General Wade's roads heads north from here to Aberfeldy, where you can join the route described above.

If you want to take any of these options, you should study your OS maps and all three of the books listed below. Christine Roche's book is an account of her journey rather than a guidebook, but the route she took was worked out with care, and sufficient detail is included to make it reasonably easy to follow.

Guidebooks

Follow the Spring North by Christine Roche, Trafford Publishing, 2004

Land's End to John O'Groats: A Choice of Footpaths for Walking the Length of Britain by Andrew McCloy, Hodder & Stoughton, 1994

Scottish Hill Tracks, edited by DJ Bennet and CD Stone, Scottish Rights of Way and Access Society, 2004 edition

DAY 40

St Cuthbert's Way

Jedburgh to Melrose (29km, 18 miles)

Once you've regained Dere Street from Jedburgh, today's route follows St Cuthbert's Way all day to its end at Melrose, so follow the 'St Cuthbert's cross' waymarks. This is a very good day's walk, varied and interesting, passing through some lovely countryside. (The other end of St Cuthbert's Way is on Holy Island, off the Northumberland coast, and the whole of this walk is highly recommended.)

The route back to Dere Street via Mount Ulston is on a quiet access road followed by a footpath, and brings you back to the Roman road on the slope down to Jed Water and the River Teviot (Day 40 Map 1). On reaching the valley bottom, if you are hungry there is the Caddy Mann tearoom/restaurant, just east of Jedfoot Bridge on the A698.

Jedburgh Abbey

The Waterloo Monument on Peniel Heugh is a prominent landmark. Begun in 1815, it collapsed in 1816 before it was finished, and was finally completed in 1824. It is dedicated to 'The Duke of Wellington and the British Army'.

There's no sign of Dere Street on the ground after crossing Jedfoot Bridge – it was obliterated by the landscaping of the Monteviot Estate, which you are now approaching. Monteviot House, the seat of the Earls of Ancrum and the earlier Earls of Lothian, was built in 1740 and largely rebuilt in 1840.

St Cuthbert's Way follows Jed Water to its confluence with the River Teviot, then follows the river up through parkland to cross an elegant suspension footbridge (Monteviot Bridge). It then continues on a tortuous route through the Monteviot House parkland and Divet Ha' Wood, until the line of Dere Street reappears in the wood. There is a good café at the Harestanes Visitor Centre near Monteviot House, open April to October.

Dere Street continues northwest across the landscape, mainly in a wide enclosure of its own, too broad to call a lane. (Turn aside to read the famous inscription on Lady Lilliard's Stone, and hope you don't meet anyone as fierce on the rest of your journey –particularly if you're English).

Gradually the line of the Roman road converges with that of the A68 trunk road (Day 40 Map 2). The path runs in trees parallel to the A68, then meets a minor road going right to Maxton. Turn right here (St Cuthbert's Way), rather than continuing on the path ahead through the woods (Dere Street).

After parting from Dere Street the route to Melrose is a lot less direct, but for the most part is worth the extra distance. At Maxton, St Cuthbert's Way meets the River Tweed and follows the bank as it meanders round towards Melrose.

The Tweed is one of the longest rivers in Britain, about 160km (100 miles), and the entire river channel is a Site of Special Scientific Interest (SSSI). This is another bit of classic riverside walking to be savoured, even if you don't have time to dawdle. The wildflowers, trees and meadows are delightful, and the river itself is a pleasure to walk beside.

St Cuthbert's Way forsakes the Tweed temporarily to walk the streets of St Boswells, which has shops and refreshments, but little else here to make the diversion worthwhile. If you need neither, St Boswells can be avoided by staying close to the river, which is the route shown on Day 40 Map 2.

Shortly after passing the suspension footbridge across to Dryburgh Abbey, St Cuthbert's Way leaves the Tweed and heads west-southwest up the side valley of Bowden Burn, before passing through Newtown St Boswells (which also has little to offer the visitor). It continues along a minor road and a pleasant track (Day 40 Map 3), before crossing Bowden Burn to the pretty little village of Bowden, at the foot of the Eildon Hills. Bowden has an excellent café but no other facilities.

'Here...arose to the still, blue bosom of the sky the three great Eildon Hills, with their heads crowned with heather as with an emerald diadem' – Elihu Burritt, *A Walk from London to John O'Groats*, 1864

All that now remains between you and the day's end at Melrose is a group of three hills, and the route crosses the col between the two highest. The climb is steady and reasonably easy, partly through woodland. If you want to belt up one of the hills, the left one is the higher (Eildon Mid Hill, 422m) and the right-hand one has the Roman signal station on it (Eildon Hill North, 404m). (And before you descend to Melrose and tell people where you've been, it would be as well to take on board that Eildons is pronounced 'Eeldons' and not 'Isledons'.)

The views are very good from the col, and you'll probably be keen to get down to the fleshpots of Melrose just below, which is where St Cuthbert's Way ends.

Melrose is the second of the principal border towns on route (Jedburgh is the first), and it gets a lot of tourists, so tends to be quite expensive, and accommodation often fills up. However, there is a campsite and a large youth hostel, and there is often room here when everywhere else is full. Burt's Hotel in the Market Square and the King's Arms Hotel in the High Street are the places to go for good beer. Melrose Abbey, in the middle of the town, is where the town started, and the abbey ruins are very photogenic and atmospheric, worth visiting in the evening sunshine (if there is any). The abbey was founded in 1136, in the reign of King David I, by Cistercian monks from Rievaulx, in Yorkshire. By the end of the 14th century English raids had pretty much destroyed it, and most of the ruins that remain are 15th and 16th century. It was abandoned in 1545. It is open all year to visitors.

DAY 41

The Southern Upland Way

Melrose to Traquair (28km, 18 miles)

Today the Trail follows the Southern Upland Way all day. This long-distance path is a connoisseur's route, running from coast to coast across southern Scotland, and generally more or less at right angles to the Trail, but for this section it runs east–west and makes a convenient link in the chain of our route. It crosses high moorland, rising to 520m crossing Minch Moor, and can be exposed, so treat this stretch with respect. Like the other Scottish national trails, the Southern Upland Way is waymarked with a thistle inside a hexagon.

The first part of the day follows the bank of the River Tweed (Day 41 Map 1), and is as good as the riverside stretch yesterday. This is followed by a rather less scenic

Melrose Abbey

march along a disused railway line through an industrial estate, then along a road past a gasometer. (Note that this section of the Southern Upland Way is likely to be diverted in the future, as there are plans to reopen part of the railway. If this does happen, the most likely new route will be on the Borders Abbeys Way along the riverbank, then across the river on the A6091 bridge (GR528347 to GR508347).)

From the gasometer things improve markedly. There is another short stretch by the river, then the Southern Upland Way starts to climb over the hills in the direction of Yair Bridge. However, for some unaccountable reason it then changes its mind and drops down again into the valley to wander around Galashiels municipal park, before climbing back up Gala Hill. There is no point in this, so instead the End to End Trail takes a shorter and more pleasant route through forestry on the south side of Gala Hill. The two routes converge shortly afterwards and climb steadily up fields to cross a pass by Hog Hill at about 200m (Day 41 Map 2), and drop back down through coverts to cross the Tweed again at Yair Bridge.

From Yair Bridge there is a steady climb through forestry, alongside Shorthope Burn, to the high moors, culminating in the summit of the Three Brethren (464m), crowned by three large cairns. The views from here are extensive, with the Eildons yet again unmistakable in the panorama, as they seem to be from every angle.

Having gained the height up to the heather moors, the benefit isn't wasted – the path heads west without dropping below 400m until the end of the day. Brown Knowe is at 523m (Day 41 Map 3), then there is a climb, along ancient Minchmoor Road, up a corridor of moorland between forestry to a similar height on the shoulder of Minch Moor. The summit, at 567m, is an easy 10-minute climb from here, and well worth the detour for the views. (Minchmoor Road was used by Edward I of England and his army in 1296 on the way to Peebles as they rampaged through Scotland.)

From Minch Moor it is a simple descent on Minchmoor Road to Traquair, passing purpose-built timber Minch Moor bothy, at GR343337, where a comfortable night can be spent. Water is available from a stream close to the path just before you reach the bothy.

There are a couple of bed and breakfasts at Traquair, but for other accommodation you will have to walk 2km (1½ miles) along the B709 to Innerleithen (crossing the Tweed again). At Innerleithen there are shops, a campsite and hotels, including the Traquair Arms, which is recommended for good food and beer.

Traquair hamlet dates back to Roman times. Its main claim to fame is Traquair House, believed to be the oldest continuously inhabited house in Scotland. It was a royal hunting lodge, and parts of it are over 1000 years old – the last monarch to hunt from here was Mary Queen of Scots in 1566. It has a working 18th-century brewery, a maze, a priest's room with a hidden staircase, and is open to visitors on summer afternoons. The famous Bear Gates into the estate that you pass on the way out of the village haven't been opened for hundreds of years, the reason for this depending on which guidebook you read.

DAY 42

Peebles and White Meldon

Traquair to West Linton (32km, 20 miles)

The Trail makes its own way northwest via Peebles to West Linton today, since the Southern Upland Way heads southwest from Traquair. To get to Peebles from Traquair, the obvious route is to follow the River Tweed, but there is no footpath for most of it, so the Trail starts along the quieter of the two roads on either side of the river, the B7062, past Traquair House's Bear Gates (see end of Day 41).

So taking the B7062 from Traquair, follow it to Old Howford (Day 42 Map 1), where you meet Cardrona Forest, a Forestry Commission plantation. The Trail leaves the road to follow tracks through the forestry, climbing to the ancient fort on Castle Knowe, the summit being bald of trees like a medieval friar's shaved head.

There are two alternative routes to Peebles from Castle Knowe. If you have the time and the energy, the Kailzie Hill alternative route entails a long, steep climb up the edge of the forestry to the top of Kailzie Hill (485m), giving a dramatic descent down Craig Head ridge, on an old drove road, into Peebles. This is a magnificent stretch to walk, and more than justifies the hard slog up the hill, but before committing yourself to Kailzie Hill, bear in mind that today is a long, hard day anyway – it's a long way to West Linton.

The shorter and easier alternative (and today's recommended Trail route) descends back down to the Tweed from Cardrona Forest, and avoids the road as much as possible, following alternative tracks and paths instead (Day 42 Map 2). It is about 1km less than the Kailzie Hill alternative (not to mention saving the strenuous 250m climb up the hill).

The River Tweed flows through the centre of Peebles, and the whole town has something of an old-fashioned air. It is the last of the three Border towns the Trail passes through, and bigger and busier than Jedburgh and Melrose. It is another ancient town of character, having been given its charter by King David II in 1367, and there are shops, banks and all services here, including a campsite on the edge of town (GR244414).

Between Peebles and West Linton the Trail follows the route described by Hamish Brown in *From the Pennines to the Highlands* (Lochar Publishing, 1992). An alternative route is outlined in *Scottish Hill Tracks*, but Hamish Brown's route has more of interest and less road walking, although it's not all easy!

Follow the riverside path up as far as Neidpath Castle (Day 42 Map 2), which overlooks the river in a dramatic position. The castle dates back to the 13th century and was besieged by Cromwell in 1650, the only time it was taken. The inside can be visited if you have time.

The Trail leaves the Tweed for the last time here, and once across the A72 heads up into the hills, initially across a golf course, then climbing over Clock Knowe, before a steep and rough climb to the summit of White Meldon (427m), a steep-sided cone of a hill with very fine views. The final climb to the summit can be avoided by a more direct descent from the ridge if you wish, but you will be missing the day's high point in more ways than one.

Recover for a while from the effort of reaching the top, then descend even more steeply down its west side to cross a minor road and enter the corner of a forestry plantation.

Just inside the trees is a forestry road (Day 42 Map 3), which leads eventually to the remote settlement at Harehope. Another climb up follows, back into forestry across Harehope Hill, then down again until you emerge from the trees on a col between Wide Hope Shank and Crailzie Hill, and look down into the valley of Flemington Burn – at this point you realise you still have a long way to go today.

Through the gate on the col the route descends to the valley, then climbs up the opposite side again, along Fingland Burn, now on a good path. Another pass is crossed, in a narrow band of forestry on a very wet path, then at last you can descend to the valley of Lyne Water. The A701 is reached near Romannobridge, but there is another 5km (3 miles) of road walking before you reach West Linton.

West Linton is an attractive village that markets itself for walkers, holding walking festivals, and the church has some intricate woodcarvings that are worth seeing. Bed and breakfast accommodation is limited, so it is a good idea to book ahead. There are shops and a post office, and also the Gordon Arms Hotel, which is recommended for both food and beer.

DAY 43

The Pentland Hills and the Union Canal

West Linton to Linlithgow (43km, 27 miles)

Today the Trail leaves the Border hills and enters the industrial lowlands of the Forth and Clyde valleys. This is a long day, but most of it is particularly easy walking. The first part of the day crosses the Pentland Hills on an ancient droving route, over a pass going by the evocative name of Cauldstane Slap. (The Pentlands are the last range of Border hills to cross, and the last moorland until Loch Lomond.)

Once you've descended Corston Hill, what follows is two days of walking through the Scottish industrial heartland, but it's surprising how rural most of this is. So much of the old heavy industry has gone, and although evidence of it usually remains, it is overgrown with regenerated woodland and grass. The Trail follows stream, river, canals and a disused railway track. The roads and housing estates are there, but you will see only a little of them from the route.

After the initial steep lane climbing out of West Linton, the gradient is easy, following Agricola's Western Way invasion road (now a tarmac farm access road) for a short distance (Day 43 Map 1). The route up to Baddinsgill is varied and interesting, on a track above the upper Lyne Water valley. Beyond Baddinsgill the moors become wild and bleak. The summit of Cauldstane Slap (435m) is a pretty godforsaken place, and marks your exit from the Borders region and entry into West Lothian.

The descent to cross the Water of Leith and the A70 is less interesting than the ascent (Day 43 Map 2), but Edinburgh and Arthur's Seat come into view for the first time, to the right on the way down, in compensation.

The best views of the day, however, are from the top of Corston Hill, the last hill on the Trail for a long way. It may be only 348m high, but Corston Hill is right on the edge of high ground, so the views are a lot more extensive than its height suggests. Ahead is the Almond valley, full of past and present industry. Look right and the valley meets the Firth of Forth, the river meeting the sea between the Forth bridges and Edinburgh, all set out below you. Also, closer at hand, are the first of the pink piles of the shale bings, slag heaps from the defunct 19th-century industry that extracted oil from the shale strata.

The descent from Corston Hill follows a line of old boundary stones to join a quiet access road to the valley and the A71 (Day 43 Map 3). Across the road there used to be a shale quarry, now the start of the Almondell and Calderwood Country Park, and what used to be desolation is now quiet and pretty woodland along the Linhouse Water valley. There is even a snack van in the car park by the A71 six days a week. The path down to Mid Calder winds through woodland and clearings, and feels as if it is miles from civilisation, although in fact it is only 300m from a housing estate at one point. The stream and path descend to go under the B7015 at Mid Calder.

A few steps from the path is the Torphichen Arms, a locals' pub, as you would expect – this is not a tourist area. The macaroni cheese is recommended and this is an excellent place to stop for lunch. There are a handful of shops and a post office here as well, and limited bed and breakfast accommodation in nearby East Calder if you need to stop overnight around here.

Continuing on the path down the river, Linhouse Water soon joins the River Almond, and good paths follow the wooded valley down towards the Firth of Forth. This part of the country park is a popular local recreation area, and rightly so – once you're past Mid Calder sewage works the rest of it is really very pretty.

A footbridge takes you across to the left-hand bank, then an artificial channel branches off the river. This feeds the Union Canal nearly 5km (3 miles) downstream, and the Trail follows it all the way, apart from a few stretches where it is culverted. The feeder crosses the river, accompanied by a footbridge, and the Trail continues down the right-hand bank of the river, then gradually rises above it. When Lin's Mill Aqueduct comes into view, carrying the canal high across the valley, it suddenly becomes clear why the feeder channel left the river so far back. At Lin's Mill the Trail joins the Union Canal.

The Union Canal was opened in 1822, joining Edinburgh to the Forth and Clyde Canal to give a fast new communications and trading link between Glasgow and Edinburgh. It started to become redundant soon afterwards, however, as the first railway link between the two cities opened in the early 1840s, and a proposed link to the Firth of Forth at the Edinburgh end was never built. The canal has recently been reopened to navigation after being closed for decades, although as yet not many boats are using it. This was funded by the National Lottery Millennium Fund, and included building a new bridge for the M8 motorway south of Broxburn. Guidebooks indicating that the towpath here is blocked to walkers are out of date.

The initial crossing of the aqueduct is spectacular – the views of the valley are lovely, although anyone with no head for heights may have other things to think about. After that the day becomes a bit more humdrum, as walking along the canal can't touch the River Almond for quality walking. The towpath through the housing estates of Broxburn is the low point of the day (Day 43 Map 4), and possibly slightly more risky than Cross Fell in poor weather. If you are walking alone and concerned about your personal security, taking a road route between bridges 23 and 27 is a safer option.

Broxburn has shops and banks, but like many of the villages and towns on the Trail today and tomorrow, it has seen better days. The decline in industry in recent decades is nowhere more obvious than around here. If you are after bed and breakfast accommodation, either head west for 2km (1½ miles) along the A899 to the Oatridge Hotel in Uphall (that's Up-hall, not Uffall), or push on 3km (2 miles) to Winchburgh.

Shale bing and the Union Canal, Niddry

Linlithgow Castle

Things look up from Bridge 27, where you leave the Broxburn estates for the shale bings ('bing' is a corruption of 'ben', as in Ben Nevis). This must have been grim when the shale was still being worked (for oil), but has now become pleasantly rural, with the added bonus of plenty of industrial archaeological remains.

Just before Winchburgh, Niddry Castle is to the right of the canal, on the other side of the railway. It's old, built in 1490, but not very big, and not open to the public. The canal passes through the middle of Winchburgh, but you hardly see anything of the town as the canal is in a deep cutting.

The canal continues in its own wooded world for another 5 or 6km (3–4 miles), then surfaces into more open country after Philpstoun for the last stretch to Linlithgow. This area isn't industrial – the nearby surroundings are pleasant farmland, and the distant views of the Ochil Hills to the north are good.

Linlithgow is an ancient and royal town. King David I built a house here in the 12th century, and subsequent kings built the royal palace, in which Mary Queen of Scots was born. It wasn't until the union of the monarchies in 1603 that its importance started to decline. The palace was gutted by fire in 1746, but is still an impressive ruin, set on the shore of Linlithgow Loch in the heart of the town, and well worth visiting. The town centre has its attractions, but also some horrendous post-war additions that should never have been given planning approval. There are pubs, shops, banks, a tourist information centre, and a range of accommodation, including a campsite just across the M9 (take the A706 Bo'ness road).

'Linlithgow, whose every stone spoke volumes of the storied past' – Robert and John Naylor, *John O'Groat's to Land's End*, 1916

DAY 44

Canal Towpaths

Linlithgow to Kilsyth (32km, 20 miles)

This is the easiest walking of the whole Trail, being on towpaths the whole way. There aren't even any locks until the end of the Union Canal, so it's absolutely level all the way to Falkirk.

The first stretch is a continuation of the rural environment on the way into Linlithgow yesterday, and includes another spectacular aqueduct, this time over the River Avon, which is where you also leave West Lothian Unitary Authority (UA) for Falkirk UA (Day 44 Map 1). It gets a bit more urban through Polmont, and the young offenders' institution on the other bank isn't the most photogenic sight of the day.

Towards the end of the Union Canal, after Bridge 61 on the approach to Falkirk, it disappears into a 631m tunnel, dug purely to appease the wealthy industrialist William Forbes, who objected to the canal being visible from his estate. The tunnel is the first high point of the day, being old and atmospheric. Water sprays out of cracks in the roof, boats nose their way past you, and at the far end the light gradually turns from a pinprick to the archway out into the daylight again. The lights in the tunnel give little illumination, but there is a railing to stop you from falling into the water (carrots the night before may be a sensible precaution).

Falkirk Tunnel on the Union Canal

If you want to visit Falkirk, leave the canal after the tunnel. Falkirk is the biggest town on the whole Trail (if you don't count Bristol) and has all services, but it's not worth visiting as a tourist.

The Union Canal joins the Forth and Clyde Canal at the Falkirk Wheel, just west of Falkirk (Day 44 Map 2). Until 1963 the canals were joined via a stair of 11 locks at Camelon, down to a canal basin by the Union Inn. For nearly 40 years after 1963 there was no connection at all, as the locks were filled in and built over. In 2002 the canals were both reopened, and the new connection between them was completed 1.5km (1 mile) further west. Instead of a flight of locks, the Falkirk Wheel, a unique new boatlift, now carries boats 25m down to the Forth and Clyde (thanks to National Lottery funding).

Just west of the Falkirk Wheel, around Rough Castle, are the best-preserved sections of the Roman Antonine Wall. This was a turf-built wall across the Forth–Clyde gap, and for a couple of decades from its construction in AD142–3 it formed a northern barrier of the Roman Empire, before the legions fell back again to Hadrian's Wall. If you want to visit this section of the Antonine Wall you will have to climb back up from the Falkirk Wheel (see Day 44 Map 2, alternative route) and head west through the woods, descending to rejoin the Trail on the

Falkirk Wheel

Forth and Clyde towpath at Bonnybridge. (You will have to take this route anyway if the Wheel complex is closed – evenings for instance – as the swing footbridge you need to cross to reach the Forth and Clyde towpath will be locked in the 'open' position, and you won't be able to cross to the towpath.)

Daniel Defoe was already pushing the idea of a canal in the 1720s, and the Forth and Clyde Canal eventually opened in 1790, linking the coasts via the two rivers after which it was named. This meant cheap bulk transport of goods and people across the country for the first time, without the long detour round the north coast. As with most canals, traffic declined with the development of railways, and it eventually closed altogether in 1963, reopening along with the Union Canal in 2002, 39 years later.

The Forth and Clyde Canal climbs on its way west, passing under the very busy A80 trunk road (Castlecary House Hotel – accommodation – is just off-route to the left near the A80 bridge).

At Wyndford Lock you join the highest stretch of the canal, at a mere 48m above sea level. The next stretch is long and straight, and the canal is wider than normal – this is Dullatur Bog. Building the canal across here was a major feat, as the embankment it is on had to be built up 16m before it settled properly into the bog. (At some point along here the canal crosses the main watershed between the River Carron and the River Kelvin, and just to prove the point, Kelvinhead is just to the right, claiming to be the source of the River Kelvin, which flows west into the Clyde.)

If you are staying at Kilsyth, either turn right at Craigmarloch Bridge (where there is no longer a drawbridge), or at Auchinstarry Bridge (where there is no longer a swingbridge).

Kilsyth itself is a rundown and desolate town, deserted by the coalmining industry that built it. There is a handful of bed and breakfasts in and around the town, and food is available at the Coachman Hotel on the A803 (GR716781).

DAY 45

Below the Campsie Fells

Kilsyth to Drymen (35km, 22 miles)

The view to the right for most of the day is dominated by the Campsie Fells – a steep escarpment rises to the north to a high plateau of moorland hills about 500m high. The Trail follows the valleys however, pushing on to join the West Highland Way at Drumgoyach Bridge towards the end of the day. (The strip maps guide you to Drumgoyach Bridge, then you will need your West Highland Way guidebook for the stretch to Drymen.)

The Forth and Clyde Canal passes into East Dunbartonshire just after Auchinstarry Bridge, and the Trail follows it past Twechar to Kirkintilloch, the next town down the valley (Day 45 Map 1). The canal and the River Kelvin continue down to Glasgow and the Clyde, but the Trail avoids the city by heading northwest from Kirkintilloch (leaving the canal at Hillhead Bridge), up the side valley of Glazert Water, along the toes of the Campsies. The Trail follows the Strathblane Railway Walkway – a disused railway that ran from Kirkintilloch to a junction at Gartness, near Drymen – all the way. There is a bed and breakfast in Lennoxtown if you need an overnight halt here (Day 45 Map 2).

Milton of Campsie Station, Strathblane Railway Walkway

The old railway bed has been turned into an official footpath, so the walking is easy, with a made surface in places, and it makes a change from the canal towpath. But despite the mainly rural situation, and the views of the Campsies, walking the railway is, as usual, inferior to walking a canal. Without water the wildlife is less varied, and the more distant views are more often obscured by trees.

Approaching Strathblane and just before passing Dunglass – a small but striking rocky hill that is probably a volcanic plug – you leave East Dunbartonshire for Stirlingshire. Strathblane has a hotel, the Kirkhouse Inn, which makes a good lunch stop.

You have to leave the line of the old railway briefly at Strathblane, but only for a few minutes. It's no longer an official footpath from here, though, and some parts are little used and it can be wet in places (it is accompanied for part of the way by an old pipeline carrying water from Loch Lomond). Despite the occasional soggy bit, this section is better than the Kirkintilloch to Strathblane section – it is more varied and there are no housing estates.

The West Highland Way joins the old railway track at Dumgoyach Bridge, after passing Dumgoyach, a steep wooded hill, so **from here until the end of this section you will need your West Highland Way guidebook**. (This part of the West

Highland Way is just an overture really. It is pleasant, but the WHW doesn't really get into its stride until tomorrow.)

Suddenly you will find yourself part of a crowd, after probably having had little company but a few dog walkers since you left Peebles on Day 42. The West Highland Way is very popular, and attracts a lot of people who have never walked a long-distance path before. You are joining these tyros as they complete the first 8km (5 miles) of their walk, and some will already be tired and sore and wondering what they've let themselves in for. You, on the other hand, have been walking every day for weeks. This is where you may well realise for the first time just how fit you have become – even when you think you are taking it easy, you will probably be overtaking people all day every day, so give them a bit of encouragement on your way past!

At Gartness, close to the site of the old railway junction, the West Highland Way leaves the old railway track and takes to minor roads to climb over the last hill and down into Drymen (which rhymes with 'women' not 'piemen').

Drymen is a pretty village, providing well for the many walkers that pass through. There are shops, amongst them an outdoor equipment shop, accommodation and pubs, including the Winnock Hotel (recommended). The campsite is at Easter Drumquhassie Farm, which is on the route nearly 3km (2 miles) before Drymen, which is a bit inconvenient if you want to eat, drink or shop in Drymen.

There is an alternative official rough camping site a bit further on in the forestry, at GR453918, but it can be a bit midgy. There are no facilities here, but if all you want is somewhere to put up your tent after an evening in Drymen, it is ideal, and recommended for a good head start for what is a very long day tomorrow (see below).

DAY 46

Loch Lomond

Drymen to Inverarnan (45km, 28 miles)

This is indeed a very long day. From Drymen the West Highland Way climbs up into the Garadhban forestry (look out for a first glimpse of Loch Lomond as you near the far edge of the plantations), over Conic Hill and up the eastern shore of Loch Lomond, through Rowardennan and Inversnaid, to Inverarnan. On the map it appears to be easy, flat walking after the initial climb over Conic Hill, but this is misleading. The northern half of the lochside path is hard work in many places, being rocky and slow to follow. (The advantage of an early start from the rough camping site in the forestry outside Drymen is a strong argument against bed and breakfast in Drymen itself at the end of Day 45, unless you choose to split Day 46 into two, with an overnight stop at Rowardennan.)

Just past the previous day's rough camping area (GR453918) the path soon emerges from Garadhban Forest onto the hillside, crosses the Burn of Mar, and climbs over Conic Hill, a steep-sided and rocky hill, 361m high, which is aptly named (the path doesn't go to the summit, and you probably haven't got time to either). The views of Loch Lomond are stunning. The path descends through another plantation, then via a big car park to Balmaha on the shore of Loch Lomond.

Loch Lomond

If you are unlucky, you will have to miss out on the excellent Conic Hill excursion and follow the B837 from Milton of Buchanan to Balmaha, as each spring the high-level route is closed to the public for four weeks at lambing time.

Balmaha is a haunt of day-trippers and best left behind quickly. The views across Loch Lomond are tremendous the whole way to Rowardennan, but for much of it the route is either too close to the road, or follows tortuous diversions to avoid it. Rowardennan has a hotel, a youth hostel, bed and breakfasts and a wild camping area.

After Rowardennan things improve, as there is no public road. The West Highland Way follows an untarred private road for the next few kilometres, which is fast and easy to walk. There is an alternative route at a lower level, but this is harder going, requiring scrambling through boulders in places. The lower route is no longer signposted as an official WHW alternative route, so if you want to follow it you will need to pay attention to pick up the start about 300m beyond Ptarmigan Lodge.

The vehicle track ends just after the two routes join again, and the path onwards is slow and rocky in places. At Inversnaid a footbridge crosses Arklet Water next to waterfalls, and you are at the Inversnaid Hotel, serviced by a road that follows Arklet Water down from Loch Arklet. The hotel allows walkers into

Rowardennan youth hostel, Loch Lomond

the bar, and is the only place for refreshments between Rowardennan and Inverarnan, above the head of Loch Lomond.

From Inversnaid the route continues along the loch shore, or close to it, and is delightful if you are not in a hurry. It is hard work and slow, though, clambering through rocky areas on steep slopes.

Two kilometres beyond Inversnaid is the three-quarter mark of the Trail, a message you may find hard to get across to anyone 'down south' who thinks you are already in the far north.

Opposite the island of I Vow the path leaves Stirlingshire and enters Argyll and Bute (which for some reason claims the slopes on the east side of the valley for a short stretch as far as Inverarnan). Towards the end of the loch the difficulties ease, and from here the route is both easy and delightful, across rough pasture and through woodland, to re-enter Stirlingshire just before reaching Beinglas Farm and the bridge across the River Falloch that gives access to the Drovers Inn at Inverarnan.

Beinglas Farm has a field for camping (walkers only), and some wooden 'wigwams' for those carrying no tent. There is also a small shop, with all the right things in, and they cook a mean breakfast – a stop here is highly recommended. Evening meals can be obtained at the Drovers Inn, an inn of (Scottish) character that is definitely worth a visit. There is limited bed and breakfast accommodation at Inverarnan, so plan ahead.

DAY 47

Glen Falloch and Strath Fillan

Inverarnan to Bridge of Orchy (29km, 18 miles)

This is the second of four full days of being sociable on the West Highland Way. Now there is no longer Loch Lomond to separate the walkers from the rest of the traffic, the fact that the West Highland Way, the Fort William railway and the busy A82 all share the same valleys has much more impact today. Having said that, the day is surprisingly good, although there is nothing particularly challenging about it. The walking is easy, on good paths and tracks, the gradients are easy and route finding is also easy.

Initially the path from Beinglas Farm follows the bank of the River Falloch, a pleasant riverside stroll with the road and the railway on the opposite bank. Soon you cross all three to join General Wade's 18th-century military road, built to pacify and control the Highlanders, and now a well-built cart track climbing above the A82.

In the first half of the 18th century there was a lot of Scottish resistance to the rule of the House of Hanover and the London parliament. In 1724, King George I sent General George Wade to the Highlands to assess the situation there and report back on what should be done about it. One of the key messages of Wade's report was the need for an improved network of forts, and connecting roads along which troops could be moved more effectively. Wade went on to plan a network of roads and forts, supervising the building of the first 250 miles of road himself before handing over construction to William Caulfeild in about 1740. These roads were well built and often underlie today's roads in the Highlands. Where the modern road takes a different line, the old road often makes a good route for walkers, and the West Highland Way follows Wade's roads in a number of places. Caulfeild's roads are also often referred to as 'General Wade's roads'.

At the head of Glen Falloch the A82 crosses a low pass, and the main Scottish watershed, over to Crianlarich and Strath Fillan. The old military road also crosses the watershed, on a slightly higher line, then instead of continuing to follow the old road straight down into Strath Fillan, the West Highland Way leaves to follow paths through forestry along the side of the valley, eventually descending to Strath Fillan valley bottom further upstream. The path then wanders easily up to Tyndrum, avoiding the road, with a railway to each side.

Tyndrum itself is a place to pass through as quickly as possible, dominated as it is by a large coach-party hotel, and what is best described as a motorway service station gone astray, although it does include an outdoor shop. There is accommodation in Tyndrum if you want to stop here overnight, though.

From Tyndrum the railways each go their own way, west to Oban and north to Fort William, and the main road divides as well, the A85 heading west to Oban and the A82 north. The West Highland Way heads north too, back on General Wade's road. The A82, the railway and WHW climb back into Argyll and Bute, to cross to the west side of the main watershed again at a pass at 315m, and descend a side valley into Glen Orchy. (Be thankful that the old road sticks closer to the quiet railway than to the busy A82.)

Bridge of Orchy is just a hamlet, but it has a post office (no groceries though), a station and the bridge, which carries the WHW over the River Orchy. More importantly for us walkers, there is also the Bridge of Orchy Hotel, which has a comfortable bunkhouse, an excellent bar and good food (recommended). There is also a second bunkhouse in the station buildings, and a wild camping area by the bridge.

DAY 48

Black Mount and the Devil's Staircase

Bridge of Orchy to Kinlochleven (33km, 21 miles)

Day three on the West Highland Way, and the route continues to follow the old military road all day, apart from a stretch on a parallel drove road from Victoria Bridge to just before Bà Bridge.

From Bridge of Orchy, the A82 and the railway head north and pass to the east of Loch Tulla, before separating to take different routes across the huge, undulating peat bog of Rannoch Moor. Here the A82 heads north and the railway northwest, and they don't meet again until Fort William. General Wade's road takes a third route, round the western side of Loch Tulla, then along the western margin of Rannoch Moor.

From Bridge of Orchy General Wade strangely took his road over the northern shoulder of Ben Inverveigh, rather than following the more natural lower route, taken by the modern minor road to the Inveroran Hotel and Victoria Bridge, at the western tip of Loch Tulla. The climb through forestry is easy enough, though, as it was engineered with reasonable gradients. (Botanists should keep their eyes open for chickweed wintergreen along here.)

From Victoria Bridge there is an excellent cart track (the drove road) heading north across remote moorland. For the first few kilometres this doesn't actually follow the line of Wade's road, which follows a parallel line up the hill to the left. Along here the main watershed is crossed again, imperceptibly, and at the same time the Trail enters the old county of Inverness-shire, and the modern Highland Region of Scotland. From here to John O'Groats the Trail is entirely in the Highland Region, which covers a huge area of largely unpopulated country. The drove road and the military road merge before the crossing of the River Bà at Bà Bridge, a beautiful and remote spot.

The old road crosses a pass (and the watershed one more time) and descends towards the A82 again, joining the road to the White Corries ski lift on the approach to the A82.

If the road wasn't here this would be as remote a location as any in the Highlands – a big, marshy area at the head of Glen Etive, many miles from anything other than mountains, heather and bog. In fact it has been an important route to the sea to the west for hundreds of years, and the Kingshouse Hotel (recommended) has been here for at least 250 of those years. The Naylor brothers passed through on their walk south in 1871: 'We walked on to a place which had figured on mileposts for a long distance named 'Kingshouse'. Here we expected to find a village, but as far as we could see there was only one fairly large house there, and that an inn.' There's little more than that here now, and it's still a small oasis in a big wet desert. Camping is permitted near the hotel, but there are no facilities other than those of the hotel bar.

The modern road to the sea from the Kingshouse goes west and down Glen Coe, and these days the route north crosses Loch Leven on the Ballachulish Bridge (there used to be a ferry). Being a military man, and short on high-tech bridge technology, General Wade instead made pretty much a beeline from the Kingshouse for the head of Loch Leven – Kinlochleven, which is now a small town. The route he took, and which the Trail follows, climbs steeply up the side of the valley a little west of the Kingshouse, a route known as the Devil's Staircase. It climbs to a sharp col at a height of 548m, the highest point on the West Highland Way. From here, without warning, the mountains to the north are suddenly all laid out ahead, the biggest of them being the biggest in the country – Ben Nevis. This is one of the best moments of the Trail, provided the weather is good enough to see the view.

From the col at the top of the Devil's Staircase the old road descends as it traverses the hillside, joining a vehicle track servicing Blackwater Reservoir, and eventually reaching Kinlochleven.

Kinlochleven is not a particularly pretty town, having been built around an aluminium plant, for which Blackwater Reservoir was built to generate electricity. The plant has closed, and any passing tourist trade vanished when the Ballachulish Bridge across Loch Leven replaced the ferry in 1975. The town is now reinventing itself to attract the tourist trade in its own right, aided by the West Highland Way. There is plenty of accommodation, including a campsite and a bunkhouse, and both a brewery and an indoor ice-climbing centre are housed in disused parts of the old aluminium works. If you want to try the excellent local Atlas Brewery beer, try the Tailrace Inn or the Antler Bar.

DAY 49

The Mamores and Glen Nevis

Kinlochleven to Fort William (23km, 14 miles)

This is the last day on the West Highland Way, and is a relatively short and easy one.

The line of Wade's road climbs up out of Kinlochleven and follows a deep trench between Beinn na Caillich on the left and the Munros of the Mamores on the right, crossing a minor watershed on the way. The valley bends north and heads for Fort William, and so does the old road, but it soon becomes a tarred motor road. Rather than follow this, the West Highland Way crosses northeast through forestry into the next valley, Glen Nevis, to the foot of Ben Nevis. In clear weather the views of the Ben on the descent are tremendous – it's a big mountain!

The route follows forestry tracks down the glen, and there are two alternative West Highland Way routes down to join the valley road, although it is actually

Descent into Glen Nevis

Ben Nevis

best to take neither, unless you are heading for the youth hostel. Where the second WHW alternative turns right off the forestry road (GR118727), keep straight on, and this will take you to the valley road further north, avoiding unnecessary walking on this busy road.

When you do join the Glen Nevis road, follow it down to the roundabout (the end of the West Highland Way). Keep left here and follow the main road into Fort William (the A82 again).

Fort William has supermarkets, outdoor shops, a TIC and loads of accommodation. The most impressive of the outdoor shops is Nevisport at the end of the High Street. The town will probably be full of visitors, many of them walkers and climbers. Fort William is the most important town serving the needs of visitors to the mountains, and before beginning Section 6 you will want to take as much advantages of it as you can.

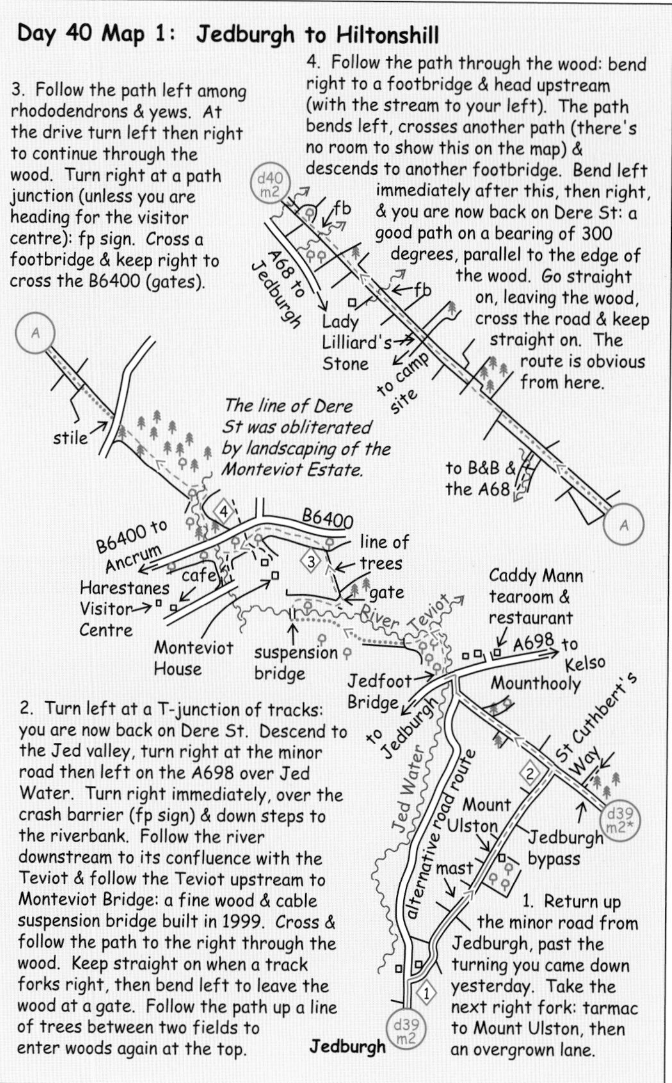
Day 40 Map 1: Jedburgh to Hiltonshill
3. Follow the path left among rhododendrons & yews. At the drive turn left then right to continue through the wood. Turn right at a path junction (unless you are heading for the visitor centre): fp sign. Cross a footbridge & keep right to cross the B6400 (gates).
4. Follow the path through the wood: bend right to a footbridge & head upstream (with the stream to your left). The path bends left, crosses another path (there's no room to show this on the map) & descends to another footbridge. Bend left immediately after this, then right, & you are now back on Dere St: a good path on a bearing of 300 degrees, parallel to the edge of the wood. Go straight on, leaving the wood, cross the road & keep straight on. The route is obvious from here.
d40 m2
fb
A68 to Jedburgh
fb
Lady Lilliard's Stone
to camp site
A
stile
The line of Dere St was obliterated by landscaping of the Monteviot Estate.
to B&B & the A68
A
4
B6400
B6400 to Ancrum
line of trees
3
cafe
Harestanes Visitor Centre
gate
Caddy Mann tearoom & restaurant
River Teviot
A698 to Kelso
Monteviot House
suspension bridge
Jedfoot Bridge
Mounthooly
St Cuthbert's Way
to Jedburgh
2. Turn left at a T-junction of tracks: you are now back on Dere St. Descend to the Jed valley, turn right at the minor road then left on the A698 over Jed Water. Turn right immediately, over the crash barrier (fp sign) & down steps to the riverbank. Follow the river downstream to its confluence with the Teviot & follow the Teviot upstream to Monteviot Bridge: a fine wood & cable suspension bridge built in 1999. Cross & follow the path to the right through the wood. Keep straight on when a track forks right, then bend left to leave the wood at a gate. Follow the path up a line of trees between two fields to enter woods again at the top.
Jed Water
alternative road route
2
Mount Ulston
Jedburgh bypass
d39 m2*
mast
1. Return up the minor road from Jedburgh, past the turning you came down yesterday. Take the next right fork: tarmac to Mount Ulston, then an overgrown lane.
1
d39 m2
Jedburgh

Day 40 Map 2: Hiltonshill to Newtown St Boswells

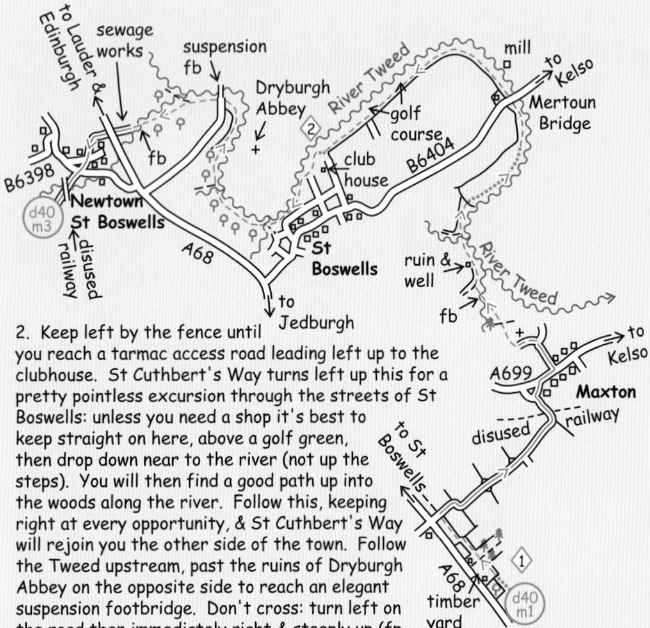

2. Keep left by the fence until you reach a tarmac access road leading left up to the clubhouse. St Cuthbert's Way turns left up this for a pretty pointless excursion through the streets of St Boswells: unless you need a shop it's best to keep straight on here, above a golf green, then drop down near to the river (not up the steps). You will then find a good path up into the woods along the river. Follow this, keeping right at every opportunity, & St Cuthbert's Way will rejoin you the other side of the town. Follow the Tweed upstream, past the ruins of Dryburgh Abbey on the opposite side to reach an elegant suspension footbridge. Don't cross: turn left on the road then immediately right & steeply up (fp sign). The path descends towards a stream: keep left here to follow the stream up through trees & across a footbridge to join an access road by a sewage works. Follow the road under the bypass & round bends between houses. Go straight across a crossroads (or right for shop & pub), down the short road opposite. Cross the main road & leave Newtown St Boswells on the road opposite, over a stream & under a disused railway.

1. After a timber yard keep right at a fork & cross a track to a stile. Continue, emerge from trees via a stile & follow a fenced path. Go left at the field corner then right & continue to a minor road: turn right along it towards Maxton, leaving Dere St for the last time, & at Maxton bending right to reach the A699. Turn right then left, signed to the church. When the road bends right go straight on (path), keeping left of all buildings & passing the old church. The path leads into a wood, down steps, over a footbridge & across a track. At a junction of paths by a wall turn right, which takes you down more steps to the River Tweed. Follow the river up to Mertoun Bridge & beyond it, bending left to reach a golf course.

Day 40 Map 3: Newtown St Boswells to Melrose

5. Climb to the Eildon ridge. There are a lot of paths on the way: St Cuthbert's Way signs show the way. Ignore the first forks left & right, keep right at the next fork, then almost immediately turn left on a small path to reach a saddle on the ridge. Cross the ridge path & descend to the right, contouring round more than you would expect from the map. When the main path goes steeply down left follow it down to the intake hedge. Descend the first field, jink right (gate) & descend steeply on a fenced path to the B6359. Turn right into Melrose.

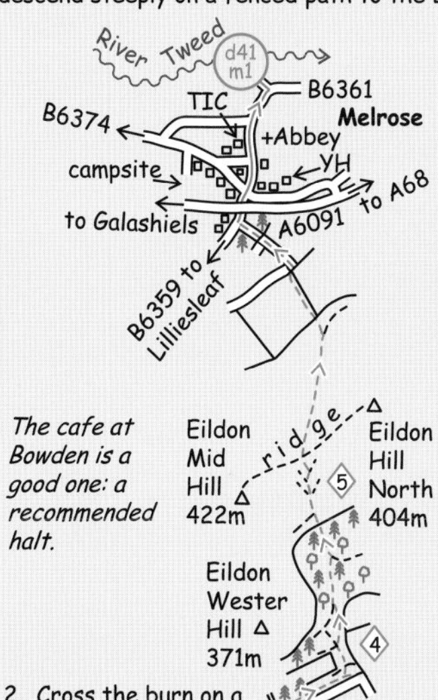

4. Field edges are visible on either side: level with the far end of the lefthand field turn right at a path junction to follow the righthand field edge. Near the end of this field the path climbs left to meet a vehicle track: turn right on this. Climb to a track junction, go left, & climb to leave the trees at a gate in the fence.

The cafe at Bowden is a good one: a recommended halt.

3. Keep to the left when you get the option on the way up the field. At the end bend left then fork right to a gate into the trees. At the end of this small plantation follow a field edge then cross a track & go up steps into a larger wood. Turn right to follow a path parallel to the track (not up the long flight of steps). The path eventually bends left & starts to climb, crossing an old track.

2. Cross the burn on a footbridge & continue upstream. The path diverges from the stream & becomes a lane. Ignore a track to the right, then keep right at the fork just afterwards. At the road turn right up to Bowden & turn right on the B6398, then first left beside the cafe. The road bends left immediately: go straight ahead through a play area to a gate & up the narrow field ahead.

1. Follow the road until it turns sharp left at a farm. Go straight on here along a good track (gates), with a fence on the left & Bowden Burn below the trees to the right. The fence bends left (gate) then forks soon afterwards: take the smaller path descending right to the stream via a small gate (not the farm gate on the lefthand track).

Day 41 Map 1: Melrose to Hog Hill

6. Turn right at the road & left at the first path. A gate leads to a field: follow its right edge up to an oak & a scots pine & veer left up the ridge to a stile into a wood. On the far side follow edges of two fields & bear left in the next: climb past a pile of stones to a post on the skyline. Cross a stile & descend a dip to join a good path along a wall.

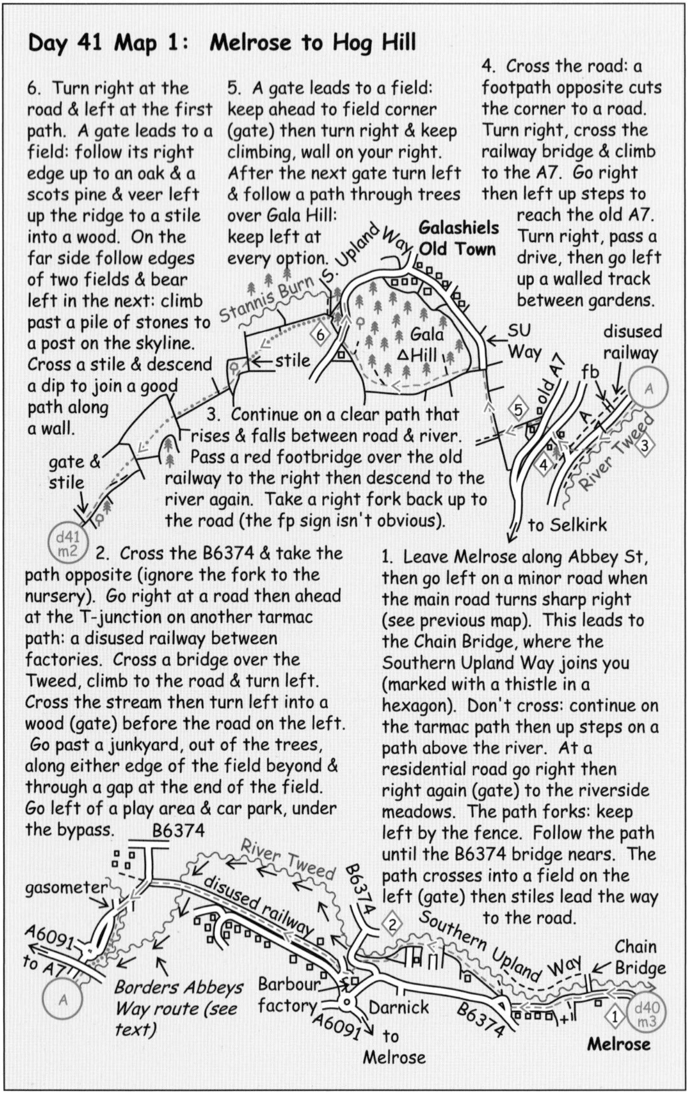

5. A gate leads to a field: keep ahead to field corner (gate) then turn right & keep climbing, wall on your right. After the next gate turn left & follow a path through trees over Gala Hill: keep left at every option.

4. Cross the road: a footpath opposite cuts the corner to a road. Turn right, cross the railway bridge & climb to the A7. Go right then left up steps to reach the old A7. Turn right, pass a drive, then go left up a walled track between gardens.

3. Continue on a clear path that rises & falls between road & river. Pass a red footbridge over the old railway to the right then descend to the river again. Take a right fork back up to the road (the fp sign isn't obvious).

2. Cross the B6374 & take the path opposite (ignore the fork to the nursery). Go right at a road then ahead at the T-junction on another tarmac path: a disused railway between factories. Cross a bridge over the Tweed, climb to the road & turn left. Cross the stream then turn left into a wood (gate) before the road on the left. Go past a junkyard, out of the trees, along either edge of the field beyond & through a gap at the end of the field. Go left of a play area & car park, under the bypass.

1. Leave Melrose along Abbey St, then go left on a minor road when the main road turns sharp right (see previous map). This leads to the Chain Bridge, where the Southern Upland Way joins you (marked with a thistle in a hexagon). Don't cross: continue on the tarmac path then up steps on a path above the river. At a residential road go right then right again (gate) to the riverside meadows. The path forks: keep left by the fence. Follow the path until the B6374 bridge nears. The path crosses into a field on the left (gate) then stiles lead the way to the road.

Galashiels Old Town
S. Upland Way
Stannis Burn
stile
Gala Hill
SU Way
old A7
fb
disused railway
A
River Tweed
gate & stile
d41 m2
to Selkirk
B6374
River Tweed
disused railway
gasometer
A6091 to A7
Borders Abbeys Way route (see text)
Barbour factory
A6091 to Melrose
Darnick
B6374
Southern Upland Way
Chain Bridge
d40 m3
Melrose

Day 41 Map 2: Hog Hill to Brown Knowe

Much of the forestry between Yair Bridge & the Three Brethren is being felled & replanted.

4. Turn left with the fence & forestry edge, & follow a good path past the end of the plantation. This is an old drove road & is generally level & dry underfoot. Gates & stiles show the way, passing right of the summit of Broomy Law, then between pines & another summit on the right, unnamed on OS maps. At the end of the pines is another gate & stile: continue, now with a wall on your right, climbing towards Brown Knowe.

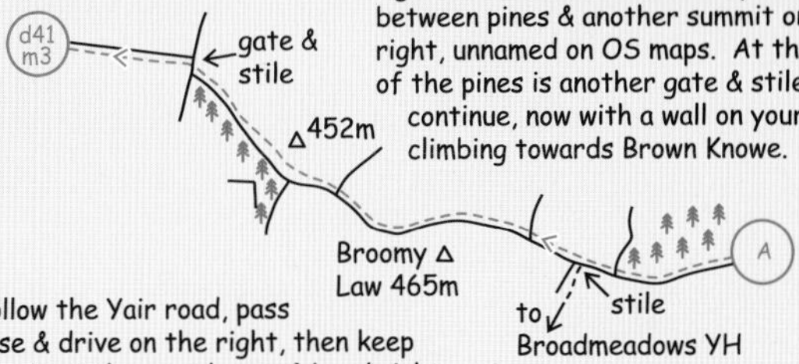

d41 m3

gate & stile

452m

Broomy Law 465m

A

stile

to Broadmeadows YH

3. Follow the Yair road, pass a house & drive on the right, then keep left again at the next house & bend right uphill behind it. Turn sharp left (fp signs) into the pines on a wide path. This climbs all the time, reaching the edge of the trees & following a wall. Eventually it bends left into the trees, emerging into a large replanted area. Continue up the valley: the stream is below to the left & a forestry track runs parallel beyond it. The path bends left & crosses both stream & track to climb steeply. Cross a second track, continuing to climb steeply, until you reach the top edge of the trees, with fence & moor on your left. Don't use the gate onto the moor: keep between fence & trees on a good path. Climb to the three cairns on the summit (the Three Brethren) & enjoy the views. This is the start of a very good high level section of the Trail: spectacular & easy (in reasonable weather).

2. At the bottom edge of the wood go left down a track between fields to cross a road & enter another wood on a fenced track. Continue down towards the A707, forking right to avoid the farmyard. Turn left on the A707, bear right over Yair Bridge, then turn right: "Private road to Yair".

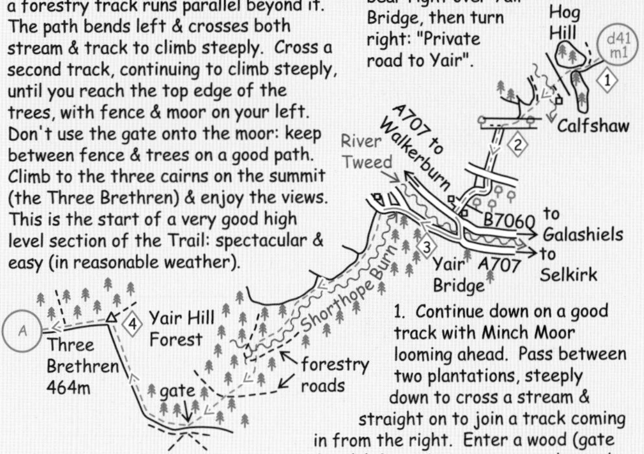

Hog Hill

d41 m1

1

Calfshaw

2

A707 to Walkerburn

River Tweed

B7060 to Galashiels

to Selkirk

3

Yair Bridge

A707

Shorthope Burn

A

4

Three Brethren 464m

Yair Hill Forest

forestry roads

gate

1. Continue down on a good track with Minch Moor looming ahead. Pass between two plantations, steeply down to cross a stream & straight on to join a track coming in from the right. Enter a wood (gate & stile) & continue on an unmade road.

Day 41 Map 3: Brown Knowe to Traquair

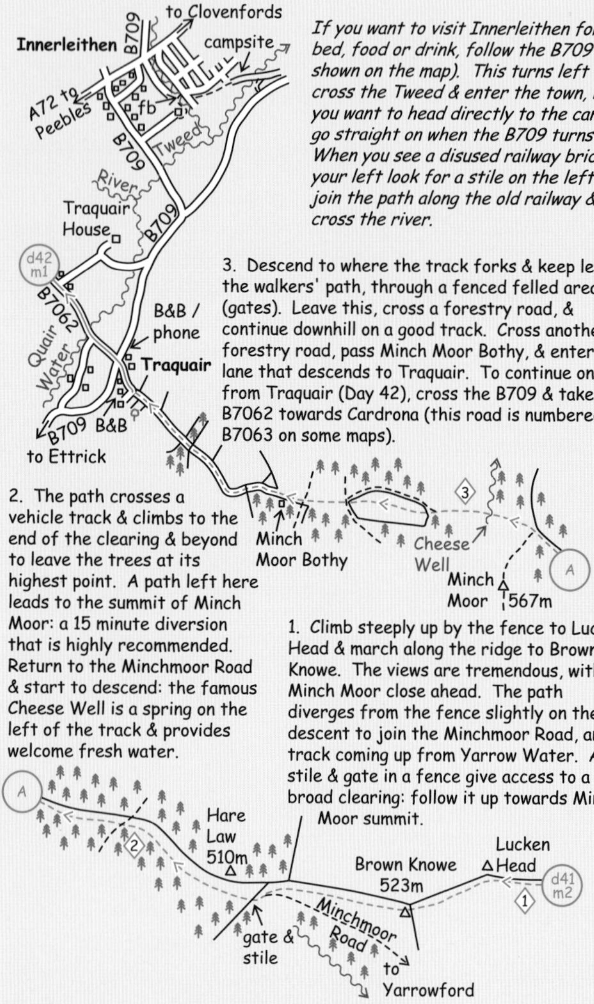

If you want to visit Innerleithen for a bed, food or drink, follow the B709 (as shown on the map). This turns left to cross the Tweed & enter the town, but if you want to head directly to the campsite go straight on when the B709 turns left. When you see a disused railway bridge to your left look for a stile on the left to join the path along the old railway & cross the river.

3. Descend to where the track forks & keep left on the walkers' path, through a fenced felled area (gates). Leave this, cross a forestry road, & continue downhill on a good track. Cross another forestry road, pass Minch Moor Bothy, & enter a lane that descends to Traquair. To continue on from Traquair (Day 42), cross the B709 & take the B7062 towards Cardrona (this road is numbered B7063 on some maps).

2. The path crosses a vehicle track & climbs to the end of the clearing & beyond to leave the trees at its highest point. A path left here leads to the summit of Minch Moor: a 15 minute diversion that is highly recommended. Return to the Minchmoor Road & start to descend: the famous Cheese Well is a spring on the left of the track & provides welcome fresh water.

1. Climb steeply up by the fence to Lucken Head & march along the ridge to Brown Knowe. The views are tremendous, with Minch Moor close ahead. The path diverges from the fence slightly on the descent to join the Minchmoor Road, an old track coming up from Yarrow Water. A stile & gate in a fence give access to a broad clearing: follow it up towards Minch Moor summit.

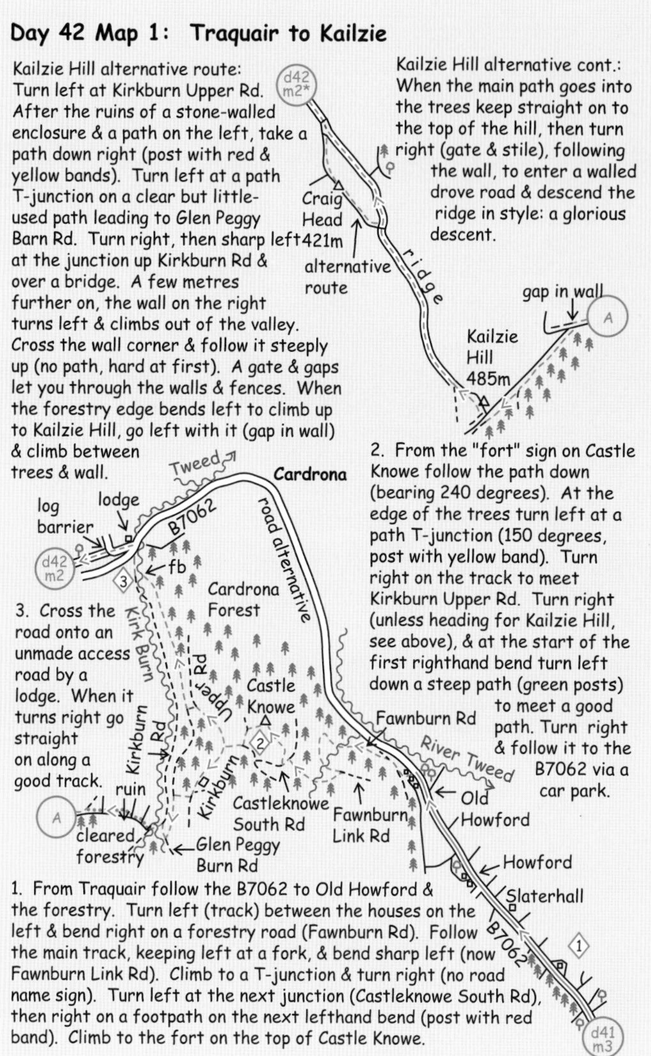
Day 42 Map 1: Traquair to Kailzie
Kailzie Hill alternative route:
Turn left at Kirkburn Upper Rd. After the ruins of a stone-walled enclosure & a path on the left, take a path down right (post with red & yellow bands). Turn left at a path T-junction on a clear but little-used path leading to Glen Peggy Barn Rd. Turn right, then sharp left at the junction up Kirkburn Rd & over a bridge. A few metres further on, the wall on the right turns left & climbs out of the valley. Cross the wall corner & follow it steeply up (no path, hard at first). A gate & gaps let you through the walls & fences. When the forestry edge bends left to climb up to Kailzie Hill, go left with it (gap in wall) & climb between trees & wall.
Kailzie Hill alternative cont.:
When the main path goes into the trees keep straight on to the top of the hill, then turn right (gate & stile), following the wall, to enter a walled drove road & descend the ridge in style: a glorious descent.
d42 m2*
Craig Head 421m
alternative route
ridge
gap in wall
A
Kailzie Hill 485m
2. From the "fort" sign on Castle Knowe follow the path down (bearing 240 degrees). At the edge of the trees turn left at a path T-junction (150 degrees, post with yellow band). Turn right on the track to meet Kirkburn Upper Rd. Turn right (unless heading for Kailzie Hill, see above), & at the start of the first righthand bend turn left down a steep path (green posts) to meet a good path. Turn right & follow it to the B7062 via a car park.
Tweed
Cardrona
log barrier
lodge
B7062
road alternative
d42 m2
3
fb
Cardrona Forest
3. Cross the road onto an unmade access road by a lodge. When it turns right go straight on along a good track.
Kirk Burn
Upper Rd
Castle Knowe
Kirkburn Rd
2
Kirkburn
Fawnburn Rd
River Tweed
A
ruin
cleared forestry
Castleknowe South Rd
Fawnburn Link Rd
Old Howford
Glen Peggy Burn Rd
Howford
Slaterhall
B7062
1
d41 m3
1. From Traquair follow the B7062 to Old Howford & the forestry. Turn left (track) between the houses on the left & bend right on a forestry road (Fawnburn Rd). Follow the main track, keeping left at a fork, & bend sharp left (now Fawnburn Link Rd). Climb to a T-junction & turn right (no road name sign). Turn left at the next junction (Castleknowe South Rd), then right on a footpath on the next lefthand bend (post with red band). Climb to the fort on the top of Castle Knowe.

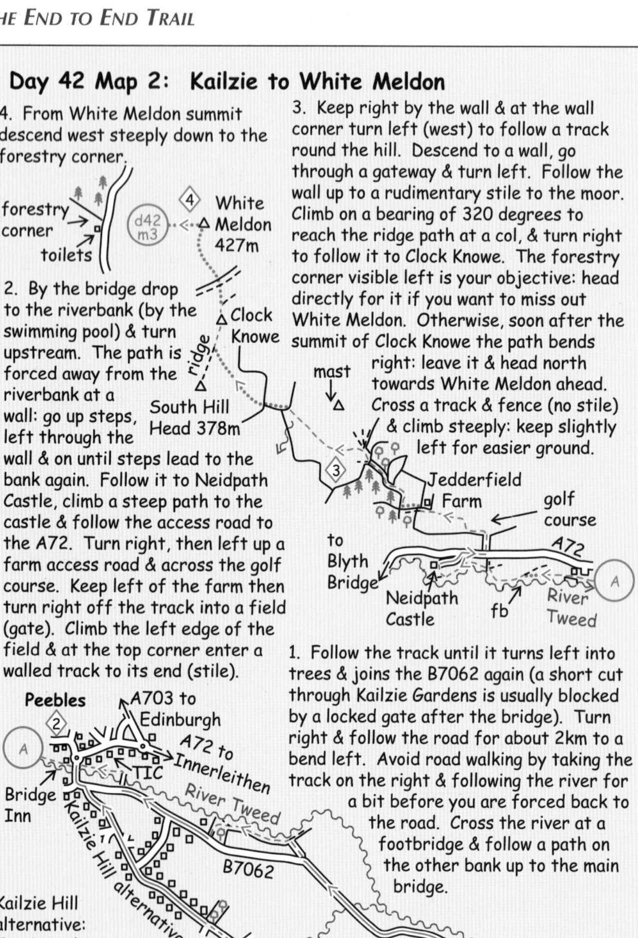
Day 42 Map 2: Kailzie to White Meldon
4. From White Meldon summit descend west steeply down to the forestry corner.
forestry corner
toilets
d42 m3
4
White Meldon 427m
3. Keep right by the wall & at the wall corner turn left (west) to follow a track round the hill. Descend to a wall, go through a gateway & turn left. Follow the wall up to a rudimentary stile to the moor. Climb on a bearing of 320 degrees to reach the ridge path at a col, & turn right to follow it to Clock Knowe. The forestry corner visible left is your objective: head directly for it if you want to miss out White Meldon. Otherwise, soon after the summit of Clock Knowe the path bends right: leave it & head north towards White Meldon ahead. Cross a track & fence (no stile) & climb steeply: keep slightly left for easier ground.
2. By the bridge drop to the riverbank (by the swimming pool) & turn upstream. The path is forced away from the riverbank at a wall: go up steps, left through the wall & on until steps lead to the bank again. Follow it to Neidpath Castle, climb a steep path to the castle & follow the access road to the A72. Turn right, then left up a farm access road & across the golf course. Keep left of the farm then turn right off the track into a field (gate). Climb the left edge of the field & at the top corner enter a walled track to its end (stile).
Clock Knowe
ridge
South Hill Head 378m
mast
3
Jedderfield Farm
golf course
A72
to Blyth Bridge
Neidpath Castle
fb
River Tweed
A
1. Follow the track until it turns left into trees & joins the B7062 again (a short cut through Kailzie Gardens is usually blocked by a locked gate after the bridge). Turn right & follow the road for about 2km to a bend left. Avoid road walking by taking the track on the right & following the river for a bit before you are forced back to the road. Cross the river at a footbridge & follow a path on the other bank up to the main bridge.
Peebles
2
A703 to Edinburgh
A
A72 to Innerleithen
TIC
Bridge Inn
River Tweed
Kailzie Hill alternative route (old drove road)
B7062
Kailzie Hill alternative: Continue down to Peebles on the old drove road. The track becomes a tarmac road & eventually meets the B7062 by the river. Turn left then bend right over the bridge to the town centre, & continue from (2) above.
gates
d41 m1*
bridge
gate
Kailzie Gardens
d41 m1
1

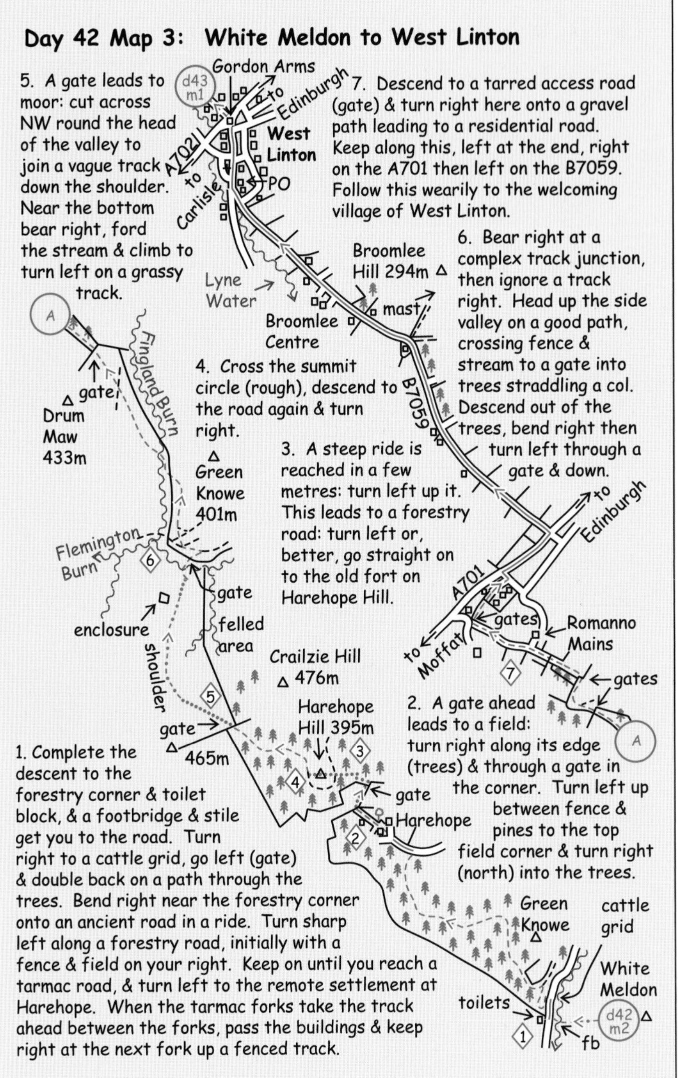
Day 42 Map 3: White Meldon to West Linton
5. A gate leads to moor: cut across NW round the head of the valley to join a vague track down the shoulder. Near the bottom bear right, ford the stream & climb to turn left on a grassy track.
d43 m1
Gordon Arms
to Edinburgh
West Linton
A702
to Carlisle
PO
7. Descend to a tarred access road (gate) & turn right here onto a gravel path leading to a residential road. Keep along this, left at the end, right on the A701 then left on the B7059. Follow this wearily to the welcoming village of West Linton.
Lyne Water
Broomlee Hill 294m
mast
Broomlee Centre
6. Bear right at a complex track junction, then ignore a track right. Head up the side valley on a good path, crossing fence & stream to a gate into trees straddling a col. Descend out of the trees, bend right then turn left through a gate & down.
A
Fingland Burn
gate
Drum Maw 433m
4. Cross the summit circle (rough), descend to the road again & turn right.
B7059
Green Knowe 401m
3. A steep ride is reached in a few metres: turn left up it. This leads to a forestry road: turn left or, better, go straight on to the old fort on Harehope Hill.
to Edinburgh
A701
Flemington Burn
6
gate
felled area
enclosure
shoulder
gates
Romanno Mains
to Moffat
7
Crailzie Hill 476m
gates
5
Harehope Hill 395m
2. A gate ahead leads to a field: turn right along its edge (trees) & through a gate in the corner. Turn left up between fence & pines to the top field corner & turn right (north) into the trees.
A
gate
465m
3
4
gate
Harehope
2
1. Complete the descent to the forestry corner & toilet block, & a footbridge & stile get you to the road. Turn right to a cattle grid, go left (gate) & double back on a path through the trees. Bend right near the forestry corner onto an ancient road in a ride. Turn sharp left along a forestry road, initially with a fence & field on your right. Keep on until you reach a tarmac road, & turn left to the remote settlement at Harehope. When the tarmac forks take the track ahead between the forks, pass the buildings & keep right at the next fork up a fenced track.
Green Knowe
cattle grid
White Meldon
toilets
d42 m2
1
fb

Day 43 Map 1: West Linton to Cauldstane Slap

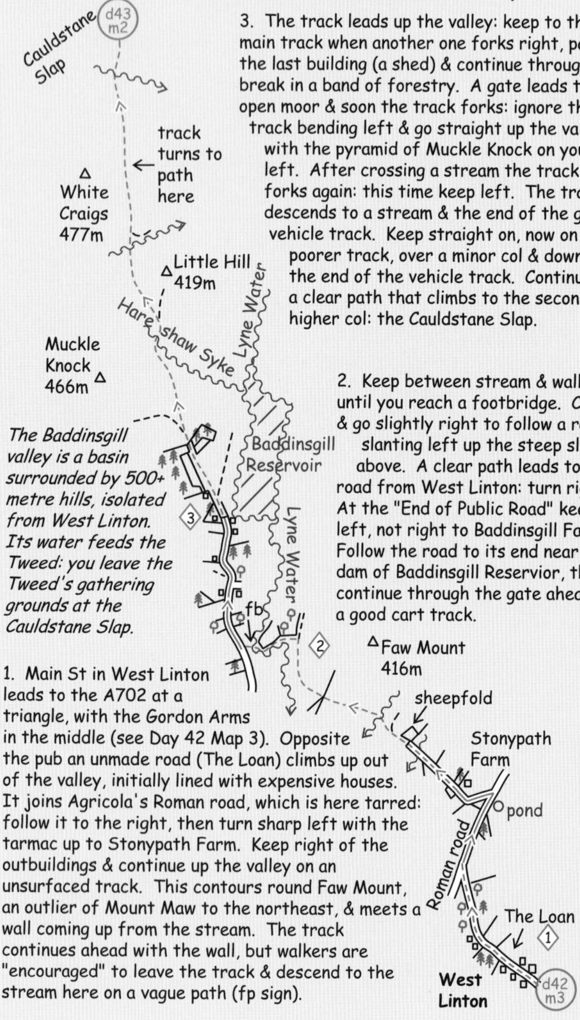

3. The track leads up the valley: keep to the main track when another one forks right, pass the last building (a shed) & continue through a break in a band of forestry. A gate leads to the open moor & soon the track forks: ignore the track bending left & go straight up the valley, with the pyramid of Muckle Knock on your left. After crossing a stream the track forks again: this time keep left. The track descends to a stream & the end of the good vehicle track. Keep straight on, now on a poorer track, over a minor col & down to the end of the vehicle track. Continue on a clear path that climbs to the second & higher col: the Cauldstane Slap.

2. Keep between stream & wall until you reach a footbridge. Cross & go slightly right to follow a ramp slanting left up the steep slope above. A clear path leads to the road from West Linton: turn right. At the "End of Public Road" keep left, not right to Baddinsgill Farm. Follow the road to its end near the dam of Baddinsgill Reservior, then continue through the gate ahead on a good cart track.

The Baddinsgill valley is a basin surrounded by 500+ metre hills, isolated from West Linton. Its water feeds the Tweed: you leave the Tweed's gathering grounds at the Cauldstane Slap.

1. Main St in West Linton leads to the A702 at a triangle, with the Gordon Arms in the middle (see Day 42 Map 3). Opposite the pub an unmade road (The Loan) climbs up out of the valley, initially lined with expensive houses. It joins Agricola's Roman road, which is here tarred: follow it to the right, then turn sharp left with the tarmac up to Stonypath Farm. Keep right of the outbuildings & continue up the valley on an unsurfaced track. This contours round Faw Mount, an outlier of Mount Maw to the northeast, & meets a wall coming up from the stream. The track continues ahead with the wall, but walkers are "encouraged" to leave the track & descend to the stream here on a vague path (fp sign).

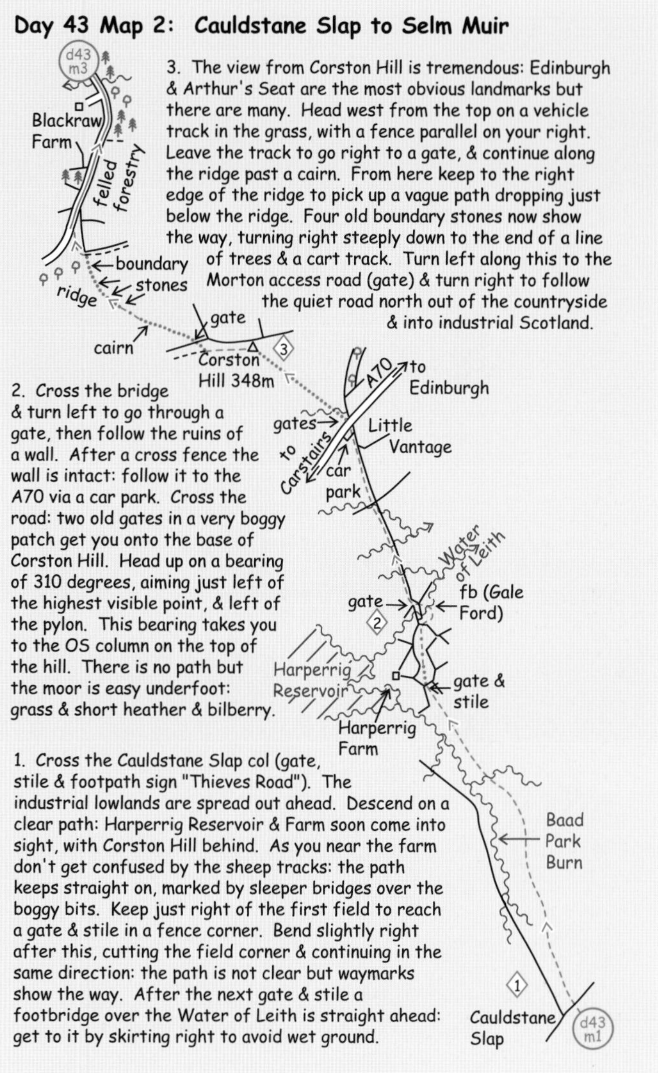
Day 43 Map 2: Cauldstane Slap to Selm Muir
d43 m3
Blackraw Farm
felled forestry
boundary stones
ridge
cairn
gate
Corston Hill 348m
3
A70 to Edinburgh
gates
to Carstairs
car park
Little Vantage
Water of Leith
gate
2
fb (Gale Ford)
Harperrig Reservoir
gate & stile
Harperrig Farm
Baad Park Burn
1
Cauldstane Slap
d43 m1
3. The view from Corston Hill is tremendous: Edinburgh & Arthur's Seat are the most obvious landmarks but there are many. Head west from the top on a vehicle track in the grass, with a fence parallel on your right. Leave the track to go right to a gate, & continue along the ridge past a cairn. From here keep to the right edge of the ridge to pick up a vague path dropping just below the ridge. Four old boundary stones now show the way, turning right steeply down to the end of a line of trees & a cart track. Turn left along this to the Morton access road (gate) & turn right to follow the quiet road north out of the countryside & into industrial Scotland.
2. Cross the bridge & turn left to go through a gate, then follow the ruins of a wall. After a cross fence the wall is intact: follow it to the A70 via a car park. Cross the road: two old gates in a very boggy patch get you onto the base of Corston Hill. Head up on a bearing of 310 degrees, aiming just left of the highest visible point, & left of the pylon. This bearing takes you to the OS column on the top of the hill. There is no path but the moor is easy underfoot: grass & short heather & bilberry.
1. Cross the Cauldstane Slap col (gate, stile & footpath sign "Thieves Road"). The industrial lowlands are spread out ahead. Descend on a clear path: Harperrig Reservoir & Farm soon come into sight, with Corston Hill behind. As you near the farm don't get confused by the sheep tracks: the path keeps straight on, marked by sleeper bridges over the boggy bits. Keep just right of the first field to reach a gate & stile in a fence corner. Bend slightly right after this, cutting the field corner & continuing in the same direction: the path is not clear but waymarks show the way. After the next gate & stile a footbridge over the Water of Leith is straight ahead: get to it by skirting right to avoid wet ground.

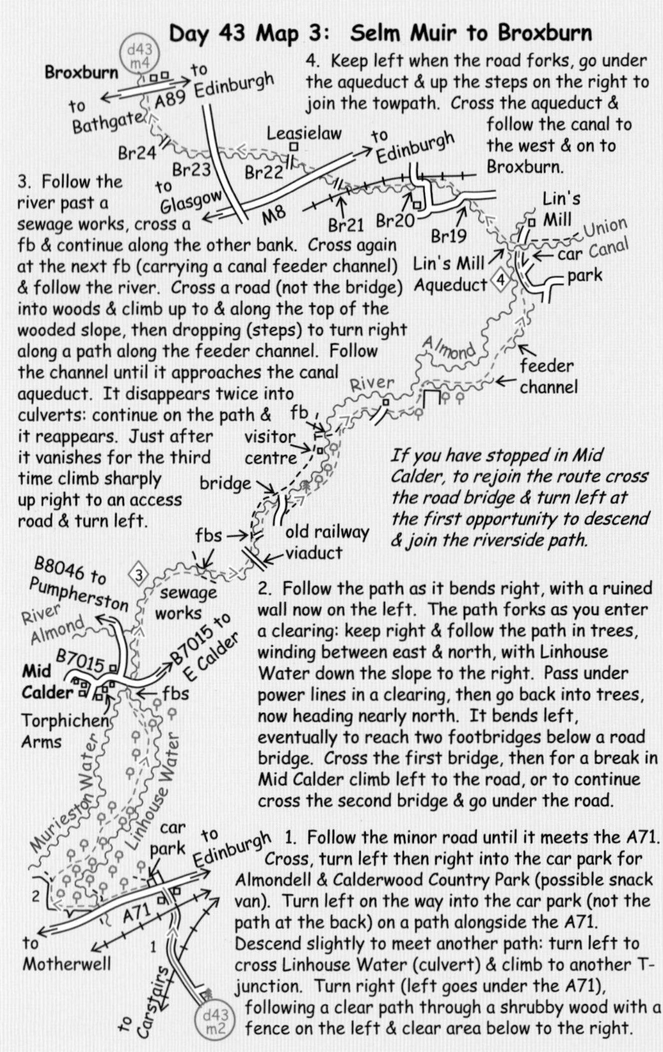
Day 43 Map 3: Selm Muir to Broxburn
4. Keep left when the road forks, go under the aqueduct & up the steps on the right to join the towpath. Cross the aqueduct & follow the canal to the west & on to Broxburn.
3. Follow the river past a sewage works, cross a fb & continue along the other bank. Cross again at the next fb (carrying a canal feeder channel) & follow the river. Cross a road (not the bridge) into woods & climb up to & along the top of the wooded slope, then dropping (steps) to turn right along a path along the feeder channel. Follow the channel until it approaches the canal aqueduct. It disappears twice into culverts: continue on the path & it reappears. Just after it vanishes for the third time climb sharply up right to an access road & turn left.
If you have stopped in Mid Calder, to rejoin the route cross the road bridge & turn left at the first opportunity to descend & join the riverside path.
2. Follow the path as it bends right, with a ruined wall now on the left. The path forks as you enter a clearing: keep right & follow the path in trees, winding between east & north, with Linhouse Water down the slope to the right. Pass under power lines in a clearing, then go back into trees, now heading nearly north. It bends left, eventually to reach two footbridges below a road bridge. Cross the first bridge, then for a break in Mid Calder climb left to the road, or to continue cross the second bridge & go under the road.
1. Follow the minor road until it meets the A71. Cross, turn left then right into the car park for Almondell & Calderwood Country Park (possible snack van). Turn left on the way into the car park (not the path at the back) on a path alongside the A71. Descend slightly to meet another path: turn left to cross Linhouse Water (culvert) & climb to another T-junction. Turn right (left goes under the A71), following a clear path through a shrubby wood with a fence on the left & clear area below to the right.
d43 m4
Broxburn
to Edinburgh
to Bathgate
A89
Leasielaw
to Edinburgh
Br24
Br23
Br22
to Glasgow
M8
Br21
Br20
Br19
Lin's Mill
Union Canal
car park
Lin's Mill Aqueduct
4
Almond
feeder channel
River
fb
visitor centre
bridge
fbs
old railway viaduct
B8046 to Pumpherston
3
sewage works
River Almond
B7015 to E Calder
B7015
Mid Calder
fbs
Torphichen Arms
Murieston Water
Linhouse Water
car park
to Edinburgh
2
A71
to Motherwell
1
to Carstairs
d43 m2

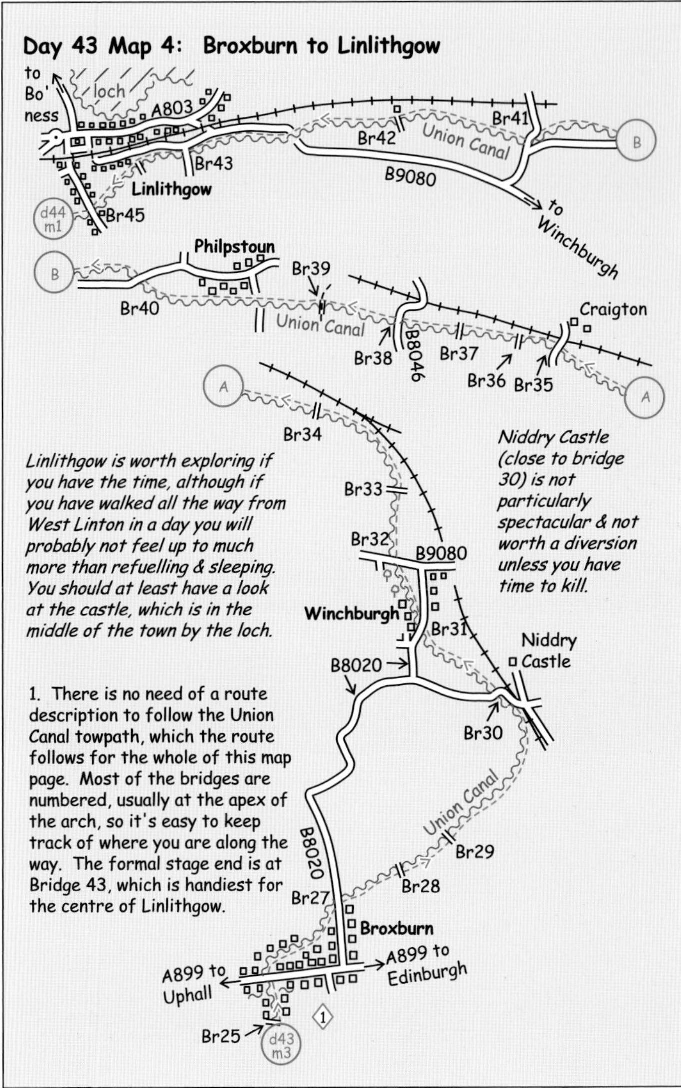
Day 43 Map 4: Broxburn to Linlithgow
to Bo' ness
loch
A803
Br41
Br42
Union Canal
Br43
B9080
Linlithgow
d44 m1
Br45
B
to Winchburgh
Philpstoun
Br39
B
Br40
Union Canal
Craigton
Br38
B8046
Br37
Br36
Br35
A
A
Br34
Br33
Br32
B9080
Winchburgh
Br31
Niddry Castle
B8020
Br30
Union Canal
Br29
Br28
B8020
Br27
Broxburn
A899 to Uphall
A899 to Edinburgh
1
Br25
d43 m3
Linlithgow is worth exploring if you have the time, although if you have walked all the way from West Linton in a day you will probably not feel up to much more than refuelling & sleeping. You should at least have a look at the castle, which is in the middle of the town by the loch.
Niddry Castle (close to bridge 30) is not particularly spectacular & not worth a diversion unless you have time to kill.
1. There is no need of a route description to follow the Union Canal towpath, which the route follows for the whole of this map page. Most of the bridges are numbered, usually at the apex of the arch, so it's easy to keep track of where you are along the way. The formal stage end is at Bridge 43, which is handiest for the centre of Linlithgow.

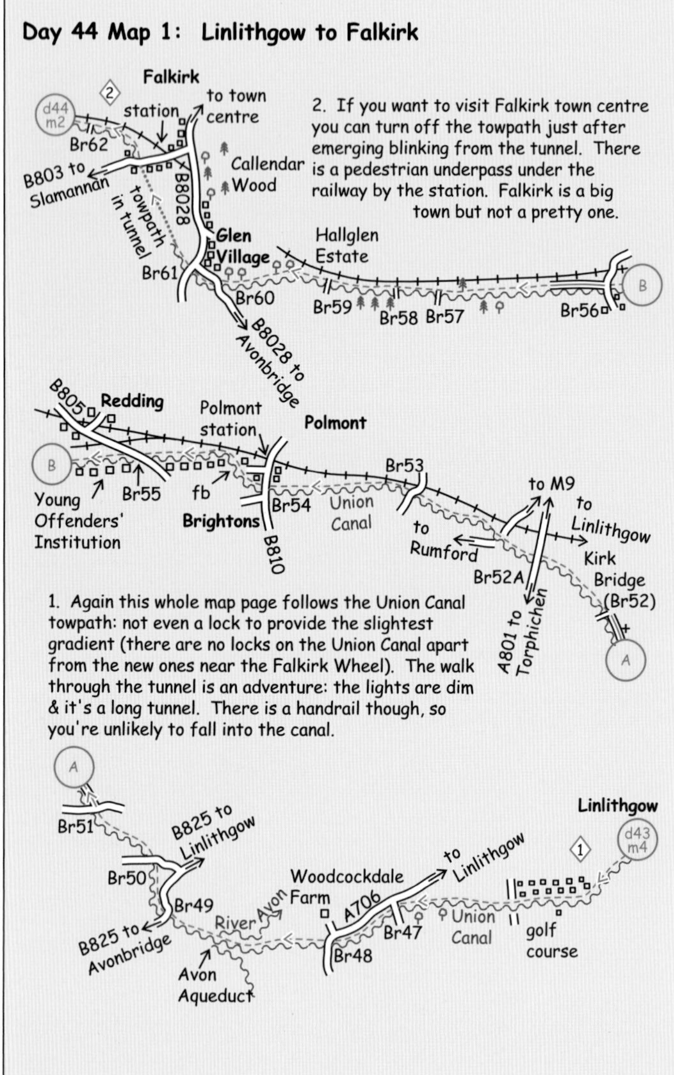
Day 44 Map 1: Linlithgow to Falkirk
Falkirk
d44 m2
station
to town centre
Br62
B803 to Slamannan
towpath in tunnel
B8028
Callendar Wood
Glen Village
Br61
Br60
Hallglen Estate
Br59
Br58
Br57
Br56
B
B8028 to Avonbridge
2. If you want to visit Falkirk town centre you can turn off the towpath just after emerging blinking from the tunnel. There is a pedestrian underpass under the railway by the station. Falkirk is a big town but not a pretty one.
B805
Redding
Polmont station
Polmont
B
Young Offenders' Institution
Br55
fb
Brightons
Br54
B810
Union Canal
Br53
to Rumford
to M9
to Linlithgow
Br52A
A801 to Torphichen
Kirk Bridge (Br52)
A
1. Again this whole map page follows the Union Canal towpath: not even a lock to provide the slightest gradient (there are no locks on the Union Canal apart from the new ones near the Falkirk Wheel). The walk through the tunnel is an adventure: the lights are dim & it's a long tunnel. There is a handrail though, so you're unlikely to fall into the canal.
A
Br51
B825 to Linlithgow
Br50
Br49
B825 to Avonbridge
River Avon
Avon Aqueduct
Woodcockdale Farm
A706
Br48
Br47
to Linlithgow
Union Canal
golf course
Linlithgow
d43 m4

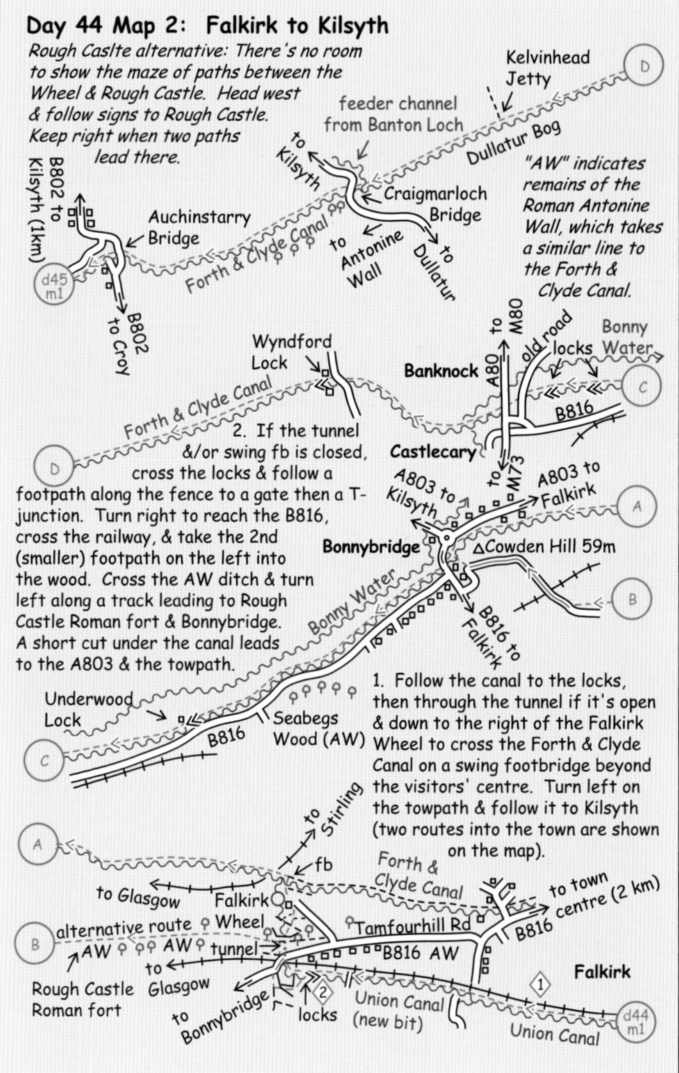
Day 44 Map 2: Falkirk to Kilsyth
Rough Caslte alternative: There's no room to show the maze of paths between the Wheel & Rough Castle. Head west & follow signs to Rough Castle. Keep right when two paths lead there.
Kelvinhead Jetty
feeder channel from Banton Loch
to Kilsyth
Dullatur Bog
"AW" indicates remains of the Roman Antonine Wall, which takes a similar line to the Forth & Clyde Canal.
B802 to Kilsyth (1km)
Craigmarloch Bridge
Auchinstarry Bridge
Forth & Clyde Canal
to Antonine Wall
to Dullatur
d45 m1
B802 to Croy
Wyndford Lock
to M80
old road
Bonny Water
locks
Banknock
A80
B816
Forth & Clyde Canal
2. If the tunnel &/or swing fb is closed, cross the locks & follow a footpath along the fence to a gate then a T-junction. Turn right to reach the B816, cross the railway, & take the 2nd (smaller) footpath on the left into the wood. Cross the AW ditch & turn left along a track leading to Rough Castle Roman fort & Bonnybridge. A short cut under the canal leads to the A803 & the towpath.
Castlecary
to M73
A803 to Kilsyth
A803 to Falkirk
Bonnybridge
△Cowden Hill 59m
Bonny Water
B816 to Falkirk
Underwood Lock
B816
Seabegs Wood (AW)
1. Follow the canal to the locks, then through the tunnel if it's open & down to the right of the Falkirk Wheel to cross the Forth & Clyde Canal on a swing footbridge beyond the visitors' centre. Turn left on the towpath & follow it to Kilsyth (two routes into the town are shown on the map).
to Stirling
fb
Forth & Clyde Canal
to town centre (2 km)
to Glasgow
Falkirk Wheel
alternative route
Tamfourhill Rd
B816
AW
AW
tunnel
B816 AW
to Glasgow
Falkirk
Rough Castle Roman fort
to Bonnybridge
locks
Union Canal (new bit)
Union Canal
d44 m1

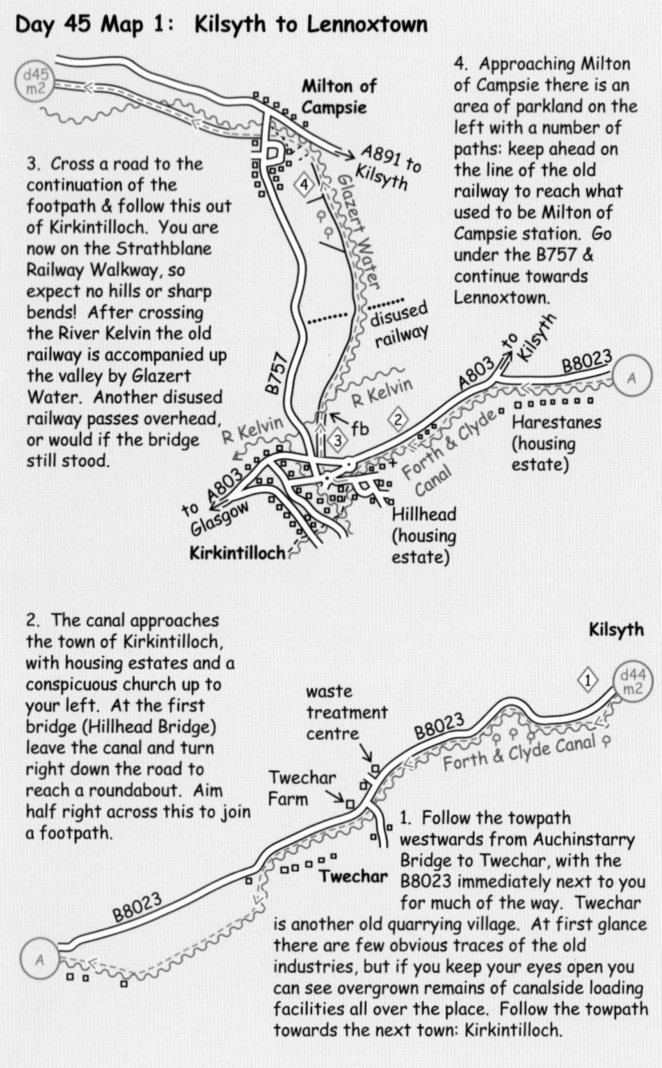
Day 45 Map 1: Kilsyth to Lennoxtown
d45 m2
Milton of Campsie
A891 to Kilsyth
Glazert Water
disused railway
B757
R Kelvin
fb
A803 to Kilsyth
B8023
A
Harestanes (housing estate)
Forth & Clyde Canal
A803 to Glasgow
Kirkintilloch
Hillhead (housing estate)
4. Approaching Milton of Campsie there is an area of parkland on the left with a number of paths: keep ahead on the line of the old railway to reach what used to be Milton of Campsie station. Go under the B757 & continue towards Lennoxtown.
3. Cross a road to the continuation of the footpath & follow this out of Kirkintilloch. You are now on the Strathblane Railway Walkway, so expect no hills or sharp bends! After crossing the River Kelvin the old railway is accompanied up the valley by Glazert Water. Another disused railway passes overhead, or would if the bridge still stood.
2. The canal approaches the town of Kirkintilloch, with housing estates and a conspicuous church up to your left. At the first bridge (Hillhead Bridge) leave the canal and turn right down the road to reach a roundabout. Aim half right across this to join a footpath.
Kilsyth
d44 m2
waste treatment centre
B8023
Forth & Clyde Canal
Twechar Farm
Twechar
B8023
A
1. Follow the towpath westwards from Auchinstarry Bridge to Twechar, with the B8023 immediately next to you for much of the way. Twechar is another old quarrying village. At first glance there are few obvious traces of the old industries, but if you keep your eyes open you can see overgrown remains of canalside loading facilities all over the place. Follow the towpath towards the next town: Kirkintilloch.

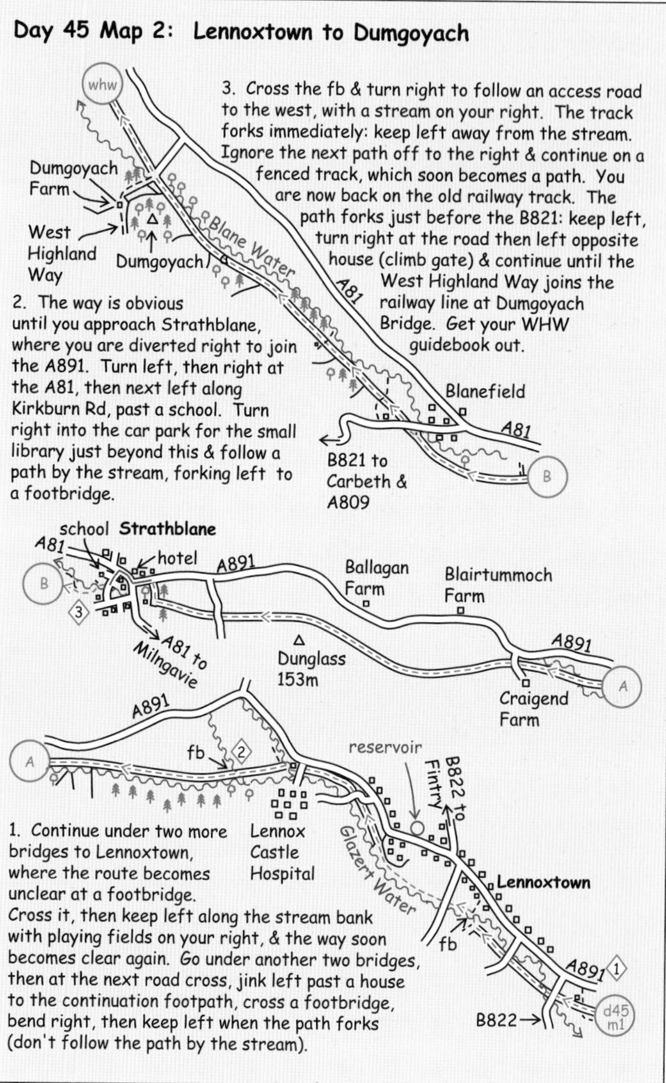
Day 45 Map 2: Lennoxtown to Dumgoyach
whw
3. Cross the fb & turn right to follow an access road to the west, with a stream on your right. The track forks immediately: keep left away from the stream. Ignore the next path off to the right & continue on a fenced track, which soon becomes a path. You are now back on the old railway track. The path forks just before the B821: keep left, turn right at the road then left opposite house (climb gate) & continue until the West Highland Way joins the railway line at Dumgoyach Bridge. Get your WHW guidebook out.
Dumgoyach Farm
West Highland Way
Dumgoyach
Blane Water
A81
2. The way is obvious until you approach Strathblane, where you are diverted right to join the A891. Turn left, then right at the A81, then next left along Kirkburn Rd, past a school. Turn right into the car park for the small library just beyond this & follow a path by the stream, forking left to a footbridge.
Blanefield
A81
B821 to Carbeth & A809
B
school
Strathblane
A81
hotel
A891
B
3
A81 to Milngavie
Ballagan Farm
Blairtummoch Farm
Dunglass 153m
A891
A
Craigend Farm
A891
A
fb
2
reservoir
B822 to Fintry
1. Continue under two more bridges to Lennoxtown, where the route becomes unclear at a footbridge. Cross it, then keep left along the stream bank with playing fields on your right, & the way soon becomes clear again. Go under another two bridges, then at the next road cross, jink left past a house to the continuation footpath, cross a footbridge, bend right, then keep left when the path forks (don't follow the path by the stream).
Lennox Castle Hospital
Glazert Water
Lennoxtown
fb
A891
1
B822
d45 m1

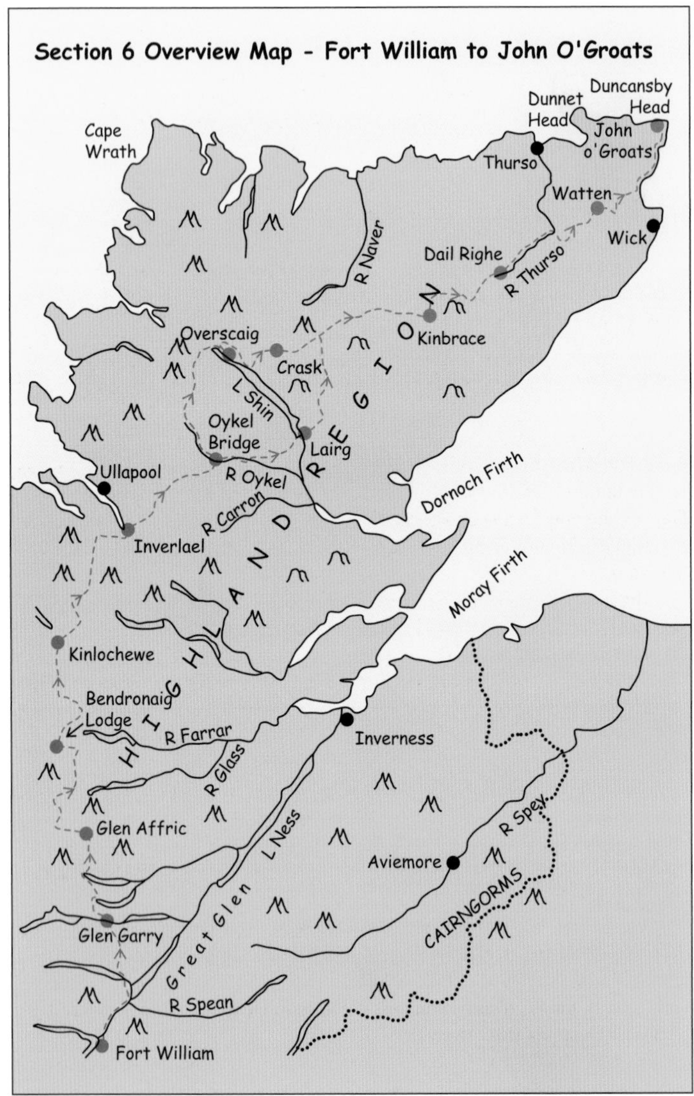
Section 6 Overview Map - Fort William to John O'Groats
Duncansby Head
Dunnet Head
John o'Groats
Cape Wrath
Thurso
Watten
Wick
R Naver
Dail Righe
R Thurso
Kinbrace
Overscaig
Crask
L Shin
Oykel Bridge
Lairg
Ullapool
R Oykel
R Carron
Dornoch Firth
Inverlael
Moray Firth
HIGHLAND REGION
Kinlochewe
Bendronaig Lodge
R Farrar
Inverness
R Glass
R Spey
Glen Affric
L Ness
Aviemore
CAIRNGORMS
Great Glen
Glen Garry
R Spean
Fort William

SECTION 6

The Northern Highlands and the Flow Country: Fort William to John O'Groats

Distance	391km (243 miles)
Road Walking	11%. This is considerably less than the average for the rest of the route; there is not much need to walk on tarred roads in the north of Scotland.
Days	12 (Main Schedule), or 18 (Alternative Schedule)
Maps	this guide, at the end of section 6

From Fort William the Trail leads northwards into the mountains, wild and largely uninhabited. In the 11 days from Fort William to Watten, at the end of Day 60, the only facilities passed are one small village with shops, five isolated hotels, a bunkhouse and a youth hostel. You also cross only 12 public roads in that time.

There are many streams and rivers to ford in this section, and alternative wet weather routes are described or indicated wherever possible, but be aware that in very wet weather even these may not be passable. If you are in any doubt about your mountain navigation and survival skills, a better course from Fort William would be to follow the Great Glen towards Inverness and take a route closer to the east coast (see the Great Glen Way and Easter Ross under Alternative Routes, below).

The valleys between Fort William and Kinlochewe, four days to the north, run mainly east–west, across the line of the Trail. This means that the route has to climb passes (bealachs) in and out of many remote glens over Days 50 –53, a significant change from the valley walking of the West Highland Way. Remote though these glens are, there are usually a few walkers about on this stretch.

A long day (Day 54) along valleys and over passes through the 'Great Wilderness' of the Kinlochewe and Dundonnel forests leads to the A835 Ullapool trunk road at the head of Loch Broom. (For the benefit of those not familiar with the Highlands, don't expect trees in Highland forests – a forest is a game reserve, not a tree reserve).

From Inverlael at the head of Loch Broom the Trail leaves the west coast for good, heading northeast towards John O'Groats. A high pass crosses the main watershed, then tracks along glens lead down to the hotel at Oykel Bridge, and up the River Oykel to the foot of the great Assynt massif. You will probably see few other walkers between here and John O'Groats.

An old stalkers' track skirts the eastern edge of Assynt above Glen Cassley, then the Trail leaves it to cut across a trackless pass to the head of Loch Shin. Continuing east, the last Highland pass leads to Loch Choire below Ben Klibreck, and then the mountains are left behind. Ahead are the lower Flow Country hills and peat bogs.

The track down from Loch Choire leads to the River Helmsdale, then a last climb over the unfrequented Knockfin Heights reaches the headwaters of the River Thurso. A path turns into a track then turns into a tarmac road as the river flows northeast. At this point the River Thurso turns north, so the Trail leaves it and the tarmac for a more direct and relatively tarmac-free route to Watten, and meets the east coast at Sinclair's Bay. The last stretch to Duncansby Head and John O'Groats follows the coast, initially on the beach then along spectacular cliff tops to finish.

Maps

1:50000 Landranger maps
41 Ben Nevis, Fort William & Glen Coe
34 Fort Augustus
33 Loch Alsh, Glen Shiel
25 Glen Carron & Glen Affric
19 Gairloch & Ullapool
20 Beinn Dearg
16 Lairg, Loch Shin
15 Loch Assynt (not needed if you take the alternative route via Lairg)
17 Helmsdale & Strath of Kildonan
12 Thurso & Wick

Recommendations

You will need all these maps, and should also consider taking information from *North To The Cape* by Denis Brook and Phil Hinchliffe, as it includes details of other potentially useful wet weather alternative routes. Because of the nature of the terrain there is little point in taking 1:25000 maps, and unlike for the earlier sections I haven't listed the complete set of those you would need to take.

To Help You On Your Way

Accommodation

These TICs are on or reasonably close to the route, and all share a common phone number and website, 0845 225 5121, www.visithighlands.com.

Cameron Centre, Cameron Square, Fort William
Cluanie Inn, Cluanie
Argyle Street, Ullapool
Ferrycroft Countryside Centre, Lairg (seasonal)
Norseman Hotel, Riverside, Wick (seasonal)
County Road, John O'Groats (seasonal)

These TICs will have local knowledge, but bear in mind that the Highland region publishes a single accommodation guide to cover the whole area. Accommodation is sparse, and advance research is recommended. Although there are bed and breakfasts along the final stretch from Keiss to John O'Groats, they often all fill up, so book ahead if you can. There is a campsite by the hotel and pier at John O'Groats.

Equipment Shops

Day 53 Moru Outdoor, Old Village Hall, Kinlochewe, tel 01445 760234 and 07780 967018. In an emergency they will open the shop out of hours if you phone.

Day 55 (off-route) North West Outdoors, West Argyle Street, Ullapool, tel 01854 613383

Food Shops

Chances to re-supply are limited after Fort William and you will have to take care not to run out of provisions.

Day 53 Kinlochewe has two general stores, and the one at the garage stays open reasonably late

Day 56L If you are taking the Lairg alternative route (see below) there is a shop at Rosehall and more in Lairg

Day 60 There is a post office/general store at Watten

Day 61 There is a general store in Keiss, and shops and a post office at John O'Groats

Alternative Routes

Via Lairg

An alternative route from Oykel Bridge via Lairg (at the foot of Loch Shin) to Loch Choire is described, avoiding the Assynt massif and the trackless pass at the head of Loch Shin. The Lairg alternative is advised if the weather is bad, if you need to re-supply, or if you just don't want to venture into a remote area. Unfortunately it involves a considerable amount of road walking on the first of the two days. The maps and description of the alternative route via Lairg days start after Day 57 and are numbered 56L and 57L.

The Great Glen Way and Easter Ross

If you are unhappy about the wilderness walking and remoteness from support and civilisation entailed by the recommended route north from Fort William, the best option is to head northeast up the Great Glen towards (but not *to*) Inverness. Then, once you are close to the east coast (north of Drumnadrochit), you will have to pick a way north to John O'Groats, avoiding roads as best you can. You will inevitably walk a fair amount of tarmac, and the scenery doesn't compare at all with the western route of the Trail. The busier roads really must be avoided as far as possible – the A82 up the Great Glen and the A9 and A99 further north are busy and dangerous.

From Fort William you can follow the Great Glen Way, a waymarked walking route that follows the glen all the way to Inverness. It takes towpaths, forestry roads and minor public roads, and since it follows the valley it gives pretty easy walking. Leaving the Great Glen Way north of Drumnadrochit, you can follow minor roads north to join the A862 across the river to Beauly. From Beauly, minor roads and tracks via Clashandorran, Aultgowrie Bridge and Moy Bridge lead to Strathpeffer, where you can leave the roads for a bit and walk along the ridge of Knock Farril to the town of Dingwall. The route so far is as described by Andrew McCloy in *The Land's End to John O'Groats Walk* (see below), and looks like the best option for this section.

From Dingwall it could be worth investigating whether a route through the hills to Strath Rusdale is feasible, although I must make clear that I have not tried this myself, and am not aware that anyone else has tried it either. This possible route goes north to cross the River Sgitheach at the bridge marked at GR531634, joining a path along the forestry edge across the slopes of Cnoc nan Each, fording the All nan

Caorach at GR548678, and crossing the River Glass by Eilanach Lodge. From Glen Glass a track over Strath Mor and a bridge at Strone (GR577746) should make it possible to join the road up Strath Rusdale. In any event you can definitely reach Strath Rusdale from Dingwall by using minor roads via Evanton and the B9176 past Alness. From Strath Rusdale there is then a hill track north from the end of the public road at Braeantra (GR569779) that crosses to the head of the Dornoch Firth at Kincardine, near Ardgay. Further details of this track are given in *Scottish Hill Tracks* (see Appendix 1).

From Ardgay it's not far up Achany Glen to Lairg, where you can rejoin the End to End Trail via the Lairg alternative (Day 56L). You can follow minor roads and the B864 all the way to Lairg if you want, but there are parallel forestry roads for parts of it that would be a better bet.

If you'd rather stick closer to the coast from Dingwall to John O'Groats you will find yourself doing a lot of road walking, although it is possible to walk along the shore at times (the cliffs between Helmsdale and Wick are particularly spectacular). Andrew McCloy's *The Land's End to John O'Groats Walk* is the best guide for this.

Guidebooks

The Great Glen Way by Jacquetta Megarry and Sandra Bardwell, Rucksack Readers, 2002
The Land's End to John O'Groats Walk by Andrew McCloy, Cordee, 2002
Follow the Spring North by Christine Roche, Trafford Publishing, 2004
Scottish Hill Tracks, editors DJ Bennet and CD Stone, Scottish Rights of Way and Access Society, 2004 edition
The Great Glen Way by Paddy Dillon, Cicerone, 2007

DAY 50

The Great Glen and Glen Garry

Fort William to Glen Garry (Loch Poulary) (37km, 23 miles)

The journey into the wilder Highlands starts deceptively easily, along the Great Glen – as far as Loch Lochy the route coincides more or less with the Great Glen Cycle Route and the Great Glen Way footpath. It then heads up into the mountains, crossing the highest of the Trail's Scottish bealachs – the Bealach Carn na h-Urchaire – and dropping down into Glen Garry.

From Fort William, 3km (2 miles) of footpaths avoids road walking for the most part to reach the Caledonian Canal at Neptune's Staircase (Day 50 Map 1). You then follow the towpath for about 11km (7 miles) northeast to Gairlochy at the foot of Loch Lochy (Day 50 Map 2). (If you want to break the journey overnight at Gairlochy, there are two bed and breakfasts and a campsite (Gairlochy Holiday Park) at Mucomir, about 1.5km (1 mile) off-route along the B8004 to the south-east.)

The Caledonian Canal follows the Great Glen (Glen Mor), which is a fault line running from coast to coast across the Highlands from Fort William to Inverness. For much of the way there were already natural lochs before the canal was dug – lochs Lochy, Oich, Ness and Dochfour. Joining them up with a canal suitable for sea-going vessels was first considered in 1726, although it wasn't until 1804 that

Neptune's Staircase, Caledonian Canal

work on building it started. The main justification for the canal was that it would give sailing ships a safer alternative to the dangerous Pentland Firth route round the north coast of Scotland, avoiding treacherous seas and even more treacherous French pirates. The canal is thus much bigger than a typical English canal designed for inland barge traffic. Each lock on the Caledonian Canal is at least 50m (170 ft) long and 12m (40 ft) wide. The point at which the route meets the canal is in the middle of Neptune's Staircase, an impressive flight of eight locks raising the canal most of the way from sea level to the level of Loch Lochy.

Construction proved difficult, and the canal wasn't opened all the way through until 1822, and even then it wasn't yet as deep as it was designed to be. Financially it wasn't a success – steamships had started to appear on the scene, and they had far less trouble with the Pentland Firth, and consequently weren't prepared to pay the canal dues. Unlike many canals, however, it managed to survive intact, and has remained open to shipping from sea to sea. It also makes a pleasant interlude on your journey through the Highlands, the towpath making for the easiest bit of walking you will get between Glasgow and John O'Groats. Moy Bridge, passed on the Trail, is the only surviving original bridge on the canal, and the bridge keeper used to have to row across to open the bridge fully.

Moy Bridge, Caledonian Canal

Between Loch Lochy and Loch Arkaig the Trail follows a track through woods past St Ciaran's Church, a pretty little building inaccessible by road, and then past Achnacarry, the home of the Camerons. The Camerons forfeited their land after the 1745 Jacobite Rebellion, but had it returned to them in 1784. Donald Cameron of Locheil then got rid of all his tenants, replacing them with sheep farmers from the lowlands. This was a classic example of the clearance of the Highlands, which took place in the 18th and 19th centuries. Once the autonomy of the clan chieftains was taken from them after 1745, they were little more than landowners, and many decamped south to Edinburgh or London and became absentee landlords. Instead of defending the territory of their extended families, they looked to maximise their incomes, and this led to the expulsion of the local population to make way for large sheep farms. This happened throughout the Highlands, and in many of the glens that are now uninhabited, or nearly so, there are many old abandoned homesteads. Your route passes many of these sites – if the political situation had been different, perhaps some of the people would still be there. Many of the glens are not that different in character to the valleys of Northumberland or the English Lake District, which have retained a local farming population.

From the foot of Loch Lochy to the foot of Loch Arkaig (Day 50 Map 2) the walking is easy, on paths, tracks and tarmac. From here (Day 50 Map 3) the character of the walk changes, as does the whole journey – today and on Days 51 to 53 the route crosses pass after pass, from valley to valley.

At the road junction at the foot of Loch Arkaig you need to consider the state of the weather and how full the streams are before going any further. The most direct route, and the best in reasonable weather, is via the Bealach Carn na h-Urchaire. This is the main Trail route, and is described first. There are however two potential drawbacks with this route. The first is that it crosses a high pathless pass that is in places quite difficult underfoot. If the cloud is down and your navigation skills are limited you should take the alternative route via Fedden, described later. The second disadvantage is that if the streams are running *at all* high, you may not be able to cross the streams once you have descended into Glen Garry, and this will mean a long detour at the end of a long day. Because this is a real danger, I have given details of the escape routes available if you do get caught out here, but if there is much water in the streams, you should avoid getting into this situation in the first place by taking the Fedden route.

Main route via the Bealach Carn na h-Urchaire (Day 50 Maps 3 and 4)

The main route from Loch Arkaig to Glen Garry crosses a major pass, the Bealach Carn na h-Urchaire, on the main watershed. At 650m this is the highest point of the Scottish part of the route, and the bealach itself is wild and pathless. For about 4km (3 miles) it is very hard work because of the nature of the terrain – steep and peaty. (David Paterson followed this route on his 'Cape Wrath Trail' and slept out on the bealach without a tent. When I was there at the end of May one year it was sleeting, and there was nowhere dry enough to consider sitting down, never mind sleeping.)

Despite the fact that you cross the bealach heading more or less northwest, you are actually crossing the watershed from west to east. The southern slopes feed into Loch Lochy and thence towards Fort William, and the northern slopes drain to Loch Ness and Inverness.

Descent from the bealach is steep and difficult to start with, but you pick up a path before the confluence with the Allt an Fhithich. From here to the bottom of the glen the walking is not too difficult but it is generally very wet underfoot. You also have two major streams to cross before reaching the valley forestry, and another to cross inside the plantation, this last being the Allt Choire a Bhalachain, which is the most difficult of the three to cross.

Alternative Wet Weather Descents from the Bealach Carn na h-Urchaire (Day 50 Maps 4, 6 and back to 4)

If the streams are high, it is possible to descend to Glen Garry without crossing any major streams, although this means an additional 10km (6 miles) of walking. To do this, cross the Allt Ailein high up (see Day 50 Map 3), then follow it down, keeping the stream on your left. There are two leaky bothies by the track at Garrygualach (Day 50 Map 6), suitable for an overnight stop if you need it.

If you get as far as the Allt Choire a Bhalachain and find that too dangerous to cross, you can also reach Garrygualach by following the main valley down – there is a path of sorts most of the way.

Alternative Wet Weather Route via Fedden (Day 50 Maps 5, 6 and 4)

If the weather is already bad when you reach Loch Arkaig, you are recommended to take a less scenic but lower-level route to Glen Garry further east, climbing up Gleann Cia-aig to the ruined farmstead at Fedden, and descending through forestry to join the Glen Garry road a few kilometres east of the Tomdoun Sporting Lodge Hotel. If you intend to visit the hotel anyway, the Fedden route doesn't involve significant additional distance.

Accommodation in Glen Garry is limited. If you want to camp, the best place is probably by the bridge over the River Garry, where the main route emerges from the forestry. There are also a couple of possible small sites by the road between the two birch groves further west. If you want a roof over your head you must make tracks for the Tomdoun (pronounced 'Tomdown') Sporting Lodge Hotel, which is 3km (2 miles) off-route along the road to the east. The hotel does bed and breakfast, serves meals, and has a bunkhouse (tel 01809 511218). You may also be able to camp near the hotel – ask.

Until 1962 the main road to Kyle of Lochalsh and Skye passed what was then the Tomdoun Inn heading west, then turned sharp right after 250m by a chapel. In 1962 Loch Loyne was dammed to make a reservoir, the road north of Tomdoun was flooded, and a new road was built between Glen Garry and Loch Cluanie, further east, going round the foot of the new Loch Loyne reservoir. This left the Tomdoun Inn marooned, but it has survived, relying on fishermen and walkers for its custom. Tomorrow the Trail meets up with the old road, which now looks like a cart track, on the other side of Glen Loyne, and follows it to Loch Cluanie.

DAY 51

Four Glens

Glen Garry (Loch Poulary) to Glen Affric (26km, 16 miles)

Today the Trail heads due north, crossing three passes that link four glens running from east to west: Glen Garry, Glen Loyne, Strath Cluanie and Glen Affric. None of the passes is particularly high, and there is only a short stretch that doesn't follow a good path. There is even a pub at lunchtime.

The path over from Glen Garry to Glen Loyne is easy to follow and easy underfoot, considering that it climbs to about 500m (Day 51 Map 1). Near the River Loyne the path disappears, however, close to where you need to cross the river. In normal weather the crossing is easy enough, but to quote *Scottish Hill Tracks*: 'This route is not possible if the River Loyne is in spate'. There is no alternative wet weather route for this section. The only guaranteed way of making progress in spate conditions would be to follow the A87 round the foot of Loch Loyne and along Loch Cluanie, which is not really much fun as a walking route, since the road is a busy one. (If the River Loyne is too full to cross safely, it *may* be practical to follow the river upstream (westwards) for 2–3km and cross higher up,

Aonach Meadhoin, A'Chralaig and Loch Cluanie

above some of the many tributaries feeding the spate, although I have not tried this and am not aware that anyone else has, either.)

Once across the Loyne (and into the old county of Ross and Cromarty) there is a good path running along the lower slope of the hillside, leading down the valley to a ruined settlement near the head of Loch Loyne. From here a steep, pathless climb up by a stream out of the valley brings you to the old Skye road, which is now a deserted and decaying track. Fast progress on the old road takes you down to the A87 and the Cluanie Inn (Day 51 Map 2).

The Cluanie Inn (tel 01320 340238) is open all day, is comfortable and serves bar meals. If you are looking for overnight accommodation, the only available beds are at the inn, which is comparatively upmarket. There are good camping spots by the old road, before reaching the A87, but an unfriendly 'no camping' sign to discourage you. There are alternative spots between the road and the loch on the way east towards the Glen Affric track.

The track over to Glen Affric is a good one most of the way to the watershed, then it deteriorates into a very wet path. Following the path from here onwards is easy, but keeping feet dry is not. The path traverses well above the River Affric, dropping down to cross a bridge near Alltbeithe youth hostel. This is the only accommodation, indeed it is the only building in sight – upper Glen Affric is a remote place. Suitable ground for pitching a tent is scarce, but there are some pitches by the Allt Beithe Garbh to the west of the youth hostel.

DAY 52

The Falls of Glomach

Glen Affric to Bendronaig Lodge (33km, 21 miles)

This is an excellent day's walking over passes and along valleys, the high point being the great chasm of the Falls of Glomach, one of the most atmospheric and impressive places in the British mountains. Some of the walking is not easy, in particular the route down the west side of Gleann Gaorsaic to the falls is slow and hard work. The effort is well rewarded though, and the rest of the day is enjoyable, mostly on good paths and tracks. There are no tarmac roads to be seen all day, and you will probably see no cars at all, as there is no public access for cars to the estate road up Glen Elchaig.

Glen Affric is remote, but probably the busiest place you will see all day, because of the youth hostel, and the number of Munros that surround it (a 'Munro' is a Scottish mountain or top at least 3000 feet high). Just about everyone else will be ticking Munros from their lists rather than following the glens and passes.

A little upstream from the hostel the main valley swings south, and a side valley comes in from the west – Gleann Gniomhaidh. There is a route from here all the way to the coast at Loch Duich, going over two passes. The Trail follows the first part of this path, initially alongside the Allt Beithe Garbh, then up the classically U-shaped Gleann Gniomhaidh between Beinn Fhada and Sgurr nan Ceathreamhnan, over the peat hags and the main watershed at its head, and down slightly to Loch a' Bhealaich at the head of Gleann Gaorsaic. The path to the coast continues west over the Bealach an Sgàirne, but the End to End Trail leaves it here to head north down the glen, which joins Glen Elchaig in a few more kilometres.

The most direct way would be to keep to the east side of the valley and follow a path that cuts a corner to join Glen Elchaig at Carnach. It may give easier walking, as well, but the Falls of Glomach must not be missed, so the Trail takes the west side of the valley, along the shore of Loch a' Bhealaich to avoid the worst of the peat hags, then for most of the way keeping close to the stream and smaller lochs. An old stalking path appears, but the going is still difficult, as the path has been neglected for a long time. The bridges across side streams are in ruin, and detours are needed to keep out of the peat bogs. Eventually the valley narrows, bends west, and you arrive at the brink of the Falls of Glomach (Day 52 Map 2).

Leave your sack at the top near the warning sign and scramble down the dead-end path below to the viewpoints. The falls are over 200m high, including a sheer drop of 90m, and the gorge is massive – the scale is alpine rather than anything you would expect to find in Britain.

Back at the top again, follow the scrambly path to Glen Elchaig, not forgetting to keep looking round for views of the falls and the gorge. This path is probably the best place to view them from other than the viewpoint path. If you are carrying walking poles it is a good idea to pack them away for this section, as you will probably want to use your hands in places.

Alternative Wet Weather Route

If the weather is bad there is an alternative route from Glen Elchaig to the Coulin Pass (Day 53 Map 2). It is described in detail in *North to the Cape* and outlined in

Glen Elchaig and Loch na Leitreach

Scottish Hill Tracks. This route is recommended if the rivers are in spate, as there is a river crossing by Loch Cruoshie on the main route that could be difficult. This alternative follows Glen Elchaig westwards to Nonach Lodge (GR935310), follows paths north up Glen Ling, then east of Loch an Iasaich and down to Loch Carron at Attadale. The valley is then followed northeast, mostly on roads, to Achnashellach, and the Trail rejoined either just below the Coulin Pass, or the other side of it if you take the route up the River Lair from Achnashellach. Strathcarron is a possible overnight stop.

To follow the **main route** of the Trail, turn right to follow Glen Elchaig upstream to the northeast. The walking is now easy on an unmade access road, and you can at last start to get moving at a reasonable pace. The road turns into a good path after the last house (Iron Lodge), then the valley and the path fork. The left fork takes you easily over a pass and down to the River Ling and good wild camping by Loch Cruoshie (Day 52 Map 3) – and Glen Affric seemed remote!

The mountain straight ahead across the valley is Beinn Dronaig, and tonight's destination is the other side of it – the Trail goes round its right-hand side. Cross the river just above Loch Cruoshie if you can – if there's too much water there is an easier crossing point 2.5km (1½miles) upstream (to the right). A pathless climb up to the shoulder of Beinn Dronaig crosses the main watershed again, then an

Tightrope bridge at the foot of Loch Calavie

entertaining wire bridge over the stream leads to a good track along the shore of Loch Calavie and over a low pass (and the watershed yet again).

The track descends slightly to the Uisge Dubh (Black Water), a tributary of the Ling, at a footbridge close to Bendronaig Lodge. Here there is a good bothy (maintained by the estate, not the MBA), or there are possible camping places near the footbridge. This is a remote place – there are no other facilities, but there are plenty of red deer.

DAY 53

Bealach Bhearnais and the Coulin Pass

Bendronaig Lodge to Kinlochewe (32km, 20 miles)

Today the Trail crosses another high pass, the Bealach Bhearnais, the climb up to which is the highlight of the day. Descent into Glen Carron and its forestry follows, to cross the Kyle of Lochalsh road and railway. A short, steep path climbs up an old pony route through forestry to the low Coulin Pass, followed by a gradual descent to Coulin Loch and more forestry. You can follow the valley from here, along the lochs then along the A896 to Kinlochewe, but an old right of way climbs up through the forestry to cut the corner off, and that's the 'official' route. You descend from the moor again to reach Kinlochewe and civilisation at last. Make the most of it – it's the last for a long way.

From Bendronaig Lodge an old stalkers' path runs up the valley to Loch an Laoigh, then climbs northeast high above the valley across the flank of Beinn Tharsuinn (Day 53 Map 1). It peters out about 2km (1½ miles) before the pass, and the next section up to the Bealach Bhearnais is rough and pathless. The bealach is a well-defined saddle pass, and at almost 600m, only the Bealach na h-Urchaire is higher on the Scottish part of the Trail.

There is a good path down from the bealach to another precarious wire bridge across the Allt a' Chonais, to join the Glenuaig Lodge access track down through the forestry into Glen Carron (Day 53 Map 2). Most of the plantation that the track goes through on the descent has been cleared and replanted quite recently.

Bendronaig Lodge

In the valley bottom a level crossing over the Inverness to Kyle of Lochalsh railway leads to the busy A890 at Craig and the first traffic since Cluanie on Day 51.

Craig is just a few houses by a busy road, but it does have a bunkhouse – the only accommodation here. There is no pub or shop, and don't bother walking east to Achnashellach looking for them there, either, as the nearest are at Strathcarron and Achnasheen, both many miles away.

About a kilometre west along the A890 from Craig, a path leaves the road to climb steeply up through cleared forestry to join the main track up to the Coulin Pass. (This path isn't marked on OS maps, but is the line of the original route, and was reopened in 1990, presumably largely thanks to the Scottish Rights of Way and Access Society.) The Coulin Pass is a low one, at 286m – the hills north of Glen Carron are not as high as those to the south.

A good track descends to Coulin (Day 53 Map 3) (joined on the way down by the Easan Dorcha track, an alternative route from Achnashellach). On the descent you can see an area of forestry straight ahead behind Loch Coulin – the line of the Trail slants up through this and can be seen clearly. On reaching the bottom of this forestry, at first there is no clear path through the trees, but the route is clear and soon a path makes the steep climb reasonably easy. Above the trees the path crosses a short stretch of moorland, then starts descending to reach the upper edge of another plantation. Shortly after this, the old right of way enters the plantation on a clear path, and here you have a decision to make (see map). *Either* skirt reasonably easily round the top of the trees without a path, *or* follow the path into the trees, and end up fighting desperately to escape from the far edge of the forest in a tangle of fallen interlocking trees (hint: choose the former).

Once the other side of the forestry you need to locate the path down the valley, then follow it to Kinlochewe.

Kinlochewe has a small outdoor shop (the last on route) and a couple of shops selling groceries. The garage near the campsite has basic food supplies and extended opening hours. There is accommodation, and the Kinlochewe Hotel (recommended) also has a comfortable bunkhouse (tel 01445 760253). Stock up well before leaving Kinlochewe, as the next shop is at Watten, at least seven days away (unless you take the alternative route via Lairg – Days 56L and 57L). There is a bothy suitable for an overnight stay at the Heights of Kinlochewe (GR071640), and wild camping is also possible in the same area.

DAY 54

The Great Wilderness

Kinlochewe to Inverlael (39km, 24 miles)

This isn't quite the longest day in terms of miles covered, but it takes longer to complete than any but the coastal switchback round Hartland Point on Day 8. You should expect today to take as long as Day 8, even if the weather is good, and longer if it isn't (*North from the Cape* takes three days to cover the same ground). You will need to start as early as possible from Kinlochewe, and then keep moving if you want to reach Inverlael in a day. After the initial easy walking to Lochan Fada the day is dominated by high mountains (if you are lucky with the weather). Lochan Fada is surrounded by Slioch, Á Mhaighdean, Beinn Tarsuinn and Mullach Coire Mhic Fhearchair. A pathless and rough section up to the Bealach na Croise leads to Loch an Nid, and a walk north down the valley, with the great slabs on the lower slopes of Sgurr Bàn dominating the view. Eventually the huge An Teallach massif comes into view ahead and continues to stamp its impact on the rest of the day's walking. A good vehicle track crosses from Strath na Sealga to the Dundonnell valley and the A832. From here an old and neglected track climbs up and crosses the moors to drop down to the Ullapool road (A835) at Inverlael, near the head of Loch Broom.

From Kinlochewe the main route gets to the foot of Lochan Fada via a good vehicle track to the Heights of Kinlochewe and up Gleann na Muice (Day 54 Map 1). By the time you get near Lochan Fada the track is a path, but the going is easy.

(There is an alternative route from Kinlochewe, further to the west, up Gleann Bianasdail from the head of Loch Maree. This is the route recommended in *North to the Cape*, so if you prefer that way, you will need to refer to the book, or follow it on the OS map. There are two reasons it is not the preferred End to End Trail route: it is slower, and it involves crossing the outflow from Lochan Fada, which is not possible in times of spate.)

From Lochan Fada to the Bealach na Croise is less than 3km (2 miles), but it is the only pathless section of the day and involves two steep climbs (Day 54 Map

The head of Loch Broom

2). First you must climb up from the loch and over featureless moor to descend to the stream flowing out of Coire Mhic Fhearchair. From here, cross the stream and ascend in prettier surroundings alongside a tributary stream to the Bealach na Croise.

The Main Route of the Trail follows a path from the bealach down to Loch an Nid, although it is rough and not quick to walk down. It also involves wading the stream above the loch, which isn't possible if the streams are up, so if this is the case you are best advised to keep to the wet weather route to the right of the stream all the way down, although the ground is rough and pathless.

On reaching Loch an Nid, review your plans. If it is any later than lunchtime, you should abandon any expectation of reaching Inverlael today, in which case staying where you are is an option worth considering. There is good camping ground by the loch, and the surroundings are idyllic. Otherwise, find your lunch and eat it on the move as you follow the path down the valley (Day 54 Map 3).

When the valley starts to bend left (to descend towards Loch na Sealga), a vehicle track cuts up out of the valley to the right. This track takes you easily across wet moorland to descend to the A832 at Corrie Hallie and the Dundonnell River (Day 54 Map 4).

Dundonnell feels very different from the environment of the past few days. For the first time since Fort William, the sea (Little Loch Broom) is very close, and the valley is much lusher and greener than anything seen so far in the Highlands. There are, however, no facilities for walkers (just the Corrie Hallie craft shop) and neither is there any obvious place to camp unobtrusively – this is a valley of neat fields full of sheep.

An old track joins the heads of Little Loch Broom and Loch Broom, and you pick this up at the edge of an old wood on the valley side. It climbs up out of the wood and the valley to cross moorland above the deep, wooded Allt a' Chairn valley, then over more undulating moorland to the edge of a steep escarpment down to Strath More, the River Broom and Inverlael. All the way across the moor there are stunning views of An Teallach behind you.

The path follows the escarpment edge briefly before dropping down and becoming intermittent on the way down to the valley. (If you are planning to camp, fill your water bottle before you reach the valley bottom.)

At Inverlael there are places where you can camp discreetly if you look carefully, and bed and breakfast is available at Clachan Farmhouse, 1km up the minor road towards Letters (GR175848, tel 01854 655209). There are no other facilities

Strath More and the River Broom

nearby. If you need to get to 'civilisation', Ullapool is about 14km (9 miles) down the A835, and the route can be rejoined from there by taking a track east from Ullapool past Loch Achall.

DAY 55

Glen Douchary and Glen Einig

Inverlael to Oykel Bridge (32km, 20 miles)

Today the Trail leaves the west coast of Scotland for good and starts to head northeast towards John O'Groats. Initially on forestry tracks, a vehicle track climbs out of the valley, and then you are on your own across rough and difficult ground, with no path until you drop down to Glen Douchary, which is a desolate and lonely place. The glen is followed north until it bends sharply to the west, at which point the Trail leaves the valley to cross a low pass (and the watershed) to descend to Loch an Daimh. From here the valley is followed, on a good track most of the way, past the loch, down the Abhainn Poiblidh and the River Einig through forestry to Oykel Bridge and the A837. (**Note** If the streams are up, an alternative route following Strath Mulzie rather than the Abhain Poiblidh is recommended instead (Day 55 Maps 2 and 3).)

From the A835 Ullapool road, at the head of Loch Broom, a track crosses a field and enters the forestry in Gleann na Sguaib (Day 55 Map 1). Twin bridges cross the River Lael, which here runs in two deep, parallel slots it has carved from the bedrock. After a couple of kilometres following forestry tracks in the valley bottom, you reach a fork in the valley. Turn left to climb up out of the forestry, and out of the valley altogether on a good vehicle track.

The built track ends high up on the boggy moorland, and the next 4km (3 miles) across the moor and down to Glen Douchary are mainly pathless and difficult. Initially the way is east up to the pass, keeping north of the boggy valley bottom, then the descent by the Allt na Lairige is rough going – the stream bank is too steep to follow, and the ground above it is difficult and peaty.

Eventually descend with relief to the broad valley of Glen Douchary and cross the river – do this as soon as you can, since the further downstream you get the deeper the river gets. Before turning downstream, though, look upstream to the head of the valley, where there is an impressive rocky cirque (Cadha Dearg), flanked by Seana Bhraigh (927m) on the left and Meall Glac an Ruighe (859m) on the right.

As you follow the river north, ruins are visible across the valley, the remains of what must have been a very isolated farming community before the Clearances (Day 55 Map 2). Shortly after this the valley bends right and narrows. Traces of a path appear occasionally, but the going is generally rough, and although sections of path appear increasingly, it never turns into anything reliable. When the stream turns sharp left and drops into a wooded gorge, the Trail turns right to cross a side stream, the Allt nan Caorach.

After crossing the stream there is a decision to make. If the streams are up, you will need to take the wet weather alternative, and follow this stream up to the southeast to pick up a path that crosses east over into Strath Mulzie. A track down Strath Mulzie leads to Duag Bridge (Day 55 Map 4) without any river crossings.

If the streams are at a normal level, a low pass to the northeast from the Allt nan Caorach crossing leads over the main watershed to Loch an Daimh. Following the shore, a good cart track is eventually picked up and takes you down the valley, past Loch an Daimh and Knockdamph to ford the Abhainn

Old Oykel Bridge (taken from the new bridge)

Poiblidh near its confluence with Rappach Water, and continue to Duag Bridge (Day 55 Map 4). (The reason for the Strath Mulzie wet weather alternative is the Abhainn Poiblidh ford. It can be difficult or impossible in wet weather, and it's a long way back round Loch an Daimh if you get here only to find you can't cross.)

Shortly after Duag Bridge the Trail enters forestry and continues down Glen Einig on a forestry road to Oykel Bridge, where the River Einig joins the River Oykel.

At Oykel Bridge there is a road, the A837, which is not exactly a major arterial route, more a minor capillary. There is also the Oykel Bridge Hotel (tel 01549 441218), which is reasonably upmarket and intended principally for anglers (the Oykel is used to fishermen rather than walkers). The hotel does bar meals, and has the only accommodation here. The best place to camp is probably in the field to your right (stile), just after crossing the River Einig, although this is about a kilometre from the hotel. There are no obvious places to camp nearer the hotel, but there are some if you head a bit further up the valley on tomorrow's route.

DAY 56

The Upper Oykel and Assynt

Oykel Bridge to Overscaig Hotel (38km, 24 miles)

This is the last day in the heart of the high mountains. The Trail follows the River Oykel north to the foot of the huge Ben More Assynt massif, then contours round its eastern flank on an old path. The objective is to get round the northeast end of Loch Shin, so once this path has taken the Trail far enough north, you need to turn off it to cross Glen Cassley. A climb over a pathless bealach and a descent to the end of Loch Shin follow, then a short road walk above the loch to the Overscaig Hotel. This is a long day in a remote setting, and there is nowhere to shelter if you find you can't make it all the way in a day. It is a good idea to be equipped for a night camping in Glen Cassley, just in case. (If the weather is bad or you need supplies, consider the Lairg alternative route (Days 56L and 57L, see below).)

At Oykel Bridge you have a decision to make. The direct route to John O'Groats is blocked by Loch Shin, 28km (18 miles) long and directly in your way, so the main Trail (Days 56 and 57) heads up the River Oykel and takes a remote mountain route round the *northwest* end of the loch, via the Overscaig Hotel, to the Crask Inn. The Lairg alternative route (Days 56L and 57L) heads down the River Oykel, away from the mountains, to go round the *southeast* end of the loch. The principal *advantages* of taking the Lairg alternative route are (1) if the weather is bad and you are not confident about navigating through pathless terrain with map and compass, it provides a route that is easier to follow, and (2) at the southeast end of Loch Shin is the small town of Lairg, which has all the facilities that you have probably been dreaming about for days, even shops. The *disadvantages* are (1) there is a lot of road walking on the way, (2) there isn't the same mountain scenery, and (3) the navigation north of Lairg to Loch Choire is as tricky as any on the whole route. This last point means that if your navigation skills are shaky you will need to follow the A836 from Lairg to Crask rather than the route for Day 57L.

From Oykel Bridge the A837 heads northwest along the left side of the valley (looking upstream), gradually diverging from the River Oykel. Luckily there is also an unmade vehicle track on the right side of the quiet valley. It is mainly used by anglers, but is just as good for walkers. (Crossing the bridge by the hotel takes you out of Ross and Cromarty and into what used to be the county of Sutherland, the river forming the boundary.)

A big forestry plantation covers the upper reaches of Glen Oykel, but a wide strip along the riverbank has been left clear of trees. Shortly after entering the second section of forestry there is a hut provided as a shelter for fishermen – if unlocked it provides a good emergency overnight shelter. (The ground hereabouts is not good for camping – too tussocky.)

Fishermen's hut, Glen Oykel

River Oykel

The track now continues further upstream than marked on OS maps, but eventually ends. The next stretch along the river is slower, but no less pleasant, on a rudimentary path through the tussocky grass. A short climb up by a stream leads to a forestry track, and in a short distance this leads to the shore of Loch Ailsh, with the Assynt mountains behind it (Day 56 Map 2). (To the right, behind Benmore Lodge, is the steep end of the ridge of Sail an Ruathair – the Trail runs beneath it.)

An estate road follows the loch shore to Benmore Lodge, then a track follows the river to where it divides. The right fork is the Allt Sail an Ruathair, and a path follows this up into a wide bowl, with Loch Sail an Ruathair to the left and the shoulder of Meall an Aonaich looming ahead. The path zigzags up this steep slope to cross the shoulder and continue its lonely way north, past Loch Carn nan Conbhairean, with Glen Cassley now apparent down to the right (Day 56 Map 3). A couple of kilometres past Loch Carn nan Conbhairean, the Trail meets the end of a vehicle track coming up from Glen Cassley.

Wet Weather Alternative

If the streams are high, you won't be able to cross the River Cassley by Loch na Sròine Luime, so turn right here and follow the wet weather alternative down into the glen, then turning left upstream to a bridge over the River Cassley by a hydro-electric power station. From here you can cross the bridge and follow the river upstream, to rejoin the main route of the Trail north of Loch na Sròine Luime. (Alternatively, if you are feeling really miserable, you can follow the power station road over Maovally and reach Loch Shin that way.)

Assuming the streams are fordable, the main Trail continues north from the vehicle track, still on the old path. When it starts to bend west, with the lochs of Glen Cassley visible below, the Trail leaves the path to cross the valley between the lochs, fording the river, and climbing up the pathless hillside to the northeast (Day 56 Map 4).

A bealach is crossed under the crags of Creag Riabhach Loch nan Sgaraig, then a beeline down the slope northeast leads to the head of Loch Shin and the power station road. An easy stroll (or limp) finds the A838, another A road with little traffic. Turn right down the road into the forestry to reach the Overscaig Hotel in 3km (2 miles).

The Overscaig Hotel has a bar, food and accommodation (tel 01549 431203). There used to be a bunkhouse here, but it is no longer open. The best place to pitch a tent is by the forestry track just after you leave the A838 – see Day 57 Map 1.

DAY 57

The Quaking Shortcut

Overscaig Hotel to Crask Inn (17km, 11 miles)

This is a very short day, but if you want to take advantage of the available accommodation there is little option. Oykel Bridge to Kinbrace in two days would be difficult, so you may as well break at the two inns. The alternatives are (1) to cut Day 56 short and camp in Glen Cassley (Day 56 Map 3), (2) to continue today and camp at the head of Loch Choire (Day 58 Map 2), or (3) to follow the Lairg alternative route (see Days 56L and 57L).

Day 57 consists of two very different sections. The first is a delightful stroll along a forestry track high above Loch Shin (Day 57 Map 1). To get to the track means

Forestry track near Overscaig

backtracking along the A838 for a few minutes from the Overscaig Hotel, but it is well worth it. The views are extensive, the track pleasant to walk on, and the alternative is dodging occasional fast cars on a narrow road (and you don't want to arrive at Crask too early anyway).

The forestry track leads from the A838 back to the A838 by Fiag Bridge (Day 57 Map 2). Here starts the second section – a pathless trudge across featureless peat bog to reach the Crask Inn. It's actually not as bad as it sounds or as it looks on the map though. The bog is blanket bog, but as peat goes it is fairly dry and fairly easy to walk on – there is little erosion. The navigation is straightforward and the altitude low, so you will be unlucky if you end up in mist. You can see the Crask Inn for miles before you get there, but if you are tired it seems to take forever to reach.

The Crask Inn (tel 01549 411241) is a simple, old-fashioned pub with reasonably priced accommodation and food. The landlord is an active MBA member, and walkers are made more than welcome, so it is recommended for an overnight stop. You can also camp nearby – ask at the Inn.

DAY 56L

Lairg Alternative

Oykel Bridge to Lairg (27km, 17 miles)

The Lairg alternative is recommended if the weather is bad or if you need to resupply. The first part of the day is a pleasant riverside stroll, but most of the remainder is on roads.

From Oykel Bridge a track follows the north bank of the River Oykel downstream, and then a footbridge crosses the river (Map 56L Day 1). The footpath on the south side of the river is better than the one on the north bank from here. (There are many signs of fly fishermen, including huts that make good emergency shelters.)

At Langwell Farm the path ends and a cart track climbs along the valley side, descending again to meet the head of a minor road at Brae Farm. From here there is only tarmac to walk on down the valley, then across it to join the A837 and follow it to Rosehall and Invercassley. Here there is accommodation, a post office/shop and the Achness Hotel, which serves bar meals.

Going through the grounds of Invercassley on what could well be the original road up the valley, but is now a quiet, unsurfaced lane, avoids a stretch of road walking along the A839. After the grounds of Invercassley, it's back to tarmac to climb out of the valley, through forestry, to join the A839 (and the road walking alternative) and follow it most of the way to Lairg. Road walking can be avoided for the last bit into Lairg by following an old path over the Ord, a small hill just outside Lairg.

Lairg has plenty of facilities, since it is the largest town, indeed the only town, for a long way. There is a tourist information centre, and shops, pubs, bed and breakfasts, a campsite and a bank (open Mon/Thu/Fri only).

DAY 57L

Lairg Alternative

Lairg to Loch Choire (28km, 17 miles)

From Lairg there are two options for rejoining the main Trail. The first is a weary 20km (12 mile) grind north up the A836 to the Crask Inn – this doesn't need a route description, other than a warning not to turn left onto the A838 by mistake. You need to follow this route if your navigation skills aren't good. The second option is to follow forestry tracks through the hills NNE of Lairg, by Loch Beannach, to Dalnessie, then follow a little-used path north from here over the hills to descend to the head of Loch Choire. This is an excellent day's walk, but the catch is that the path from Dalnessie to Loch Choire is indeed 'little used', and not always easy to follow. In mist you would be more likely to lose it than not.

From Lairg minor roads and a path climb out of the valley to a forestry access road past Loch Dola and into the forestry plantation (Day 57L Map 1). A brief descent down an old track leads to Loch Tigh na Creige, a loch now surrounded by the plantation. The track disappears, and you walk round the shore of the loch to a stile, wondering if there is a way out at all. A short climb up a narrow path through the trees and you are once more on a proper forestry track, which is followed all the way to the edge of the plantation, passing Loch Beannach, and up to the isolated houses at Dalnessie (Day 57L Map 2). This is a bleak place in poor weather.

The path north from Dalnessie is an old one, and at one time was carefully built – there are signs of this all the way to Loch Choire. The Trail takes the left fork of the valley along the Allt Gobhlach then continues north at the head of the valley, climbing up onto the broad featureless ridge of Meall an Fhuarain (Day 56L Map 3).

Careful route finding will lead to the correct way down the northern slopes, which are much more interesting than the featureless southern side, and down a side valley to the picturesque head of Loch Choire. This is an excellent place to camp, and there is a hut for shelter if needed. You are now back on the main Trail route, 11km (7 miles) into Day 58 (see Day 58 Map 2).

DAY 58

Farewell to the Highlands

Crask Inn to Kinbrace (40km, 25 miles)

Today's route crosses the last bealach, passes the last Munro, and follows the shore of the last mountain lochs in the last glen of the journey. The second half of the day follows an estate road out of the mountains and into upper Helmsdale and the Flow Country hills.

A good path leads up Srath a' Chraisg from the Crask Inn. The valley is wide and featureless, with forestry to the right. As the outlying foothills of Ben Klibreck (961m) draw nearer, the path climbs the hillside and bends to the left to reach Bealach Easach, and you feel a very different atmosphere. The slopes are steep, the pass narrow, and the descent to Loch a' Bhealaich is to be savoured, not hurried over (Day 58 Map 1). (The pass marks another crossing of the main watershed, since the water from Loch Choire flows to the north coast along Strathnaver – another sign that journey's end in approaching.)

At the shore of Loch Choire (Day 58 Map 2) there is a choice to be made. Turn left and you will follow a good track along the northwest side of the loch to Loch Choire Lodge. Much better, however, is the path on the southeast side, reached by turning right instead, which skirts round the head of the loch. There are bridges to cross the two streams, idyllic camping grounds, and a hut suitable for emergency shelter or cooking away from the midges. This is where the Lairg alternative rejoins the main route of the Trail. From here the path along the loch potters through patches of old woodland and a constantly changing environment (the path on the northwest side is rather boring by comparison).

At the foot of the loch is Loch Choire Lodge, quite impressive as shooting lodges go, and you can follow the estate access road from here to the B871 if you wish. The Trail, however, follows what is presumably the original line of the road for the first 3km (2 miles). This old track keeps higher up the hillside and is much pleasanter to walk (Day 58 Map 2), although eventually it descends to meet the estate road again (Day 58 Map 3), and from here there is no alternative but to plod along it to Loch Badanloch, the River Helmsdale and the B871 (Day 58 Map 4), in the process crossing the watershed imperceptibly again into the Helmsdale gathering grounds.

Wild camping at Kinbrace

Kinbrace is a further 7km (4 miles) eastwards along the B871, but rather than take the road the Trail follows the line (more or less) of an old track above and parallel to the road – this is a pleasant route, and reaches Kinbrace avoiding all but a few metres of road walking.

The day ends at a footbridge over Bannock Burn just outside the village. This is an excellent place to camp, and camping is the only option here. At Kinbrace there is a railway station, a 'main road' (the single track A897) and a school, but no longer a shop or accommodation.

DAY 59

The Knockfin Heights and Glutt Water

Kinbrace to the River Thurso (Dail Righe) (26km, 16 miles)

Today the Trail climbs up to the soggy plateau of the Knockfin Heights, then descends to follow Glutt Water from its source down the long valley until it becomes the River Thurso. Although the altitude is not great, the country is wild and remote. You are unlikely to see another walker, and may not see another person all day after crossing the road north of Kinbrace.

For the first 3km (2 miles) the Trail follows Bannock Burn up the valley north from Kinbrace, parallel to the road and railway (Day 59 Map 1). (The road is a quicker alternative if you are missing walking on tarmac and dodging the occasional car.) After crossing the railway and the A897 you follow the burn northwest, away from the road, across moorland, to reach the remains of the abandoned clearance village of Knockfin, at the base of the steep flank of the Knockfin Heights. As well as the ruins and some idyllic camping, there is a fully restored circular sheepfold, showing what all the others you have seen must have looked like at one time.

It is important to locate the ruined village before climbing onto the plateau, unless your navigation skills are pretty good. The Knockfin Heights consist of a featureless, flat plateau of wet peat bog covering a huge area. (If you lose your way, you are likely to stay lost until you have descended into one valley or another and regained your bearings.) The Trail follows a stream up from Knockfin to approach the Ordnance Survey column on the Knockfin Heights (438m) –

Circular sheepfold at Knockfin

about the only sure landmark on the whole plateau. (It is only the summit in the sense that there are no obvious higher points among the acres of alternative candidates for the title.)

At the OS column the Trail leaves Sutherland and enters Caithness (Day 59 Map 2). (Around the same point you cross the watershed again – Glutt Water flows eventually to the north coast at Thurso.) From the top it is important to descend towards the east, not further south. On this featureless ground it is vital to rely on map and compass, even in clear weather, as poor judgement here could mean a descent into Berriedale before you have realised your mistake.

Once running water has been picked up between the peat hags, following it downhill eventually leads to valley scenery rather than moorland tops. For the first time all day an old track appears – this is stalking country.

Just before you meet the track 'chalybeate springs' is marked on the 1:25000 OS map. Chalybeate, according to the Oxford English Dictionary, means 'impregnated or flavoured with iron', so the springs appear to be a source of natural, if rather flat, Irn Bru. The spa at Harrogate is based on chalybeate springs, but so far the crowds have not flocked to Glutt Water with quite the same fervour.

The old track leads to a rough parking area and a vehicle track shortly afterwards, and this track can be followed all the way down to Glutt Lodge and its outbuildings. For part of the way to Glutt, a path nearer the burn is recommended instead, which is pleasanter to walk on than the vehicle track, and also gives a good view of the bijou Eas Gluta waterfall.

An untarred access road continues down the valley from Glutt Lodge, past the house at Dalganachan, where Glutt Water turns into the River Thurso. Shortly after this, and before Dalnawillan Lodge comes into view (Day 60 Map 1), you reach a flat, grassy field by the river. This is called Dail Righe, and is one of the best places to put up a tent between Land's End and John O'Groats (you will have to share it with the oystercatchers though).

DAY 60

The River Thurso and Acharole

Dail Righe to Watten (33km, 20 miles)

Today the Trail continues on the access road down the Thurso valley, with the valley becoming wider and flatter all the time. Shortly after the road turns to tarmac, the Trail takes to the riverbank, following it in pleasant meadows to the point where a tributary, the Little River, joins it. You leave the Thurso here for a quarry track up the Little River in wild surroundings, fording the river when you can to reach the A9 Thurso trunk road. A forestry track and a pleasant stroll through meadows leads to the end of a minor road running down the valley into the village of Watten, and the end of the penultimate day.

From the recommended camping ground at Dail Righe, near Dalnawillan Lodge, the access road continues past Dalnawillan (the lodge itself is derelict, but a house and noisy kennels are still very much occupied) (Day 60 Map 1).

As you continue downriver the valley opens out, with Loch More coming into view. The surroundings are still very much peat moors, but are becoming flatter and flatter – typical Flow Country. The road makes for easy walking. It passes a number of gravel pits, dug to make the road, but other features are few and far between.

Peat and sand beach, Loch More

Eventually the forestry at the end of Loch More is reached, and a short walk through the trees leads to the metalled public road from Lochmore Cottage. (There is a stream just off-route in the forestry to replenish your water bottle. Reliable drinking water is hard to find between here and Watten, so don't pass this by unless you are sure you won't regret it later.)

If you want to, you can stay on the tarmac – keep straight on and the road leads directly to Watten, today's objective. The Trail, however, takes to the riverbank after the first houses (Strathmore Lodge), taking a much more interesting and enjoyable route (Day 60 Map 2). The ground by the River Thurso varies between rough moorland and green pastures, but the latter predominate, making this a very pleasant stretch after the long walk on the access road.

Just before the river changes direction from eastward to northwest, two bridges carry a track over it. This track continues southeast, parallel to the Little River, and leads to Knockdoo quarries, where a lot of sand and gravel has been extracted over the years. The first quarried area, a section about 1km long, is reached soon after crossing the Thurso. Here the quarrying has been done relatively recently, along the line of the track (you can feel a bit like Frodo walking through Mordor).

At the end of this rather unpleasant section the track rises up an artificial ramp to continue across the moorland. This stretch has clearly had little traffic for a long time, and puts the smile back on your face. When you reach the next quarries, at the end of the track, it is plain they have not been active for many years.

You now have to cross the Little River to get to the A9 (formerly the A895). Depending on how much water there is in the river you have three options. (1) If the water is low you can cross at the point where it turns south, to the ruined building at Torran, which is the shortest route. (2) If it is not absolutely clear that it is safe to cross here, then there's a tractor ford below Tacher farm, about 500m further south. (3) If you can't cross safely here, either, you should continue south for another kilometre to the first bridge (also a ford) at GR171459. (There is good ground for wild camping here, if you have enough water with you, and bed and breakfast at Tacher Farm (tel 01593 741313).) Whichever way you cross, as soon as you have done so, make straight for the A9 (the ground is difficult, and a cross-country route to avoid the road is impractical).

The A9 is busy, and you have to follow it north until you can enter the forestry on the right, crossing the watershed for the last time, and also the Trail's last 100m contour in the process.

Once among the trees the busy road is forgotten in moments. The forestry road is soon following the eastern edge of the plantation, with Halsary Burn alongside, and when the burn turns east away from the forestry, the Trail follows it. This is a lovely walk alongside a 'babbling brook', accompanied by yellow flags (irises) in season – a good place to camp if you want to stop.

At Shielton, the highest farm in the Acharole valley, the Trail joins the farm access road, which becomes a minor road to Watten. The road is quiet (and what appears to be a possible alternative route along the bank of the burn is not a through route). After passing Achingale Mill the Trail takes to the meadows again for the last short stretch to the crossroads in Watten.

Watten is a village with a post office/shop and the Brown Trout Hotel, which stands at the crossroads. The hotel is the only accommodation actually in the village, and not expensive. It can fill up with anglers, however, so ringing ahead is worth considering (tel 01955 621354). If it's full, there's a bed and breakfast 10 minutes' walk along the A882 towards Wick. Alternatively, you should be able to find somewhere discreet to pitch a tent by the Wick river a bit further along the Trail, or you can continue a bit further downstream to Bilbster House (Day 61 Map 1, GR282534), which does bed and breakfast.

DAY 61

The Butt

Watten to John O'Groats (Duncansby Head) (37km, 23 miles)

Here is my journey's end, here is my butt,
And very sea-mark of my utmost sail.
Othello, *William Shakespeare*

This is the last day. It is also the most varied day, one of the two toughest days, and one of the very best days. Having said all that, it comes with a health warning. For half the day the Trail follows the cliff tops along the east coast, and for much of this there is no path. Between Keiss and Freswick Bay the route is mainly between the cliff-top fence and the cliff top, and these are occasionally uncomfortably close to each other. If you have no head for heights, it's probably not a good route to take (and certainly not suitable for young children or dogs). If you don't want to follow the cliff edge, the best option is to follow the road route north from Watten via Lyth – the road is quiet, but boring. If you head for the coast, then decide not to follow the cliffs, your only real option is the busy A99, but this would be a poor way to end your Land's End to John O'Groats journey.

From Watten the first section of the day follows the Wick river downstream (Day 61 Map 1). This is a popular angling river, so it is possible to follow the bank for most of the way. Some of it is along the edge of crops, some through pasture, until you reach the hamlet of Bilbster. Here the Trail leaves the river to head northeast for Sinclair's Bay and the sea. It crosses the railway and follows the B874 briefly to take a track into the forestry, emerging at the other side in the Moss of Killimster, a spectacularly soggy area of flat, heather-covered peat bog at an altitude of only 20m.

Keiss Castle

Crossing the Moss of Killimster is difficult. To start with, the Trail follows north a stream that is flanked by particularly wet ground and tall reeds. The recommended approach is to cross the stream, with a flying leap, as soon as you get to it, then follow the edge of the (comparatively) drier heather, with the boggier 'valley bottom' to your left. This is a mass of reeds and yellow flag – pretty to look at, but very difficult to walk through. (You are more likely to see red deer close up crossing the Moss of Killimster than anywhere else on the Trail. The reeds hide the deer, and they often don't see you until you are very close.)

Eventually you reach the Burn of Killimster, a straight-dug drain with solid banks, very different from the other burn. Following it is not much easier, though, due to the reeds. Detours to the right help in places and make it worse in others. You also risk missing the right place to cross the burn if your detours are too enthusiastic. By the time you make it to the cart track and the road, you are likely to be in need of a rest.

The next short section is along the road from Killimster to Westerloch, from where the disused undersea pipeline assembly line is visible ahead (Day 61 Map 2). (That's 'line' as in 'railway line' – 8km (5 miles) of dual railway tracks head inland in a straight line from the shore. Lengths of pipeline used to be brought up the A99 and added onto the end of the pipeline, which was mounted on bogies on the railway line.)

The Trail reaches the A99 (formerly the A9) at Westerloch, by the pipeline works, crosses sand dunes, and suddenly you are on the beach – the sands of Sinclair's Bay. The next section is a pleasant stroll along the sands to Keiss, as the beach is long, scenic, sandy, and usually deserted. The sands end just before Keiss, and from the end of the beach a good track above the shore leads to the village.

Keiss has a pretty little harbour, a shop, a post office, the Sinclair Bay Hotel and other bed and breakfast accommodation. John O'Groats via the Trail is a long and strenuous way from here, so if you aren't going to make it today, then Keiss is probably the best place to stop for the night. If you want to camp, you can find a good place for a tent by the cliff-top path between the harbour and the castle.

From Keiss to Freswick Bay the Trail follows the cliff top, and as far as the picturesque ruins of Keiss Castle (Day 61 Map 3) there is a path.

Keiss Castle is a typical Scottish cliff-top castle, and over 300 years old. Built on the cliff edge for defence, it was obviously designed to repel enemies. The Victorian 'Keiss Castle' inland from the ruin is also typical of its period. Many ugly Victorian buildings, such as this and the John O'Groats Hotel, were put up along the Caithness coast once the railway had made access easier.

From Keiss Castle to Freswick Bay the cliffs are less frequented and there is no clear path. Whenever a stream or field drain reaches the cliff edge, there is a patch of nettles, and sometimes there is no room between fence and cliff top to avoid them. Long trousers are essential, and the going is slow.

The cliff scenery, on the other hand, is some of the best in Britain. The situation of the ruins of Bucholly Castle, in particular, is astonishing, and the contorted strata below the castle just have to be seen. Every geo is also worth investigating. (For the uninitiated, a geo is an inlet in the cliffs, often very narrow. They are called 'zawns' in Wales and the southwest of England, and there are a lot of them along this eastern coast of Caithness, giving plenty of very atmospheric places to peer down into.)

At Freswick Bay the Trail passes Freswick Castle, a 17th-century fortified house built on the foundations of a 12th-century Viking building. Viking remains have been found in Freswick Bay, including that of the only known long house in Scotland.

At the far end of the beach the Trail abandons the cliffs for a while – a fence has been put up too close to the edge for comfort. Instead, a lane leads to a minor road that is followed east through the hamlet of Skirza to reach the coast again by Skippie Geo (Day 61 Map 4). There is a bed and breakfast at Skirza (The Farmhouse, tel 01955 611254).

Following the coast north from here to Duncansby Head is straightforward, if not always quick underfoot. Nowhere are you constrained uncomfortably between fence and cliff top. The cliff scenery continues to be spectacular to the end, and although alternative shortcuts away from the cliffs are sometimes possible, they are disappointing in comparison. There is a clear path for the last stretch, with alternatives as you get closer to Duncansby Head. Again, the best views are to be had from closer to the cliffs, which rise to over 60m.

Duncansby Head is logically the end of the route, although the Trail continues to John O'Groats, following a path to end at the pier and the John O'Groats House Hotel. From Duncansby Head the views to the north across the Pentland Firth are wonderful, and there is a panorama diagram showing which island is which. The nearest island is Stroma, with the Orkneys behind and the Pentland Skerries over to the right. Over to the left is St John's Point, with Dunnet Head behind it, the most northerly point of the Scottish mainland.

The End: John O'Groats

Approached this way, John O'Groats feels less of an anticlimax than if approached by road, which is what cyclists and most walkers do. Principally, it is because you meet Duncansby Head, its OS column, its lighthouse and its cliffs before you meet the village itself.

As you reach John O'Groats the path forks – keep left to enter the campsite, or right for the pier and the hotel. If you want accommodation or a meal, there is a tourist information centre here, with addresses and phone numbers in the window. In any event, your best bet is to follow the road inland for a few minutes. Meals and accommodation are available at Caberfeidh Guest House and the Seaview Hotel, and there are other bed and breakfasts close by. The John O'Groats House Hotel itself will probably not be open for accommodation, as it seems to have been 'closed for renovation' for most of the past ten years or more. It has a bar (the Groats Inn), but this doesn't serve meals.

Sort out your accommodation, get something to eat, and have a drink or two, and if you want, you can register your achievement at the Groats Inn or the Seaview Hotel. You are entitled to sit back with a self-satisfied grin on your face – you've made it.

John O'Groats has a long history (although most of what is here now is due to the growing number of tourists over the past 100 years or so). James IV of Scotland wanted to set up a regular ferry service to connect his new territory, the Orkneys, to the Scottish mainland, to consolidate his hold on them. He engaged three Dutchmen, possibly brothers, to set up the ferry, and they turned up in the wilds of Caithness in 1496. They ran the ferry service to the Orkneys from the location that was most practical, close to the northeast corner of the mainland. One of the three Dutchmen was called Jan de Groot, which led to the wilderness location from which they ran the ferry becoming known as John O'Groats. Today it's still next to nothing in the middle of nowhere, but the ferry continues to run, half a millennium later.

The legend of Jan de Groot building an octagonal house with an octagonal table in it to resolve family hierarchy squabbles appears to be no more substantiated than King Arthur's suspiciously similar round table at Tintagel. Elihu Burritt found little evidence of it in 1863, which was before the new hotel was built nearby.

The Huna Inn is where Elihu Burritt and the Naylor brothers stayed on the earliest Land's End–John O'Groats walks. At that time there was nothing much at John O'Groats but the vague marks on the ground where John O'Groat's house had been – the Huna Inn was a mile or two to the west by the shore of the Pentland Firth. In 1875, four years after the Naylors were here, the John O'Groats House Hotel opened.

How to Leave John O'Groats

The rest of this book is about how to get to John O'Groats, but all you need is a short paragraph to get you away again. For times of the buses from John O'Groats to Wick, phone Highland Country on 01847 893123 (the bus stop is in the car park by the TIC). There are four or five buses a day, but none on Sundays. From Wick you can catch a train south, but don't forget you're a long way north. It is likely to take you more than a day to get home, if home isn't in Scotland.

Recognition of Your Feat

There is nothing 'official' about walking between Land's End and John O'Groats, but there are two organisations you can register your achievement with if you wish, whether you have walked, cycled or driven End to End. For both you need to collect evidence of your journey, in the form of signatures of witnesses along your route.

The Land's End John O'Groats Association

This is an independent association run by its members. If you send them £15 for your first year's membership, together with evidence of your journey, they will send you a certificate, a car sticker, and a magazine three times a year. Continuing membership is £15 annually, there is an annual dinner and presentation weekend, and other social events. And you may even win a trophy – the Shanks Pony Trophy is awarded annually to 'the individual/s who achieve the best performance on foot'. Address: Mr Richard Elloway, Clovelly, 4 Seymour Street, Wellington, Somerset TA21 8JT www.landendjohnogroats.com.

The Land's End John O'Groats Club

This is run by the Land's End and John O'Groats Company Ltd, which owns and manages Land's End and John O'Groats. If you send them the evidence of your journey and £10, they will send you a certificate, a card entitling you to a year's free parking at Land's End and free admission to the Land's End amenities, and a brief newsletter twice yearly. They also make awards annually. Address: The Administration Office, The Land's End John O'Groats Club, The Custom House, Land's End, Sennen, Cornwall TR19 7AA www.landsend-landmark.co.uk.

Registration

You can pick up a registration form for the Club at the hotel reception in the Land's End complex or at the Groats Inn, depending on where you start, and you can get it stamped at the other end when you finish. Follow the instructions on collecting evidence of your journey on the way. For the Association you can similarly register at Land's End youth hostel at Sennen or John O'Groats youth hostel (at Canisbay), or the First and Last Shop or the Seaview Hotel at John O'Groats. If you want to join both, the Association will accept a photocopy of the Club's form as evidence, so you don't have to collect two separate sets of signatures.

The Falls of Glomach, Day 52

Day 50 Map 1: Fort William to Torcastle

4. In the housing estate keep parallel to the railway. Cross the end of the first road, follow the path between houses (& under two!), join another road, & at its end go straight ahead to a stile behind a small play area. Follow the path to the right, under the railway. Bear half left across waste ground to meet the road in Blar Mhor Industrial Estate. Follow the road round to the left to join the A830, cross the road & turn left. When the road starts to bend left, look out for a small path on the right leading to the old line of the road, now overgrown. Go straight on along this until you meet the locks on the Caledonian Canal. Turn right along the towpath towards Gairlochy (don't cross the canal).

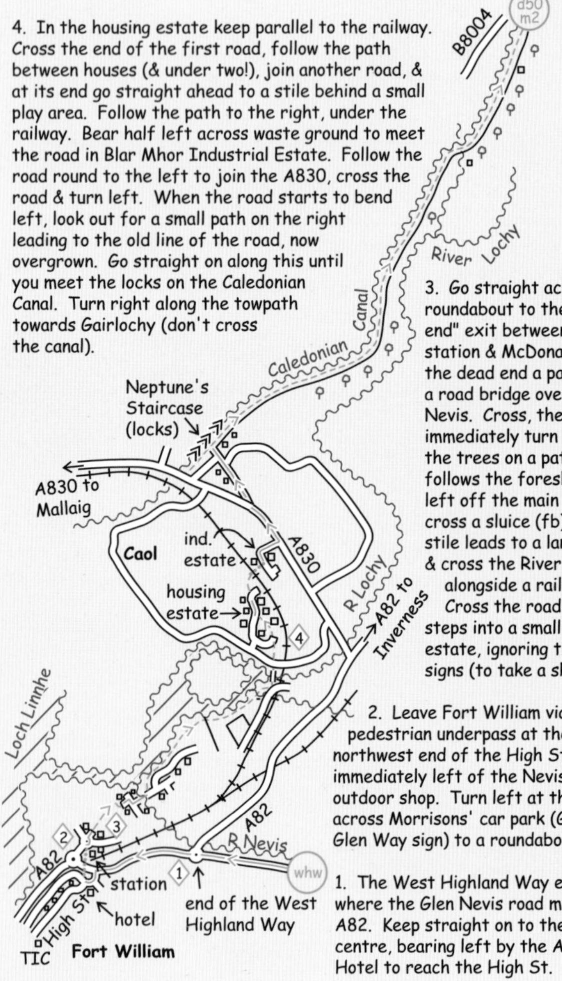

3. Go straight across the roundabout to the "dead end" exit between a petrol station & McDonalds. From the dead end a path leads to a road bridge over the River Nevis. Cross, then immediately turn left into the trees on a path that follows the foreshore. Turn left off the main path to cross a sluice (fb), then a stile leads to a lane. Go left & cross the River Lochy (fb) alongside a railway bridge. Cross the road & descend steps into a small housing estate, ignoring the GGW signs (to take a shortcut).

2. Leave Fort William via the pedestrian underpass at the northwest end of the High St, immediately left of the Nevisport outdoor shop. Turn left at the station across Morrisons' car park (Great Glen Way sign) to a roundabout.

1. The West Highland Way ends where the Glen Nevis road meets the A82. Keep straight on to the town centre, bearing left by the Alexandra Hotel to reach the High St.

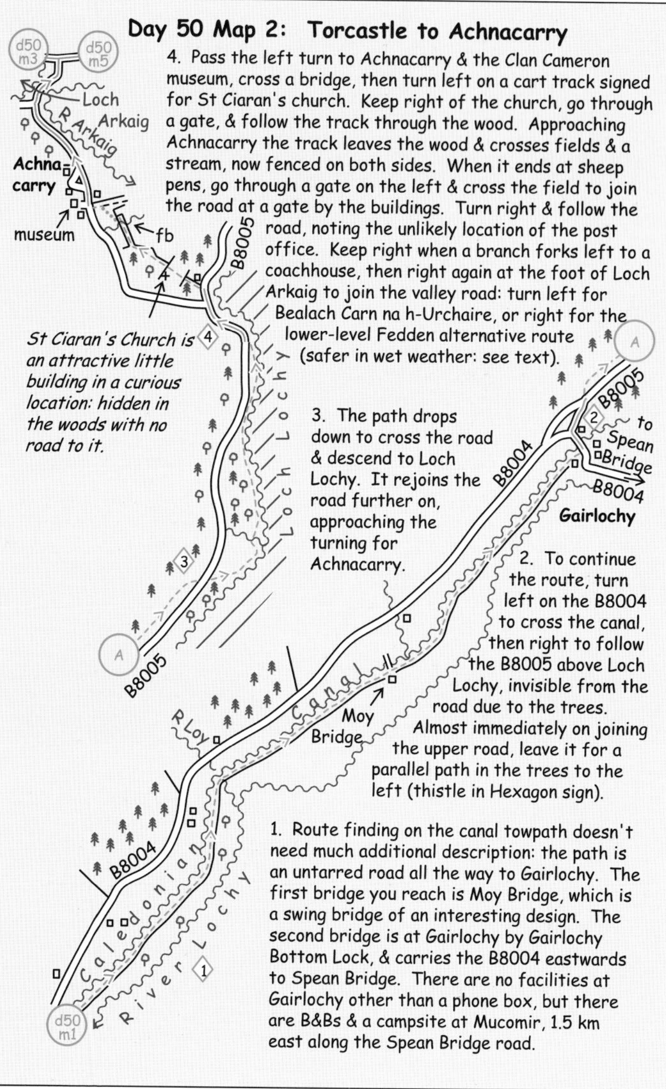
Day 50 Map 2: Torcastle to Achnacarry
4. Pass the left turn to Achnacarry & the Clan Cameron museum, cross a bridge, then turn left on a cart track signed for St Ciaran's church. Keep right of the church, go through a gate, & follow the track through the wood. Approaching Achnacarry the track leaves the wood & crosses fields & a stream, now fenced on both sides. When it ends at sheep pens, go through a gate on the left & cross the field to join the road at a gate by the buildings. Turn right & follow the road, noting the unlikely location of the post office. Keep right when a branch forks left to a coachhouse, then right again at the foot of Loch Arkaig to join the valley road: turn left for Bealach Carn na h-Urchaire, or right for the lower-level Fedden alternative route (safer in wet weather: see text).
St Ciaran's Church is an attractive little building in a curious location: hidden in the woods with no road to it.
3. The path drops down to cross the road & descend to Loch Lochy. It rejoins the road further on, approaching the turning for Achnacarry.
2. To continue the route, turn left on the B8004 to cross the canal, then right to follow the B8005 above Loch Lochy, invisible from the road due to the trees. Almost immediately on joining the upper road, leave it for a parallel path in the trees to the left (thistle in Hexagon sign).
1. Route finding on the canal towpath doesn't need much additional description: the path is an untarred road all the way to Gairlochy. The first bridge you reach is Moy Bridge, which is a swing bridge of an interesting design. The second bridge is at Gairlochy by Gairlochy Bottom Lock, & carries the B8004 eastwards to Spean Bridge. There are no facilities at Gairlochy other than a phone box, but there are B&Bs & a campsite at Mucomir, 1.5 km east along the Spean Bridge road.
d50 m3
d50 m5
Loch Arkaig
R Arkaig
Achnacarry
museum
fb
B8005
Loch Lochy
A
B8005
to Spean Bridge
B8004
Gairlochy
Canal
Moy Bridge
R Loy
B8004
Caledonian
River Lochy
d50 m1

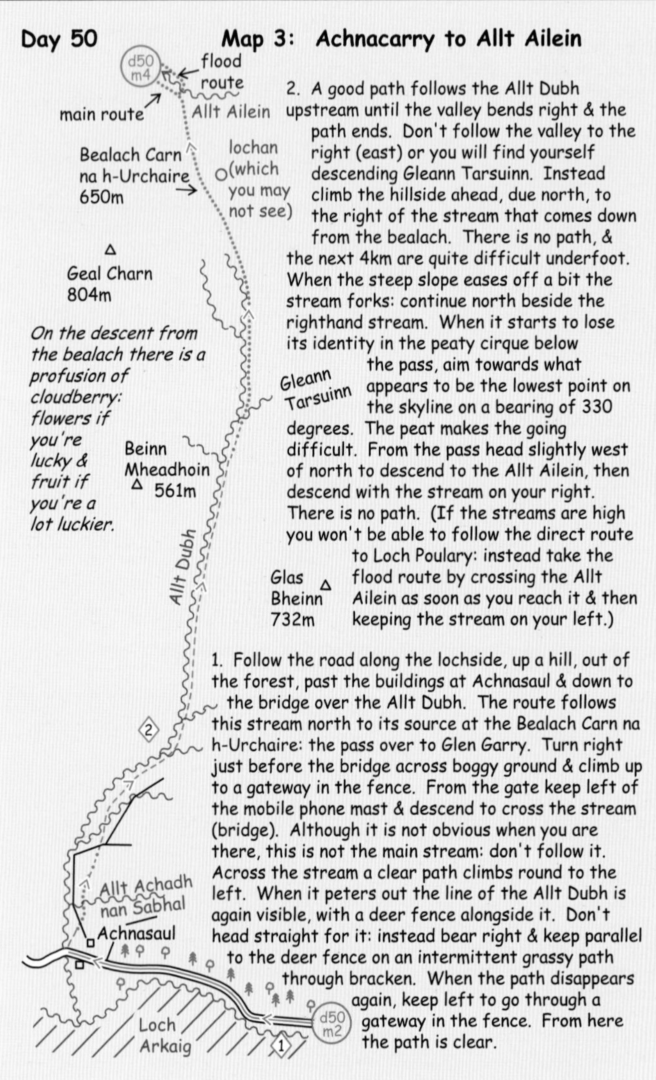
Day 50
Map 3: Achnacarry to Allt Ailein
d50 m4
flood route
main route
Allt Ailein
Bealach Carn na h-Urchaire 650m
lochan (which you may not see)
Geal Charn 804m
On the descent from the bealach there is a profusion of cloudberry: flowers if you're lucky & fruit if you're a lot luckier.
Gleann Tarsuinn
Beinn Mheadhoin 561m
Allt Dubh
Glas Bheinn 732m
2
Allt Achadh nan Sabhal
Achnasaul
Loch Arkaig
1
d50 m2
2. A good path follows the Allt Dubh upstream until the valley bends right & the path ends. Don't follow the valley to the right (east) or you will find yourself descending Gleann Tarsuinn. Instead climb the hillside ahead, due north, to the right of the stream that comes down from the bealach. There is no path, & the next 4km are quite difficult underfoot. When the steep slope eases off a bit the stream forks: continue north beside the righthand stream. When it starts to lose its identity in the peaty cirque below the pass, aim towards what appears to be the lowest point on the skyline on a bearing of 330 degrees. The peat makes the going difficult. From the pass head slightly west of north to descend to the Allt Ailein, then descend with the stream on your right. There is no path. (If the streams are high you won't be able to follow the direct route to Loch Poulary: instead take the flood route by crossing the Allt Ailein as soon as you reach it & then keeping the stream on your left.)
1. Follow the road along the lochside, up a hill, out of the forest, past the buildings at Achnasaul & down to the bridge over the Allt Dubh. The route follows this stream north to its source at the Bealach Carn na h-Urchaire: the pass over to Glen Garry. Turn right just before the bridge across boggy ground & climb up to a gateway in the fence. From the gate keep left of the mobile phone mast & descend to cross the stream (bridge). Although it is not obvious when you are there, this is not the main stream: don't follow it. Across the stream a clear path climbs round to the left. When it peters out the line of the Allt Dubh is again visible, with a deer fence alongside it. Don't head straight for it: instead bear right & keep parallel to the deer fence on an intermittent grassy path through bracken. When the path disappears again, keep left to go through a gateway in the fence. From here the path is clear.

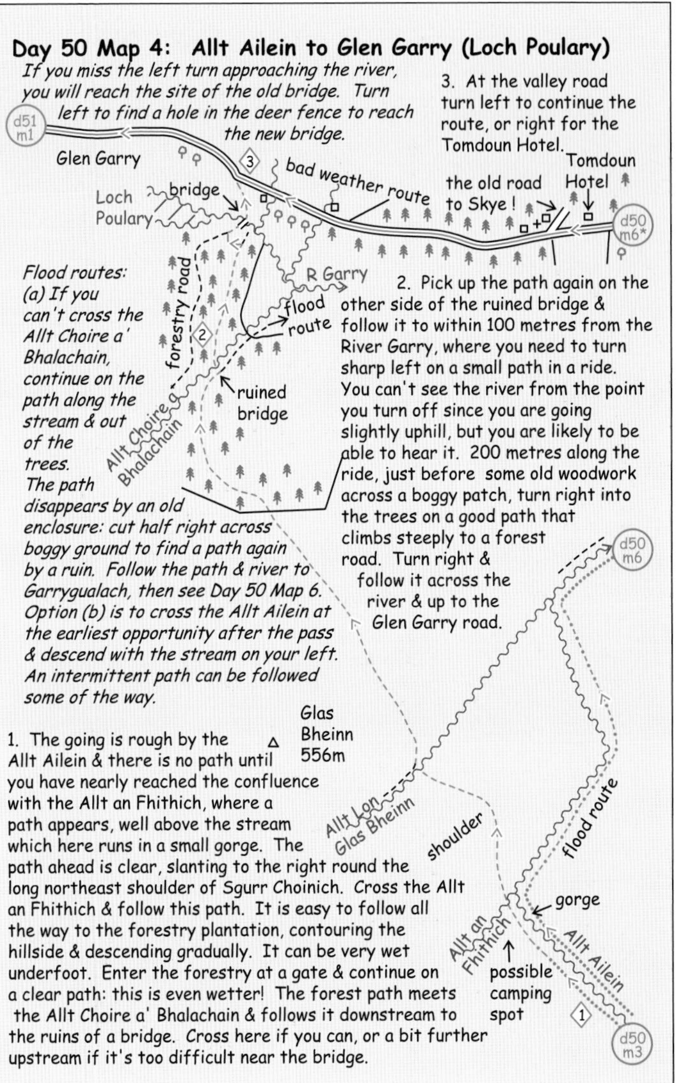
Day 50 Map 4: Allt Ailein to Glen Garry (Loch Poulary)
If you miss the left turn approaching the river, you will reach the site of the old bridge. Turn left to find a hole in the deer fence to reach the new bridge.
3. At the valley road turn left to continue the route, or right for the Tomdoun Hotel.
d51 m1
Glen Garry
3
bad weather route
the old road to Skye !
Tomdoun Hotel
Loch Poulary
bridge
d50 m6*
forestry road
R Garry
flood route
2
2. Pick up the path again on the other side of the ruined bridge & follow it to within 100 metres from the River Garry, where you need to turn sharp left on a small path in a ride. You can't see the river from the point you turn off since you are going slightly uphill, but you are likely to be able to hear it. 200 metres along the ride, just before some old woodwork across a boggy patch, turn right into the trees on a good path that climbs steeply to a forest road. Turn right & follow it across the river & up to the Glen Garry road.
Flood routes:
(a) If you can't cross the Allt Choire a' Bhalachain, continue on the path along the stream & out of the trees.
The path disappears by an old enclosure: cut half right across boggy ground to find a path again by a ruin. Follow the path & river to Garrygualach, then see Day 50 Map 6.
Option (b) is to cross the Allt Ailein at the earliest opportunity after the pass & descend with the stream on your left.
An intermittent path can be followed some of the way.
ruined bridge
Allt Choire a' Bhalachain
d50 m6
Glas Bheinn 556m
1. The going is rough by the Allt Ailein & there is no path until you have nearly reached the confluence with the Allt an Fhithich, where a path appears, well above the stream which here runs in a small gorge. The path ahead is clear, slanting to the right round the long northeast shoulder of Sgurr Choinich. Cross the Allt an Fhithich & follow this path. It is easy to follow all the way to the forestry plantation, contouring the hillside & descending gradually. It can be very wet underfoot. Enter the forestry at a gate & continue on a clear path: this is even wetter! The forest path meets the Allt Choire a' Bhalachain & follows it downstream to the ruins of a bridge. Cross here if you can, or a bit further upstream if it's too difficult near the bridge.
Allt Lon Glas Bheinn
shoulder
flood route
gorge
Allt an Fhithich
possible camping spot
Allt Ailein
1
d50 m3

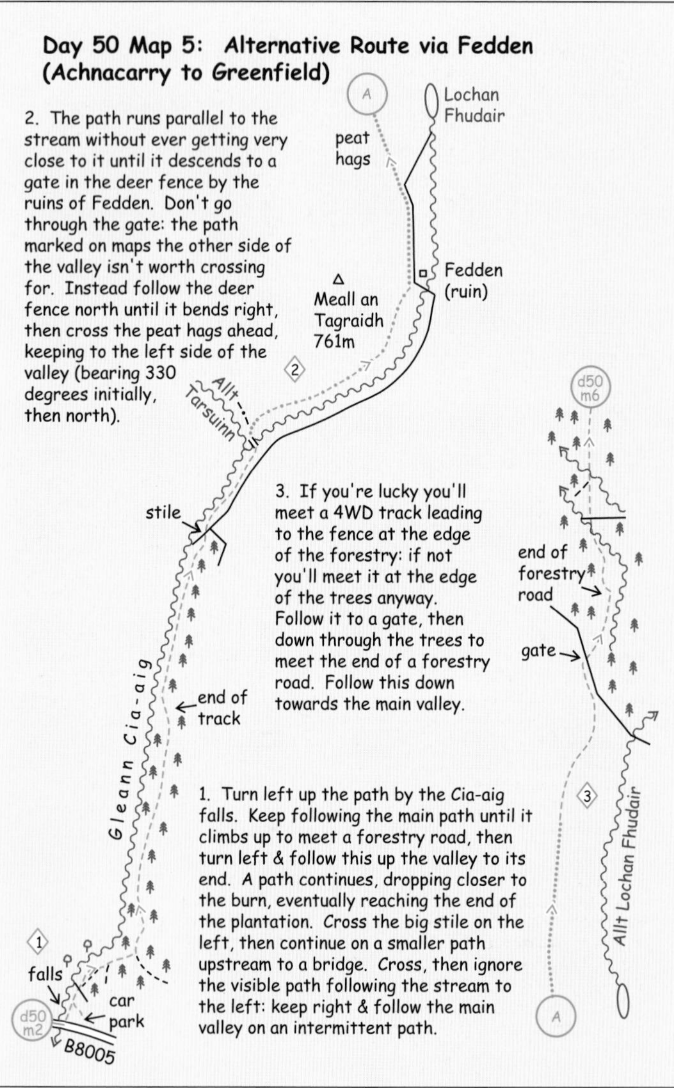
Day 50 Map 5: Alternative Route via Fedden
(Achnacarry to Greenfield)
2. The path runs parallel to the stream without ever getting very close to it until it descends to a gate in the deer fence by the ruins of Fedden. Don't go through the gate: the path marked on maps the other side of the valley isn't worth crossing for. Instead follow the deer fence north until it bends right, then cross the peat hags ahead, keeping to the left side of the valley (bearing 330 degrees initially, then north).
A
Lochan Fhudair
peat hags
Fedden (ruin)
Meall an Tagraidh 761m
2
Allt Tarsuinn
d50 m6
stile
3. If you're lucky you'll meet a 4WD track leading to the fence at the edge of the forestry: if not you'll meet it at the edge of the trees anyway. Follow it to a gate, then down through the trees to meet the end of a forestry road. Follow this down towards the main valley.
end of forestry road
gate
end of track
Gleann Cia-aig
1. Turn left up the path by the Cia-aig falls. Keep following the main path until it climbs up to meet a forestry road, then turn left & follow this up the valley to its end. A path continues, dropping closer to the burn, eventually reaching the end of the plantation. Cross the big stile on the left, then continue on a smaller path upstream to a bridge. Cross, then ignore the visible path following the stream to the left: keep right & follow the main valley on an intermittent path.
3
Allt Lochan Fhudair
1
falls
car park
d50 m2
B8005
A

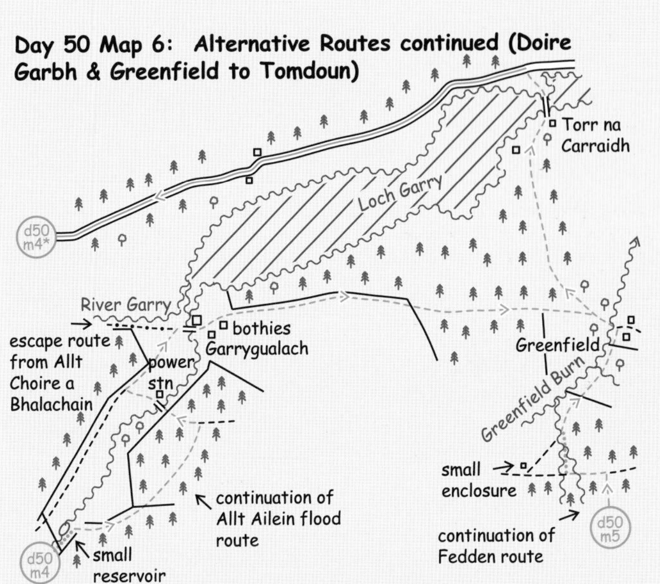

Route from the Allt Ailein: Follow the stream down until you reach a deer fence which you must climb. Just after this is a small reservoir, where you meet a forestry track. Downstream from here the stream is very difficult to follow in dense heather and bracken, so instead join the forestry track. You may have a gate or fence to climb: the track was still under construction in November 2005. Follow the track through the trees to a junction of tracks & turn left to descend to a bridge by a small power station. Follow the track up to a T-junction & turn right to descend to cross the stream again on an old bridge at Garrygualach. Follow the rough road to a junction near Greenfield & turn left, joining the route described below.

Fedden route: Follow the forestry road to a T-junction & turn left. The track crosses one small stream then another at the edge of a felled area on the right. Turn off the track before this bridge & follow the stream down to where an old track fords it. Turn right here & follow this track down to meet an untarred road by houses at Greenfield. Turn left across the bridge & follow the road to a big bridge across Loch Garry & the tarmac of the valley road. Turn left to the Tomdoun Hotel & beyond to rejoin the main route at the end of Loch Poulary.

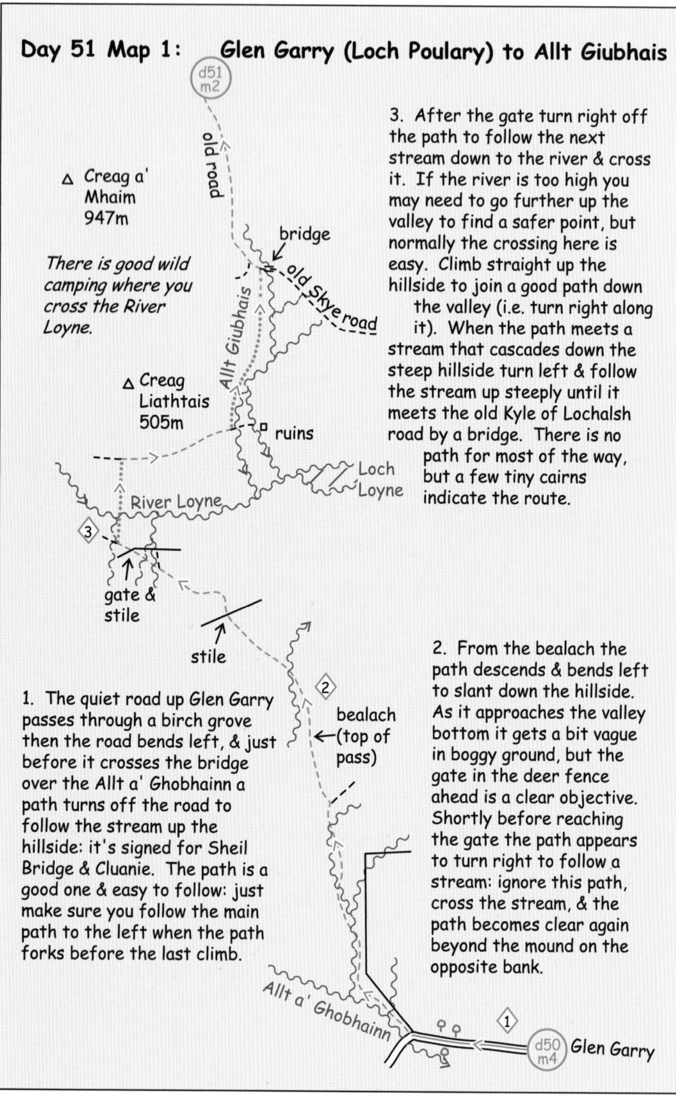
Day 51 Map 1: Glen Garry (Loch Poulary) to Allt Giubhais
d51 m2
old road
Creag a' Mhaim 947m
3. After the gate turn right off the path to follow the next stream down to the river & cross it. If the river is too high you may need to go further up the valley to find a safer point, but normally the crossing here is easy. Climb straight up the hillside to join a good path down the valley (i.e. turn right along it). When the path meets a stream that cascades down the steep hillside turn left & follow the stream up steeply until it meets the old Kyle of Lochalsh road by a bridge. There is no path for most of the way, but a few tiny cairns indicate the route.
bridge
There is good wild camping where you cross the River Loyne.
old Skye road
Allt Giubhais
Creag Liathtais 505m
ruins
Loch Loyne
River Loyne
3
gate & stile
stile
2. From the bealach the path descends & bends left to slant down the hillside. As it approaches the valley bottom it gets a bit vague in boggy ground, but the gate in the deer fence ahead is a clear objective. Shortly before reaching the gate the path appears to turn right to follow a stream: ignore this path, cross the stream, & the path becomes clear again beyond the mound on the opposite bank.
2
bealach (top of pass)
1. The quiet road up Glen Garry passes through a birch grove then the road bends left, & just before it crosses the bridge over the Allt a' Ghobhainn a path turns off the road to follow the stream up the hillside: it's signed for Sheil Bridge & Cluanie. The path is a good one & easy to follow: just make sure you follow the main path to the left when the path forks before the last climb.
Allt a' Ghobhainn
1
d50 m4
Glen Garry

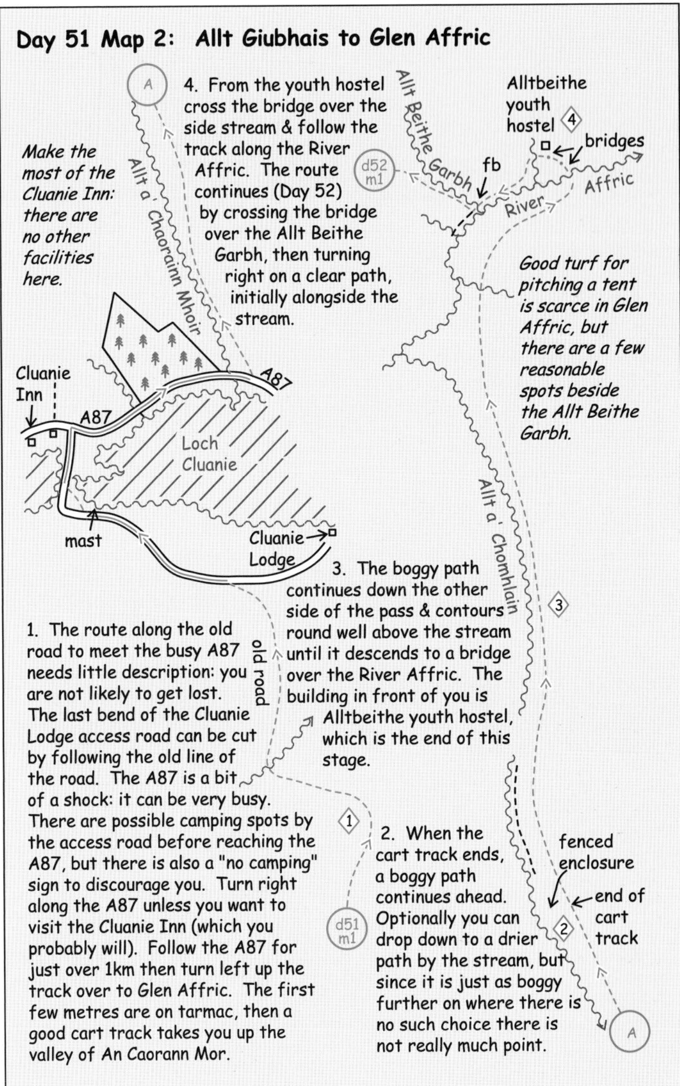
Day 51 Map 2: Allt Giubhais to Glen Affric
A
4. From the youth hostel cross the bridge over the side stream & follow the track along the River Affric. The route continues (Day 52) by crossing the bridge over the Allt Beithe Garbh, then turning right on a clear path, initially alongside the stream.
Allt Beithe Garbh
Alltbeithe youth hostel
4
bridges
fb
d52 m1
River
Affric
Make the most of the Cluanie Inn: there are no other facilities here.
Allt a' Chaorainn Mhoir
Good turf for pitching a tent is scarce in Glen Affric, but there are a few reasonable spots beside the Allt Beithe Garbh.
Cluanie Inn
A87
A87
Loch Cluanie
mast
Cluanie Lodge
Allt a' Chomhlain
3. The boggy path continues down the other side of the pass & contours round well above the stream until it descends to a bridge over the River Affric. The building in front of you is Alltbeithe youth hostel, which is the end of this stage.
3
old road
1. The route along the old road to meet the busy A87 needs little description: you are not likely to get lost. The last bend of the Cluanie Lodge access road can be cut by following the old line of the road. The A87 is a bit of a shock: it can be very busy. There are possible camping spots by the access road before reaching the A87, but there is also a "no camping" sign to discourage you. Turn right along the A87 unless you want to visit the Cluanie Inn (which you probably will). Follow the A87 for just over 1km then turn left up the track over to Glen Affric. The first few metres are on tarmac, then a good cart track takes you up the valley of An Caorann Mor.
1
2. When the cart track ends, a boggy path continues ahead. Optionally you can drop down to a drier path by the stream, but since it is just as boggy further on where there is no such choice there is not really much point.
fenced enclosure
end of cart track
2
d51 m1
A

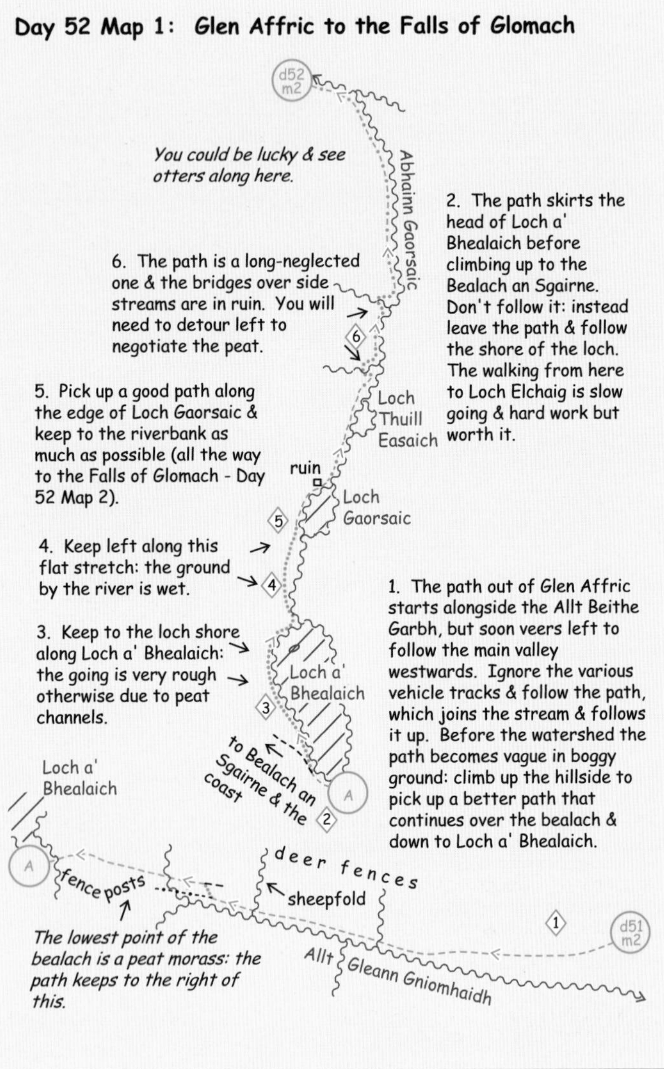
Day 52 Map 1: Glen Affric to the Falls of Glomach
d52 m2
You could be lucky & see otters along here.
Abhainn Gaorsaic
2. The path skirts the head of Loch a' Bhealaich before climbing up to the Bealach an Sgairne. Don't follow it: instead leave the path & follow the shore of the loch. The walking from here to Loch Elchaig is slow going & hard work but worth it.
6. The path is a long-neglected one & the bridges over side streams are in ruin. You will need to detour left to negotiate the peat.
6
5. Pick up a good path along the edge of Loch Gaorsaic & keep to the riverbank as much as possible (all the way to the Falls of Glomach - Day 52 Map 2).
Loch Thuill Easaich
ruin
Loch Gaorsaic
5
4. Keep left along this flat stretch: the ground by the river is wet.
4
1. The path out of Glen Affric starts alongside the Allt Beithe Garbh, but soon veers left to follow the main valley westwards. Ignore the various vehicle tracks & follow the path, which joins the stream & follows it up. Before the watershed the path becomes vague in boggy ground: climb up the hillside to pick up a better path that continues over the bealach & down to Loch a' Bhealaich.
3. Keep to the loch shore along Loch a' Bhealaich: the going is very rough otherwise due to peat channels.
Loch a' Bhealaich
3
to Bealach an Sgairne & the coast
A
2
Loch a' Bhealaich
A
deer fences
fence posts
sheepfold
1
d51 m2
The lowest point of the bealach is a peat morass: the path keeps to the right of this.
Allt Gleann Gniomhaidh

Day 52 Map 2: Falls of Glomach to the Allt na Sean-luibe

2. The path down from the falls to Glen Elchaig is steep in places & involves the use of hands on a rocky section. Bridges across the Allt a' Ghlomaich & the River Elchaig take you to the access road up the glen. Turn right unless you have had enough of the hills & want to explore an alternative route nearer the coast. The road briefly has an old tarmac surface but soon becomes unsurfaced.

3. Follow the road past Loch na Leitreach & the farm buildings at Carnach as far as its end near Iron Lodge, now a modern estate cottage with a pretty waterfall behind it. Don't cross the stream to the lodge: keep straight on along a clear track up the valley. When the track forks keep left & follow this branch up the An Crom-allt & over the pass to Maol-bhuidhe & Loch Cruoshie (see Day 52 Map 3).

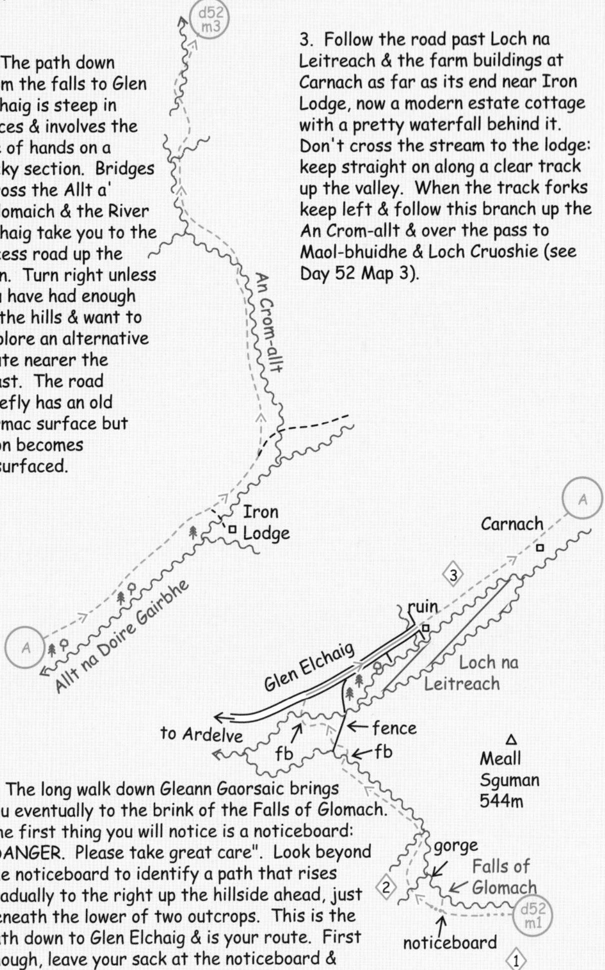

1. The long walk down Gleann Gaorsaic brings you eventually to the brink of the Falls of Glomach. The first thing you will notice is a noticeboard: "DANGER. Please take great care". Look beyond the noticeboard to identify a path that rises gradually to the right up the hillside ahead, just beneath the lower of two outcrops. This is the path down to Glen Elchaig & is your route. First though, leave your sack at the noticeboard & descend the lower path carefully to get a good view of the falls: tremendous!

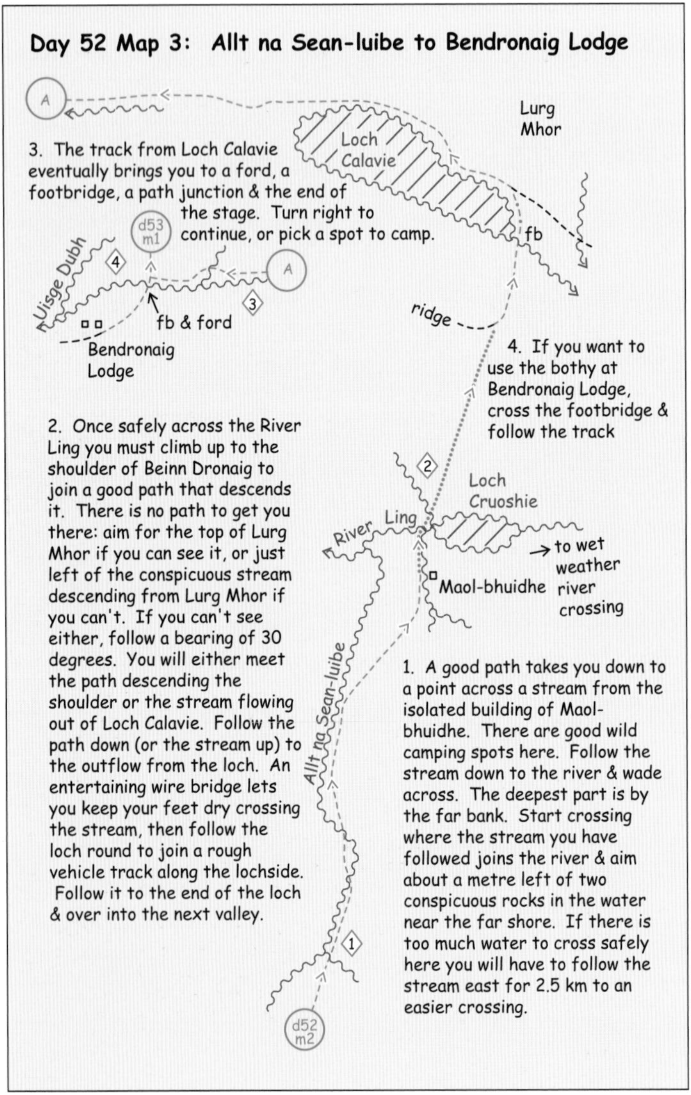

Day 52 Map 3: Allt na Sean-luibe to Bendronaig Lodge

A
Lurg Mhor
Loch Calavie

3. The track from Loch Calavie eventually brings you to a ford, a footbridge, a path junction & the end of the stage. Turn right to continue, or pick a spot to camp.

d53 m1
fb
Uisge Dubh
4
A
3
fb & ford
ridge
Bendronaig Lodge

4. If you want to use the bothy at Bendronaig Lodge, cross the footbridge & follow the track

2. Once safely across the River Ling you must climb up to the shoulder of Beinn Dronaig to join a good path that descends it. There is no path to get you there: aim for the top of Lurg Mhor if you can see it, or just left of the conspicuous stream descending from Lurg Mhor if you can't. If you can't see either, follow a bearing of 30 degrees. You will either meet the path descending the shoulder or the stream flowing out of Loch Calavie. Follow the path down (or the stream up) to the outflow from the loch. An entertaining wire bridge lets you keep your feet dry crossing the stream, then follow the loch round to join a rough vehicle track along the lochside. Follow it to the end of the loch & over into the next valley.

2
Loch Cruoshie
River Ling
→ to wet weather river crossing
Maol-bhuidhe
Allt na Sean-luibe

1. A good path takes you down to a point across a stream from the isolated building of Maol-bhuidhe. There are good wild camping spots here. Follow the stream down to the river & wade across. The deepest part is by the far bank. Start crossing where the stream you have followed joins the river & aim about a metre left of two conspicuous rocks in the water near the far shore. If there is too much water to cross safely here you will have to follow the stream east for 2.5 km to an easier crossing.

1
d52 m2

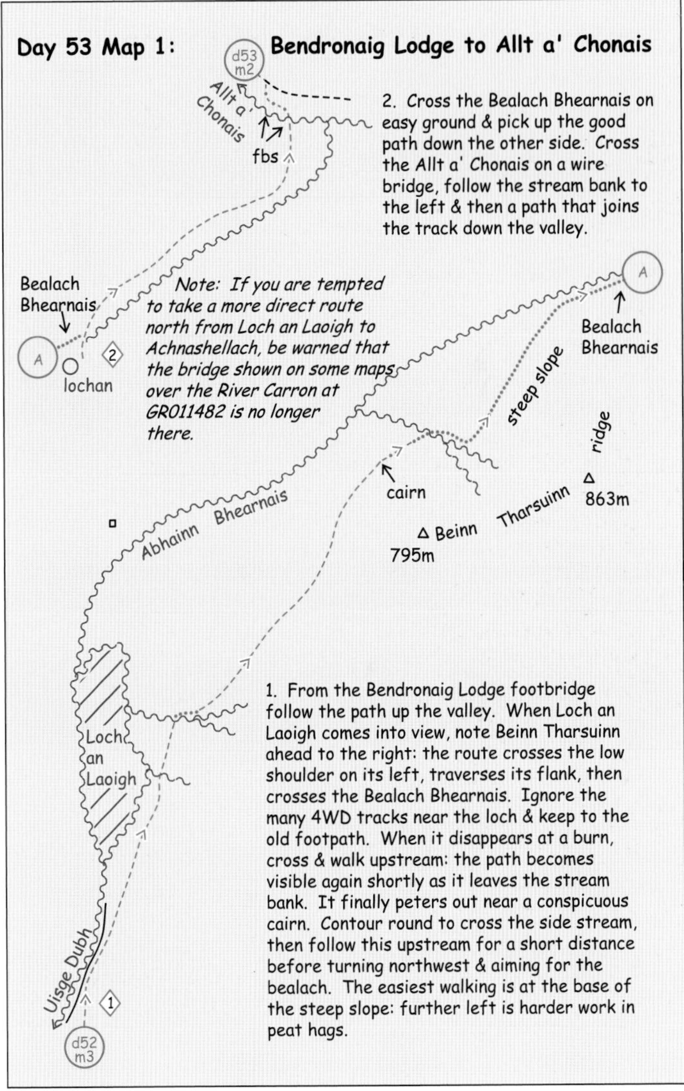

Day 53 Map 1:
Bendronaig Lodge to Allt a' Chonais
d53
m2
Allt a' Chonais
fbs
2. Cross the Bealach Bhearnais on easy ground & pick up the good path down the other side. Cross the Allt a' Chonais on a wire bridge, follow the stream bank to the left & then a path that joins the track down the valley.
Bealach Bhearnais
A
2
lochan
Note: If you are tempted to take a more direct route north from Loch an Laoigh to Achnashellach, be warned that the bridge shown on some maps over the River Carron at GR011482 is no longer there.
A
Bealach Bhearnais
steep slope
ridge
cairn
863m
Beinn Tharsuinn
795m
Abhainn Bhearnais
Loch an Laoigh
1. From the Bendronaig Lodge footbridge follow the path up the valley. When Loch an Laoigh comes into view, note Beinn Tharsuinn ahead to the right: the route crosses the low shoulder on its left, traverses its flank, then crosses the Bealach Bhearnais. Ignore the many 4WD tracks near the loch & keep to the old footpath. When it disappears at a burn, cross & walk upstream: the path becomes visible again shortly as it leaves the stream bank. It finally peters out near a conspicuous cairn. Contour round to cross the side stream, then follow this upstream for a short distance before turning northwest & aiming for the bealach. The easiest walking is at the base of the steep slope: further left is harder work in peat hags.
Uisge Dubh
1
d52
m3

Day 53 Map 2: Allt a' Chonais to the River Coulin

2. Follow the road for just over 1km, past one parking area on the left. Just before a second signposted parking area, turn right on a small path into the forestry. It would be easy to miss, if not for the sign by the road: "Coulin Pass Old Pony Track. This historic route was, until the coming of the railway, the direct route from Glen Torridon to the droving stance at Craig & was used by Thomas Hogg, the Ettrick Shepherd, during his tour of the Highlands, whilst travelling between the inn at Craig & Kinlochewe in June 1803." The path enters the forestry, bends left, & climbs diagonally up the hillside, with discreet marker posts where needed. Much of this hillside has been felled in recent years. The path passes the end of one forestry road (a post marks a turn to the right here), then it climbs further to the next forestry road. Turn right along this to follow it out of the plantation, over the Coulin Pass & down.

Thanks are due to the Scottish Rights of Way and Access Society for reopening & marking the Old Pony Track.

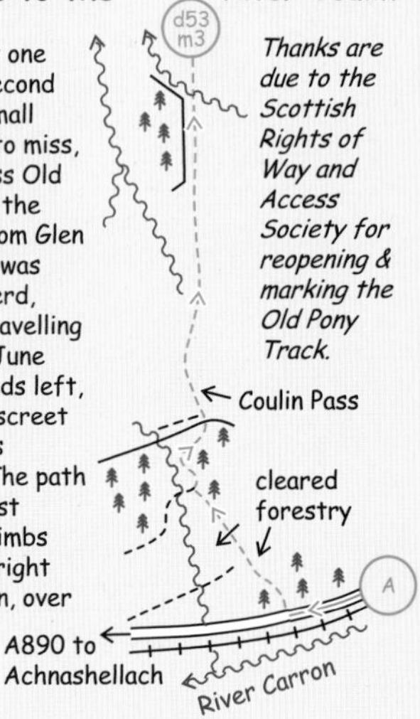

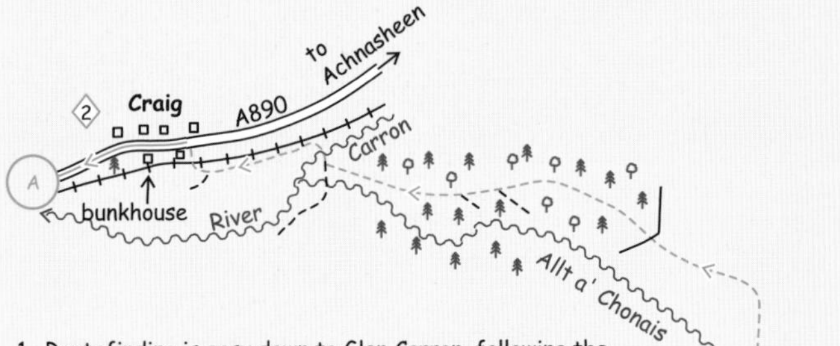

1. Routefinding is easy down to Glen Carron, following the main track all the way. Most of the forestry along this side of the Allt a' Chonais has been felled in recent years. Keep right at the valley bottom to cross the River Carron, then the track bends left, parallel to the railway. There are possible camping places by the track here, although since it is a bit close to "civilisation" it may be advisable to enquire locally for permission. Just after a track joins from the left the main track bends right: follow it up to cross the railway & turn left along the busy A890 into the hamlet of Craig. The railway is the most northerly of the lines to the west coast, running from Dingwall to the Kyle of Lochalsh.

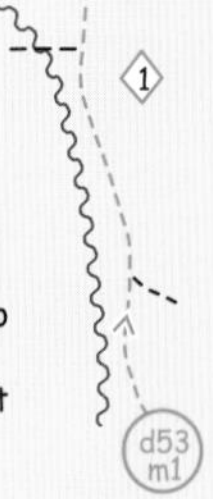

Day 53 Map 3: River Coulin to Kinlochewe

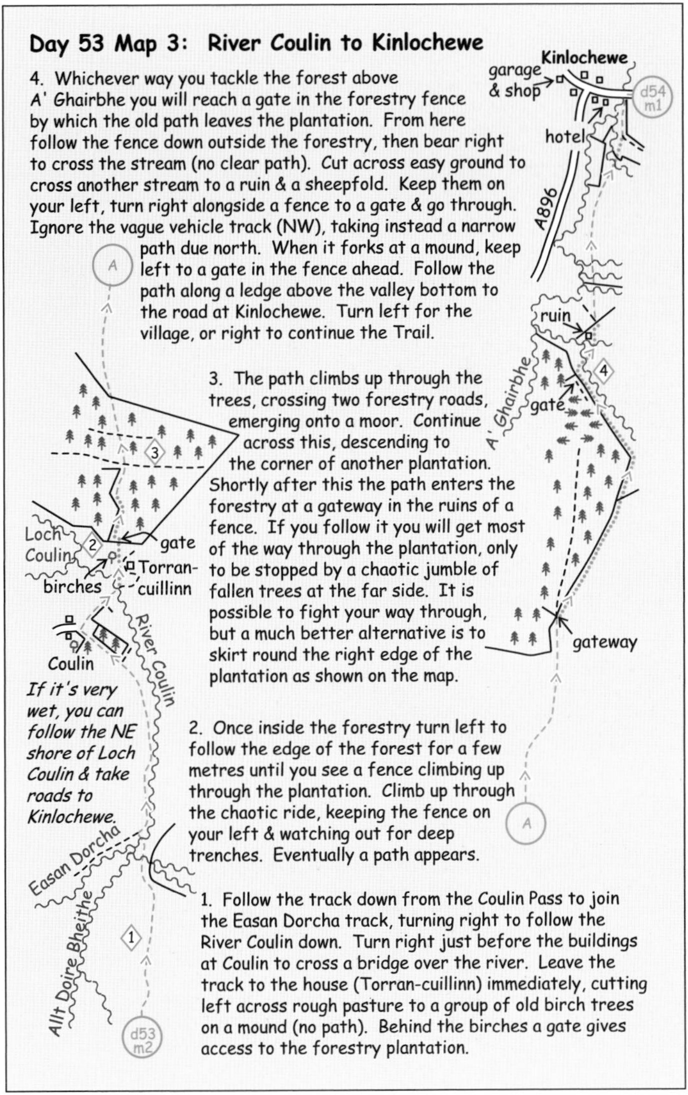

4. Whichever way you tackle the forest above A' Ghairbhe you will reach a gate in the forestry fence by which the old path leaves the plantation. From here follow the fence down outside the forestry, then bear right to cross the stream (no clear path). Cut across easy ground to cross another stream to a ruin & a sheepfold. Keep them on your left, turn right alongside a fence to a gate & go through. Ignore the vague vehicle track (NW), taking instead a narrow path due north. When it forks at a mound, keep left to a gate in the fence ahead. Follow the path along a ledge above the valley bottom to the road at Kinlochewe. Turn left for the village, or right to continue the Trail.

3. The path climbs up through the trees, crossing two forestry roads, emerging onto a moor. Continue across this, descending to the corner of another plantation. Shortly after this the path enters the forestry at a gateway in the ruins of a fence. If you follow it you will get most of the way through the plantation, only to be stopped by a chaotic jumble of fallen trees at the far side. It is possible to fight your way through, but a much better alternative is to skirt round the right edge of the plantation as shown on the map.

If it's very wet, you can follow the NE shore of Loch Coulin & take roads to Kinlochewe.

2. Once inside the forestry turn left to follow the edge of the forest for a few metres until you see a fence climbing up through the plantation. Climb up through the chaotic ride, keeping the fence on your left & watching out for deep trenches. Eventually a path appears.

1. Follow the track down from the Coulin Pass to join the Easan Dorcha track, turning right to follow the River Coulin down. Turn right just before the buildings at Coulin to cross a bridge over the river. Leave the track to the house (Torran-cuillinn) immediately, cutting left across rough pasture to a group of old birch trees on a mound (no path). Behind the birches a gate gives access to the forestry plantation.

Kinlochewe
garage & shop
d54 m1
hotel
A896
ruin
A' Ghairbhe
gate
gateway
A
Loch Coulin
gate
Torran-cuillinn
birches
Coulin
River Coulin
Easan Dorcha
Allt Doire Bheithe
d53 m2

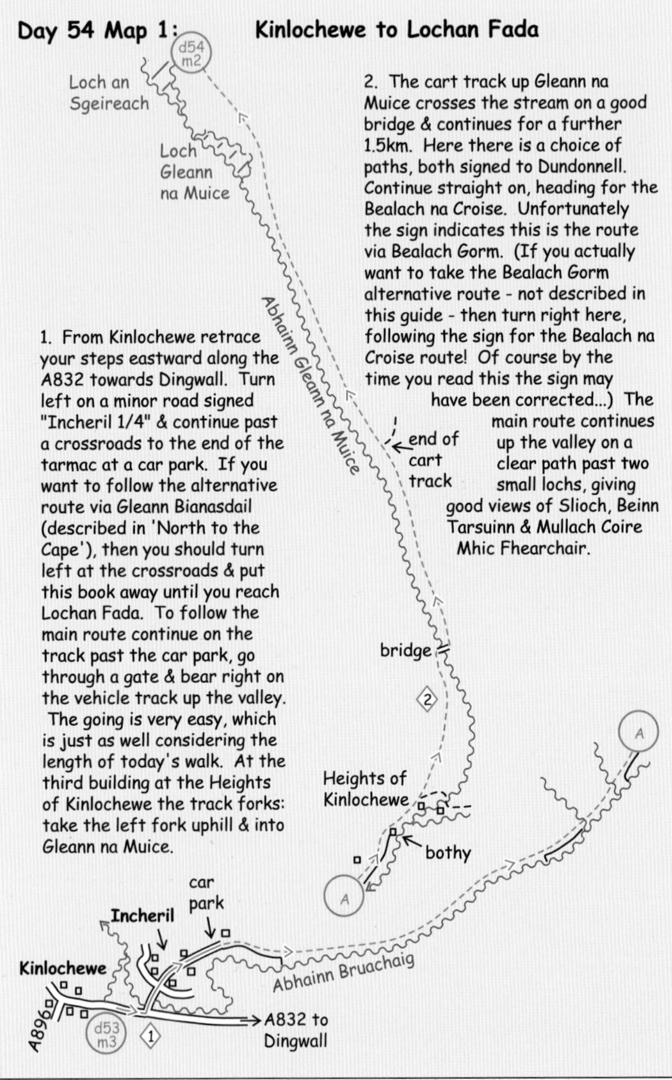
Day 54 Map 1: Kinlochewe to Lochan Fada
d54 m2
Loch an Sgeireach
Loch Gleann na Muice
Abhainn Gleann na Muice
2. The cart track up Gleann na Muice crosses the stream on a good bridge & continues for a further 1.5km. Here there is a choice of paths, both signed to Dundonnell. Continue straight on, heading for the Bealach na Croise. Unfortunately the sign indicates this is the route via Bealach Gorm. (If you actually want to take the Bealach Gorm alternative route - not described in this guide - then turn right here, following the sign for the Bealach na Croise route! Of course by the time you read this the sign may have been corrected...) The main route continues up the valley on a clear path past two small lochs, giving good views of Slioch, Beinn Tarsuinn & Mullach Coire Mhic Fhearchair.
end of cart track
1. From Kinlochewe retrace your steps eastward along the A832 towards Dingwall. Turn left on a minor road signed "Incheril 1/4" & continue past a crossroads to the end of the tarmac at a car park. If you want to follow the alternative route via Gleann Bianasdail (described in 'North to the Cape'), then you should turn left at the crossroads & put this book away until you reach Lochan Fada. To follow the main route continue on the track past the car park, go through a gate & bear right on the vehicle track up the valley. The going is very easy, which is just as well considering the length of today's walk. At the third building at the Heights of Kinlochewe the track forks: take the left fork uphill & into Gleann na Muice.
bridge
2
A
Heights of Kinlochewe
bothy
A
car park
Incheril
Kinlochewe
Abhainn Bruachaig
A896
d53 m3
1
A832 to Dingwall

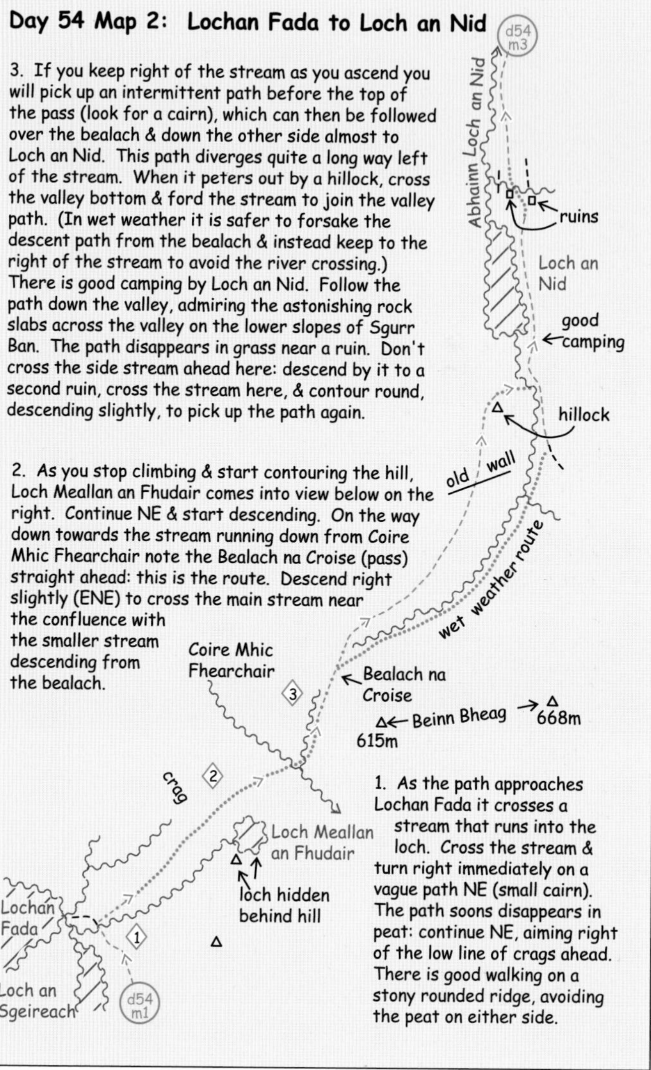
Day 54 Map 2: Lochan Fada to Loch an Nid
3. If you keep right of the stream as you ascend you will pick up an intermittent path before the top of the pass (look for a cairn), which can then be followed over the bealach & down the other side almost to Loch an Nid. This path diverges quite a long way left of the stream. When it peters out by a hillock, cross the valley bottom & ford the stream to join the valley path. (In wet weather it is safer to forsake the descent path from the bealach & instead keep to the right of the stream to avoid the river crossing.) There is good camping by Loch an Nid. Follow the path down the valley, admiring the astonishing rock slabs across the valley on the lower slopes of Sgurr Ban. The path disappears in grass near a ruin. Don't cross the side stream ahead here: descend by it to a second ruin, cross the stream here, & contour round, descending slightly, to pick up the path again.
2. As you stop climbing & start contouring the hill, Loch Meallan an Fhudair comes into view below on the right. Continue NE & start descending. On the way down towards the stream running down from Coire Mhic Fhearchair note the Bealach na Croise (pass) straight ahead: this is the route. Descend right slightly (ENE) to cross the main stream near the confluence with the smaller stream descending from the bealach.
1. As the path approaches Lochan Fada it crosses a stream that runs into the loch. Cross the stream & turn right immediately on a vague path NE (small cairn). The path soons disappears in peat: continue NE, aiming right of the low line of crags ahead. There is good walking on a stony rounded ridge, avoiding the peat on either side.
d54 m3
Abhainn Loch an Nid
ruins
Loch an Nid
good camping
hillock
old wall
wet weather route
Coire Mhic Fhearchair
Bealach na Croise
Beinn Bheag
615m
668m
crag
Loch Meallan an Fhudair
loch hidden behind hill
Lochan Fada
Loch an Sgeireach
d54 m1
1
2
3

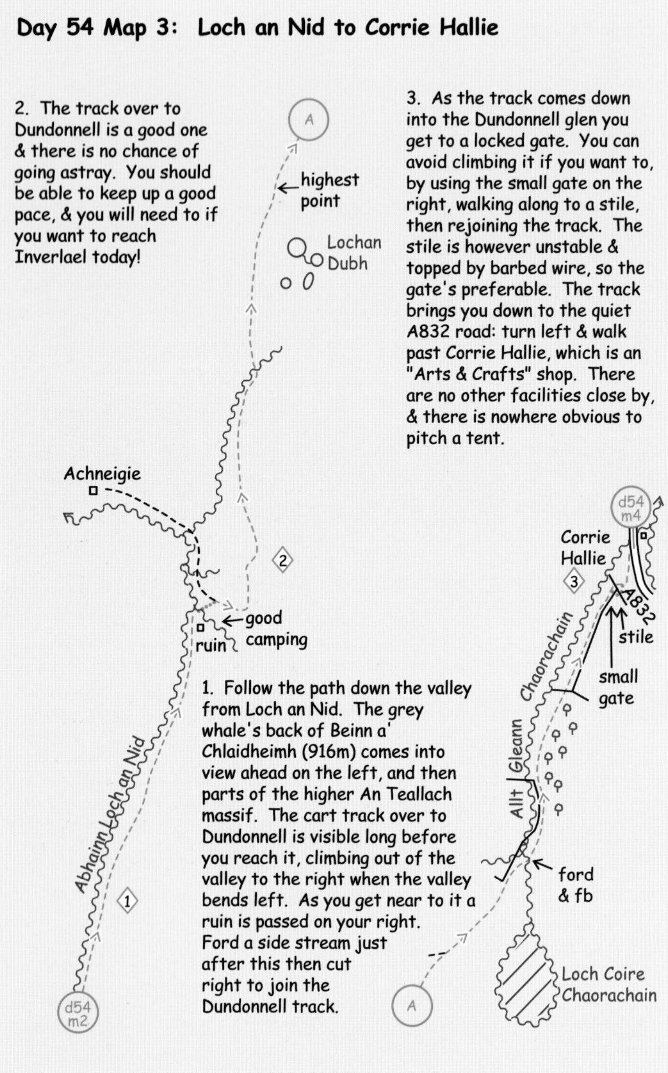
Day 54 Map 3: Loch an Nid to Corrie Hallie
2. The track over to Dundonnell is a good one & there is no chance of going astray. You should be able to keep up a good pace, & you will need to if you want to reach Inverlael today!
A
highest point
Lochan Dubh
3. As the track comes down into the Dundonnell glen you get to a locked gate. You can avoid climbing it if you want to, by using the small gate on the right, walking along to a stile, then rejoining the track. The stile is however unstable & topped by barbed wire, so the gate's preferable. The track brings you down to the quiet A832 road: turn left & walk past Corrie Hallie, which is an "Arts & Crafts" shop. There are no other facilities close by, & there is nowhere obvious to pitch a tent.
Achneigie
2
good camping
ruin
d54 m4
Corrie Hallie
3
A832
stile
small gate
Chaorachain
Allt Gleann
ford & fb
Abhainn Loch an Nid
1
1. Follow the path down the valley from Loch an Nid. The grey whale's back of Beinn a' Chlaidheimh (916m) comes into view ahead on the left, and then parts of the higher An Teallach massif. The cart track over to Dundonnell is visible long before you reach it, climbing out of the valley to the right when the valley bends left. As you get near to it a ruin is passed on your right. Ford a side stream just after this then cut right to join the Dundonnell track.
d54 m2
A
Loch Coire Chaorachain

Day 54 Map 4: Corrie Hallie to Inverlael

Turn round as you cross the moorland & take in the tremendous view behind you of An Teallach & its satellites standing on a huge plinth of grey slabs.

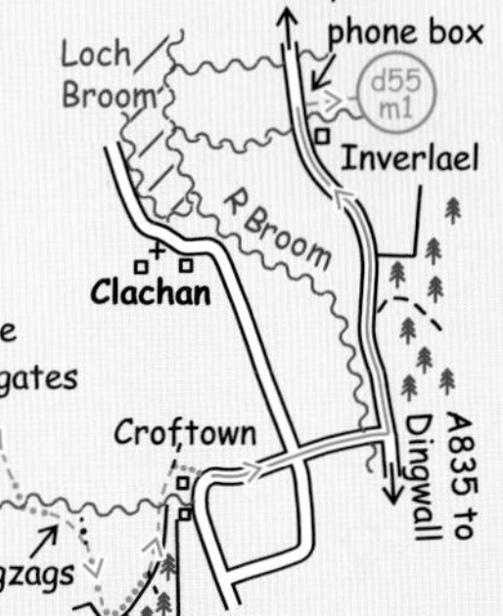

3. The track across the moorland from Dundonnell to Inverlael is clearly an old one, but it is little used now. Although wet in places it is easy to follow until it reaches the edge of the steep drop to the valley & Loch Broom. The path follows the edge of the escarpment for a while before starting to descend, becoming indistinct by a small stream. If you intend to camp in the valley this is the last chance to fill your water bottle, although it can dry up in very dry weather. Drop down a little here to pick up the path again, which zigzags down to meet another old track. Follow this to the righthand end of the plantation visible ahead, then turn sharp left to follow the edge of the trees down steeply. Pass above cottages & some gorse bushes then turn right off the path to descend & bear right again to a gate by a barn. This leads to an access road then a minor road: turn left & follow it to the A835, then turn left.

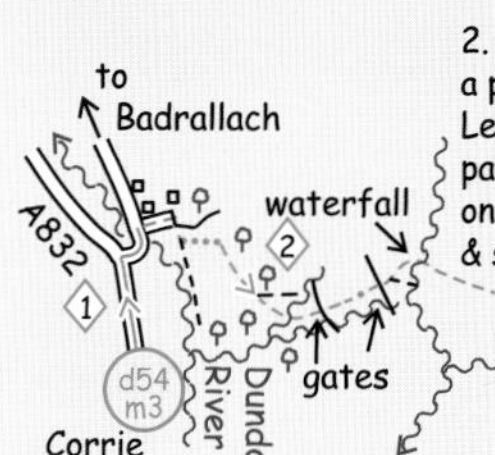

2. Follow the track SE through the wood, ignoring a path to the left just before crossing a stream. Leave the wood at a gate & continue east on a faint path. Soon a clear section of path is visible ahead on the left at a steep section leading to a waterfall & stream crossing. At a fork before the waterfall keep left. Cross by the falls & continue on a clear track.

1. Turn right off the A832 on a minor road signed to Badrallach, cross the river & a cattle grid then turn right immediately down an unsurfaced lane. When it forks turn right through a gate into a field, then leave the track to climb uphill (due east) to the birch woods. Pick up a clear track at the edge of the trees.

Day 55 Map 1: Inverlael to Douchary

3. Continue east across the hillside aiming for a prominent cairn. Ignore the vehicle tracks to the right: they are in wet peat & best avoided. Continue east past the cairn, following 4WD tracks here if they are dry enough. Descend parallel to the burn: if you keep your distance from it you are more likely to pick up stretches of vehicle tracks that will assist in crossing what is difficult ground in places. The tracks disappear for the last steeper section down to join the River Douchary: pick your way down as best you can. Once you are near the flat bottom of the valley cut across to the river & ford it at the first chance you get: it's a lot deeper further down. Follow the river down the valley.

The ruins of the settlement at Douchary are not marked on the 1:50000 OS map but are obvious on the ground. This is a bleak place to have lived.

d55 m2
ruins
River Douchary
Allt na Lairige
3
cairn
A
4WD tracks

2. Once out of the plantation a good track continues for a further 2km uphill. Just after crossing a stream in a boggy area turn left (NE) off the vehicle track on a vague path (small cairn). When the path gives out continue NE then east once clear of the wet ground near the stream.

1. Turn right off the busy A835 at Inverlael, between the house & the phone box on a good track (gate). Follow it into the forestry (gate) & turn left at the first opportunity to cross the River Lael (twin bridges over gorges). Turn right along the forestry road along the far bank. Ignore the first left turn, pass a ruin & a sluice as the road bends left, & pass between a pair of gateposts. When the road starts to bend right again keep straight on to follow a zigzag track up the felled hillside, across another forestry road & up to a gate out of the forestry (which you may need to climb).

A

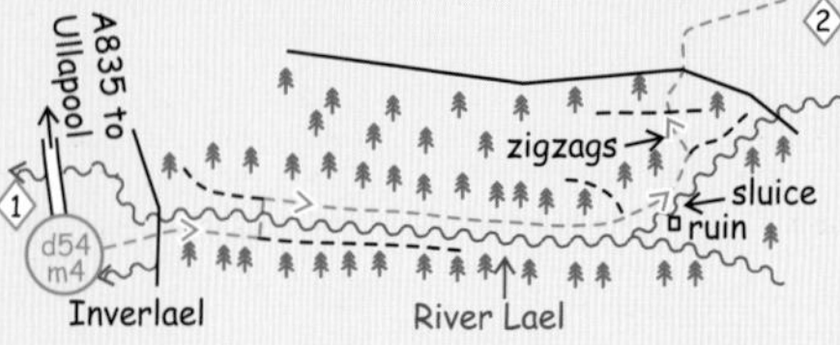

Day 55 Map 2: Douchary to the Abhainn Poiblidh

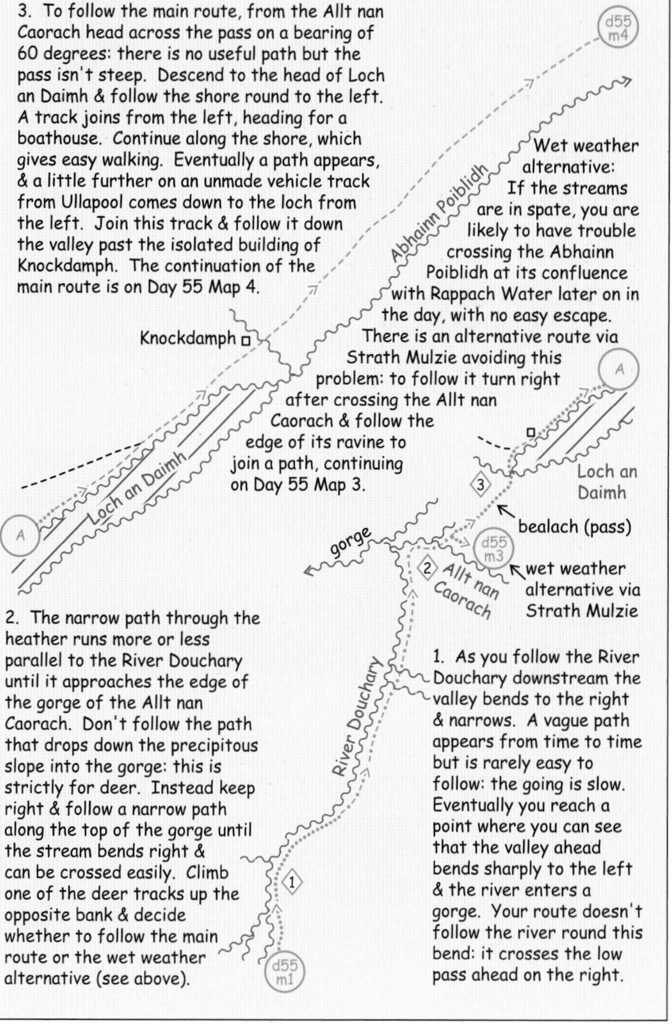

3. To follow the main route, from the Allt nan Caorach head across the pass on a bearing of 60 degrees: there is no useful path but the pass isn't steep. Descend to the head of Loch an Daimh & follow the shore round to the left. A track joins from the left, heading for a boathouse. Continue along the shore, which gives easy walking. Eventually a path appears, & a little further on an unmade vehicle track from Ullapool comes down to the loch from the left. Join this track & follow it down the valley past the isolated building of Knockdamph. The continuation of the main route is on Day 55 Map 4.

Wet weather alternative: If the streams are in spate, you are likely to have trouble crossing the Abhainn Poiblidh at its confluence with Rappach Water later on in the day, with no easy escape. There is an alternative route via Strath Mulzie avoiding this problem: to follow it turn right after crossing the Allt nan Caorach & follow the edge of its ravine to join a path, continuing on Day 55 Map 3.

2. The narrow path through the heather runs more or less parallel to the River Douchary until it approaches the edge of the gorge of the Allt nan Caorach. Don't follow the path that drops down the precipitous slope into the gorge: this is strictly for deer. Instead keep right & follow a narrow path along the top of the gorge until the stream bends right & can be crossed easily. Climb one of the deer tracks up the opposite bank & decide whether to follow the main route or the wet weather alternative (see above).

1. As you follow the River Douchary downstream the valley bends to the right & narrows. A vague path appears from time to time but is rarely easy to follow: the going is slow. Eventually you reach a point where you can see that the valley ahead bends sharply to the left & the river enters a gorge. Your route doesn't follow the river round this bend: it crosses the low pass ahead on the right.

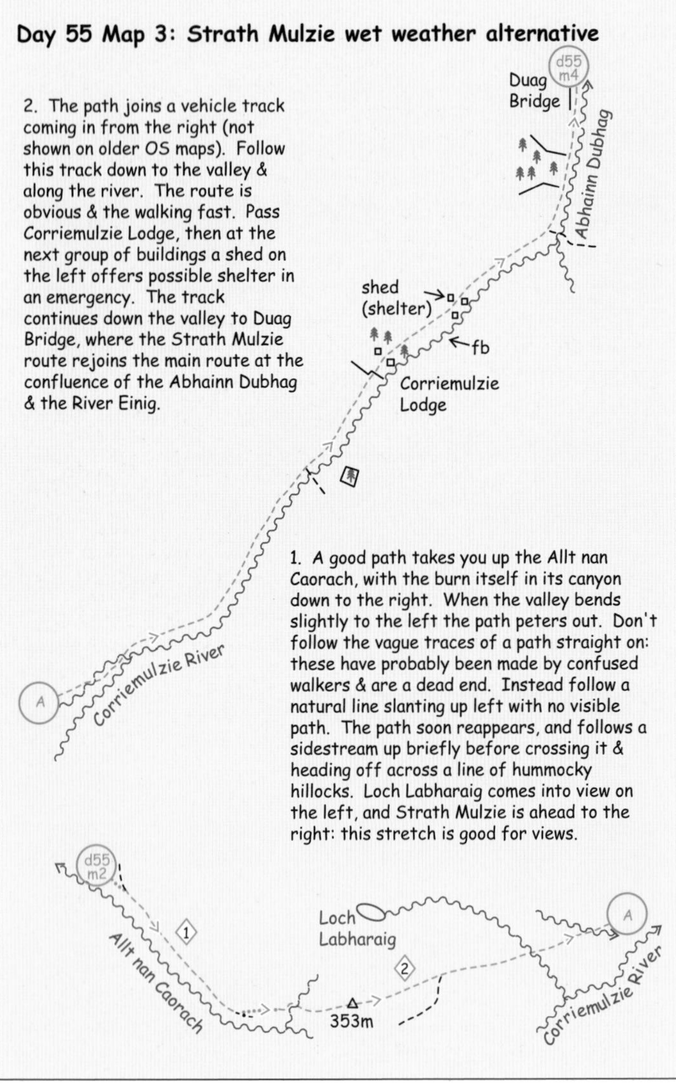
Day 55 Map 3: Strath Mulzie wet weather alternative
d55
m4
Duag
Bridge
Abhainn Dubhag
2. The path joins a vehicle track coming in from the right (not shown on older OS maps). Follow this track down to the valley & along the river. The route is obvious & the walking fast. Pass Corriemulzie Lodge, then at the next group of buildings a shed on the left offers possible shelter in an emergency. The track continues down the valley to Duag Bridge, where the Strath Mulzie route rejoins the main route at the confluence of the Abhainn Dubhag & the River Einig.
shed
(shelter)
fb
Corriemulzie
Lodge
A
Corriemulzie River
1. A good path takes you up the Allt nan Caorach, with the burn itself in its canyon down to the right. When the valley bends slightly to the left the path peters out. Don't follow the vague traces of a path straight on: these have probably been made by confused walkers & are a dead end. Instead follow a natural line slanting up left with no visible path. The path soon reappears, and follows a sidestream up briefly before crossing it & heading off across a line of hummocky hillocks. Loch Labharaig comes into view on the left, and Strath Mulzie is ahead to the right: this stretch is good for views.
d55
m2
1
Allt nan Caorach
Loch
Labharaig
2
353m
A
Corriemulzie River

Day 55 Map 4: Abhainn Poiblidh to Oykel Bridge

3. The track eventually leaves the forestry at a cattle grid: shortly after this bear left to cross a bridge over the river. A stile on the right here gives access to a field that is probably the best place to pitch a tent in the area. Otherwise, continue on the track, keep right at the junction, & continue past houses, now on a surfaced road, to a junction with the A837 at Oykel Bridge. Turn left for the hotel, right for the Lairg alternative route (Day 56L Map 1), or go straight on for the main route.

A lot of the forestry shown here has been felled recently: it may or may not have been replanted.

2. Cross Duag Bridge & continue down the track. Ignore the first (minor) left fork downhill: it just leads to the meadow by the river. At the next fork you can take either route: the lower slightly uphill route enters the forestry, & the upper (steeply uphill initially) follows the upper edge of the forestry for about 2km before joining the lower route in the plantation. If you choose the upper route, which is marginally a better one, keep left at the next two track junctions then straight on to a gate then a junction with the lower route just before the bridge over the Allt nan Caisean. After the bridge keep left at the next track junction.

As you approach Duag Bridge on the main route, a steep track is visible straight ahead up a hill with the unpromising name of Cnoc nam Bad Bog. You will be pleased to know that is not your route.

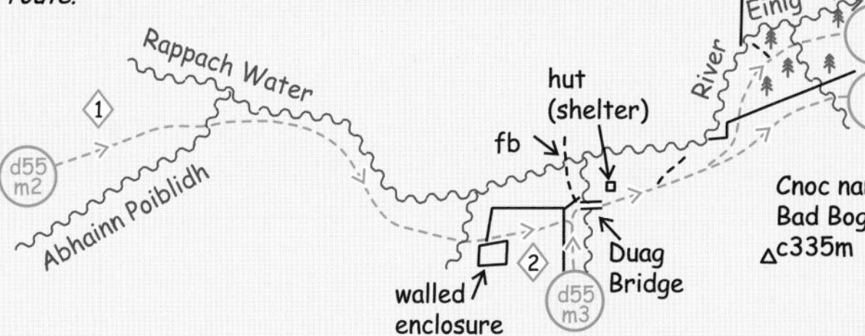

1. The route from Loch an Daimh to Oykel Bridge is all on cart tracks & forestry roads down the valley, so the routefinding is easy. Continue on the track above the Abhainn Poiblidh & ford it just before it joins Rappach Water. As mentioned on Day 55 Map 2 this crossing can be a problem in very wet weather.

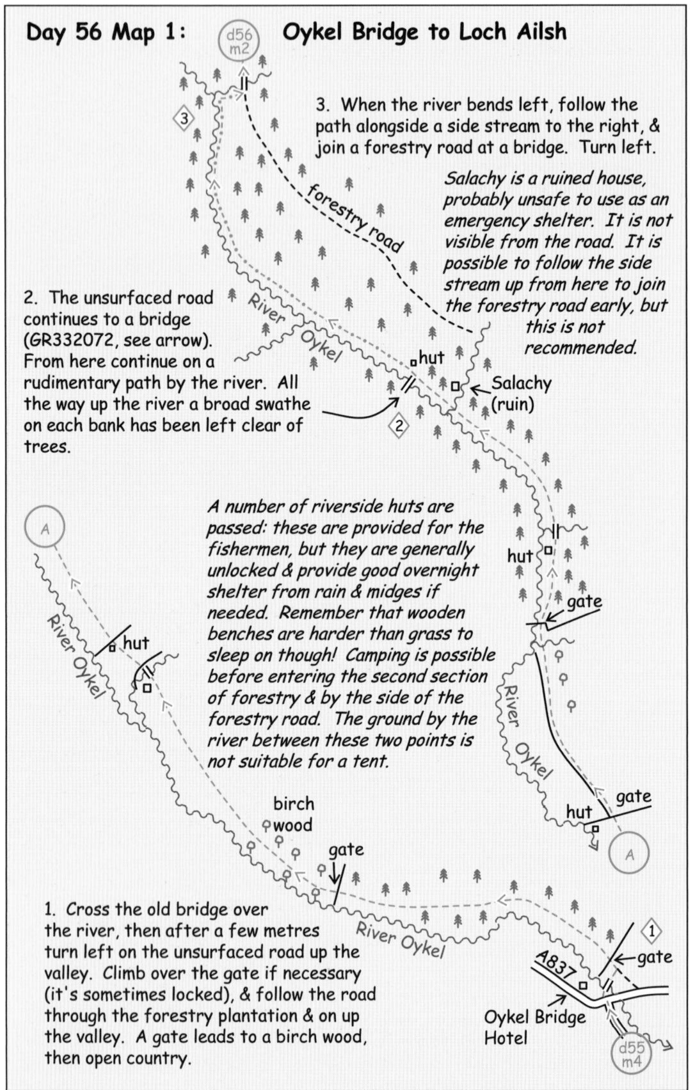
Day 56 Map 1:
d56 m2
Oykel Bridge to Loch Ailsh
3. When the river bends left, follow the path alongside a side stream to the right, & join a forestry road at a bridge. Turn left.
Salachy is a ruined house, probably unsafe to use as an emergency shelter. It is not visible from the road. It is possible to follow the side stream up from here to join the forestry road early, but this is not recommended.
forestry road
2. The unsurfaced road continues to a bridge (GR332072, see arrow). From here continue on a rudimentary path by the river. All the way up the river a broad swathe on each bank has been left clear of trees.
River Oykel
hut
Salachy (ruin)
A number of riverside huts are passed: these are provided for the fishermen, but they are generally unlocked & provide good overnight shelter from rain & midges if needed. Remember that wooden benches are harder than grass to sleep on though! Camping is possible before entering the second section of forestry & by the side of the forestry road. The ground by the river between these two points is not suitable for a tent.
A
hut
gate
River Oykel
hut
River Oykel
gate
hut
A
birch wood
gate
1. Cross the old bridge over the river, then after a few metres turn left on the unsurfaced road up the valley. Climb over the gate if necessary (it's sometimes locked), & follow the road through the forestry plantation & on up the valley. A gate leads to a birch wood, then open country.
River Oykel
A837
gate
Oykel Bridge Hotel
d55 m4

Day 56 Map 2: Loch Ailsh to Meall an Aonaich

Note: Benmore Lodge is the last building you will see for many hours, & you may see no-one else all day. This is very remote country, so make sure you are equipped for survival before you set out, & have told someone where you are going.

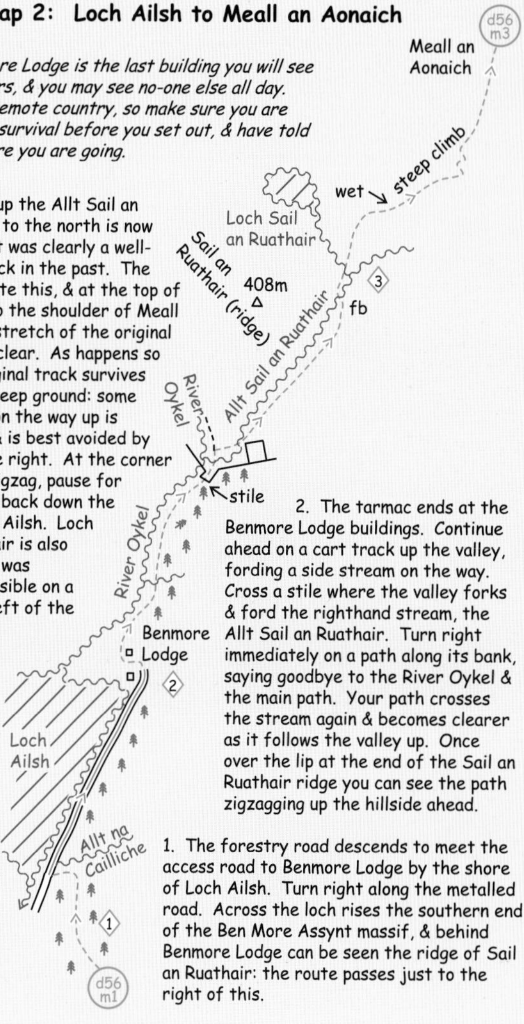

3. This path up the Allt Sail an Ruathair & on to the north is now little used but was clearly a well-build cart track in the past. The zigzags indicate this, & at the top of the climb onto the shoulder of Meall an Aonaich a stretch of the original track is very clear. As happens so often the original track survives less well on steep ground: some of the track on the way up is waterlogged & is best avoided by keeping to the right. At the corner of the first zigzag, pause for breath & look back down the valley to Loch Ailsh. Loch Sail an Ruathair is also visible now: it was previously invisible on a shelf to the left of the path.

2. The tarmac ends at the Benmore Lodge buildings. Continue ahead on a cart track up the valley, fording a side stream on the way. Cross a stile where the valley forks & ford the righthand stream, the Allt Sail an Ruathair. Turn right immediately on a path along its bank, saying goodbye to the River Oykel & the main path. Your path crosses the stream again & becomes clearer as it follows the valley up. Once over the lip at the end of the Sail an Ruathair ridge you can see the path zigzagging up the hillside ahead.

1. The forestry road descends to meet the access road to Benmore Lodge by the shore of Loch Ailsh. Turn right along the metalled road. Across the loch rises the southern end of the Ben More Assynt massif, & behind Benmore Lodge can be seen the ridge of Sail an Ruathair: the route passes just to the right of this.

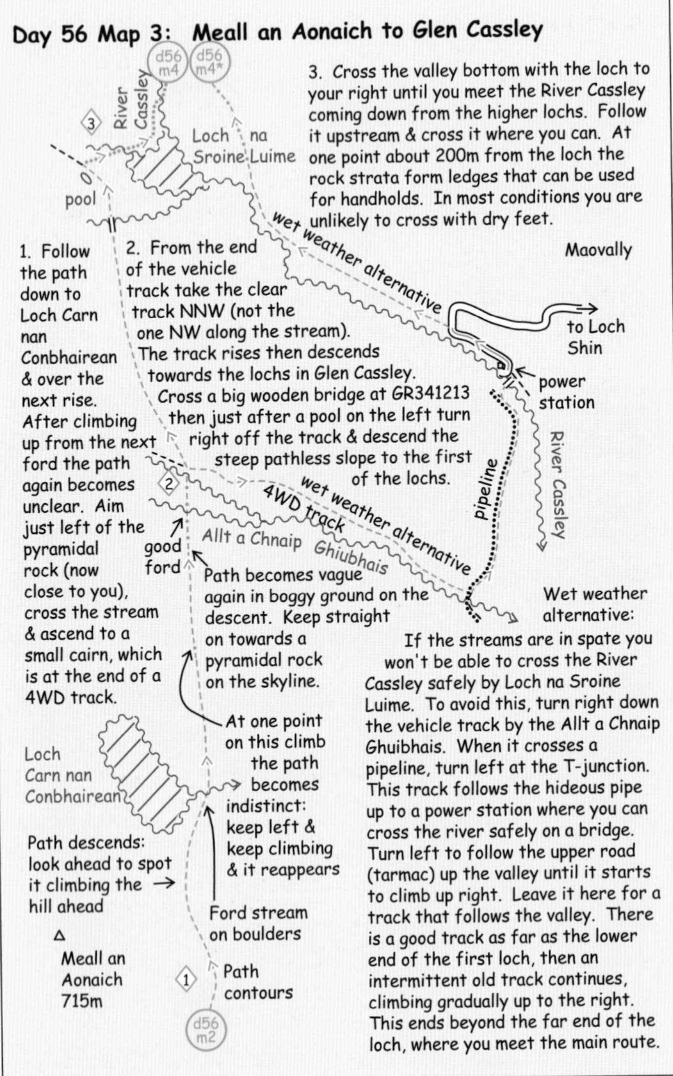
Day 56 Map 3: Meall an Aonaich to Glen Cassley
d56 m4
d56 m4*
3. Cross the valley bottom with the loch to your right until you meet the River Cassley coming down from the higher lochs. Follow it upstream & cross it where you can. At one point about 200m from the loch the rock strata form ledges that can be used for handholds. In most conditions you are unlikely to cross with dry feet.
River Cassley
3
Loch na Sroine Luime
pool
wet weather alternative
Maovally
to Loch Shin
power station
1. Follow the path down to Loch Carn nan Conbhairean & over the next rise. After climbing up from the next ford the path again becomes unclear. Aim just left of the pyramidal rock (now close to you), cross the stream & ascend to a small cairn, which is at the end of a 4WD track.
2. From the end of the vehicle track take the clear track NNW (not the one NW along the stream). The track rises then descends towards the lochs in Glen Cassley. Cross a big wooden bridge at GR341213 then just after a pool on the left turn right off the track & descend the steep pathless slope to the first of the lochs.
pipeline
River Cassley
2
wet weather alternative
4WD track
Allt a Chnaip Ghiubhais
good ford
Path becomes vague again in boggy ground on the descent. Keep straight on towards a pyramidal rock on the skyline.
Wet weather alternative:
If the streams are in spate you won't be able to cross the River Cassley safely by Loch na Sroine Luime. To avoid this, turn right down the vehicle track by the Allt a Chnaip Ghuibhais. When it crosses a pipeline, turn left at the T-junction. This track follows the hideous pipe up to a power station where you can cross the river safely on a bridge. Turn left to follow the upper road (tarmac) up the valley until it starts to climb up right. Leave it here for a track that follows the valley. There is a good track as far as the lower end of the first loch, then an intermittent old track continues, climbing gradually up to the right. This ends beyond the far end of the loch, where you meet the main route.
Loch Carn nan Conbhairean
At one point on this climb the path becomes indistinct: keep left & keep climbing & it reappears
Path descends: look ahead to spot it climbing the hill ahead →
Ford stream on boulders
Meall an Aonaich 715m
1
Path contours
d56 m2

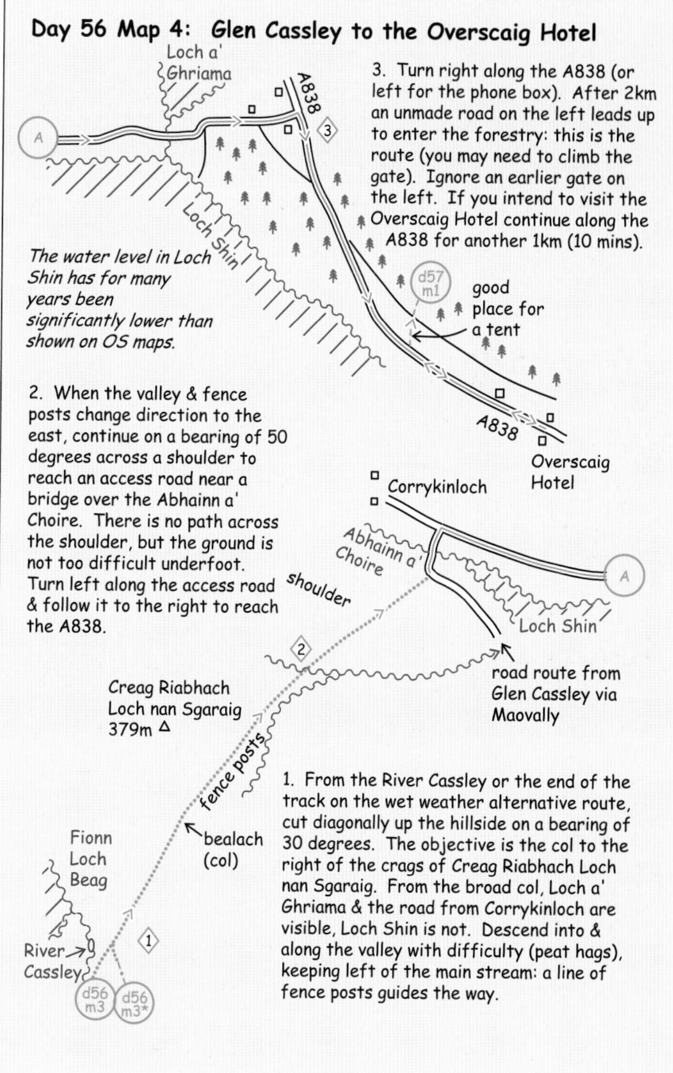
Day 56 Map 4: Glen Cassley to the Overscaig Hotel
Loch a' Ghriama
A838
3
3. Turn right along the A838 (or left for the phone box). After 2km an unmade road on the left leads up to enter the forestry: this is the route (you may need to climb the gate). Ignore an earlier gate on the left. If you intend to visit the Overscaig Hotel continue along the A838 for another 1km (10 mins).
A
Loch Shin
The water level in Loch Shin has for many years been significantly lower than shown on OS maps.
d57 m1
good place for a tent
A838
Overscaig Hotel
Corrykinloch
2. When the valley & fence posts change direction to the east, continue on a bearing of 50 degrees across a shoulder to reach an access road near a bridge over the Abhainn a' Choire. There is no path across the shoulder, but the ground is not too difficult underfoot. Turn left along the access road & follow it to the right to reach the A838.
Abhainn a' Choire
shoulder
A
Loch Shin
2
road route from Glen Cassley via Maovally
Creag Riabhach Loch nan Sgaraig 379m
fence posts
1. From the River Cassley or the end of the track on the wet weather alternative route, cut diagonally up the hillside on a bearing of 30 degrees. The objective is the col to the right of the crags of Creag Riabhach Loch nan Sgaraig. From the broad col, Loch a' Ghriama & the road from Corrykinloch are visible, Loch Shin is not. Descend into & along the valley with difficulty (peat hags), keeping left of the main stream: a line of fence posts guides the way.
Fionn Loch Beag
bealach (col)
1
River Cassley
d56 m3
d56 m3*

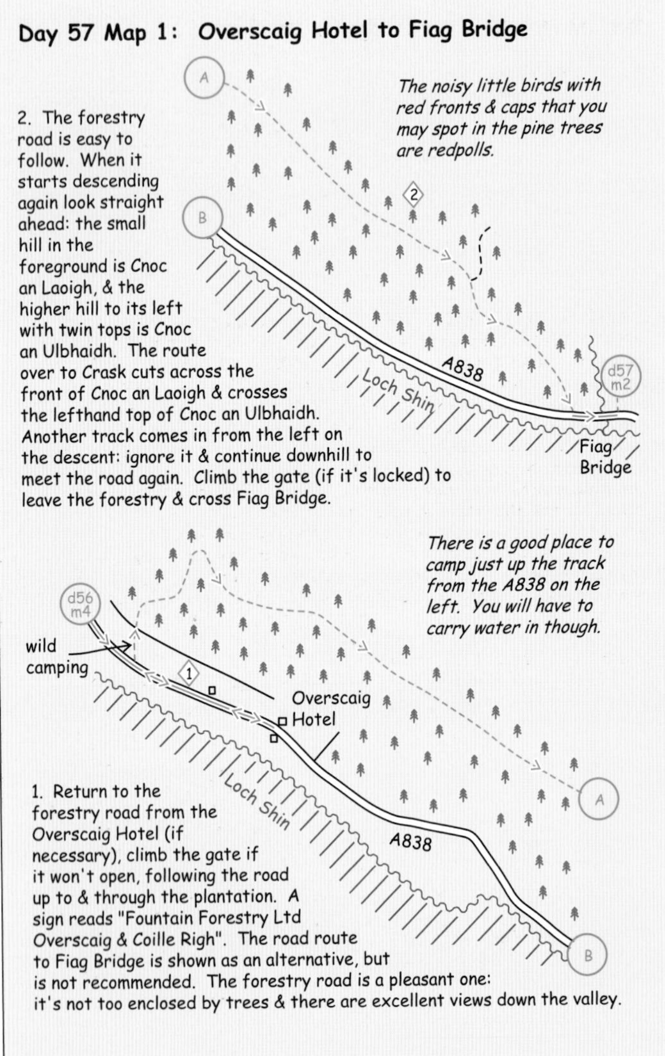
Day 57 Map 1: Overscaig Hotel to Fiag Bridge
A
The noisy little birds with red fronts & caps that you may spot in the pine trees are redpolls.
2. The forestry road is easy to follow. When it starts descending again look straight ahead: the small hill in the foreground is Cnoc an Laoigh, & the higher hill to its left with twin tops is Cnoc an Ulbhaidh. The route over to Crask cuts across the front of Cnoc an Laoigh & crosses the lefthand top of Cnoc an Ulbhaidh. Another track comes in from the left on the descent: ignore it & continue downhill to meet the road again. Climb the gate (if it's locked) to leave the forestry & cross Fiag Bridge.
2
B
A838
Loch Shin
d57
m2
Fiag
Bridge
There is a good place to camp just up the track from the A838 on the left. You will have to carry water in though.
d56
m4
wild
camping
1
Overscaig
Hotel
Loch Shin
A838
A
B
1. Return to the forestry road from the Overscaig Hotel (if necessary), climb the gate if it won't open, following the road up to & through the plantation. A sign reads "Fountain Forestry Ltd Overscaig & Coille Righ". The road route to Fiag Bridge is shown as an alternative, but is not recommended. The forestry road is a pleasant one: it's not too enclosed by trees & there are excellent views down the valley.

Day 57 Map 2: Fiag Bridge to Crask

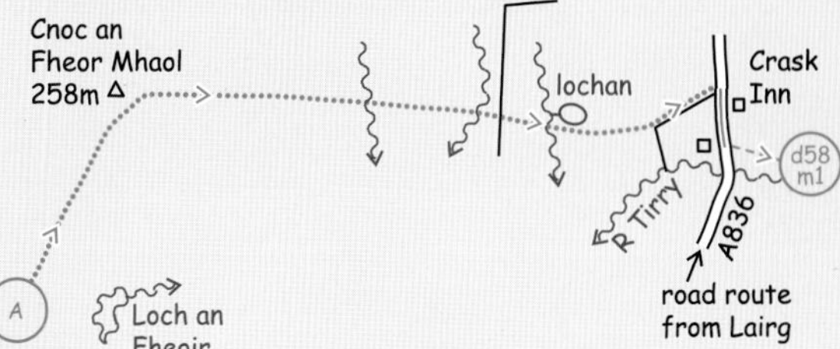

1. Cross Fiag Bridge then turn left (kissing gate) onto the track heading north. A parallel fence on the right soon comes into view: when it bends away from the track turn right to follow it until it turns sharp right. Follow a bearing of 50 degrees from here to reach the lefthand (northwest) summit of Cnoc an Ulbhaidh. On the way look out for deep drainage ditches, & keep left of the obvious "notch" in a hummocky area on the ascent: there is a boggy area in front of it. From the summit (no cairn) you can see the Crask Inn, Loch an Fheoir & Cnoc an Fheor Mhaol, which is the next objective. Beyond the Crask Inn is Ben Klibreck, the last Munro the Trail approaches. It's well worth looking back the way you've come as well: the view is impressive for such a modest hill. Leave on a bearing of 35 degrees to Cnoc an Fheor Mhaol: Loch an Ulbhaidh comes into view almost immediately. Skirt the summit of Cnoc an Fheor Mhaol & head due east, aiming for the Crask Inn. Climb a fence & skirt to the right of a lochan to reach the A836 and the inn.

A
Loch an
Ulbhaidh
292m
Cnoc an
Ulbhaidh
292m
hum mocks

This section is 7km across pathless blanket bog & is tedious apart from the views. The Crask Inn is in view from the top of Cnoc an Ulbhaidh & almost continuously thereafter, but it never seems to get any closer. The two saving graces are (i) that many bogs are a lot wetter than this one, & (ii) that the Crask Inn is welcoming when you reach it.

River
Fiag
1
d57
m1
Fiag
Bridge
pylon
A838
Cnoc an Laoigh
Loch Shin

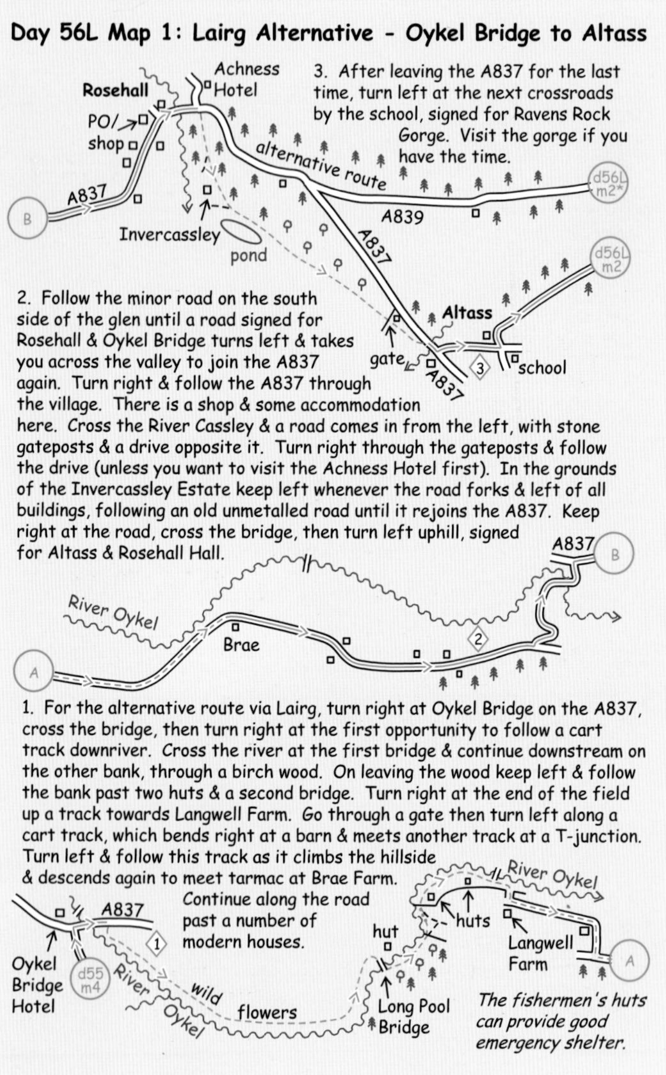
Day 56L Map 1: Lairg Alternative - Oykel Bridge to Altass
Achness Hotel
Rosehall
PO/ shop
A837
B
Invercassley
pond
alternative route
A839
A837
d56L m2*
d56L m2
Altass
gate
school
3
3. After leaving the A837 for the last time, turn left at the next crossroads by the school, signed for Ravens Rock Gorge. Visit the gorge if you have the time.
2. Follow the minor road on the south side of the glen until a road signed for Rosehall & Oykel Bridge turns left & takes you across the valley to join the A837 again. Turn right & follow the A837 through the village. There is a shop & some accommodation here. Cross the River Cassley & a road comes in from the left, with stone gateposts & a drive opposite it. Turn right through the gateposts & follow the drive (unless you want to visit the Achness Hotel first). In the grounds of the Invercassley Estate keep left whenever the road forks & left of all buildings, following an old unmetalled road until it rejoins the A837. Keep right at the road, cross the bridge, then turn left uphill, signed for Altass & Rosehall Hall.
A837
B
River Oykel
Brae
2
A
1. For the alternative route via Lairg, turn right at Oykel Bridge on the A837, cross the bridge, then turn right at the first opportunity to follow a cart track downriver. Cross the river at the first bridge & continue downstream on the other bank, through a birch wood. On leaving the wood keep left & follow the bank past two huts & a second bridge. Turn right at the end of the field up a track towards Langwell Farm. Go through a gate then turn left along a cart track, which bends right at a barn & meets another track at a T-junction. Turn left & follow this track as it climbs the hillside & descends again to meet tarmac at Brae Farm.
Continue along the road past a number of modern houses.
A837
1
Oykel Bridge Hotel
d55 m4
River Oykel
wild flowers
hut
Long Pool Bridge
huts
River Oykel
Langwell Farm
A
The fishermen's huts can provide good emergency shelter.

Day 56L Map 2: Lairg Alternative - Altass to Lairg

Lairg is not a big town, but it is the biggest for a long way & has an importance out of proportion to its size. There are shops, pubs, a bank, a chemist, a post office, a campsite & a number of B&Bs. The campsite, the Nip Inn & most of the shops are in Main St.

If you want to visit the Tourist Information Centre you can take a path branching left off the track down from the Ord, before you reach the housing estate. The path leads directly to the TIC.

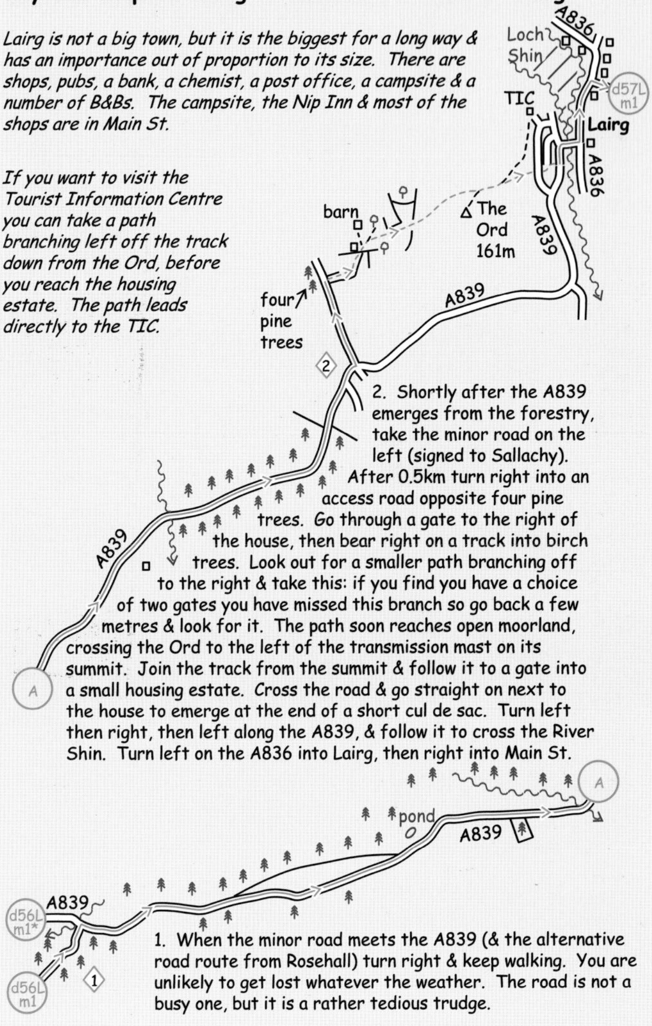

2. Shortly after the A839 emerges from the forestry, take the minor road on the left (signed to Sallachy). After 0.5km turn right into an access road opposite four pine trees. Go through a gate to the right of the house, then bear right on a track into birch trees. Look out for a smaller path branching off to the right & take this: if you find you have a choice of two gates you have missed this branch so go back a few metres & look for it. The path soon reaches open moorland, crossing the Ord to the left of the transmission mast on its summit. Join the track from the summit & follow it to a gate into a small housing estate. Cross the road & go straight on next to the house to emerge at the end of a short cul de sac. Turn left then right, then left along the A839, & follow it to cross the River Shin. Turn left on the A836 into Lairg, then right into Main St.

1. When the minor road meets the A839 (& the alternative road route from Rosehall) turn right & keep walking. You are unlikely to get lost whatever the weather. The road is not a busy one, but it is a rather tedious trudge.

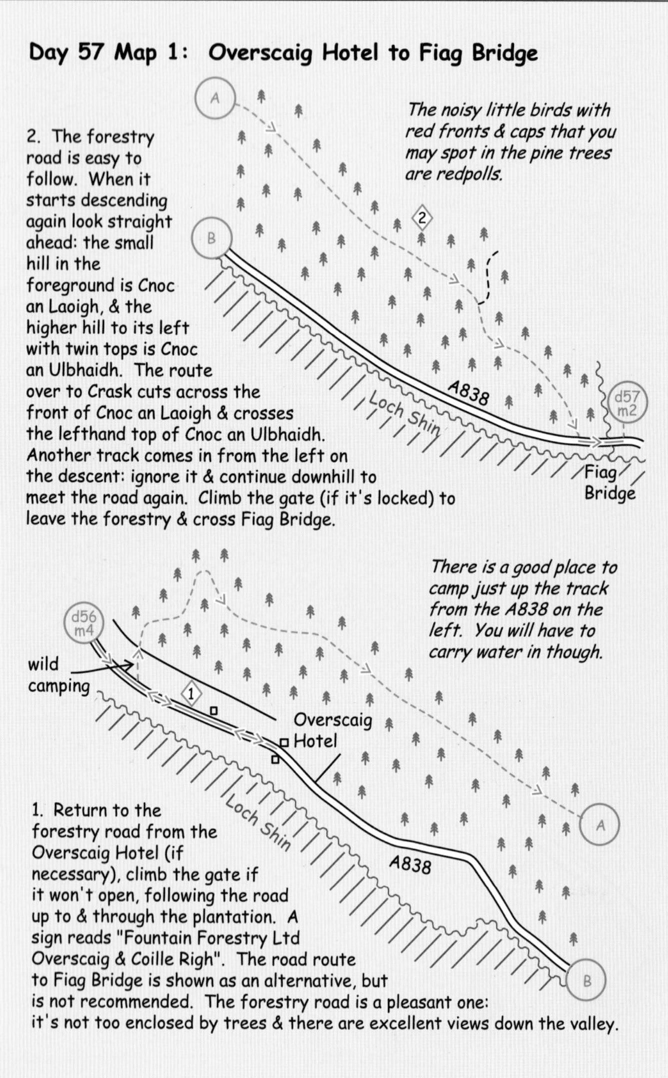
Day 57 Map 1: Overscaig Hotel to Fiag Bridge
A
The noisy little birds with red fronts & caps that you may spot in the pine trees are redpolls.
2. The forestry road is easy to follow. When it starts descending again look straight ahead: the small hill in the foreground is Cnoc an Laoigh, & the higher hill to its left with twin tops is Cnoc an Ulbhaidh. The route over to Crask cuts across the front of Cnoc an Laoigh & crosses the lefthand top of Cnoc an Ulbhaidh. Another track comes in from the left on the descent: ignore it & continue downhill to meet the road again. Climb the gate (if it's locked) to leave the forestry & cross Fiag Bridge.
2
B
A838
Loch Shin
d57
m2
Fiag
Bridge
There is a good place to camp just up the track from the A838 on the left. You will have to carry water in though.
d56
m4
wild
camping
1
Overscaig
Hotel
Loch Shin
A838
A
B
1. Return to the forestry road from the Overscaig Hotel (if necessary), climb the gate if it won't open, following the road up to & through the plantation. A sign reads "Fountain Forestry Ltd Overscaig & Coille Righ". The road route to Fiag Bridge is shown as an alternative, but is not recommended. The forestry road is a pleasant one: it's not too enclosed by trees & there are excellent views down the valley.

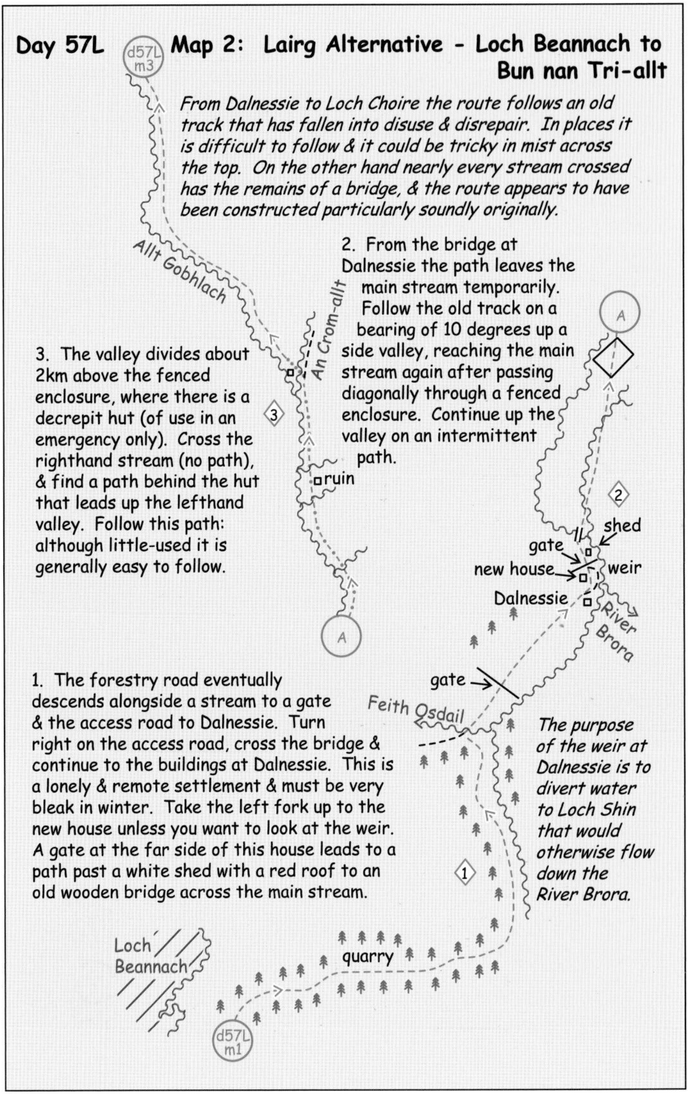
Day 57L
d57L m3
Map 2: Lairg Alternative - Loch Beannach to Bun nan Tri-allt
From Dalnessie to Loch Choire the route follows an old track that has fallen into disuse & disrepair. In places it is difficult to follow & it could be tricky in mist across the top. On the other hand nearly every stream crossed has the remains of a bridge, & the route appears to have been constructed particularly soundly originally.
Allt Gobhlach
An Crom-allt
2. From the bridge at Dalnessie the path leaves the main stream temporarily. Follow the old track on a bearing of 10 degrees up a side valley, reaching the main stream again after passing diagonally through a fenced enclosure. Continue up the valley on an intermittent path.
A
3. The valley divides about 2km above the fenced enclosure, where there is a decrepit hut (of use in an emergency only). Cross the righthand stream (no path), & find a path behind the hut that leads up the lefthand valley. Follow this path: although little-used it is generally easy to follow.
3
ruin
2
shed
gate
new house
weir
Dalnessie
River Brora
A
1. The forestry road eventually descends alongside a stream to a gate & the access road to Dalnessie. Turn right on the access road, cross the bridge & continue to the buildings at Dalnessie. This is a lonely & remote settlement & must be very bleak in winter. Take the left fork up to the new house unless you want to look at the weir. A gate at the far side of this house leads to a path past a white shed with a red roof to an old wooden bridge across the main stream.
gate
Feith Osdail
The purpose of the weir at Dalnessie is to divert water to Loch Shin that would otherwise flow down the River Brora.
1
Loch Beannach
quarry
d57L m1

Day 57L Map 3: Lairg Alternative - Bun nan Tri-allt to Loch Choire

The head of Loch Choire is a lovely place to camp overnight

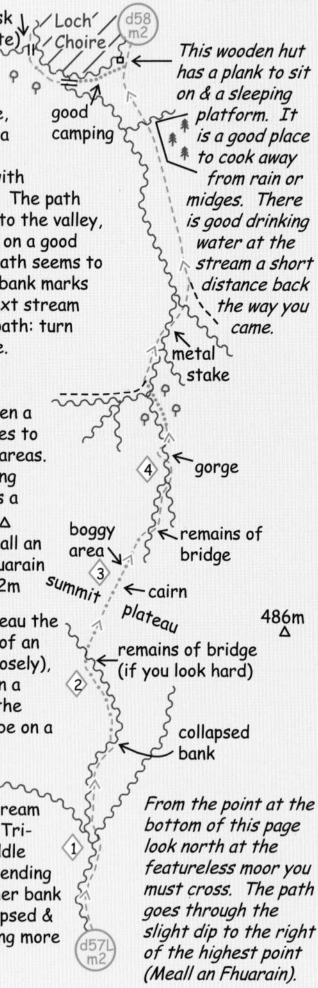

from Crask (main route)

Loch Choire

d58 m2

This wooden hut has a plank to sit on & a sleeping platform. It is a good place to cook away from rain or midges. There is good drinking water at the stream a short distance back the way you came.

good camping

4. The stream enters a small gorge, & the path crosses the stream for a while, crossing back again at the bottom of the gorge & continuing with the stream once more on your left. The path peters out in trees: continue down to the valley, cross the main stream & turn right on a good path. Cross the stream when the path seems to end: a metal stake on the opposite bank marks the spot. Cross the valley & the next stream (bridge or ford) to meet a better path: turn left & follow it down to Loch Choire.

metal stake

3. On the far side of the summit plateau there is a small cairn, & then a boggy area in which the path weaves to some extent to avoid the wettest areas. It still keeps to a 30 degree bearing overall until it bends right to cross a stream at the wreckage of another bridge. Follow the stream down.

gorge

4

Meall an Fhuarain 502m

boggy area

remains of bridge

3

summit plateau

cairn

486m

2. When you near the summit plateau the path crosses the stream (remains of an old bridge are visible if you look closely), & continues as an indistinct path on a bearing of about 30 degrees. On the summit ridge the path appears to be on a wide disused track.

remains of bridge (if you look hard)

2

collapsed bank

1. At the head of the valley the stream divides into three (hence "Bun nan Tri-allt"). The path stays with the middle stream, initially northwards then bending to the right. It crosses to the other bank at a point where the bank has collapsed & continues near the stream, becoming more difficult to follow.

1

From the point at the bottom of this page look north at the featureless moor you must cross. The path goes through the slight dip to the right of the highest point (Meall an Fhuarain).

d57L m2

Day 58 Map 1: Crask to Loch a' Bhealaich

2. The eastern side of the pass is very different. Instead of the rounded contours of the western side, the eastern prospect is of a narrow & deep valley with crags on each side. When the path crosses a stream there is an ideal place for pitching a small tent: atmospheric, good turf, running water & probably less midgy than the valley bottom. The path continues down to contour above Loch a' Bhealaich, becoming a rough 4WD track.

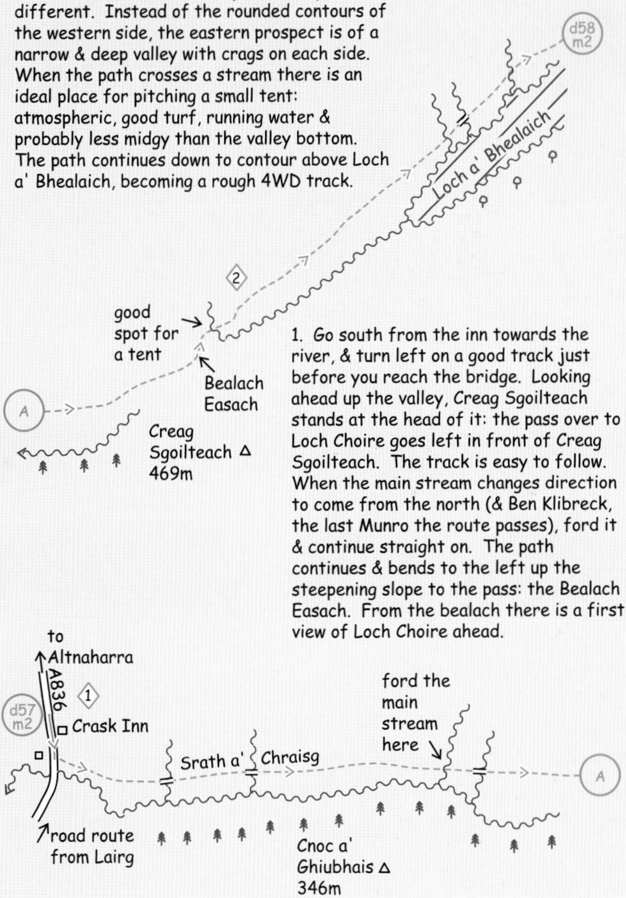

1. Go south from the inn towards the river, & turn left on a good track just before you reach the bridge. Looking ahead up the valley, Creag Sgoilteach stands at the head of it: the pass over to Loch Choire goes left in front of Creag Sgoilteach. The track is easy to follow. When the main stream changes direction to come from the north (& Ben Klibreck, the last Munro the route passes), ford it & continue straight on. The path continues & bends to the left up the steepening slope to the pass: the Bealach Easach. From the bealach there is a first view of Loch Choire ahead.

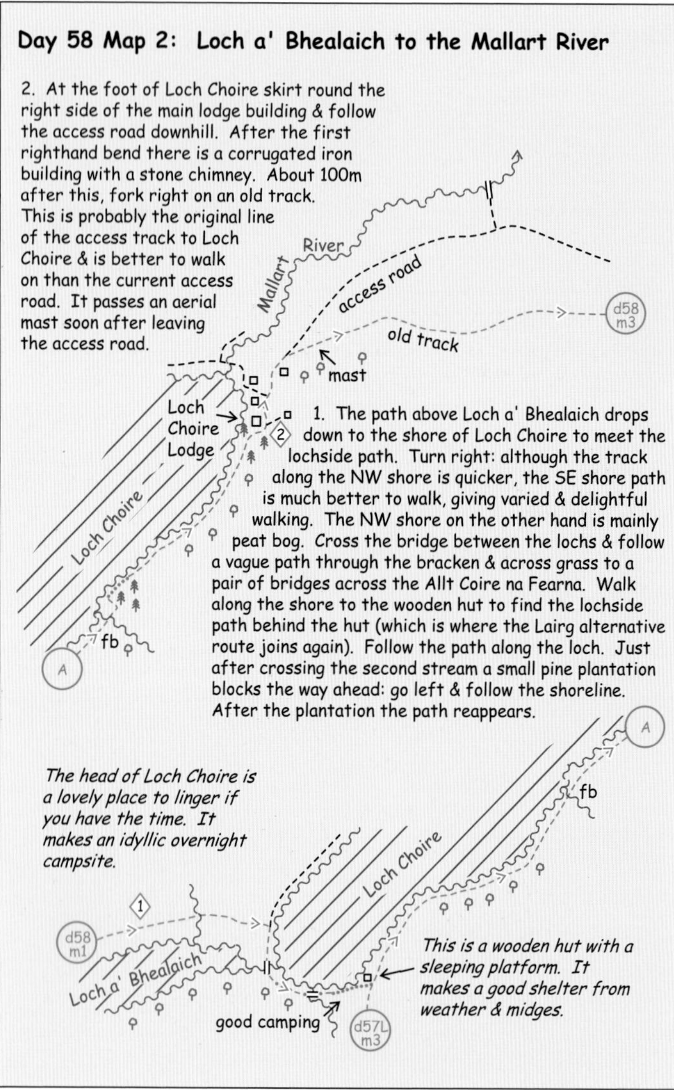
Day 58 Map 2: Loch a' Bhealaich to the Mallart River
2. At the foot of Loch Choire skirt round the right side of the main lodge building & follow the access road downhill. After the first righthand bend there is a corrugated iron building with a stone chimney. About 100m after this, fork right on an old track. This is probably the original line of the access track to Loch Choire & is better to walk on than the current access road. It passes an aerial mast soon after leaving the access road.
River
Mallart
access road
d58
m3
old track
mast
Loch
Choire
Lodge
2
1. The path above Loch a' Bhealaich drops down to the shore of Loch Choire to meet the lochside path. Turn right: although the track along the NW shore is quicker, the SE shore path is much better to walk, giving varied & delightful walking. The NW shore on the other hand is mainly peat bog. Cross the bridge between the lochs & follow a vague path through the bracken & across grass to a pair of bridges across the Allt Coire na Fearna. Walk along the shore to the wooden hut to find the lochside path behind the hut (which is where the Lairg alternative route joins again). Follow the path along the loch. Just after crossing the second stream a small pine plantation blocks the way ahead: go left & follow the shoreline. After the plantation the path reappears.
Loch Choire
fb
A
A
fb
The head of Loch Choire is a lovely place to linger if you have the time. It makes an idyllic overnight campsite.
Loch Choire
1
d58
m1
Loch a' Bhealaich
This is a wooden hut with a sleeping platform. It makes a good shelter from weather & midges.
good camping
d57L
m3

Day 58 Map 3: Mallart River to Badanloch Lodge

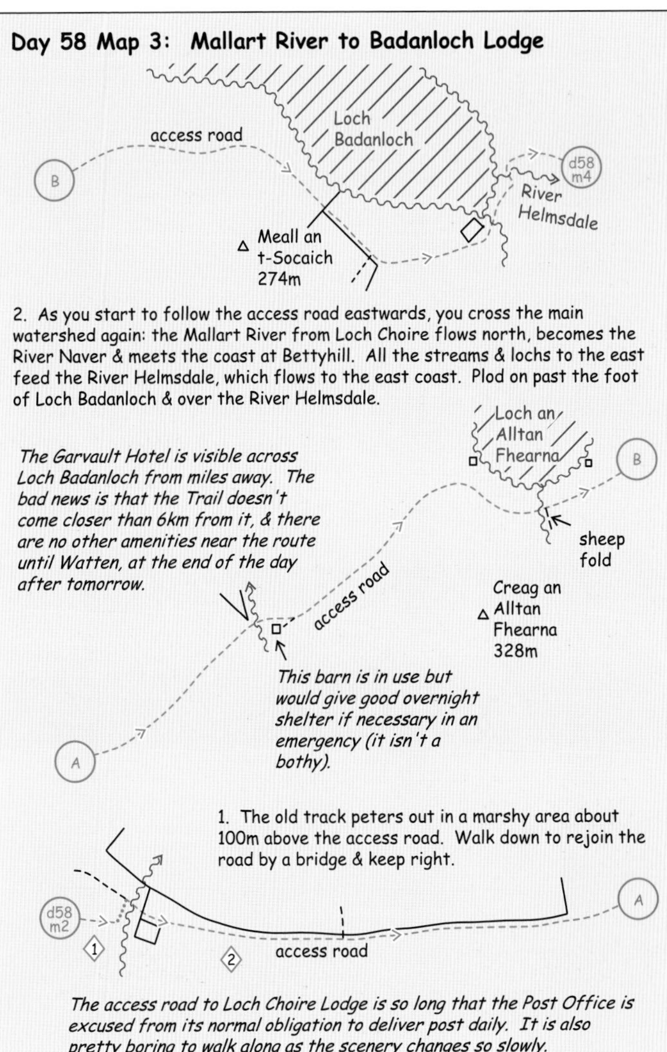

2. As you start to follow the access road eastwards, you cross the main watershed again: the Mallart River from Loch Choire flows north, becomes the River Naver & meets the coast at Bettyhill. All the streams & lochs to the east feed the River Helmsdale, which flows to the east coast. Plod on past the foot of Loch Badanloch & over the River Helmsdale.

The Garvault Hotel is visible across Loch Badanloch from miles away. The bad news is that the Trail doesn't come closer than 6km from it, & there are no other amenities near the route until Watten, at the end of the day after tomorrow.

This barn is in use but would give good overnight shelter if necessary in an emergency (it isn't a bothy).

1. The old track peters out in a marshy area about 100m above the access road. Walk down to rejoin the road by a bridge & keep right.

The access road to Loch Choire Lodge is so long that the Post Office is excused from its normal obligation to deliver post daily. It is also pretty boring to walk along as the scenery changes so slowly.

Day 58 Map 4: Badanloch Lodge to Kinbrace

4. Follow the ditch through two fields on a clear path. At the end of the second field go through the gate ahead then immediately left through another gate. Cut diagonally across the field to the bottom edge of a section of wall: there is a gate where wall & fence meet. Continue diagonally down the next field to a gate at the forestry corner. Head towards the river then bend left to reach a footbridge over the Bannock Burn, inside a ruined walled enclosure. Camping is good by the bridge: the water in Claggan Burn is probably the safest to drink hereabouts. A route from here to the village is shown on the map in case you need it.

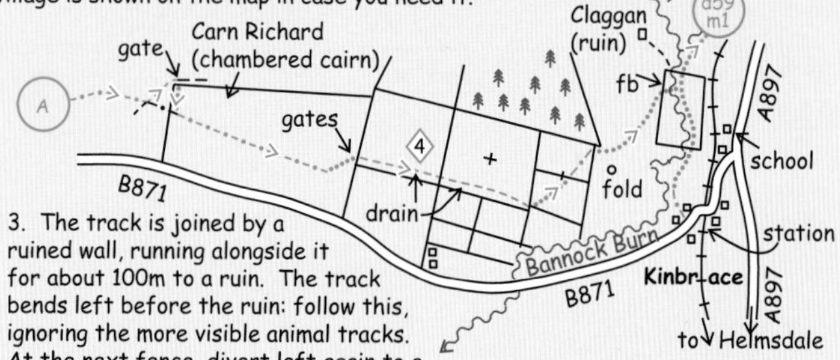

3. The track is joined by a ruined wall, running alongside it for about 100m to a ruin. The track bends left before the ruin: follow this, ignoring the more visible animal tracks. At the next fence, divert left again to a gate, then rejoin the track. Continue to contour until you reach a wall: go up to the left slightly to go through the lefthand (larger) of two gates. Follow the field edge, with a drainage ditch soon joining you.

2. From the forestry corner head along the contour across the moor on a bearing of 140 degrees, just to the right of the alignment of the bottom of the forestry behind you. You should pick up the line of a long-abandoned cart track which you can then follow, contouring. When a fence blocks the way, detour left slightly to a gate then regain the track.

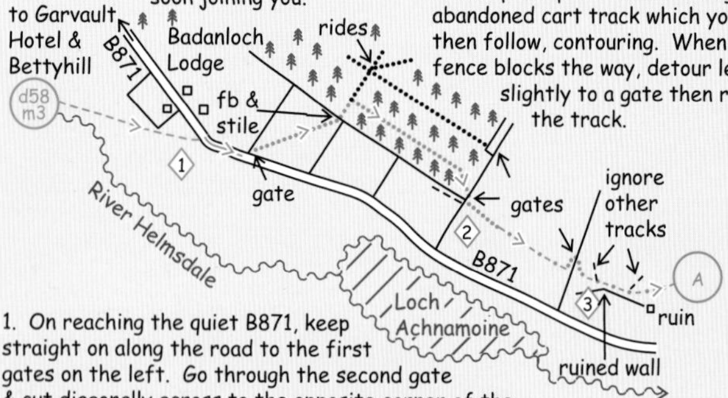

1. On reaching the quiet B871, keep straight on along the road to the first gates on the left. Go through the second gate & cut diagonally across to the opposite corner of the field. A stile gives access to the forestry: climb up the ride until you see a narrow gap on the right. This leads to a gate at the bottom corner of the plantation, above Loch Achnamoine.

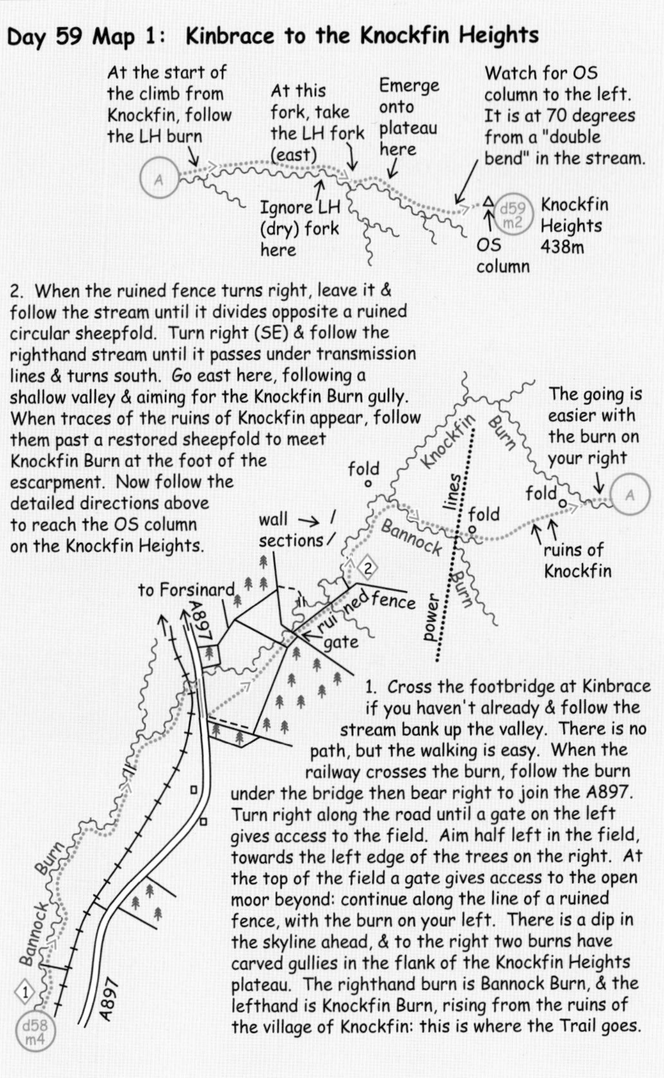
Day 59 Map 1: Kinbrace to the Knockfin Heights
At the start of the climb from Knockfin, follow the LH burn
At this fork, take the LH fork (east)
Emerge onto plateau here
Watch for OS column to the left. It is at 70 degrees from a "double bend" in the stream.
A
Ignore LH (dry) fork here
d59 m2
Knockfin Heights 438m
OS column
2. When the ruined fence turns right, leave it & follow the stream until it divides opposite a ruined circular sheepfold. Turn right (SE) & follow the righthand stream until it passes under transmission lines & turns south. Go east here, following a shallow valley & aiming for the Knockfin Burn gully. When traces of the ruins of Knockfin appear, follow them past a restored sheepfold to meet Knockfin Burn at the foot of the escarpment. Now follow the detailed directions above to reach the OS column on the Knockfin Heights.
The going is easier with the burn on your right
Knockfin Burn
fold
lines
fold
fold
A
wall sections
Bannock Burn
ruins of Knockfin
2
to Forsinard
A897
ruined fence
gate
power
1. Cross the footbridge at Kinbrace if you haven't already & follow the stream bank up the valley. There is no path, but the walking is easy. When the railway crosses the burn, follow the burn under the bridge then bear right to join the A897. Turn right along the road until a gate on the left gives access to the field. Aim half left in the field, towards the left edge of the trees on the right. At the top of the field a gate gives access to the open moor beyond: continue along the line of a ruined fence, with the burn on your left. There is a dip in the skyline ahead, & to the right two burns have carved gullies in the flank of the Knockfin Heights plateau. The righthand burn is Bannock Burn, & the lefthand is Knockfin Burn, rising from the ruins of the village of Knockfin: this is where the Trail goes.
Bannock Burn
1
d58 m4
A897

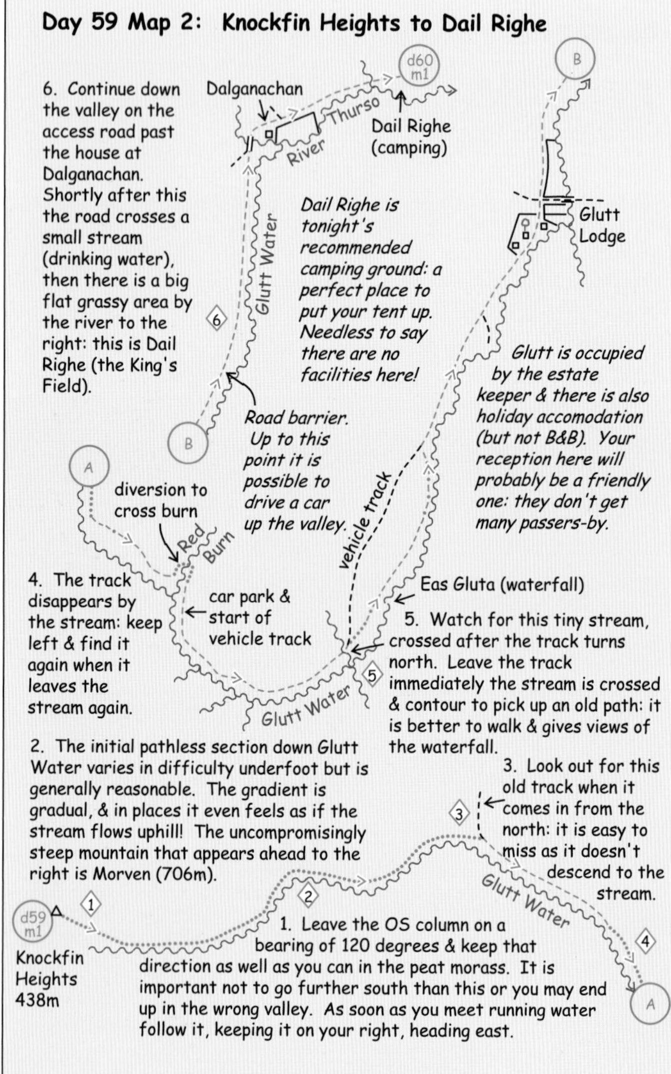
Day 59 Map 2: Knockfin Heights to Dail Righe
6. Continue down the valley on the access road past the house at Dalganachan. Shortly after this the road crosses a small stream (drinking water), then there is a big flat grassy area by the river to the right: this is Dail Righe (the King's Field).
Dalganachan
d60 m1
River Thurso
Dail Righe (camping)
B
Dail Righe is tonight's recommended camping ground: a perfect place to put your tent up. Needless to say there are no facilities here!
Glutt Water
6
Glutt Lodge
Glutt is occupied by the estate keeper & there is also holiday accomodation (but not B&B). Your reception here will probably be a friendly one: they don't get many passers-by.
Road barrier. Up to this point it is possible to drive a car up the valley.
B
A
diversion to cross burn
Red Burn
vehicle track
4. The track disappears by the stream: keep left & find it again when it leaves the stream again.
car park & start of vehicle track
Eas Gluta (waterfall)
5. Watch for this tiny stream, crossed after the track turns north. Leave the track immediately the stream is crossed & contour to pick up an old path: it is better to walk & gives views of the waterfall.
5
Glutt Water
2. The initial pathless section down Glutt Water varies in difficulty underfoot but is generally reasonable. The gradient is gradual, & in places it even feels as if the stream flows uphill! The uncompromisingly steep mountain that appears ahead to the right is Morven (706m).
3. Look out for this old track when it comes in from the north: it is easy to miss as it doesn't descend to the stream.
3
2
1
d59 m1
Knockfin Heights 438m
Glutt Water
4
1. Leave the OS column on a bearing of 120 degrees & keep that direction as well as you can in the peat morass. It is important not to go further south than this or you may end up in the wrong valley. As soon as you meet running water follow it, keeping it on your right, heading east.
A

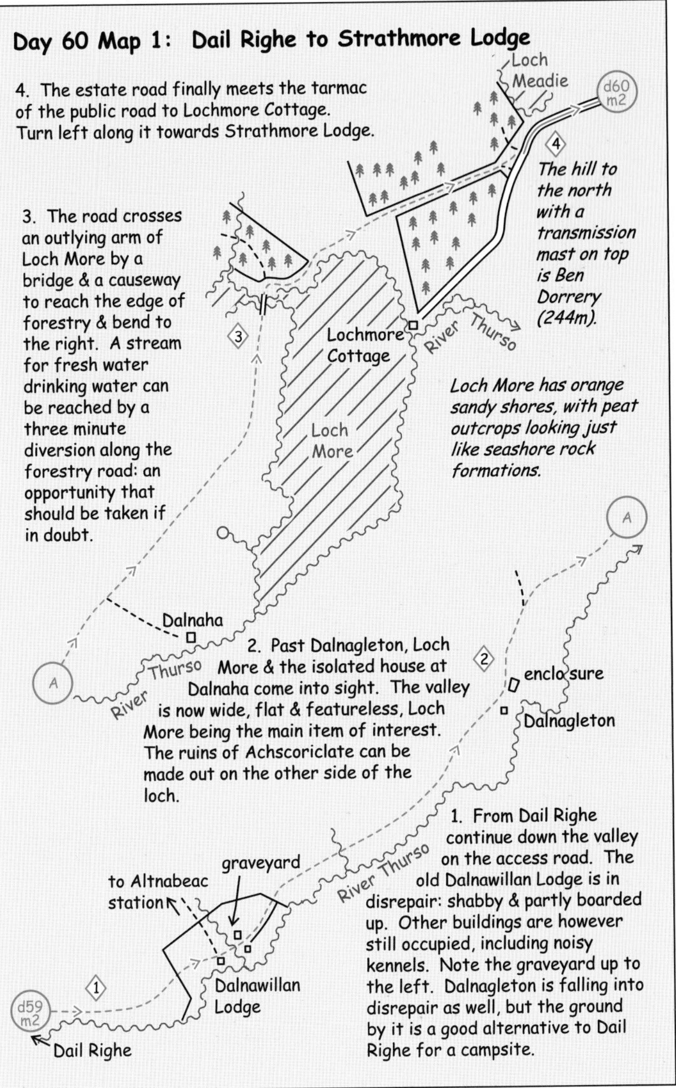
Day 60 Map 1: Dail Righe to Strathmore Lodge
4. The estate road finally meets the tarmac of the public road to Lochmore Cottage. Turn left along it towards Strathmore Lodge.
Loch Meadie
d60 m2
4
The hill to the north with a transmission mast on top is Ben Dorrery (244m).
3. The road crosses an outlying arm of Loch More by a bridge & a causeway to reach the edge of forestry & bend to the right. A stream for fresh water drinking water can be reached by a three minute diversion along the forestry road: an opportunity that should be taken if in doubt.
3
Lochmore Cottage
River Thurso
Loch More
Loch More has orange sandy shores, with peat outcrops looking just like seashore rock formations.
A
Dalnaha
A
River Thurso
2. Past Dalnagleton, Loch More & the isolated house at Dalnaha come into sight. The valley is now wide, flat & featureless, Loch More being the main item of interest. The ruins of Achscoriclate can be made out on the other side of the loch.
2
enclosure
Dalnagleton
1. From Dail Righe continue down the valley on the access road. The old Dalnawillan Lodge is in disrepair: shabby & partly boarded up. Other buildings are however still occupied, including noisy kennels. Note the graveyard up to the left. Dalnagleton is falling into disrepair as well, but the ground by it is a good alternative to Dail Righe for a campsite.
graveyard
to Altnabeac station
River Thurso
1
d59 m2
Dalnawillan Lodge
Dail Righe

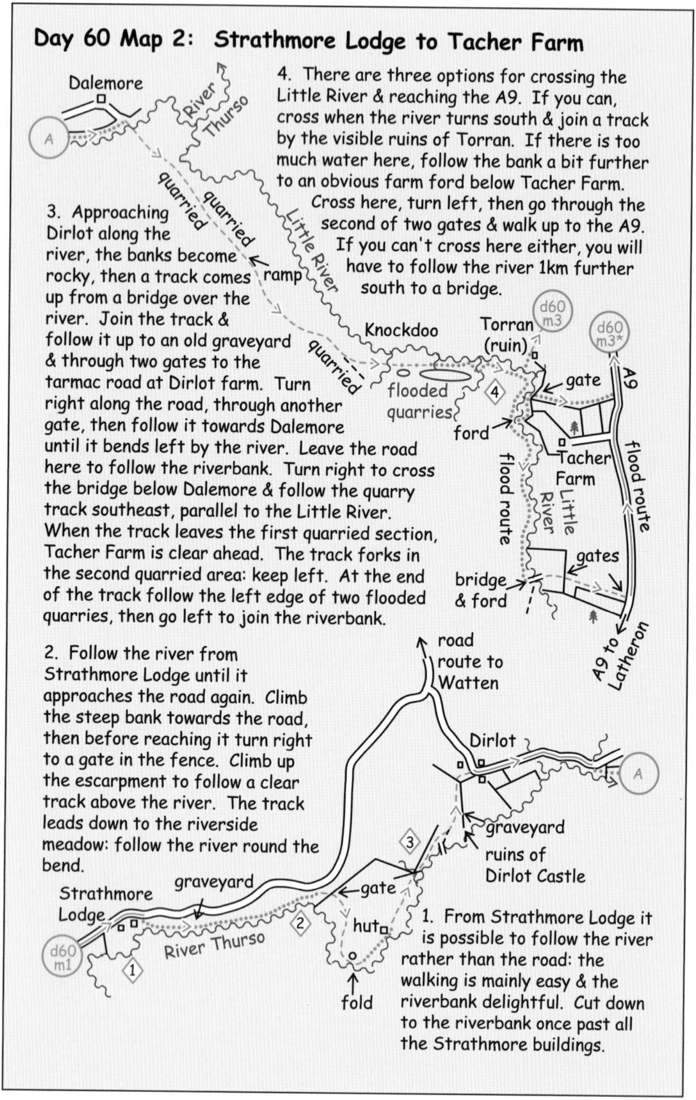
Day 60 Map 2: Strathmore Lodge to Tacher Farm
4. There are three options for crossing the Little River & reaching the A9. If you can, cross when the river turns south & join a track by the visible ruins of Torran. If there is too much water here, follow the bank a bit further to an obvious farm ford below Tacher Farm. Cross here, turn left, then go through the second of two gates & walk up to the A9. If you can't cross here either, you will have to follow the river 1km further south to a bridge.
3. Approaching Dirlot along the river, the banks become rocky, then a track comes up from a bridge over the river. Join the track & follow it up to an old graveyard & through two gates to the tarmac road at Dirlot farm. Turn right along the road, through another gate, then follow it towards Dalemore until it bends left by the river. Leave the road here to follow the riverbank. Turn right to cross the bridge below Dalemore & follow the quarry track southeast, parallel to the Little River. When the track leaves the first quarried section, Tacher Farm is clear ahead. The track forks in the second quarried area: keep left. At the end of the track follow the left edge of two flooded quarries, then go left to join the riverbank.
2. Follow the river from Strathmore Lodge until it approaches the road again. Climb the steep bank towards the road, then before reaching it turn right to a gate in the fence. Climb up the escarpment to follow a clear track above the river. The track leads down to the riverside meadow: follow the river round the bend.
1. From Strathmore Lodge it is possible to follow the river rather than the road: the walking is mainly easy & the riverbank delightful. Cut down to the riverbank once past all the Strathmore buildings.
Dalemore
A
River Thurso
quarried
quarried
Little River
ramp
quarried
Knockdoo
Torran (ruin)
d60 m3
d60 m3*
A9
gate
flooded quarries
4
ford
Tacher Farm
flood route
flood route
Little River
gates
bridge & ford
A9 to Latheron
road route to Watten
Dirlot
A
graveyard
ruins of Dirlot Castle
3
gate
hut
fold
graveyard
Strathmore Lodge
d60 m1
1
2
River Thurso

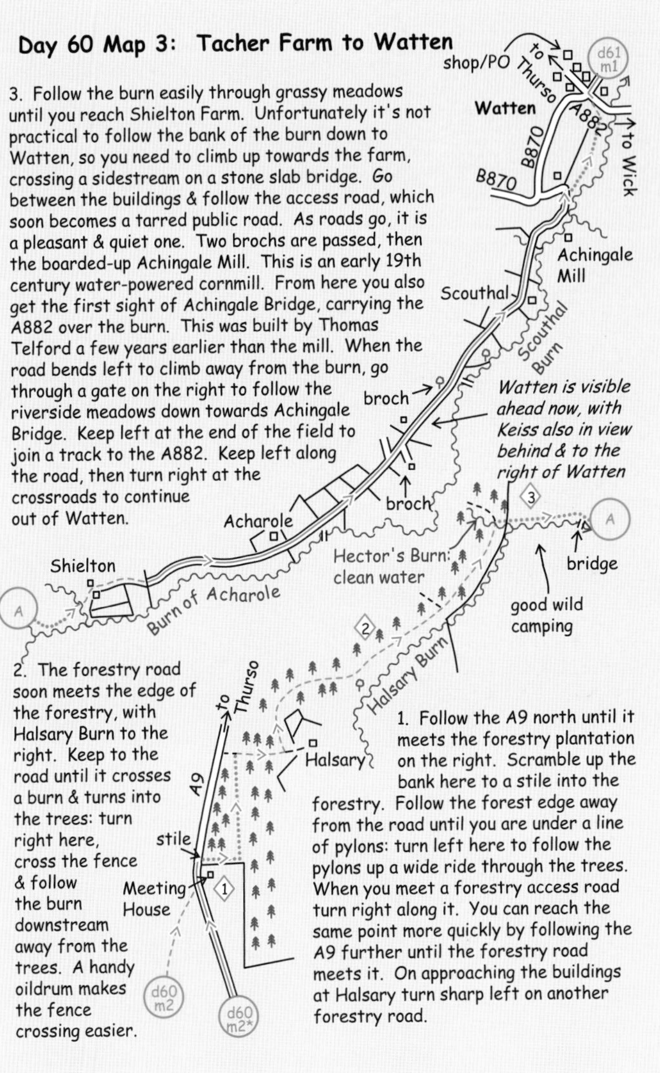
Day 60 Map 3: Tacher Farm to Watten
3. Follow the burn easily through grassy meadows until you reach Shielton Farm. Unfortunately it's not practical to follow the bank of the burn down to Watten, so you need to climb up towards the farm, crossing a sidestream on a stone slab bridge. Go between the buildings & follow the access road, which soon becomes a tarred public road. As roads go, it is a pleasant & quiet one. Two brochs are passed, then the boarded-up Achingale Mill. This is an early 19th century water-powered cornmill. From here you also get the first sight of Achingale Bridge, carrying the A882 over the burn. This was built by Thomas Telford a few years earlier than the mill. When the road bends left to climb away from the burn, go through a gate on the right to follow the riverside meadows down towards Achingale Bridge. Keep left at the end of the field to join a track to the A882. Keep left along the road, then turn right at the crossroads to continue out of Watten.
shop/PO
to Thurso
d61 m1
Watten
A882
to Wick
B870
B870
Achingale Mill
Scouthal
Scouthal Burn
broch
Watten is visible ahead now, with Keiss also in view behind & to the right of Watten
broch
3
A
Acharole
Hector's Burn: clean water
bridge
Shielton
A
Burn of Acharole
good wild camping
2
Halsary Burn
2. The forestry road soon meets the edge of the forestry, with Halsary Burn to the right. Keep to the road until it crosses a burn & turns into the trees: turn right here, cross the fence & follow the burn downstream away from the trees. A handy oildrum makes the fence crossing easier.
to Thurso
A9
Halsary
stile
Meeting House
1
d60 m2
d60 m2*
1. Follow the A9 north until it meets the forestry plantation on the right. Scramble up the bank here to a stile into the forestry. Follow the forest edge away from the road until you are under a line of pylons: turn left here to follow the pylons up a wide ride through the trees. When you meet a forestry access road turn right along it. You can reach the same point more quickly by following the A9 further until the forestry road meets it. On approaching the buildings at Halsary turn sharp left on another forestry road.

Day 61 Map 1: Watten to Killimster

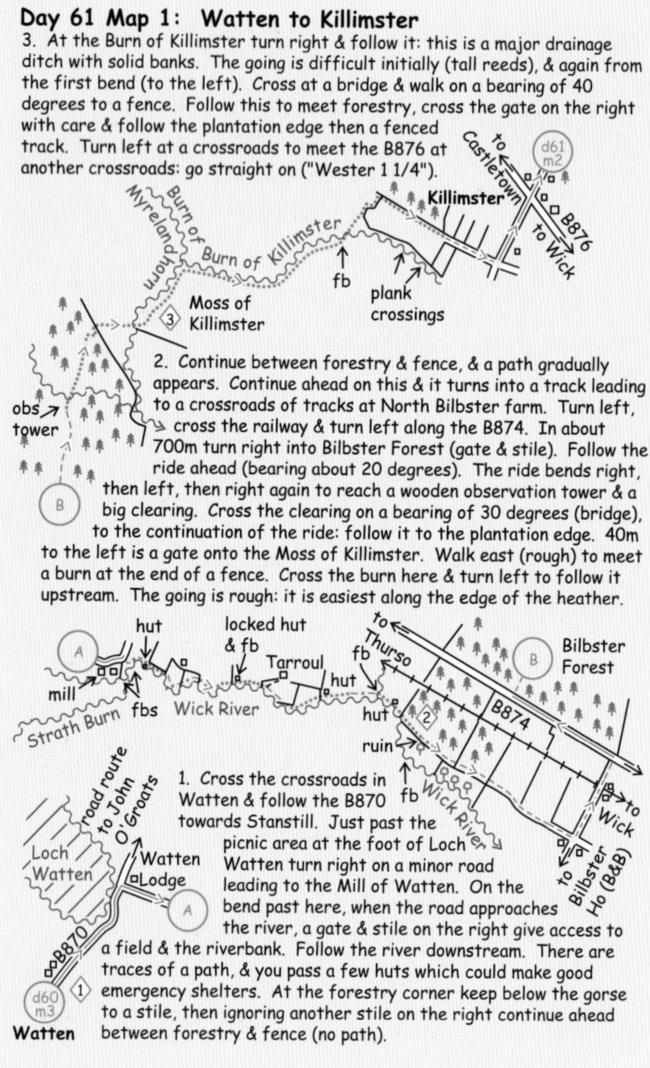

3. At the Burn of Killimster turn right & follow it: this is a major drainage ditch with solid banks. The going is difficult initially (tall reeds), & again from the first bend (to the left). Cross at a bridge & walk on a bearing of 40 degrees to a fence. Follow this to meet forestry, cross the gate on the right with care & follow the plantation edge then a fenced track. Turn left at a crossroads to meet the B876 at another crossroads: go straight on ("Wester 1 1/4").

2. Continue between forestry & fence, & a path gradually appears. Continue ahead on this & it turns into a track leading to a crossroads of tracks at North Bilbster farm. Turn left, cross the railway & turn left along the B874. In about 700m turn right into Bilbster Forest (gate & stile). Follow the ride ahead (bearing about 20 degrees). The ride bends right, then left, then right again to reach a wooden observation tower & a big clearing. Cross the clearing on a bearing of 30 degrees (bridge), to the continuation of the ride: follow it to the plantation edge. 40m to the left is a gate onto the Moss of Killimster. Walk east (rough) to meet a burn at the end of a fence. Cross the burn here & turn left to follow it upstream. The going is rough: it is easiest along the edge of the heather.

1. Cross the crossroads in Watten & follow the B870 towards Stanstill. Just past the picnic area at the foot of Loch Watten turn right on a minor road leading to the Mill of Watten. On the bend past here, when the road approaches the river, a gate & stile on the right give access to a field & the riverbank. Follow the river downstream. There are traces of a path, & you pass a few huts which could make good emergency shelters. At the forestry corner keep below the gorse to a stile, then ignoring another stile on the right continue ahead between forestry & fence (no path).

Day 61 Map 2: Killimster to Keiss Castle

2. In the dunes, pick up a track heading northeast behind the main sandhills, & when it peters out cross the dunes & climb down onto the beach of Sinclair's Bay. Turn left & walk north along the sand. At the end of the beach look for a "footpath" sign up to the left. Climb up to it & follow a track between a fence & the stony shore. The track passes some houses, then bends left & heads inland. A few metres further on, a fenced signed footpath on the right leads to the village of Keiss. Turn right at the road (South St) & follow it round to meet the High St. If you turn left here you will find the post office, the shop, the hotel & the A99. The Trail, on the other hand, turns right to the picturesque little harbour. When the road doubles back towards the harbour, keep straight on (gate) on a path through the grass above the shore.

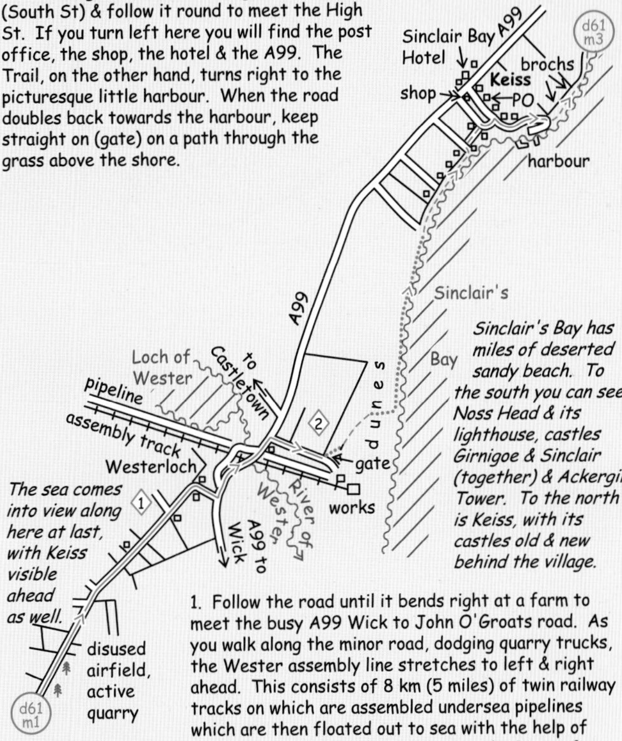

Sinclair's Bay has miles of deserted sandy beach. To the south you can see Noss Head & its lighthouse, castles Girnigoe & Sinclair (together) & Ackergill Tower. To the north is Keiss, with its castles old & new behind the village.

The sea comes into view along here at last, with Keiss visible ahead as well.

1. Follow the road until it bends right at a farm to meet the busy A99 Wick to John O'Groats road. As you walk along the minor road, dodging quarry trucks, the Wester assembly line stretches to left & right ahead. This consists of 8 km (5 miles) of twin railway tracks on which are assembled undersea pipelines which are then floated out to sea with the help of barges. Turn left on the A99, cross the River of Wester, & continue past a house to the tarmac access road for the works. Turn right here, ignoring the "no access" sign, & at the first bend go through a gate on the left into the dunes.

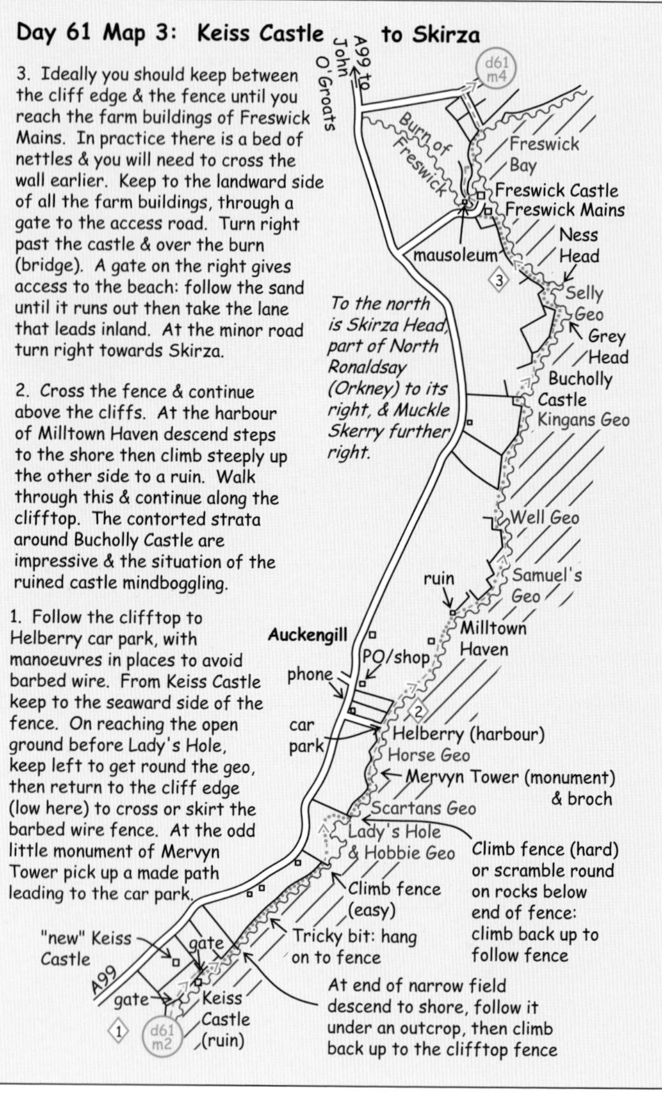
Day 61 Map 3: Keiss Castle to Skirza
3. Ideally you should keep between the cliff edge & the fence until you reach the farm buildings of Freswick Mains. In practice there is a bed of nettles & you will need to cross the wall earlier. Keep to the landward side of all the farm buildings, through a gate to the access road. Turn right past the castle & over the burn (bridge). A gate on the right gives access to the beach: follow the sand until it runs out then take the lane that leads inland. At the minor road turn right towards Skirza.
2. Cross the fence & continue above the cliffs. At the harbour of Milltown Haven descend steps to the shore then climb steeply up the other side to a ruin. Walk through this & continue along the clifftop. The contorted strata around Bucholly Castle are impressive & the situation of the ruined castle mindboggling.
1. Follow the clifftop to Helberry car park, with manoeuvres in places to avoid barbed wire. From Keiss Castle keep to the seaward side of the fence. On reaching the open ground before Lady's Hole, keep left to get round the geo, then return to the cliff edge (low here) to cross or skirt the barbed wire fence. At the odd little monument of Mervyn Tower pick up a made path leading to the car park.
A99 to John O'Groats
d61 m4
Burn of Freswick
Freswick Bay
Freswick Castle
Freswick Mains
mausoleum
Ness Head
3
Selly Geo
Grey Head
To the north is Skirza Head, part of North Ronaldsay (Orkney) to its right, & Muckle Skerry further right.
Bucholly Castle
Kingans Geo
Well Geo
ruin
Samuel's Geo
Milltown Haven
Auckengill
PO/shop
phone
2
car park
Helberry (harbour)
Horse Geo
Mervyn Tower (monument) & broch
Scartans Geo
Lady's Hole & Hobbie Geo
Climb fence (hard) or scramble round on rocks below end of fence: climb back up to follow fence
Climb fence (easy)
Tricky bit: hang on to fence
"new" Keiss Castle
gate
A99
gate
Keiss Castle (ruin)
1
d61 m2
At end of narrow field descend to shore, follow it under an outcrop, then climb back up to the clifftop fence

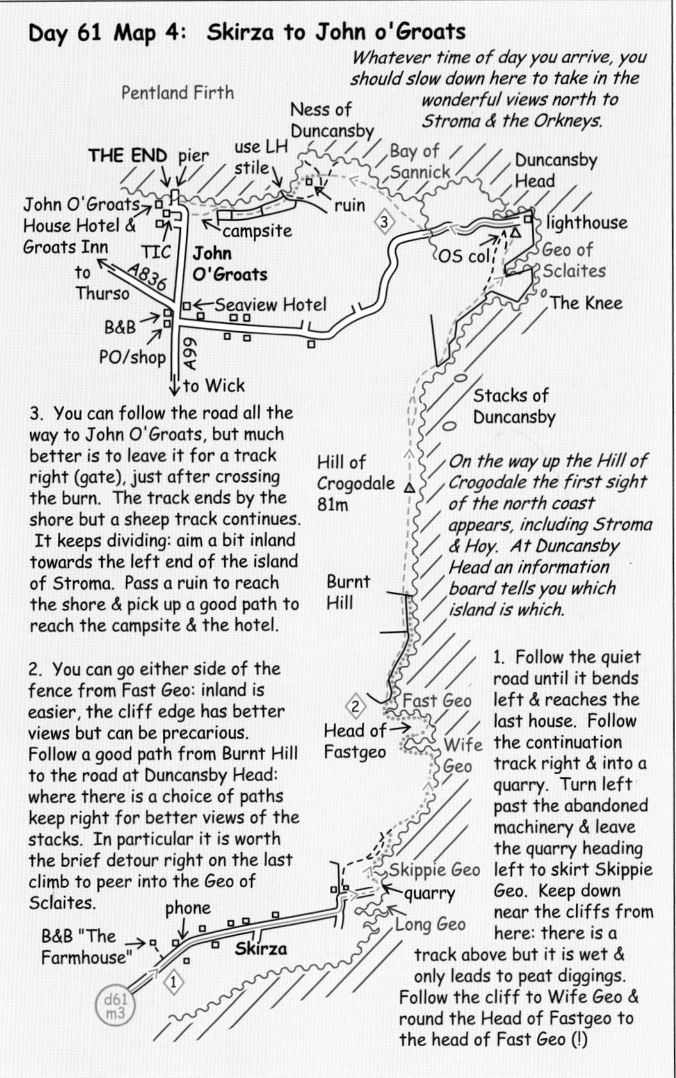
Day 61 Map 4: Skirza to John o'Groats
Whatever time of day you arrive, you should slow down here to take in the wonderful views north to Stroma & the Orkneys.
Pentland Firth
Ness of Duncansby
Bay of Sannick
Duncansby Head
THE END
pier
use LH stile
ruin
John O'Groats House Hotel & Groats Inn
campsite
3
lighthouse
OS col
Geo of Sclaites
The Knee
TIC
John O'Groats
to Thurso
A836
Seaview Hotel
B&B
PO/shop
A99
to Wick
3. You can follow the road all the way to John O'Groats, but much better is to leave it for a track right (gate), just after crossing the burn. The track ends by the shore but a sheep track continues. It keeps dividing: aim a bit inland towards the left end of the island of Stroma. Pass a ruin to reach the shore & pick up a good path to reach the campsite & the hotel.
Stacks of Duncansby
Hill of Crogodale 81m
On the way up the Hill of Crogodale the first sight of the north coast appears, including Stroma & Hoy. At Duncansby Head an information board tells you which island is which.
Burnt Hill
2. You can go either side of the fence from Fast Geo: inland is easier, the cliff edge has better views but can be precarious. Follow a good path from Burnt Hill to the road at Duncansby Head: where there is a choice of paths keep right for better views of the stacks. In particular it is worth the brief detour right on the last climb to peer into the Geo of Sclaites.
1. Follow the quiet road until it bends left & reaches the last house. Follow the continuation track right & into a quarry. Turn left past the abandoned machinery & leave the quarry heading left to skirt Skippie Geo. Keep down near the cliffs from here: there is a track above but it is wet & only leads to peat diggings. Follow the cliff to Wife Geo & round the Head of Fastgeo to the head of Fast Geo (!)
2
Fast Geo
Head of Fastgeo
Wife Geo
Skippie Geo
quarry
Long Geo
phone
B&B "The Farmhouse"
Skirza
1
d61 m3

APPENDIX 1

Route Summary Tables

The following tables summarise the daily stages of the two schedules, the Main Schedule and the three-month Alternative Schedule. Some key points are as follows.

1 Distances are given to the nearest kilometre and nearest mile, measured from 1:50000 OS maps with mapping software.

2 The road walking is an estimate of the proportion of the day's distance that must be walked on tarmac, including private access roads. Some of this can be avoided on the South West Coast Path by taking to the beaches, provided the tides are out far enough. In any event, virtually all the roads followed are either very quiet lanes in the country, or roads in villages and towns with good pavements. There is very little traffic dodging.

3 The ascent per day is given in metres, again measured with mapping software.

4 The accommodation and other key facilities listed are usually within a few minutes walk of the stage end. Exceptions to this are explained in the main text of the book.
The hotels indicated are usually reasonably inexpensive – exceptions are noted in the main text of the book.

5 Where a pub or pubs are indicated at a stage end, there will be at least one pub that normally serves evening meals. Be aware, however, that many pubs do not serve meals on Sunday or Monday nights.

Main Schedule

Day	Stage end	Km	Miles	% on roads	Metres of ascent	B&B/hotel	Hostel/bunkhouse	Bothy	Campsite	Wild camping	Pub	Café/ restaurant	Grocer	Post office	Outdoor shop	Bank	ATM	Public phone
	Land's End (& Sennen)					•	•		•		•	•	•	•				•
1	Zennor	26	16	3	1120	•	•		•		•	•						
2	Gwithian	26	16	25	720	•			•		•	•						•
3	Perranporth	31	19	13	1530	•	•		•		•	•	•	•		•	•	•
4	Mawgan Porth	27	17	16	1020	•			•		•	•						•
5	Wadebridge	28	17	18	670	•			•		•	•	•	•	•	•	•	•

Day	Stage end	Km	Miles	% on roads	Metres of ascent	B&B/hotel	Hostel/bunkhouse	Bothy	Campsite	Wild camping	Pub	Café/ restaurant	Grocer	Post office	Outdoor shop	Bank	ATM	Public phone
6	Boscastle	30	19	14	1390	•	•				•	•	•					•
7	Bude	26	16	6	1440	•	•		•		•	•	•	•	•	•	•	•
8	Clovelly	37	23	3	2390	•			•		•	•	•	•	•			•
9	Barnstaple	37	23	21	1110	•					•	•	•	•	•	•	•	•
10	Warren Farm/ Simonsbath	34	21	31	1140	•				•	•				•			•
11	Roadwater	29	18	15	650	•					•		•	•				•
12	Bridgwater	36	22	23	920	•					•	•	•	•	•	•	•	•
13	Cheddar	32	20	33	180	•	•		•		•	•	•	•	•	•	•	•
14	Easton-in-Gordano/Pill	44	27	19	940	•					•	•	•	•			•	•
15	Chepstow	30	19	41	370	•			•		•	•	•	•		•	•	•
16	Monmouth	27	17	12	950	•			•		•	•	•	•	•	•	•	•
17	Pandy	26	16	26	620	•	•		•		•							•
18	Hay-on-Wye	26	16	11	750	•			•		•	•	•	•		•	•	•
19	Knighton	45	28	20	1500	•			•		•	•	•	•		•	•	•
20	Craven Arms	23	14	26	700	•					•	•	•	•		•	•	•
21	Ironbridge (& Coalport)	37	23	9	760	•	•				•	•	•	•				•
22	Penkridge	37	23	35	380	•					•	•	•	•		•	•	•
23	Abbots Bromley	26	16	14	290	•					•		•	•				•
24	Thorpe	35	22	11	650	•			•		•							•

Day	Stage end	Km	Miles	% on roads	Metres of ascent	B&B/hotel	Hostel/bunkhouse	Bothy	Campsite	Wild camping	Pub	Café/ restaurant	Grocer	Post office	Outdoor shop	Bank	ATM	Public phone
25	Youlgreave	26	16	20	780	•	•				•	•	•	•				•
26	Hathersage (& North Lees)	29	18	11	840	•	•		•		•	•	•	•	•	•	•	•
27	Dunford Bridge	33	21	2	1120													•
28	Hebden Bridge	45	28	15	1500	•					•	•	•	•	•	•	•	•
29	Thornton in Craven	36	22	10	1310	•												•
30	Horton in Ribblesdale	41	25	15	1210	•	•		•		•	•	•	•	•			•
31	Hawes	22	13	8	520	•	•		•		•	•	•	•	•	•	•	•
32	Keld	20	12	15	710	•			•			•						•
33	Middleton-in-Teesdale	33	21	4	800	•			•		•	•	•	•	•		•	•
34	Dufton	32	20	5	710	•	•		•		•		•	•				•
35	Alston	31	19	4	1070	•	•		•		•	•	•	•	•	•	•	•
36	Greenhead	26	16	3	600	•	•		•		•	•						•
37	Bellingham	34	21	14	940	•	•		•		•	•	•	•		•	•	•
38	Byrness	24	15	4	550	•		•	•		•	•						•
39	Jedburgh	31	19	22	830	•			•		•	•	•	•	•	•	•	•
40	Melrose	29	18	22	590	•	•		•		•	•	•	•		•	•	•
41	Traquair	29	18	8	990	•		•										•
42	West Linton	32	20	34	1020	•					•	•	•	•		•	•	•
43	Linlithgow	44	27	9	720	•			•		•	•	•	•		•	•	•

Day	Stage end	Km	Miles	% on roads	Metres of ascent	B&B/hotel	Hostel/bunkhouse	Bothy	Campsite	Wild camping	Pub	Café/ restaurant	Grocer	Post office	Outdoor shop	Bank	ATM	Public phone
44	Kilsyth (Auchinstarry)	33	20	0	260	•					•	•	•	•		•	•	•
45	Drymen	35	22	14	330	•			•	•	•	•	•	•	•	•	•	•
46	Inverarnan (via Conic Hill)	45	28	9	1440	•	•		•		•	•						
47	Bridge of Orchy	29	18	1	730	•	•			•	•			•				•
48	Kinlochleven	33	21	13	980	•	•		•		•	•	•	•			•	•
49	Fort William	23	14	12	710	•	•		•		•	•	•	•	•	•	•	•
50	Glen Garry (Loch Poulary & Tomdoun)	37	23	16	930	•	•			•								•
51	Glen Affric	26	16	20	910		•	•		•								
52	Bendronaig Lodge	34	21	3	920			•		•								
53	Kinlochewe	32	20	4	1010	•	•	•		•	•	•	•	•	•			•
54	Inverlael	39	24	6	1390	•				•								•
55	Oykel Bridge	32	20	6	790	•				•	•							•
56	Overscaig	38	24	16	780	•				•								•
57	Crask	18	11	8	420	•				•								
58	Kinbrace	40	25	1	490					•								
59	River Thurso (Dail Righe)	26	16	1	420					•								
60	Watten	33	20	22	140	•					•		•	•				•
61	John O'Groats	37	23	24	640	•			•		•	•	•	•				•

Alternative Three-month Schedule

Day	Stage end	Km	Miles	Metres of ascent	B&B/hotel	Hostel/bunkhouse	Bothy	Campsite	Wild camping	Pub	Café/ restaurant	Grocer	Post office	Outdoor shop	Bank	ATM	Public phone
	Land's End (& Sennen)				•	•		•		•	•	•	•				•
A1	Pendeen	16	10	660	•			•		•	•	•	•				•
A2	St Ives	21	13	900	•	•		•		•	•	•	•		•	•	•
A3	Portreath	28	17	800	•	•				•	•	•	•			•	•
A4	Perranporth	19	12	1040	•	•		•		•	•	•	•		•	•	•
A5	Newquay	18	10	600	•	•		•		•	•	•	•	•	•	•	•
A6	Trevone	25	16	850	•					•	•	•	•				•
A7	Port Isaac	23	14	430	•					•	•	•	•			•	•
A8	Boscastle	20	12	1170	•	•				•	•	•					•
A9	Bude	26	16	1440	•	•		•		•	•	•	•	•	•	•	•
A10	Hartland Quay (& Stoke)	22	14	1320	•			•		•							•
A11	Clovelly	15	9	1040	•			•		•	•	•	•	•			•
A12	Westward Ho!	18	11	930	•					•	•	•	•			•	•
A13	Barnstaple	21	13	200	•					•	•	•	•	•	•	•	•
A14	Challacombe	21	13	750	•					•		•	•				•
A15	Warren Farm (& Simonsbath)	14	8	390	•				•	•				•			•
A16	Luxborough	24	15	510	•					•							•
A17	Bicknoller Post	16	10	480	•					•		•	•				•

Day	Stage end	Km	Miles	Metres of ascent	B&B/hotel	Hostel/bunkhouse	Bothy	Campsite	Wild camping	Pub	Café/ restaurant	Grocer	Post office	Outdoor shop	Bank	ATM	Public phone
A18	Bridgwater	25	15	580	•					•	•	•	•	•	•	•	•
A19	Blackford[1]	20	13	80						•							•
A20	Sandford	27	17	660	•					•		•					•
A21	Easton-in-Gordano (& Pill)	28	17	380	•					•	•	•	•			•	•
A22	Chepstow	30	19	370	•			•		•	•	•	•		•	•	•
A23	Monmouth	27	17	950	•			•		•	•	•	•	•	•	•	•
A24	Pandy	26	16	620	•	•		•		•							•
A25	Hay-on-Wye	26	16	750	•			•		•	•	•	•		•	•	•
A26	Kington	23	15	710	•	•		•		•	•	•	•		•	•	•
A27	Knighton	22	13	780	•			•		•	•	•	•		•	•	•
A28	Craven Arms	23	14	700	•					•	•	•	•		•	•	•
A29	Much Wenlock	29	18	600	•			•		•	•	•	•		•	•	•
A30	Shifnal	21	13	350	•					•	•	•	•		•	•	•
A31	Penkridge	26	16	200	•					•	•	•	•		•	•	•
A32	Abbots Bromley	26	16	290	•					•		•	•				•
A33	Thorpe	35	22	650	•			•		•							•
A34	Youlgreave	26	16	780	•	•				•	•	•	•				•
A35	Baslow	13	8	300	•					•	•	•					•
A36	Moscar[2]	19	12	620													•

Day	Stage end	Km	Miles	Metres of ascent	B&B/hotel	Hostel/bunkhouse	Bothy	Campsite	Wild camping	Pub	Café/ restaurant	Grocer	Post office	Outdoor shop	Bank	ATM	Public phone
A37	Flouch	22	14	770	•					•	•						
A38	Marsden	26	16	690	•					•	•	•	•			•	•
A39	Hebden Bridge	24	15	860	•					•	•	•	•	•	•	•	•
A40	Cowling	25	16	890	•			•		•	•	•	•				•
A41	Malham	28	17	760	•	•		•		•	•			•			•
A42	Horton in Ribblesdale	24	15	880	•	•		•		•	•	•	•	•			•
A43	Hawes	22	13	520	•	•		•		•	•	•	•	•	•	•	•
A44	Keld	20	12	710	•			•			•						•
A45	Baldersdale	23	14	500	•	•		•									
A46	Langdon Beck	23	14	590	•	•				•							
A47	Dufton	20	12	420	•	•		•		•		•	•				•
A48	Alston	31	19	1070	•	•		•		•	•	•	•	•	•	•	•
A49	Greenhead	26	16	600	•	•		•		•	•						•
A50	Twice Brewed	11	7	380	•	•		•		•							
A51	Bellingham	24	15	610	•	•		•		•	•	•	•		•	•	•
A52	Byrness	24	15	550	•		•	•		•	•						•
A53	Jedburgh	31	19	830	•					•	•	•	•	•	•	•	•
A54	Melrose	29	18	590	•	•		•		•	•	•	•		•	•	•
A55	Traquair	29	18	990	•		•										•

Day	Stage end	Km	Miles	Metres of ascent	B&B/hotel	Hostel/bunkhouse	Bothy	Campsite	Wild camping	Pub	Café/ restaurant	Grocer	Post office	Outdoor shop	Bank	ATM	Public phone
A56	Peebles	12	8	270	•			•		•	•	•	•	•	•	•	•
A57	West Linton	20	12	750	•					•	•	•	•		•	•	•
A58	Broxburn (& Uphall)	30	18	590	•					•	•	•	•		•	•	•
A59	Falkirk (B803)	28	17	290	•					•	•	•	•		•	•	•
A60	Lennoxtown	31	20	200	•					•	•	•	•			•	•
A61	Drymen	22	13	220	•					•	•	•	•	•	•	•	•
A62	Rowardennan (via Conic Hill)	23	15	760	•	•			•	•							•
A63	Inverarnan	22	13	670	•	•		•		•	•						
A64	Tyndrum	19	12	580	•	•		•		•	•	•		•		•	•
A65	Kingshouse	30	18	670	•				•	•							
A66	Kinlochleven	14	9	460	•	•		•		•	•	•	•			•	•
A67	Fort William	23	14	710	•	•		•		•	•	•	•	•	•	•	•
A68	Gairlochy (Mucomir)	15	10	120	•			•									•
A69	Glen Garry (Loch Poulary & Tomdoun)	24	15	830	•	•			•								•
A70	Glen Affric	26	16	910		•	•		•								
A71	Loch Cruoshie	26	16	720			•		•								
A72	Craig	23	14	690		•			•								
A73	Kinlochewe	16	10	500	•	•	•		•	•	•	•	•	•			•

Day	Stage end	Km	Miles	Metres of ascent	B&B/hotel	Hostel/bunkhouse	Bothy	Campsite	Wild camping	Pub	Café/ restaurant	Grocer	Post office	Outdoor shop	Bank	ATM	Public phone
A74	Loch an Nid	18	11	610					•								
A75	Inverlael	22	13	780	•				•								•
A76	Knockdamph	18	11	630			•		•								
A77	Oykel Bridge	13	8	160	•				•	•							•
A78	Glen Cassley	28	17	630					•								
A79	Overscaig	10	6	150	•				•								•
A80	Loch Choire	29	18	600					•								
A81	Kinbrace	29	18	310					•								
A82	River Thurso (Dail Righe)	26	16	420					•								
A83	A9 (Halsary)	22	14	100	•				•								
A84	Keiss	29	18	110	•				•	•		•	•				•
A85	John O'Groats	19	12	570	•			•		•	•	•	•				•

Notes

1 There is no accommodation in Blackford itself – see the main text for details of a number of nearby options.

2 There is no accommodation at Moscar either. Again, refer to the main text for a discussion of your options.

APPENDIX 2
Bibliography

These are a few of the many books I have read while researching Land's End to John O'Groats. They have all been included because either they include valuable information, or they are thought provoking, or because they are (in my opinion) good books. Some are all three, but be warned that they are not all good literature. Many more people have written End to End books – for a more complete bibliography visit the website www.longwalks.org.uk.

Some of these books are out-of-print, but may be available from your local library for a small fee if you ask the librarian to track them down for you. Other than that, you'll have to search the secondhand bookshops, or websites such as www.abebooks.co.uk and www.bookfinder.com.

Essential Guidebooks

If you want to follow a guidebook all the way from End to End you will need the following – they contain maps and detailed route descriptions that are not included in this guidebook.

The South West Coast Path by Paddy Dillon, Cicerone, 2003

Walking Offa's Dyke Path by David Hunter, Cicerone, 2001

The Pennine Way by Martin Collins, Cicerone, 2nd edition 2003

The West Highland Way by Terry Marsh, Cicerone, 2nd edition 2003

Recommended End to End Books

A Tour Through the Whole Land of Great Britain by Daniel Defoe, 1724–6

Penguin Classics published an abridged version in 1986. This isn't really an End to End book, but does purport to document a series of journeys Defoe made, including to Land's End and John O'Groats. It's well worth reading.

A Walk from London to John O'Groat's by Elihu Burritt, Sampson Low, Son & Marston, 1864

A Walk from London to Land's End and Back by Elihu Burritt, Sampson Low, Son & Marston, 1865

Elihu Burritt was appointed US Consul to Birmingham by Abraham Lincoln. In 1863 he walked from London to John O'Groats, and the following year he completed his End to End walk by walking from London to Land's End and back. He tends to concentrate on the grand buildings he sees and their wealthy and/or aristocratic owners, rather than the walking or the scenery – the books were written with an American agriculturalist audience in mind. It is perhaps not too surprising that his writing doesn't chime well with modern walkers, as his motivation was very different.

Having said all that, he probably has to be given the credit for coming up with the idea of walking between Land's End and John O'Groats. He did it in two parts only because he couldn't start early enough in 1863. The second book improves a lot once he gets away from 'civilisation'.

From John O'Groat's to Land's End by RN and JN (Robert and John Naylor), Caxton Publishing Co Ltd, 1916

This is a fascinating account of what may well have been the first continuous walk between Land's End and John O'Groats. The Naylor brothers were well-to-do young men from Cheshire who were presumably inspired to attempt the walk by the writings of Elihu Burritt, although they don't actually say so in their account of their walk. Although the book was published in 1916, they actually did the walk in 1871. John Naylor wrote up and published the account from their earlier notes after the death of his brother, 45 years after their expedition! The book is well written, and the Naylors had a modern approach to their walking that is easy to identify with today -- they were doing it for a challenge, and to see as much of the country as they could. They refused to take ferries, and walked every step of the way. There is rather a lot of interspersed historical fact, and also some historical myth, which is how the book ends up weighing in at 659 pages, but there is plenty of personal account in it as well.

Cross Country by Theo Lang, Hodder & Stoughton, 1948

Theo Lang was a journalist and novelist who walked a rambling route from Land's End to John O'Groats in 1946, just months after the end of the Second World War. He set off on 17 March and finished just under five months later, having walked about 1500 of the 2200 miles he travelled. He wrote articles as he went for the Sunday Chronicle, and later wrote them up into a book. The account is an entertaining one by a professional writer, and has a similar feeling to John Hillaby's account (see below). If you enjoy that, then this is worth seeking out.

The Big Walk by A Walker, Prentice-Hall, 1961

This is an account of the race from John O'Groats to Land's End organised and sponsored by Billy Butlin, the holiday camp entrepreneur. It's a hilarious read, and full of mind-boggling examples of what not to do. Billy Butlin conceived the idea of sponsoring a race after the publicity given to Dr Barbara Moore's 22-day walk, presumably as a publicity stunt for his holiday business. The race was on roads all the way, and started from the John O'Groats Hotel at 5pm on 26 February 1960 – not the ideal time of year for the racers, but nicely timed before the start of the Butlin's holiday season. Of the 715 starters, only 138 finished, and many of the competitors had no idea of what they were embarking on, only competing to win the £1000 prizes for the first man and woman to finish. The anonymous (presumably) author of the book didn't quite finish the race, so isn't included in the list of finishers. He did, however, write a very good account.

Journey Through Britain by John Hillaby, Constable, 1968 (widely reprinted)

The book that must have inspired a thousand attempts at walking from Land's End to John O'Groats. John Hillaby did the journey in the late 1960s, mainly avoiding walking on roads, and wrote this extremely entertaining book about it. The only official long-distance path at the time was the Pennine Way, which he incorporated into his route (more or less). He also followed parts of what later became the Offa's Dyke Path and the West Highland Way.

Turn Right at Land's End by John Merrill, Oxford Illustrated Press, 1979

John Merrill is probably the most prolific long-distance walker in Britain, and this book is his account of the longest walk in Britain -- following the coast all the way round. He set off on 3

January 1978, finished on 8 November, and estimated the distance he walked at 6824 miles. Naturally the walk included joining Land's End to John O'Groats, walking 3800 miles between the two. Oh yes, and he also walked Land's End to John O'Groats three months earlier for a warm up. This walk qualifies for a 'don't try this at home' warning, and you wouldn't have thought it would have had many repeats, although a number of accounts have been written of similar walks since. The walk was obviously very hard both mentally and physically, and included a lot of unavoidable road walking and urban and industrial areas. It is well worth reading for his approach to preparation, and his experience of how to cope with very long walks. Where else are you going to get statistically valid estimates of the life expectancy of boots and socks, for instance?

Hamish's Groat's End Walk by Hamish Brown, Victor Gollancz, 1981 (also Paladin paperback)

This is Hamish Brown's account of his 1979 walk from John O'Groats to Land's End with his Shetland collie, Storm. The route was an indirect one, taking in mountains in Scotland (to complete his sixth round of Munros), England, Wales and Ireland, and the trip took about five months to complete. He generally kept to the mountains where he could, camping wild a lot, and making up for this by staying in comfortable hotels from time to time (a good way to travel, I think). The book is a very readable account which I found difficult to put down, and I have to recommend it strongly as excellent pre-walk mental preparation. There is also plenty of practical information in the book. It has a very good section on what he took and why, and an extensive bibliography.

Land's End to John O'Groats by Andrew McCloy, Hodder & Stoughton, 1994 (also Coronet paperback)

An excellent book in which the author outlines three different off-road walking routes. This is a guidebook rather than an account of his journeys, and a recommended read for anyone planning to walk off-road from Land's End to John O'Groats. It doesn't give a lot of detail of the routes, so you would still need to do a lot of planning or improvising to follow one of them. The End to End Trail coincides in part with two of the routes.

One Woman's Walk by Shirley Rippin, Shirley Rippin/Logaston Press, 1998

A well-written and relaxed account by an experienced walker. The route includes the Pennine Way and the West Highland Way.

One Pair of Boots by Tony Hobbs, Logaston Press, 2000

An account of the author's walk from Land's End to John O'Groats in 1997, this is well worth reading. He set out to follow one of Andrew McCloy's routes, having done minimal preparation, and buying guidebooks and maps as he went along. The book is full of things such as his account of squeezing pus out of his toes, and a list of every pint of beer comsumed on the trip (285 pints of 83 varieties). Therapeutic reading for anyone who tends to overplan their life.

A Walk for Jim by Sally Thomas, published privately, 2001

A moving and readable account of Sally Thomas's walk from Land's End to John O'Groats in aid of leukaemia research – her son had died of leukaemia shortly before her walk. Her route was largely off-road and avoided hilly country, so is worth considering if you don't want to climb many hills.

The Land's End to John O'Groats Walk by Andrew McCloy, Cordee, 2002

This is a more detailed description of one of the three routes (the 'Central Route') outlined in Andrew McCloy's earlier book. It is still not a detailed route description, though, and to follow the route described will require detailed planning with maps for the sections not covered by waymarked routes.

No Fixed Abode by Douglas Legg, Colby Press, 2002

An account of a 5000-mile coastal walk that in many respects bore more resemblance to the journeys of an old-fashioned 'man of the road' than a modern long distance walk.

Follow the Spring North by Christine Roche, Trafford Publishing, 2004

An account of a backpacking End to End walk, following a route that had been well researched. Worth reading for some of the route suggestions. Although this is an account of a walk, there is enough information about the route to be able to follow it accurately most of the way.

Other End to End Books Referenced in This Guidebook

A Ride from Land's End to John O'Groats by Evelyn Burnaby, Sampson Low, Marston & Co, 1893
Land's End to John O'Groats by G H Allen, Fowler, 1905
2000 Miles on Foot by E W Fox, Walter Scott Publishing, 1911
On Old-World Highways by Thos D Murphy, L C Page & Co (Boston USA), 1914
From Land's End to John O'Groats by Jessie Barker Gardner, published privately (USA), 1930
From Land's End to John O'Groats by Colin Howard, Blackie, 1939
The Great Backpacking Adventure by Chris Townsend, Oxford Illustrated Press, 1987

Recommended General Information Books

The Long Distance Walkers' Handbook, A&C Black, 7th edition, 2002

This is the Long Distance Walkers' Association's directory to the UK's long-distance paths. A must-have for anyone interested generally in long-distance walking in the UK.

Beyond Backpacking by Ray Jardine, AdventureLore Press (USA), 2001

This is an updated and generalised edition of Ray's classic Pacific Coast Trail Hiker's Handbook, and is the best book in existence on how to travel light. The importance of Ray Jardine to the current ethic of lightweight hiking can't be overemphasised. Large amounts of the material written in the UK outdoor magazines, and a lot of the products on the market, have been influenced significantly by Ray, either directly or indirectly. Buy this book and you will end up with a lighter rucksack as a result. Don't take everything in it as gospel, though, as things that work in America don't necessarily work over here. Anyone trying to use an umbrella in a typical Pennine rainstorm, or sleep under a tarp in the Highland midge season, is likely to regret it!

The Independent Hostel Guide, Backpackers Press (distributed by Cordee), revised annually

This lists independent bunkhouse accommodation throughout the British Isles.

Youth Hostels in England & Wales, YHA, revised annually

Scottish Youth Hostels, SYHA, revised annually

These give locations, opening dates and booking information for all the youth hostels on and near the route. The booklets are free to members, or can be bought in bookshops.

Good Beer Guide, CAMRA Books, revised annually

This is an annual guide to the best British pubs and best traditional British beer. It is indispensable to a certain class of walker, of which I am most definitely one. (CAMRA is the pressure group that saved the tradition of British beer in the 1970s, and is still providing sterling service today.)

A Journey to the Western Islands of Scotland by Samuel Johnson, 1775

The Journal of a Tour to the Hebrides by James Boswell, 1786

These two classic accounts of a trip through the Scottish Highlands in 1773 have been republished by Penguin Classics in a single volume. They are both fascinating books, and include a lot of detail that conveys vividly what it must have been like to travel in Scotland in the days of the clearances. Boswell's book also gives enormous insight into the personalities involved, many of them larger than life. The Penguin edition is recommended reading to carry with you for the Scottish part of the walk -- good value in words per ounce, relevant, and brilliant writing.

Romany Hints for Hikers by Gipsy Petulengro, Methuen, 1936

This is a well-written and entertaining book of backpacking and camping tips from an early practitioner who knew what he was talking about, and had the right attitude right down the line. I've included some of the best tips in this guidebook, to save you the effort of trying to find a copy.

Scottish Hill Tracks, Scottish Rights of Way and Access Society, revised 4th edition, 2004

An invaluable publication giving brief description of over 300 routes in the Scottish hills and mountains. It concentrates on routes between places, rather than bagging peaks, which makes it much more useful for our purposes than most other Scottish walking guides. I have followed a number of the paths described in this book – it saved me a lot of research time. If you plan to walk in Scotland again, you should get a copy.

Other Publications Referenced in this Book

The South West Coast Path, South West Coast Path Association (revised annually)

South West Coast Path National Trail: Poole Harbour to Minehead, South West Coast Path Association, 2004

Walking in Somerset by James Roberts, Cicerone, 1997

Macmillan Way West, Macmillan Way Association, 2001

The Tarka Trail – A Walker's Guide by Richard and Henry Williamson, Devon Books, 1992

The Limestone Link, Yatton Ramblers, 2001 (reprint)

The Cotswold Way by Kev Reynolds, Cicerone, 2005

The Heart of England Way by Richard Sale, Aurum Press, 1998

Where to Stay – Offa's Dyke Path and Glendwr's Way, Offa's Dyke Association, revised annually

Offa's Dyke Path Backpackers' and Camping List, Offa's Dyke Association, revised annually

The Wye Valley Walk by Anthony Burton, Aurum Press, 1998

Offa's Dyke Castles Alternative Route, Offa's Dyke Association, revised 1994

Guide to the Maelor Way by Gordon Emery, via Wrexham Borough Council, revised 2003
The South Cheshire Way: Grindley Brook to Mow Cop, Mid-Cheshire Footpath Society
Etherow-Goyt Valley Way, Tameside Countryside Warden Service
Trans Pennine Trail Map 1 West – Southport to Penistone, Barnsley MBC
The North Cheshire Way, Mid-Cheshire Footpath Society, 2006
A Cestrian Link Walk by John N Davenport, Westmorland Gazette, 1983 with 1986 amendment sheet
Walking the Limestone Way by Ron and Elizabeth Haydock and Bill and Dorthy Allen, Scarthin Books, 1997
The Alternative Pennine Way by Denis Brook and Phil Hinchliffe, Cicerone, 1992
The Pennine Way Accommodation and Camping Guide, ed. John Needham, Pennine Way Association, revised periodically
Pennine Way Accommodation and Public Transport Guide, The Countryside Agency
St Cuthbert's Way Official Trail Guide by Roger Smith and Ron Shaw, The Stationery Office, 1997
From the Pennines to the Highlands by Hamish Brown, Lochar, 1992
Exploring the Edinburgh to Glasgow Canals by Hamish Brown, Mercat Press, 2nd edition 2006
The West Highland Way Pocket Companion, Loch Lomond and the Trossachs National Park Authority, revised annually
The Highland High Way by Heather Connon and Paul Roper, Mainstream, 1996
The Rob Roy Way by Jacquetta Megarry, Rucksack Readers, 2002
The Great Glen Way by Jacquetta Megarry and Sandra Bardwell, Rucksack Readers, 2002
The Cape Wrath Trail by David Paterson, Peak Publishing, 1996
North to the Cape by Denis Brook and Phil Hinchliffe, Cicerone, 1999

APPENDIX 3

Other sources of information

Land's End John O'Groats Association

To quote their website: 'The Land's End John O'Groats Association is an exclusive membership of those who have completed the epic journey from Land's End to John O'Groats, or vice versa, by means of a single trip. It exists to celebrate members' achievements.'

Membership Secretary: Don Dyer, 18 Coberley Avenue, Davyhulme, Manchester M41 8QE www.landsendjohnogroats.com

Long Distance Walkers Association

The aim of the LDWA is 'to further the interests of those who enjoy long-distance walking'. Among other things, they organise long-distance walking events and publish a useful newsletter.

Membership Secretary, 4 Chestnut Way, Formby, Merseyside, L37 2DP www.ldwa.org.uk

South West Coast Path Association

The SWCPA is a volunteer 'user group' that promotes use and improvements on the South West

Coast Path. Membership includes newsletters and the annual handbook.
Contact the SWCPA Administrator, Windlestraw, Penquit, Devon PL21 0LU, tel 01752 896237 www.swcp.org.uk

Offa's Dyke Association

The Offa's Dyke equivalent of the SWCPA, although the ODA came first, having been founded in 1969. Membership includes newsletters and an accommodation guide.
Offa's Dyke Association, West St, Knighton, Powys LD7 1EN, tel 01547 528753 www.offasdyke.demon.co.uk. This includes a comprehensive accommodation list.

Pennine Way Association

The PWA publishes an accommodation guide, and sends newsletters to their members.
Tony Jones, Membership Secretary, 19 Bywell Avenue, Hexham, Northumberland NE46 1JA www.pennineway association.co.uk

Youth Hostels Association

Runs hostels and camping barns in England and Wales.
YHA, Trevelyan House, Dimple Rd, Matlock, Derbyshire DE4 3YH, tel 01629 592700 www.yha.org.uk.

Scottish Youth Hostels Association

Runs hostels in Scotland.
SYHA, 7 Glebe Crescent, Stirling FK8 2JA, tel 01786 891400 www.syha.org.uk.

Independent Hostel Guide

Information about all their independent hostels is online at www.independenthostelguide.co.uk

Mountain Bothies Association

The MBA maintains bothies, most of which are in Scotland. They publish regular newsletters.
c/o Henderson Black & Co, Edenbank House, 22 Crossgate, Cupar, Fife KY15 5HW www.mountainbothies.org.uk

West Highland Way

The official West Highland Way website is highly recommended. It includes comprehensive accommodation listings www.west-highland-way.co.uk

Scottish Rights of Way and Access Society

24 Annandale Street, Edinburgh EH7 4AN www.scotways.com

Stanfords

The Long Acre shop is the best map shop in the UK, and they also have shops in Manchester and Bristol.
12–14 Long Acre, London WC2E 9LP (near Covent Garden), tel 0207 836 1321 www.stanfords.co.uk

www.longwalks.org.uk

This is my own website, and among other things it features the latest updates to this book, and further Land's End to John O'Groats information. If you come across anything incorrect or out of date in this guidebook, please email me via www.longwalks.org.uk so that I can put the information onto the website.

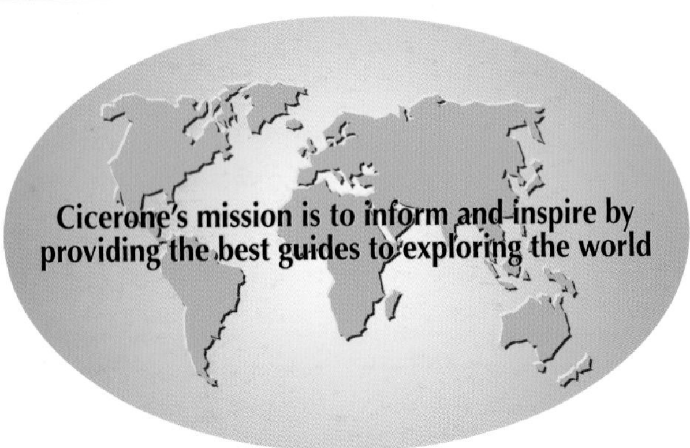

Since its foundation over 30 years ago, Cicerone has specialised in publishing guidebooks and has built a reputation for quality and reliability. It now publishes nearly 300 guides to the major destinations for outdoor enthusiasts, including Europe, UK and the rest of the world.

Written by leading and committed specialists, Cicerone guides are recognised as the most authoritative. They are full of information, maps and illustrations so that the user can plan and complete a successful and safe trip or expedition – be it a long face climb, a walk over Lakeland fells, an alpine traverse, a Himalayan trek or a ramble in the countryside.

With a thorough introduction to assist planning, clear diagrams, maps and colour photographs to illustrate the terrain and route, and accurate and detailed text, Cicerone guides are designed for ease of use and access to the information.

If the facts on the ground change, or there is any aspect of a guide that you think we can improve, we are always delighted to hear from you.

Cicerone Press

2 Police Square Milnthorpe Cumbria LA7 7PY

Tel:01539 562 069 Fax:01539 563 417

e-mail:info@cicerone.co.uk web:www.cicerone.co.uk